N

Extend Your Lifespan

How You Can Live a Long and Healthy Life

Extend
Your Lifespan

How You Can Live
a Long and Healthy Life

By

Gary A. Holt, Ph.D., R.Ph.
Mac McCrory, Ed.D.
Gerald Norris, M.D.
Jack Sandler, Ph.D.

MANCORP PUBLISHING, INC.
Tampa, Florida

Mancorp Publishing, Inc.
P.O. Box 21492
Tampa, FL 33622

Cover and book design: JA Studios
Typesetting: JA Studios

Printed in the United States of America

Library of Congress Cataloging-in-Publication Data

Extend your lifespan: how you can live a long and healthy life/by Gary A. Holt ... [et al.].
      p.   cm.
      Includes bibliographical references and index.
      ISBN 0-931541-52-2
      1. Medicine, Popular. 2. Medicine, Preventive. 3. Health.
4. Longevity. I. Holt, Gary A.
613--dc20   94-11320
                                                                         CIP

AUTHORS

GARY A. HOLT, Ph.D., R.Ph.

Fellow of the American Society of Consulting Pharmacists; Pharmacy and Public Health; College of Pharmacy and Health Sciences, Northeast Louisiana University, Monroe, Louisiana

MAC McCRORY, Ed.D.

Wellness Center; Health Promotion, Wellness and Stress Management; Oklahoma State University, Stillwater, Oklahoma

GERALD NORRIS, M.D.

Physician; Diplomate, American Board of Internal Medicine, Birmingham, Alabama

JACK SANDLER, Ph.D.

Professor of Clinical Psychology; University of South Florida, Tampa, Florida

CONTRIBUTORS

The publisher and the authors are grateful for information and contributions in the form of articles and/or reviews of all or portions of the manuscript of this book before publication, by:

AMERICAN CANCER SOCIETY, Inc.
New York, New York

AMERICAN HEART ASSOCIATION
Dallas, Texas

AMERICAN PUBLIC HEALTH ASSOCIATION
Washington, D.C.

CAROL A. ANDRUS
President, Write On Target, New York, New York

RAY BULLMAN
Deputy Executive Director, National Council on Patient Information and Education, Washington, D. C.

DONNA COHEN, Ph.D.
Professor and Chair, Department of Aging and Mental Health; Director, Institute on Aging, University of South Florida, Tampa, Florida

TIM COVINGTON, Pham.D., R.Ph.
Bruno Professor of Clinical Pharmacy and Pharmacy Practice, Samford University, Birmingham, Alabama

LEONARD Y. COSMO, M.D., F.C.C.P.
Pulmonary Associates of Tampa; Investigator and Chief Operating Officer, Medical Research Associates; Tampa, Florida

EDWIN HALL, Ph.D., R.Ph.
Professor of Pharmacy Administration and Pharmacy Practice, Samford University, Birmingham, Alabama

JOHN HARDY, Ph.D.

Director, Suncoast Alzheimer's Disease Laboratory, University of South Florida, Tampa, Florida

KAY HOLT, M.Mus., Ph.D.

Education, Vocal Performance and Vocal Health; Northeast Louisiana University, Monroe, Louisiana

GARY H. LYMAN, M.D., M.P.H.

Professor, Director of Medical Oncology, Department of Internal Medicine, University of South Florida College of Medicine, Tampa, Florida

JEAN MAGUIRE

Director, Health and Nutrition, *Family Circle Magazine*, New York, New York

ROBERT L. MASSON, M.D.

Department of Neurosurgery, Memorial Clinic, Olympia, Washington

NATIONAL CANCER INSTITUTE

Bethesda, Maryland

NATIONAL INSTITUTE ON AGING

Bethesda, Maryland

LUCINDA L. MAINE, Ph.D.

Senior Director for Pharmacy Affairs, American Pharmaceutical Association, Washington, D.C.

ROGER PARKER, Ph.D., R.Ph.

Professor of Pharmacology, Samford University, Birmingham, Alabama

VALORIE G. WEAVER

Editor-in-Chief, *Remedy Magazine*, Westport, Connecticut

FOREWORD

For centuries human beings have searched the world over for the "fountain of youth." It appears that the fountain of youth is not in a magical paradise on some inaccessible mountain top or in a secluded primeval forest, nor is it in magic bullets.

Scientists and medical researchers are working feverishly to understand and manipulate molecules in the cells of human beings hoping to control the aging process. There is no evidence that biotechnology has succeeded as yet in this regard. Nevertheless, advancement in science and medicine is undergoing exponential growth. Innovations in medical procedures and cures ranging from the mundane to the more serious are discovered and used. These advances will offer one component to healthy living with an expanded lifespan.

Will we live to be 300 years or more? Based on what is known, it is clear that at present no magic bullets exist that will guide us through a lifespan of 300 years. Until that time when medical science unravels the mysteries of the aging process, what are our options? It turns out that we are to take charge of our health. This book will show *you* how, through simple changes in lifestyle, *you* can add years to *your* life. More importantly, you can live not only longer but better.

This comprehensive book offers a *personalized*, *interactive* and *realistic* program for *quality life extension*. It provides outlines for understanding the major diseases and, based on the latest available information, guides you through programs for managing stress and for lowering the risk of cancer, heart attack and AIDS. An extensive section is provided for the understanding of drugs and herbs. What works and what doesn't, including side effects, are discussed.

The reader is encouraged to complete the Health Status Evaluation found on page 49. And remember, *"the road to a healthier you is a journey that cannot be delegated to someone else."* Read along and enjoy a healthy long life.

M. N. Manougian, Ph.D.
Publisher

ACKNOWLEDGMENTS

This work reflects the efforts of many scholars, past and present. I am indebted to all of my teachers and my patients who have helped me to discover the art of medicine and health care. I am especially grateful to Dr. Edwin Hall, friend, mentor and a true scholar whose wisdom and patience have helped many to weather the storms of academic and intellectual endeavors; to Dr. Tim Covington, under whose masterful guidance and wisdom a great many students and colleagues have come to better understand both the science and art of medicine, therapeutics and professionalism; and to Dr. Roger Parker, whose rare blending of scholarship and wit was a continual source of inspiration for our creative endeavors together.

I am especially indebted to *The American Cancer Society* and *The American Heart Association* for the information provided. It is the tireless and humanitarian commitment of organizations such as these that have enhanced public and professional understanding of two of the significant causes of premature death and disability. The wealth and quality of information from these organizations, including preventive interventions, was invaluable to us in our efforts to compile and organize a more complete prescription for healthy living.

I am indebted to the Wellness Center at Oklahoma State University for its informational support. This is a center where people learn daily how to live healthier lives and how to rehabilitate from potentially devastating illnesses and injury.

I am indebted to my parents who engendered a love of learning and discovery within me, a commitment to help others and a belief in all that is fair and true.

This project has been a labor of love for over two years. To my mother, Lillian Holt, this project became known as "The Book." In every conversation with her she would offer encouragement and support and ask, "So, how's *the book* coming along?" It is to my great regret that she died just weeks before the project was completed. I dedicate this book to her.

Finally, I dedicate this book to you, the reader. I encourage you to commit to a healthier lifestyle and a healthier environment.

Gary A. Holt, Ph.D., R.Ph.

CONTENTS

SECTION FOUR

SECTION FIVE

APPENDICES

OUTLINES

SECTION ONE

Introduction to a Healthier You

SECTION TWO

Aging

SECTION THREE

Diseases and Interventions of the 20th Century

SECTION FOUR

Drugs and Health

SECTION ▍ *FIVE*

Becoming an Informed Consumer

TABLES ▍

SECTION ONE

Introduction to a Healthier You

I. HEALTH AND DISEASE

"Supposedly, we have the highest standard of living
in any country in the world. Do we, though? It
depends on what one means by high standards."

— Henry Miller

It's 6 a.m. and the caffeine from my first cup of coffee has not yet kicked in. The TV is on (force of habit), when suddenly . . . there she is! A seemingly well-preserved woman (they claim she's 60 years old!) in workout tights and cheer leading a stunned, (i.e.,post-somniferous) audience through a series of exercises guaranteed to wake us up and rout our archenemy . . . cellulite!

As she easily bends over to touch her toes, she states casually, "Exercise is the way to better health." After a short burst of toe touches she asks, "Now don't you want to be healthy?"

Of course I do! But now wait a minute. I'm already healthy. I have no symptoms; no signs of health problems. In fact, just last week my doctor checked me over, stem to stern. All was well.

So, having confirmed my positive health status, I returned to my coffee. However, the message of the "health" merchants is an unrelenting crusade. Over on Channel 17 a celebrity is touting the latest exercise gadget; on Channel 24 there are four ladies who look like members of the Dallas Cheerleaders, attired in the latest sweat togs and pump-up tennis shoes (with mix-n-match shoe laces). They giggle as they bounce up and down, all the while pitching an enticing offer, "These wonderful workout togs are only available through this special TV offer, but order now because they won't last long!" And after all, they have only been offering this incredible special for the past forty seven weeks, so they are bound to be running low by now.

Then there's the chap on Channel 33 who looks like he could easily bench press the workout machine he's promoting . . . with me on it! He looks directly at me and asks, "You do want health, good health, don't you? Of course you do!" Well, at least he answered for me, so I didn't have to think about it for long.

"And, if you order the new and improved "Gimcrack Exerciser" from this special TV offer (for the amazingly low price of $19.99 per month for the rest of your natural life), we'll send, at no extra charge, a 5-gallon bucket of "Metaboflab," the high-potency vitamin, mineral, anti-oxidant, anti-aging, energy-producing laxative used by . . . a whole bunch of regular people."

OK, so if I order one "Gimcrack Exerciser", what do I gain?

"Health!" is the resounding retort.

Well, is it possible to be a bit more specific? After all, if I am going to purchase this stuff in spite of the fact that I have already been declared to be "healthy," just what is this nirvana of health for which I am now being encouraged to invest my retirement fund? In fact, now that I think about it, just what is health anyway?

As it turns out, no one knows . . . at least, we can't seem to agree on a single definition. There are different philosophies and orientations about health (see Outline 1). This is a reflection of the fact that even health scholars can't agree on a definition. But is it really important that we agree on the meaning of the term? Well, as it turns out . . . it is!

The way we define "health" is an outcome of the cultures and societies in which we exist. For example, farmers and ranchers living in rural areas are more likely to tolerate or ignore certain symptoms and diseases than do urban residents. Their definition of health (i.e., what it takes before you go to a doctor) may differ from that of people living in cities where health care is readily available. This is more than a simple matter of convenience. People in rural areas may define the seriousness of their symptoms differently than people in urban areas.

Part of the problem in the search for a "health" definition is that we engage in contradictory practices. For example, many people who criticize the FDA (Food and Drug Administration) for a failure to release more drugs more quickly, are first in line at the attorney's office when something goes wrong with the drugs that they demanded the right to have! Ah . . . that's "health" in America. We demand the right to damage our own health with poor lifestyle choices . . . then we demand someone else to blame if illness occurs.

Our personal definitions for health, of course, reflect our individual beliefs about it. For some people, health is a "Gimcrack Exerciser" and a bucket of "Metaboflab." For others, it is a walk around the block; and for still others, it is watching seven hours of TV each day.

As long as we are unable to agree on a definition, it is unlikely that we will have agreement on what constitutes a healthy lifestyle.

OUTLINE I

DIFFERING PHILOSOPHICAL VIEWS ABOUT HEALTH[1]

❦ Health and Quality of Life

Meaningful life experiences and the achievement of desirable accomplishments affect our quality of life, and so, health may be viewed as a state of competence which allows us to achieve a desirable quality of life.

❦ Health as a Freedom to Achieve

Health may be viewed as the ability or freedom to do what we want to do, to become what we want to become, or to achieve desirable lifestyles and aspirations even when we have disease. Donald Ardell discusses health in terms of physical, emotional and mental freedoms (see Outline 2). Poor health may prevent us from achieving all the things that we would like to achieve.

❦ Health as a Lack of Disease

The most common view of health asserts that we are "healthy" as long as we are not sick. So, the onset of symptoms marks the beginning of disease.

❦ Health as a Potential for Adaptation

This view refers to our ability to adapt to our environments (e.g., home, work). Rene Dubos describes this as a *creative adaptation*, which requires conscious participation and the making of healthy lifestyle choices.

❦ Health as a State of Balance

Health may depend upon our ability to achieve an equilibrium or balance between our internal environments (i.e., body organs and systems) and our external environments (e.g., air and water pollution).

1. See references 1-12

```
OUTLINE 2
```

SUMMARY OF THE FREEDOMS OF WELLNESS AS PROPOSED
BY DONALD ARDELL[2]

Component of Health	Description	Level of Freedom
Physical	A state of well-being.	Freedom from pain and the limitations of illness.
Emotional	A state of calm, serenity and zest for living.	Freedom from disabling stress and excess passion.
Mental	A state of compassion and purpose.	Freedom from selfishness and aimlessness.

"You view wisdom as if it is a flower to be plucked
. . . It is a mountain to be climbed."

— Cain (Kung Fu)

In our hectic lives, a "Gimcrack Exerciser" and a spoonful of "Metaboflab" are as easily promoted as the flowers to be plucked for instant health.

Onward Through the Fog

The dictionary defines health as:

- Physical and mental well-being;
- Freedom from defect, pain or disease;
- Normality of mental and physical functions; and
- A universal good condition.

So, we are healthy as long as we are not sick. This is the way most people view health, and it is also the orientation of professional health care. The problem with this view is that we tend to ignore our health status until it has already been threatened in some way. We are even willing to engage in high risk behaviors which endanger our health for short-term benefits (e.g., the weekend athlete; playing golf in lightning storms because it's our only day off and we really want to play; smoking to relax; eating foods high in cholesterol and fats because they taste better than those healthy alternatives). If "health" means no disease, it is easy to believe that our lifestyle choices are safe as long as we experience no symptoms.

Unfortunately, we are easily deceived. The absence of symptoms may only mean that disease is not yet apparent. We may feel "normal" even when our blood pressure is at dangerously high levels. And, it is difficult to convince smokers to kick the habit when the negative outcomes of smoking may not appear for 20 years. The trouble with this approach is that by the time symptoms appear it is often too late to undo the damage.

The health community has not helped much in this regard. Professional health care is fragmented and strongly oriented to the "health as the absence of disease" philosophy. The medical specialists divide the human body into "practice territories." A hospital patient becomes "the gallbladder patient in Room 219." We take our moles to one doctor and our hemorrhoids to another. As the objects of medical specialization, we are no longer a whole human being, but instead, a collection of biological parts. As long as all of our parts are free of symptoms, we are declared to be "healthy."

This "Dr. Goodwrench" philosophy has some merit. The ability of doctors to successfully treat symptoms, control disease and reassemble our parts (e.g., following disease or injury) is indeed miraculous. Even when a disease cannot be cured, it can often be made more tolerable. As a result, it is easy to develop a dependency upon doctors and drugs as an antidote for virtually every discomfort.

We prefer this orientation. Over the years we have given responsibility for our health to health care professionals. We often live carelessly, convinced that if disease or injury occurs, medicine can fix us. We have come to believe that as long as there is enough medical care, we will be healthy.

We expect too much of medicine and become frustrated if doctors cannot undo the damage of our lifestyle choices. So, protesters carry signs in front of the FDA demanding the release of new medications before they have been adequately tested. Yet, there are no sign carriers who encourage the healthy lifestyle choices that would allow them to avoid the need for these medications in the first place.

Disease and Illness

We use the terms *disease* and *illness* to mean the same thing. However, many health professionals use *disease* to refer to the physical changes that occur as a result of a *disease* process of some kind. *Illness* refers to our perceptions of disease or the way we experience disease in the context of family and society.[3]

Each of us can experience a disease or health problem differently. For example, pregnancy can be a wonderful and meaningful experience for some women and an intolerable one for others.   PMS has existed as one of the great enigmas of modern medicine because of the myriad ways in which women respond to it.

In most cases we do not usually experience the actual cause of disease (e.g., organ malfunction or an infecting organism), but rather, the symptoms which result from disease. For example, we do not actually feel a cold virus, but we do feel the symptoms of a cold. However, cold symptoms are similar to the symptoms of a dozen other diseases in their early stages (e.g., measles, pneumonia). So, whenever cold-like symptoms occur, we assume that it is a cold because that is our experience with those symptoms.

Illness begins when we decide that we no longer feel "normal." Since each of us responds to symptoms differently, the same problem may be debilitating to one person, but not to another. And in fact, an illness can exist without disease (e.g., patients sometimes have no actual physical problem even though they insist that something is wrong).

We respond to the illness, while health professionals respond to the disease. When doctors correctly treat the disease, but fail to treat the illness, we may insist that the doctor has misdiagnosed the problem, or we may disagree with the therapy that has been suggested. In either case, we are less likely to follow our doctor's advice. For example, a college professor denied the diagnosis of his heart condition and refused to take his medicines because he was afraid that to do so would cause him to become an invalid. Once he realized that this was not the case, he began to take his medications.

---

3. See reference 11.

In a similar way, we usually prefer to "experience" the medications we are taking. Historically, people have tended to judge drug activity in terms of side effects. When side effects are absent, it is easy to believe that the drug is not working.

Despite our efforts to clarify the meaning of health, there appears to be an inescapable reality:

> However much a definition of health takes into account common sense, philosophy, and science, we are generally accustomed to defining it in our own terms.[4]

Therein lies the rub. Each of us defines health in our own terms. Each of us decides whether or not certain behaviors are healthy. Each of us *is* the problem, and each of us is, potentially, the solution.

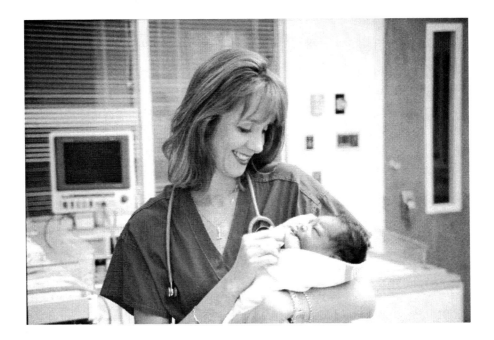

---

4. See reference 8.

CASE STUDY

LESSONS FROM REAL LIFE— FRED

Fred was diagnosed with an ulcer by his physician, who prescribed a new drug. This drug is associated with few side effects when used appropriately for short time periods. Fred took the drug for a few days, then returned to the pharmacy.

Fred: "I want my money back on this prescription," he demanded of the pharmacist.

RPh: "What's the problem, Fred?"

Fred: "This stuff doesn't work! I want a refund!"

RPh   "How's your stomach doing?"

Fred: "My stomach is fine, but I don't feel a thing when I take this drug!"

This is a true example. Historically, most medications have produced side effects. Most of the "stronger" pain medications cause sedation or euphoria; many of the older stomach medications also caused significant drowsiness, dry eyes and blurred vision. Thus, the illness experience of most patients is that if medications work, they should cause you to feel "medicated." Most of these experiences however are due to side effects of the drug and not the purpose for which the drug was actually being taken. So, when a drug is prescribed which has few side effects, people sometimes feel that they have not been effectively treated. For Fred, it was ironic that his therapy had actually worked, but he was judging the outcome by the absence of medication side effects, not by the fact that his problem had improved.

HOW ABOUT YOU?

How do you judge the effectiveness of therapy?

2. WELLNESS

"The daily habits of people have a great deal more to do with what makes them sick and when they die than do all the influences of medicine."

Dr. Lester Breslow

The concept of "wellness" has been popularized by writers such as Donald Ardell in his book, *High Level Wellness* (see Outline 3). An appropriate definition for our purposes is:

Wellness is an active process, whereby you make choices that affect your health and well-being.

Several terms within this definition help to expand our understanding of this concept:

Active means that each of us must deliberately participate in decisions and actions related to our own health status. For example, engaging in exercise is active and intentional. Nutritional choices require that we consciously select what and how much we eat. Choosing a healthy meal at a fast food restaurant is, perhaps, the best example of a positive decision.

Process means that wellness behaviors begin today and will last a lifetime. Exercising one time will not cause you to be physically "fit." Eating one low-fat meal does not constitute nutritional consciousness. Wellness is an ongoing process that requires "active" effort every day of your life.

Individuals practice wellness. Each of us is responsible for our own well-being. No one can do this for us.

Choice is a key concept. We make thousands of choices every day. Some of these choices have a major impact on health and well-being. Smoking, eating fatty foods, being sedentary and misusing or abusing drugs are behaviors which have a negative impact on our quality and quantity of life. The choice to not use tobacco products, to eat properly, exercise and use medication products wisely, will have a positive impact on both our quality and quantity of life.

OUTLINE 3

WELLNESS CONCEPTS, GUIDELINES AND SKILLS
BY DONALD ARDELL

❦ Acceptance of Life

It is possible to be "well" in the midst of illness, or even dying. This involves an acceptance of life and a continual striving for optimal good health that enables you to achieve the fullest existence within your present scenario.

❦ Barrier Removal

Identify and eliminate *your* barriers to health and wellness.

❦ Communication Skills

Learn to express your emotions (e.g., sadness, fears, anger, enthusiasm, needs and desires) in healthy ways, rather than suppressing them or letting them control you.

❦ Creativity

Take advantage of your creative abilities and talents toward health and a meaningful life. Suppressing your natural gifts and talents can be unhealthy.

❦ Health Promotion

Health promoting activities in one area of your life will encourage the adoption of other healthy behaviors. The more positive things you do for your body, the fewer negative things you will want to do against it.

❦ Loving Yourself

Seek a greater sense of self-worth and self-acceptance. It's OK to like who you are.

❦ Patience

Wellness is achieved over time; it is not achieved suddenly.

❦ Prevention

We spend vast sums of money to treat diseases that could have been prevented for free.

OUTLINE 3 cont'd

❦ Relaxation Techniques
Identify and practice relaxation techniques and methods for reducing stress and tension.

❦ Self-Awareness and Self-Repair
Become aware of your mind-body connection. Your body is often capable of self-healing and self-repair, but it has a limited capacity to overcome years of misuse and neglect. Healthy lifestyles enhance your natural resistance to ill health.

❦ Self-Responsibility
Modern medicine is wonderful, with two exceptions: (1) We expect too much of it; and (2) We expect too little of ourselves. Wellness activities seek to help people take charge of their lives and to feel good about themselves. The only tyrant you face is your own inertia and the absence of a commitment; that is, a belief that you are too busy to take responsibility for your own well-being and that the pursuit of a wellness-promoting lifestyle is too hard, complicated or inconvenient. Discover the ways by which you contribute to your own health problems and life stresses. Identify desirable lifestyle changes and ways to achieve them. Health professionals can assist you, but you are ultimately responsible for you.

❦ Stop Searching for "Magic Bullets" and "Fountains of Youth"
Don't spend your life being victimized by your own unhealthy lifestyle decisions and then seeking "miracle" treatments after your health has been threatened. Aging is natural. It is not a disease to be cured.

❦ Wellness Lifestyles
Wellness lifestyles and improved environments reduce the risks for disease, premature aging and unnecessary suffering; reduce health care costs; provide for a life of greater satisfaction, increased serenity and greater interests in the future.

❦ Wellness is More Fun Than Illness.
Is an explanation here really necessary?

Who Is in Control?

Each of us has direct control over certain aspects of our lives. Some of these are major components of wellness, including:[5]

- Career, job and professional choices
- Hobby and recreational choices
- Community
- Safety and prevention
- Diet, nutrition and weight control
- Social and cultural factors
- Environmental factors
- Stress management and relaxation
- Exercise and physical activity
- Use, misuse and abuse of substances
- Family

To ignore these factors and their impact on our health, or to focus on only a few, disregarding the rest, would be naive. Exercise, nutrition, stress management and the use of substances are considered in greater detail in later sections of the book. Several others are mentioned here.

Health and well-being should become the avocation of everyone. These efforts should include physical activity, nutritional awareness, stress management and the wise use of substances. How we spend our leisure time determines to a large extent our state of wellness and health. "Couch potatoes," whose hobbies consist of watching TV and eating snacks, are on the "short track" of life. People who opt for active, healthy hobbies in their spare time are on the "long track" of life.

The environment is where we live (e.g., home, workplace, community and even our planet). Volumes have been written about the decay of the Earth. The choices which we make can increase or reduce this decay. Recycling, conservation and pollution controls are examples of how we can protect the environment. In turn, a healthy environment (air, water, temperature, humidity, pollution, population control)

5. See references 1-12

promotes our health and well-being.

The family is a significant influence in our lives, but family members are not responsible for the choices *we* make. Ultimately, each of us is responsible for our own choices and behaviors. The influence which family members have on us can be powerful, as can the influence which we have on our family. It is easier to make healthy lifestyle decisions if the entire family is willing to commit to them. And a family is more likely to become health conscious when individuals within the family opt for positive health choices.

Our social and cultural contacts in life can range from a small network of family and friends to a federal bureaucracy. We usually have more influence on family and friends than on the federal government. And, our family and friends can have a tremendous influence on our behavior. For example, adult role models and peer pressure influence the drug taking behaviors of young people. This represents a social or cultural influence on individual behaviors.

For many adults, work and career influences can be detrimental to health or even deadly. Much of our time is spent at work or thinking about work. This "stress energy" can lead to health problems if it is not counteracted in some way. If you are in a stressful job environment, activities such as exercise, family outings, reading, hobbies and so on, might reduce the level and effects of stress.

A Force of One

A study of 7000 men and women in California conducted by Dr. Lester Breslow and Dr. Nedra Belloc showed that physical well-being and lifespan were significantly affected by seven lifestyle practices (see Outline 4). These have come to be known as "The Breslow 7." The study found that the physical health status of people who adhered to these practices was about the same as that of people who were 35 years younger, but who did not follow these practices. The results of this study indicate that we *can* increase our lifespan by adopting these lifestyle practices.

These simple lifestyle choices have more impact on health and lifespan than most of the technology of modern medicine. Because these simple practices are not as sensational as the advancements of medicine, they tend to be overlooked. We are enamored with high-tech medicine. Many tend to assemble "pharmacies" of herbs and medicines at home, turn to medical references, but are reluctant to eat three rational meals a day.

OUTLINE 4

THE BRESLOW 7: LIFESTYLE BEHAVIORS WHICH CAN IMPROVE YOUR QUALITY AND QUANTITY OF LIFE[6]

❦ **Eat Breakfast Every Day**
Literally means to "break the fast." Eat the right kind of foods within an hour of arising. Eating Grandma's sausage, biscuits and gravy (high fat foods) every day is not a good idea. High carbohydrate foods (e.g., cereals, breads and grains) are a much better way to start your day.

❦ **Eat 3 Meals / Day at Regular Intervals With Limited Snacking**
It is important to eat regular meals (e.g., 3 to 4 times each day). Eating between meals increases daily calorie intake. Snack foods are usually counter productive (i.e., high fat, low nutrient content).

❦ **Maintaining a Desirable Body Weight**
Healthy diets and physical activity (e.g., exercise) are important.

❦ **Avoid Excessive Alcohol Consumption**
It's best to avoid alcohol products. However, studies have shown that alcohol in moderation (e.g., no more than 4 ounces / day) may actually provide some health benefits (e.g., reduced risk of heart disease). Limit alcohol consumption to no more than 2 drinks per day. Alcohol use in higher amounts has been linked to the development of cancer (e.g., breast cancer in women; oral and intestinal cancers in men and women).

❦ **Regular Exercise**
Exercise and physical activity help to maintain ideal body weight; reduce disease (e.g., heart disease, cancer) and stress; and extend life.

❦ **No Tobacco Products**
Tobacco use is associated with heart disease, cancer, strokes, high blood pressure and birth defects. What else needs to be said . . . the use of tobacco products will kill you!

❦ **Sleep 7-8 Hours Each Night**
Sleep is extremely important for health maintenance. Yet, it can be as unhealthy to sleep too much (9+ hours daily) as it is to sleep too little (less than 6 hours).

6. See reference 9.

Table 1 shows the estimated years one can expect to live depending on age and number of lifestyle practices adopted. For example, a 45-year-old man who adopts six lifestyle practices can expect to live to the age of 78. A 55-year-old woman who adopts four lifestyle practices can expect to live to 80. The reader may wish to estimate his/her own lifespan depending on current age and the number of lifestyle practices adopted.

TABLE I

ESTIMATED YEARS YOU CAN EXPECT TO LIVE IF YOU ARE FOLLOWING TRAITS LISTED IN THE BRESLOW 7

	By Following 0 - 3 of the Breslow 7	By Following 4 - 5 of the Breslow 7	By Following 6 - 7 of the Breslow 7
MEN (at age)			
45	22	28	33
55	14	20	25
65	11	14	17
WOMEN (at age)			
45	29	34	42
55	20	25	28
65	12	17	20

Quality Versus Quantity of Life

We are obsessed with our length of life, and scurry to the very corners of the globe on a quest for virtual immortality. And, there is no end to the books at your local bookstore that will provide you with the latest (but heretofore unknown to medicine) "secret formula" guaranteed to increase your lifespan. Many of these offerings are simply hype. For the price of the book they will tell you what you want to hear, but not necessarily what is true.

Ah, but while we prepare our herbal baths (with just a pinch of powdered wing of bat and eye of newt) specially formulated to remove those awful wrinkles that cause us to look our age, perhaps we would do well to give a fleeting thought to another issue: Should we be more concerned with *quantity* of life or *quality* of life?

Quantity does not equal *quality*. Even if we could do it, we might well question the wisdom of increasing our lifespan to 150+ in a youth-oriented culture that has not yet learned to deal responsibly and humanely with our elderly.

What conditions of life await us in a world that presently squanders both natural and man-made resources without regard for future consequences? Should we not become concerned about the health of our world before the air and waters are so polluted that recovery is beyond hope? Are we to hold death at bay via the "miracles" of medicine, only to succumb to the consequences of "soiling our own nest"? In fact, should we not rethink our acceptance of death as the final stage of life, rather than hiding behind a shield of medical denial?

The adoption of healthy lifestyles *will* increase lifespan somewhat. More importantly, however, is the realization that a healthy lifestyle *can* vastly improve our quality of life. And that, it seems to us, is a vastly more important issue.

3. LESSONS FROM HIPPOCRATES

"It is true that faith in the healing power of ancient gods has somewhat weakened, but faith itself has lost no ground to reason. Men want miracles as much today as in the past. If they do not join one of the new cults, they satisfy this need by worshiping at the altar of modern science."

— Rene Dubos

We consider ourselves to be the most enlightened society in the history of the Earth ... a nation of science and reasoning that has given up its ghosts, goblins, myths and folklore. Yet, we need only to look as far as the tabloids at the grocery store, to the TV advertisements for psychic interventions, or to the $100 billion per year health fraud industry to reaffirm the existence of our own myths and folklore.

The history of medicine is abundant with myths, potions and magic. At times the contributions of myths have been positive and at times negative, and they have helped people cope with a bewildering and often hostile world. Even today our beliefs about health reflect a blend of science, religion, faith, witchcraft, hope, wishful thinking, and the supernatural. Our actions and interpretations reflect bits and pieces of the past and present.

Myths and folklore become more influential when people are desperate. Faced with an incurable illness, we will travel to the other side of the planet to try "an ancient potion." But even when the problem being "treated" is not serious we may resort to mythical cures. For example, consider the sales of quack products which promise to enhance appearance in some way. The allure of bulging muscles, a larger male organ or female breasts make insecure teens or adults an easy target.

Actually, this is nothing new. Our incessant search for "magic bullet" solutions is at least 2500 years old. Many people continue today to seek supernatural and related interventions (e.g., herbs, cults, psychic interventions) as a substitute for self-responsibility, healthy lifestyles or professional medicine.

Throughout history myths have provided supernatural explanations for ordinary life events (e.g., birth, death, health, disease, economic depressions, war, famine, disease). When a rational explanation is unavailable, supernatural explanations are always available to fill in the gaps. Today, our concepts of health retain elements of our ancient heritage. Examples of this are reflected in the philosophies of Asclepius, Hygeia and Hippocrates (see Outline 5). These are three of the most important health figures in all of human history. Yet they are little remembered today. Their beliefs remain as a reminder of our inextricable link to the past.

Asclepius and Hygeia represent a never ending conflict between two different points of view. In one form or another, these two views have always existed simultaneously in all civilizations.

The wisdom of Hygeia has been largely ignored throughout history, just as it is today. Disease and injury are more spectacular, and so, they receive more attention. The banal normalcy of health goes unnoticed, so that the thousands of lives saved by improved sanitation systems receives no mention in the news. Television shows champion the Marcus Welbys, Ben Caseys, and even such absurd offerings as a Doogy Howser. Yet, we would laugh at a show which featured a public health worker.

Prevention is boring as compared to the bells and whistles of modern medical technology. Indeed, when prevention is most effective, nothing happens (i.e., no disease or injury). This scenario is simply not the preferred fodder of the grinding wheels of the media. But this should come as no surprise since the lack of human interest in prevention has changed very little over the past 2500 years.

The focus of curative medicine is one of "doing something" that produces an observable effect. Every society throughout history, no matter how primitive, has demanded curative medicine. Prevention lacks the glamour and cultural appeal of extracting people from the "jaws of death." This, of course, is the foundation for TV doctor shows (No family practitioner in the history of the world ever saw the mix of patients seen by Marcus Welby in a single TV season!).

This orientation is also reflected in our unwillingness to support preventive services. Consider, for example, the National Influenza Immunization Program launched on October 1, 1976. This public health program was implemented because the virus was similar to the one which in the winter of 1918 killed 20 million people worldwide (500,000 people died in the U.S.). Influenza is a disease of major concern, especially since it is largely preventable. Pandemics (i.e., worldwide epidemics) occur periodically when the flu virus mutates into a form for which people have no natural immunity. For example, 45 million people in the U.S. became ill with the Asian Flu in 1957 (70,000 died), and 20% of the U.S. population was infected with the Hong Kong Flu in 1968 (30,000 died and the cost of the disease was estimated that year to be $3.9 billion). The projected 1976 virus would have been the first time in our history that a nation was able to anticipate and prepare for a disease of potentially pandemic proportions.[7]

The 1976 flu season proved to be less disastrous than health officials had anticipated. One would think that this might be a cause for celebration. Not so! In fact both public health officials and the government were criticized despite their success. "See there, nothing happened! You guys just wasted our tax dollars!"

Say, have we forgotten something? After all, the intent of the program was to avoid the flu. And for the most part, that's just what we did! We will never know exactly what impact this program had on the epidemic. At the very least, the national attention paid to the Swine Flu may have caused people to be more careful (e.g., avoiding contacts with others who had the flu).

We are willing to pay for crisis intervention, but not prevention. So, if five times the amount spent on the Swine Flu Vaccination Program had been spent to treat people after becoming ill, the effort would have been applauded.

This lack of concern for prevention is also apparent in most insurance programs, which tend only to pay for problems after they occur. Because curative medicine is expensive, insurance companies dictate what will be covered. So, both medicine and consumers are progressively becoming the pawns of a brand of insurance "medicine" with profit margins (rather than humane and rational health care) as the primary concern.

It is difficult to know what the impact of health care reform will be, but it seems reasonably clear that we have yet to rediscover the wisdom of Hygeia and Hippocrates as the most effective health care orientations.

---

7. See reference 5.

OUTLINE 5

IMPORTANT FIGURES OF ANTIQUITY THAT HAVE INFLUENCED OUR CONCEPTS OF MEDICINE AND HEALTH THROUGHOUT HISTORY[8]

❦ Hygeia (about 1500 B.C.)

Hygeia was a goddess who guarded the health of Athens, and was likely a personification of Athena, the goddess of reason. Her name was derived from an abstract word meaning "health." She was more of a concept than an actual person and never had as much impact as Asclepius did. Hygeia represented the earliest philosophical orientations to health, even though she was not actually involved in the treatment of the sick. She symbolized a belief that people can remain well if they live their lives wisely. Health was viewed as a natural order of things, so that the basic function of medicine was to discover the laws of nature which help to ensure a healthy mind and body and then to teach these laws to others. It is worth noting at this point that the term "doctor" did not originally refer to a healer, but rather to a teacher.

❦ Asclepius (about 1200 B.C.)

According to legend Asclepius was the first Greek physician. He achieved fame through his mastery of the knife and a knowledge of the curative powers of plants. And, it was his training of others in these curative skills that popularized his philosophy of medicine. In most representations he appears as a handsome, self-assured young god, accompanied by two maidens. One was Hygeia (discussed above) and Panakeia. Panakeia is described as a healing goddess (via her knowledge of medicinal substances). Her philosophy is alive and well today, as reflected in our unending search for drug panaceas. The basic medical sciences (e.g., anatomy, physiology, biochemistry) found their beginnings in the discoveries and followers of Asclepius. This accounts for the immense volume of useful knowledge of therapeutics that had accumulated long before our modern scientific era. According to the philosophy of Asclepius, the primary role of the physician was to promote health by treating disease as it occurred and

8. See references 1-4 and 6-9.

OUTLINE 5 cont'd

correcting the imperfections of the body . . . an orientation that characterizes medicine to this day.

❧ Hippocrates (5th Century B.C.)

Hippocrates was a Greek physician. Little is actually known about him as an individual. Many of the writings which are associated with him may have actually been written by other authors. Still, he serves as an important figure for many of our medical and health beliefs. In many ways he represents a blending of the views of Asclepius and Hygeia. He promoted rational thinking based on knowledge rather than myths and supernatural influences. Ancient physicians were students of the natural order of things and sought to discover how health is affected by diet, occupations, and lifestyles. The role of medicine was to promote healthy environments and lifestyles. With this in mind, it is interesting to note that the word "physician" comes from a Greek word meaning "nature." Hippocrates was holistic in his thinking. He believed that mind and body affect each other and that physicians should treat the whole person.

4. HOLISM —A CONCEPT IN SEARCH OF A DEFINITION

"To heal does not necessarily imply to cure. It can simply mean helping people to achieve a way of life compatible with their individual aspirations —to restore their freedom to make choices —even in the presence of continuing disease."

—Rene Dubos

Over the past decade or so, the term *holism* has become a popular buzz word for health books and discussions. Like the term health itself however, the concept of holism has been largely misunderstood and lacks a universal definition.

Contemporary holism is associated with the phrase, "the whole is greater than the sum of its parts," which suggests that we cannot completely understand people by an analysis of their separate organs. This type of reasoning is not new. In fact, holistic thinking appears here and there throughout history and can be traced back to the ancient Chinese.

The most significant historical event involving holistic thinking in the 20th Century was a book, *Holism and Evolution,* written by Jan Smuts and published in 1926. Smuts was a South African scientist, philosopher, lawyer, politician, statesman, soldier and, as if that was not enough to keep him busy, an author. Although the book is tedious reading, it does offer some profound insights regarding holism. Some people have dubbed Smuts the "father" of holism and also of holistic health. In fact, he was neither. Holistic thinking predates Smuts by at least 5000 years, and his writings have little to do with health. Nonetheless, we are indebted to Smuts for two contributions. To begin with, he coined the term "holism" from the Greek word for "whole" (and by the way, the original term was "holism" and not "wholism"). Secondly, his writings organized and consolidated the myriad thoughts and philosophies which had existed for thousands of years related to this concept.

Smuts was primarily concerned with holism in nature rather than health. In fact, his book does not actually deal with health care at all, but it does address the quality of life in general and many of his ideas can be applied to health care.

Holism and Health Care

Holism as applied to health care considers the whole individual and involves the merger of older ideas and practices with newer knowledge and techniques. This newer perspective (see Outline 6), enables us to formulate a reasonable definition:

> Holism is a model of health care which involves you and health care professionals in a cooperative effort to establish and maintain optimal health and well-being as a whole person in your environments by using any technique or method of prevention, diagnosis, therapy or rehabilitation which is capable of fulfilling your particular health needs.[9]

Because holism has been misunderstood many people have been unwilling to accept such approaches to health care. This confusion is the result of attempts to include or exclude certain techniques and practices as "holistic." For example, is yoga holistic? Acupuncture? This confusion is easily reconciled when we realize that the objective of holism is to promote optimal health and well-being, and not whether any specific technique should or should not be included in our definition.

OUTLINE 6

BASIC CONCEPTS WHICH CHARACTERIZE HOLISTIC HEALTH CARE

❦ Acceptance of Limitations

We must learn to accept and understand the health problems which we experience, as well as realistic limits of therapy. Holism is an optimistic philosophy, but it also emphasizes a need to accept limitations (e.g., of self and modern medicine). Given a serious health problem some people can never expect to fully recover, and

---

9. See reference 1

OUTLINE 6 cont'd

may even face death. In any event, each of us is encouraged to understand our life situation as it relates to health and disease.

❦ Balance

In order for us to be healthy, each aspect of our being must be in balance or harmony with others (e.g., mind / body / spirit; individual / environments). Disease is thought to occur when there is an imbalance of these interrelating components. Holism attempts to restore harmony.

❦ Body, Mind and Spirit

Holism recognizes that we have mental, emotional, spiritual and social needs in addition to our physical needs. All of these aspects of our being must be healthy in order for optimal health to exist. Holistic health approaches attempt to restore *all* of these to a healthy state.

❦ Environments

Holism considers the ways in which environmental factors can affect our well-being. Environmental factors which impact our health can include external factors (e.g., pollution, noise, smoking), social environments (e.g., stresses of culture and society, work environment stresses, family lifestyle stresses) and other environments to which we are exposed.

❦ Long-Term Process

Holism is a long-term process, not a one-time technique. It strives to discover health skills and behaviors which can promote a lifetime of well-being and freedom from disease and infirmities.

❦ Patient/Practitioner Roles

As a patient in holistic health care we assume the role of an active learner and form a partnership with health care professionals. Health professionals should serve as guides, counselors, facilitators and teachers. They should encourage us to assume greater responsibility for self-care and allow opportunities for us to discover our inherent capabilities and resources. In this way, the health professional is not one who makes us well, but rather assists us in our efforts to achieve optimal health and well-being.

OUTLINE 6 cont'd

❦ Prevention

Holism emphasizes prevention. Symptoms appear only after health has been threatened in some way. Optimal well-being is not likely to occur if we only treat symptoms as they appear. Effective prevention reduces the need for therapeutic interventions.

❦ Quality of Life

Holism is concerned with our quality of life. It encourages optimal well-being by promoting self-control and self-understanding of our life situation as it relates to health. It encourages changes in our behaviors and beliefs that are associated with health problems.

❦ Self-Responsibility

Holism encourages self-responsibility for health, self-awareness and self-understanding. This helps us to discover the behavioral choices, actions and attitudes necessary for better health and well-being. Each of us is encouraged to be an active participant in the healing process and not merely a passive recipient of professional care. Each of us has potentials, resources and energy which can be tapped as a source of therapeutic power and healing. Holism seeks to teach us how to take advantage of our own therapeutic potentials.

❦ Therapeutic Tolerance

Holism promotes the use of ANY health or therapeutic approach that can satisfy the health needs of the whole person. It promotes the use of both traditional and nontraditional health practices as long as they are effective. It is a philosophy that basically states, "If it works ... use it!"

❦ Wellness (versus the absence of disease)

Holism is oriented to people, not disease. It seeks to satisfy all of our needs in an effort to achieve optimal well-being.

❦ Wholes

The basic premise of holism is that the whole is greater than the sum of its parts. This means that health care activities should consider the whole person and not specific body parts. Each of us is unique, so that generalizations about health may not be appropriate for every person.

5. UPSET SYSTEMS – MAN IS NOT AN ISLAND

"Life is an adventure in a world where nothing is static; where unpredictable and ill-understood events contribute dangers that must be overcome, often blindly and at great cost; where man himself, like the sorcerer's apprentice, has set in motion forces that are potentially destructive and may someday escape his control."

— Rene Dubos

A *system* is an organized "whole" comprised of individual parts which interact in various ways. Your car is an organized system of auto parts. If a part ceases to function normally, the entire system can break down, which is a more or less common occurrence with cars. When one part is repaired, the system may function normally again. When the parts of a system are arranged in an order of increasing complexity, a hierarchy is created (see Outline 7).

Health problems can also be considered from a systems perspective. This allow us to better understand the various factors which can affect health (e.g., environmental, social, cultural, behavioral, biological). Our state of health at any given level is continually changing because of a "ripple effect" that occurs throughout the system. Positive events at any given level will tend to improve health throughout the system, while negative events threaten health throughout the system.

Consider a cigarette smoker (see Outline 8). Initially, smoking damage occurs at the lower biological levels (molecules and cells). Continued smoking will damage tissues, organs and organ systems. Eventually, major health problems can occur (e.g., disability, premature death).

The family is always affected by the illness of one of its members. In turn, communities and organizations will suffer because of increases in time lost from work and increased employee benefit costs. This places a greater cost burden on society, since all healthy workers must spend a portion of their income (e.g., through taxation, insurance payments, out-of-pocket expenses) to pay for the damages caused by the behaviors of smokers.

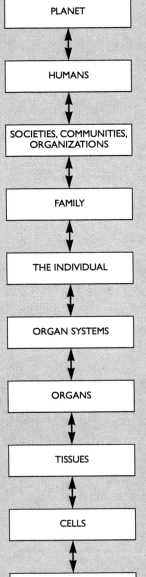

OUTLINE 7

A SYSTEMS HIERARCHY

PLANET

HUMANS

SOCIETIES, COMMUNITIES,
ORGANIZATIONS

FAMILY

THE INDIVIDUAL

ORGAN SYSTEMS

ORGANS

TISSUES

CELLS

MOLECULES

OUTLINE 8

CIGARETTE SMOKING FROM A SYSTEMS PERSPECTIVE

PLANET	Social irresponsibilities in one area tend to encourage irresponsibility in others. In the long run, the planet suffers.
HUMANS	Economic and social costs to society are tremendous.
SOCIETIES, COMMUNITIES, ORGANIZATIONS	Increasing health costs become a burden for society as a whole. Ironically, society subsidizes the tobacco industry and promotes tobacco use via advertising.
FAMILY	Economic costs (for tobacco use, health costs): loss of income if individual dies or cannot work; secondary health threats from tobacco exposure to other family members.
THE INDIVIDUAL	The individual decides to smoke; economic costs to support habit and pay for health problems.
ORGAN SYSTEMS	
ORGANS	Damage to cells, tissues, organs, organ systems as a result of oxygen depletion, and effects of tobacco toxins over time.
TISSUES	
CELLS	
MOLECULES	Damage at the molecular level as a result of tobacco toxins.

Negative events which disturb the system are called *disruptions*. Those which cannot be corrected are of the greatest concern. For example, long-term smoking will eventually cause enough damage to the lungs and other organs that the body cannot repair itself.

The systems view depicts health problems as a sequence of related events. Each level is the object of different disruptions and each provides different opportunities for interventions. In the smoking example, science may eventually be able to design drugs to prevent or correct tobacco damage. Education and smoking cessation programs at both the individual and family level may encourage people not to use tobacco products. Health care costs associated with tobacco use may cause policy development at the society and community levels to discourage tobacco use.

The systems view reminds us that individual behaviors affect the health and well-being of others. Without this view it is easy to believe that our life choices are no one else's business.

A View From the Top — World Health

As we struggle with health care reform, criticize the FDA for its efforts to protect us from questionable products, curse the high costs of medicine, while enjoying the "benefits" of a high-risk lifestyle . . . it is of merit to consider the health of individuals and societies from a broader perspective.

We take for granted the advantages which we have. We are the wealthiest and most educated country in the world. We have available to us freedoms that are inconceivable to people in some parts of the world. And yet, we are not the healthiest nation in the world by any standard. But then, our many freedoms include the freedoms to live unwisely, to value profits far more than health care and to sacrifice the environment if there is a profit to be made.

Health Care in the World

In Ethiopia there is one doctor for every 58,490 people. In the U.S., there is one doctor for every 250 people. About 40% of the world has no access to health care (yet consider how we take our health and health care for granted here in the U.S.).

The cost of providing primary health care worldwide was estimated in 1989 to be about $50 billion each year. Sounds like a lot? It is about 67% of what the world spends on tobacco products each year and about 7% of worldwide military expenditures. There is a soldier for every 43 people in the world, but only one physician for every 1000 people. And, it is estimated that three million vaccines could be purchased for the cost of a single fighter plane. Any questions about where our priorities are?

Suffer the Little Children . . .

In Algeria, 10% of babies die before their first birthday. In some developing countries, as many as 80% of children never survive childhood. So, there is another "Hiroshima" every three days in terms of child deaths in the world.

Water, Water Everywhere . . . And Not a Drop to Drink

About 25,000 people die every day due to unclean drinking water. In Bangladesh, about 60% of rural children have cholera, typhoid, parasites, or other diseases transmitted by their water.

An Ounce of Prevention . . .

In some developing countries it is estimated that 5 million children under the age of five die of diarrhea diseases each year. Death from diarrhea is caused by dehydration and the loss of essential fluids and salts from the body. These deaths could be prevented by the use of inexpensive oral fluid preparations that restore fluids and electrolytes to the body while the diarrhea stops naturally.

More than 26 million people have been blinded by preventable or treatable eye diseases (e.g., cataracts), including those that are prevented by adequate daily doses of Vitamin A. In fact, malnutrition is the most common cause of blindness in some parts of the world.

After age five, the most common causes of death in both industrialized and nonindustrialized countries are heart disease, cancers and accidents. And, the majority of premature deaths are preventable with appropriate lifestyle changes (e.g., diet, exercise, safety and public health interventions, no smoking). Health officials estimate that tobacco will soon be the leading cause of cancer in the world. In the United Kingdom, each day one person will be murdered, six people will be killed in traffic accidents and 250 will die of tobacco-related diseases for every 1000 adult males who smoke.

The American Way

Worldwide, our lifestyles (including our risk behaviors) are being copied as fast as the media can transmit our ideas, images and profit schemes to these other countries. Our lifestyle influences are a major cause for the increases in cancer, sexually-transmitted diseases, and accidents in developing countries.

The systems view reminds us that our health and lifestyle decisions can have a far reaching impact. For example, consider the problems and issues which both individuals and societies will have to address in the near future:

- Accidents
- Population growth
- Hunger
- Childhood diseases
- Sanitation
- Infant health
- Demographic trends
- Health
- Teen health
- Malnutrition
- Disability
- Urbanization
- Men's health
- Drug use (legal and illegal)
- Water supplies (safe)
- Occupational health
- Exercise
- Alcohol use
- Risk behaviors
- Industrialization
- Contagious diseases
- Sexual/reproductive
- Insurance coverage
- Life expectancy
- Diet and nutrition
- Unemployment
- Maternal health
- Disability
- Violence
- Mental health (including stress)
- Employee health
- Women's health

6. PASS THE ASPIRIN — SELF-CARE IN AMERICA

"A healing attitude is not superficial. It involves a deep inner knowledge that we are not victims of the world. Rather, we have the authority to respond to adversity in any way we choose. By taking responsibility for our health and for our entire lives, we gain a sense of mastery over what we previously perceived as beyond our control."

— Richard Carlson and Benjamin Shield

Health Care Decision Making

When illness occurs there are a number of different reactions possible. We can simply tolerate the problem, or we can opt for one of the domains of health care in our society: popular, folk, or professional (see Outline 9).

Our choice of any of one of these alternatives is based upon many factors (see Outline 10). The most common initial response is, of course, self-care. Even if we turn to the folk or professional alternative, we still depend heavily upon self-care.

When we engage with health professionals for treatment this alternative involves certain "negotiations" including possible differences in beliefs, attitudes, values, and expectations. If we disagree with health professionals we are less likely to follow their advice. For example, parents sometimes ask pharmacists to recommend cold products for infants or small children. Unfortunately, these products are usually inappropriate for young children, and for this reason, the pharmacist may advise the parents to take the child to a physician. Yet, the parents often insist on using a self-care product anyway. The negotiation in this case involves a belief on the part of the parents that a self-care product is adequate (and a doctor's fee is avoided) versus a belief by the pharmacist that the child should be seen by a physician. A major role of health professionals is to think and act objectively in our behalf so that the best possible decisions are made. There's an old saying that goes:

He who treats himself . . .
has a fool for a physician!

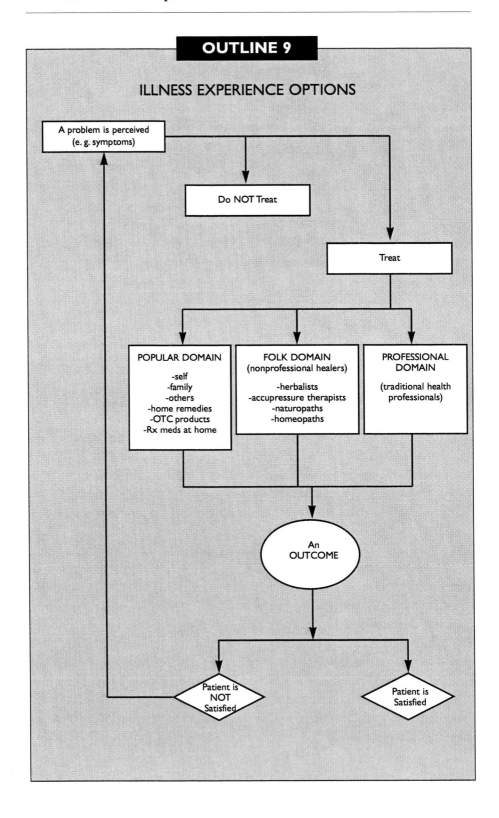

OUTLINE 9

ILLNESS EXPERIENCE OPTIONS

A problem is perceived
(e. g. symptoms)

Do NOT Treat

Treat

POPULAR DOMAIN

-self
-family
-others
-home remedies
-OTC products
-Rx meds at home

FOLK DOMAIN
(nonprofessional healers)

-herbalists
-accupressure therapists
-naturopaths
-homeopaths

**PROFESSIONAL
DOMAIN**

(traditional health
professionals)

An
OUTCOME

Patient is
NOT
Satisfied

Patient is
Satisfied

OUTLINE 10

FACTORS WHICH IMPACT OUR HEALTH BELIEFS AND DECISIONS

Cultural Influences

Demographic Characteristics

- Aging population
- Birth rates (e.g., increasing in lower class; decreasing in middle and upper class)
- Gender differences (e.g., more women entering work force)

The Economy

- Health care costs
- Standards of living

Miscellaneous

- Cultural assumptions and beliefs (e.g., about health problems and therapy)

Health Care Options

Professional Health Care Facilities and Services

- Availability
- Distribution

Alternate Approaches to Health Care

- Awareness of self-care options
- Awareness and acceptance of folk domain options (e.g., herbalism, homeopathy)

Individuals

Attitudes and Beliefs

- Acceptance of available options
- Belief in prevention and planning for health and health care
- Emphasis on health and fitness
- Faith
- Frustrations with and distrust of professional health care
- Perceived benefits, barriers, costs for taking action
- Perceived seriousness of the problem
- Self-responsibility for health

OUTLINE 10 cont'd

❦ Values (including changing values due to cultural influence)
Education and Sophistication

❦ Availability of health information
❦ Awareness of available options
❦ Educational level and sophistication
❦ Media messages (e.g., advertisements)
❦ Quality and quantity of information available
❦ Quality and frequency of interactions with health professionals
❦ Symptom interpretation
❦ Understanding about health and health problems

Products

❦ Availability and type of new products
❦ Competition
❦ Effectiveness and safety
❦ Packaging and labeling

Symptom Experience

How the Symptoms are Perceived

❦ Accuracy of diagnosis by others (e.g., family, friends, co-workers)
❦ Accuracy of self-diagnosis
❦ Denial
❦ Seriousness
❦ Competing interpretations of the symptoms

Disruptive Nature of the Symptoms

❦ Disruption of social functioning (e.g., family, work, leisure activities)
❦ Frequency of disruptions
❦ Persistence of symptoms
❦ Tolerance of symptoms

Often it is difficult for us to think and act objectively in our own behalf despite our belief to the contrary. There are times when we need a professional who can make an objective diagnosis and recommendations. Some people "doctor hop" (i.e., they search for a doctor who will tell them what they want to hear and prescribe whatever drugs they want). This is NOT objective health care.

Factors Which Affect Our Decision Making

Our decision to choose self-care or to opt for other options is affected by many factors. A brief consideration is helpful in our efforts to better understand why we make the choices that we do.

We the People

Self-care practices are affected by the characteristics of our population. The number of elderly has been increasing since 1900, while the number of individuals 19 and under has declined. This is significant, since health problems tend to vary with age. For example, adults under 55 are more likely to experience minor cuts and scratches, colds, sinus problems, acne, lip and dental problems than those who are over 55 years of age. Older adults on the other hand are more likely to experience arthritis; rheumatism; problems involving the back, ears, feet; and sleeping difficulties. Resorting to self-care is directly related to these age/problem factors. Furthermore, it is very clear that advertising and promotional practices, as well as the availability of certain types of products, recognize these differences.

Another factor of some concern involves birth rates. Population growth continues to increase in lower classes in this country, while it has leveled off or is declining for the middle and upper classes. This may be increasingly important in years to come, especially regarding health care cost concerns. This trend will cause people in the middle and upper classes to bear an increasing health cost burden for the lower class. The implications of this trend for health care programs of the future and for decision-making can only be speculated.

Gender is also an important cultural consideration. Women are more likely to make medication purchases for the family, contact health professionals and to use nonprescription drug products. Women are often responsible for family health care matters, especially regarding care for children. They are also popular targets for advertising (e.g., the "woman's gentle laxative") which may influence choice-making.

Moreover, men and women report different problems for which self-medication may be used. This is often a reflection of career choices and cultural roles. For example, women are more likely to report problems associated with emotional stresses (e.g., anxiety, stomach and indigestion, headaches, fatigue, sleep), arthritis, and lifestyle (e.g., the lips and skin, weight control). Men are more likely to report problems associated with physical injury (e.g., muscle aches and pains, minor cuts and scratches), colds, and lack of attention to personal care (e.g., dental problems). It is interesting to note that women begin having physical examinations on a regular basis during their teen years. These examinations are related to their reproductive health and continue regularly throughout their reproductive years. Men, on the other hand, may have few regular checkups until middle age, when they typically begin to experience more health problems. So, women in our culture become oriented early in their lives to regular examinations, while men are conditioned to avoid them. These differences also impact decision making related to health care.

The Economy

In general, self-care is less expensive than professional care. Hospital charges, professional fees and costs of other health-related products and services have risen significantly. As a result, we are demanding alternatives which are less expensive.

Four times as many health problems are treated with nonprescription drugs than are taken to physicians, and as much as 95% of all illness episodes are initially treated with some form of self-care. Although 60% of medications purchased by American consumers are nonprescription, these purchases account for less than 2% of U.S. health care expenses. Self-medication is cost-effective. How ironic that at a time when third-party programs (e.g., insurance) are interested in reducing costs, their programs do not encourage self-care efforts.

Self-care also saves time. Traditional health care involves time lost from work, time for physician visits, and time required to obtain prescriptions from a pharmacy. Self-medication can reduce many of these time investments.

Finally, the decision to self-medicate may be largely a matter of convenience. Nonprescription products can be purchased at more than 700,000 locations (e.g., convenience stores, grocery stores, gas stations, pharmacies), as compared to only about 70,000 pharmacies. Even so, the input of a pharmacist can be valuable when needed.

Accessibility / Availability Considerations

The availability of health services and products can influence the health care choices which we make. For example, people may be unwilling to travel long distances to a doctor unless they think that their problem is serious.

We do not have unlimited access to professional care, especially for minor problems. Our demands far exceed the available resources of the health care industry. If only a small percentage of self-medicating consumers were to suddenly seek professional care, the increase in demand would overwhelm the medical system as it currently exists. This could become an important issue in dealing with universal health coverage. Self-care practices discourage the trivial use of health professionals, who can devote their attention to those individuals who have a greater need for professional care.

Attitudes and Beliefs

We may self-medicate to avoid health professionals. For example, children may be afraid they will be given injections; adults may fear threats to their normal lifestyles; we have negative perceptions about some health problems and may actually welcome others, as long as they are not too serious (e.g., an ulcer as the hallmark of the "hard working, Type A" personality). And of course, there are concerns about expenses. Regardless of the reasons, self-medication allows us to avoid some anxieties and frustrations. While this can represent a naive or even hazardous viewpoint, it is a very real component of our beliefs about health.

In more recent years, we have all seen more TV shows which promote health and fitness (at least to the extent that you are willing to buy the product which they are promoting). Some religious groups will deny professional care for their followers, even if it means death for a patient that could have been saved.

Our decisions to select professional care, self-care or a folk option also reflect our frustrations and distrust of health professionals, as well as the barriers and benefits which we perceive to exist. Or, we may opt for one domain or another based upon how serious we believe the problem to be.

Education and Sophistication

It is interesting to note that there were over 5,000 self-help books available in American bookstores by 1980 (a reflection of our preoccupation with health matters). Although the accuracy of many of these books is questionable, our interest in health care is very real. And, many people have indeed become more knowledgeable regarding the care of health problems.

Most of us have gathered bits and pieces of information from health professionals, advertisements, friends, relatives, books, magazines and a variety of other sources. However, the *accuracy* of medical and health information available to consumers can vary considerably depending upon the source.

One study of 1,233 Americans, for example, indicated that 35% use the *Physicians' Desk Reference* (PDR) for information about drugs. Even though the PDR is not written for consumers, it can be found in most major bookstores. It is important to realize, however, that one can acquire information without understanding and this can lead to poor self-care decisions. And while some people have become more informed in the last few decades, there are also those who remain misinformed. For example, many people still believe that antibiotics and cold products can "cure" or prevent a cold. Others believe that a daily bowel movement is required for good health. These examples represent the types of cultural myths which can result in disappointments, frustrations and health care problems.

Misinformation can also cause the inappropriate use or misuse of products. All medications, including self-care products, can be misused (e.g., deliberate misuse, pleasure seeking, or escape from daily stress) and can cause health problems to become worse.

Products

Self-care products are designed to be safe and effective when used appropriately. In reality, however, no drug is *absolutely* safe, and, in fact, can cause significant side effects, mask health problems, or interact in harmful ways with foods, drugs, and laboratory tests. The bottom line is that most self-care products *are relatively safe if used as directed.* Side effects should be minor and predictable so that you can adapt to them.

To varying degrees, nonprescription products have always been effective. Even poorly formulated products can be "successful" if you are treating problems that would improve anyway. Many illnesses have no specific remedies (e.g., the common cold, many allergies). Many patients who see physicians have minor problems which do not actually require professional attention.

As a result of the FDA Review program of over-the-counter (OTC) products, the switch of some prescription products to nonprescription status (see Chapter 33), and changes in federal regulations over the years, nonprescription products have become increasingly effective for self-care.

Symptoms

Most people are simply not trained to accurately diagnose health problems. Diseases can mimic each other, so that potentially serious conditions may be misdiagnosed. We prefer problems that are simple, easy to comprehend and easily treated by self-care efforts. So, if we have symptoms that could be either a cold or pneumonia, we will normally opt for the cold. We must learn to acknowledge the limits of our abilities to self-diagnose and self-treat, as well as the risks of exceeding those limits.

We sometimes delay seeking professional help while we wait to see if the problem will improve or become worse. Similarly, the use of OTC products can mask symptoms that would normally warn us of a more serious problem.

Self-Care

Self-care refers to anything that we do for ourselves or others (e.g., family, friends, co-workers, significant others) to promote or improve health. This can include anything from reading about health to actual health promotion, prevention, traditional and nontraditional medical practices. We like self-care because it allows us to take an active role in our own care or the care of those around us. There is a little "doctor" in all of us. Still, self-care should not be a substitute for professional help when it is needed.

Our demand for self-care is deeply rooted in our society. Threats to our cherished cultural values (e.g., independence) are deeply resented. We often complain that health care professionals have too much control and restrict our access to desirable medications and health products. Yet, we have also entrusted health care professionals with the obligation to ensure public health. So, access to some products and services must be restricted in order to preserve public well-being (including a decrease in health care costs!)

Self-Medication

Self-medication is defined by the Nonprescription Drug Manufacturers Association as:

> The act of properly and responsibly treating ourselves with nonprescription medications in the management of easily recognizable conditions that can be safely treated without professional help.

Nonprescription products, as defined, do not require a prescription and are usually used without medical supervision. However, you should consult a health professional (e.g., your pharmacist) anytime you have a question about the appropriate selection and use of a nonprescription product.

On the average Americans experience 2 to 3 problems each week for which self-care can offer some benefit. About 90% of us report being "a little under the weather" at some time during each month.

We learn self-medication practices early in our lives (e.g., the majority of children under age two have been given a nonprescription drug at least once). Most of us have nonprescription drugs at home and we may supplement prescription therapy with self-prescribed products. We tend to opt for self-care when we think that the problem is not serious, or if health professionals are not needed.

Nonprescription Drugs

Nonprescription drugs are also known as *over-the-counter* (OTC) or *nonlegend* products. Historically, they have also been referred to as "patent medicines" or as "proprietary medicines," although both of these terms are now obsolete.

No one actually knows how many OTC products are available to us. In part, this is because some manufacturers and health fraud promoters distribute "health" products without approval of the Food and Drug Administration (FDA). Some authorities estimate that there may be as many as 600,000 OTC products (although 300,000 is the number quoted most often) manufactured by 12,000 firms. Despite the large number of products, however, there are only about 800 active ingredients in all of them. So, there are many duplications.

Nonprescription drugs are considered to be safe and effective as long as people read and follow label directions and warnings. Outline 11 summarizes the pros and cons associated with self-care and self-medication. This outline can help you make realistic and objective self-care decisions.

OUTLINE 11

THE PROS AND CONS OF SELF-MEDICATING

PROS	CONS
1. OTC medications are relatively safe.	1. There are many potent OTC products available today.
	2. Dangerous substances may be introduced into home and society.
	3. Potential for adverse drug reactions.
	4. May compromise the health of the individual, family or society.
2. Consumers are better educated today regarding their health care needs.	5. Misinformation and inaccurate beliefs regarding medications, therapy and health care are still prevalent.
	6. Inaccurate clinical assessments by the consumer.
	7. Inappropriate selection and use of OTC products.
	8. Misuse or abuse of OTC products.
	9. It is difficult for any individual to think and act objectively in his/her own behalf or for significant others.
	10. Inappropriate use of medical references can lead to poor self-care decisions (e.g., PDR, which is available in most major bookstores).
3. OTC medications are effective for many conditions.	11. Self-care practices may weaken consumer trust in health care professionals by decreasing demand for high quality care.
4. Reduced costs (e.g., time and money)	12. Competition by OTC manufacturers in an aggressive market environment can actually increase the costs of OTC products.
	13. Inappropriate self-care practices can result in an increase in health care problems, and ultimately, in costs.
5. Represent a form of health care that is relatively convenient and available.	14. Convenience and availability can discourage consumers from seeking professional care at times when it is truly needed.
6. Reinforces consumer	15. Overconfident and uninformed consumers

---

OUTLINE II cont'd

responsibility for self and others.

7. People have an innate desire to self-medicate.

8. Self-care is perceived to be an inalienable right.

9. The patient is more aware of his/her body and how it feels than can usually be communicated to a health professional.

10. Allows for the avoidance of disappointments, anxieties, suspicions or concerns regarding health care professionals and the health care industry.

11. Reduced requirement for professional manpower.

are often willing to accept responsibility for self-care at times when it is not truly in their best health interests.

16. Demands for self-care products and practices sometimes far exceeds reasonable therapeutic expectations for the products which are available.

17. How an individual feels does not always correlate accurately to the individual's actual health status.

18. Individuals may avoid health care professionals at times when they truly need to be clinically evaluated.

The Folk Domain — Alternate Approaches to Health

During the past three decades there has been an increase in alternate health care approaches. This is particularly true regarding the Folk Domain, as well as approaches which have been legitimized by traditional health care (e.g., holism, wellness, midwives, natural childbirth). People have come to realize that health information and services need not be restricted to physicians, especially since health professionals are not always able to produce "health."

The Business of Self-Care

Ours is a free-enterprise culture. The manufacturers of OTC products compete with each other with an intensity and aggressiveness which is not seen anywhere else in the world. This creates some concern regarding ethical drug promotion practices.

Advertising

It's estimated that the average American is exposed to 1,500 advertisements each day (e.g., television, radio, billboards and signs, newspapers, magazines and other publications). Advertising is expensive and increases the cost of self-care products. So, the most heavily advertised products tend to be the most expensive.

Advertisers insist that their efforts offer advantages to the consumer. According to this view, advertisements increase our awareness of products, explain product benefits, stimulate comparisons, encourage us to select and use products wisely and stimulate the development of new and better products.

Despite this endorsement, many advertisements are deceptive and inaccurate. These include efforts to conceal the identity of active ingredients (e.g., "the ingredient that 4 out of 5 doctors recommend"); the creation of new markets by creating new "diseases" (e.g., the "blahs," the "stubborn cold," "combination skin"); misuse of science to suggest that one product is better than another (e.g., the inappropriate use of charts and graphs, distortion of the results of legitimate studies), the association of products with product-based "health agencies" (e.g., the "Sineaid Society," the "Ponds Institute"); and unjustified therapeutic claims.

It is reasonable to assume that irresponsible advertising practices can result in confusion about products and encourage drug misuse. For example, is it possible that children might learn inappropriate drug taking behaviors from watching television?

Moreover, as a result of staying abreast of one's competition, drug manufacturers have become preoccupied with the development of "me-too" products, rather than the development of new and different products. Assume, for example, that there are 400,000 OTC products available in the U.S. Since there are only about 800 OTC ingredients, then there is an average of 500 products per ingredient! It would appear that the manufacturers are spending a great deal more effort and money on the development of new product packages and advertising campaigns, than they are on the development of truly new products.

In any case, the potential impact of advertising (in particular, TV ads) on self care decisions emphasizes a need for control. Consider the fact that the average person watches about 7 hours of television each day, which reaches 99% of all U.S. households. Space and time restrictions limit the ability of advertising to serve the same purpose as product labels, and it would appear that advertisers have ignored many of their ethical obligations to the public.

Labels

OTC labels should provide the right kind of information so that you can properly select and use products without the advice of a health professional.   And in fact, labeling language is an important factor regarding whether or not a drug product can be given OTC status.

FDA and manufacturer officials insist that current label language is adequate for consumers to make appropriate decisions. This view is supported by FDA regulations which require that labeling must be "stated in terms that are likely to be read and understood by the average consumer, including those of low comprehension under customary conditions of purchase and use." In other words we should have no problems in selecting and using nonprescription products and the advice of health professionals should not be needed for such decisions.

However, studies indicate that people do have difficulty reading labels (e.g., because of inappropriate color combinations used on labels, small print size, or because the language is simply difficult to understand).   Many labels are written at a ninth grade reading level or higher (some are written at a college level).   But, the average consumer reads at about a sixth to eighth grade level and 20% of American adults are reading below a fifth-grade level.   Other studies show that people may misinterpret labels, and in fact, it may be impossible to write error-free labels.

Cultural Responsibilities and Roles

Successful self-care requires responsibility on the part of all concerned.   The three major components of self-care are industry, consumers and health professionals.   Among health professionals, pharmacists are most frequently involved with the selection and use of self-care products.   So, it is appropriate to consider the responsibilities which have been proposed for these groups.

Industry

There is no doubt that the OTC industry will continue to provide us with new products (and especially "new" versions of old products).

These should be named, designed and packaged in a responsible manner. The product name issue is significant since we are easily misled by names which sound alike (e.g., Tylenol #3, which contains codeine versus Anacin 3, which does not). In a similar way, ethical (i.e., non-deceptive) and responsible advertising and promotional practices should be the norm.

It would be helpful if manufacturers would place an identifying trademark on all of their tablets and capsules. This would be useful in cases of accidental poisonings. Also, it would help you to know when you are buying a brand name versus a generic product.

Labeling should be written in such a way that virtually everyone can select and use these products appropriately. Packaging should reduce the risks for accidental poisoning in children and tampering and should insure stability of the contents under normal home storage conditions.

Consumers

We all have a responsibility to read and follow label directions, to communicate with health professionals regarding any questions which we have about appropriate use and to avoid misuse or abuse of all drug products.

Pharmacists

The profession of pharmacy is attempting to expand the role of pharmacists in providing information and health counseling. Pharmacies are attempting to position themselves as education centers in their communities. Because pharmacists continually review the drug literature, they are in an ideal position to provide current information on all drug products and to promote safe and effective products and self-care practices.

Pharmacists are the most available of all health professionals. There are more U.S. communities with a pharmacy than any other type of health professional. And, studies have shown that pharmacists are the most trusted of all professionals.

Pharmacists can help to prevent misuse and abuse of self-care products and drug interactions with prescription drugs. Pharmacy record systems help to insure the safe and effective use of all drug products. Also, we will likely see more pharmacy programs which provide various types of patient monitoring and physician referral services, as well as a variety of professional services (e.g., home health care, blood pressure monitoring).

The Future of OTCs

In the future we will have more sophisticated products, more prescription-to-OTC switches, more self-diagnostics and a greater variety of products for older Americans.

New products are forthcoming as a result of biotechnology and many of these will eventually be switched to OTC status. In the long run, OTCs will likely continue to offer safe and effective products that can increase the quality of life for those who use them responsibly.

7. YOUR HEALTH STATUS —
AN EVALUATION

The main purpose of this book is to provide *you* with accurate and up-to-date information concerning health and health care issues. Above all, the book's intent is to provide *you* with a realistic personalized program for a healthy extended lifespan. As we proceed in the book, it will become apparent that to attain a long and healthy life, *you* will have to adopt a lifestyle that *promotes* health and deals with disease in terms of *prevention* on a continued basis and *intervention* when the need arises.

At this point you have an opportunity to determine your relative well being. Over the years health scientists have been able to develop various types of health risk appraisals. These instruments estimate your relative age based upon lifestyle behaviors. For example, a person who is 50 years old and who has a relatively unhealthy lifestyle may have a lifestyle-adjusted age of 60. Yet, a 50-year-old person who has healthy lifestyle behaviors may have a lifestyle-adjusted age of 40.

Health-risk appraisals are based upon data from agencies such as the Centers for Disease Control (CDC) in Atlanta. The CDC has collected data for years about morbidity (disease) and mortality (death), and this information was correlated with lifestyle behaviors. Then, over time it was possible to predict the impact that certain lifestyle behaviors have on the age to which you can expect to live.

The following health-risk appraisal is an instrument which can help you determine your relative well being. It is reprinted with permission from the National Wellness Institute, Inc., Stevens Point, WI. If you wish to receive your personal wellness assessment report, follow the instructions below.

Instructions

1. Print your name and address. An incomplete report cannot be processed. It is important that you complete all questions and record only one answer.

2. Read each question carefully and mark your answers using dark and heavy marks.

3. Erase clearly any answers you change.

4. Sign and date the Questionnaire under the Release of Information section.

5. The accuracy of the Personal Wellness Assessment report that you will receive depends on the accuracy of your answers as well as on the completeness of the Questionnaire that you send in.

6. Tear the Questionnaire along the dotted line, include a $15 processing fee and mail to:

Dr. Leonard Cosmo, M.D.
Director, Wellness Assessment Division
Mancorp Publishing, Inc.
P. O. Box 21492
Tampa, FL 33622

7. Allow 4-6 weeks for processing.

Confidentiality and Use of Information

The information which is obtained will be treated as privileged and confidential and will not be released or revealed to anyone without your expressed written consent. Information will, however, be treated in an aggregate manner to provide group information for research or statistical purposes. The professional/medical staff may contact you for follow-up education.

PLEASE NOTE: The report generated from this questionnaire is an awareness tool only. It is not diagnostic in nature, and is in no way intended to replace the advice of your personal physician. If you have questions about this questionnaire, please contact the Director of the Wellness Assessment Division.

t here

WELLNESS ASSESSMENT QUESTIONNAIRE

Exam Date_____ Soc. Sec. No. _____ - _____ - _____

Last Name _____ First Name _____ M.I._____

Home Address _____

City _____ State _____ Zip _____

1. Sex   ❑ Male   ❑ Female

2. Please mark your ethnic group: (Note: this program is operated in compliance with all laws and regulations regarding Civil Rights. Questions on ethnic origins are asked to gain information on diseases and conditions which may be more common in certain races and ethnic groups.

   ❑ White   ❑ African American   ❑ Hispanic   ❑ Asian

   ❑ American Indian   ❑ Other: specify _____

3. Date of birth: Mo._____ Day _____ Yr _____

4. Height: _____ft _____in.   5. Weight: _____ lbs

6. What is your body frame size?

   ❑ Small   ❑ Medium   ❑ Large

7. What is your marital status?

   ❑ Married   ❑ Widowed   ❑ Separated

   ❑ Divorced   ❑ Single   ❑ Cohabitating

8. Have you ever been diagnosed as having diabetes (or sugar diabetes)?

   ❑ Yes   ❑ No

9. Does your natural mother, father, sister, or brother have diabetes?

   ❑ Yes   ❑ No   ❑ Not sure

10. Did either of your parents die of a heart attack before age 60? If your parents are younger than 60, mark No.

    ❑ Yes, one   ❑ Yes, both   ❑ No   ❑ Not sure

11. Are you now taking medicine for high blood pressure?

    ❑ Yes   ❑ No

12. What is your blood pressure now?

    Systolic (high) _____ Diastolic (low) _____

13. If you do not know your blood pressure, select the answer that best describes your blood pressure.

    ❑ High   ❑ Normal or Low   ❑ Don't know

14. What is your TOTAL cholesterol level (based on a blood test)?

    ❑ _____   ❑ I do not know

15. What is your High Density Lipoprotein (HDL) cholesterol level (based on a blood test)?

    ❑ _____   ❑ I do not know

16. Approximately how many cigars do you usually smoke per day?

    ❑ None   ❑ 1   ❑ 2 - 3   ❑ 4 or more

17. How many pipes of tobacco do you usually smoke per day?

    ❑ None   ❑ 1   ❑ 2 - 3   ❑ 4 or more

18. How many times per day do you usually use smokeless tobacco (chewing tobacco, snuff, pouches, etc.)?

    ❑ None   ❑ 1   ❑ 2 - 3   ❑ 4 or more

19. How would you describe your cigarette smoking habits?

    ❑ Never smoked   ❑ Used to smoke   ❑ Still smoke
    (Go to Question 22.)   (Go to Question 21.)   (Go to Question 20)

t here

✂

20. How many cigarettes per day do you smoke?

   ❑ 1 - 9   ❑ 10 - 19   ❑ 20 - 29   ❑ 30 - 39   ❑ 40 or more

21. As an ex-smoker:
   a. How many years has it been since you smoked regularly? _____
   b. What is the average number of cigarettes per day you smoked in the two years before you quit smoking?

   ❑ 1 - 9   ❑ 10 - 19   ❑ 20 - 29   ❑ 30 - 39   ❑ 40 or more

22. In the next year, how many thousands of miles will you travel by each of the following?

   a. Car/truck/van _____   b. Motorcycle _____

23. On a typical day, how do you usually travel?

   ❑ Walk   ❑ Bicycle
   ❑ Motorcycle   ❑ Sub-compact/Compact car
   ❑ Mid-size/Full-size car ❑ Truck/Van
   ❑ Bus/Subway/Train   ❑ Usually stay at home

24. What percent of the time do you usually buckle your safety belt when driving or riding?

   ❑ High   ❑ Normal or Low   ❑ Never

25. On the average, how close to the speed limit do you usually drive?

   ❑ Within 5 m.p.h. of limit   ❑ 6 - 10 m.p.h. over limit
   ❑ 11 - 15 m.p.h. over limit   ❑ More than 15 m.p.h. over limit

26. How many times in the last month did you drive after drinking too much alcohol or ride when the driver had perhaps too much alcohol to drink?

   ❑ _____   ❑ None

27. On the average, how many alcoholic drinks do you consume in a typical week?

   ❑ _____   ❑ None

FOR MEN ONLY, GO DIRECTLY TO QUESTION 37

FOR WOMEN ONLY

28. At what age did you have your first menstrual period?

29. How old were you when you gave birth to your first child? If you have not had children, mark none).

    ❑ _____   ❑ None

30. How long has it been since your last breast x-ray (mammogram)?

    ❑ less than 1 year   ❑ 1 year   ❑ 2 years

    ❑ 3 or more years   ❑ Never

31. How many women in your natural family (mother and sisters only) have had breast cancer?

32. Have you had a hysterectomy?

    ❑ Yes   ❑ No

33. How long has it been since you had a pap smear test?

    ❑ less than 1 year   ❑ 1 year   ❑ 2 years

    ❑ 3 or more years   ❑ Never

34. How often do you examine your breasts for lumps?

    ❑ Monthly   ❑ Every few months   ❑ Rarely or never

35. About how long has it been since you had your breasts examined by a physician or nurse?

    ❑ less than 1 year   ❑ 1 year   ❑ 2 years

    ❑ 3 or more years   ❑ Never

33. About how long has it been since you had a rectal exam?

    ❑ less than 1 year   ❑ 1 year   ❑ 2 years

    ❑ 3 or more years   ❑ Never

GO TO QUESTION 41

FOR MEN ONLY

37. About how long has it been since you had a rectal or prostate exam?

    ❏ Less than 1 year   ❏ 1 year   ❏ 2 years

    ❏ 3 or more years   ❏ Never

38. Do you know how to properly examine your testes for lumps?

    ❏ Yes   ❏ No   ❏ Not sure

39. How often do you examine your testes for lumps?

    ❏ Monthly   ❏ Once every few months   ❏ Rarely or never

40. About how long has it been since you had your testes examined by a physician or nurse?

    ❏ Less than 1 year   ❏ 1 year   ❏ 2 years

    ❏ 3 or more years   ❏ Never

41. How many times in the last year did you witness or become involved in a violent fight or attack where there was a good chance or a serious injury to someone?

    ❏ 4 or more times ❏ 2 or 3 times ❏ 1 time or never ❏ Not sure

42. Considering your age, how would you describe your overall physical health?

    ❏ Excellent   ❏ Good   ❏ Fair   ❏ Poor

43. In an average week, how may times do you engage in physical activity (exercise or work which lasts at least 20 minutes without stopping and which is hard enough to make you breathe heavier and make your heart beat faster)?

    ❏ Less than 1 time per week   ❏ 1 or 2 times each week

    ❏ At least three times each week

44. If you ride a motorcycle or all-terrain vehicle (ATV), what percent of the time do you wear a helmet?

    ❏ 75 to 100%   ❏ 25 to 74%   ❏ Less than 25%   ❏ Does not apply

45. Do you eat some food every day that is high in fiber, such as whole grain bread, cereal, fresh fruits, or vegetables?

    ❏ Yes   ❏ No

46. Do you eat foods every day that are high in cholesterol or fat, such as fatty meat, cheese, fried foods, or eggs?

    ❏ Yes   ❏ No

47. In general, how satisfied are you with your life?

    ❏ Mostly satisfied   ❏ Partly satisfied   ❏ Not satisfied

48. Have you suffered a personal loss or misfortune in the past year that had a serious impact on your life? (For example, a job loss, or the death of someone close to you).

    ❏ Yes, one serious loss or misfortune   ❏ Yes, two or more

    ❏ No

RELEASE OF INFORMATION

My answers and statements are correct, complete and true to the best of my knowledge and belief. You are authorized to release all data obtained from this questionnaire for processing and forwarding my Wellness Assessment Report.

Signature _____ Date _____

SECTION TWO

Aging

AGING AWARENESS QUIZ

Take the following quiz to see how knowledgeable you are about growing older.

TRUE OR FALSE?

____ 1. If you live long enough, you will eventually become "senile."

____ 2. We Americans have abandoned our elderly.

____ 3. Depression is a serious problem among older people.

____ 4. The number of elderly in our society is growing.

____ 5. Most elderly are self-sufficient.

____ 6. Mental confusion is pretty much unavoidable as we grow older.

____ 7. Our intelligence declines as we grow older.

____ 8. Our ability to perform sexually, as well as our sexual desires, decline with aging.

____ 9. If you have already been smoking for 30 years or more, there really is no reason to quit. The damage is already done.

____ 10. As you grow older, rest more and reduce your activity and exercise levels.

____ 11. Vitamin and mineral supplements are more important as you grow older.

____ 12. After age 50, calcium supplements offer few benefits.

____ 13. Temperature extremes (heat or cold) can be especially dangerous to older people.

____ 14. As you age, you are more likely to be injured in preventable accidents.

____ 15. Women tend to live longer than men.

____ 16. The number of deaths due to heart disease and strokes seems to be declining.

____ 17. We tend to take more medications as we grow older.

____ 18. Medical quacks (products and promoters) are common today and elderly are frequent targets.

____ 19. Our personality tends to change with aging.

____ 20. Vision problems are a common aging problem.

[Answers are found on page 109]

8. AGING

It Is Never Too Late

"It is too late? Ah, nothing is too late
till the tired heart shall cease to palpitate.
Caso learned Greek at eighty; Sophocles
Wrote his grand Oedipus and Simonides
Bore off the prize of verse from his compeers,
When each had numbered more than four-score years ...
Chaucer, at Woodstock with the nightingales,
At sixty wrote the Canterbury Tales;
Goethe at Weimar, toiling to the last,
Completed Faust when eighty years were past.
There were indeed exceptions, but they show
How far the guilt-stream of our youth may flow
Into the arctic regions of our lives . . .
For age is opportunity no less
Than youth itself, though in another dress . . ."

- - Longfellow

What does it mean to grow old in America? What causes aging? Will we ever be able to live to be 200? 400?

These are some of the questions that people ask about aging. And as more people reach old age, our questions seem evermore to reflect an optimism that science will someday discover the elusive *fountain of youth.*

In fact, there is reason for optimism, although it may not be exactly identical to what most people seem to be searching. Many elderly are quite active, pursuing hobbies, interests and even new careers after retirement. Middle-aged and even younger people often look forward to retirement as a new beginning in their lives. Despite the bad press associated with aging, the fact is many elderly are quite healthy and many more are able to live quality lives in spite of diseases and impairments.

Nevertheless, America is an energetic, youth-oriented society that is preoccupied with vigor and beauty. As we have discovered that it is possible for more people to reach old age, we have also become increasingly preoccupied with extending our lifespan with the use of medicine to achieve this objective. It is ironic that the miracles of modern medicine which have allowed more people to reach old age have also generated unrealistic demands upon medicine as an antidote for our unhealthy lifestyle choices.

We hear it said often that "people are living longer today" than they did at the turn of the Century. Yet, this is not entirely true. What has happened is more of a mathematical phenomenon than an actual age-extension fact. To truly comprehend this circumstance, we must appreciate the difference between the *absolute age* lifespan versus the *average age* lifespan to which people can expect to live.

The absolute age (i.e., the highest age to which humans can live) has not changed a great deal for thousands of years. And in fact, there is little evidence that the absolute age for humans has ever really changed throughout history. The Bible mentions people who lived to be 70 years old (i.e., "three score and ten"), and in all likelihood, there were many who lived far beyond that. Most of us today cannot expect to live more than a century, even if we live our lives wisely.

Legends and rumors abound regarding certain groups of peoples around the world who, supposedly, live to be exceptionally old. In particular, there are three groups with members who supposedly live to be 150. These consist of a group in the Vilcabamba region of southern Ecuador, the Hunzukuts in Pakistan and the Georgian Republic of Russia. The explanations for their longevity have included heredity, an exceptionally healthy diet, hard work and a vigorous sex life. Yet, careful review of the facts indicate that these people may not actually live longer than anyone else! For example, the Hunzukuts in Pakistan have no written language, and therefore, no birth records, and a church fire destroyed important records of the people of Vilcabamba. Even so, intensive studies of the evidence and records (e.g., marriage records) available seems to clearly indicate that none of these individuals are older than 100.

A lack of reliable birth records and exaggeration is also thought to account for the reported old ages of the Soviet Georgians. And, in this case, there has been an additional motive . . . draft dodging! It appears that many Russians used the records of their fathers in order to avoid military service during World War I and the Russian Revolutionary War by reason of old age. Eventually, these "remarkable" individuals were identified as "heroes" of the Soviet Union (i.e., as examples of the life-prolonging effects of Communism). The attention this brought also increased tourism to the area, which provided yet another reason to continue the masquerade. Exaggeration is a common problem, especially when people become the object of attention.

But what about our trend here in America for an increasing average age? The answer is found in the triumphs of both modern medicine and public health. In the early part of the 20th Century there was a much higher infant mortality rate and a much higher rate of mothers who died while giving birth. Many infectious diseases were also uncontrolled at that time. So, with more women and children dying at younger ages, there were fewer people reaching old age. Mathematically, this means that the average age to which people could expect to live was reduced.

Many of the diseases of children and young adults at the turn of the century were caused by sanitation problems (e.g., contaminated water). Public health measures improved waste disposal and water supplies, as well as food supplies (e.g., milk). The result was an almost instant decline in the incidence of many disease-related deaths. Since the 1930s medicine has discovered more and more antibiotics which also served to extend life. Finally, over time, surgical and medical techniques reduced the risk of death during childbirth.

The result of all of this medical progress was that more people survived childhood and young adulthood and therefore reached old age, even though the absolute age to which people could expect to live had not really changed at all. Mathematically, the average age increased and many people interpreted these advances as proof that decades were added to our lifespan. In fact, this is not an accurate perception.

Nevertheless, medicine has certainly improved the quality of life of older Americans. Moreover, while it is not possible to actually cure many of our chronic diseases, medicine has been able to make them more tolerable. Finally, never lose hope that medicine will one day be able to discover ways in which to add years to our absolute lifespan.

Aging: Just What Is It Anyway?

Actually, no one really knows the answer to that question. However, there is much that we do know. Aging is technically called the *period of senescence*; that is, a complex process that is associated with the passage of time. With aging, certain predictable changes occur in our bodies, many of which are quite visible. Naturally, we tend to view aging in terms of these visible changes (e.g., gray hair, wrinkles), and there is no limit to the products promoted to help us avoid these visible changes. Some advertisers even boast that their products have "anti-aging" properties! (Don't invest your life savings just yet!)

A more accurate position is to consider aging as a normal part of our life cycle that is affected by many influences, such as heredity, stresses and strains, injuries, infections and disease, immunologic changes, nutritional deficiencies, metabolic disturbances, neglect and abuse, lifestyles and behaviors, and environments in which we live. Even though heredity is an important factor in the aging process, it appears to be less important after age 70.

On the other hand, there is a strong correlation between lifespan and lifestyles, habits and personal actions that favor survival. This is good news, since it suggests that we can play a significant role in both our quality of life and our quantity of lifespan if we live our lives in healthy ways (remember Hygeia?).

Still, aging is not well defined and appears to have no single cause. People grow older at different rates and at different ages. Stanley Holt, a parent of one of the authors, did not turn gray until he was in his 80s. Yet, we have all known other individuals who turned gray at early ages.

Aging and Disease

In the U.S., because we are an energetic and youth-oriented culture, many of us associate aging with the development of chronic diseases and an inability to engage in youthful activities. This association is so strong for most of us that we regard disease as an unavoidable consequence of aging. The good news is that this is an inaccurate exaggeration.

Disease involves disorders in body functioning that may occur within a broad age range. Aging involves changes that are related solely to the passage of time. Age-related changes and disease-related changes are biologically different. In order to better understand aging, it is important for us to separate the effects of aging from the effects of disease. Unfortunately, the effects of aging and disease are intertwined in such a way that they are difficult to untangle. Some changes related to aging are also involved in some diseases. Consequently, some changes which we now view as normal aging may eventually come to be viewed as a disease of some type. And, the physiological, social and psychological effects of aging and disease are even more highly intermingled. For example, natural declines in hearing, vision and balance can increase the likelihood of falls and injury. Moreover, both aging and disease can cause recovery to be delayed.

It is true, of course, that older people are more likely to be affected by chronic illnesses than by acute illnesses and are more likely to have disabilities. Even so, however, studies indicate that many elderly do not suffer severe restrictions in their abilities to get around in the community, and this includes creative adaptations and a tolerance for some inconveniences and discomforts.

Studies have also shown correlations between income and disabilities among elderly. People with higher income may be less likely to have disabilities than those with lower income. These types of studies are difficult to interpret, since chronic illness can result in

OUTLINE 12

MAJOR CAUSES OF DEATH FOR 1900 AND 1993

1900	%	1993	%
Pneumonia & Influenza	12	Heart*	38
Tuberculosis	11	Cancer*	22
Heart*	8	Stroke*	8
Stomach	8	Accidents*	5
Stroke*	7	Lung Diseases*	4
Kidney	5	Pneumonia & Influenza	4
Accidents*	5	Diabetes	3
Early Infancy	5	Suicide*	2
Cancer*	4	Liver (Cirrhosis)*	2
Diphtheria	3	Arteriosclerosis*	2
Typhoid	2	Homicide*	1

Summary

Infectious Diseases	28	Infectious Diseases	4
Lifestyle Diseases (*)	24	Lifestyle Diseases (*)	84

costs to the individual, and having a chronic illness may decrease one's financial resources. Individuals with lower incomes are more likely to have impaired vision, high blood pressure, arteriosclerosis, lung diseases and heart diseases. In part, this circumstance may reflect an inability to pay for medicines or health care. Interestingly, however, arthritis does not appear to be related to income levels.

Causes of death are also helpful to our understanding of aging, and for improving our health. Outline 12 summarizes information

OUTLINE 13

IMPACT OF VARIOUS FACTORS ON LIFESPAN[1]

Factor	Impact on Lifespan (years)
1. Medicine: Declines in childhood diseases	+ 15
2. Ideal blood Lipoprotein levels	+ 10
3. Heredity-1: Both mother and father lived to age 90	+ 7
4. Living in the country (instead of the city)	+ 5
5. Being married (instead of single, widowed, divorced)	+ 5
6. Heredity-2: 4 Grandparents who lived to be 80	+ 4
7. Heredity-3: Father lived to age 90	+ 4
8. Heredity-4: Both mother and father lived to age 80	+ 4
9. Heredity-5: Mother lived to age 90	+ 3
10. Heredity-6: 2 Grandparents who lived to be 80	+ 2
11. Heredity-7: Mother or father lived to age 80	+ 2
12. Average blood Lipoprotein levels	0
13. Heredity-8: Mother or father died by age 60	- 1
14. Heredity-9: Both mother and father died by age 60	- 2
15. Being 25 - 35% overweight	- 4
16. Being 45% overweight	- 7
17. Smoking-1 (1 pack of cigarettes / day)	- 7
18. High blood Lipoprotein levels	- 7
19. Being 55% overweight	- 11
20. Smoking-2 (2 packs of cigarettes / day)	- 12
21. Being 67% overweight	- 15
22. Highest Lipoprotein levels	- 15

1. See reference 8.

regarding deaths in 1900 and in 1993. The percentages are estimates, but allow us to make important observations. Note the tremendous decline in deaths due to infections and the tremendous increase in deaths associated with lifestyles and the environments in which we live. This emphasizes the impact which lifestyle and behavior changes can have in promoting health if we choose for them to have such an impact.

Outline 13 summarizes various factors which seem to be correlated with longevity. It is not possible to alter hereditary factors such as the age to which parents lived. However, it is possible to make healthy lifestyle choices which can offset the negative impact of some of the other factors. Note that at least 12 of the factors in Outline 13 (55% of them!) CAN be affected by dietary, exercise and medication interventions.

CASE STUDY

LIFE EXTENSION USING OUTLINE 13

Sylvia is a 39-year-old, married librarian living in a small Midwestern town. Her parents are still alive at ages 67 and 68. Sylvia's maternal grandmother is still alive at 91, but her maternal grandfather died at 59. Her paternal grandparents died in a train accident when they were in their fifties. Sylvia is slightly overweight at 5'4" and 139 pounds and she is down to one pack of cigarettes a day. On her last physical, her Lipoprotein level was in the average range. Applying this information to the list in Outline 13 yields the following.

Factor		Plus	Minus
1.	Medicine	15	
2.	Ideal Lipoprotein		
3.	Heredity 1		
4.	Country Living	5	
5.	Married	5	
6.	Heredity 2		
7.	Heredity 3		
8.	Heredity 4		
9.	Heredity 5	3	
10.	Heredity 6		
11.	Heredity 7	2	
12.	Average Lipoprotein		
13.	Heredity 8		1
14.	Heredity 9		
15.	Overweight 1		4
16.	Overweight 2		
17.	Smoking 1		7
18.	High Lipoprotein		
19.	Overweight 3		
20.	Smoking 2		
21.	Overweight 4		
22.	Highest Lipoprotein		
	Total	**+30**	**-12**

CASE STUDY cont'd

Net gain   30 - 12 = 18

Although Sylvia cannot change any of the heredity factors, note that if she stops smoking, loses ten pounds and acheives ideal Lipoprotein levels, she can expect to add 21 years to her lifespan.

On the next page, use Outline 13 and the Case Study above to determine if years can be added to your lifespan through changes in lifestyle.

OUTLINE 14

ESTIMATE YOUR LIFESPAN EXTENSION

	Factor	Plus	Minus
1.	Medicine	_____	_____
2.	Ideal Lipoprotein	_____	_____
3.	Heredity 1	_____	_____
4.	Country Living	_____	_____
5.	Married	_____	_____
6.	Heredity 2	_____	_____
7.	Heredity 3	_____	_____
8.	Heredity 4	_____	_____
9.	Heredity 5	_____	_____
10.	Heredity 6	_____	_____
11.	Heredity 7	_____	_____
12.	Average Lipoprotein	_____	_____
13.	Heredity 8	_____	_____
14.	Heredity 9	_____	_____
15.	Overweight 1	_____	_____
16.	Overweight 2	_____	_____
17.	Smoking1	_____	_____
18.	High Lipoprotein	_____	_____
19.	Overweight 3	_____	_____
20.	Smoking 2	_____	_____
21.	Overweight 4	_____	_____
22.	Highest Lipoprotein	_____	_____
	Total	_____	_____

Net   _____ – _____ = _____

Current age   _____

Can you extend your lifespan?

9. AGING THEORIES

"To live forever . . .
acquire a chronic disease and take care of it."

— Griffin's Law, John Peers

Aging is a normal part of the human condition. Even so, there is a great deal about aging that is poorly understood. Much of our attention involves ways in which we can slow the aging process. Advances in medicine will continue to address chronic diseases more effectively, so that some years will be added to the human lifespan as a result. Yet, as we indicated earlier, there are likely natural limits to the length of time that can be added to the human lifespan. Similarly, there appear to be no natural limits to our incessant drive to discover "fountains of youth."

While we await such discoveries, it is of merit to consider several of the more popular theories of aging that have been offered. These serve to enlighten us about the aging process. And, they help to explain our interests in many of the anti-aging medications and viewpoints which are being promoted to the public.

The Theories of Aging

Some theories of aging have achieved popular status on television talk shows, radio shows and popular magazines. For example, the theory that antioxidants can reduce aging is consistent with our search for *"magic bullet cures"* for aging. Yet, there are actually many other theories that have also been promoted. None of them can totally explain the process of aging, but each makes a contribution to our understanding. We can say that aging is the result of numerous processes acting together, rather than a specific cause. Ultimately as we increase our understanding of aging and the aging process, a unified theory will emerge that will enable us to:

- Modify the aging process
- Develop anti-aging drugs
- Extend our lifespan

- ❧ Provide for a better quality of life

- ❧ Formulate a different social concept of aging

- ❧ Gain a more clear understanding of disease as it relates to aging

Accumulation of Wastes Theory

The body often produces certain substances which exceed the amount required for the formation of tissues. This excess is broken down and excreted in the urine and feces. "Waste theories" suggest that we age because our cells, organs and systems are slowly poisoned or hampered in their function as a result of the accumulation of these waste products. However, many examples of waste accumulation are thought to be more a symptom of aging, rather than a cause. While these theories seem to explain some of the "nuisance" aspects of aging, they do not adequately explain the true causes of degenerative diseases.

Aging Center Theory

Some authorities believe that there may be a center in the brain that serves as a control center for hormonal activity in the body. This center may receive signals from the brain and major body systems which stimulate it to regulate hormonal secretions in various ways. As the signals to this control center change over time, the hormonal response may change as well. This outcome would explain some of the observed changes associated with aging.

Auto-Immunity Theories

A number of the leading causes of death (e.g., cancer, diabetes, heart diseases) have been linked (although loosely in some cases) to auto-immune disorders as well as degenerative diseases (e.g., arthritis). Some aging theories argue that this production of inappropriate antibodies tends to increase with age and are therefore related to death from disease. This theory is an attractive one to scientists because it can be experimentally tested and lead to agents that could modify the aging process. Even so, the theory may also involve symptoms of disease more than causes.

One variation of this theory emphasizes the Thymus Gland, which plays an important role in the normal immune process. This gland tends to atrophy after sexual maturity, which could be related to a decrease in certain immune responses with age, as well as to an increased susceptibility to auto-immune processes and cancer.

Cellular Aging Theory

A common misconception of aging is that the cells of the body begin to die at a faster rate than they are produced. Consequently, this process continues until there are no longer enough cells to function and death occurs.

Although it is true that some cells seldom or never reproduce (e.g., brain, central nervous system, muscle), most cells continue to reproduce themselves. Theoretically this would enable an individual to live indefinitely.

It is also argued that cells may age in the sense that they reproduce only a finite number of times. In time, they may reproduce imperfectly or "errors" may occur in the reproductive process. Such errors in cell reproduction might impair normal cell function and division and accelarate the aging process.

Counterpart Theory

This theory suggests that certain processes that are adaptive for younger ages may actually have a negative impact in older people. For example, some cells of the central nervous system are not replaced when they die. In the brain this allows humans to have an enhanced memory and learning ability, which increases our chances for survival. However, this fact would also prevent indefinite functioning and could result in disease, since damaged cells would not be replaced.

Cross-Linkage Theories

Cross-linkage theories of aging are based on research which suggests that proteins and nucleic acids necessary for metabolism lose their ability to maintain good health because of the development of linkages that join them together. This "cross-linking" then may occur as a result of normal biochemical processes in the body but, its long-term effect leads to aging.

Collagen is an example of fibrous connective tissue protein. It is formed slowly in some tissues and eliminated slowly or not at all. Collagen buildup and cross-linking cause tissues to become more rigid. This in turn interferes with normal organ functioning and contributes to such characteristics of aging as the formation of skin wrinkles and slow wound healing seen in older people.

Lipofuscins are another group of substances that buildup in some nerve cells with aging. This gives rise to pigments in these cells and may be involved in the decline of nerve function in some way. Evidence that aging pigments cause defects in cell function or limit lifespan, however, are not very convincing.

Calcium shifts from bone to tissues. This shifting effect can contribute to the formation of eye cataracts, arterial calcification, wrinkled skin and the formation of brittle bones. Once again, however, calcium shifts are not thought to be a major cause of aging.

Cross-linkage theories are related to numerous consumer practices which attempt to "purge the system of wastes" in order to maintain good health. For example, some individuals are convinced that they should drink vinegar on a regular basis as a means of "cleaning out the system." Perhaps the rationale here is that something that works for coffee pots should also offer some advantages to humans.

Cybernetic Pacemaker Theory

This theory proposes that the central nervous system is the pacemaker for age-related changes. These changes may also be dependent upon endocrine changes controlled by the hypothalamus. Thus, the nervous system and endocrine system (i.e., hormones), which are the two messenger systems in the body, are responsible for aging mechanisms. In this context, for the body to function normally, organs and organ systems must communicate with each other in order to maintain a balance of functioning. The science of communication and the interaction of different elements of a system with one another is called *cybernetics*.

As we age, it may be that the nervous and endocrine systems become less efficient in transmitting messages. Thus, the body functions less efficiently and diseases sometimes arise as a result.

Error Catastrophe Theory

This theory proposes that cellular aging occurs because of an increase in error rates in the translation of the genetic code for protein synthesis and also in the number of defective enzymes required by the cell for normal functioning. Thus, cell damage, malfunction and death could occur as a result of the accumulation of random errors in protein synthesis. Over the years there have been conflicting results from well-designed studies attempting to explore this possibility.

External Factors

Aging is influenced by factors which are external to the individual. These are best viewed as potentials that may support longevity, or which may threaten to shorten lifespan. For example, environmental factors can terminate life regardless of genetic potentials (e.g., accidents, lightening, disease, radiation). Some of these factors may be affected by the resistance of the individual as determined by genetic makeup (e.g., some people seem to be more resistant to the development of certain diseases).

Diet

It does not appear that the absolute age to which people can expect to live is determined by diet alone. However, there is little doubt that dietary habits may predispose us to more or less healthy lives, which may impact individual lifespan.

Interest in diet as an aging factor has resulted from many different observations. Some of the most dramatic have involved the three cultures of people mentioned earlier who are reported to live well beyond 100 years in age. These groups (Russian Caucasus, Himalayan Hunza and Ecuadorian Vilcabamba) apparently consume a lower caloric intake and percentage of proteins than other groups in their regions. Similarly, studies have indicated that the lifespan of animals can be extended when their caloric intake is reduced, especially during early life.

Still, research has not demonstrated that our lifespan can be extended by dietary restrictions alone. Other lifestyle factors complicate such conclusions. For example, the three groups mentioned above have other lifestyle characteristics that are significantly different from Americans (e.g., exercise, low stress levels, a more simple existence).

Geography

It is the mountains of the world that seem to be most associated with the largest groups of 100+ year old residents (e.g., the high valleys of the Himalayas, the Caucasus and the Andes). As we have seen, however, the actual age of people in these regions is difficult to assess because of a lack of accurate birth records. Also, these tribes tend to be relatively isolated, so that inbreeding is likely. This in turn might lend an advantage of genetic predispositions for long life and would explain why longevity varies from one mountain group to another.

Lower oxygen levels at higher altitudes may also serve to slow metabolic rates, especially in children before puberty. This might serve as a protective influence in a similar way to dietary restrictions.

The nature of the terrain, and the fact that these tribes are farmers and herdsmen, requires considerable exercise. Many ascend and descend significant distances on the mountain slopes several times a day. Thus, their exercise levels are considerably more rigorous than the average sedentary American.

Population Density

Studies over the years have indicated that people living in more densely populated areas (e.g., urban areas) may have shorter lifespan than those living in less densely populated areas (e.g., rural areas). This does not suggest a need for total isolation, since it appears that population density is beneficial up to a certain point.

In American culture there is little doubt that urban areas are associated with a greater risk for crime, accidents, environmental pollution, high stress and other factors that are associated with greater numbers of people.

Financial Status

There does appear to be some correlation between income and lifespan. This probably occurs because food intake, housing, sanitation, medical facilities, education and other factors are purchased with money to varying degrees. Thus, our quality of life is often associated with income. However, this relationship is not a perfect one, since considerable variations exist between people with similar incomes. It is also worth noting that the preoccupation of Americans with materialistic gains can result in considerable stresses and can predispose us to unhealthy lifestyles (e.g., accidents, drugs and other unhealthy coping behaviors).

* * * * *

The conclusion to be made here is that lifespan is probably affected by various external factors, even though internal factors are considered to be more important. It may be that external factors influence internal factors (e.g., amplify negative internal factors or detract from positive internal factors) in various ways. It is also apparent from research that no single external factor can explain aging or lifespan. It is far more likely that external factors operate together with internal factors in a synergistic way to impact health and aging.

Finite Cell Division Theory

This theory suggests that cells have a "clock" or "program" that directs a cell's capacity to reproduce itself. Accordingly, cell aging and death are genetically programmed. In this context, aging involves inevitable changes that are built into the pattern of all living things. As we progress from one stage of our lives to another, the aging phenomenon occurs in a predetermined way.

Some studies have demonstrated that cultured cells will indeed undergo a finite number of cell divisions and then stop. Moreover, if the culture is frozen quickly during the division process and then thawed it will complete the normal finite cycle, then stop. These cells then seem to be programmed to divide only a certain number of times, suggesting that cells are not designed for perpetual activity, or to significantly increase lifespan. Since both dividing and nondividing cells are involved in aging, some scientists have suggested that tissue aging is caused by a transition of cells from an active phase to an inactive phase.

Additional studies involving lifespan, twins and heredity (e.g., the relationship between the lifespan of parents and their children) also seem to support this view. Thus, the cell division theory seems to explain many observations about aging.

Free Radical Theory

A free radical is a very unstable molecule. Stable molecules on the other hand have a symmetrical pair of electrons in their outer orbital which balance the molecule by exerting opposite directions of spin. Since free radicals lack one of these balancing electrons, they seek to obtain an additional electron by taking one from a stable molecule in the body. When this happens the result leaves inactive products which accumulate in the body (e.g., age pigments, lipofuscin).

The products which are formed by free radicals are of little use to the cells and tissues in which they accumulate. However, they can interfere with normal physiological functions and can contribute to the development of diseases. Moreover, some studies have shown that the effects of free radicals can increase with age. Yet, there is little evidence to suggest that age pigments contribute to cellular malfunctions, especially in the brain where accumulations of these substances might be expected to result in increased problems with mental functioning. Still, this theory has led to a search for "Geroprotectors" or antioxidants which could slow the aging process.

Genetic Theories

Many authorities have suggested that genetic characteristics may control the aging process at the organ or even cellular level. Consequently, the genes we inherit may cause certain age-related changes to occur at certain times as we age.

Another genetically-related theory rests on the fact that gene products (e.g., RNA, DNA, proteins) may only be produced in limited quantities in early life. Therefore, the concentration of these products is reduced throughout life when individual molecules are lost because of injuries of various kinds or because they are used and not replaced. As a result, the biological processes which depend upon these gene products would be altered. Similarly, the loss of genetic information over time could cause some genes to function improperly. In theory, as these genes cease to function properly, they may "turn on" other genes which attempt to compensate in various ways.

The fascination with gene theories for us is that it may be possible to eventually identify the genes associated with aging, alter them and delay the aging process. On the other hand it seems likely that many genes are involved in such changes and not merely a single "aging" gene. Over time, some genes may switch "on," while others "switch" off. If so, alteration of aging through gene manipulation would require that scientists identify the numerous genes involved in the aging process. Moreover, in many cases it appears that genetic aging occurs as a result of certain physiological changes over time. Thus, researchers must not only identify which genes are involved, but the ways in which their functions interact. To merely switch some genes "on" and others "off" without regard for the systematic way in which they impact each other could have serious consequences for normal functioning.

Heredity

It is reasonably clear that there is a hereditary connection involved in the lifespan of many organisms. In general, lifespan is related to the size of the animal:

TABLE 2	
Animal	*Lifespan*
Indian Elephant	60 yrs
Horse	50 yrs
Hippopotamus	50 yrs
Whales	30 - 50 yrs
Dolphins	30 - 50 yrs
Cats (large)	30 yrs
Bears	30 yrs
African Elephant	30 yrs
Primates	30 yrs

There are a number of exceptions:

Humans*	70 yrs
Tortoise	up to 150 yrs

*Try not to be insulted here. Humans are classified as "animals" by virtue of the fact that they are not plants!

Additionally, some owls, cockatoos, eagles, parrots, condors and pelicans may live for more than 50 years.

Another related factor is that the ratio of brain weight to body weight is highly correlated to lifespan. In this context, the larger size of the human brain may be an important biological advantage that contributes to longevity. Perhaps our ability to think has better prepared us to survive and to evolve in such a way that lifespan has continued to increase. However, studies which have attempted to correlate brain weight and body size with lifespan have not been confirmed in humans.

Most animal species cannot expect to live much beyond their reproductive years. Yet, humans can expect to live at least 25 years past menopause and 45 years past the birth of the last child. Perhaps the human aging process evolved in such a way to allow for parents to insure the survival of children and grandchildren through social mechanisms (e.g., teaching children and grandchildren to survive), rather than through biological mechanisms.

Twins also offer insight into the hereditary component of aging. Identical twins tend to have a more similar lifespan than fraternal twins, which indicates again the importance of genetic factors. Finally, this theory is supported by the common observation that the children of parents and grandparents who have long lifespan are also more likely to have longer lifespan.

Homeostatic Imbalance Theory

This theory proposes that the homeostatic mechanisms that maintain a vital physiologic balance are central to the aging process. Thus, aging involves an increase in homeostatic "faults."

Consider the fact that the ability to maintain homoestasis is similar at rest in both younger and older individuals. However, readjustments back to normal after periods of stress is more difficult for older individuals and can even threaten survival. These stressors can include both physical (e.g., heart attacks due to physical overexertion) and social (e.g., emotions associated with the death of a spouse). As a result of these changes, stress takes a greater toll in the elderly.

This theory is possibly the most general of all the theories and provides a clear link between physiological, social and psychological aspects of aging. Yet, as with the Wear and Tear Theory, stress alone does not completely explain the cause of aging.

Immunological Theories

Some investigators have attempted to correlate changes in the immune system with aging. For example, there is a decline in functioning of various cells and organs of the immune system (e.g., thymus gland, T-cells, immune response) over time. These changes seem to be associated with the development of certain diseases (e.g., lupus erythematosus, multiple sclerosis, and cancers). Such observations have been supported by animal studies in which the thymus gland was removed. Afterwards, the animals developed more diseases which occur as a result of decreased immune function and they seemed to age more quickly.

Normally, the immune system recognizes the tissues of the body and does not react to them. If the immune system fails to recognize these tissues, it would begin to react to them just as it would any other "foreign" tissues. On the other hand, it is possible that a decline in immune function actually protects us. For example, as the immune system declines, it would be less able to react to normal tissues of the body. Even so, declining immune functions combined with reactions to normal body tissues may interact in ways to increase the likelihood of disease and aging.

Rate of Living Theory

This is one of the oldest of all the aging theories and proposes that each individual has a certain reserve of vitality. This resource may be used up quickly (leading to a shorter life) or more slowly (leading to a longer life). This theory serves as a basis for our cultural concerns with "Type A" personalities and people who seem to "work themselves to death."

Again, there is some research to support this theory. A number of studies have shown a direct relationship between metabolic rates (i.e., energy production and utilization rates in the body) and lifespan. For example, mice have a metabolic rate which is about 30 times greater than that of humans and the lifespan of mice is 2 to 3 years, while that of humans is substantially longer.

Running Out Theory

This theory proposes that aging occurs because our genetic program simply "runs out" or comes to its natural end. The greater mental abilities of humans may simply have allowed people to live longer. Our later years may be analogous to a rocket that was programmed to place a satellite in orbit but then continues to orbit for some time after accomplishing its programmed task. Accordingly, people could not expect to live beyond the time that is "programmed" into their genetic makeup. In this context, even if diseases were eliminated, people would not live to be 400.

Somatic Mutation Theory

This theory proposes that spontaneous mutations occur in cells that can lead to changes in normal cell functioning. The changes that occur could include uncontrolled growth characteristics (e.g., cancer), altered cholesterol metabolism (e.g., arteriosclerosis) and altered immune mechanisms (e.g., arthritis). Although this theory cannot explain the entire aging process, and is no longer accepted by many people, it did lead to the development of the "error theories" mentioned previously.

Wear and Tear Theory

This is possibly the most common sense theory of aging. It suggests that in time we simply "wear out." This theory is commonly expressed among elderly who say, "I'm just old and worn out." According to this theory, aging results from a gradual deterioration of the various organs which are essential for life. It is this view that has encouraged an interest in organ replacement surgeries (e.g., heart, kidney, joints). Yet, many scientists feel that there is an integral interrelationship of the various body systems which is more important than the failure of any particular organ. Thus, merely replacing "parts" may be helpful when a single organ is diseased and not likely to recover, but not particularly helpful in increasing lifespan to an appreciable degree.

Despite the seemingly logical nature of this theory, there is little evidence to suggest that either hard work, stress or other factors that could contribute to wear and tear are actually responsible for reducing one's lifespan. The effects of hard work and stress are largely removed by periods of rest. Even the impact of severe chemical stress (e.g., alcohol, smoking) will not impact lifespan if they are removed before permanent damage occurs. As long as stresses do not overwhelm the physiological capacity of the individual to recover, they appear to be limited in their impact on aging, per se.

When all is said and done, we can summarize by saying that the aging process is still only minimally understood, and we are left but with one conclusion: reduce as many health risks as possible and engage in as many favorable health practices as possible. You will, at least, have the satisfaction of knowing you have certainly enhanced your life style and even extended your longevity.

10. AGE-RELATED CHANGES AND INTERVENTIONS

"I have everything I had 20 years ago . . .
except now it's all lower."

— Gypsy Rose Lee

Physical changes occur with aging. While it is unrealistic to avoid these physical changes completely, there are creative adjustments to age related changes which allow us to improve our quality of life, and to varying degrees, our length of life. The youth orientation of Americans is one of obsession and denial. To counter this focus, it is becoming increasingly important for us to accept and even celebrate aging as something that is valued and not as something to dread. We must accept ourselves as worthwhile individuals at whatever stage of life we find ourselves. To seek to maximize our quality of life regardless of age is healthy. Trying to turn back the hands of time, or somehow stop the clock, is to seek certain frustration.

Learn to like yourself!

It is in that context that we should consider the changes which aging produces and what options are available to us once they occur.

Appearance

Body Contours and Features

Changes occur in our general body features because of a redistribution of fat tissue, which normally fills and rounds out the body. Without fat, bony prominences and hollows become more prominent. Exercise helps to tone muscles and promote a more normal, healthy and youthful appearance. Appropriate nutrition is important in maintaining health and normal percentages of fat and muscle.

Facial Appearance

Changes in facial appearance occur due to atrophy of facial bones, recession of gums, loss of teeth and a loss of skin elasticity, moisture and supporting fat. Regular dental checkups and professional dental care can help to insure healthy gums and teeth, including a natural facial appearance.

Fat Distribution

We hear a great deal of negative information about fat. Yet, fat is not all bad, and in fact, it is necessary for health. Not only is fat required to make hormones and other essential components of our body, it also contours our shape, provides insulation and padding. It is also true that there are changes in fat distribution that occur with aging. From about age 40 on, our percentage of body fat increases as our rate metabolism begins to decrease. As these changes occur, we begin to notice various changes in appearance.

For example, some of these changes are in part responsible for the development of wrinkles or "new" fat around the chin, waist, hips and bottom. As we age, males experience an increase in abdominal fat above the umbilicus ("belly button"), and females below the umbilicus. Also in females, there is a decrease in breast fat, which results in a sagging appearance.

Changes in appearance can be minimized by exercise, which promotes a healthy and more youthful appearance. Aerobic exercise burns excess fat and calories, while strength training increases muscle tone.

Nutrition is also important. An appropriate diet helps to maintain your weight at desirable levels for a more attractive and healthy appearance. Also, appropriate nutrition helps to offset changes in fat distribution.

Hair

Probably the most common sign of aging with which everyone is familiar is graying of our hair which occurs because of normal decreases in hair pigments. Genetic factors also play a role in graying. We all know people who seem to gray unusually early or unusually late. Such deviations from the norm can usually be explained by hereditary differences between one individual and another.

Balding also occurs with age because of a gradual decrease in secretions of the adrenal glands after age 20 and decreased blood circulation to the scalp. Simultaneously, facial hair becomes more obvious.

So, what's wrong with turning gray? Becoming bald? Not a thing! Acceptance is possibly the most important intervention. Here again, appropriate nutrition will promote general health and delay the negative effects of hair-related changes with age.

Height

A loss of 1 to 2 inches can occur as we age due to a number of changes. For examples, changes can occur in the discs between vertebrae and the spine itself can begin to bend. Emphysema causes changes in the chest cavity (i.e., a more barrel-chested appearance) with a slight decrease in overall height. Also, flexing of the legs sometimes occurs, which gives the arms a longer appearance.

If there is a panacea for this problem . . . it would be exercise. Exercise promotes healthy muscles, bones and skeletal integrity. Strength and flexibility exercises, especially those that strengthen the abdominal muscles and lower back, promote flexibility and posture.

Creative adaptations can also be helpful in this connection. New ways of doing old chores may help one to function more normally. For example, consider moving kitchen items that you use often to lower shelves in your cabinets. Identify new tools that can help you to function more efficiently and don't be shy about asking for assistance from others.

Appropriate nutrition promotes healthy muscles and bones, and should include an adequate intake of calcium and vitamin D. However, don't overdo these. *Too much vitamin D can be toxic.* Ask your doctor, nurse or pharmacist to help you select an appropriate product and dose.

Nails

Our nails tend to grow more slowly as we age. Other changes in our nails such as wrinkling and unusual thickness can occur. Some nail changes can reflect diseases, so regular checkups are important. Exercise improves circulation throughout the body, including the hands and feet. Nutrition promotes health and counters the negative effects which we associate with aging. Vitamin and other supplements may also be helpful here.

Nail care programs, conditioning and polishing kits can promote healthy and attractive nails and help to prevent nail infections and other nail problems.

Skin

The skin is the largest organ of the body, although we tend not to view it that way. In fact, we usually consider it merely as the "wrapper" of the human "package." However, the skin is the most visible human organ, and like other body systems, skin changes occur with aging. These begin by about age 40 when the skin tends to become more pale, especially those areas that have been exposed most often to the sun. Changes in texture, loss of elasticity and dryness may also develop. The first sign of skin change which many people notice is the appearance of new spots. These can include pigmentation spots and red patches on the backs of hand and forearms due to the harmless rupture of small blood vessels. "Liver spots" appear on nearly 90% of people by the time they reach their 50s. These spots are also known as senile lentigo, lentigines, or melanotic freckles. They tend to appear most frequently on the face, neck and back of the hands. "Ruby Spots" (cherry angioma or senile angioma) are another type of spot which people begin to notice. Other changes in the skin include a decrease in the size and number of sweat and sebaceous glands and a loss of fat padding, which can lead to pressure sores and decreased insulation.

Since sunlight is considered to be the major culprit regarding the development of skin cancers and premature skin aging, it is best to avoid excessive exposure to the sun. Also, use sunscreens with a Sun Protection Factor (SPF) of at least 15 and wear clothing that protects you from the sun. In addition, lotions and moisturizers may help to offset the effects of dry skin and damage from sun exposures.

As we have indicated nutrition promotes general health, including healthy skin. And, regular checkups are important for the early detection of skin cancers. Some skin lesions (e.g., liver spots, ruby spots) can be surgically removed.

Weight

Our weight tends to remain relatively constant up to about age 70, then begins to decline. Exercise helps to maintain an ideal weight, but regular checkups are important if you begin to experience any sudden weight changes.

Circulatory System

Heart and Blood Pressure

The ability of the heart to respond to stress tends to decline with aging. So, older people may function well under normal circumstances, but not so well when dealing with stressful events. Blood pressure also tends to increase with age, but some people experience occasional drops in blood pressure (hypotension) due to changes in the heart and circulation. This can be a cause for concern, since sudden decreases in blood pressure may result in dizziness or fainting (especially when rising too quickly from a seated or lying position). This in turn, increases the risk for falls and injuries.

To reduce these risks, home and work environments can be rearranged so that falls are less likely to occur. Another simple measure involves getting up more slowly from seated and lying positions. It is also possible through relaxation and other techniques to reduce stress levels in order to reduce stress on the heart. Finally, if you have heart problems, always check with a physician, nurse or pharmacist before taking any medications.

Of all the various adjustments and options available to you, exercise is most important since it strengthens the heart and cardiovascular system, improves blood pressure levels, stamina and the ability to withstand stress (especially in conjunction with relaxation techniques). However, it is always best to check with a doctor before beginning any exercise program.

In terms of diet, reducing sodium (salt) intake is most important. Use salt sparingly at the table and eliminate it completely from cooking. You will tend to use less salt that way. Use lemon as a salt substitute if it is compatible with the foods that you are eating, since lemon can fool the taste buds and you won't miss the salt as much.

Pseudo-Hypertension

"Hardening of the arteries" can give the impression that high blood pressure exists, when in fact, the pressure is relatively normal. This occurs because it takes more pressure from the blood pressure cuff to obtain the reading. Have regular checkups so that your physician can more carefully monitor your condition and identify health problems as they occur.

Digestive System

This is the system that is considered to be least affected by aging. Although changes do occur throughout the digestive tract with age, digestive functioning is usually maintained at adequate levels. The stomach and intestinal problems which do occur are often not serious health threats.

An appropriate diet is important with this system. Nutrition promotes general health, including a healthy digestive system. A high-fiber, low-fat diet can help to prevent intestinal cancers and lower cholesterol and fat levels. Vitamin/mineral supplements may help to insure that all nutritional needs are being met.

Exercise is another important intervention, since appropriate exercise helps to insure normal bowel functioning.

Appetite

Some people experience a decrease in their appetite as they get older because of a reduction in smell and taste, or as a result of normal reductions in activity levels. In as much as eating typically involves an important social component, and older people sometimes become more isolated over time (e.g., death of a spouse, or health problems that discourage social interactions) loss of appetite can contribute to this problem. To reduce this risk, one should identify ways in which meals can be socially meaningful, as well as nutritionally meaningful (e.g., Meals on Wheels, Senior Citizen Centers, eating with friends or family).

Mouth and Throat

a. Mouth. Age-related changes in the mouth include a reduction in the flow of saliva, which can make swallowing more difficult, reduce the effectiveness of sublingual medications (i.e., those that are placed under the tongue) and can cause food to be less enjoyable. Changes in the mouth tissues can also result in oral problems, including mouth irritations and a longer time for oral sores to heal. The use of hard candy or gum can increase salivation. Increasing your fluid intake can assist swallowing and cause foods to be more enjoyable.

b. Taste and Smell. The number of taste buds decreases with age, in particular, those involved with the detection of sweet and salty substances. As a consequence, more taste and smell stimulation is required to achieve the same taste effect. Such changes probably explain why older people often complain that food does not taste as good as it used to. Moreover, they may overseason foods (e.g., salt), which can lead to other health problems, or find eating to be less enjoyable (possibly resulting in malnutrition). Disease can also have a negative impact on taste and smell.

It is important to remember that food preferences are learned. We can relearn to like foods, make appropriate substitutions, or at least accept some of our favorites that now taste differently. If necessary, use salt at the table, but not in cooking. You will tend to use less salt that way. Also, as indicated earlier, lemon can be used to "fool" the taste buds. "New" foods should be attempted to identify new "favorites." Some nutrients (e.g., zinc) can improve taste and smell. Avoid smoking, since it can interfere with taste and smell. Most importantly do not avoid eating just because food tastes differently. Good nutrition is required for general health and well-being.

c. Teeth and Dentures. Although loss of teeth is commonly associated with aging, this problem is almost totally preventable. Teeth require lifetime care, proper diet and occasional repair. This is an important consideration, since your natural teeth are far more effective than dentures for chewing.

There is no substitute for daily flossing and brushing. Proper nutrition promotes general health of the teeth and gums, and prevents tooth damage. Regular dental checkups are also important, since teeth require regular evaluation and maintenance by dental professionals.

Poorly fitting dentures can result in the swallowing of air and the development of excessive stomach and intestinal gas. People tend not to eat as well with dentures, so proper nutrition becomes a serious consideration. Make a special effort to eat healthy! Have regular dental checkups to insure that dentures are fitting properly over time.

d. Throat and Esophagus. About 75% of people over the age of 50 have hiatal hernias. This can result in esophagitis (heartburn) and other discomforts. Hiatal hernias usually produce no symptoms or only occasional symptoms (e.g., pain, difficulty swallowing, emotional distress). In any event this problem can often be treated with medications (e.g., antacids, and other stomach medications) or by surgery in more extreme cases.

Acceptance of this problem is important since in most cases we simply have to learn to live with it. However, there are ways to adjust to the discomfort. For example, elevating the head of the bed is sometimes beneficial. Increase your fluid intake, avoid foods that seem to aggravate the problem, eat more slowly, chew your food thoroughly and avoid eating just before bed. It is also important to have regular checkups to insure that your symptoms are not actually caused by something else.

Stomach

Age-related decreases in stomach acid production can result in some digestive problems and an increased risk for stomach cancer. This may include decreases in nutrient absorption (including vitamins and minerals). Equally important, stomach changes can increase the likelihood of other problems (e.g., irritations, indigestion).

In such cases some dietary changes may be in order, so it is important for us to accept them. Since, as we have suggested, most of our dietary preferences are learned, we can also learn to like alternatives. The key is to alter dietary patterns in healthy ways by eating a balanced diet and avoiding irritating foods (e.g., alcohol, spicy foods).

Exercise and other stress reduction techniques can help to reduce stress levels, thereby reducing your risk for stomach problems. So, give your lifestyle some thought.

Intestines

Aging may also result in some loss of normal intestinal functioning. Nevertheless, this is usually not a problem. The incidence of ulcers and diverticula (pouches in the intestine which become inflamed, much like an inflamed appendix) is greater in older people than in younger people. But in general, intestinal health is promoted by a healthy diet (e.g., high fiber, low fat). Again, exercise is also generally beneficial, both in reducing stress and in promoting normal intestinal functioning.

a. Constipation. Constipation is not really the common household problem that advertising and cultural myths would have us believe. Older people do appear to complain more about it than younger people. However, much "constipation" is really nothing more than normal changes in bowel habits. For example, the need to defecate tends to occur less frequently with aging. Thus, a person who was accustomed to having a bowel movement every day, may only have one every 2 to 3 days. This is NOT constipation if everything else is basically functioning normally and no symptoms of discomfort exist.

Once again, proper nutrition and exercise are important preventive measures. A high-fiber, low-fat diet promotes natural functioning of the intestines. Also increased fluid intake can be beneficial. Some people might consider using one of the bulk laxatives (e.g., Metamucil) on a regular basis but should check with their doctor first! Bulk laxatives are healthy for the digestive system and have been shown to help lower cholesterol levels. However, it is best to avoid the use of any laxative products other than the bulk type, unless instructed differently by a physician.

b. Liver. Normally the liver is not as affected by aging as many other organs or organ systems. However, there may be some loss of functioning of normal enzyme systems regulated by the liver. Since these systems are necessary for drug metabolism, people must use drugs with caution as they age. Drugs can work more or less effectively, depending upon how they are normally metabolized.

In any event, use drugs carefully as you age. Liver impairments due to either aging or other diseases may decrease your tolerance for some medications. Report any new side effects to your doctor. Also, some drugs can cause liver damage (e.g., acetaminophen) if taken in excessive amounts. There is evidence that some B vitamins may help to protect the liver from damage. Finally, regular checkups are important to identify liver diseases or losses of normal functioning.

Endocrine

Hormones are chemical messengers in the body that are carried through the blood stream. Changes in hormones and the endocrine system can result in decreased insulin production, decreased ability to handle sugars and changes in thyroid function.

The primary intervention in such cases is regular medical checkups. Most health problems associated with hormone dysfunction are due to diseases which require professional medical intervention. Appropriate nutrition and exercise will help to maintain general health, including that of the endocrine system, but these do not replace professional care.

Feet

Our feet are the object of a great deal of wear and tear throughout our lives. Problems can include bunions, calluses, corns and toenail problems (e.g., ingrown, overgrown and thickened), some of which may increase with age. Circulation problems of the feet can also develop with aging. This increases the risk for more serious problems of the feet unless appropriate professional care is received.

Learn to accept the possibility of feet-related problems. Then consider ways to deal with or prevent them. For example, allow yourself the luxury of not attempting to maintain the same activity levels as you did when you were younger. Buy appropriate shoes. Consider foot massagers or other devices which pamper your feet. See if you can find ways to take care of your various responsibilities while seated, rather than always standing.

Appropriate nutrition promotes general well-being, including the health of your feet. Try to maintain an ideal weight, since extra pounds will weigh heavily on your feet. Have regular checkups from your physician or podiatrist regarding any problems you are having with your feet.

Immune System

The immune system may have a significant role in aging, although its functions in this capacity are not well understood. We do know it serves to protect us from harmful external factors (e.g., bacteria and viruses) and internal factors (e.g., cancer formation). Some diseases (e.g., arthritis, diabetes) may result from a breakdown of our normal immune functioning.

Changes in immune functioning can be due to a variety of factors, other than aging including:

❧ Poor nutrition	❧ Drugs
❧ Poor health in general	❧ Exercise (lack of)
❧ Stress	❧ Ionizing radiation

It is important to emphasize that exercise promotes general health and well-being, including a healthy immune system. Similarly, good nutrition promotes general health and well-being. Again, regular checkups are important to identify diseases of the immune system or diseases which may negatively affect immune functioning. Here too, drugs should be used cautiously, since excessive drug use can compromise the immune system.

Muscular and Skeletal Changes

Muscles

Much of the muscle weakness reported by older individuals is actually associated with disuse. Other causes can include vitamin deficiencies, changes in the nervous system and hormonal functioning, and decreases in normal muscle mass and tissue composition. As a result of any of these factors, we can experience atrophy, weakness and a decreased ability for rapid movements.

Skeleton

As we age there are a number of skeletal changes which can occur. The backbone tends to droop, causing a sagging appearance of the stomach. Some joint changes may occur as a result of wear and tear, diseases (e.g., arthritis, osteoporosis) and changes in bone composition (e.g., calcium losses). These joints may become enlarged, inflamed or deformed.

Appropriate nutrition and exercise are absolutely essential to prevent these types of occurrences, and to minimize their effects once they occur.

Warm soaks (e.g., baths, hot tubs) can promote circulation and reduce inflammation and discomfort of joints. While it is not a panacea, the benefits of warm water therapy were in use long before the emergence of modern medicine. However, there are two important cautions. As we age our tolerance for temperature extremes may decline. So, check with your doctor before spending time in a hot tub. Secondly, the water temparature should be comfortable. This is *not* a "no pain, no gain" activity. Water that is too hot can be dangerous to your health.

Nervous System

In general, normal functioning of the nervous system declines with age in various ways. Muscle tremors are more common and reaction time decreases due to decreased reflexes. Reduced blood circulation to and within the brain can result in a decreased ability to respond to stress.

Despite these changes, and in contrast to popular myths, brain functioning remains relatively normal unless you are exposed to stresses of some kind (e.g., emotional stresses, physical stresses, poor nutrition, inappropriate drug use). Changes in other body systems can impact brain functioning (e.g., nervous system functioning in general, heart and circulation).

Becoming aware of these possible changes enables us to cope with them effectively. Consequently, reducing stress levels becomes important. Exercise improves general health, increases resistance to disease, and improves blood flow to the brain. Similarly, good nutrition promotes health in general and helps to counter the negative effects of aging and disease on all systems including the nervous system.

Balance and Falls

Problems with our sense of balance can cause impairment in the sense of position and movement, which in turn may result in injury due to falls (these are more common in women than men). Changes in vision, ear infections and decreased blood flow to the inner ear can also increase the risk of falls and injury, as can changes in gait. Similarly, older people do not tend to lift their feet as high when walking and sway more when they walk, which also increases the risk of falls. Moreover, our ability to avoid falls once we lose our balance decreases with aging.

Intervention may include a number of measures. Furniture may be rearranged (at home and work) so that falls are less likely to occur. Handrails (especially in bathrooms) can be installed as needed. Select floor coverings that have less risk for tripping, slipping or falls (e.g., nonstick surfaces, carpets with short fiber). Medications should be used carefully, since many drugs can cause dizziness, sedation or decreased coordination. Finally, have regular checkups to identify any health problems that may contribute to falls.

Hearing

Hearing impairments which increase with age can be due to problems with the auditory nerve, brain centers and ear structures. They also can be caused by exposure to loud noises (e.g., rock music, work noises) during earlier years. The obvious solution to some of these conditions is a hearing aid. However, hearing losses due to problems beyond the middle ear (i.e. ear structures) cannot be corrected by these devices.

For some hearing problems, talking louder will NOT be helpful. In these cases it is important to face the individual, speak slower and allow them to watch your lips as you speak.

Whatever the cause of the loss, it is important to recognize it as a natural process and allow yourself the freedom to adapt and take corrective measures. Be aware of the types of changes that are occurring. Learn to listen more carefully. Look at people when they speak. Educate others around you regarding hearing problems so that they can help you (e.g., by speaking in a different way that better allows you to hear). Protect your hearing throughout your life (e.g., avoid loud music, wear ear protection if you must be around loud machinery). Have regular checkups to accurately assess hearing changes and to provide for appropriate corrective measures. Some television sets now have closed captions for the hearing impaired. Also, it is often possible to attach electronic devices to televisions so that hearing impaired individuals can listen through headphones.

Pain Perception

Tolerance for pain also seems to increase as we age. This may be due to changes in the central nervous system which increase our pain threshold. Or, perhaps over time we experience more aches and pains (and expect to in the future), and so, simply learn to tolerate them.

Whatever the cause, it is best to avoid stimuli that seem to result in pain or discomfort (e.g., temperature extremes, activities), but in any event, pain is a signal that something is wrong. Don't ignore it . . . check it out!

Senses

Our senses (e.g. hearing, sight, touch, etc.) are the means for receiving information from the world around us. Sensory impairment can result in a number of problems beyond those listed above (e.g., problems in normal daily functioning, mental health problems, social isolation, increased likelihood of falls and injury). Some decrement in sensory ability as a result of aging is unavoidable, but adaptations to those circumstances are also available.

Regular checkups by qualified health professionals (e.g., optometrists, ophthalmologists, ear/nose/throat doctors) are important in identifying diseases or impairments that result in sensory disturbances, and to provide appropriate therapy as needed. In addition what can we do ourselves in such cases? Consider the way in which your home is arranged   For example, are there ways to reorganize things in your home so that you can find them more easily? Can you reorganize in such a way so that you are still able to follow routines on a regular basis? The point here is that reduced sensory ability should not necessarily impair daily activities

Sensorimotor Functioning

As we age, increased time is required to respond to stimuli and to perform certain sensorimotor tasks such as tracking moving targets, adjusting dials or operating a car. This condition is accompanied by a greater risk for work-related accidents, as well as for accidents or injuries related to rapid evasive movements or falls. More importantly, these changes decrease the ability to perceive dangers, process input from the external environment or to respond quickly.

Adjusting to these changes requires some planning and initiative. For example, explore new tools and techniques for attending to normal job and home demands. Rethink tasks to see if there are alternate ways of doing things. Delegate some tasks to others. Identify new tasks that are easier to perform. Avoid unnecessary risks. Identify and reduce the stresses in your life. Get plenty of rest.

Correct as many sensory problems as possible as they occur (e.g., vision, hearing). Insure that problems reflect normal age-related changes and not diseases that require therapy of some kind.

Sleep

Sleep patterns and disturbances also increase with age. These changes may cause the individual to feel more tired than before. On the other hand, older people may require less sleep due to decreases in activity. Nevertheless, they may force themselves to stick to their old routines and insist that they are not sleeping "normally." Sleep disturbances and feelings of being tired are often compensated by spending more time in bed (e.g., naps during the day).

Before jumping to any such conclusions, rethink your sleep patterns. They may change over time, but this is normal, and it's OK! Allow yourself the freedom to change with your body's natural patterns as they emerge. In fact, new sleep patterns may prove to be even more restful (e.g., daytime naps, going to bed earlier or later, getting up earlier or later) than older ones. If you awaken in the middle of the night "wide awake," do something fun and creative. Use your time in productive or satisfying ways (e.g., watch an old movie if one is on).

In addition, consider starting an exercise program. This promotes health in general, more restful sleep, and reduces stresses and depression that may interfere with normal sleep patterns. However, vigorous exercise just before going to bed can increase sleep latency (i.e., it takes longer for you to fall asleep once you have gone to bed), while relaxation exercises (e.g., yoga, deep breathing, meditation) can decrease sleep latency (i.e., you fall asleep more quickly once in bed).

Avoid foods that contain caffeine (e.g., coffee, cola beverages) within 4 to 6 hours before going to bed. And, of course, have regular checkups to identify health problems that may interfere with sleep.

Touch and Dexterity

Some reduction in touch and dexterity occur due to disease, as well as age-related changes. Abilities to use hands in performing tasks may decline as a result of changes in muscles and the nervous system.

Here again, you may want to identify new ways of doing old things as well as the use of new equipment that help you with your normal routines and activities.

Vision

Presbyopia (an inability to focus on both near and far objects) is a common visual problem that develops with aging. In some cases, this change occurs in the late 30s and early 40s. Presbyopia can also decrease one's ability to see in less bright light or to distinguish between certain colors (e.g., dark blue versus black socks). This can make it difficult to distinguish between medications with similar colors. Aging also results in a decreased ability of light to penetrate the lens and other eye structures and in less tolerance for bright light and glare. Aging is also associated with increases in the incidence of cataracts, glaucoma and irreversible degeneration of the retina.

Some of these changes are normal. Even a healthy eye for example requires significantly more light to perform the same tasks at age 60 as compared to age 20. Thus, more time is required for the eyes to adapt when moving from an area of light to an area that is darker.

In any event, visual changes can be frustrating, as can the need to purchase new visual aids (e.g., bifocal glasses). The need to adjust to these changes is paramount. First, of course, learn to accept, then consider how to adapt. One obvious solution is to use corrective lenses including bifocals. Sort clothing according to colors so that you do not have to strain to distinguish between them. Provide better lighting. Use sunglasses when in the sun. Vitamin A helps to prevent some visual problems (e.g., night blindness). Exercise care. Vitamin A can be toxic in large doses. Large print books are available for individuals with visual impairments.

Finally, we all need regular visual checkups as we age. Immediately report any unusual visual changes to an eye care professional. Remember, most eye problems can be corrected.

Voice

Voice changes are inevitable with aging. This may include changes in our rate, quality and vitality of speaking. There are also declines in vocal intensity, power and ability to sustain sound. Vocal pitch may change due to changes in the vocal cords or because of changes in the central nervous system in general. Speech may slow and is more likely to quaver. There are declines in muscle function of the throat and vocal cords.

Once again, it's OK for such changes to occur. Once you notice the changes that have occurred, make a committment to adapt. You may need to speak some words differently. Does speaking more loudly or softly seem to help? Pay attention to how you are breathing when you talk. You may be able to improve the voice by adopting more effective use of air.

Increase fluid intake, since this helps to keep the vocal cords moist. And, as in all such cases, regular checkups can help to identify health problems that may impact the voice and need effective treatment.

Respiratory System

Age-related changes in muscle tone and lung tissues can impact breathing and response to stresses (e.g., physical and emotional). By age 60 your maximum breathing capacity will have decreased by 50%. Moreover, lung diseases and problems are more common with aging.

You can deal with these factors in a number of ways. Avoid stressful activities that exceed your physical capacity. Also, regular exercise improves the natural elasticity of lung tissues and increases total lung volume and flow. Increase fluid intake. This helps the lungs to thin respiratory secretions and eliminate debris and other accumulations.

It is important to identify health problems early which involve the respiratory system (e.g., lung cancer can often be successfully treated if diagnosed early).

Sexual Functioning

Age-related changes occur in hormone levels that are associated with normal sexual functioning and sexual characteristics. Even so, individual sexual activity varies considerably and is probably more influenced by health, desire and social environments.

Females

Decline in hormone levels (estrogen and progesterone) can result in increases in bone loss and brittle bones.

The vagina decreases in length and width and the lining becomes thinner. Also, its ability to expand decreases and the cervix and uterus decrease in size. In general, these changes increase the likelihood that the vagina can become irritated or injured during intercourse.

Some remedies for these problems are readily available. For example, use sexual lubricants during intercourse (e.g., K-Y Jelly). This can help to reduce painful intercourse and irritation or injury to vaginal tissues. Be sensitive to changes in your sexual drive, as well as those of your sexual partner. Identify sexual activities that are mutually satisfying, without being irritating. Regular checkups can help to identify diseases that may occur, prevent problems or initiate appropriate therapy.

Males

Males also have declines in normal hormonal levels.

The prostate typically enlarges after age 50. The primary causes of such enlargement are: (1) Benign prostatic hypertrophy (i.e., noncancerous enlargement); and (2) Cancer (see "Prostate Cancer in Chapter 12). The symptoms of enlargement are:

- Difficulty urinating
- Frequent urgency to urinate
- Inability to empty bladder
- Urinary discomfort

Diets high in fat appear to be associated with the development of prostate cancer. It is extremely important to identify and diagnose prostate problems early. Prostate cancer can be effectively treated when diagnosed early. It can be deadly if left untreated.

Sexual Dysfunction

The causes of sexual dysfunction include:

❦ Alcohol	❦ Fear of failure in sexual performance
❦ Certain drugs	❦ Norms and cultural beliefs about older people
❦ Disease	❦ One's partner
❦ Emotional problems	❦ Overeating
❦ Fatigue	❦ Social factors

In our hectic world with its never-ending conflicts and demands upon us, it is easy to understand why people have trouble finding the time for intimacy. But this can be easily resolved. Create quality, uninterrupted time to be with your partner. Regular exercise can increase libido by improving endurance and muscle tone and by enhancing a zest for living. Reduce alcohol intake. Contrary to popular belief, alcohol is NOT an aphrodisiac. It can lower inhibitions, but can also reduce your ability to perform sexually.

Finally, it is important to identify health problems that may contribute to sexual dysfunction. Check with your doctor or pharmacist to see if the medications that you are taking could be involved.

Stress Adaptation

Aging is associated with a general decline in our ability to adapt to stress. This can have serious consequences. Aging results in a decreasing ability to regulate:

- ❦ Blood chemistry levels (e.g., sugar, acid/base, oxygen levels)
- ❦ Blood pressure
- ❦ Oxygen consumption
- ❦ Pulse

However, many of our previous recommendations are also beneficial in this case. Regular exercise, for example, serves to "flush out" the chemicals and by-products of our metabolism that are produced in response to stress. Relaxation exercises (e.g., yoga, meditation, self-hypnosis) can provide a "break" from a hectic day and allow you to redirect your energies and efforts in healthier and more productive ways. Nutrition promotes general health and well-being and increases our tolerance for stress.

Urinary

Bladder

As we age, decreases may occur in the ability of the bladder to empty. This in turn can increase the likelihood of urinary tract infections. Drinking cranberry juice is no panacea, but it has been found to reduce the incidence of bladder infections in some people by altering the urine so that bladder infections are less likely to occur. Also, increasing fluid intake helps to dilute the urine and promotes flushing of the bladder.

Kidneys

Age-related changes in the kidneys occur even in the absence of disease. Fortunately, these organs have tremendous reserves unless affected by disease, injury or other problems. Conditions such as high blood pressure, diabetes and chronic infections can increase the risks for kidney problems.

Probably the most important selfcare practice, however, is to increase fluid intake. Your body needs adequate fluids to promote normal kidney functioning. Also, as kidney function declines with aging the body becomes less able to excrete drugs normally, so medications should be taken with this fact in mind. Contact your doctor or pharmacist if new or unusual symptoms or side effects of medications occur. Don't adjust the dosage of your medications without consulting a health professional.

Intellectual Function

It is a general myth that intellectual functions decline with age. Research does not support this belief. Rather, most studies indicate that when older people are confronted with tasks that do not depend upon speed and youthful dexterity, they show little or no decrements in performance, speed or accuracy. In fact, intelligence test scores may actually improve with age, rather than decline. Continuous intellectual activity and sufficient stimuli (mental and physical) serve to maintain intellectual functioning (unless it is affected by other diseases in some way). Diseases seem to be the primary cause of intellectual problems, not aging changes. Factors that contribute to declines in IQ performance:

- Disease
- Educational levels
- Nearness to death
- Personal losses
- Social class

Areas of little or no change:

- Breadth of knowledge
- Language dexterity
- Practical judgment
- Verbal memory
- Vocabulary

Age-Related Intellectual Losses

Performance speeds may decline, as can some powers of concentration. Some abilities associated with reasoning may become more difficult:

- Abstract reasoning or conceptualizing
- Adaptations to new situations
- Ability to register or store new information (e.g., due to visual and hearing losses)
- Coding and storing information for long perods of time.

The biggest problem in this area is the stereotyping of the elderly and our resistence to acknowledging our strengths and our weaknesses. Be honest with yourself about age-related changes. If you find old tasks more difficult, then identify new ways to do them. New activities that are meaningful, but create fewer problems are always an option: learn a foreign language; enroll in a computer class; do your own tax return, take a music or writing class, etc. Most of all, it is important to differentiate between normal, age-related changes versus health problems that interfere with normal functioning.

Creativity

Some of the most brilliant creative works have been produced late in life. Clearly, many people continue to grow and achieve their optimal creativity long after they have retired. Creativity is difficult to measure and comparisons are hard to make. But, in any event, the more active one's life style the greater the opportunity to create. Declines in creativity are often related to:

- Decreases in physical vigor
- Decreases in senses (e.g., hearing, vision)
- Diseases (including mental health problems)
- Preoccupations with practical concerns (e.g., retirement, illness of spouse)
- Less favorable conditions for concentration
- Less intense curiosity
- Unfavorable habits
- Also, people who have already achieved prestige may try less hard to achieve additional successes.

Learning

Some learning impairments may occur as we age. However, there is much evidence to suggest that learning abilities are not seriously impaired as a result of aging. Again, we seem to be dealing more with a stereotype than actual reality here. Many 70 year olds perform just as well as younger individuals on learning tasks. Learning new tasks may take a bit longer for an older person but this may be more a matter of "pacing" rather than a specific learning deficit.

Some factors that seem to influence learning more than aging include:

- Educational background
- General health
- Individual differences
- Motivation

Memory

Although many older people complain about memory losses, there is much evidence to suggest that these complaints do not actually correlate with memory performance. Memory loss may be due to:

- ❧ Disuse of Information

- ❧ Some memories interfere with others as the individual collects more and more memories over time.

- ❧ Changes in the brain and nervous system cause the brain not to store or retrieve the information effectively.

- ❧ Changes in the senses (e.g., vision and hearing) prevent the individual from receiving the information in the first place.

Rely on devices that can help you to remember the things that you need to (e.g., to-do lists, calendars, notes on refrigirator door). If the problem is related to hearing losses, consider a hearing aid. Enlist the aid of others to help you.

As we have emphasized before, exercise and nutrition promote general health and well-being, including increased blood flow to the brain, mental health and intellectual functioning. Regular checkups identify health problems that may contribute to memory problems (e.g., hearing). Medications are available which have been shown to be beneficial for some individuals with senility or other cognitive dysfunctioning. This option can be discussed with your physician.

Senility and Alzheimer's

Senility is a chronic disease process, not a consequence of aging, per se. Signs and symptoms include declines in:

❧ Cognitive abilities	❧ Memory
❧ Creativity	❧ Normal functioning

General Interventions and Prevention

Acceptance

It is OK to be yourself and it is especially OK not to be 25 years old all of your life. Allow yourself to age and change. Celebrate life, as well as the experiences and wisdom you've gained over time.

Creative Adaptations

Discover new ways of doing things. Let go of tasks and responsibilities that are too demanding or difficult. Pick up new tasks and activities that are more in keeping with your present situation. Learn how to cope with the changes of aging in healthy and acceptable ways.

Exercise

Exercise tones muscles, improves strength and appearance, reduces depression, energizes, reduces the risk for disease in general, improves general fitness (especially heart and lungs), can lower blood pressure and improve general well-being. Aerobic exercises burn off calories and fat, while strength training improves muscle tone and overall strength. Exercise helps to offset the negative consequences of age-related changes. Always check with your physician before beginning an exercise program in order to identify exercises that will be safe and beneficial for you.

Nutrition

There is no substitute for a balanced and healthy diet. This includes eating at regular intervals and limiting snacks and alcohol consumption. Vitamin supplementation is OK, but there is limited evidence to support the use of massive doses. And, Vitamins A, D and K can result in toxicity if taken in excessive quantities. Mineral supplements may also be beneficial, especially calcium for women. Avoid excessive use, but insure that you are getting at least the recommended daily allowance. Appropriate nutrition promotes healthy tissues, organs and organ systems, decreases body fat and helps to offset the negative consequences of age-related changes. In general, decrease the amount of fat in the diet and increase fiber and complex carbohydrates.

Regular Checkups

Consult with a health professional regarding the appearance of any unusual symptoms or problems. Regular checkups will help you to avoid health problems and provide opportunities for the initiation of appropriate therapy when need

OUTLINE 15

COPING STRATEGIES FOR AGE-RELATED CHANGES

Factor	Acceptance	Adaptation	Checkups	Exercise	Nutrition	Stress Reducton
Adapting to Stress	X	X		X	X	X
Appetite	X	X	X	X	X	
Balance	X	X	X		X	
Bladder	X	X	X		X	
Body Contours and Features	X			X	X	
Circulatioin	X	X	X	X	X	X
Colon	X	X	X	X	X	X
Constipation	X	X	X	X	X	
Eating	X	X	X	X	X	X
Endocrine System	X	X	X	X	X	X
Esophagus	X	X	X		X	
Facial Appearance	X		X		X	
Fat Redistribution	X			X	X	
Feet	X	X	X		X	
Hair	X				X	
Hearing	X	X	X			

OUTLINE 15, cont'd

Factor	Acceptance	Adaptation	Checkups	Exercise	Nutrition	Stress Reducton
Heart	×	×	×	×	×	×
Height	×	×	×	×	×	
Intellectual Funtioning	×	×	×	×	×	
Intestines	×	×	×	×	×	×
Kidneys	×	×	×		×	
Liver	×		×		×	×
Memory	×	×	×	×	×	
Mouth	×	×	×		×	
Muscle	×	×	×	×	×	
Nails	×		×		×	
Nervous System	×	×	×	×	×	×
Pain Perception	×	×	×			
Respiration	×	×	×	×		
Senses	×	×	×		×	
Sexual Functioning	×	×	×	×	×	
Skeletal	×		×	×	×	
Skin	×	×	×	×	×	
Sleep	×	×	×		×	×
Stomach	×	×	×		×	×

OUTLINE 15, cont'd

Factor	Acceptance	Adaptation	Checkups	Exercise	Nutrition	Stress Reducton
Taste & Smell	X	X			X	
Teeth	X	X	X		X	
Throat	X	X	X		X	
Touch & Dexterity	X	X	X			
Vision	X	X	X		X	
Voice	X	X	X		X	
Weight	X		X	X	X	

VIEWPOINT

AGING—THE NEW FRONTIER FOR LIVING

by

Donna Cohen, Ph.D.
Professor and Chairman
Department of Aging and Mental Health
and
Director, USF Institute on Aging

Robert Heinlein made a remarkable prediction in a letter to his agent in 1949 — that our future will be profoundly affected by genetics, geriatrics, and atomic energy.[1] Who else other than a master of science fiction could have imagined that human aging would be such a dramatic force. For the first time in the history of hu(wo)mankind the aging of the human species has fundamentally altered the aging of the world population.[2] Population aging has replaced population growth in the industrialized countries as well as the developing countries of the world. This demographic revolution is occurring because mortality rates are declining for all age groups and it will create compelling social, economic, and ethical choices that will shape the health, well-being, and quality of life of society well into the next century.[3]

We are now within a few years of the beginning of the 21st Century, and if Robert Heinlein were alive, what might he predict about the future? I believe he would describe a world where growing old is accompanied by increasing productivity and those who are old are seen as having great aesthetic, economic, and social value. Does that sound strange to you? Can you imagine what it would be like to live out the biblical prescription of 120 years? Some of you will shudder at the thought. Others will deny that you will live so long, and still others will pray for good health and try to live a long and happy life.

The new age of aging is upon us and the facts are clear. Short of an accident or untimely death from AIDS, cancer, or another disease, most of us will grow old. Currently, 20% of the population dies after age 80, and by the beginning of the next century more than 50% will die after age 80.[4] Furthermore, our children's chances of living to 100 will increase as research breakthroughs uncover the secrets of longevity, health and emotional well-being.

All of us, regardless of what our age is now, have the responsibility to define what it means to grow up and grow old and to discover the productive potential of our lives. We are creating the images of age that our children and our children's children will either admire and emulate or fear and reject. The responsibility we share as members of a rapidly aging world community is to discard the fears of later life and reframe our attitude and expectations to be productive and generative throughout the decades of our life as we ascend what Samuel Ullman called the "summit of years."[5]

There is a reason for living a long life. The answer is revealed in Robert Heinlein's book *Time Enough For Love.* The message is also captured in the title. Growing old is necessary because we need a long time to learn how to survive, how to heal and how to love. Only with this knowledge will we be able to the define the goals of our life as we ascend the summit. John Denis has described the following goals for the many decades of life. The years from birth to 30 are characterized as a period of development, 30 until 60 as a period of expansion, 60 to 90 as a period for continued contributions, and 90 until 120 as a period of contemplation and wisdom.

Yes, aging is creating a new frontier for living. The way we value ourselves and others as we live longer together will affect people of all ages and ultimately our vitality, health, productivity and security in a changing and increasingly interdependent world.

Footnotes

1. Heinlein, Virginia (Ed.) *Robert Heinlein Grumbles from the Grave.* New York: Ballantine, 1989.

2. Olshansky, S. Jay, Carnes, Bruce, & Cassel, Christine. The aging of the human species. *Scientific American* 1993 268:46-52.

3. Cohen Donna (Ed.) Towards a 1991 White House Conference on Aging. Chicago: University of Illinois at Chicago, 1989.

4. Brody, Jacob & Cohen, Donna. Epidemiologic aspects of Alzheimer's disease: Facts and Gaps. *Journal of Aging and Health,* 1989, 1: 139147.

5. DeWitt, Karen. Work of obscure poet bonds a city and Japan. *New York Times,* 1991.

ANSWERS TO THE AGING QUIZ

1. FALSE

Brain diseases (e.g., Alzheimers) only occurs in 25% of less of older individuals. In fact, some cognitive functions actually increase with aging in some individuals. According to aging and medical scholars, the term "senility" is an unofficial term which lacks meaning. They recommend that it should be removed from our vocabulary.

2. FALSE

The family is still the primary caretaker of older relatives. Many elderly live close to their children and see them often. About 80% of men and 60% of women live in family settings. Cultural concerns do exist regarding our youth orientation and nursing home care.

3. TRUE

Depression, loneliness, loss of self-esteem, anxiety and other problems are more common as we age. This can result from the loss of family and friends, loss of independent functioning, and retirement. Fortunately, these emotional problems are treatable.

4. TRUE

It is estimated that about 12% of the American population is over the age of 65. By the year 2030 it is estimated that 20% of the population will be over this age.

5. TRUE

Only about 5% of elderly live in nursing homes. The rest are basically healthy and self-sufficient.

6. FALSE

There are many health problems that can cause problems in mental functioning (e.g., head injury, high fever, poor nutrition, adverse drug reactions, strokes, depression). Alzheimers is only one of many problems that can result in incurable problems in mental functioning.

ANSWERS TO THE AGING QUIZ, cont'd

7. FALSE

You intelligence does not decline unless there is a health problem of some kind to cause it. Intelligence is maintained in most folks and can even increase in some.

8. FALSE

Most people can have meaningful sexual relationships as they age. Consider creative adaptations (e.g., sexual lubricants) if sexual activities are uncomfortable.

9. FALSE

Stop smoking at any age! You body begins to heal immediately. After about 10 years of no tobacco use, your risk for health problems is probably no greater than that of nonsmokers.

10. FALSE

Exercise is beneficial at any age. Many older people enjoy and benefit from regular exercise (e.g., walking, swimming, bicycle riding). Not only will exercise strengthen your heart and lungs, but it can also lower your blood pressure. Be sure and check with your doctor before beginning any exercise activity.

11. FALSE

Your need for appropriate nutrition (including vitamins and minerals) does not decline with aging. However, the key is really one of a balanced diet, not an excessive intake of individual nutrients. Intake of some nutrients may need to be decreased (e.g., sweets, fats, salt, high calorie diets, alcohol). Check with your doctor about any special diets which may be beneficial for you.

12. FALSE

As above, there is a need for a balanced diet. However, we usually require fewer calories as we age. Otherwise, we will tend to gain weight. Calcium supplements are considered to be beneficial (especially for women). Calcium helps to prevent osteoporosis and broken bones due to falls.

ANSWERS TO THE AGING QUIZ, cont'd

13. TRUE

The ability of our body to adapt to temperature extremes declines with age (including the temperature regulating ability of our "thermostat" in the brain). So, dress appropriately for the weather outside.

14. TRUE

In particular, there is a much greater risk for falls and broken bones as we age. So, creative adaptations are very important (e.g., remove items that can trip you, use a cane, install nonskid carpets, use safety mats in the tub or shower, rearrange the furniture so that you have clear paths).

15. TRUE

Women tend to outlive men by about 8 years. By age 65, there are 1/3 fewer men than women. By age 85, there are about 60% fewer men. This trend may be changing, since proportionally more women are smoking and since both sexes have become more aware of lifestyle changes which help to reduce risks for heart disease and cancer.

16. TRUE

Fewer people are dying from strokes and heart disease. This increases your chances for surviving to old age (assuming, of course, that you make appropriate lifestyle changes).

17. TRUE

We tend to develop more health problems as we age, and so, take more medications. So, the 12% of the American population that is over the age of 65 is taking about 25% of the medications. This increases their risk for adverse drug reactions.

18. TRUE

Health fraud (i.e., medical quackery) may be a $100 billion industry. DON'T BUY HEALTH AND MEDICAL PRODUCTS THROUGH THE MAIL! Always check with a doctor, nurse or pharmacist before purchasing health products from medial advertisements (e.g., TV, radio, magazines).

ANSWERS TO THE AGING QUIZ, cont'd

19. FALSE

Personality doesn't change with age. There can be mood changes associated with life changes that occur with aging (e.g., retirement, inability to participate in some activities). However, emotional problems can often be treated.

20. FALSE

Although changes in vision are common with aging, they are considered to be the result of diseases and not aging, per se. Many vision problems can be corrected. So, see an eye care professional if you are having problems seeing clearly.

SCORE YOURSELF

18 +	=	Excellent! You know your stuff!
16 - 17	=	That's real good!
14 - 15	=	Not bad, but could be better.
13 or less	=	Well, the good news is that you are in for some pleasant surprises!

Reference: National Institutes on Aging

SECTION THREE

Diseases and Interventions of the 20th Century

11. TAKE HEART
...AND YOUR HEALTH

"States of health or disease
are the expressions of the successes or failures
experienced by the organism in its efforts
to respond adaptively to environmental challenge."

— Rene Dubos

Modern medicine, health education and public health measures have all helped to increase the average person's lifespan. Many elderly people now live with diseases that would have resulted in premature deaths in previous generations of history.

In modern times our major killers are related to lifestyles and environmental factors (see Outline 12). An understanding of these factors and the health problems they represent does not mean that we will likely increase our absolute lifespan, but we can identify guidelines by which we are more likely to reach our maximum lifespan and by which we can increase our quality of life.

"In the future, I think therapists should become much more conscious of helping people change their lifestyles and habits in such a way that they don't get sick in the first place. I am not overwhelmingly impressed with technological "miracles" like artificial hearts. If scientists can figure out how to keep people from getting heart attacks in the first place, this will be a real achievement."

— Sun Bear, Medicine Chief

The cardiovascular system (heart and blood vessels) are responsible for carrying oxygen and nutrients to all parts of the body. These components are the "food" that your body needs in order to function normally. This system also removes waste products that occur as a part of metabolism, digestion and other processes in the body. These waste products are eliminated by a filtering process that occurs in the kidneys, liver and lungs.

The heart is the pump which forces blood flow throughout the body. It is a muscle that must beat in an organized manner in order to function normally. This pulse or beating is coordinated by electrical impulses that travel throughout the nerves in the heart.

Because the heart is of such critical importance to health, it is important to consider diseases which affect the heart and blood vessels. Consider the following facts: Diseases of the heart and blood vessels kill someone every 32 seconds (that's nearly 1 million people each year). Heart diseases account for 43% of all deaths. One out of every four Americans has some type of disease involving the heart or blood vessels. It is estimated that 11% of women and 17% of men (age 45 - 64) have some form of heart disease or stroke. Finally, more than 17% of all people who die from heart and vascular diseases are under the age of 65.

Atherosclerosis and Arteriosclerosis

The walls of blood vessels become thicker as a result of normal aging. Consequently, they become more rigid and weak. When arteries (i.e., the vessels that carry blood away from the heart to the body tissues and organs) are damaged, major problems may occur. Veins are the vessels through which blood is returned to the heart.

Arteriosclerosis is the term which refers to the thickening and hardening of the arteries. This process can cause the arteries to rupture or clog, which interrupts blood flow to vital organs. Strokes and heart attacks are common outcomes of these problems.

Atherosclerosis is characterized by deposits of fats, cholesterol, cellular waste products, calcium and other deposits inside the blood vessels. This buildup of debris in the blood vessels is called plaque. Plaque formation can interfere with normal blood flow to certain tissues and can result in bleeding from the vessels or in clot formation. Strokes and heart attacks can occur when a clot breaks loose and travels to other tissues (e.g., the heart, brain, lungs), where it blocks blood flow to these tissues.

Plaque formation is more common at some sites in the body than others. Blood travels more slowly in some vessels than others, which allows plaque formation to develop more quickly. Plaque formation often begins in childhood and may have a hereditary basis. However, it is also certainly related to our diets. Plaque formation proceeds more rapidly in some people than it does in others. Some people develop problems by the time they reach their 30s, while others may not have problems until old age.

Cholesterol and Fats

Cholesterol is a fat-like substance that is used by the body to make other substances which it needs. Your body requires cholesterol for normal functioning. However, most of the cholesterol we need is manufactured by the liver, so that the amount of fat and cholesterol in the average American diet is excessive. These substances become a problem if the body is unable to eliminate them in healthy ways.

Like other substances needed by the body, cholesterol is transported in the blood stream to the sites in the body where it is needed. *Hypercholesterolemia* is the term for high cholesterol levels in the blood stream.

Cholesterol and other fats do not dissolve in the blood ("oils and water cannot mix"). So, fats combine with proteins and are carried in the bloodstream as special substances called *lipoproteins*. There are two types of lipoproteins, *high density lipoproteins* (HDLs) and *low density lipoproteins* (HDLs).

LDLs are the major carrier for cholesterol in the blood, and if there is too much LDL cholesterol in the blood, fatty deposits are more likely to occur. It is the LDLs that are known as "bad" cholesterol. Lower LDL levels are beneficial to health.

Cholesterol deposits increase plaque formation and atherosclerosis. Plaque formation tends to begin in the aorta, arteries of the heart and arteries which deliver blood to the brain. This process typically increases with age. Eventually, a highly cholesterol-laden "goo" develops that is very difficult for the body to remove and transport.

Blood vessels, especially arteries, are composed of several distinct layers of tissue. Some of these layers are quite delicate. The thickening and damage that occurs to the various layers can be compared to a termite infestation that weakens the foundation of a house. As the thickening and damage continues, arteries can weaken, "balloon" out (i.e., an aneurysm), or bleed. The blood that seeps out forms a clot. As clots enlarge, they can block blood flow in the artery. Scar tissue forms because of damage to the vessels and includes calcium deposits which contribute to the thickening process.

The damage that occurs to the blood vessels can result in clot formation, ruptures and bleeding. Any of these problems can result in abnormal blood flow patterns and occlusive diseases (e.g., strokes, heart attacks, and peripheral vascular diseases).

HDLs appear to be able to absorb excess cholesterol and carry it back to the liver for reprocessing and excretion. HDL may even be able to remove some cholesterol and fatty deposits from vessel walls. Since HDL is able to reduce your risk for heart diseases, it is often referred to as "good" cholesterol (remember "H" for "heart" or "health"). Doctors usually measure cholesterol, LDL and HDL levels in order to obtain a more accurate picture of your overall heart health. Women tend to have higher HDL levels than men because the female sex hormone estrogen tends to raise HDL levels. Since estrogen levels are highest before menopause, women of childbearing age tend to have fewer heart problems.

As people age, fat levels (i.e., triglycerides) in the blood usually increase. The term for high triglyceride levels in the blood is *hypertriglyceridemia*. Some people with high triglyceride levels do not seem to develop heart and vessel problems. Still, there is a strong association between triglyceride levels and the development of heart and blood vessel diseases. So for most people, it is important to monitor these levels.

The term "fat" is commonly used, but not commonly understood, especially when reading food labels. There are basically two types of fats: (1) saturated; and (2) unsaturated (see Outline 16). Saturated fats are the primary problem for dietary health. This type of fat is largely derived from animals and some plants. It is saturated fats and dietary cholesterol that raise blood cholesterol levels.

Unsaturated fats tend to be of vegetable origin. They may help to lower your blood cholesterol levels when used instead of saturated fats in your diet. Even so, all fats should be used in moderation regardless of type.

During food processing, fats may undergo a process known as *hydrogenation*. This is done to harden margarine, for example, so that it can be molded into tubs or sticks, or to provide shortening with a creamy consistency. Hydrogenation also increases the shelf-life of these products so that they do not become rancid as quickly as they otherwise would.

OUTLINE 16

SOURCES OF FATS [1]

Saturated (higher risk)

- Beef
- Beef fat
- Butter
- Cheeses
- Cocoa butter
- Coconut oil
- Cream
- Lamb
- Lard
- Milk
- Palm kernel oil (tropical oils)
- Palm oil
- Pork
- Poultry fat
- Veal
- Whole milk products

Unsaturated Fats (lower risk)

- Avocados
- Canola
- Corn
- Nuts
- Olive
- Peanut oils
- Safflower
- Seeds
- Sesame
- Soybeans
- Sunflower seeds

Ischemic Heart Disease

Approximately 250,000 people die each year from ischemic heart disease (heart problems which arise from a decreased blood flow to the heart). Heart disease is the leading cause of death in men older than 35, and in all persons older than 45. Premature heart disease (i.e., before age 65) can also result in reduced productivity and enjoyment of life. The risk factors for ischemic heart disease are:

- Cigarette smokers (10+ / day)
- Decreased HDL (< 40 in men or < 45 in females)
- Diabetes mellitus
- Family history of ischemic heart disease (before age 55 in parents or siblings)
- High blood pressure

---

1. See references 34, 36.

   ❦ Increased LDL (160+; or 130+ with 2 or more of the other risks)

   ❦ Increased lipoprotein A (LpA)

   ❦ Males

   ❦ Obesity (greater than 30% over ideal weight)

Increases in heart disease are clearly linked to increases in LDL cholesterol. The first defense in reducing your heart risks is to reduce your dietary intake of cholesterol and saturated fats. Dietary restrictions can lower LDL cholesterol by about 10% (which reduces the risks for heart disease by more than 20%). This is true even when these dietary changes are begun late in life. Dietary changes are indicated if:

1. LDL cholesterol is 160+ mg/dl in the absence of other risk factors.

2. LDL cholesterol is 130+ mg/dl and 2 or more other risk factors exist.

Dietary changes should not result in malnutrition. In our attempts to modify our diets via self-regulation, we sometimes delete essential nutrients. Consider enlisting the aid of a dietitian in order to insure a balanced diet.

Drug treatment for heart problems is often necessary for individuals who have a considerable risk for these conditions, based on the characteristics described. "Young elderly" (i.e., age 70 or less) tend to be better candidates for this therapy than older individuals.

The average age at which heart disease becomes a concern has increased over the last few decades and the number of deaths due to heart disease has actually declined since 1963. Even so, heart disease remains the most important health problem of elderly. The probability of having a heart attack is related to the numbers and sizes of atherosclerotic plaques. Cigarette smoking, high blood pressure, increased cholesterol levels and diabetes are also important risk factors. Fortunately, these are also the ones most likely to respond in a positive way to lifestyle changes. Cholesterol control is important, since atherosclerotic plaque formation begins in the teen years and accumulates throughout life. Prevention includes appropriate diet, regular exercise, maintaining an appropriate weight and no smoking. Health authorities believe that premature heart disease would be rare if these preventive measures were followed.

High Blood Pressure

Blood pressure refers to the amount of pressure which blood forces against the blood vessels as it is pumped throughout the body. It is related to the pumping force of the heart, the volume of blood being pumped, viscosity of the blood and the resistance (i.e., elasticity) of the blood vessels.

High blood pressure (or *hypertension*) occurs when the blood exerts too much force on the blood vessels over a period of time. This condition can cause tissue damage (including organs damage), bleeding, clot formation, an enlarged heart and heart strain. Hypertension can ultimately result in strokes, heart attacks, kidney failure (e.g., about 10% of deaths related to hypertension result from kidney damage) and other problems if it is not treated. Increased blood pressure can also damage the delicate blood vessels of the eyes and result in permanent visual damage.

"Normal" blood pressure is typically viewed as a reading less than 140/90. The first number is called the systolic reading and represents the highest pressure exerted against vessel walls when a wave of blood passes through a blood vessel. The second number is called the diastolic reading and represents the minimal pressure exerted against the blood vessels as blood flows through the vessels. Readings greater than 140/90 fall into the hypertension category.

High blood pressure is a "silent" disease because most people do not actually feel any symptoms (they feel "normal" because they have become accustomed to it). Health problems occur much later as a result of the damage caused over time. So, it is important to have periodic blood pressure checks.

Blood pressure can vary from one reading to another. For example, a physician may detect a high reading during an examination, even though the patient ordinarily has normal blood pressure. This is known as *labile hypertension*. In fact, a condition known as "white coat hypertension" can occur in people who become anxious about medical exams (their blood pressure readings are only elevated when they are at the doctor's office).

Most high blood pressure is classified as *essential hypertension*, which means that no specific cause can be found. More than 90% of people with high blood pressure have this type, which tends to run in families. Most cases of essential hypertension occur after the age of 35. *Secondary hypertension* is associated with other disease or health problems (e.g., thyroid, kidney, liver). So, regular checkups are important.

High blood pressure (hypertension) killed nearly 33,000 Americans in 1990 and contributed to the deaths of thousands more. Men have a greater risk of high blood pressure than women until age 55, then the risk becomes equal. After age 65, the risk increases for women. More than 46% of people with high blood pressure do not realize that they have it.

Of all people with high blood pressure, 67% are not on therapy (diet or drugs) at all, 22% are on inadequate therapy and 11% are adequately controlled. People with lower educational and income levels have a greater risk for high blood pressure.

Diets which are high in sodium contribute to high blood pressure levels. On the average we eat about 10 times as much salt as our body actually needs. Excessive salt intake tends to cause fluid retention in the body. In turn, this increases blood pressure. Give some thought to cutting back on your salt intake. One way to begin is to eliminate salt when cooking. People tend to use less when it is only used as a seasoning at the table.

There are a great many medications which are used to treat high blood pressure. Basically, they work by one of three ways:

1. Alter the heart in some way (e.g., slow it down or cause it to pump more efficiently). In essence, this is a matter of altering the "pump" (e.g., beta-blockers, digitalis)

2. Dilate the blood vessels so that the pressure of the blood against them is reduced (e.g., Minipress, Apresoline, Lonitin).

3. Reduce the amount of fluid in the blood vessels (e.g., diuretics or "water pills"), so that there is less pressure being exerted against the vessels.

People usually feel worse for a few days after beginning therapy for hypertension. This is because the body has become accustomed to a higher blood pressure. When it is suddenly lowered, the patient must become accustomed to a new "normal." People may feel tired during this time, or just not "normal." They may stop taking their medication because they think it is "too strong," or "not the right medication." In fact, they feel worse because the medication is working! Over a period of a few days or weeks the patient will begin to feel "normal" again. So, it is important to continue the medication during this initial adjustment phase.

In addition to medications, there are many lifestyle changes that help to reduce blood pressure. These include diet, exercise, and stress reduction. And in fact, it is sometimes possible to reduce blood pressure levels without the use of medications at all!

Increased systolic blood pressure was long thought to be a "natural" phenomenon of the elderly caused by stiffening of the artery walls that occurs with aging. This *isolated systolic hypertension* was observed to occur in as many as 20% of elderly. More recent studies have shown that the risk for organ damage can occur as a result of increases in either diastolic or systolic blood pressure. Isolated systolic hypertension is the most frequent type of hypertension that occurs in people over 65. In these cases, the diastolic pressure is less than 90, but the systolic pressure is greater than 160. There is a feeling among some physicians that a "high normal systolic blood pressure" (between 140 - 160) may indicate the need for treatment, especially if other risk factors exist. The risk for strokes and heart problems are reduced when hypertension is controlled. Additionally, diabetic eye diseases seem to occur more often in patients with isolated systolic hypertension.

Medication doses are adjusted carefully to identify the most effective dose with the fewest side effects. Doses which are too high can result in dizziness, fainting and falls. Although all beneficial lifestyle changes should be part of the treatment plan, certain lifestyle modifications are especially important (e.g., low salt diets, relaxation exercises, weight control).

Heart Attacks and Angina

Heart attacks are the number one killer of both men and women in America. This year 1.5 million people will have a heart attack and one-third of them will die. Approximately 45% of heart attacks occur in people under age 65 (5% of heart attacks occur in people less than 40). Many heart attacks are not fatal. However, many people who do die might have been saved if they had known what to do (300,000 will die before they reach a hospital). The average heart attack victim denies what is happening, and 50% of them will wait for two hours or more before seeking help.

Heart attacks occur when one or more of the major blood vessels to the heart becomes blocked due to plaque, fatty deposits, or a blood clot. Heart tissues (a type of muscle) are damaged and can even die when they do not receive an adequate blood supply. The result can be an irregular heart beat (i.e., *arrhythmia*, which can be quite dangerous), or the heart may stop pumping. The medical term for heart attack is *myocardial infarction* or "MI." Symptoms include:

- ❦ Chest discomfort (e.g., uncomfortable pressure, fullness, squeezing or pain lasting more than a few seconds)
- ❦ Sweating
- ❦ Lightheadedness
- ❦ Nausea
- ❦ Pain that spreads to the shoulders, neck or arms
- ❦ Shortness of breath
- ❦ Fainting

These symptoms can be deceptive because they can mimic other health problems which are less serious. The symptoms can subside, then return. Pain is the most common complaint and is often described as a squeezing or crushing sensation. It is usually in the central part of the chest or upper abdomen. In approximately one-third of cases it radiates to the arms (especially the left arm), but can also radiate to the back, jaw and neck. The pain usually does not go below the umbilicus (i.e., "belly button") or above the base of the skull. Nausea, vomiting, sweating, shortness of breath and anxiety also occur. As much as 30% of heart attacks are painless ("silent" heart attacks). The absence of pain may be caused by a weakness of the nerves that transmit pain signals (especially in diabetics and elderly). The pain of both heart attacks and angina can occur without exercise and often occurs in the morning (possibly due to normal daily variations in hormonal levels and natural physiological rhythms at that time of day). The presence of pain beneath the breastbone and sweating for more than 30 minutes is suggestive of a heart attack.

A heart attack can happen to anyone, anywhere, anytime. When it occurs, there is no time for delay. Early intervention is important with heart attacks, since immediate therapy can help to dissolve clots and prevent additional damage to heart tissues. Heart attack patients may be given "clot dissolvers" if they are diagnosed early. These medications can reduce deaths from heart attacks if given within one to six hours of symptoms. The problem is that people deny the possibility of a heart attack and may insist that it is just "indigestion."

Clot dissolvers may not be an option in patients with a recent stroke, since bleeding and damage to the brain could become worse because of the blood-thinning effects of clot dissolvers. High blood pressure increases the risk for strokes with these agents. People who have had ulcers or colon lesions may also not be ideal candidates for this therapy because of an increased risk for bleeding. And finally, individuals who are older than 75 are at a greater risk for stroke formation and are not ideal candidates for this type of therapy.

The use of clot dissolvers is intended to limit heart damage *during the heart attack*. Once the immediate crisis is over, a major focus of therapy becomes one of behavior modification and reduction of heart attack risks. Survival after heart attacks has improved because of medications (e.g., beta-blockers, calcium channel blockers, aspirin, and others). Many of these drugs improve heart function. This is important, since heart attacks often weaken the heart and increase the risk for more problems. The use of estrogens in post-menopausal women appears to decrease the risk of heart problems, probably because of its impact on cholesterol and stroke risks. The control of other diseases (e.g., diabetes) is also important.

Aspirin has received a great deal of attention regarding its potential to prevent heart attacks. However, preventive therapy with aspirin should not be a self-care measure. Aspirin can actually increase the risk of brain hemorrhages and bleeding of the stomach and intestines. It should only be implemented by physicians who are familiar with your complete medical and health history.

Antioxidants (e.g., beta-carotene, Vitamin C, Vitamin E, Selenium) may inhibit the formation of plaque. Plaque formation may be increased by diabetes, which would explain why diabetics have a greater risk for heart disease. And in general, heart disease can be reduced by aggressive control of diabetes (e.g., weight reduction, careful glucose monitoring, appropriate insulin therapy).

Heart attacks can result in the development of scar tissues that can be detected by electrocardiograms (EKGs). This is an important diagnostic procedure since many people (about 25%) have "silent" heart attacks (i.e., those without the usual symptoms). When chest pains occur, physicians often recommend a treadmill test to detect changes in the EKG when the heart is stressed. Other tests (e.g., coronary arteriograms) may be recommended to identify heart problems in individuals who are having symptoms, but have normal exercise test results. Procedures such as coronary catheterization allow doctors to dilate arteries constricted by heart disease with a balloon-like instrument (a *percutaneous transluminal coronary angioplasty*, or PTCA). This procedure, while sometimes beneficial, is not necessarily a "cure," since a significant percentage of these arteries can become blocked again. High-tech procedures also include the use of lasers to vaporize clots in the arteries and special microscopic catheters which contain scalpels to remove cholesterol blockage.

Angina pectoris refers to chest pain that occurs when the heart is not receiving a sufficient blood supply. Angina is not a heart attack, per se, but it can be a warning sign that a heart attack could occur. Since the heart needs more oxygen when it is working harder, many people have angina attacks when exercising in some way (e.g., walking, swimming, etc.).

It is also possible to have silent ischemia (angina without pain). Many people have this problem and then eventually experience a heart attack with little warning. There are tests to diagnose this problem, so it is important to have regular checkups after age 40.

Studies show that certain lifestyles increase the risk for heart attacks. Almost all of the major risk factors can be controlled or even eliminated, which means that we can significantly reduce our risk for heart attacks!

The Big four risk factors are:

🐛 Elevated cholesterol	🐛 Lack of exercise
🐛 Elevated blood pressure	🐛 Smoking

Other risk factors include:

🐛 Diabetes	🐛 Excess weight
🐛 Family history of heart disease	🐛 Oral contraceptives (in women with other risk factors)

Some of these factors may have a hereditary component, but, even so, lifestyle choices (e.g., diet and exercise) can help to offset their potential hazards.

One risk factor worth mentioning is alcohol consumption. Some studies have indicated that alcohol in moderation may actually protect the heart. This occurs because small quantities of alcohol seem to raise HDL levels. Unfortunately, this small protective factor is easily lost with overconsumption. And, Americans are prone to drink more than the small amounts associated with heart protection. The heart-protective level is no more than two drinks/day. The negative effects of excessive consumption can be hazardous to your health:

- ❦ Auto accidents
- ❦ Diseases of the nervous system
- ❦ Pancreas disease
- ❦ Increased triglyceride levels
- ❦ Liver disease
- ❦ Heart failure
- ❦ Increased blood pressure

Arrhythmias and Sudden Cardiac Death

An *arrhythmia* is an irregular heart beat. Arrhythmias can include an unusually rapid pulse (*tachycardia*) or slow pulse (*bradycardia*), which cause little discomfort or danger. However, some arrhythmias result in such chaotic heart rhythms that the heart cannot function normally. When this occurs, neither the heart or the other tissues of the body receive an adequate blood supply.

Arrhythmias can occur because the nerve signals to the heart are not being conducted in an organized way. When this happens the heart muscles do not contract in sequence like they should. Arrhythmias can also occur if the heart tissues are damaged (e.g., from a lack of blood supply). Thus, even if the nerve signal reaches the tissues, the muscle is simply not able to respond.

Sudden Cardiac Death refers to a sudden loss of heart function (i.e., cardiac arrest). This can occur in people who are known to have heart problems, but also occurs in people with no history of heart disease.

Medications are available to treat most heart problems. People can be successfully treated and live nearly normal lifespans if they comply with therapy. Unfortunately, many people do not take their medications as directed, nor do they make recommended lifestyle changes.

Prevention is the most important and effective weapon we have, since most heart problems are avoidable. The adoption of healthier lifestyles from early ages could save countless lives and medical expenses.

Strokes

Strokes are the leading cause of disability in the U.S. It is estimated that about 5% of the population over age 65 has been affected by a stroke. However, this condition is not restricted to this age group, since approximately 28% of people who suffer strokes are under the age of 65. About 500,000 people suffer a stroke each year and more than 3 million stroke victims are alive today. After age 55, the incidence of stroke more than doubles each ten years.

A stroke occurs when a blood vessel is blocked by a blood clot, fat particle or cholesterol buildup, rupture of an aneurysm, or abnormal heart function (e.g., cardiac arrest). The actual damage that occurs depends upon the tissue that is being deprived of blood (e.g., heart, brain, lung). For example, brain damage can be permanent, since damaged brain cells cannot be replaced. The outcomes of strokes include:

- Loss of ability to read
- Loss of awareness
- Changes in behavior
- Difficulty chewing or swallowing
- Clumsiness (e.g., bumping into things)
- Depression
- Loss of feeling in arms or legs
- Muscle weakness
- Paralysis (usually one-sided)
- Loss of recognition or ability to use common objects
- Changes in thinking, thought patterns and memory
- Inability to understand speech
- Speech problems
- Loss of vision

As much as 80% of strokes occur in the brain, and in fact, the term *stroke* is normally reserved for clots involving the brain. Other terminology is used to describe clot formation in other organ sites. Clots in the small vessels of the brain cut off blood supply, oxygen and nutrients to important nerve centers. These vessels can rupture and bleed and are associated with much higher fatality rates.

Transient ischemic attacks (TIAs) refer to nervous system damage that improves after the "attack." The area of the body affected by this event depends upon the area of the brain involved. Most defects clear up completely (usually within 24 hours) and can be traced to blockage of certain arteries. A TIA is a warning sign which indicates that a major stroke could occur. There are other health problems that can cause similar symptoms (e.g., migraine, hypoglycemia, certain types of seizures, some drugs). Any symptoms which could suggest a stroke should be evaluated immediately by a physician:

- Changes in behavior
- Dizziness
- Emotional lability
  (e.g., sudden mood swings, emotional outbursts, sudden changes in emotion)
- Sudden severe headaches with no apparent cause
- Changes in mental functioning
  (e.g., memory, attention span, learning ability)
- Loss of speech, trouble talking or difficulty understanding speech
- Difficulty swallowing
- Unsteadiness or sudden falls
- Sudden dimness or loss of vision (especially of one eye)
- Sudden weakness or numbness of the face, arms or legs (esp. on one side of the body)

The risk factors for strokes include:

- Birth control pills
- Elevated cholesterol
- History of "mini-strokes" (Transient Ischemic Attacks, or TIAs)

❦ Excessive alcohol use

❦ Heart disease

❦ High blood pressure

❦ Tobacco use

❦ Migraine headaches (esp. in women on birth control pills)

❦ Overweight

Elderly individuals have an increased risk for brain hemorrhages that can result in abnormal brain function. Since the brain ordinarily shrinks with age, the vessels that line the brain can be stretched, rupture and bleed. Falls, which are more common among older people, can injure these delicate vessels, result in slow bleeding and promote a gradual build-up of pressure around the brain. This can cause decreases in alertness and ability to concentrate. *Aneurysms* are blood-filled pouches that occur as a result of weak blood vessels and are aggravated by high blood pressure. They are not always dangerous, but can be if they rupture.

Treatment depends upon the type of stroke involved and its location in the brain. Control of risk factors is important (prevention is always more desirable than "cures," even if cures are possible). TIAs are sometimes treated by surgical procedures which remove plaque from the carotid arteries in the neck. Once an actual stroke occurs, treatment attempts to reduce bleeding and swelling in the brain. Some brain hemorrhages can be removed surgically.

Aspirin has been used to prevent the risk of occlusive strokes, but can also increase the risk of bleeding. Thus, it is important that this type of therapy be prescribed by a physician. Self-medicating to prevent strokes can be hazardous. Other blood thinners (e.g., Coumadin) may be prescribed for patients with certain types of health problems (e.g., heart diseases that could result in clot formation).

Congestive Heart Failure (CHF)

CHF occurs because the heart muscle is damaged or overworked. It can result from high blood pressure, heart attack, atherosclerosis, congenital heart defects, lung diseases and other problems. When the heart becomes damaged it may not be able to pump blood as efficiently. Blood returning to the heart may begin to back up, causing swelling (edema) and congestion. Fluid accumulations in the lungs can result in breathing difficulties. Heart failure can interfere with normal kidney function and can result in disturbances of electrolyte balance.

Common signs of CHF are swelling of the legs and ankles, difficulty breathing, and weight gain due to accumulated fluids. Treatment usually requires rest, diet, modified daily activities, and medications. For the most part CHF can be treated successfully and most patients can lead relatively normal lives.

Peripheral Vascular Disease

Blockage of blood flow can occur in arteries that supply organs such as the kidneys, sexual organ, and extremities (e.g., arms and legs). The scenario is essentially the same as that for strokes. However, the medical term applied to this problem is called peripheral vascular disease.

Use of tobacco products constricts the arteries and can contribute to the development of this problem. Impaired blood flow can result in pain to the buttocks, thighs and calves, especially during exercise. Diabetes can result in problems involving the small arteries in the feet. So, foot care is especially important for diabetics (e.g., avoiding restrictive shoes). Gangrene (tissue death) is another risk which must be considered.

There are a number of medical procedures which can be used to detect and treat reduced blood pressure in the legs and other body sites. Also, ultrasound can be performed to detect blockage in arteries. Therapy includes appropriate exercise to enhance circulation and medications (e.g., blood vessel dilators, blood thinners) to increase blood flow. Surgery (e.g., angioplasty or balloon dilation; artery bypass surgery) is sometimes indicated.

Weight, Fat, Diet and Prevention

Up to this point, the focus of the discussion has involved specific heart problems. However, our weight, fat composition and diet are general problems that impact all heart diseases and which are very much under our control.

Excess weight and the heart

Being overweight is a risk factor for heart problems in general. The only healthy approaches to weight control involve a healthy diet and exercise program. Approximately 25% of the American population is 20+% over a desirable weight. People who are 30% or more over their ideal body weight are considered to be obese and are more likely to develop health problems (e.g., heart disease, strokes). The risks of excess weight and your health include:

- ☙ Decreased HDL levels
- ☙ Extra strain on the heart
- ☙ Increased cholesterol levels
- ☙ Increased triglyceride levels
- ☙ Increased blood pressure
- ☙ Increased risk for diabetes
- ☙ Increased risk for gallstones
- ☙ Increased risk joint diseases

Body Shape and Heart Problems

Body shape can be an indicator of potential heart and other problems. In general, waist measurements should not exceed hip measurements. For men, the waist measurement should not be more than 90% of the hip measurement [e.g., a man with a 40 inch hip measurement should not have more than a 36 inch (40 x .90 = 36) waist measurement]. For women, the waist measurement should not be more than 80% of the hip measurement [e.g., a woman with a 36 inch hip measurement should not have more than a 29 inch (36 x .80 = 28.8) waist measurement].

There are many methods by which health professionals can measure body composition and make body fat determinations:

Body Impedance

Electrodes are placed on the body and a small, imperceptible electrical charge is passed through the body. The calculation of body fat is based on the resistance to the electricity and is based on the fact that fat, water and bone conduct electricity at different rates, which can be measured. The test is time consuming, it requires that the patient must lie down for a period of time while the test is being conducted, and the equipment involved is expensive. People who are unusually lean or fat may have unreliable readings.

Circumference Measures

This test is conducted by using a measuring tape to measure various parts of the body. It is a simple test which is considered to be reasonably accurate unless the subject is unusually muscular.

Height and Weight Charts

This evaluation method uses height and weight charts to determine whether an individual is overweight as compared to norms for the general population. It is a simple method, but can be unreliable, especially if the individual is unusually muscular.

Hydrostatic (Underwater) Weight

In this test the patient is submerged in water and the displacement (i.e., density) is calculated and compared with a table of known values of fat percentage. This test is quite accurate when conducted by a trained expert. However, it is time consuming and requires a hydrostatic weight tank or swimming pool designed for this purpose. It can also be unpleasant for the patient, who must exhale all air in the lungs then be completely submerged underwater for several seconds while a reading is being taken.

Infrared Light

An infrared light wand is placed over an area of muscle and fat (e.g., upper arm). The instrument measures the thickness of fat and calculates a percentage of body fat. These instruments are very popular in health fairs because they are quick and easy. However, this technology is expensive and sometimes unreliable.

Skinfold Test

This test is conducted by using skinfold calipers, which are used to pinch and measure fatty areas of the body (e.g., arms, back, waist). Formulas are used to estimate body fat, and the test requires expertise on the part of the person doing the test. This is considered to be a fast and reliable test, and is probably the most widely used test in clinics and health clubs.

The "Pinch and Inch" Method

More recently, a popular cereal advertisement stated that if you can pinch an inch of fat above your hip, you need to be eating their cereal. The area of the body to which this advertisement refers is known as the supra iliac, located just above the hip bone (i.e., the "love handles"). There is some validity to this technique. If you actually can pinch an inch or more of fat in the waist line area, you may need to consider healthy weight loss efforts.

OUTLINE 17

PREVENTING HEART ATTACKS [2]

❦ Alcohol in Moderation

It appears that no more than 2 drinks per day can help to protect your heart. However, many drinkers do not stop at this level. More than 2 drinks per day are associated with a great many health problems. So, if you don't drink ... don't start! If you do drink, do so in moderation.

❦ Have Regular Medical Checkups

Many of the risk factors for heart disease have no symptoms in their early stages (high cholesterol, high blood pressure and diabetes). Regular checkups allow your physician to detect these problems early and to prevent problems later on. It is especially important for women taking oral contraceptives to have regular checkups.

❦ Eat an Appropriate Diet

Diets with saturated fats and cholesterol promote atherosclerosis and other heart problems. High-fat diets are also associated with the development of cancer. Our dietary "tastes" are acquired. We can all learn to eat healthy ... and enjoy it!

❦ Increase Your Levels of Exercise and Regular Physical Activity

Try to include activities in your lifestyle that give your heart and lungs a workout for 30 to 60 minutes 3 to 4 times each week. Even if you can't achieve these levels, try something! Every bit helps!

❦ Reduce Stress

Be aware of yourself. If stress is affecting you in negative ways, try to do something about it.

❦ Avoid Tobacco Products

Tobacco products are directly associated with so many health problems that it is an enigma of our culture that so many people continue to use them. So, if you don't use tobacco products, continue to avoid them. If you do use tobacco products ... QUIT!

2. See references for Chapter 11.

```
┌─────────────────────────────────────────────────┐
│              ███ OUTLINE 17 cont'd ███            │
│                                                   │
│  ❦ Maintain an Ideal Body Weight                  │
│      Being overweight increases your chances for  │
│      having high choles-                          │
│      terol, high triglyceride levels, low HDL     │
│      levels, high blood pressure                  │
│      and diabetes.                                │
│                                                   │
└─────────────────────────────────────────────────┘
```

Diet

As with other health problems discussed in this book, a healthy diet must be an integral part of lifestyle if we are to improve our quality and quantity of life. Outline 18 summarizes guidelines from the American Heart Association. As you will see in other sections of the book (e.g., cancer, nutrition), there are repeating themes. There is a reason for that . . . they make a difference!

An Ounce of Prevention

Obviously, it is better to prevent heart problems than to treat them once they occur. Also learn how to perform Cardiopulmonary Resuscitation (CPR) from the Red Cross or American Heart Association. Many lives are saved each year because someone knew what to do.

```
┌─────────────────────────────────────────────────┐
│                 ███ OUTLINE 18 ███                │
│                                                   │
│        DIETARY GUIDELINES OF THE AMERICAN HEART   │
│                    ASSOCIATION [3]                │
│                                                   │
│   Food Labels                                     │
│        ❦ Read food labels.  Learn what you are    │
│          buying.                                  │
│                                                   │
│   Avoid:                                          │
│        ❦ Bakery goods        ❦ Foods high in fats │
│        ❦ Fatty meats         ❦ Whole milk dairy   │
│                                 products          │
│                                                   │
└─────────────────────────────────────────────────┘
```

3. See references for Chapter 11.

OUTLINE 18 cont'd

Breads, Grains, Cereals
- Eat 6+ servings per day.

Cholesterol and Fat Intake
- Low cholesterol diets do NOT necessarily mean giving up desirable foods. Many favorite foods are already part of a healthy diet.
- Intake should be no more than 300 milligrams (mg) per day (and less if possible).
- Chill soups and stews after cooking so that you can remove the hardened fat from the top before serving.
- Consume no more than 8 teaspoon servings of fats and oils per day. These should be limited to cooking and baking and in salad dressings and spreads.
- Drain off fat after cooking before the dish is put onto the table.
- Favor recipes and cooking that require little or no fat (e.g., boil, broil, bake, roast, poach, steam, saute, stir-fry or microwave).
- Monosaturated fat should be no more than 15% of total calories.
- Polyunsaturated fat intake should be no more than 10% of total calories.
- Saturated fat intake should be less than 10% of calories.
- Total fat intake should be less than 30% of total calories.

Dairy Products
- Milk

  Whole milk contains more cholesterol and saturated fats (about 45% of the calories in whole milk come from saturated fat) as compared to skim milk or low fat milks. Instead of whole milk, use 1% milk (only 14% of its calories come from saturated fats), or skim milk (which has even less calories from saturated fats). Both 1% and skim milk are rich in protein, calcium and other nutrients without being high in fat.
- Butter, Cream and Ice Cream

  Reserve these products for special occasions, since they contain more fat than whole milk. Be careful about the butter and cream

OUTLINE 18 cont'd

hidden in many casserole and other dishes. Generally, use unsaturated vegetable oils and polyunsaturated margarine instead of lard or butter.

❦ Cheese

Many people eat cheese instead of meat because it is high in protein. However, cheeses also tend to be high in fats (as much as 70% of the calories in cheese may come from butter fat, which is as high as ice cream). Instead of regular cheese, select low-fat cottage cheese, and other low-fat cheese products.

❦ Eggs

The American Heart Association recommends that you should eat no more than 4 egg yolks each week, including those used in cooking. Egg whites are good protein sources without cholesterol. Substitute 2 egg whites for each egg yolk in recipes that call for eggs. Eat only cooked eggs and egg whites, not raw ones.

Fruits

❦ Eat more fruits (5+ servings per day). Substitute fruits for desserts and salads higher in fats and cholesterol.

Meats

❦ Eat no more than 6 ounces (cooked) per day of lean meat, fish and skinless poultry.

❦ Create "low meat" meals by combining lean meats with pasta, rice, beans or vegetables.

❦ It is best to teat lean cuts of meat. Trim off as much of the visible fat as possible before cooking.

❦ Fish products can be either fatty or lean, but represent a healthy protein source. Fish products may contain some cholesterol, but they tend to be lower in saturated fats.

❦ Organ meats (e.g., liver, kidney, brain, heart) are high in cholesterol. It is best to limit your intake of these meats.

❦ Poultry products contain most of their fats in the skin. So remove the skin before cooking. Also, chicken and turkey have lower fat contents than duck or goose.

OUTLINE 18 cont'd

- Processed meats (e.g., sausage, bologna, salami, hot dogs) tend to be high in fats (as much as 80% of their calories from fats). Even those with "reduced fat" labels may be excessively high in fats. Substitute turkey products where possible (e.g., turkey sausage, turkey ham, etc.).

- Red meat is not a problem if eaten in moderation.

Sodium

- Should be no more than 3 grams (3000 milligrams) per day. That's equal to less than 1.5 teaspoons of salt. (For what it's worth, the average American consumes 10 times the amount of salt that our bodies actually need!)

Vegetables

- Eat 5+ servings per day.

- Opt for main dishes which feature vegetables, beans, rice or pasta.

12. CANCER

"We often think of people who are ill as *victims* of disease, and this reinforces their sense of helplessness."

Patricia Norris

Even though heart disease kills more people each year, cancer is more dreaded. And, there are many reasons for us to better understand why and what we can do about this problem:

🐛 Cancer is the second leading cause of death in the U.S.

🐛 Cancers are primarily related to lifestyles, and

🐛 80% of cancers are preventable!

There is no nationwide cancer registry, so there is no way of accurately knowing how many new cases of cancer occur each year. Even so, reasonable estimates can be made based upon the facts and figures from a variety of organizations.

What is Cancer?

The term *cancer* actually refers to a *group* of diseases which are characterized by the uncontrolled growth and spread of abnormal cells. Death can occur if the spread is not controlled in some way.

There are three general categories of these causes:

1. Heredity;

2. Viral infections (certain types); and

3. Environmental hazards (including lifestyle choices).

The various factors that can contribute to cancer formation can act independently, or they may combine to increase the risk for developing certain types of cancer. For example, the combination of smoking and heavy caffeine use may increase the risk for developing cancer of the pancreas. Since many smokers also drink beverages which contain caffeine (e.g., coffee), it is difficult to separate the impact which each has on the development of this type of cancer.

Problems also exist because of the length of time which can occur between causative factors and the development of cancer. Smokers may not develop lung (and other) cancers for 20 years. During the interim they may be relatively free of symptoms. As described in the introductory section, there is no universal definition for "health." People tend to view themselves as being "healthy" unless symptoms or disease appear. Thus, people may engage in high risk behaviors without regard for the damage which they are doing to themselves because they have no symptoms to warn them. By the time symptoms appear, effective treatment is often too late.

The early detection and treatment of cancers increases the chances for positive outcomes. As logical as this sounds, there are still many of us who ignore the warning signs. Many men, for example, have died prematurely from prostate cancer because of their reluctance to acknowledge symptoms or to undergo a simple rectal examination.

Authorities estimate that 90% of the 700,000 skin cancers that will be diagnosed this year can be prevented by appropriate protection from the sun's rays. Virtually all cancers associated with smoking and heavy alcohol intake could be avoided (about 180,000 lives each year). Nearly half of all new cancer cases will involve the breast, tongue, mouth, colon, rectum, cervix, prostate, testes and skin. These and other cancerous conditions would be treatable if we engaged in preventive lifestyles, regular screening and self-examinations. As many as 100,000 people would survive each year if their cancers had been detected at earlier stages. These are minimal estimates. In fact, we really don't know how many more would be saved annually if prevention was more important to us.

Anyone can develop cancer, although the incidence is higher as we age. During the 1980s there were more than 4.5 million cancer deaths, more than 9 million new cancer cases, and 12 million people under medical care for cancer. Approximately one-third of us can expect to develop some form of cancer.

Despite these grim statistics, the news is not all bad. More than 8 million Americans who are alive today have a history of cancer. The majority of these are "cured" (i.e., they have no evidence of the disease) and have the same life expectancy as people who have not had cancer. In most cases, five cancer-free years without symptoms (i.e, remission) indicates that the individual has been cured. For some forms of cancer, the patient must be observed for a longer time period.

OUTLINE 19

CANCER PREVENTION GUIDELINES [4]

❦ Alcohol

Heavy alcohol drinkers are at a greater risk for the development of certain types of cancer (e.g., oral, liver). This is especially true for smokers who drink.

❦ Diet (see discussion in this chapter)

❦ Estrogen

Estrogen therapy in postmenopausal women appears to increase the risk of cancer of the uterus. If progesterone is included, the risk appears to be minimized. Women who are interested in estrogen replacement therapy should discuss this therapy with their physician in an effort to accurately evaluate risks and benefits.

❦ Occupational Hazards

Exposure to certain industrial agents (e.g., nickel, chromate, asbestos, vinyl chloride, benzene) appears to be associated with a higher risk for the development of certain types of cancer (e.g., lung), especially among smokers.

❦ Sun and Ionizing Radiation

Ionizing Radiation

Excessive exposure to ionizing radiation can increase cancer risk. Most medical and dental X-rays are adjusted to deliver the lowest possible dose needed to provide diagnostic information.

Radon

Radon exposure in the home may increase lung cancer risks, especially in smokers. It is a good idea to have homes evaluated for radon levels.

Sun Exposure

Sun exposure is related to nearly all of the 700,000+ nonmelanoma types of skin cancer, and is a major factor in the development of melanomas. It is best to limit sun exposures (e.g., wearing protective clothing, not staying in the sun too long). We need to rethink

4. See references for Chapter 12.

OUTLINE 19 cont'd

our orientation to the "tan is beautiful" belief. Use skin protectants with Skin Protectant Factors (SPFs) higher than 15.

☙ Avoid Tobacco Products
Tobacco use is responsible for about 87% of lung cancer cases and is associated with nearly 1/3 of all cancers. People who smoke 2+ packs of cigarettes a day are as much as 25 times more likely to die from lung cancer than non-smokers.

It is estimated that nearly 2 million new cancer cases will be diagnosed this year. More than 500,000 people will die of cancer (about 1,400 people per day), and 1 out of 5 deaths in the U.S. is from cancer.

The Costs of Cancer

The overall costs for cancer were estimated to be $104 billion in 1990. This included $35 billion for direct medical costs, $12 billion for lost productivity and $57 billion for death related costs. Cancer is responsible for about 10% of the total cost of disease in the U.S. and about 18% of all causes of premature death. The costs of screening add another $4 billion to the overall cost picture.

Causes of Cancer

Although there is much that still needs to be learned about cancer, our knowledge has increased considerably in the past several decades. Cancers appear to occur as a result of multiple factors, both external (e.g., chemicals, radiation, viruses) and internal (e.g., hormones, status of the immune system, heredity). In any one case it is often difficult to know exactly which factors are the primary cause. However, there are three categories of factors which seem to emerge most frequently, and these are well worth our consideration.

Heredity

Some people inherit a risk for certain types of cancers. For this reason, if you have a family history of cancers, you should have regular checkups to identify problems early. A family history indicates that you may have a genetic predisposition for the development of certain types of cancers. Consequently, it is imperative to avoid other risk factors. A family history of cancer does not necessarily mean, of course, that you will develop cancer. Rather, it only means that your risk is greater if you are exposed to other risk factors. This component is the object of many of the biotechnological advances, particularly regarding gene manipulations.

Viruses

Viruses appear to be involved in the development of certain types of cancer. Some viruses appear to be direct causes of certain types of cancer (certain herpes viruses, Epstein-Barr virus). Other viruses affect you in negative ways that predispose you to cancer formation (e.g., HIV).

Environmental Damage

There is little doubt that environmental damage is the greatest causative factor of cancer in industrialized nations, such as the U.S. Environmental causes include such factors as pollution and destruction of the ozone layer. However, environmental risks also include lifestyle choices (e.g., smoking, heavy caffeine use, excessive sun exposure, high fat diets). The importance of this observation is that the majority of cancers can be prevented if people are willing to make appropriate lifestyle changes.

Diet and Cancer

The relationship between diet and cancer is more controversial than some of the other risk or protective factors. Even so, there is growing evidence that diet can impact the potential for certain types of cancers in either positive or negative ways. The importance of this information is also clear. Each of us can increase or reduce risk factors by the diets we choose. Thus, some understanding of dietary impact on cancer can serve as a valuable guide to cancer prevention.

Evidence for dietary influences on cancer can be seen in geographic distributions of certain types of cancers in different parts of the

---

OUTLINE 20

SUMMARY OF DIETARY GUIDELINES FOR
REDUCING CANCER RISKS [5]

❦ Maintain a desirable body weight.

❦ Eat a varied diet.

❦ Include a variety of both vegetables and fruits in your daily diet.

❦ Eat more foods high in fiber (e.g., whole grain cereals, legumes, vegetables, fruits).

❦ Reduce your dietary fat intake.

❦ Reduce your consumption of alcoholic beverages ... if you drink at all.

❦ Reduce your consumption of foods that are salt-cured, smoked, or preserved with nitrates.

---

world. Various cultures often have dramatically different dietary patterns. For example, prior to World War II Japan had one of the lowest breast cancer rates in the world. This was probably due to the low fat intake of the Japanese people, since their diet consisted largely of fish, rice and vegetables. Since World War II, however, the Japanese have been significantly influenced by Western cultural traditions. Many have moved to the U.S., attended universities here, or have been exposed to our culture in other ways including a diet that is higher in fat. As a result, for example, breast cancer rates for Japanese women have increased drastically in the last few decades. Similarly, breast cancer rates in the Netherlands have historically been high, presumably because of diets which have always been high in fats.

Health authorities have been studying the relationship between diet and cancer for more than 20 years in an effort to better understand this phenomenon. Even though correlations exist, it is almost impossible to accurately assign risks and benefits of dietary behaviors. Still, the research is sufficiently clear to justify evaluation of our dietary habits. Rather than waiting for definitive confirmation or for a cure,

---

5. See references for Chapter 12.

we should adopt healthier lifestyles, including healthier diets, in an effort to reduce our risks for cancer.

Foods, as they are related to cancer, can be generally assigned to two categories: (1) promoters, which increase the risk for cancer development and the rates at which cancers may grow; and (2) anti-promoters, which inhibit the development of cancers in some way.

Promoters: Fats

Diets which are high in fat appear to be associated with a higher risk for the development of certain types of cancer (e.g., breast, colon, prostate). Most of the concern has involved saturated fats, but even some unsaturated fats have been shown to promote tumor formation. In the case of colon cancer, the fats are presumed to damage colon tissue over time and to cause the development of cancerous cells. Here again, the cancer may be discovered only late in its development.

Anti-promoters

Calcium

Calcium apparently binds with bile and fatty acids, thereby preventing cancer development in certain tissues (e.g., colon). For this reason some people have advocated adding calcium supplements to our diet in order to prevent cancer. Although some studies have indicated that higher intakes of milk (a natural source of calcium) may lower cancer risks, the benefits from calcium supplements remain unclear.

Calorie Restriction

Reducing calorie intake appears to counteract the effects of aging, increases lifespan and may also inhibit cancer development. People (and cultures) that have a higher calorie intake tend to be taller, but they also appear to have a greater risk for developing certain cancers (e.g., colon, rectal, lung, leukemia, Hodgkin's Disease, bone). This relationship may involve the total number of body cells and the rates at which they divide. At any rate, the maintenance of an appropriate weight and reduced calorie intake should be considered as measures to prevent cancer formation.

Fiber

Dietary fiber is thought to protect the colon by a number of mechanisms. It speeds the passage of the intestinal contents, lowers the concentration of cancer-producing substances and impacts the digestibility of the intestinal contents. Ironically, research on dietary fiber is conflicting, but seems to suggest that certain types of fiber (e.g., from fruits and vegetables) may inhibit cancer development (e.g., lung, colon, breast). Some studies have suggested that fiber may actually promote the formation of colon tumors in their initial stages. Even so, fiber does not appear to be a cancer promoter by itself, but rather, may act with other cancer-producing substances in some way. At present, the general consensus among health authorities is that fiber is healthy and serves to protect you from cancer, not promote it.

Fruits

Vegetables and fruits should be included in everyone's daily diet, since they are associated with a decreased risk of developing certain types of cancers (e.g., lung, prostate, bladder, esophagus, colon, rectal and stomach). Desirable fruits include:

❦ Apricots	❦ Mango	❦ Plantain
❦ Blackberries	❦ Nectarines	❦ Prunes
❦ Cantaloupe	❦ Oranges	❦ Raspberries
❦ Grapefruit	❦ Papaya	❦ Strawberries
❦ Lemons	❦ Peaches	❦ Tangerines
❦ Limes	❦ Persimmons	❦ Tomatoes

Vegetables

Vegetables contain certain enzyme inhibitors called protease inhibitors. These substances may counteract the actions of cancer-producing substances and prevent the development of tumors. Plants also contain substances known as sterols which, like calcium, may protect colon tissue from injury by damaging substances. Desirable vegetables include:

❦ Asparagus	❦ Collard greens	❦ Potatoes
❦ Beet greens	❦ Dandelion greens	❦ Pumpkin
❦ Bok choy	❦ Garden cress	❦ Radish greens
❦ Broccoli	❦ Green pepper	❦ Rutabagas
❦ Brussels sprouts	❦ Horseradish	❦ Spinach
❦ Cabbage	❦ Kale	❦ Turnips
❦ Carrots	❦ Kohlrabi	❦ Upland cress
❦ Cauliflower	❦ Mustard	❦ Watercress

Varied Diet

A varied diet eaten in moderation also offers preventive advantages regarding cancer development. If for no other reason, it increases the likelihood that you will eat healthy foods from all of the groups listed as anti-promoters.

Vitamins

Certain antioxidant vitamins (e.g., A, C and E) are being widely promoted as cancer-protective agents. The mechanism proposed for these substances is that they may be able to pick up free-radicals in the body which are capable of causing certain types of cellular damage. The actual scientific evidence of this position, however, is not as convincing as the promotional hype. It seems reasonably clear that the adoption of healthy lifestyles in general is far more beneficial than increasing your intake of a few "magic bullet" vitamins.

There are other facts to be considered in this connection. For example, many vitamins taken in large quantities can be toxic, and research suggests that excessive vitamin supplementation is not desirable. Foods are considered to be much more effective sources as a risk reduction measure, since they offer other risk reduction components (e.g., fiber) in addition to vitamins.

Vitamin E is able to collect certain free-radicals in the body that cause several types of cellular damage, but its impact on cancer prevention is unclear. Vitamin C may prevent the formation of certain types of cancer-producing substances in the stomach, but again its beneficial effects are unconfirmed. The foods which contain carotene or Vitamin A (e.g., dark green and deep yellow vegetables, certain fruits) may offer some protection against certain types of cancer (e.g., throat, lung, cervix). However, Vitamin A supplements taken in large quantities can be toxic.

Weight

As we have emphasized, it is important to maintain a desirable weight for a number of reasons. In particular, the risk of certain cancers is higher if you are overweight (e.g., colon, breast, prostate, gallbladder, ovary and uterus).

Mixed Reviews

Food Additives

The relationship between food additives and cancer has received considerable attention in the media. Typically, additives are considered to be harmful and we are encouraged to avoid them. Yet, research involving these substances is conflicting. Some may actually offer protection against colon cancer, while others seem to promote cancer formation (e.g., esophagus, stomach). Obviously more research is needed to sort this one out. In the meantime, it is probably best to limit your intake of salt-cured, smoked and nitrite-cured foods.

Diet and Specific Cancers

Breast Cancer

Breast cancer rates in women are so significant that even a small drop in rates would spare many lives. Even though breast cancer appears to be related to a number of risk factors (e.g., heredity, reproductive factors, age at onset of menstrual cycle and menopause, etc.), diet may offer an easily controllable factor to help prevent development of this type of cancer.

Dietary fat has been implicated as a risk factor in the development of breast cancer, but the results of scientific research have been conflicting. At least one significant study indicated that fat intake is a greater risk factor for women after menopause. Other studies have suggested that total calories per day is the real risk factor, not fat alone. This issue is difficult to clarify, since total fat intake is often related to the total calories consumed per day. Other studies have suggested that a reduction in saturated fats (10% or less of total daily calories) and an increase in consumption of fruits and vegetables could reduce breast cancer rates by 16% for women before menopause and 24% for women after menopause.

Excessive weight, especially obesity, has been implicated as a risk factor, yet the actual degree of risk is controversial. In part, problems in clarifying these findings arise because there is disagreement regarding how to measure how much "overweight" a person is, or whether or not one is "obese." Regardless of the controversies however, there is little doubt that maintaining an appropriate body weight is a healthy thing to do.

Prostate Cancer

As with breast cancer, the actual role of diet in the development or prevention of prostate cancer is controversial. At least one study has indicated that whole milk increases the risk for prostate cancer (as compared to low-fat milk or no milk intake). If this observation is eventually confirmed, this could represent a significant, but easy, lifestyle change in reducing the risk of developing this form of cancer. It is worth noting that whole milk represents the second major source of saturated fat in the diet of the average American adult (hamburgers are #1).

The protective ability of vitamins (A, C and beta-carotene) are also controversial. Apparently, fruits and vegetables which contain these vitamins have been shown to be correlated with lower risk. Even so, at present it would appear that dietary modifications are more beneficial than vitamin supplements.

Alcohol and coffee have not been specifically identified as risk factors in prostate cancer. Weight, as with breast cancer, is controversial because of the different ways in which health researchers define "overweight" and "obesity."

Colon Cancer

Health researchers seem to generally agree that increasing dietary fiber reduces your risk for developing colon and rectal cancer. This is achieved by increasing your dietary intake of vegetables, grains and fruits. Not all studies have indicated these results (a few have indicated no protective value and some have even suggested that fiber may increase risk for cancer development). Still, the overwhelming majority of studies support this view and health authorities are comfortable with the recommendation of increasing dietary fiber.

There appears to be little doubt that the adoption of healthy diets (i.e., fewer promoters and more anti-promoters) as a part of a healthier lifestyle is far more rational than the search for "magic bullets" (e.g., drugs, herbs, etc.) for which we Americans are famous. Dietary changes represent a desirable approach to reducing cancer risks, since it primarily involves simple changes in dietary habits, rather than major lifestyle changes. Chapter 18 (Nutrition) includes outlines dealing with healthy shopping, meal planning and eating out.

Specific Cancers

We use the term cancer as if it referred to a single disease. In reality, not all cancers are alike. They can vary in cause, symptoms, treatments and rate of cures. The differences between one cancer and another can impact our individual efforts to avoid them. So, it is helpful to review some basic information about some of the cancers which are of concern to us.

Bladder Cancer

More than 52,000 new cases of bladder cancer occurred in 1993. The incidence is 4 times more likely in men than women and is higher among whites than blacks. Nearly 10,000 deaths are anticipated annually.

Warning signs include blood in the urine and an increased frequency of urination. Since similar symptoms can also occur with prostate cancer, it is important for males to have a checkup at the first sign of these symptoms.

Smoking is the greatest risk factor in bladder cancer. Other risk factors include exposure to dyes, rubber or leather. Early detection requires physician examination for diagnosis. The importance of this is reflected by the fact that the 5-year survival rate is 90% when detected early.

Breast Cancer

About 1 out of 9 women will develop breast cancer by age 85. There are more than 180,000 new cases each year, including 1000 cases that occur in men. Approximately 46,000 women and 300 men will die of breast cancer each year. Warning signs include:

- Breast changes that don't go away
- Dimpling
- Distortion
- Lumps
- Nipple tenderness
- Pain
- Retraction
- Scales
- Skin irritation
- Swelling
- Thickening

The risk factors for breast cancer are:

- Age (especially over 40)
- Age at birth of last child
- Diet (e.g., high fat intake; however, this is controversial)
- Never had children
- Family history of breast cancer
- Higher socioeconomic status
- Higher education
- Late age at menopause
- Early onset of menstrual cycle

Risk factors are more important in identifying people who are likely to develop breast cancer, than they are in identifying prevention behaviors. So, here again, early detection is important, since many adult women cannot practically alter some of their risk factors.

Women between the ages of 20 to 40 should have a physical examination of the breast every 3 years, and every year after age 40. Monthly self-exams are recommended for all women over 20. A base line mammogram is recommended before age 40, and another every one to two years until age 50. After age 50, women should have a mammogram every year.

Most breast lumps are NOT cancers, but only a physician can make this determination. The 5-year survival rates are quite good if the cancer is detected early (93+%). If the cancer has spread, the survival rates decline significantly, especially if the cancer has spread to distant sites.

OUTLINE 21

BREAST SELF-EXAMS [6]

Breast self-exams are an easy procedure. The more you do it, the better you become at it. By learning how your breasts feel normally, you are more likely to notice changes.

Best Time to do Self-Exams

- Right after your menstrual period, when the breasts are not tender or swollen.
- If your periods are not regular, or you sometimes skip a month, do it on the same day each month.

Procedure

1. Lie down and put a pillow under your right shoulder. Place your right arm behind your head.
2. Use the finger pads of your 3 middle fingers on your left hand to feel for lumps or thickenings in the right breast. Your finger pads are the top third of each finger.

---

6. See reference 20.

OUTLINE 21 cont'd

3. Press firmly enough to know how your breast feels. Learn how your breasts feel and look most of the time. A firm ridge in the lower curve of each breast is normal.
4. Move around the breast in an organized way. Do it the same way each time. This will help to insure that you cover the entire breast each time, and that you learn how it normally feels.
5. Use your right hand finger pads to examine your left breast by repeating steps 1 - 4.
6. Stand in front of a mirror. See if there are any changes in the way your breasts look (e.g., dimpling of the skin, changes in the nipple, redness, swelling).
7. Notify your doctor if you notice any changes.

Alternate Approach

An alternate approach is to do the self-exam while in the shower. Soapy hands glide more easily over wet skin. This makes it easier to check how the breasts feel.

Colon and Rectal Cancer

Approximately 110,000 new cases of colon cancer and 43,000 new cases of rectal cancer are reported each year. The incidence appears to be declining for all groups of people, except for black males. There are 50,000 deaths per year from colon cancer and 7,000 from rectal cancer.

Warning signs include:

❦ Blood in the stool   ❦ Persistent abdominal cramping

❦ Changes in bowel habits   ❦ Rectal bleeding

The risk factors for colon and rectal cancer are a family history of this type of cancer, inflammatory bowel disease and diets which are high in fats or low in fiber. Early detection can be made by a physician with a digital exam. There are also simple test kits which can be performed at home to test for blood in the feces. When these initial measures indicate the need for additional testing, the physician may perform a *proctosigmoidoscopy* by inserting a hollow tube into the rectum to inspect the rectum and lower colon.

The 5-year survival rates are quite high (85+%) for these cancers when they are detected early. Survival rates drop significantly once the disease has spread.

Leukemia

Approximately 29,000 new cases and 19,000 deaths were reported in 1993 for leukemia. The warning signs include:

- Bleeding (esp. unexplained)
- Paleness
- Bruising easily
- Repeated infections
- Fatigue
- Weight loss
- Nosebleeds

The disease occurs in both sexes and all age groups. Symptoms can appear suddenly in children or slowly in chronic leukemia.

Risk factors include Down Syndrome, excessive exposure to ionizing radiation, excessive exposure to certain chemicals (e.g., benzene), and certain viruses (e.g., HTLV-I, the Human T-Cell Leukemia / Lymphoma Virus-1). The actual cause of most cases, however, is unknown. Early diagnosis is often difficult because the symptoms mimic other less serious conditions. Diagnosis requires an examination by a physician. The 5-year survival rates vary from 37% to 72% depending upon the type of leukemia involved and the stage at which it is diagnosed.

Lung Cancer

There are 170,000 new cases and 150,000 deaths of lung cancer reported each year. The rate appears to be decreasing in men and increasing in women (we can probably thank advertising practices, such as . . . "You've come a long way baby!" for this trend). Women are now more likely to die from lung cancer than breast cancer as a result of tobacco use. The warning signs include:

- Chest pain
- Recurring lung problems
- Persistent cough
- Sputum streaked with blood

Risk factors consist primarily of toxic environmental exposures, such as smoking, industrial toxins (e.g., arsenic, asbestos), radiation exposures (e.g., occupational, medical, outside exposures), residential radon exposure and exposure to the smoke from smokers.

Since symptoms may not appear until the disease is advanced, early detection can be difficult. If smokers quit before cancerous changes occur to the lungs, damaged tissues may return to normal over time. The 5-year survival rate is only 13% in all patients, regardless of the stage of the cancer when it is diagnosed. This is because lung cancer tends to be diagnosed too late in the progression of the disease for effective interventions. This is a sad scenario, since most lung cancers are preventable.

Lymphoma

Approximately 51,000 new cases (8,000 cases of Hodgkin's Disease and 43,000 cases of non-Hodgkin's) are reported each year. The incidence of Hodgkin's Disease has declined and the incidence of non-Hodgkin's lymphoma has increased since the early 1970s. The warning signs are:

❧ Anemia	❧ Itching
❧ Enlarged lymph nodes	❧ Night sweats
❧ Fever	❧ Weight loss

The risk factors are largely unknown. However, reduced immune function, certain types of infections (e.g., certain viruses), organ transplants (due to reduced immune system functions) and exposures to certain chemical (e.g, herbicides, industrial solvents, vinyl chloride) appear to increase your risks. The overall 5-year survival rate for Hodgkin's is 77%, and for non-Hodgkin's is 51%, although it can vary significantly depending upon the type and stage of the disease.

Oral Cancers

About 30,000 new cases and 8,000 deaths due to oral cancer are reported each year. The incidence is more than two times as high in men, and is most frequent in men over 40. Warning signs include:

- ❧ Difficulty in chewing, swallowing, or moving the tongue or jaws

- ❧ Lumps or thickenings

- ❧ Red or white patches that persist

- ❧ Sores that bleed and don't heal

Risk factors include smoking, smokeless tobacco products and excessive use of alcohol. Dentists and primary care physicians are most likely to catch cancerous changes during routine examinations.

Survival rates vary considerably (23% to 93%) depending upon the tissues involved and the stage of development of the cancer.

Cancer of the Ovary

About 1 out of 65 women will develop ovarian cancer by age 85. It accounts for about 4% of all cancers among women and causes more deaths than any other cancer of the female reproductive system. There may be few or no symptoms until the disease has progressed. Enlargement of the abdomen may occur because of fluid accumulation. Abnormal vaginal bleeding occurs rarely. Vague digestive disturbances (e.g., stomach discomfort, gas, distention) can also occur. These can persist and are not explained by other causes.

The risk factors for ovarian cancer include age (the highest rates are in women over 60), having never had children, breast cancer, heredity and living in industrialized nations. The overall 5-year survival rate for ovarian cancer is about 39% because the disease is often advanced by the time it is detected. Early diagnosis increases the survival rate to about 89%. Conversely, early detection is made by having pelvic examinations on a regular basis. Women over the age of 40 should have a cancer-related checkup every year.

Cancer of the Pancreas

There are about 28,000 new cases of pancreas cancer and 25,000 deaths each year in the U.S. This disease is 30% more common in men than in women and 40% more common in blacks than whites. There are usually no symptoms until the disease is advanced. Little is known about the causes of the disease or how to prevent it. Risk factors that are thought to exist include age (more common after 50, and most cases occur between 65 to 79), smoking, chronic pancreatitis, diabetes (unconfirmed), cirrhosis (unconfirmed), and a diet high in fat.

Presently, a diagnosis of pancreatic cancer can only be confirmed with a biopsy. Unfortunately, the need for a biopsy may only become apparent after the disease is in advanced stages. Current research is exploring new ways to diagnose the disease before it becomes too advanced. Only about 3% of patients live more than 5 years after a diagnosis is made.

Prostate Cancer

Approximately 10% of men develop prostate cancer by age 85. There are 165,000 new cases and 35,000 deaths each year due to this condition. Prostate cancer is the second leading cause of cancer death among men. Rates are higher in black men than white men. Warning signs include:

- Blood in the urine
- Difficulty starting or stopping the urine flow
- Difficulty urinating
- Need to urinate frequently (especially at night)
- Pain in the lower back, pelvis or upper thighs
- Pain or burning on urination
- Weak or interrupted flow of urine

Many of these symptoms can mimic urinary infections of various kinds or benign prostate enlargement. However, only a physician can tell the difference. More than 80% of all prostate cancers are diagnosed in men over 65. Other risk factors include diets high in fat and a family history of prostate cancer. Environmental factors are also thought to be a risk factor, although the exact nature of this link is not clear.

Every man over 40 should have a digital rectal exam every year. Men over 50 should also have an annual prostate-specific antigen blood testing. It is estimated that 58% of all prostate cancers are discovered before they have a chance to spread to other sites. The 5-year survival rates for these individuals is 91%. Survival rates for all stages of prostate cancers have improved over the past 30 years.

Skin Cancer

More than 700,000 highly curable cases of skin cancer occur each year. Melanoma is the most serious skin cancer and about 32,000 cases are diagnosed each year. The incidence of this disease has been increasing by about 4% each year. About 9,000 deaths will occur each year due to skin cancers (7,000 due to melanoma and 2,300 due to other skin cancers). Warning signs include:

- A change in size or color of a mole or other darkly pigmented spot

- A change in skin sensation of a particular area of the skin

- Any unusual skin condition

- Itching

- Pain

- Scaling, oozing, bleeding or change in the appearance of a bump or nodule

- Tenderness

- The spread of pigmentation beyond its border

Risk factors include excessive exposure to ultraviolet radiation, a fair complexion and exposure to certain chemicals (coal tar, pitch, creosote, arsenic, radium). All skin cancers are highly curable if detected early. Malignant melanoma can spread to other areas of the body very quickly, so that early detection is very important. Practice self-examination once a month. Any suspicious lesions should be examined by a physician.

OUTLINE 22

THE ABCD SCREENING GUIDE FOR MELANOMA

A = **Asymmetry**
One half of the mole or lesion does not match the other half.

B = **Border**
The border is irregular. The edges are ragged, notched, or blurred.

C = **Color**
The pigmentation is not uniform.

D = **Diameter**
The diameter is greater than 6 millimeters.

Cancer of the Uterus and Cervix

Approximately, 44,500 new invasive cases (cervix = 13,500; uterus = 31,000) are reported each year. The incidence of invasive cervical cancer has steadily decreased over the years. Precancerous conditions of the cervix are now more frequent than invasive cancer, especially in women under 50. Cancer of the uterus is more common among women over 50. Deaths have decreased over the past 40 years due to regular checkups and the use of the PAP test. Warning signs include:

ᵂ Bleeding outside of the normal menstrual period

ᵂ Bleeding after menopause

ᵂ Unusual vaginal discharge

The risk factors for each are:

Cervical Cancer	**Uterine Cancer**
ᵂ Early age at first intercourse	ᵂ Early onset of the menstrual cycle
ᵂ Multiple sex partners	ᵂ Estrogen or tamoxifen therapy
ᵂ Smoking	ᵂ Failure to ovulate
ᵂ Sexually transmitted diseases	ᵂ History of infertility
ᵂ Obesity	ᵂ Late menopause

An annual PAP test and pelvic examination are recommended after age 18 (or sooner, if sexually active). After three or so normal examinations, these examinations may be performed less frequently at the discretion of the physician. Women over 40 should have an annual pelvic examination. Women with a higher risk for uterine cancer should have an evaluation of tissue samples at menopause. If caught early, the 5 year survival rate for cervical cancer is nearly 100% (94% for uterine cancer).

Cancer in Children

Cancer is rare as a childhood disease, but is still the chief cause of death by disease in children under 14 (8,000 new cases per year). Cancers in children are often difficult to recognize, so children should have regular checkups. The 5-year survival rates vary considerably depending upon the type of cancer involved and the stage at which it is detected. Parents should be alert to any unusual symptoms that persist:

- An unusual mass or swelling, unexplained paleness
- Eye or vision changes (esp. sudden)
- Fever (prolonged or unexplained)
- Headaches (frequent)

- Illness (prolonged or unexplained)
- Limping
- Loss of energy
- Pain (persistent or localized)
- Tendency to bruise
- Weight loss (excessive or rapid)

OUTLINE 23

RECOMMENDATIONS FOR CANCER SCREENING IN PEOPLE WITHOUT SYMPTOMS*

Site	Procedure	Age	Frequency
Breast	Breast Self Exam	20 and over	every month
	Physician Exam	20-40	every three years
		over 40	every year
	Mammography	40 - 49	every 1-2 years
		50 and over	every year
Uterus	Pelvic Exam	18 and over	every year
	Pap Smear	18 and over	every year †
Colon/Rectum	Digital Rectal Exam	40 and over	every year
	Stool Slide Test	50 and over	every year
	Sigmoidoscopy	50 and over	every 3-5 years
Prostate	Prostate Exam	50 and over	every year

OUTLINE 23 cont'd

	Prostate Specific Antigen (PSA)	50 and over	every year
Cancer Check Up	Above plus exam of thyroid, testes, mouth, ovaries, skin, lymph nodes	20-40 over 40	every 3 years every year

* Current recommendations from the American Cancer Society

† Every 1-3 years after three consecutive normal annual exams

TABLE 3

A SHORT, SIMPLE SELF-SCREENING TEST FOR CANCER RISK

Although there is no substitute for a professional assessment of your risk for cancer, if all or most of the following circustances apply to you, the need for medical consultation and for lifestyle change is particularly urgent.

	Yes	No
1. Family history of one or more cancer conditions	❏	❏
2. Sixty plus years of age	❏	❏
3. Moderate to heavy smoker	❏	❏
4. High fat diet, foods high in nitrates, preservatives	❏	❏
5. Excessive exposure to direct sun	❏	❏
6. Excessive exposure to industrial toxins	❏	❏
7. Excessive exposure to radiation	❏	❏
8. History of high-risk viral infections	❏	❏
9. Excessive alcohol consumption	❏	❏

Note: Individuals characterized by all nine circumstances may lead a cancer-free life, and others who are not characterized by any of the above may contract cancer. Other things being equal, however, more of the former will develop cancer than will those who fall into the second category.

VIEWPOINT

CANCER—PREVENTION, DETECTION AND TREATMENT

by

Gary H. Lyman, M.D., MPH
and
Nicole M. Kuderer

H. Lee Moffitt Cancer Center and Research Institute
at The University of South Florida
Tampa, Florida

Evidence of cancer in man dates back to the ancient Egyptians and Greeks and probably occurred among earliest man. However, over the centuries and with western industrialization, cancer seems to have increased substantially. Cancer is now the second leading cause of death in the United States and represents a major health problem throughout the world. Risk for the fifteen most common cancers in this country is summarized in the Table below. Cancer mortality depends not only on how common a cancer is but also on how fatal it is following diagnosis. For example, lung cancer is the most lethal cancer in the United States for both men and women even though prostate cancer and breast cancer are more common.

Cancer is a disease characterized by the uncontrolled growth and proliferation of cells altered by either genetic or environmental factors. Additional features of cancer are the ability to invade surrounding tissues and the capacity to metastasize throughout the body by spreading to other organs. The cancer cell represents a normal host cell that has undergone a change in the genetic material contained in the chromosomes of the cell's nucleus. Most spontaneous changes in the cell's chromosomes do not result in cancer. However, if a set of specific chromosomal alterations occurs (initiation) followed by stimulation of cell growth (promotion), a cancer may develop. Some cancers arise from exposure to an initiating factor first followed by subsequent exposure to a separate promoting factor. In the case of cigarette smoking, both initiating and promoting effects occur from the same exposure. Following a prolonged precancerous period during which initiation and promotion take place, a single or small number of cancer cells may emerge.

Each of these divides into two cells, passing on the genetic change in the chromosomal DNA that allows for the uncontrolled growth and spread characteristic of cancer.

Cancer Prevention

Mutations in the cell's genetic material which are necessary to form a cancer may be inherited (10%) or acquired (90%) by virtue of exposure to environmental factors. Recognized environmental cancer causing factors, known as carcinogens, include chemicals, radiation and certain viruses. Chemical exposures may occur in the home, in the workplace and in the medical setting. The most common exposures are the result of certain lifestyles such as cigarette smoking and certain eating habits. Tobacco products not only cause 80% of all lung cancers but also significantly increase the risk for head and neck cancer, bladder cancer, pancreatic cancer and probably for leukemia and several other malignancies. Excess consumption of alcohol, dietary fat and overall calories along with a deficiency of dietary fiber and certain vitamins have been linked to specific cancers.

Radiation occurs in the form of natural radiation from space and in the soil or it may be man-made and used in the occupational and medical setting. The longer and more intense the exposure to radiation, the greater the risk of cancer. A challenging problem for medicine is the fact that it takes a long time following radiation exposure for a cancer to become apparent. Natural sources account for more than 80% of radiation exposure with radon representing the greatest single component. Radon is a radioactive gas which results from the decay of uranium in the soil and causes intense radiation damage in the lung if inhaled. Regrettably, while aimed at the diagnosis and treatment of disease, medical uses represent the second leading source of radiation exposure for the U.S. population.

While viruses cause many cancers in animals, their role in human malignancies is only starting to be understood. The viruses responsible for infectious mononucleosis, infectious hepatitis and AIDS, among others, appear to be capable of producing cancers under very specific circumstances.

Current suggestions for cancer prevention relate directly to the risk of cancer associated with the exposures discussed above. People who avoid cigarette smoking reduce their risk of getting cancer the most. Dietary recommendations with considerable support include reduced fat, alcohol and overall caloric intake as well as increased dietary fiber. While studies are limited at present, the consumption of specific antioxidants including beta carotene, vitamin E, and vitamin C may represent additional ways of fighting cancer. With regard to skin cancer, the sun should be enjoyed in moderation. Common sense dictates that limiting exposure to chemicals and radiation in any form may be advisable. Physicians should think carefully about the need for specific medical tests and treatments.

Cancer Detection

In those in whom cancer has already developed, early detection holds the greatest promise for effective treatment and survival. It is important to understand that for most malignant tumors, it requires at least one billion cancer cells to become clinically apparent. Approximately 30 cell doublings are necessary for a single tumor cell to reach this point. This represents most of the natural history of a cancer and for most types occurs over a period of a few years. Cancer generally develops and spreads in a systematic and predictable fashion from one or a few cells through the earliest stages of detectability. These tumors metastasize to other parts of the body only during the later stages of development. The value of cancer screening is based on the ability to identify malignant tumors at a relatively early stage when the chance for successful treatment and cure is greatest. For some cancers either the spread pattern is too unpredictable or available tests are too insensitive or expensive to be practical for screening the general population. Therefore, it is important to be aware of the current recommendations for cancer screening from the American Cancer Society summarized in Outline 23.

Many investigators are trying to unlock the secrets of the biology and natural history of cancer. The new techniques of molecular biology are being intensively studied in an effort to enhance available screening methods. Specific markers in the blood for various cancers are being sought which might improve our ability to detect cancers at a stage when they are still highly curable. Research into improved cancer-screening methods also includes the identification of high risk groups for certain cancers in order to meet their special needs.

Treatment and Supportive Care

The choice of treatment depends on the specific type of cancer found and the stage of disease. This often involves several modalities including surgery, radiation therapy, chemotherapy, hormone therapy and the use of substances to modify the patient's immune response. The optimal care of the cancer patient involves active support through the complications of treatment including infection, bleeding and organ failure. Even when chemotherapy and other measures are no longer effective, a patient's quality of life can be greatly improved through the use of effective pain control methods and other supportive techniques.

Selection of cancer treatment depends on both the type of cancer and whether it remains localized or has spread to other areas. If a cancer is diagnosed early, surgical removal may prove curative. In more advanced cases, surgery is not sufficient and needs the additional support of radiation and chemotherapy. Most patients who die from cancer have evidence of distant spread of their disease to other organs through the blood stream or lymphatic channels. Therefore, there is great interest in the use of systemic therapies which are effective throughout the body, such as chemotherapy, hormone therapy and modifiers of the immune system. Chemotherapy functions by attacking cells and disrupting critical molecular processes. The effectiveness as well as the toxicity of chemotherapy increases in direct proportion to the intensity of treatment. Modern cancer treatment uses selected doses, schedules and combinations of agents designed to minimize injury to normal cells while destroying as many cancer cells as possible. The principle toxicity of chemotherapy is on blood cell production in the bone marrow resulting in weakness, infection and bleeding. Recently, researchers have been successful in producing blood growth stimulating factors which are used to reduce the incidence of infection and anemia in cancer patients receiving chemotherapy. Hormone therapy can also be very helpful in selected cancers such as those of the breast, uterus and prostate.

Most cancer treatments to date have been based on fighting cancer cells either through removal (surgery) or through directly destroying them (chemotherapy and radiation). The damaging effect of such treatments on normal cells has lead in recent years to a new approach which involves stimulating the growth and function of the patient's immune system cells by various biologic response modifiers, including the interferons and interleukins. The toxicity of intensive systemic treatment may also be altered by replacing damaged normal cells through bone marrow transplantation.

Considerable advances have occurred in the ability to support patients during and following cancer treatment. These include a wide variety of effective antibiotics for infections, the use of specific blood components, and the use of anti-nausea medications. Other natural products such as the vitamin A derivative, retinoic acid, have been found to stimulate leukemia cells to grow normally.

Through the use of modern cancer treatments, the survival of patients with most cancers have increased over the past two decades, as shown in the Figure below. While some of this progress may be due to earlier detection and better results from already available treatments, much is undoubtedly due to improved methods of cancer treatment and supportive care.

When standard cancer treatment fails or is not appropriate, patients may enroll in one of a large number of investigational programs at cancer centers throughout the country. A centralized registry of currently available studies is maintained at the National Cancer Institute. Careful oversight of these studies assures that they represent promising areas of investigation and that patients receive the best treatment available for their disease. Only through the support of such studies can we continue to make meaningful progress against this dread disease. To what extent alternative medicine is capable of treating cancer or relieving symptoms is still unknown. It is hoped that some of these methods may find a role along with traditional treatments. It must always be remembered that there is a great deal that can be offered to patients to improve the quality of life by relieving symptoms such as pain, fatigue, nausea, constipation, itching and malnutrition. The use of hospice or home support services is aimed at keeping patients at home and as comfortable as possible. The importance of the emotional support of family, friends, and all who come in contact with the patient is unquestioned.

CANCER TABLE

NEW CASES OF CANCER IN USA IN 1994*†

	Males†	Females†	Total†
Digestive Organs	123,000 (19.5)	110,200 (19.1)	233,300 (19.3)
Prostate	200,000 (31.6)	————	200,00 (16.6)
Respiratory System	112,800(17.8)	76,200 (13.2)	189,900 (15.7)
Breast	1,000 (0.2)	182,000 (31.6)	183,000 (15.1)
Urinary System	55,000 (8.7)	23,800 (4.1)	78,800 (6.5)
Lymphoma/Myeloma	35,900 (5.7)	29.700 (5.2)	65,600 (5.4)
Uterus	————	46,000 (8.0)	46,000 (3.8)
Skin (melanoma)	17,000 (2.7)	15,000 (2.6)	32,000 (2.7)
Head and Neck	19,800 (3.1)	9,800 (1.7)	29,000 (2.4)
Leukemia	16,200 (2.6)	12,400 (2.2)	28,6000 (2.4)
Ovary	————	24,000 (4.2)	24,000 (2.0)
Brain/ Nervous Sys	9,600 (1.5)	7,900 (1.4)	17,500 (1.4)
Bone/Soft Tissue	4,400 (0.7)	3,600 (0.6)	8,000 (0.7)
Testes	6,800 (1.1)	————	6,800 (0.6)
Other	30,400 (4.8)	35,400 (6.1)	65,800 (5.4)
TOTAL	**632,000 (100)**	**576,000 (100)**	**1,208,000 (100)**

* Estimates provided by the American Cancer Society

† Numbers in parentheses represent the percentage of all cancers in males, females or both.

( ) Indicates percent

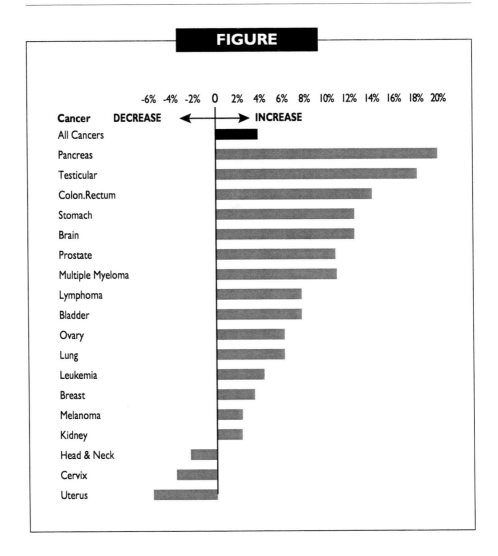

FIGURE

13. DIABETES MELLITUS

"The symptoms of illness often can be seen as signals for attention or ways of making us aware of
needs that are not being met."

— Martin Rossman

Diabetes mellitus is an abnormality of sugar metabolism. This process is controlled by the pancreas, which produces insulin as needed to maintain normal blood-sugar levels. Insulin, in turn, functions in the body like a key, unlocking the door to the cells in our body. Once this door is open, the cell has access to the sugar it needs for fuel and energy. In diabetes, normal sugar metabolism is impaired. Instead of being absorbed into the cells, sugar levels increase in the blood and the cells are deprived.

Diabetes is classified into two different types: (1) Type I (Insulin Dependent Diabetes) in which the body is unable to produce sufficient insulin for its needs; and (2) Type II (Non-insulin Dependent Diabetes) in which the body is able to produce some insulin, but less than what is needed for normal functions. Type I is defined as an autoimmune disease and usually begins in childhood or adolescence. People with this type of diabetes must take daily insulin injections and monitor their blood sugar levels frequently. Fortunately, this type accounts for only about 5% of diabetics. Type II diabetes is defined as a metabolic disorder in which the body is unable to produce enough insulin for its needs, or is unable to effectively use the insulin that has been produced. So, it can often be treated with medications that stimulate the pancreas to produce more insulin. Type II diabetes tends to occur after age 30, but can progress to Type I diabetes.

As a disease, diabetes is the fourth leading cause of death in the U.S. with an annual death rate of approximately 160,000. It is estimated that more than 13 million people have diabetes, but more than half of these are undiagnosed. As an example of its high incidence, a new diabetic patient is diagnosed every 49 seconds.

Since the complications of diabetes increase over time, it is particularly important to consider its relationship to the aging process. In mild forms diabetes can go undetected for years, even though its harmful effects may continue. In particular, its potential to cause longterm health problems (e.g., blindness, kidney disease, nerve damage, damage to blood vessels, heart disease, stroke and amputations due to poor circulation) makes it of vital importance to all of us.

Diabetes is the leading cause of blindness in people under the age of 74. Approximately 10% of diabetics will develop kidney disease and it is the most frequent cause of lower limb amputations not due to a traumatic injury of some kind. Diabetics are also 2 to 4 times more likely to have heart disease and five times more likely to suffer a stroke. Studies indicate that there is a strong relationship between lack of blood sugar control and blood vessel diseases in Type I (insulin-dependent) diabetes. In fact, more than 80% of diabetics die of some form of heart disease. Diabetes damages the heart by causing abnormal cholesterol and lipoprotein levels and by increasing the risk for atherosclerosis. The symptoms of diabetes include weight changes and increases in urination, thirst and hunger. These symptoms are the result of increasing urine and sugar losses.

Adequate control of diabetes involves a program of frequent blood sugar testing, diet, exercise, appropriate medications and regular checkups. Ironically, many diabetics do not take good care of themselves. So, the disease remains a significant health threat. Effective blood glucose monitoring is very important, since either low or high blood sugar levels can result in serious health problems. Appropriate insulin therapy appears to significantly reduce the risk of heart disease and prevents damage to other organs.

Drug treatment involves the traditional medications (i.e., insulin and oral hypoglycemics), as well as a new class of drugs, called aldoreductase inhibitors. These new drugs hold particular promise for decreasing the pain and disability associated with the nerve damage that is sometimes associated with diabetes. It is this complication, as well as damage to arteries, that is responsible for many of the health problems associated with diabetes over time (e.g., kidney failure, visual damage, heart disease and impotence in males). Other categories of drugs (e.g., calcium channel blockers, ACE Inhibitors) may protect kidney function and decrease protein losses that many diabetics experience.

Most recently, a new drug has been approved for Type II (noninsulin dependent) diabetes. This new drug, Metformin (brand name: Glucophage) has a different type of action than the drugs currently available. Rather than stimulating the pancreas to produce more insulin, Metformin increases the body's response to its own insulin.

So, hypoglycemia (low blood sugar) and weight gain are not as likely to occur with this treatment. Side effects include temporary loss of appetite (anorexia), abdominal discomfort, diarrhea and nausea. Metformin has also been associated with a more serious problem called lactic acidosis (an accumulation of lactic acid). Symptoms can include malaise, rapid breathing, shortness of breath, severe weakness, mental confusion, coma and fatalities (rare). Although the incidence of lactic acidosis appears to be very low, all patients should be carefully monitored. If symptoms appear, a physician should be contacted immediately. The drug should not be used by people with impaired kidney or liver function, children, or women who are pregnant or breast feeding.

The American Diabetic Association (ADA) is the leading nonproft health organization in the U.S. dedicated to the prevention and cure of diabetes. Its membership includes more than 265,000 diabetics, families and health professionals (e.g., physicians, nurses, dietitians, pharmacists and social workers), scientists and educators. Its efforts are supported by more than a million volunteers and include educational classes, counseling, support groups, advocacy services, referral services and educational materials.

CASE STUDY

PERSONAL PROFILE: AGE-ONSET DIABETES

Walt is a 68-year-old mechanical engineer who has been in good health all of his life. Several weeks ago he started waking up several times a night because of his need to urinate. At about the same time, he also developed an excessive thirst and started drinking 7 or 8 glasses of water a day. He also noticed that his eyesight, especially for objects at a distance, was becoming blurred. Finally, due to his wife's urging, Walt made an appointment to see his doctor. A blood test taken at that time revealed a blood-sugar content severely above normal levels. His doctor also elicited the information that Walt's father had been diagnosed with diabetes at about the same age, although Walt had forgotten this. After explaining the significance of his findings, the doctor arranged for Walt to attend an educational program at a local hospital. The staff taught him how to recognize the signs of high and low blood sugar levels, how to monitor this through the use of a simple home-care kit, the importance of diet and exercise, etc. Walt has put these lessons into practice and all of his readings have been around the normal level for blood sugar. His doctor has taken him off the medicine and Walt has been able to maintain the proper sugar level just on the basis of diet and exercise. He can now look forward to leading a normal life without the fear of any of the usual side-effects as long as he practices the simple rules provided by his doctor and the hospital staff.

14. OSTEOPOROSIS

> "Every manifestation of existence is a response to stimuli and challenges, each of which constitutes a threat if not adequately dealt with. The very process of living is a continual interplay between the individual and his environment, often taking the form of a struggle resulting in injury or disease."
>
> — Rene Dubos

Osteoporosis is a major cause of disability and death in postmenopausal women in our society. Moreover, this disease affects 25 million Americans and these numbers are expected to increase. With life expectancy currently for women at about 80 years, and menopause typically occuring at around age 50, women can expect to live at least 30 years at risk for this problem. It is estimated that one-third of women over the age of 65 will have at least one fracture of the vertebrae (a major outcome of osteoporosis), and 20% of these victims will die within the following year.

The costs associated with osteoporosis are also a concern. At present it costs about $10 billion to treat the 1.5 million fractures that occur each year. However, this figure is expected to double over the next 30 years as the number of elderly increase.

Osteoporosis is characterized by a loss of bone tissue. This condition results in weaker bones, increasing the possibility of fractures. Under normal circumstances our bones undergo a continuous change in which older bone tissue is replaced by new bone tissue, a process that insures stronger bones. This process is affected by a number of factors, including:

❦ Calcium levels	❦ Insulin
❦ Estrogen levels	❦ Interferons
❦ Exercise (weight-bearing)	❦ Prostaglandins
❦ Growth hormones	❦ Thyroid hormones
❦ Hormone activity	❦ Vitamin D

Of these factors, estrogen, calcium, Vitamin D and exercise are the elements which are easiest for us to control. Estrogen helps to insure a balance between new bone formation and old bone elimination. As women age, their natural levels of estrogen decrease (bone mass decreases at a rate of about 2% per year during the first 5 years after menopause and at a rate of about 1% for the next 20 years). Consequently, new bone formation lags behind the loss of bone tissue, and the bones become more brittle. Generally, women lose more bone mass than men.

Bone mass is optimal at about age 35 in both men and women, but even then, women have about 30% less bone mass than men. At about age 40 the bone mass begins to decline for both sexes, but at a faster rate in women. This occurs because of decreased absorption of calcium by the digestive system, a decrease in Vitamin D activity (which is needed for effective absorption of calcium from the diet) and as a result of changes in bone formation.

The term osteoporosis is used to encompass all such types of bone tissue loss. However, health professionals recognize 3 types of osteoporosis (see Outline 24). Risk factors can be viewed as being either controllable or uncontrollable. This is an important distinction because it identifies opportunities for prevention. Examples of these risk factors include:

Controllable Factors	**Uncontrollable Factors**
❧ Alcohol use (high)	❧ Body frame (thin, small)
❧ Caffeine intake (high)	❧ Gender (being female)
❧ Calcium (low intake)	❧ Heredity (a family history of osteoporosis)
❧ Disease & health problems (anorexia, bulimia, digestive, kidney, liver, thyroid, some cancers, hormonal)	❧ Menopause (early)
	❧ Race (caucasian or asian)
❧ Exercise (low levels)	❧ Weight (low)
❧ Tobacco use	

Controllable risk factors represent those which are readily available to treatment. For example, excessive alcohol intake is associated with diets poor in calcium and vitamin D. Also, alcohol may directly interfere with bone formation. Caffeine intake (more than 2 cups of coffee per day) is also associated with increased bone loss. However, if you drink at least 1 glass of milk daily, you may offset some of the negative impact of caffeine. An adequate intake of calcium (1000 to 1500 mg per day) and vitamin D (400 mg per day; as high as 800 mg per day after menopause) can also help to offset bone losses. Moreover, it is best to obtain calcium and vitamin D from a balanced diet, with use of supplements as indicated. Appropriate calcium intake reduces the

---

OUTLINE 24

TYPES OF OSTEOPOROSIS

	TYPE I (postmenopausal)	TYPE II (senile)	TYPE III (Secondary)
CAUSE	This type occurs as a result of changes that occur after menopause.	This type occurs as result of imbalance between new bone formation and old bone loss.	This type occurs secondary to disease (e.g., kidney, liver, thyroid, digestive) or the use of medications (steroids, long-term anti-convulsant therapy, high dose heparin therapy, some diuretics, insulin, thyroid, antacids that contain aluminum).
TYPICAL AGE AT DIAGNOSIS	50 to 70	70+	any age
GENDER RATIO (women to men)	6 : 1	2:1	about equal
TYPICAL FRACTURE SITES	vertebrae wrist	hip	vertebrae hip esxtremeties
RATE OF BONE LOSS	less than 3% / year	less than 0.5% / yr	varies

risk for excessive losses of bone mass. There are times in the lives of women when calcium supplementation is particularly important. For example, pregnancy and breastfeeding place a considerable demand on normal calcium stores in the body. Vitamin D helps the body to utilize calcium more effectively. Adequate sun exposure can also help the body to produce sufficient Vitamin D through normal physiological processes. Smokers will likely have greater bone losses than non-smokers.

Weight-bearing exercise (e.g., walking, jogging, running, biking, weight lifting, climbing stairs) stimulates bone formation. They are also more effective when there is adequate calcium and vitamin D in the diet. Exercise in moderation is more beneficial than excessive exercise, which can actually increase your risk for fractures.

Estrogen replacement therapy (ERT) is recommended by many physicians. This hormone appears to be able to reduce bone losses and helps to preserve bone density. But it is not for everyone. For example, women with a history of certain types of cancer (uterine, breast), diabetes, depression, high blood pressure, severe varicose veins and liver or kidney diseases must be monitored carefully for use of ERT. Recently, this type of therapy has received negative press because of the risks. On the other hand, any drug therapy requires an evaluation of the risk to benefit ratio. The cancer risk has been reduced by the addition of progestin to the ERT regimen, and the risk of developing breast cancer is only slightly larger than the risk in women who are not on ERT. Estrogen therapy can also increase the risk for gallbladder problems and can interfere with diabetes control, but these problems are minimized by careful monitoring. Given these circumstances, effective and safe estrogen therapy is available but requires periodic evaluations by the physician (e.g., breast exams, mammograms, Pap smears, pelvic exams).

Early intervention for osteoporosis is vital for a number of reasons. First, there are often no symptoms for many years. Over time some individuals experience pain (e.g., back). Symptoms of progressive problems include fractures, decreased height, hump back, reduced lung capacity, protruding abdomens and chronic pain. Fractures are the major problem of osteoporosis. Tiny fractures of the vertebrae of the back, for example, can lead to severe bending of the upper back (i.e., "Widow's Hump"). Loss of height is fairly common, and scoliosis (an abnormal curvature of the back) occurs in many individuals. Hip fractures tend to occur later than fractures of the spine and occur more often in women than men (e.g., in 33% of women versus 17% of men who live to age 90). About half of women who have a hip fracture are permanently disabled and many of these will spend their last years in a long term care facility of some type.

Unfortunately, the negative press related to ERT has affected the use of this important form of treatment for osteoporosis. Studies indicate that as much as 30% of women who receive a prescription never fill it. Of those who fill it, 10% do not take it as directed and 20% stop taking it within the first nine months of therapy. The reasons for this noncompliance include a fear of developing cancer. Yet, this risk is often lower than women realize.

It is easy to overlook the skeleton as a vital organ system that must be maintained by healthy lifestyles. With increased knowledge and the availability of both preventive and treatment options we can now begin to look forward to a time when the problems of osteoporosis will no longer be regarded as an inevitability of the aging process.

15. DEMENTIA

"Complete freedom from disease and from struggle
is almost incompatible with the process of living."

— Rene Dubos

Dementia is defined as a permanent or progressive decline of various aspects of intellectual ability that interferes substantially with one's normal life activities. Alzheimer's Disease which involves dementia (first identified by Alois Alzheimer) is not an inevitable consequence of normal aging. It is characterized by certain types of changes in normal brain tissues and cells.

Despite the popular view above, many elderly retain normal intellectual functioning in their 90s and beyond. Some studies do indicate that 10% of people over the age of 65 and half of those over the age of 85 may have some signs of Alzheimer's, but this simply confirms the fact that most elderly are not adversely affected. There is a clear genetic predisposition for Alzheimer's, especially families with early onset of dementia. Alzheimer patients become progressively worse, although the symptoms and impairments of the disease can vary significantly from one person to another. The long term care of these individuals can involve tremendous costs.

Diagnosis of Alzheimer's is often delayed due to the slow onset of the disease (symptoms may occur over a period of eight to ten years after onset). The incidence tends to increase with age, and there is a 25 to 48% prevalence for persons over the age of 85. So, the risk factors for Alzheimer's are increasing age and a family history. Head trauma may also pose an increased risk.

The cause of Alzheimer's disease is complex. A loss of nerve cells in the brain is associated with this condition. The connections between nerve cells and nerve centers in the brain are destroyed or disrupted by a process that is not currently understood. Since damage occurs more commonly in areas of the brain associated with memory, Alzheimer patients experience memory and intellectual dysfunction (see Outline 25).

OUTLINE 25

SYMPTOMS OF ALZHEIMER'S DISEASE[7]

Symptoms	Example Behavior Problems
❦ Calculations	Inability to handle calculations as in the past.
❦ Confusion	Misplaces objects
❦ Depression	Mood and behavior changes.
❦ Disorientation	
◊ people	Misidentification of relatives and friends.
◊ place, time	Inability to keep appointments.
❦ Hallucinations	
❦ Language Problems	Difficulty following conversations or instructions. Failure to initiate communication. Inability to communicate effectively.
❦ Learning	Difficulty learning new tasks (the patient may be able to perform previously familiar tasks)
❦ Memory Loss	Difficulty remembering names, places, etc. (especially short-term memory).
❦ Mood or Personality Changes	Aggressiveness Delusions Depression Mood Swings Anxiety
❦ Poor Judgment	Carelessness Inappropriate behavior
❦ Thinking	Thinking becomes more difficult.
❦ Unpredictability	Impulsive, erratic behavior.
❦ Visual/Spatial	Difficulty getting around in a new environment. Difficulty operating simple appliances.

7. See references 1, 2.

An exact diagnosis of the disease is usually made only after the patient dies and an autopsy is performed. So, a diagnosis can be difficult.

Physicians and psychologists conduct basic mental status and physical examinations in an effort to determine orientation, attention, calculation ability, recall, language use and some motor skills. Scoring is done in an objective way that provides the professional with a measure of intellectual functioning.

Since other health problems can mimic the signs and symptoms of Alzheimer's (e.g., brain tumors, blood clots in the brain, thyroid disease, liver disease, an imbalance of calcium or sodium, Vitamin B12 deficiency), it is important to see a physician so that an accurate diagnosis can be made. Multiple small strokes can cause multi-infarctional dementia and can be detected by MRI or CAT scans. Also, depression in the elderly can result in behavioral changes and intellectual impairments that mimic Alzheimer's disease. Finally, medications can impair normal cognitive functioning by chronic drug intoxication.

The diagnosis of Alzheimer's is usually made by excluding other possible problems. Technological advances in the future will likely offer new methodologies for making an accurate diagnosis. For example, the use of SPECT Scans (Single-Photon Emission Computerized Tomography) are already available. By combining these results with objective clinical evaluations, the diagnostic accuracy is estimated to be greater than 85%. In addition, the objective criteria which clinicians use to evaluate their patients are being refined to more accurately make a diagnosis.

The treatments available depend upon the cause of the dementia. For example, if the problem is due to multiple strokes, treatment involves efforts to prevent additional strokes. Therapy includes management of cholesterol, blood pressure and other diseases which pose a risk (e.g., diabetes). Lifestyle changes are recommended as needed (e.g., smoking cessation, dietary changes), and drug therapy may be prescribed (e.g., low dose aspirin therapy, other blood thinners). The physician may assess the status of the carotid arteries (which carry blood to the brain) to determine if there is a need for surgery. The heart will be carefully examined, since *arrhythmias* (irregular heart rhythms) can contribute to the formation of strokes. This type of problem can be treated with appropriate medications which thin the blood and regulate the rhythm of the heart.

There are also treatment options for Alzheimer's disease. Some medications can improve functioning and delay progress of the disease for a time. Unfortunately, it is not presently possible to cure the disease or to prevent progressive damage over time.

Deprenyl, a drug used to retard progression of Parkinson's disease, can sometimes help Alzheimer patients. Apparently the drug is able to slow changes and enhance the action of the remaining brain cells.

Some researchers have noted a similarity between Alzheimer's and thiamine deficiencies. This suggests a need for additional studies to see if the role of thiamine may be related to the development of Alzheimer's in some way. Large doses of thiamine have not proven to be beneficial for Alzheimer patients.

Drugs that potentiate the supply of a neurotransmitter called acetylcholine (ACH) have proven to be beneficial in some patients with Alzheimer's disease. These drugs have to be given carefully, since toxicity and side effects can occur. Close observation by the physician (weekly lab tests) are important during the early stages of therapy. These drugs include Tacrine, which has received some attention by the media. Apparently it improves the efficiency of brain cells which have not been damaged. Given the almost inevitable decline of Alzheimer's patients, family members and caretakers are strongly advised to become involved in a total treatment plan that may differ in each patient's case.

VIEWPOINT

ALZHEIMER'S DISEASE

by
John Hardy, Ph.D.

Director, Suncoast Alzheimer's Disease Laboratory,
Tampa, Florida

Descriptions of elderly people with dementia date from ancient Greek literature with examples also in the Bible and in Shakespeare. Becoming "feeble minded" has been thought to be an inevitable consequence of becoming old. It is only very recently that dementia was realized to be the result of disease processes, and not an inevitable consequence of growing old.

At the turn of the century, in southern Germany, a doctor, Alois Alzheimer, who was both a psychiatrist and a pathologist (an unheard of combination in these days of medical specialization) had a patient, a middle-aged woman in her early 50s, who had become demented. She started off by forgetting things, but gradually, as her memory problems became more severe, she began to become paranoid and believed that her husband was stealing her things and hiding her belongings. She became progressively demented, finally became bedridden, and died at age 52.

Alzheimer performed an autopsy on his patient and examined her brain. When he stained sections of her brain with silver salts, a new technique invented a few years before to help in the examination of microscopic sections, he saw two types of pathology: plaques, which are fibrous lumps of scar tissue, each about a tenth of a millimeter across; and tangles, flame-shaped lumps of abnormal protein that appeared to gum up a lot of the nerve cells.

Alzheimer made the important step of saying that this pathology was what caused his patient's dementing illness. He was the first person to recognize that the process which had led the woman to become demented was abnormal. For this reason, the disease was named after Dr. Alois Alzheimer.

Unfortunately, Alzheimer's first case, and the subsequent cases examined by other pathologists, were all reasonably young people. This was because of the prejudice that elderly persons with dementia were inevitable and therefore, not worth examining. Thus, from 1907 until the mid 1960s Alzheimer's disease was regarded as a neurological curiosity: a fairly rare disease occurring in middle age and leading to dementia and death, with a distinctive pathology. It was only in 1963 that a British research group, Blessed (a psychiatrist), Tomlinson (a pathologist) and Roth (another psychiatrist) started to publish their observations on the brains of elderly people. They realized that about half the elderly people who had become demented actually had Alzheimer's disease. The other half had had multiple strokes, or other causes of dementia, or a mixture of causes. For the first time, therefore, researchers realized that dementia was not inevitable, but rather that it was caused by disease, and that about half of it was caused by Alzheimer's disease. It takes some time for the medical education process to work effectively and so it wasn't until the mid 1970s that this realization reached most medical practitioners. For this reason, people who died before about 1970 were rarely correctly diagnosed. They were described as being demented, or senile, or (wrongly) as having hardening of the arteries.

Research into the causes and treatment for Alzheimer's disease actually began in earnest when it was finally realized that, far from being just a neurological curiosity or a rare dementing disease of middle age, Alzheimer's disease was actually a major cause of dementia in the elderly. We now know that Alzheimer's disease affects about 5% of the population over 65, an estimated 2 million Americans. This number is growing as the number of elderly in the population increases.

When I started to work on Alzheimer's disease in 1979, there were only about 15-20 groups with perhaps a hundred people in total working on the disease. Now, the biennial Alzheimer research meeting attracts about 1,000 people, perhaps a tenth of those who actually work on the disease.

Much of the early work on the disease in the 1970s centered on the examination of the nerve cells which were damaged and lost during the disease process. This research was aimed at finding out what chemical the damaged nerve cells used as its chemical messenger. It was hoped that therapies that helped the brain make more of these "lost" chemicals might help alleviate the disease symptoms. In the 1960s this approach had been spectacularly successful in Parkinson's disease. In Parkinson's disease, pathologists showed that most of the nerve cells damaged by the disease used a chemical called dopamine as their messenger. This led to the use of a chemical called DOPA, which the brain turns into dopamine, called DOPA, for treatment of the disease. However, this approach has been less successful with Alzheimer's disease, probably because many different types of nerve cells are damaged. However, cells that use acetyl-choline are particularly hard hit, so this has led to the testing of drugs that inhibit the breakdown of acetyl choline by the brain as a possible treatment for Alzheimer's disease. One of these drugs, Tacrine (Cognex), is presently the only approved drug treatment for Alzheimer's disease, although for the reasons outlined above, it seems that it is only marginally effective in some patients.

Since Alzheimer's day there had been argument and discussion as to what part of the pathology he described was the cause of the disease and what was the consequence. Some people thought that the nerve cell death was the first event and that plaques and tangles were just scar tissue, marking where damage had occurred. Others thought that plaques were at the center of the disease process. Yet others thought tangles were more important. This argument is important because in order to understand any disease process, it is vital to understand the order in which things happen. It is only by understanding the order and sequence of a disease process that you can try to design rational treatments. Studying pathology does not give you the order of the process because all you see is a still picture of the final consequence of the disease.

In a few families, the disease is inherited as a simple genetic disease. In these families, the disease has the same clinical symptoms as the typical Alzheimer case and the same pathology. The only unusual feature is that the disease has an early onset (typically from 30-50 years) and is fairly constant within a family. Our group felt that if we could use the techniques of molecular biology to find the defective gene in these families, this would give us a clue as to what might cause the disease in other cases.

We started this work in 1986. The principle of the molecular genetic approach is very simple. Molecular biological techniques are used to follow the inheritance of genetic material, DNA, through families with this form of the disease. The defective gene must be inherited by all the people in the family with the disease, but not by those who haven't got the disease. While the principle is very simple, in practice there is an enormous amount of work to do to find the defective gene. Our work was complicated by the fact that at first we assumed that all the genetic cases would have the same defective gene. We now know this is an incorrect assumption. This mistake cost us (and other groups doing the same type of experiments) about three years work. However, in 1991, the work paid off and we found the first genetic mistake that causes Alzheimer's disease. This mistake was in a gene called the amyloid gene. Amyloid is a protein which is found in the center of the plaque in Alzheimer's disease. This genetic finding showed that in these individuals at least, the amyloid plaque is not a consequence of the disease, but rather it is the cause of the disease process. This work has been confirmed by us and by many other groups, and now a series of mutations in the amyloid protein has been found which causes Alzheimer's disease. Each of these mutations is very rare, and together they account for less than 1% of the total number of Alzheimer cases. The effects of the mutations have been studied by many groups. All that the different mutations have in common is that they each lead to cells producing more insoluble amyloid. So the importance of the discovery of these mutations is that in these rare cases, we can be sure that the amyloid plaque causes the disease. By analogy, we expect that other causes of the disease must also lead to plaque build-up.

This idea that amyloid build-up is the cause of the disease process led a group of researchers led by Roses at Duke University in 1993 to try to find what proteins were involved in removing amyloid from the brain. They found that a protein called ApoE could bind to amyloid. This protein is genetically variable with three common variants called ε2, ε3 and ε4. Each of us inherits two copies of the ApoE gene, one from our father and one from our mother. This means that we can be ε2ε2, ε3ε3, ε4ε4, ε2ε3, ε2ε4 or ε3ε4. ε3 is the most common variant and about half the population is ε3ε3. The Duke group also showed that the ε4 version of the protein stuck to amyloid very tightly and that the 15% of the population who are ε3ε4 had a three-fold increase in their risk of developing Alzheimer's disease. The 3% of people who are ε4ε4 had an eight-fold increase in their risk of developing the disease. We have extended this work and shown that people with an ε2 version of the gene are less likely to get Alzheimer's disease. These findings are very important. Since this protein binds amyloid, the results confirm the idea that amyloid is central to the cause of the disease. Also, in all the cases we know so far, amyloid build-up is the key.

What does this mean for the future? What does it mean for the treatment of the disease? First, it means that it should now be easier to find out the specific causes of Alzheimer cases. We know that other genetic causes are involved in some cases, but we also suspect that there must be some environmental causes of the disease. We don't know what these are yet for certain, but there is evidence that severe head injury can play a role. Boxers, for example, can develop a type of Alzheimer's disease. Most important though, understanding the disease process helps researchers to think in detail about the disease and to think where in the disease process it might be possible to intervene. For example, researchers are now studying in detail how amyloid can build up, and how this build-up can be prevented. They're also studying why and how the amyloid build-up damages the nerve cells to see if this damage can be prevented.

How long will it be before we have an effective treatment for the disease? This is a very difficult question to answer. The official goal of the National Institutes of Health is to be able to slow the disease process by the year 2000. This is a difficult but possibly achievable goal. Certainly the rapid pace of research over the last 5-10 years is a very hopeful sign that perhaps this generation will be the last which has to face the devastation wrought by this horrible disease.

16. SEXUAL DYSFUNCTION

"Faulty ideas create faulty experience."

— Robert Anthony

Our culture is one that values youthful energy and sexual prowess. So, sexually-related issues are frequent topics of the media and lay press and are frequently misleading. Changes in sexual functioning frequently occur with aging. However, aging alone does not prevent older individuals from having meaningful sexual relationships. Still, there are a number of sexually-related problems that merit consideration in this context, as described below.

Impotence is defined as a failure to achieve or sustain an erection satisfactory for normal sexual intercourse. The causes of impotence are many and sometimes complex. Problems with normal hormone production for example can cause impotence if sufficient testosterone is not produced or if problems occur with the pituitary gland.

Similarly, many drugs can interfere with normal sexual functioning (see Outline 26), including alcohol, if they are taken in significant amounts over time.

Diseases of the penis can affect erections. For example, Peyronie's Disease is characterized by fibrous plaques in the shaft of the penis which interferes with normal erections by causing pain or abnormal curvature.

Compression of the nerves leading from the spine to the penis occurring as a result of herniated discs in the spine or from bony spinal spurs can also cause impotence. Nerve fibers can also be damaged as a result of diseases (e.g., diabetes, multiple sclerosis) or surgery (e.g., prostate gland or bladder).

In fact, since erections are dependent on a flow of blood to the penis, any blockage of arteries in the pelvis can cause impotence, including cholesterol deposits and the constriction of arteries due to certain medications or tobacco use.

Finally, anxiety or depression can lead to impotence and many of the antianxiety and antidepressant drugs can interfere with normal sexual functioning. The drug, Yohimbine, is sometimes used to prevent this side effect of other medications.

These observations make it important to distinguish between psychological and physical impotence. One reliable diagnostic sign involves the ability of the penis to achieve a normal erection. For example, a phenomenon called nocturnal erection normally occurs many times each night and indicates that the nerve fibers and blood flow to the penis are satisfactory, so that psychological causes in such cases should be investigated.

For physical factors clinicians depend upon a variety of diagnostic indicators to assess impotence. A medical history may reveal drug use, diabetes, circulatory problems or prior surgeries which contribute to sexual problems in some way. Physical examinations focus on the nervous system, circulatory system and sexual organs. Tests can also include the measurement of hormone levels, blood pressure of the penis and psychological evaluation.

Treatment for impotence depends upon the cause of the problem. Male hormone (e.g., testosterone) can be given to men with testicular failure. Surgery to restore blood flow to the penis can benefit some men with circulatory, nerve or even psychological problems.

Vacuum devices can also be used for the purpose of drawing blood into the penis. Once the penis is engorged with blood, a rubber band is applied to sustain the erection. Prosthetic devices can actually be surgically inserted into the penis to cause rigidity. These devices include malleable rods and inflatable balloons.

Sexual dysfunction in females typically involves painful intercourse or an inability to achieve orgasms. Vaginal lubrication is reduced in cases of estrogen deficiency, inadequate foreplay or psychological factors (e.g., disinterest). Females that have a diminished libido (i.e., sex drive) can occasionally be successfully treated with small doses of testosterone prescribed by a physician.

Since the causes of sexual dysfunction are myriad, it is important to have a complete physical exam by a physician whenever problems develop.

OUTLINE 26

DRUG CATEGORIES ASSOCIATED WITH VARIOUS TYPES OF SEXUAL DYSFUNCTION [8]

Drug products can interfere with normal sexual functioning. However, human sexuality is quite complex. The fact that a drug category appears in this list does not mean that it will necessarily interfere with normal sexual functioning, but only indicates that it is possible. Any changes in normal sexual functioning, or unusual symptoms associated with the reproductive organs should be referred to a physician for evaluation of possible causes.

Examples of Sexual Problems Reported in the Medical Literature

- Breast (decrease in size)
- Breast (enlargement)
- Breast (secretions)
- Breast (tenderness)
- Ejaculation (delayed)
- Ejaculation (premature)
- Erection (difficulty maintaining)
- Erection (painful)
- Impotence
- Menstruation (changes in normal cycle)
- Menstruation (changes in normal flow)
- PMS-like symptoms
- Sex drive (changes in normal patterns)
- Sexual functioning (changes in normal patterns or abilities)

Categories of Drug Products Associated with Sexually-Related Problems

- Amphetamines
- Anorexiants (i.e., amphetamine -like weight loss drugs)
- Anti-acne (e.g., accutane)
- Anti-anxiety
- Anti-cholesterol agents
- Anti-depressants
- Anti-parkinsons agents
- Anti-psychotic agents
- Anti-seizure agents
- Antihistamines
- Benzodiazepine tranquilizers (e.g., Valium)
- Beta-blockers
- Blood Pressure Medications
- Birth control pills
- Diuretics
- Estrogens
- H2 Blockers (e.g., Tagamet)
- Heart medications
- Hormones
- Migraine prevention agents
- Muscle relaxants
- Nonsteroidal antiInflammatory agents (NSAIDs; e.g., ibuprofen, naprosyn)
- Progestins
- Steroids
- Tranquilizers
- Calcium Channel Blockers

---

8. See references 1 - 3.

17. HIV and AIDS

"Human beings long for new experiences. For the
sake of adventure, they commonly expose themselves to situations to which they are biologically
or socially ill-adapted."

— Rene Dubos

Worldwide, HIV-related illnesses are having profound medical,
social and economic consequences. Since its identification about fifteen years ago this virus has spread rapidly in previously unaffected
populations, ignoring geographical and social boundaries. The rate of
infection in the U.S. continues to grow, especially in women and
minorities. The boundaries between high-risk versus low-risk groups
is becoming less distinct and we must accept the possibility that
almost no one is entirely free from risk. Suffice it to say that HIV has
had more impact than any other disease of modern times.

We have learned a great deal about HIV since it was first isolated.
And in fact, so much new information is published almost daily that it
is difficult to keep up with all of these developments, even for health
professionals.

Health Concerns Prior to AIDS

Until the early 1980s there were few infectious diseases that were
a major health concern. At that point in time our major health threats
were noninfectious problems associated with lifestyles, environmental
threats and aging (e.g., heart disease, cancers, degenerative diseases,
chronic diseases, accidents). All of this changed with the appearance
of HIV.

The Historical Origins of HIV

To appreciate the magnitude of this problem, we can start by
understanding its origin. Reviewing these circumstances offer an
opportunity to reflect on how we respond to disease (or fail to!) and
how we contribute to its continued development. At the very least,
this may help to prevent or better address future epidemics.

In 1981

The first AIDS cases were diagnosed in 1981 among young homo-sexual men in the U.S. The only medically common factor among them was an impaired immune system. As a result, they became infected by organisms that normally cause no problems for us. Many explanations for this development were proposed, but the most likely explanation for the cause was a new infection of some type. Reports to the Centers for Disease Control (CDC) in Atlanta indicated the emergence of a number of unusual health problems:

❑ Pneumocystis carinii Pneumonia

Over an 8-month period five cases of this extremely rare type of pneumonia (caused by the protozoan, Pneymocystis carinii) had been diagnosed in the Los Angeles area. This pneumonia is an opportunistic infection that tends to occur only in individuals whose immune systems have been impaired by cancer or by powerful immuno-suppressive drugs. The disease was so uncommon that the drug given to treat it, pentamidine isethionate, was considered to be experimental and could only be obtained from the CDC. Records indicated that between November, 1967 and December 1979, there had been only two requests for this drug. These five new cases had involved young homosexual men whose immune system had no apparent reason to malfunction.

❑ Kaposi's Sarcoma

At about the same time, the CDC also received reports of an increase in the incidence of a type of cancer known as Kaposi's Sarcoma. In a 30-month period 26 cases had been diagnosed among young homosexual men in New York and California. This cancer had been seen only rarely in the U.S. and then only in elderly men and patients receiving immunosuppressive therapy.

❑ Chronic Lymphadenopathy

The incidence of this condition, characterized by enlarged lymph nodes, began to increase among homosexual men.

❑ Non-Hodgkin's Lymphoma

A relatively rare malignancy.

In 1982

These health problems were recognized as an entirely new syndrome that became known as Acquired Immuno-deficiency Syndrome (AIDS). Evidence indicated that the disease was transmitted by some type of infectious agent and that it was transmitted through sexual relations among homosexually active men. Researchers had already noted that the number and frequency of sexual contacts was a related factor in AIDS patients.

By 1982 AIDS cases were also being reported for people who had been injected with blood or blood products (e.g., people with hemophilia, recipients of blood transfusions and IV drug users who had shared needles), but had no other risk factors . This was the first significant evidence that AIDS can be transmitted by nonsexual means.

In 1983

In January of 1983 AIDS cases were being documented in heterosexual partners of male IV drug abusers. This indicated that AIDS could be transmitted to either a heterosexual or homosexual partner of an infected individual.

Later in 1983, a number of AIDS cases were first recognized in people from central Africa and Haiti who had no history of homosexuality or IV drug abuse. It was now becoming evident that AIDS was a sexually transmitted disease and that the most important risk factor was the number of different sexual partners. It was also apparent that the extent of homosexual versus heterosexual transmission varied from country to country.

Retrovirus: The Most Likely Cause

The knowledge of retroviruses and their cancer-causing ability had been known for a long time. In fact, researchers had identified certain transmissible agents in animals at the beginning of this century that were capable of causing leukemias (cancers of the blood cells) and other tumors. Over the years such retroviruses were identified in many animal species. Yet, little was known about their life cycle until the 1970s. No retroviruses had been found in humans by the mid 1970s, and it was believed by many that none would ever be found. Although most animal retroviruses had been fairly easy to find none had ever been discovered in humans. Unfortunately, we were soon to find that this was not a correct assumption.

Human T-Lymphotropic Virus (HTLV)

By 1980 a team effort led by Robert Gallo (Chief of the Laboratory of Tumor Cell Biology at the National Cancer Institute) isolated the first human retrovirus, which was called Human T-Lymphotropic Virus Type 1 (or HTLV-1) and infects T lymphocytes (a type of white blood cell that has an important role in the immune response). This virus causes a rare and highly malignant cancer (Adult T-cell Leukemia, or ATL) that had been reported in parts of Japan, Africa and the Caribbean, but is now spreading to other regions of the world as well.

Two years later the same scientists discovered a second virus which was a close relative of the first. They called it Human T-Lymphotropic Virus Type 2 (or HTLV-2). This virus is thought to cause leukemias (e.g., Hairy-cell Leukemia) and lymphomas of a different type than those linked to HTLV-1.

HTLV-1 and HTLV-2 share several important features. They are spread by blood, by sexual intercourse and from mother to child.

Both cause disease after a long latency period (i.e., a period of time during which there are no symptoms of the illness) and both infect T-lymphocytes.

Although the AIDS virus proved not to be a close relative of HTLV-1, the initial belief that they might be similar stimulated scientific research that eventually led to the discovery of HIV.

Human Immunodeficiency Virus (HIV)

This new virus was isolated in early 1983 and was originally called HTLV-3 by American scientists and LAV (Lymphadenopathy-Associated Virus) by French scientists. The name was later changed to HIV by an international commission in order to eliminate confusion caused by the two names and to acknowledge that the virus was indeed the cause of AIDS.

In 1985 it was determined that the virus in Western Africa was different than the one affecting people in central Africa, the U.S. and Europe. So, the original HIV was called HIV-1 and the new strain was called HIV-2. The discovery of HIV-2 raised the possibility that other undiscovered viruses might also exist and, consequently, represented a source of great concern.

HIV-1 and HIV-2 were found to be similar and both could cause AIDS (although HIV-2 posed a less serious human health threat). The origins of HIV-1 are more mysterious than those of HIV-2, but it is now estimated that HIV-1 has infected humans for more than 20 years but probably less than 100 years.

The reason for the relatively long time for HIV to reach epidemic proportions was because the virus was likely present in small, isolated groups (e.g., in central Africa and elsewhere) for many years before being introduced to the world at large. With increasing contact from these isolated communities to urban centers, the virus began to spread indiscriminately.

The Search for Answers in Monkeys

Of the many leads that have been pursued in the search for answers to HIV, one that is of interest stems from the fact that wild monkeys may harbor pathogens that are a key source of human infections. Some authorities believe that viruses related to the AIDS epidemic may have originally infected both people and African primates. In this view HIV may have spread to America via the slave trade and to the southwestern islands of Japan (the virus's other endemic area) by oceangoing Portuguese traders.

Subsequently, research involving Asian Macaque monkeys began in 1984 and resulted in the discovery of Simian Immunodeficiency Virus (SIV), which is related to HIV. At about the same time, veterinarians at several primate research centers in the U.S. were reporting outbreaks of an AIDS-like disease called Simian AIDS (SAIDS) in captive Macaque monkeys. As with HIV, these infected monkeys suffered from a depressed immune system and ultimately died of opportunistic infections very similar to those seen in human AIDS. This similarity was of interest, since these monkeys could serve as a potential model for the testing of drugs for HIV. Subsequent research indicated that the Macaque Monkey was not the natural host for SIV, but rather, it appeared that these monkeys had been exposed to SIV while in captivity.

In a related finding, SIV infections were also discovered in up to 70% of African Green Monkeys (similar rates were not discovered in other species). Yet, these monkeys did not show signs of immunosuppression or SAIDS. SIV then appears to occur naturally in this species, but seems to do them no harm.

The finding that SIV occurred in the Green Monkey (Africa) but caused no harm, yet adversely affected the Macaque (Asian), suggested that the virus was only a risk when exposed to the right host (e.g., the Macaque monkey). The African Green monkey had possibly evolved in such a way to avoid disease (i.e., SAIDS).

This difference between the Green and Macaque monkeys also seemed to mirror the difference between people and chimpanzees with regard to AIDS. Chimpanzees, for example, can be experimentally infected with the HIV isolated from AIDS patients. Yet, the virus does not seem to cause fatalities in chimpanzees as it does in humans. Here again, perhaps, chimpanzees might have somehow acquired resistance to HIV.

In nature, retroviruses tend to coexist with their hosts, allowing both to survive. This occurs because these viruses can evolve in such a way that they eventually cause no disease. The ability of both HIV and SIV to mutate rapidly could result in some strains which are highly dangerous and others that are not. The similarity between the viruses which have been identified suggests that infections may have spread to humans from monkeys (or vise versa).

The Virus

HIV operates in novel ways. So, an understanding of HIV may not only hold the key to the control of AIDS, but also to an understanding of how our cells normally regulate their own growth and activity.

Like other viruses, retroviruses must take over the "machinery" of a "host" cell in order to reproduce themselves. The interaction between HIV and its host cell is complex and depends upon the kind of host cell infected, as well as its own level of activity.

Under ordinary circumstances HIV can lie dormant indefinitely in the T cells of the immune system. Thus, it is bound to the cell, but remains hidden from the immune system. When HIV becomes active it can destroy the T cell in a burst of replication. In other cells the virus grows continuously, but slowly. The cells are spared, but their functions are altered.

OUTLINE 27

HIV RISK FACTORS [9]

Behaviors

- Most risk factors associated with HIV transmissions are behavioral (e.g., sexual practices, sex with prostitutes, IV drug abuse).

Drug Use

- The use of intoxicants (e.g., alcohol and other illicit drugs) does not directly increase the risk of transmissions. However, it may reduce normal inhibitions and restraints so that individuals are more likely to engage in other risky behaviors.
- The most dangerous drug-related activity is the exchange of sex for drugs.

Frequency of Exposure

- More frequent participation in risk behaviors results in a greater risk of contact with an HIV-infected individual (e.g., multiple sex partners, frequent sharing of dirty IV needles).

Geographic Location

- Engaging in risk behaviors in areas of the country where the incidence of infections is higher (e.g., New York City, Los Angeles) or with individuals who are from high risk areas increases the risk for infection.

Population Subgroups

- There are no populations or subgroups that have a "natural" risk for HIV infections. The members of some groups may be more likely to participate in certain high-risk behaviors than other people. However, merely being a member of a certain group is not the risk factor.

Type of Exposure

- HIV transmission requires direct access to the bloodstream. So, practices that provide this access are the most dangerous (e.g., IV drug abuse, sex). This type of risk is increased when precautions are not observed (e.g., failure to use condoms). A related factor could involve males who have not been circumcised, since lack of circumcision may increase the risk for certain types of sexually-transmitted diseases.

9. See references 7, 9, 12, 19, 21, 22, 27, 31, 36.

Transmission of HIV

There are three documented routes by which the HIV can be transmitted from one person to another:

1. Sexual;

2. Parenteral (e.g., sharing needles, transfusions); and

3. Perinatal (i.e., from mother to child).

All three routes involve the direct transfer of body fluids (e.g., blood, semen or vaginal fluids) containing the live virus from an infected person. No new routes of transmission have been identified since 1984. HIV is considered to be a "fragile" virus, that is, it does not live long outside of a host cell. It is only found in certain tissues and cells, so transmissions can only occur in certain ways.

Sexual Transmission

Sexual transmission is the most common route of HIV infection. Since the first reports of AIDS in 1981, over 70% of all AIDS cases have been traced to sexually-related transmissions. Heterosexual activities account for a smaller percentage of HIV infections in the U.S. Even so, AIDS is currently spreading faster among heterosexuals than among homosexuals. Heterosexual transmission represents the major mode of transmission in many African countries. Infection may be transmitted from males to females or from females to males after a single heterosexual encounter.

Homosexual activities initially received the greatest attention regarding the HIV problem. This fact caused many Americans to ignore the disease until it had already reached epidemic proportions. Among male homosexuals or bisexuals the high incidence of HIV infection is related to multiple sex partners, which increases the odds of being exposed to the virus; and to unprotected anal intercourse, which causes injury of the rectal tissue and provides a direct route of transmission to the bloodstream. By the nature of their practices, lesbians are not usually considered to have a high risk for HIV transmission. Even so, transmission in this population might be possible with certain sexual activities.

OUTLINE 28

RELATIVE SAFETY OF CERTAIN SEXUAL PRACTICES

Safe Sex Practices

- Body-to-body contact (excluding mucous membranes)
- Hugging
- Intercourse between two uninfected partners in a monogamous relationship
- Massage
- Mutual masturbation
- Social ("dry") kissing

Intermediate Safety Practices

- Intercourse (anal or vaginal) with latex condoms
- French ("wet") kissing
- Oral sex

Unsafe Sex Practices

- Exchange of or contact with blood
- Intercourse (anal or vaginal) without a condom
- Manual anal penetration ("fisting")
- Oral contact with semen or urine
- Oral/anal contact ("rimming")
- Sharing sex toys

The receptive partner in sexual encounters is at greater risk than the insertive partner. This is because there is a high concentration of HIV in male ejaculate, and because both vaginal and rectal injury during intercourse can create an opportunity for the virus to get to the bloodstream.

Kissing is generally considered to be a safe practice, since there is little HIV present in saliva. Also, there is little opportunity for the virus to get to the bloodstream unless mouth sores are present.

Merely kissing on the lips involves less risk than kissing practices which involve the tongue.

Having multiple sex partners is possibly the single most important risk factor regarding transmission of all sexually transmitted diseases (STDs), including HIV.

The presence of genital ulcerations from STDs (e.g., syphilis, chancroid, herpes, anogenital warts) creates a "portal of entry" for HIV. This increases the risks of HIV infection during sexual contact with a partner who is HIV-positive.

The risk for oral sex is uncertain. These types of sexual practices still involve the transfer of potentially infected sexual secretions. Thus, it essentially involves the same conditions that promote HIV transmissions in vaginal or anal intercourse. Intact oral mucosa is not likely to be penetrated by HIV, which is why there appear to be few cases of AIDS transmitted by oral sexual practices. Still, the use of a condom is recommended to reduce risk.

Celibacy or a monogamous relationship between two uninfected partners are the safest and most socially acceptable alternatives. Yet it is naive to believe that people will limit themselves to these alternatives. In a culture in which individuals engage in a wide array of sexual preferences, sex education is critical for the prevention of this disease.

OUTLINE 29

RISK OF TRANSMISSION OF HIV FROM SELECTED BODY FLUIDS AND SECRETIONS

Location	Safety	Comments
Blood	Unsafe	Large amounts of HIV are likely found here. The cells infected by HIV are found in large numbers in the blood.
Breast Milk	Unsafe	HIV is probably present in smaller numbers, but breast milk is still considered to be unsafe.

OUTLINE 29 cont'd

Coughing	Safe	Available evidence does not suggest that the virus can be transmitted this way.
Feces	Unsafe	HIV may be present if blood cells are present in the feces.
Saliva	Safe	Contain almost no HIV. The amount that is present is so small that saliva is considered to be safe. Additionally, there is little opportunity for the virus to be transmitted via this route.
Semen	Unsafe	Large amounts of HIV are likely found here. The cells infected by HIV are found in large numbers in semen.
Sneezing	Safe	Available evidence does not suggest that the virus can be transmitted this way.
Sweat	Safe	This route is not considered to pose a risk for HIV transmission.
Tears	Safe	This route is not considered to pose a risk for HIV transmission.
Urine	Unsafe	HIV is probably present in smaller numbers, but urine is still considered to be unsafe.
Vaginal Secretions	Unsafe	Large amounts of HIV are likely found here. The cells infected by HIV are found in large numbers in vaginal secretions.

The presence of HIV in donor sperm from sperm banks has been responsible for a few cases of AIDS. Even so, improved screening procedures have reduced this risk.

OUTLINE 30

COMMON SOURCES WHICH ARE NOT CONSIDERED TO BE A THREAT FOR HIV TRANSMISSION [10]

- Air we breathe
- Animals
- Casual contacts with others
- Eating in a restaurant
- Food handled by HIV-positive individuals
- Hair dressers
- Hot tubs
- Insect bites (e.g., mosquitoes)
- Living with or near an HIV-infected individual
- Objects around us
- Public toilets
- Riding a bus
- Schoolchildren who are HIV-positive
- Shaking hands
- Swimming pools
- Working with HIV-infected individuals

Parenteral Transmission

Transmission from blood transfusions has declined dramatically since 1985 due to improvements in the screening of blood donors. The risk of HIV infection from a unit of blood is extremely low (about 1:38,000 to 1:300,000). These low risk estimates, however, do not decrease the importance of other preventive measures, such as limiting the use of transfusions and encouraging the use of autologous (pre-saved) blood donations. Similarly, organ transplants were responsible for a few cases of AIDS, but this risk has also declined due to improved screening procedures.

In addition to homosexual transmission, IV drug abuse has been

10. See references 1, 7, 8, 12, 19, 21, 31.

the other publicized route of transmission since the epidemic began in this country. Particles of blood that remain in or on the needle and syringe can transmit the virus. Since IV drug abusers often engage in sharing of needles, this practice allows the virus to be directly injected into the bloodstream.

Occupational exposures have become a major concern for health workers who are exposed to blood (e.g., physicians, nurses, emergency personnel, dentists). Accidental sticks from needles used on HIV individuals, invasive procedures (e.g., surgery, drawing blood) and the handling of laboratory specimens are the concerns. In the majority of occupational cases that have been reported, transmission occured from exposure to sharp instruments which had been contaminated with infected blood or body fluids. Hollow needles are more likely to result in transmission than solid sharp objects. Since health workers may not actually know if an individual is HIV-positive, it has become necessary to take certain precautions with all patients.

The actual extent of occupational transmission risk is not known. It may be much greater than estimates indicate because many cases go unreported and because of a lack of formal programs for the surveillance of occupational transmissions. There were approximately 100 occupational transmissions reported between 1982 to 1992 among the one million healthcare workers who occasionally work with HIV-infected patients. The risk of HIV infection from a single puncture exposure has been estimated to be less than 1%. The overall risk for health care workers who are highly exposed to HIV-positive individuals is less than 0.1% per year of exposure. Nurses who work fulltime on an AIDS ward and sustain the average accidental punctures for all nurses (roughly 0.1 needlestick / year) have the highest risk.

Perinatal Transmission

Most infants born to mothers with HIV infections will test positive at birth because the mother's antibodies are transmitted to the child. Approximately 1/3 of these infants will actually become HIV-infected and eventually develop AIDS. The other 2/3 are not actually infected with the virus and will eventually test negative after their own immune system develops and the mother's antibodies are eliminated. Most cases of AIDS in children less than 6 years old are caused by transmissions from an infected mother. Transmissions can occur to infants through breastfeeding, especially if the mother was recently infected.

Assessing Risks

The risk for transmission from one person to another depends upon many factors, so it is virtually impossible to calculate actual risk rates in any given case. People who are infected with HIV are capable of transmitting the infection for the remainder of their lives since, at present, there is no medical way to stop the virus.

The extended time between initial infection and the appearance of symptoms increases the risk. In the absence of symptoms, infected individuals typically continue to engage in high risk behaviors and interact with noninfected individuals.

High-Risk People Versus High-Risk Behaviors

The HIV infection is related to behaviors that promote transmission. So, the transmission of HIV is not so much a matter of high-risk groups of people, but rather, high-risk behaviors in which people engage (e.g., IV drug abusers are only at risk if they share needles, homosexual males are only at risk if they engage in high-risk sexual activities).

HIV — The Disease

HIV by itself does not usually kill. Rather, the body becomes unable to fight off other potentially fatal diseases. The severity of HIV diseases is directly related to the degree of immune suppression. The specific clinical picture varies from one individual to another. Unlike other epidemic diseases in the past, HIV does not involve unique symptoms that identify the initial infection.

HIV Disease Classification Scheme

The development of a classification scheme promotes optimal diagnosis, medical care and prevention. It also emphasizes that most people infected with HIV follow a similar progression of the disease from stage to stage.

OUTLINE 31

A SUMMARY OF HIV CLASSIFICATION SCHEMES [11]

Stage 0:   Exposure to the Virus

The Walter Reed Scheme lists this stage to emphasize the importance of HIV exposure as an important factor.   It refers to exposure via any of the known routes of transmission. HIV usually causes no symptoms at first, and it can be as long as a year before it can be detected by laboratory tests.   Exposure awareness encourages early testing and diagnosis, and helps to prevent additional transmissions by educating individuals to avoid spreading the disease to others.

Stage 1:   Acute Illness Stage

Typically occurs within 1 week to 1 year of initial infection.   This stage may or may not be associated with symptoms.   Studies indicate that individuals who experience more significant symptoms, or who experience symptoms for two weeks, may have a greater risk for developing AIDS within three years (as compared to individuals who experience no symptoms, or only mild symptoms). Symptoms at this stage may resemble mononucleosis or the flu.   Because of its similarity to the flu, patients tend to ignore it and fail to seek medical assistance. The cause of the symptoms is not entirely clear, and they usually subside within a few weeks. Symptoms include:

diarrhea	muscle aches
fever	nausea
fatigue	rash (face or trunk)
headache (severe)	sore throat
joint pain	swollen lymph nodes
malaise	

Stage 2:   Asymptomatic Carrier Stage

This stage typically lasts for several years (e.g., 2-5).   It is nearly always

---

11. See references 15, 33.

the longest stage. During this stage patients feel well and may have no symptoms of the disease, even though subclinical signs may exist (e.g., lab values). Patients may have chronically swollen lymph nodes, which may be the first sign of immune system dysfunction. This occurs because of an ongoing HIV stimulation of B cells, which are abundant in the lymph nodes and which results in a flood of antibodies. This hyper-activity is not beneficial, since the activation of large numbers of B cells reduces the number that can produce antibodies in response to new pathogens.

Seroconversion

This refers to the point at which the patient "converts" from a negative to positive test for HIV antibodies. Sufficient HIV antibodies are now present to result in a positive serologic test for the disease. Antibodies to HIV usually develop within 6-48 weeks. Antiviral therapy may have maximum potential during this phase. The risk of progressing to advanced stages of the disease may be reduced if viral replication can be checked before it has a chance to cause significant damage to the immune system.

Stage 3: Early Symptomatic Disease

This stage typically lasts about 18 months. The beginning of this stage is marked by a drop in the CD4 cell count, which is an indication that the immune system is no longer functioning normally. This stage is characterized by a wide array of symptoms and problems associated with HIV disease:

> CNS symptoms
>
> Constitutional symptoms
>
> Herpes zoster
>
> Oral hairy leukoplakia
>
> Persistent generalized lymphadenopathy (PGL)
>
> Skin disorders

OUTLINE 31 cont'd

Stage 4: Advanced Symptomatic Disease

Includes AIDS, which is the terminal and ultimately fatal stage of HIV infections.

Other manifestations:

Malignancies:

Kaposi's Sarcoma

Non-Hodgkins Lymphoma

Opportunistic Infections:

Candidiasis	Leukoplakia (oral hairy)
Cytomegalovirus	Mycobacteriosis
Cryptococcosis	Pneumocystis carinii pneumonia
Herpes simplex	Salmonella
Herpes zoster	Toxoplasmosis

As the disease becomes more serious, patients may develop unusually severe or persistent infections (e.g., viral or fungal) of the skin and mucous membranes.

This classification underscores the grim reality that nearly all people who are infected with HIV will eventually progress to the final stages and die prematurely.

AIDS — The Disease

A	=	Acquired	(i.e., not inherited)
I	=	Immune	(i.e., affecting the body's defense system)
D	=	Deficiency	(i.e., a decrease in normal cell counts and functioning)
S	=	Syndrome	(i.e., a collection of signs, symptoms and diseases)

For reporting purposes, the Centers for Disease Control (CDC) defines AIDS as an illness characterized by one or more indicator diseases (e.g., opportunistic infections, cancers, HIV Encephalopathy, HIV Wasting Syndrome).

The progression of HIV may not follow a well-defined path, even though it generally proceeds along the classification scheme described above. For example, a patient may progress directly to AIDS without previous symptoms of infection. Some HIV-infected people may not progress to AIDS for several years, while others progress more quickly. AIDS cannot develop unless there is HIV infection, however AIDS does not develop just because there is HIV infection. Certain cofactors likely affect development of the diseases associated with AIDS, and may serve as a "trigger" for HIV activity.

The slow progress of the disease has been an issue of great interest to scientists. Some people have speculated that HIV might initially pose little danger to cells, but later changes into a more active and dangerous form. It is also possible that HIV is active in the body throughout the infection, but it is held in check for a time by the immune system. This theory is based upon observations that initially there is a vigorous immune response to HIV, which includes the production of antibodies and direct activation of the immune system. Thus, the immune system appears to be able to limit viral activity for some time, but eventually, the virus overcomes these barriers. At this point the immune system can no longer function sufficiently to keep the infection under control.

Yet another theory proposes that there is a gradual rise in the amount of virus in the body over time (rather than an initial low level followed by a sudden rise later on). This view is supported by the observation that with each successive stage of the disease there is an increase in the amount of virus that can be detected. As the amount of virus increases, so does the infection.

Although it is impossible to know whether a given patient will be symptom-free for years or progress rapidly to advanced disease and death, there are clinical and laboratory indicators associated with more rapid disease progression. These signs can assist practitioners in making decisions regarding treatment and monitoring. AIDS usually occurs quite late in HIV infections.

Variations in the disease seen in patients may occur as a result of differences in viral strains. Mutations of viral strains may explain why some strains are more likely to cause problems, while others do not.

OUTLINE 32

SYMPTOMS AND HEALTH PROBLEMS ASSOCIATED WITH HIV [12]

❦ AIDS-Related Complex (ARC)

A "pre-AIDS" syndrome. It is typically diagnosed when an HIV-infected individual experiences one or more symptoms and signs (e.g., laboratory) beyond Stage 3. Many health authorities suggest that there is not really an ARC disease state, per se. Accordingly, it may be better to refer to this stage as "advanced HIV disease" rather than "ARC".

❦ AIDS Dementia Complex.

The most common complication of HIV infection involves the central nervous system. This is characterized by abnormal mental functioning, problems with motor functioning and changes in behavior. Some patients reach a point at which they cannot walk or communicate effectively. They may have to keep lists in order to complete normal activities. Complex tasks may need to be broken down into steps. Patients may lose interest in their work and other activities, which may be mistaken for depression.

Early in the Course of the Disease

Apathy	Motor deficits
Behavioral changes	(e.g., loss of balance, leg weakness)
Depression	Slowness of thought
Forgetfulness	Social withdrawal
Loss of concentration	

Later in the Disease

Agitation	Motor weakness
Ataxia	Psychomotor retardation
Delusion	Psychosis
Hallucinations	Unstable mood
Incontinence	

12. See references: 2, 5, 7, 8, 13, 15, 21, 23, 27, 31, 33.

OUTLINE 32 cont'd

❦ Constitutional Symptoms

Diarrhea   Night sweats

Fever   Weight loss (unexplained)

Fatigue

❦ Herpes Zoster (Shingles)

❦ Neurological Signs

Dementia   Myelopathy

Peripheral neuropathy

❦ Oral Hairy Leukoplakia

Possibly viral in origin. It is characterized by painless, velvet-like white plagues on the sides of the tongue.

❦ Persistent Generalized Lymphadenopathy (PGL)

Characterized by enlarged lymph nodes in 2 different sites (besides the groin area), which last for at least 2 months and has no other apparent causes. Occurs in about 50% of all HIV patients.

❦ Skin Disorders

❦ HIV Wasting Syndrome ("Slim Disease")

Symptoms include:

Profound Involuntary Weight Loss (> 10% of baseline body weight)

Chronic weakness

Chronic diarrhea (2+ loose stools / day for 30+ days)

Fever (intermittent or constant for 30+ days)

These symptoms occur in the absence of some other illness or condition other than HIV that could explain them.

Changing Natural History of HIV Disease

The earlier pattern characteristic of HIV disease has recently changed because of earlier use of antiviral drugs and because of better therapy and prevention for opportunistic infections. As a result, patients are living longer and better lives. HIV disease is beginning to be viewed and treated as a chronic viral illness. The availability of more effective therapies may encourage high-risk individuals to be tested and seek early treatment. Even though the number of patients will continue to increase for some time, it is hoped that a greater proportion will be treated earlier in the course of their infection. The difficulties associated with both the disease and public education result in two types of HIV epidemics:

1. An epidemic modified by medical intervention and individual prevention; and

2. An epidemic that continues to run the natural course of unmodified HIV infection.

HIV Therapy and Treatment

The treatment of HIV patients can be complex. Just as one disease or problem is diagnosed and treated, a new problem can emerge. Outline 33 summarizes treatments of HIV-related diseases. Some of the more common categories and examples of drugs currently in use are discussed below.

OUTLINE 33

SUMMARY OF HIV-RELATED DISEASES AND THE DRUGS USED TO TREAT THEM (INCLUDING INVESTIGATIONAL AGENTS AND THERAPIES) [13]

Condition	Medication
Anemia due to Zidovudine	Erythropoietin

13. See references: 5,7,8,11,17,20,21,23,28,29,30,31,33,34,38.

Aphthous Stomatitis	Chlorhexidine	Nystatin
	Diphenhydramine	Prednisone
	Hydrocortisone	
Candidiasis	Amphotericin B	Ketoconazole
	Clotrimazole	Nystatin
	Fluconazole	
Coccidiomycosis	Amphotericin B	Ketoconazole
Cryptococcal Disease	Amphotericin B	Flucytosine
	Fluconazole	
Cryptosporidiosis	Paromomycin	Zentel
	Sandostatin	Zithromax
	Spiramycin	
Cytomegalovirus (CMV)	Filgrastim	Sargramostim
	Foscarnet	Zidovudine
	Ganciclovir	
Folliculitis	Dicloxicillin	
Fungal Infections	Amphotericin B	Flucytosine
	Clotrimazole	Ketoconazole
	Fluconazole	Nystatin
Herpes	Acyclovir	Foscarnet
Histoplasmosis	Amphotericin B	Sporanox
	Ketoconazole	
HIV	2,3, butyl DNJ	Didanosine
	AL-721	Dideoxycytidine
	Alpha Interferon	Dideoxyinosine
	AzdU	Penosan Polysulfate

OUTLINE 33 cont'd

	BI-RG-587	Protease Inhibitors
	CD4 (recombinant)	Ribavirin
	Compound Q	TIBO Derivatives
	D4T	Zalcitabine
	Dextran Sulfate	Zidovudine
Kaposi's Sarcoma	Adriamycin	Vinblastine
	Bleomycin	Vincristine
	Interferon alfa-2a	
Impetigo	Dicloxacillin	
Isosporiasis	TMP / SMX	
Microsporidia	Paromomycin	Zental
	Sandostatin	
Mycobacterial Infections	Amikacin	Ethambutol
	Ansamycin	Isoniazid
	Ciprofloxacin	Pyrazinamide
	Clarithromycin	Rifampin
	Clofazimine	Streptomycin
Mycobacterium Avium	Amikacin	Ethambutol
	Ciprofloxacin	Rifabutin
	Clarithromycin	Rifampin
	Clofazimine	
Neutropenia	G-CSF	GM-CSF
Periodontal Disease	Chlorhexidine	Povidone Iodine
Pneumocystis carinii pneumonia (PCP)	Dapsone	Primaquine
	Eflornithine	Pyrimethamine / Sulfadoxine
	Pentamidine	TMP-SMZ

OUTLINE 33 cont'd

Pneumocystis pneumonia	Cleocin	Pentamidine
	Dapsone	Isethionate
	Leucovorin	TMP-SMZ
		Trimetrexate
		Glucuronate
Salmonella	Ampicillin	TMP-SMZ
	Amoxicillin	
Septicemia	Ampicillin	TMP-SMZ
	Amoxicillin	
Sinusitis (recurrent)	Human Immunoglobulin	Penicillins
Syphilis	Penicillins	
TB	Ansamycin	Isoniazid
	Clofazamine	Pyrazinamide
	Ethambutol	Rifampin
Toxoplasma gondii	Cleocin	Pyrimethamine
	Leucovorin	Sulfadiazine
Toxoplasmosis	Cleocin	Pyrimethamine
	Leucovorin	Sulfadiazine
Varicella Zoster	Acyclovir	

Aminoglycoside Antibiotics

❦ Amikacin sulfate ❦ Streptomycin sulfate

❦ Aromomycin sulfate

Aminoglycosides cause death of bacteria by interfering with protein synthesis and cause a misreading of the genetic code.

Anti-fungals

❦ Amphotericin B   ❦ Itraconazole

❦ Clotrimazole   ❦ Ketoconazole

❦ Fluconazole   ❦ Nystatin

Most antifungals appear to interfere with the normal synthesis of fungal cell membranes. This allows increased permeability and leakage of cellular components.

Anti-infectives (miscellaneous)

❦ Trimethoprim / sulfamethoxazole (TMP/SMZ)

Both ingredients interfere with normal biosynthesis of essential nucleic acids and proteins. Studies indicate that bacterial resistance develops more slowly with this combination than with either ingredient used alone.

Anti-malarial

❦ Primaquine phosphate   ❦ Pyrimethamine

The antimalarials appear to cause structural changes and create a major disruption in the metabolic processes of the organism.

Anti-protozoals

❦ Eflornithine HCl   ❦ Pentamidine isethionate

Eflornithine interferes with normal cell differentiation and division. Pentamidine is thought to interfere with nuclear metabolism and inhibits the synthesis of DNA, RNA, phospholipids and protein synthesis.

Anti-TB Agents

❦ Ethambutol HCl   ❦ Rifampin

❦ Isoniazid   ❦ Streptomycin sulfate

❦ Pyrazinamide

Most of these agents interfere with normal cellular metabolism and enzyme activities. These activities lead to decreased cell multiplication and cell death.

Anti-virals

- Acemannan
- Acyclovir
- AIDS vaccine
- AL-721
- Ansamycin
- Azidouridine
- CD4 (human recombinant)
- CD4-IgG
- D-ala-peptide T
- Deoxynojirmycin
- Dextran sulfate
- Didanosine
- Dideoxycytidine
- Fiacitabine
- Fluorothymidine
- Foscarnet sodium
- Ganciclovir sodium
- HIV vaccine
- Iscador
- Isoprinosine
- Monoclonal antibody
- Nevirapine
- Protease inhibitor
- Ribavirin
- Rifabutin
- SCD4-PE40
- Stavudine
- T4 (human recombinant)
- Trichosanthin
- Zalcitabine
- Zidovudine

Although the various agents are relatively specific for certain types of virus, their modes of action are similar. Most work by interference with normal viral DNA synthesis. In some cases the agent may be directly incorporated into viral DNA. The DNA chains are terminated and viral replication is inhibited.

Cytokines

- Alpha interferon
- Interferon alfa-2a
- Interferon alfa-2b
- Interferon alfa-n3
- Interferon beta

- Interleukin-2
- Interleukin-2 PEG
- Interleukin-3 (recombinant human)
- Sargramostim

Cytokines act as powerful signals between cells. Although they affect a variety of cellular activities, their primary function is regulation of the immune system. The exact mechanism by which these agents are able to exert antitumor actions is not known. However, they appear to produce multiple immunological effects, which include activation of cellular immunity and inhibition of tumor growth. For example, the antiviral activity of interferons involves their ability to interfere with viral replication. An infected cell releases interferons, which signals neighboring cells to begin producing antiviral substances.

Fluoroquinolone

- Ciprofloxacin

The fluoroquinolones kill bacteria by interfering with enzymes needed for the synthesis of bacterial DNA.

Folic Acid Derivative (blood modifier)

- Leucovorin calcium

Leucovorin is a derivative of folic acid. It is useful as an antidote to drugs which act against folic acid antagonists. It is also used to enhance the therapeutic and toxic effects of certain cancer agents.

Hematopoietics

- G-CSF
- GM-CSF

These agents are the products of recombinant DNA technology. Colony stimulating factors act on blood-producing cells. They may stimulate the proliferation of certain cells types, differentiation of cells into needed blood cell types and may activate the functions of some cell types. Neutropenia associated with idovudine therapy is a difficult problem to manage. These agents stimulate production of neutrophils from human bone marrow and are under investigation.

Immunomodulators

- ❦ Ampligen
- ❦ AS-101
- ❦ Bropirimine
- ❦ Diethyl-dithiocarbamate
- ❦ Immune globulin IV
- ❦ Imreg-2
- ❦ Isoprinosine
- ❦ Lentinan

- ❦ Methionine-enkephalin
- ❦ Muramyl-tripeptide
- ❦ Oxothiazolidine carboxylate
- ❦ Roquinimex
- ❦ Thymic humoral factor
- ❦ Thymopentin
- ❦ Thymostimuline
- ❦ Tumor necrosis factor

All of the agents in this list are in various stages of clinical trials. In general, the intent of research in this arena is one of finding ways of regulating the immune response. Eventually, agents may be identified which are able to stimulate the host's immune system.

Leprostatics

- ❦ Clofazimine
- ❦ Dapsone

The mechanism of action is not generally known. Clofazimine appears to inhibit bacterial growth and binds to bacterial DNA. It also has anti-inflammatory properties.

Lincosamide Anti-biotics

- ❦ Clindamycin

Lincosamides suppress protein synthesis.

Macrolide Antibiotics

❦ Azithromycin   ❦ Clarithromycin

Macrolide antibiotics inhibit RNA-dependent protein synthesis.

Red Blood Cell Stimulator

❦ Epoetin alfa

Epoetin alfa stimulates red blood cell production.

Sulfonamides

❦ Sulfadiazine

Sulfonamides are bacteriostatic and exert their action by interference with folic acid synthesis. Thus, these agents are only useful for treating organisms that require an external source of folic acid.

Prevention

The longer people are infected with HIV and the more immune-deficient they become, the more likely they are to pass HIV to others. People are also more likely to infect others early on in the infection before the immune system is activated. This information emphasizes the importance of early diagnosis and medical followup, which allows for public health measures (i.e., individual, family and community) to prevent spread of the disease.

Sexual Transmissions

Sex transmissions comprise the greatest risk for the continuing spread of the HIV epidemic. Obviously, abstinence is the only 100% method of avoiding infection. Yet, sexual activities are a normal and meaningful component of human relationships, and it is unrealistic to believe that most people will abstain. Consequently, the next alternative involves "safe sex" practices. Even though the risk for infection still exists in such cases, safe sex practices are regarded as the appropriate approach for individuals who do choose to engage in sexual activities.

OUTLINE 34

REDUCING THE RISK OF SEXUAL TRANSMISSIONS [14]

Abstinence

This is the only method that is 100% effective.

Latex Condoms

These are NOT 100% effective, but their use does reduce the risk as compared to unprotected sex. Effectiveness is higher when condoms are used and stored appropriately.

Sexual intercourse between noninfected individuals.

e.g. Mutually monogamous sex between partners who are not involved in IV drug use. This approach only offers protection to the extent that partners are faithful to each other sexually and refrain from other risk behaviors.

Avoid sexual intercourse with individuals who:

- Engage in other high risk behaviors
- Use IV drugs
- Have had sex with other individuals who use IV drugs
- Engage in anal sex
- Have many sex partners
- Have other sexually transmitted diseases (STDs)
- You don't know well

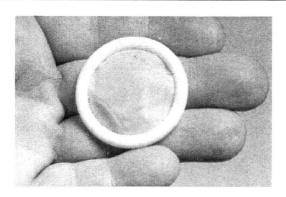

14. See references: 1, 3, 7, 8, 12, 17, 27, 19, 21, 22, 25, 26, 31, 34, 36.

OUTLINE 35

COMPARISON OF LATEX AND
NATURAL SKIN CONDOMS [15]

Latex Condoms	Natural Skin Condoms
Composition of the majority of condoms currently available in the U.S.	Composition of only about 5% of the condoms currently available in the U.S. The "skin" condoms are made from lamb cecum, a pouch which forms a portion of the lamb's large intestine.
Lower Cost	Higher cost. Only one condom can be made from each sheep. Thus, production is limited to the number of animals killed.
Better protection against sexually-transmitted diseases.	Less effective protection against sexually-transmitted diseases.
Provide for a snug fit onto the penis. This serves to reduce the risk of slipping off (and therefore, contraceptive failure and a failure to protect against sexually-transmitted diseases).	Do not fit as snugly onto the penis, and therefore, slip off more easily.
Microscopic evaluation indicates that the surface appears bumpy, but does not show any pores even when stretched. This prevents even the smallest molecules from passing through, including viruses (e.g., hepatitis B and HIV).	The intertwining fibrous layers of the membrane provide for strength, but can also allow for the formation of pores. These pores are smaller than a sperm, but are much larger than viruses (e.g., hepatitis B, HIV).

The FDA does not allow these condoms to carry the disease prevention labeling which latex condoms carry. |
| Less expensive brands tend to be thicker and have been criticized as reducing the physical sensations associated with intercourse (e.g., reduce transmission of body heat).

More expensive brands tend to be thinner, resulting in increased physical sensations. | Proponents claim greater physical sensations are associated with this type of condom. Supposedly, they transmit more heat and sensation and provide for a more "natural" feeling. |

15. See references: 1, 3, 7, 8, 21, 25, 31.

OUTLINE 36

BASIC INFORMATION ABOUT CONDOMS [16]

Characteristics

- ❦ Condoms are available in a wide array of styles and features:
    - colors (e.g., transparent, colors, opaque)
    - composition (e.g., latex rubber, animal skin)
    - shapes (e.g., rippled or pagoda shaped, contoured)
    - surface variations (e.g., flocked with a rough rubber surface, dry, lubricated)
    - tip variations (e.g., plain-end or reservoir tip)

Use as Contraceptives

Both latex and natural skin condoms are effective as contraceptives. Both provide a mechanical barrier that collects the semen and prevents sperm from entering the uterus and fertilizing the egg. Effectiveness rates approach 100% when they are used correctly. Failure rates may be as high as 15% when they are not used correctly. The majority of failures are due to "operator problems" and not product defects.

Use to Prevent Sexually-Transmitted Diseases (STDs)

- ❦ The proper use of condoms can reduce, but not eliminate, the risk of STDs (including HIV).
- ❦ Latex condoms are more effective in the prevention of STDs (including HIV) than natural skin condoms.
- ❦ Transmission of the following pathogens can be reduced significantly by the use of latex condoms:
    - Chlamydia Trichomatis   - Herpes Simplex
    - Cytomegalovirus   - HIV
    - Hepatits B   - Neisseria Gonorrhea
- ❦ It has also been proposed that latex condoms may be able to reduce the risk for infertility and cervical cancer.

Use Guidelines

- ❦ Don't open condom packages until you are ready to use them.
- ❦ Condoms should be handled with care to prevent puncture or damage.
- ❦ The condom should be placed on the penis before any genital contact occurs in order to prevent possible exposure to infectious fluids.
- ❦ If condoms are used which have no reservoir end, leave about 1\2 inch

---

16. See references: 1, 3, 7, 8, 21, 25, 31.

OUTLINE 36 cont'd

of space at the tip to collect the semen.

❦ Pinch the tip of the condom before application to squeeze out the air. Then, unroll the condom until the length of the penis is covered.

❦ Generously lubricate the outside of the condom with a water-based lubricant.

❦ The use of condoms containing spermacides may provide additional protection against STDs. However, additional applications of spermacides is likely to provide greater protection.

❦ Withdraw the penis before losing erection (preferably before ejaculation), holding onto the base of the condom to prevent it from slipping off.

❦ Remove the condom and dispose of it properly.

❦ Condoms should never be reused.

❦ Wash the genital area with soap and water following use.

Storage Guidelines for Condoms

❦ Condoms should be stored in a cool, dark, dry place.

❦ Condoms should not be stored in wallets.

❦ Avoid use of condoms from damaged packages, or those that show obvious signs of deterioration (e.g., discoloration, drying out, stickiness).

❦ Do not purchase condoms if an expiration date is not printed on the package, or if the expiration date has passed.

❦ Condoms should not be used if they were purchased more than 3 months earlier.

❦ Certain environmental substances can damage condoms:

- air pollution   - ozone
- heat   - ultraviolet light
- humidity

❦ Signs of deterioration

- discoloration   - stickiness
- drying out

❦ Expiration dates

Manufacturers estimate the shelf life of condoms to be approximately 3 to 5 years under optimal conditions. Stability can be reduced by exposure to adverse environmental conditions (so that expiration dates on packages are probably useless).

Condoms and Spermacides

❦ Spermacides can inactivate STD organisms in addition to sperm and may provide additional protection against STDs in the event of condom leak-

OUTLINE 36 cont'd

age. However, when condoms break there may not be sufficient spermacide to prevent either pregnancy or diseases. For additional protection, use extra spermacide.

❧ Nonoxynol-9

Safe and effective as a vaginal spermacide. Also inhibits the growth of:

- Chlamydia
- Neisseria gonorrhea
- Herpes simplex
- Treponema
- HIV

Condom Lubricants

❧ General comments

Condoms may be dry or lubricated. Both products are competitively priced and are effective as contraceptives and as barriers against STDs. There is some evidence that lubrication can decrease the risk of condom breakage by reducing friction. Lubricated condoms are advisable if there is difficulty with penetration or if there is excessive irritation of the vagina.

❧ Safe Lubricants

- Corn Huskers Lotion
- Today Personal Lubricant
- Gynol II
- Water-Based Products (i.e., contain no oils)
- K-Y Jelly

❧ Lubricants which weaken latex condoms

- Baby Oil
- Mineral Oil
- Cold Cream
- Petroleum Jelly
- Hand Lotions
- Vegetable Oil

For example, a one-minute exposure to mineral oil can cause a 90% decrease in the strength of latex condoms. A 15-minute exposure allows for passage of HIV.

Needle Use

It is well documented that people who share IV needles are at a greater risk of becoming HIV-infected. The sharing of unclean needles allows for direct exchange of blood from one person to another. While drug use may be a cofactor for the development of AIDS (e.g., by damaging general health or the immune system), it is the sharing of needles that causes actual transmission. IV drug use flourishes in areas that are burdened by:

- Crime
- Homelessness
- Prostitution
- School dropout
- Teenage pregnancy
- Unemployment
- Welfare dependency

These conditions may represent scenarios for which drug use serves as a coping mechanism for social stress (e.g., escape from loneliness and stress, a source of income). They are intertwined and cannot be solved without providing improvements in the basic community infrastructure (e.g., jobs, schools and housing). Such improvements are necessary to increase individual self-respect, dignity and hope for the future in such a way that there is a decreased dependency upon drug use as a source of income and coping.

Needle exchange programs provide clean needles and syringes in exchange for used ones. These programs experienced some success in Europe. However, one must be careful in extrapolating this observation to our own, since cultural differences can significantly affect outcomes. At the very least, this approach is controversial. Critics oppose the appearance of drug use that is "sanctioned" by the states. Advocates argue that the preservation of life is a higher value and that it is worth a try. Also, it is unlikely that even if we adopted such practices IV drug use will stop. Addicts and recreational drug users WILL likely continue high risk practices, and the disease will likely continue to be transmitted in this population despite such interventions.

The "sharing" of needles occurs anytime that the same needle is used by more than one person. People sometimes assume that they are not "sharing" needles when they are being used with others who are close to them (e.g., friends, close acquaintances, family, etc). Yet, anyone can be HIV-infected if they are involved in high-risk behaviors. And, these individuals may not be aware that they are infected.

OUTLINE 37

IV DRUG USE GUIDELINES [17]

❦ Avoid Drug Use

Obviously, not using IV drugs is the only 100% effective method for avoiding HIV transmission via IV drug routes.

❦ Drug Rehabilitation and Related Programs

IV drug users should be encouraged to participate in drug rehabilitation and other programs designed to assist people in not using drugs. This should also include programs designed to reduce stress and enhance self-esteem, so that drugs are not used as a coping mechanism.

❦ Avoid Sharing Needles

If people insist on using IV drugs, encourage them not to share needles, since this increases the risk for HIV infection.

❦ Clean Needles if They Are to be Shared

If people insist on sharing needles, they should clean needles between uses. Cleaning needles and syringes with chlorine bleach kills the virus. However, the effectiveness of this approach depends upon the willingness of IV drug users to appropriately clean used needles. These same concepts apply to shared needles for purposes of ear piercing and tattooing.

Cleaning Procedure:

1. Mix bleach with water in a ratio of 1:10 to 1:100.
2. Flush the needle and syringe twice in the bleach.
3. Rinse the needle and barrel twice in clean water.

Use only fresh bleach (less than 24 hours old). A small amount of bleach entering the body is not likely to cause significant harm. Certainly, it poses less risk than an HIV infection.

---

17. See references: 7, 12, 17, 19, 21, 22, 27, 31, 36.

OUTLINE 38

PUBLIC HEALTH OBJECTIVES AND STRATEGIES [18]

Objectives

I. CARE

- Provision of compassionate, effective and cost-sensitive care to people with HIV.
- Committed and well-trained health professionals.
- A responsive health care financing system.

2. PREVENTION

- Prevent further transmission of the disease.
- Education
- Judicious use of available public health measures.
- Special attention to minorities, IV drug users, etc.

3. RESEARCH

- Support of research that may lead to more effective prevention, diagnosis and treatment.
- The development of new human and institution capacities.
- Balancing basic and applied objectives.
- Design of coherent research plans.

Strategies

- Leadership

  To inspire, direct and organize interventions at local, state, national and international levels.

- Financial Resources

  Adequate financial resources (both public and private) to do the job.

- Legal Protection

  Legal protection against discrimination. (It's time to put our bias aside . . . and deal with this damned thing!).

---

18. See reference: 12.

OUTLINE 38 cont'

❦ Surveillance

We need a surveillance system that can track and project the status of the epidemic. This is important because the future course of the epidemic is uncertain and we must keep pace with changing trends.

Reducing Individual Risks

❦ Knowledge of HIV (e.g., how it is transmitted)

❦ A sense of personal susceptibility ("it could happen to me!)

❦ Skills for changing behavior (e.g., safe sex skills)

❦ A sense of personal competence ("I can change!)

❦ HIV reduction efforts at all levels of society (e.g., community, legal, social)

Perinatal Transmissions

The baby of a woman who has HIV has a 30% chance of becoming infected from the mother before or during its birth. The only known way of prevention is for HIV-positive women to avoid pregnancy. However, premarital screening for HIV represents another controversial proposal, although it has been considered by legislatures in more than 30 states. Opponents argue that universal premarital screening could be counterproductive. For example, inaccurate test results could give people a false sense of security, and screening programs require human and other resources. Results in states such as Illinois, where it was legislated, seem to support the concerns of public health officials that there are more problems than benefits realized from this approach.

OUTLINE 39

SOURCES OF ADDITIONAL INFORMATION

Organizations and Hotlines

- AIDS Hotline
  U.S. Public Health Service
  Atlanta, GA (24 hours daily)
  (800) 342-AIDS or (800) 342-2437

- American Association of Physicians for Human Rights
  P.O. Box 14366
  San Francisco, CA, 94114
  (415) 558-9353

- AIDS Project
  American Civil Liberties Union
  132 West 43rd St.
  New York, NY   10036
  (212) 944-9800

- American College Health Association
  15879 Crabbs Branch Way
  Rockville, MD   20855

- American Foundation for AIDS Research
  1515 Broadway, Suite 3601
  New York, NY   10036
  (212) 719-0033

- American Psychological Association
  1200 17th St., NW
  Washington, DC,   20036
  (202) 955-7600

- American Red Cross
  AIDS Education Office
  1730 D St., NW
  Washington, DC,   20006
  (202) 737-8300

OUTLINE 39 cont'd

❦ Centers for Disease Control
AIDS Activity Office
1600 Clifron Rd.
Atlanta, GA   30333
(404) 329-2550

❦ Gay Men's Health Crisis
PO Box 274
132 West 24th St.
New York, NY, 10011
(212) 807-6655

❦ Health Education Resource Organization (HERO)
101 West Read St., Suite 812
Baltimore, MD, 21201
(301) 945-AIDS or (301) 685-1180

❦ Hispanic AIDS Forum
c/o APRED
853 Broadway, Suite 2007
New York NY, 10003
(212) 870-1902 or (212) 870-1864

❦ Lambda Legal Defense and Education Fund
132 West 43rd St.
New York, NY, 10036
(212) 995-8585

❦ Minority Task Force on AIDS
c/o New York City Council of Churches
475 Riverside Dr., Rm 456
New York, NY, 10015
(212) 749-2816

❦ Mothers of AIDS Patients (MAP)
3403 E. St.
San Diego, CA   92102
(619) 234-3432

OUTLINE 39 cont'd

❦ Mothers of AIDS Patients (MAP)
PO Box 1763
Lomita, CA, 90717-9998
(213) 541-3134;   (213) 530-2109
(213) 450-6485;   (818) 794-1455
(805) 251-2448

❦ National AIDS Hotline
(800) 342-AIDS

❦ National AIDS / Pre-AIDS Epidemiological Network
2676 N. Halsted St.
Chicago, ILL, 60614
(312) 943-6600, ext. 424, 389

❦ National Association of People with AIDS (NAPWA)
PO Box 65472
Washington, DC, 20035

❦ National Gay and Lesbian Task Force
1734 14th St., NW
Washington, DC, 20009
(202) 332-6483

❦ National Gay Health Coalition
206 N. 35th St.
Philadelphia, PA, 19143
(215) 386-5327

❦ National Hemophilia Foundation
National Resource and Consultation Center
The Soho Building
110 Greene St., Rm 303A
New York, NY, 10012
(212) 219-8180

OUTLINE 39 cont'd

❦ National Institute of Allergy and Infectious Disease
9000 Rockville Pike
Bethesda, MD, 20892
(301) 496-4000

❦ National Institute of Mental Health
5600 Fishers Lane
Rockville, MD 20857
(301) 443-4515

❦ National Institute on Drug Abuse
5600 Fishers Lane
Rockville, MD, 20857

❦ Planned Parenthood Federation of America
810 Seventh Ave.
New York, NY, 10036
(212) 541-7800

❦ Project Inform: Newsletter and Information
Drug hotline: (800) 822-7422

❦ PWA Coalition
31 West 26th St.
New York, NY, 10010
(212) 532-0290

❦ San Francisco AIDS Foundation
333 Valencia St., 4th Floor
San Francisco, CA, 94103
(415) 863-AIDS

❦ Sex Information and Education Council of the U.S. (SIECUS)
80 Fifth Ave.
New York, NY, 10011
(212) 929-2300

OUTLINE 39 cont'd

❧ U.S. Public Health Service
Public Affairs Office
Hubert H. Humphrey Building, Rm 725-H
200 Independence Ave., SW
Washington, DC, 20201
(202) 472-4248
(800) 342-AIDS

Sources of Information

❧ ETR Associates / Network Publications
Catalog and sample pamphlets are available (free).
Call (800) 321-4407.

❧ Institute of Medicine, National Academy of Sciences;
National Academy Press, 2101 Constitution Ave., NW,
Washington, D.C., 20418.

❧ National AIDS Information Clearinghouse
A variety of publications are available; many are free of charge.
Call (800) 458-5231 for a list of holdings and samples.

❧ San Francisco AIDS Foundation   (SFAF)
Free catalog of materials.   Call   (415) 861-3397.

Publications

❧ AIDS: A SELF-CARE MANUAL.
AIDS Project Los Angeles
(213) 450-6485

❧ AIDS ALERT: THE MONTHLY UPDATE FOR HEALTH
PROFESSIONALS;
AIDS GUIDE FOR HEALTH CARE WORKERS;
AIDS CLINICAL DIGEST
American Health Consultants
(800) 554-1032

OUTLINE 39 cont'd

❦ AIDS CLINICAL CARE
Monthly update of practical information. Feature articles writ-
ten by leading clinicians. Published by the Medical Publishing
Group of the Massachusetts Medical Society (publishers of
The New England Journal of Medicine). Call (800) 843-6356.

❦ AIDS Clinical Trials Information
(800) TRIALSA

❦ AIDS EDUCATION AND PREVENTION:
AN INTERDISCIPLINARY JOURNAL
Official publication of the International Society for AIDS
Education (ISAE). The executive office is at the University of
South Carolina School of Public Health. Contains articles from
authors world-wide, a community bulletin, book and film
reviews. Published quarterly. Call (803) 777-5231.

❦ AIDS Educator
San Francisco AIDS Foudation
(415) 861-3397

❦ AIDS Patient Care: A Magazine for Health Care Professionals
c/o Mary Ann Liebert, Inc.
(212) 289-2300

❦ AIDS Products — Update in Development
Pharmaceutical Manufacturers Association
(202) 835-3400

❦ AIDS Treatment News
ATN Publications
(800) TREAT-1-2

❦ AmFAR Directory of Experimental Treatments
American Foundation for AIDS Research (AmFAR)
(212) 719-003

OUTLINE 39 cont'd

❧ ANAC: Association of Nurses in AIDS Care
704 Stony Hill Rd., Suite 106
Yardley, PA 19067

❧ ATIN (AIDS Targeted Information Newsletter)
William and Wilkins
(800) 638-6423

❧ BETA: BULLETIN OF EXPERIMENTAL TREATMENT FOR AIDS
Published quarterly by the SFAF. Free to San Francisco residents; $25 / year to others. Call (800) 458-5231.

❧ CALIFORNIA AIDS CLEARINGHOUSE REVIEWER
Available from ETR Associates / Network Publications; published quarterly. A catalog of other materials is also available. Free to education and prevention projects funded by the Office of AIDS ($48 to others). Call (800) 321-4407.

❧ CARING FOR THE PATIENT WITH HIV INFECTION
Written for health care professionals. C.E. credit is available. Offered by GLAXO (free). Call (800) 334-0020; Ask for the Division of Continuing Education.

❧ DOES AIDS HURT?
Suggestions for teachers, parents and other care provides for children up to 10 years of age. Available from ETR Associates/Network Publications ($15). A catalog of other materials is also available. Call (800) 321-4407.

❧ Focus: A Guide to AIDS Research and Counseling
AIDS Health Project, University of California, San Francisco
(415) 476-6430

❧ HIV / AIDS SURVEILLANCE
Published monthly by the U.S. Dept. of Health and Human Services: Public Health Service Centers for Disease Control, Center for Infectious Diseases, Division of HIV/AIDS. Available free of charge from the National AIDS Information Clearinghouse. Call (800) 458-5231.

OUTLINE 39 cont'd

❧ LYNDA MADARAS TALKS TO TEENS ABOUT AIDS: AN ESSENTIAL GUIDE FOR PARENTS, TEACHERS AND YOUNG PEOPLE
96 pages; Available from ETR Associates/Network Publications ($6). A catalog of other materials is also available. Call (800) 321-4407.

❧ PWA Coalition Newsline
Surviving and Thriving with AIDS
(212) 532-0290

❧ SEX, DRUGS AND AIDS
Appropriate for parents, teenagers and organizations. Available from ETR Associates / Network Publications ($4). A catalog of other materials is also available. Call (800) 321-4407.

❧ SFAF AIDS Hotline Training Manual
Manual covers many topics, including definitions for "street" terms regarding sex and drugs. Available from SFAF ($25). A catalog of other materials is also available. Call (415) 861-3397.

❧ SFAF SPEAKERS BUREAU MANUAL
A manual which addresses specific topics and audiences. Available from the SFAF ($20). A catalog of other materials is also available. Call (415) 861-3397.

❧ Surviving and Thriving with AIDS
(212) 532-0290

❧ TEACHING AIDS: A RESOURCE GUIDE
Resource information and lesson plans for educational pro-grams involving young people from junior high to junior college; 163 pages; Available from ETR Associates/Network Publications ($20). A catalog of other materials is also available from the SFAF; Call (415) 861-3397.

❧ THE AIDS CHALLENGE: PREVENTION EDUCATION FOR YOUNG PEOPLE
Suggestions for the development of AIDS education programs in

OUTLINE 39 cont'd

a variety of community settings; 526 pages; Available from ETR Associates/Network Publication; paperback ($25) or hardback ($35); A catalog of other materials is also available. Call (800) 321-4407, or the SFAF at (415) 861-3397.

❧ THE AIDS KNOWLEDGE BASE
1100 pages ($89); Published by The Medical Publishing Group, Waltham, MA (1990). Call (800) 843-6356.

❧ THE HIV HANDBOOK FOR PHYSICIANS, OTHER HEALTH CARE WORKERS AND HEALTH EDUCATORS
241 pages; Available from ETR Associates/Network Publications ($20). A catalog of other materials is available. Call (800) 321-4407.

❧ THE MEDICAL MANAGEMENT OF AIDS
Textbook which covers the treatment of a variety of HIV-related problems. W.B. Saunders Company (1990); about $45.

❧ THE PARENT-TEEN AIDS EDUCATION PROJECT
Produced by the SFAF, KPIX Television Station, and Education Programs Associates. Program includes and implementation manual that covers a comprehensive range of topics; a 27-minute video ("Talking with Teens" with Jane Curtin); 25 copies of an educational brochure ("Talking with Your Teens About AIDS"). Available from the SFAF ($150). Components of the program can be ordered individually. Call (415) 861-3397.

❧ TRAINING EDUCATORS IN HIV PRESENTATION: AN INSERVICE MANUAL
Available from ETR Associates / Network Publications ($40); 150 pages; A catalog of other materials is also available. Call (800) 321-4407.

❧ UNDERSTANDING AND PREVENTING AIDS: A BOOK FOR EVERYONE
Written as a reference for health professionals, AIDS-service organizations, AIDS patients, and laymen; 240 pages. Available from ETR Associates/Network Publications ($25). A catalog of materials is also available. Call (800) 321-4407.

19. NUTRITION AND WEIGHT LOSS

"The more man becomes civilized or at least urbanized, the more he is likely to lose the experience of honest physiological hunger and to replace it by nonphysiological needs born out of the pleasure of eating. The pleasure soon becomes an end in itself, replacing the physiological purpose from which it originated."

— Rene Dubos

The principles involved in good nutrition and weight loss are really quite simple. Applying these concepts in any given case, however, is more difficult, since so many Americans are overweight and the majority of us consume almost twice as much fat as recommended by health professionals.

Nutrition Basics

Foods are divided into three basic groups:

1. Carbohydrates

2. Proteins

3. Fats

The definitions of each are complex and based on their chemical and structural characteristics. We can better define these groups by identifying the foods in each category (see Outline 40). But many foods (for example, meat), include some combination of carbohydrates, fats and/or proteins in them.

Carbohydrates are further divided into two groups, *simple* and *complex*. Simple carbohydrates have a sweet taste and are readily soluble in water. They include sugars, fruits, vegetables and honey. Complex carbohydrates are often bland tasting and are relatively insoluble. Rice, cereals, pasta, flour and breads are examples.

OUTLINE 40

EXAMPLES OF FOODS IN THE THREE FOOD CATEGORIES

Carbohydrates	Fats	Proteins
Rice	Red meats	Meats
Cereals	Eggs	Chicken
Pasta	Lard	Fish
Legumes (beans/peas)	Oils	Milk
Breads & crackers	Some nuts	Yogurt
Fruits	Whole milk	Beans
Vegetables	Cheese	Nuts
All forms of sugars		Cheese

Most authorities recommend that a healthy diet should contain 60% carbohydrates, 30% fats and 10% protein (the 60/30/10 rule). Unfortunately, a typical diet in this country averages 43% fat.

The New Pyramid

The United States Department of Agriculture sets the recommended standards for the American diet. In 1990, they published the "The Eating Right Pyramid" (see Outline 41), a simple model for understanding the recommended daily portions of the basic food groups.

Following these recommended daily guidelines and participating in regular exercise will allow most of us to achieve an ideal body weight. Unfortunately, many Americans consume more food (calories) than needed and fail to exercise enough to burn off the excess.

Essential Nutrients

Carbohydrates, fats and proteins are all nutrients that contain calories, while other nutrients essential to the body (e.g., minerals, vitamins and water) do not contain calories.

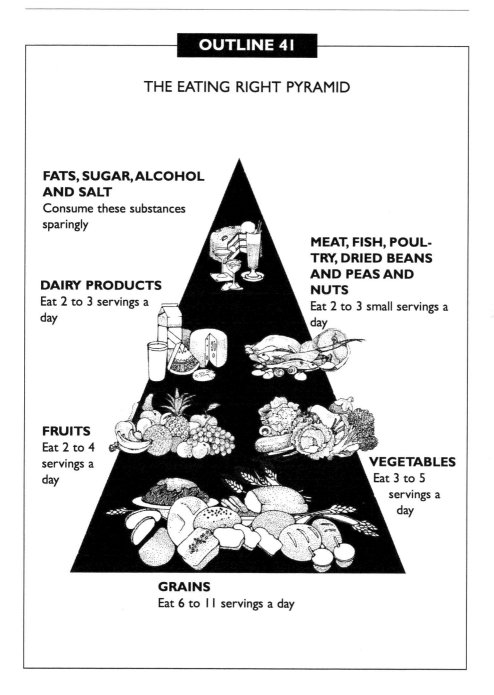

OUTLINE 41

THE EATING RIGHT PYRAMID

FATS, SUGAR, ALCOHOL AND SALT
Consume these substances sparingly

MEAT, FISH, POUL-TRY, DRIED BEANS AND PEAS AND NUTS
Eat 2 to 3 small servings a day

DAIRY PRODUCTS
Eat 2 to 3 servings a day

FRUITS
Eat 2 to 4 servings a day

VEGETABLES
Eat 3 to 5 servings a day

GRAINS
Eat 6 to 11 servings a day

Vitamins

Vitamins warrant special consideration because they have become the object of so much attention. So much has been written about them that it is often difficult to separate the myths from the realities.

The name "vitamin" is actually a misnomer. At one time, we recognized that vitamins were "vital" elements of nutrition, but they were all erroneously thought to belong to a category of chemicals called "amines." Thus, the name "vitamine" was introduced, and then eventually shortened to "vitamin" when it was recognized that not all vitamins are amines. Regardless of the chemical class to which they belong, vitamins are required in our diets for normal physiological functioning. Over the centuries, physicians have noted that certain diseases would occur if certain vitamins were missing from the diet.

Vitamin and mineral products which are promoted for sale without a prescription to supplement the diet are regulated as "foods" by the FDA. However, vitamins which are promoted for the prevention or treatment of diseases and health problems are regulated as "drugs" by the FDA. Many consumers do not agree with this distinction. Yet, it is important to remember that drugs must be proven to be safe and effective for their promoted uses. This law prevents unethical manufacturers and promoters from making false claims about drug products and is designed to protect the consumer in a culture where health fraud is rampant.

The water-soluble vitamins include the B-vitamins and vitamin C. The fat-soluble vitamins include vitamins A, D, K and E (see Outline 42). A primary distinction between water-soluble vitamins and fat soluble is that the water-soluble vitamins are more easily excreted when too much is consumed in the diet. The fat-soluble vitamins are less easily eliminated by the body and are more likely to result in vitamin toxicities.

Many people are critical of the Recommended Daily Allowances (RDAs). Some have even gone so far as to suggest that the FDA and the health community are attempting to withhold the "truth" about vitamins from the public. Nothing could be farther from the truth. The FDA has no desire to withhold useful information from the public. And, it is certain that if vitamins were the panacea for health that they are often promoted to be, drug manufacturers would have already exploited the fortunes to be made from them. In truth, of course, vitamins are not a panacea for all of life's ills.

The concept of the RDA warrants clarification because it is misunderstood by the public and misrepresented in the media. In many countries throughout the world there are committees of health scientists who periodically evaluate the best available scientific evidence

OUTLINE 42

ESSENTIAL VITAMINS AND MINERALS WITH THE RECOMMENDED DAILY ALLOWANCE (RDA) IF ESTABLISHED

Minerals

7 Macrominerals	15 Microminerals	
Calcium (1000-1500 mg)	Arsenic	Manganese
Chlorine	Boron	Molybdenum
Magnesium (280-400 mg)	Cobalt	Nickel
Phosphorus (800-1200 mg)	Copper	Selenium (40-70 mcg)
Potassium	Chromium	Silicon
Sodium	Fluorine	Sanadium
Sulfur	Iodine (150 mcg)	Zinc (12-15 mg)
	Iron (10-15 mg)	

Vitamins

Fat Soluble	Water Soluble
Vitamin A (1000 IU)	Vitamin C (60 mg)
Vitamin D (400 IU)	Vitamin B_1 (1-1.5 mg)
Vitamin E (12-15 IU)	Vitamin B_2 (1.2-1.7 mg)
Vitamin K (45-80 mcg)	Vitamin B_6 (1.4-2 mg)
	Vitamin B_{12} (2 mcg)
	Folate (150-200 mcg)
	Niacin (13-20 mg)

regarding the amount of vitamins and minerals we need in order to prevent deficiency diseases. In this country, assessments of nutritional supplements are made by the Food and Nutrition Board of the National Academy of Sciences. These guidelines may not be appropriate for everyone, since individual lifestyles (e.g., diet, certain diseases) can affect our need for certain nutrients. However, the RDA is only intended to serve as a general guideline for the majority of individuals.

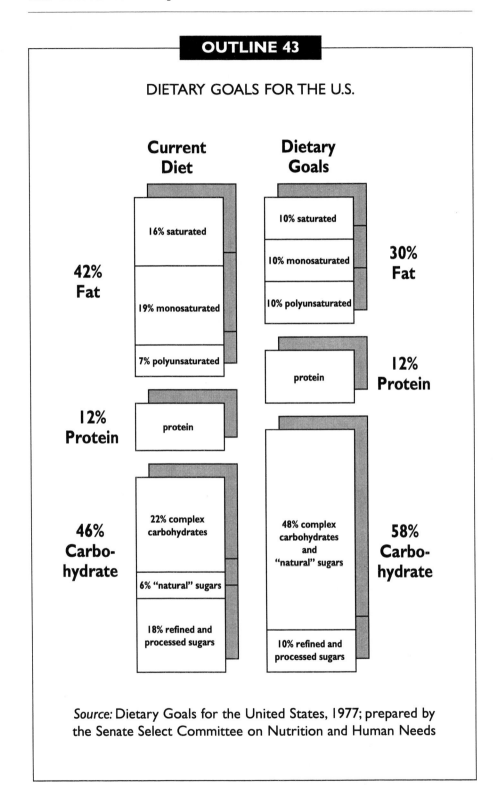

OUTLINE 43

DIETARY GOALS FOR THE U.S.

Current Diet

Dietary Goals

42% Fat

- 16% saturated
- 19% monosaturated
- 7% polyunsaturated

30% Fat

- 10% saturated
- 10% monosaturated
- 10% polyunsaturated

12% Protein

protein

12% Protein

protein

46% Carbo-hydrate

- 22% complex carbohydrates
- 6% "natural" sugars
- 18% refined and processed sugars

58% Carbo-hydrate

- 48% complex carbohydrates and "natural" sugars
- 10% refined and processed sugars

Source: Dietary Goals for the United States, 1977; prepared by the Senate Select Committee on Nutrition and Human Needs

The RDAs are often criticized by various individuals on the grounds that the recommended levels are too low to "prevent colds" and other diseases. These criticisms are incorrect, since this is NOT the purpose of the RDAs. The RDAs merely reflect the nutritional needs of the body to avoid deficiency diseases. They were never

---

OUTLINE 44

VITAMIN NAMES

Name	Alternate Name	Type
Ascorbic Acid	Vitamin C	Water-Soluble
Beta-Carotene	Provitamin A	Fat-Soluble
Bioflavonoids	Vitamin P	Water-Soluble
Cyanocobalamin	Vitamin B12	Water-Soluble
Niacin	Vitamin B3	Water-Soluble
Nicotinic Acid	Vitamin B3	Water-Soluble
PABA	Para-Aminobenzoic Acid	Water-Soluble
Pyridoxine	Vitamin B6	Water Soluble
Retinol	Vitamin A	Fat-Soluble
Riboflavin	Vitamin B2	Water-Soluble
Thiamine	Vitamin B1	Water-Soluble
Vitamin A	Retinol	Fat-Soluble
Vitamin B_1	Thiamine	Water-Soluble
Vitamin B_2	Riboflavin	Water-Soluble
Vitamin B_3	Niacin, Nicotinic Acid	Water-Soluble
Vitamin B_5	Calcium Pantothenate, Pantothenic Acid	Water-Soluble
Vitamin B_6	Pyridoxine	Water-Soluble
Vitamin B_{12}	Cyanocobalamin	Water-Soluble
Vitamin C	Ascorbic Acid	Water-Soluble
Vitamin D	Ergocalciferol, Cholecalciferol	Fat-Soluble
Vitamin D_2	Ergocalciferol	Fat-Soluble
Vitamin D_3	Cholecalciferol	Fat-Soluble
Vitamin E	Tocopherol	Fat-Soluble
Vitamin P	Bioflavonoids	Water-Soluble

intended to be therapeutic guidelines for the treatment of other diseases. In fact, vitamins can be toxic when taken in amounts that are greater than what is needed by the body. Outlines 45 to 60 summarize the deficiency and toxicity problems which have been identified for a number of the vitamins and minerals.

A study reported in the American Journal of Public Health in 1986 emphasized the benefits of a healthy lifestyle (as compared to vitamins) in promoting health. In this case, scientists were attempting to discover if Vitamin C could indeed prevent premature deaths due to cancer, heart diseases and other causes as suggested by various authors over the years. The project involved more than 3,000 people who were studied for 10 years. The subjects consumed daily amounts of Vitamin C which ranged up to 5,000 mg each day, far beyond the RDA. The results clearly showed that Vitamin C was not able to prevent cancer or any other causes of death. However, the lifestyles of the participants in the study were related to death rates. In fact, the health habits that offered the greatest protection from disease were:

- No smoking
- Regular physical activity
- Moderate or no use of alcohol
- 7 to 8 hours of sleep each night
- Maintaining an appropriate weight.

Notice the similarity between these health habits and the "Breslow 7" (see Outline 4), as well as other healthy habits listed in this book.

In our search for "magic bullets" as a solution to our health problems, we are attracted to vitamins, herbs and any other substances that might serve as a substitute for healthy lifestyle changes (e.g., we don't want to eliminate favorite foods from our diets; we are dependent upon gadgets that eliminate physical activity; we frequently turn to drugs, such as alcohol, as a coping mechanism for a stressful existence, etc.) but, to date, no "magic bullet" has been discovered.

Contemporary research does seem to suggest that vitamins, especially the antioxidants (Vitamins A, C and E), may offer some previously undiscovered health benefits. Yet, it is unlikely that vitamins or any other "pills" will ever be a substitute for a rational lifestyle.

Even so, the wisdom of Hygeia continues to be overshadowed by our preoccupation with a search for the "magic bullets" of Asclepius.

OUTLINE 45

VITAMIN A

Deficiency

- Dry eyes
- Unstable movement or gait
- Wasting away
- Red eyes
- Decreased hormone production
- Defective bone formation
- Birth defects
- Thickening of bones
- General decline in health and growth
- Separation of the fetus from the womb
- Growth failure
- Increased pressure in the brain
- Skin problems
- Lowered resistance to infections
- Degeneration of the cornea
- Night blindness
- Growth retardation

Excess

- Abdominal discomfort
- Hair loss
- Loss of appetite
- Blurred vision
- Bone pain or tenderness
- Bone deterioration
- Thickening of bones
- Brittle nails
- Liver damage
- Constipation
- Diarrhea
- Dizziness
- Double vision
- Drowsiness
- Dry, flaking or itching skin
- Dry mucous membranes
- Swelling of lower extremities
- Toxicity of embryos
- Fatigue
- Fractures
- Headache
- Enlargement of the liver
- Enlargement of the spleen
- Increased calcium levels
- Decreased menstrual bleeding
- Increased pressure in the brain
- Increased skin pigmentation
- Inflammation of the tongue, lips, gums
- Irritability
- Jaundice
- Joint pain
- Lethargy
- Cracks in the lips
- Malaise
- Sore or stiff muscles
- Nausea / vomiting
- Night sweats
- Eye problems
- Thirst
- Frequent urination
- Itching
- Redness or swelling of skin
- Skin peeling or scaling
- Pimples (e.g., shoulder and back)
- Skeletal abnormalities
- Skin discoloration
- Slow growth
- Skin thickening
- Vertigo
- Increased fluid pressure of the spine

OUTLINE 46

VITAMIN B₁ (THIAMINE)

Deficiency

Beriberi

- Loss of appetite
- Unsteady movement or gait
- Mental deficits
- Enlarged heart
- Digestive problems
- Mental confusion
- Heart symptoms
- Shortness of breath

- Muscle wasting
- Muscle weakness
- Paralysis of the eye muscles
- Nerve involvement
- Paralysis
- Rapid pulse
- Swelling / fluid accumulations
- Palpitations

Wernicke's Encephalaopathy

- Abnormal eye movements
- Unsteady movement or gait

- Nerve palsy
- Confusion

Other

- Constipation
- Headache
- Insomnia

- Irritability
- Weakness

Excess

- Feeling of warmth
- Rash or hives
- Sweating
- Restlessness
- Swelling or fluid accumulation
- Health collapse
- Upset of the stomach or intestines

- Itching
- Weakness
- Nausea
- Tightness of the throat
- Bleeding in the digestive tract
- Death

OUTLINE 47

VITAMIN B2 (RIBOFLAVIN)

Deficiency

- Inflammation of the mouth
- Itching of the eyes
- Burning of the eyes
- Swollen, cracked lips
- Skin irritations (seborrhea)

- Inflammation of the tongue
- Spasms of the eye lids
- Sensitivity to light
- Roughness of the eyelids

OUTLINE 48

VITAMIN B6 (PYRIDOXINE)

Deficiency

- Amnesia
- Depression
- Irritability
- Inflammation of the mouth and tongue
- Abnormal electrical activity of the brain
- Weakness or numbness of the hands and feet

- Convulsions
- Anemia
- Lesions of the eyes, nose and mouth

Excess

- Unsteady movement or gain
- Nervousness
- Numb feet
- Numbness around the mouth
- Drowsiness
- Abnormal electrical activity of the brain
- Decreased sensation to touch, temperature and vibrations

- Impaired memory
- Tremors
- Awkwardness of hands
- Numbness of hands and fingers

OUTLINE 49

VITAMIN B12

Deficiency

❧ Pernicious anemia

Excess

❧ Digestive problems
❧ Anemia

❧ Irritation of the tongue
❧ Nerve damage

OUTLINE 50

VITAMIN C

Deficiency

❧ Scurvy (degeneration of blood vessels, bone and connective tissues)
❧ Anemia
❧ Loss of appetite
❧ Bleeding gums
❧ Faulty bone and teeth development
❧ Inflammation of the gums
❧ Easy bruising
❧ Weakness

❧ Loose teeth
❧ Skin hemorrhaging
❧ Poor wound healing
❧ Prominent hair follicles
❧ Bleeding of the mouth and digestive tract
❧ Joint and muscle aches

Excess

❧ Serious toxicity is uncommon
❧ Can trigger diabetes
❧ Diarrhea
❧ Thinning of mucus of the uterus
❧ Abnormal laboratory tests
❧ Kidney stones
❧ Dental problems (with chewable tablets)
❧ Fainting or dizziness (with rapid IV administration)
❧ "Rebound scurvy" after stopping long-term intake of large doses

OUTLINE 51

VITAMIN D

Deficiency

- Bone pain
- Deformity
- Difficulty in walking
- Growth problems
- Hearing loss

- Low calcium levels
- Low phosphate levels
- Muscular weakness
- Brittle bones
- Rickets

Excess

- Abnormal urine
- Acidosis
- Anemia
- Loss of appetite
- Brittle bones
- Calcium deposits
- Irregular pulse
- Cataracts
- Central nervous system changes
- Constipation
- Convulsions
- Diarrhea
- Dry mouth
- Fatigue
- Reduced growth (in children)
- Headache
- Increased phosphorous levels
- Death (due to kidney or heart failure)

- Kidney damage and failure
- Kidney stones
- Liver damage
- Malaise
- Mental retardation
- Metallic or bad taste in the mouth
- Nausea / vomiting
- Frequent urination at night
- Peptic ulcers
- Thirst
- Protein in the urine
- Vague aches and stiffness
- Muscle and bone pain
- Weakness
- Weight loss
- Increased calcium levels
- Increased blood pressure

OUTLINE 52

VITAMIN E

Excess

- Abdominal cramps
- Fatigue
- Increased blood pressure
- Hives or rash
- Breast tenderness
- Elevated blood sugar levels
- Muscle problems

OUTLINE 53

VITAMIN K

Deficiency

- Easy bruising
- Nose bleeding
- Bleeding in the digestive tract
- Blood disorders
- Increased tendency to bleed
- Blood in the urine

Excess

- Chest pain
- Shortness of breath
- Flushing
- Skin rash
- Hives or rash
- Kidney damage
- Lver damage
- Abnormal increase in red blood cells
- Enlarged spleen
- Blood disorders

OUTLINE 54

FOLIC ACID

Deficiency

- Diarrhea
- Forgetfulness
- Irritability

- Anemia
- Sore mouth

Excess

- Irritability

- Sleep disturbances

OUTLINE 55

NIACIN

Deficiency

- Confusion
- Dementia

- Skin inflammations
- Diarrhea

Excess

- Abnormal blood sugar tolerance
- Abnormal liver function
- Diarrhea
- Dizziness
- Flushing
- Headache
- Peptic ulcer
- Skin dryness
- Vascular changes
- Irritation of the stomach and intestines

- Increased uric acid levels in the urine
- Lowered blood pressure
- Increased intestinal activity
- Itching
- Skin problems
- Liver damage
- Nausea
- Heartburn

OUTLINE 56

CALCIUM

Deficiency

- Convulsions
- Muscle spasms and twitching
- Spasms of the throat
- Muscle cramps
- Numbness of extremities

Excess

- Loss of appetite
- Constipation
- Dry mouth
- Frequent urination
- Nausea / vomiting
- Abdominal pain
- Thirst

OUTLINE 57

MAGNESIUM

Deficiency

- Changes in muscles
- Reduced calcium levels
- Reduced potassium levels
- Calcium deposits in the kidneys

Excess

- Confusion
- Changes in normal brain activity
- Lowered blood pressure
- Muscle weakness
- Sedation

OUTLINE 58

POTASSIUM

Deficiency

- Abnormal heart function
- Changes in normal brain activity
- Fatigue
- Paralysis
- Reduced reflexes
- Intestinal obstruction
- Urinary problems

- Abnormal muscle function
- Numbness of extremities
- Thirst
- Respiratory distress
- Muscle spasms or twitching
- Weakness

Excess

- Decreased reflexes
- Irregular pulse
- Changes in normal brain activity
- Paralysis
- Abnormal heart function
- Lowered blood pressure

- Listlessness
- Mental confusion
- Respiratory difficulty
- Weakness
- Weakness or heaviness of legs
- Numbness of extremities

OUTLINE 59

SODIUM

Excess

- Abdominal cramps
- Diarrhea
- Dizziness
- Headache
- Swelling or fluid accumulation
- Irritability
- Weakness

- Muscle twitching
- Nausea / vomiting
- Dulled sensitivity
- Respiratory distress
- Restlessness
- Rapid pulse

OUTLINE 60

ZINC

Deficiency

- Hair loss
- Loss of appetite
- Inflammation of the eyelids
- Skin problems
- Skin rash
- Retarded growth
- Enlarged spleen
- Inflammation of the skin surrounding the nails
- Impaired function of testes or ovaries
- Impaired hearing
- Impaired taste
- Dwarfism
- Inflammation of the mouth or tongue
- Changes in vision or smell
- Enlarged liver

Excess

- Dehydration
- Diarrhea
- Drowsiness
- Lethargy
- Rash
- Restlessness
- Nausea / vomiting
- Changes in normal enzyme levels

Electrolytes

Every cell in the body contains fluids and nutrients required for metabolic processes. Those that are dissolved in body fluids are called solutes. Electrolytes make up some of these solutes, including chloride, bicarbonate, phosphate, sulfate, sodium, potassium, calcium and magnesium.

To understand the importance of electrolyte balance in the human body, we must first understand our necessity for water. Water serves the body in several critical ways. It is involved in the regulation of body temperature, serves as a solvent for biochemicals (e.g., enzymes, hormones and waste products), acts as a lubricant (e.g., digestion, joints, eyeballs and other body parts) and is actively involved in other body processes.

CASE STUDY

LESSONS FROM REAL LIFE —
"HERE FATHER, HAVE I GOT A GREAT DEAL FOR YOU!

Kathy had become interested in selling vitamin products as a means of earning some extra money. She had no formal training in health, but the home sales organization that sponsored the vitamin products (and a variety of other household items, as well) emphasized that this was not necessary, since they would provide her with the "appropriate" information she needed. She went to meetings scheduled by the organization and was given literature and information regarding the product line.

Kathy's elderly father purchased a bottle of vitamins and a bottle of minerals. These products were relatively expensive compared to most commercial vitamin and mineral products. The father was instructed by his daughter to take 2 tablets daily of each product.

However, this would have provided 1600 units of Vitamin D each day and would have eventually resulted in Vitamin D toxicity. Fortunately, the father consulted a health professional, who instructed him not to take the products as directed by his daughter.

The daughter had not read the products labels, and was unaware that many mineral products also contain Vitamin D (in order to increase calcium absorption). The daughter indicated that the sales meetings which she attended had related the "benefits" of vitamin and mineral supplementation, but never mentioned the adverse reactions that can occur from overdosages.

To be used by the muscles for energy, food (glycogen) must pass into the cells through the cell membranes. It does this by osmosis, which is the movement of fluid molecules through the membranes. The types and concentration of electrolytes on either side of a membrane control this movement. If the electrolyte balance is abnormal, cells do not function properly.

Electrolytes and water are lost from the body through urine, feces, expired air and perspiration. Extreme water loss from any of these sources will result in an electrolyte imbalance. Diarrhea for example, may cause sodium depletion. Vomiting causes a loss of hydrochloric acid, sodium and potassium. Profuse sweating causes the loss of sodium and chloride (salt).

"Sports drinks" and salt tablets have been recommended by coaches, athletes and advertising media as a necessary replacement for heavy exercise. However, the actual facts are somewhat different. Sports drinks are actually absorbed into the system more slowly than water, and salt tablets are simply too much, too quick. If you sweat profusely during exercise or work, drink plenty of water, and don't wait until you are thirsty. You might consider adding a little extra salt to your food, but you probably won't need salt tablets. If you do use sports drinks, either dilute them (half & half with water) or drink more water than sports drink.

Just as electrolyte losses can be dangerous, excessive electrolytes can also be unhealthy. The body will attempt to maintain its electrolyte balance no matter what you do to it. If you take in too much salt, the body will retain more fluid (water) to balance the high concentration of salt. This can lead to a higher fluid volume of the blood and an increase in blood pressure. It can also lead to increases in the water contained in fat and muscles.

Weight Control

Weight control refers to loss, gain or maintenance. Weight control is based on a very simple theory:

$$\text{Calories IN} - \text{Calories OUT} = \text{Weight (GAIN or LOSS)}$$

If you take in more calories than you use, you will gain weight. If you burn more calories than you eat, you will lose weight. And, if the calories you consume equal the calories you burn off, your weight will remain constant.

A calorie is actually a measure of heat. It is the basic measure of nutritional energy. In terms of nutrition, the basic unit is a kilocalorie (1000 calories), written with a capital 'C' (Calorie). A Calorie is defined scientifically as the amount of energy (heat) required to raise one liter of water from 15 to 16 degrees Celsius temperature.

The food you eat is used for energy or heat production in a variety of ways. Some energy is needed just to process the food and is called "specific dynamic effect". The largest percentage of energy is used in the normal maintenance of everyday, bodily functions. It is called basal metabolic rate (BMR). Physical activity and exercise account for the remainder of the energy utilized.

The rate at which the body uses energy can be measured using a variety of scientific methods, and it is influenced by many factors, which include age, sex, hormonal status, body size, nutritional state and other factors. The average American consumes 3300 Calories per day, excluding alcohol. So, gaining weight is easy to do.

Theories of Obesity and Overweight

There are several theories regarding obesity that have been researched and promoted in recent years. As with the theories of aging, no single theory seems to be completely adequate, and additional research is needed to better understand obesity and weight gain.

Malfunctioning Hypothalamus Theory

The hypothalamus gland is located at the base of the brain, and it regulates the appetite and satiety. If the hypothalamus is malfunctioning, an individual could receive incorrect hunger signals, which would prompt continued eating with a resultant weight gain.

There are blood tests for thyroid function that can check for endocrine malfunctions, but only a very small percentage of the population would likely have a malfunctioning of the hypothalamus. A physician can determine whether or not these tests are indicated.

Sluggish Metabolism Theory

This theory refers to factors that influence your basic metabolic rate (the rate at which the body uses energy). A lower metabolic rate means that the body will be less likely to burn off calories, while a higher metabolic rate means that the body will be more likely to burn off calories. Factors which affect the basal metabolic rate (BMR) include:

1. *Age and Gender*
Younger people tend to have a higher BMR than older adults. As we age the BMR tends to decrease, which increases our tendency to gain weight. The BMR for men is approximately 6-7% higher than that for women.

2. *Size*
Smaller people tend to have a lower BMR than larger people. People who have more fat tend to have a lower BMR than the same

size person who has a lower percentage of body fat. This is because lean muscle tissue uses energy (i.e., burns calories). Fat does not use energy.

3. *Hormones*

Certain hormones affect the BMR. Only a physican can check to see if a normal hormonal balance exists.

4. *Nutritional Status*

A severe restriction in caloric intake (less than 1200 calories /day for females; less than 1500 calories/day for males) may cause a decrease in the BMR. For this reason, fasting diets are not as effective (and certainly not as healthy) as people tend to believe.

OUTLINE 61

HOW TO ESTIMATE YOUR DAILY METABOLIC RATE AND CALORIE NEEDS

Procedure:
  1. Weight (in pounds) divided by 2.2 = weight in kilograms.
  2. Weight in kilograms multiplied by 22 (for women) or 24 (for men).
  3. The result represents daily nutritional need (in calories), excluding exercise.

An example
  Consider a man who weighs 180 pounds:
  1. Divide 180 by 2.2   = 81.8 kilograms
  2. 81.8 kg multiplied by 24   = 1964 calories

   This man will need 1964 calories daily for normal functioning. If he eats more calories per day (e.g., 2500) he will gain weight. If he consumes 500 more calories per day than needed, he will gain a pound each week (This is because a pound of fat equals 3500 calories. He will accumulate this many extra calories every 7 days). If he reduced his caloric intake and increased his caloric expenditure (30 minutes of exercise = 300 calories out), so that he lost 500 calories each day, he could lose a pound of weight each week.
   By using this information, find out where you stand by completing the table below.

```
┌─────────────────────────────────────────────────────────────┐
│                    ████ TABLE 4 ████                          │
│                                                               │
│              ESTIMATE YOUR DAILY METABOLIC RATE               │
│                    AND CALORIC NEEDS                          │
│                                                               │
│   1. Your weight in kilograms            ——— lbs ÷ 2.2 = ———  │
│                                                               │
│   2. Multiply your weight in kilograms                        │
│      by 22 (for women) or 24 (for men)   ——— kg x — = ———     │
│                                                               │
│   3. Your daily nutritional need is                   ———     │
│                                                               │
│   4. Your daily caloric intake is                     ———     │
│                                                               │
│   5. Your weekly caloric intake is                    ———     │
│                                                               │
│   6. Your estimated weekly caloric expenditure is     ———     │
│                                                               │
│   7. Net gain (or loss) in weekly calories            ———     │
│                                                               │
│              *Can you improve your lifestyle?*               │
└─────────────────────────────────────────────────────────────┘
```

5. *Exercise*

Regular exercise helps to keep the BMR at a higher level. Not only will exercise burn more calories, but your metabolism tends to remain elevated for an extended time after the exercise bout. The BMR will probably be significantly higher in people who exercise, than in those who do not.

Brown Fat Theory

Brown fat is located in the back, chest and abdomen. It amounts to less than 1% of body weight (as opposed to adipose, or white fat) which accounts for as much as 25% of the weight of a normal person. White fat stores excess calories. Brown fat burns calories to produce heat (thermogenesis). Studies in laboratory rats indicate that when lean rats eat an excess number of calories, their brown fat can burn these calories more efficiently than can the brown fat of obese rats. Brown fat is normally stimulated by excessively low temperatures (<28°F) and caloric intake. Brown fat tends to diminish with age. It is not really known what role it plays in weight control.

Fat Cell Theory

The number of fat cells in the body is fixed (approximately 30 billion), although the number of fat cells increases at certain ages (e.g., birth to 5, and 7 to 11). It was generally believed that the number remained constant once adulthood was reached. Now it is believed that the size and number of fat cells will increase in response to significant weight gains. This would make it more difficult to lose weight, but not impossible. Typically, changes in weight (fat) result in changes in fat cell size, not their number.

Set Point Theory

This theory suggests that there is a unique "ideal weight" for each of us. Our ideal weight may not be in agreement with ideal weight charts which are available from many sources. Research of starvation and overeating indicate that once the experiments are over people tend to return to their "normal" eating patterns and a weight (i.e., their set weight) which appears to be "normal" for them.

• • • •

No single theory adequately explains weight problems. In all likelihood, obesity occurs as a combination of factors, and most people who diet return to their pre-diet weight within a year or so, regardless of the weight reduction program selected. Whatever the validity of any given theory it is no excuse for unhealthy lifestyles, overeating and sedentary living. Eating right and regular exercise are absolutely essential to insure that you maintain your ideal weight and body composition.

Diet versus Weight Control

Most people associate the term "diet" with restricted eating. So, no more hot fudge sundaes, no more sausage, biscuits and gravy, eat only "rabbit food" etc. No wonder it's so hard for the average American to lose or maintain "proper" weight. Dieting is a negative concept and most people are simply unwilling to accept the "necessity" that is implied.

Nevertheless, in order to control weight, maximize health and live longer, eating "right" is critical. This, however, does NOT mean giving up all the foods we like, but it does mean being smart about what, how much and how often we eat. Hot fudge sundaes are still allowed, but not every day. Moreover, it is probably best to limit them to a single dip. The bottom line in eating: we should consume only about 1800 calories per day, and these calories should reflect a balance between the food groups (i.e., 30% from fats, 60% from carbohydrates and 10% from proteins).

Bad Diets

Most people view a diet as being a temporary state of restricted eating in order to lose weight. According to this view, all diets are "bad." In fact, any diet that restricts our caloric intake to 1200 calories (women) or 1500 calories (men) is not only unpleasant, but also unhealthy (unless prescribed and monitored by a physician). The best approach is one in which you lose no more than 1 to 2 pounds of weight per week. Any more than that may result in loss of tissue other than fat (e.g., muscle), and the whole idea is to lose the excess fat. People with weight problems due to metabolic disorders of some type should consult their physician about a proper weight reduction program.

Diets that overemphasize or restrict certain food groups are not a good idea either. The body must have all of the food groups in order to function normally. When it is deprived of certain nutrients, it has to actually "build" those that are missing. So, when people opt for a diet that is high in protein but low in carbohydrates and fats for example, (as some popular weight loss programs recommend) the body uses the protein to make the carbohydrate and fat components that it needs. Unfortunately, this is an imperfect "manufacturing" process. The by-products of this type of metabolism can be toxic if they accumulate in the body, and people have actually died from high protein diets.

Today's diet fad is one of high carbohydrate and protein intake, and low fat intake. Although this may be less risky, it still does not insure that good eating habits are replacing poor ones. The key to good nutrition remains one of balance rather than the overemphasis of some food groups to the exclusion of others.

Diets that use powdered foods, special packaged foods or liquid replacement foods are also probably unhealthy. In this case, you may lose weight rapidly, but some of this weight loss may not be fat. And, most people who use such fad or "crash" diet programs and products gain back the weight they have lost after they finish using the product and return to their old eating habits.

Weight Control Medications

Weight control medications (either prescriptions or nonprescription) are designed to promote rapid weight losses by one of two basic methods. The first involves the use of diuretics to help flush water from the system. Since 60-75% of body weight is water, losing water certainly can result in dramatic changes in scale weight in a short amount of time. Unfortunately, it is important to realize that with this method you are not losing fat, only water.

The second method uses some kind of appetite suppressant, such as caffeine or amphetamine-like substances (these include decongestants that are found in most cold and allergy products). These products do often suppress the appetite and increase metabolism. They may work while a person is taking the drug (although their effectiveness tends to decrease over time). Unfortunately, the use of such drugs for weight loss rarely results in lifestyle changes (i.e., diet and exercise habits). Consequently, when the person stops taking the drug, he regains the weight that was lost. And, this problem does not even include the fact that such drugs can have unhealthy side effects (e.g., sleeplessness, heart palpitations, high blood pressure and stomach problems).

Eating Right

As we have stressed above, a "good" diet is a matter of eating the right mix of carbohydrates, fats and proteins (60% /30% /10%) and should add up to no more than 1200-2000 calories per day . . . give or take a few. So why is it so difficult for most of us to eat within these limits? For one reason, in our society food is an important component of our social lives. Dinner parties, dinner and a show, dinner and dancing, backyard barbecue and romantic dinners are the norm. For most of us, our lifestyles involve many activities that are associated with eating.

Counting

Many diets emphasize the importance of counting calories. Unfortunately, most of us resist this practice and, consequently, reject the whole notion of weight management. Actually, it is not really necessary to count calories or fat grams forever in order to eat right. However, counting is initially helpful in starting on a weight program until you realize what eating right means for you. Afterward, the changes become second nature, and counting calories is no longer necessary. Moreover, most foods are labeled with their content of calories, carbohydrates, protein and fat per serving, which makes the practice relatively easy.

Portion or serving sizes are critical to eating right. A sixteen ounce T-bone steak, for example, is enough red meat for four days in terms of our recommended allowance. Conversely, it is easy to learn what a 3 to 4 ounce piece of meat looks like. This is more than sufficient at any given meal. Of course, you may have to weigh the portion at first until you realize how big a 3 to 4 ounce portion really is. Similarly, you will need to measure certain foods with a measuring cup until you realize what 1/2 cup or 2 ounces of cereal looks like in a bowl.

Once you become familiar with portion size, then you can go on to the next step. In order to better understand the 60/30/10 concept for example, it is necessary to know how many calories are contained in a gram of each of the food types and how to use them. Outline 62 shows how to calculate the percentage of calories derived from the fat content of foods. Since fat is the major dietary culprit in terms of bad eating habits, it serves as a good example. The idea is to limit Calories from fats to 30% or less per day. Just because butter is 100% fat, does not mean you can never eat it. But, if you spread it on a croissant (a high fat bread), as opposed to a bagel (no fat), you will exceeded the 30% fat target for that course of your meal.

Consider a man who wants to eat no more than 1800 calories per day. If 30% of the 1800 calories are derived from fat, then no more than 540 calories (1800 x 30%) or 60 grams of his calories per day should come from fats. One cup of milk and a tablespoon of butter would represent 1/4 of his daily fat allowance!

Cooking

Cooking is just as critical to the "eating right" concept as the foods you eat. Traditionally, "good cooks" (like Grandmas) deep fried most everything (usually in animal lard) from meat and potatoes to vegetables (e.g., okra, squash and tomatoes). Chicken fried steak, fried potatoes, fried okra, biscuits (made with bacon fat) and whole milk were the ingredients of many typical American meals. A leading hamburger franchise made the "best" French fries in the world according to kids everywhere . . . deep fried in 100% lard. And, those wonderful cookies with chocolate on the outside and a creamy center that you

---

OUTLINE 62

CALCULATING THE FAT PERCENTAGE
OF THE FOODS YOU EAT

Caloric Content of the Three Basic Food Groups:

Carbohydrates = 4.5 calories / gram

Proteins = 4.5 calories / gram

Fats = 9 calories / gram

Examples

A butter container states that 1 tablespoonful = 63 calories and 7 grams of fat. What percent of the calories are derived from the fat in this product?

Since there are 9 calories / gram, and 7 grams of fat, then 9 x 7 = 63 calories contained in the 7 grams. Thus, in this example ALL of the calories are from fat.

One cup of whole milk contains 150 calories and 8 grams of fat. What is the percentage of calories from fat?

9 calories / gram of fat = 9 x 8 grams = 72 calories from the fat. So, 72 divided by 150 total calories = 48% of the calories are from fat.

Now You Try It:

A processed meat package states that each serving is 180 calories and 10 grams of fat. What percentage of the calories are derived from the fat?

[Answer = 50%]

---

pulled apart to eat were made from lard.

One reason our Grandmas used to cook everything in grease was because they did not have the types of cooking utensils that we now enjoy. Non-stick surfaces on skillets require less fat (oil) in cooking. Now, instead of frying, we can saute food for a much healthier cooking style. Using non-stick skillets and low fat cooking sprays (or very little oil) will reduce the number of calories and fat grams in the food we prepare. And baking, broiling or boiling without oils eliminates even more calories and fat.

Healthy cooking also involves common sense. Meat, milk, eggs and oils are major sources of fat in our diets. So, if a recipe calls for meat, limit the portion size to no more than 4 ounces. Trim off excess fat and skin. Use 1/2% or 1% milk instead of whole milk. Use egg whites instead of the whole egg and use oils sparingly. It is often possible to use half the oil indicated by recipes without sacrificing any noticeable difference in the flavor or texture.

One problem sometimes encountered in healthy cooking is that individual family members may have different dietary needs and preferences from a health perspective. Women may have more difficulty eating right when they are preparing meals for husbands who are unwilling to cooperate with dietary changes. Conversely, when husbands are interested in "eating right," or willing to change, wives have fewer problems converting the family (and cooking habits) to healthy alternatives.

Obviously, then, in order to facilitate healthy cooking practices, the entire family should discuss their lifestyle and eating habits. Agree on common goals and make a commitment. Discuss meal options, plan menus and ways in which you can reward yourselves periodically for achieving common healthy eating goals. Celebrate the "victories" of each family member.

Recipes

There are literally thousands of recipes contained in newspapers, magazines and cook books that offer assistance in learning to eat right. Many recipes print the calories, fat grams, cholesterol and sodium (salt) content for each ingredient. There are several cook books on the market that emphasize low fat recipes, including publications by the American Heart Association and American Cancer Society. In fact, any cook book that publishes the calories and fat grams per serving can be used to achieve healthy eating styles. Ultimately, however, each of us must choose and cook only those recipes that conform to our new "eating right" policy.

OUTLINE 63

HEALTHY EATING: RECIPES, SHOPPING, COOKING AND MEAL PLANNING

General

🍂 Prepare more meatless meals (e.g., beans, peas, tofu, cooked grains, brown rice, pasta).

🍂 Use non-stick cookware with spray cooking products, rather than oils.

🍂 Be sure to check the sodium content of the products you purchase (if salt is a concern).

🍂 Use herbs instead of salt (or lemon in appropriate foods).

🍂 Buy frozen entrees rather than dinners. Dinners frequently come with sauces or desserts.

🍂 Beware of the terms, "Lite", "Light" or "Low Fat." These terms often mean that the product is lower in fat than it used to be, and not that the product is a healthy alternative.

🍂 Many of the new frozen dinners that promote low fat are healthy alternatives. However, you should still read the label to make sure that it fits your dietary program.

Breads, Cereals, Pasta

🍂 Buy whole grain breads, cereals & pastas and be sure to check the fat content.

Dairy

🍂 Choose low-fat dairy products when available. There are even fat free cheeses and spreads available.

🍂 Use nonfat or low-fat margarine products rather than butter.

🍂 Use egg substitutes or egg whites instead of whole eggs.

🍂 Use low-fat or skim milk instead of whole milk.

🍂 Use evaporated skim milk instead of cream.

🍂 Use low-fat cottage cheese instaed of full fat or ricotta cheese.

🍂 Use nonfat yogurt or nonfat sour cream instead of sour cream.

OUTLINE 63 cont'd

Desserts

🐞 Reduce desserts (a hiding place for fats). If you have a dessert, limit the size.

🐞 Opt for low-fat desserts like raisin or cinnamon breads. There are many recipes for low-fat desserts (Many of these are very good!).

Fats

🐞 Cook with cooking sprays instead of frying in fat.

🐞 Reduce fats in recipes. Fat in most recipes can be easily reduced by as much as 50% or more. This works especially well in casseroles and quickbreads.

🐞 Opt for healthy snacks (e.g., fresh or dried fruits, fresh vegetables) and avoid the dips!

🐞 Avoid cream sauces and gravies. On those occasions when sauces are indicated, limit the amount you use or place some on the side of your plate rather than on top of the food. Prepare gravies and sauces using the Paste Method (Add flour or cornstarch to cold liquid slowly, then blend well. This eliminates the need for fat).

🐞 Read labels! Opt for products with reduced levels of fats and oils.

🐞 Use fat-free salad dressings.

🐞 Use half the oil or butter indicated by recipes.

🐞 Use pureed fruit instead of oil-baked items.

Fruits

🐞 Buy fresh fruit or dried fruit. If you buy canned fruit, choose those packed in water or light syrup, not heavy syrup.

Meats

🐞 Choose meats that are lean (not much visible fat).

🐞 If you don't like to skin the chicken, buy it pre-skinned.

🐞 Be sure to check portion sizes of meats.

🐞 Use smaller amounts (a 3 oz portion is about the size of the palm of your hand).

🕊 Opt for low-fat cooking methods (e.g., bake, boil, broil, grill, poach, roast, simmer, steam).

🕊 Select meats which are leaner or contain less fat (e.g., fish or poultry).

🕊 Substitute complex carbohydrates and vegetables for meats.

🕊 Trim away all visible fat before meal preparation.

🕊 Use herbs and spices to flavor meats instead of fats.

🕊 Refrigerate soups or stews which contain meat or poultry. This will allow the fats to solidify on the surface so that they can be removed easily before heating and serving.

🕊 Use skinless chicken or turkey for red meat.

Vegetables

🕊 Buy fresh vegetables. There's not much difference in canned versus frozen vegetables.

🕊 Avoid vegetables in sauces or creams.

🕊 Steam or boil vegetables in water.

🕊 Prepare vegetables with herbs and spices, rather than butter or sauces.

Shopping

Healthy eating and healthy cooking require that you buy the right kinds of foods to begin with. So, shopping becomes a critical component of your life extension program (see Outline 63). The key to shopping is learning to read and interpret the labels. Serving size, calories, fat grams and other necessary information are now required on the labeling of most food products. If foods are not labeled, don't buy them! You can also write to the company that prepares your favorite foods for the labeling information, or consult with a local dietitian for help in determining the necessary information.

Meats and produce are often not labeled, so this information must be obtained elsewhere. Most fruits and vegetables are "fat-free" (i.e., less than 1 gram of fat per 100 grams of weight). An apple, for

```
┌─────────────────────────────────────────────────────┐
│                    CASE STUDY                         │
│                                                       │
│            LESSONS FROM REAL LIFE —                   │
│         THE AUTHOR AT THE GROCERY STORE               │
│                                                       │
│   One of the authors (GH) was at the grocery store    │
│ recently. He noticed a package of "lite" frankfurters.│
│ They looked great. But then he looked at the label    │
│ and noticed the following information:                │
│                                                       │
│            Calories / Serving  =  140                 │
│                         Fat  =  12 grams              │
│                                                       │
│   Is this bad? Well, let's see. Since there are 9     │
│ calories associated with each gram of fat, then:      │
│                                                       │
│               12 x 9  =  108 calories                 │
│                                                       │
│   This means that of the 140 calories / serving, 108  │
│ of them are from the fat contained in this product.   │
│ So:                                                   │
│                                                       │
│               108 / 140  =  77%                       │
│                                                       │
│   Ah, so now we know that 77% of the calories /       │
│ serving in this product come from fat. Even thought   │
│ this is a "lite" product, it still has a dispropor-   │
│ tionate amount of fat calories.                       │
│   So, the author opted for another brand in which     │
│ the fat only accounted for about 26% of the calories  │
│ / serving.                                            │
└─────────────────────────────────────────────────────┘
```

instance, contains only 0.6 grams of fat in 100 grams of weight, but is considered to be fat free.

Be wary (i.e., read labels!) of cereals and snack bars, especially those that promote whole grain and high fiber. The grain is desirable, but these products are frequently high in fat content. Also, there are many new products that are identified as fat-free, or reduced calorie foods. Here again, it's best to read the ingredients to determine what these often misleading terms actually mean.

Eating Out

Our love of "eating out" is a contributing factor to our weight control difficulties. Not only is this a socially desirable behavior, but eating out often saves time in our busy lifestyles especially where both husbands and wives work. Yet, fast food establishments can be the downfall of every "eating right" program. These are establishments where foods are cooked fast, eaten fast and burned off slow. Moreover "fast" is almost universally synonymous with "fried." Thus, most fast foods are high in calories and very high in fat. For example, a breakfast biscuit with bacon, egg and cheese can contain 35 grams of fat, more than half the daily allowance for the man who is consuming 1800 calories per day.

OUTLINE 64

HEALTHY EATING: EATING OUT

Before Going Out

❦ Eat a light, low-fat snack before dining out.

Appetizers

❦ Instead of canapes or other high fat hors-d'oeuvre, select bread sticks or fresh vegetables.

Salads

❦ Avoid adding meat or cheese to salad.

❦ Be careful at salad bars. Creamy salads (e.g., macaroni salad) tend to be loaded with fat.

❦ Ask for salad dressings and sauces "on the side." This allows you to better determine how much you will use.

Breads

❦ Opt for unbuttered breads and toast.

❦ Choose bagels, muffins or bread sticks rather than croissants, biscuits, rolls or cakes.

❦ Use fruit spreads on bread instead of butter.

Main Entrees

❦ When ordering, be in control. Don't be afraid to make special requests.

OUTLINE 64 cont'd

❧ Ask how the meat entrees are prepared. Leave off sauces or gravies, or at least have them put on the side.

❧ Order leaner cuts of meat. Choice cuts are leaner than prime cuts.

❧ Choose chicken or fish instead of meat.

❧ Avoid fried foods (they are always higher in fat content than the same foods that have been baked, simmered, or roasted). See if menus offer baked, broiled, grilled or poached dishes. These are better than fried. If they are not on the menu, ask if they can be special-ordered in these ways.

❧ Opt for foods without sauces, gravies or butter . . . they have less fat.

❧ Eat vegetables without butter, margarine, sauces or cream.

❧ Order a la carte. One chicken enchilada is better than the enchilada dinner that comes with refried beans and guacamole.

❧ Order thin crust pizza with vegetable toppings, and limit the cheese.

❧ If you are going to a Mexican restaurant, watch out for fried dishes like flautas. Guacamole and cheese dips are high in fat. Choose bean burritos or chicken enchiladas with salsa instead of cheese toppings.

❧ Watch out for condiments like tartar sauce or Hollandaise . . . they are loaded with fat.

❧ Leave enough food to necessitate a "doggy bag". Your pet will love you (although these foods are not really healthy for animals either), or you'll have another meal tomorrow.

Desserts

❧ Desserts are the major contributors of fat in our diets. Opt for low-fat alternatives (e.g., fruit, ice milk, sorbet, low-fat yogurt, angel food cake, plain or fruit gelatin). If you must get the cheese cake, at least share it with your dinner partner(s).

Snacks

❧ Keep low-fat, high-fiber snacks at work and in the car. This will allow you to opt for "smart snacks."

Airlines

❧ Check with airlines before you fly. Many offer low-fat meals.

There are smarter selections on many fast food menus if we are willing to make the right choices. Ordering a salad is usually smart, no matter how unsatisfying this might seem, at first. Of course if you then load the salad with high fat dressings, meats and cheeses you have defeated the purpose.

Even chicken breast sandwiches which are touted as healthy choices can be deceiving. Chicken does sound healthier than hamburgers, but a fried, breaded chicken breast has more fat than a grilled hamburger.

The smartest way to eat right at fast food establishments is to limit the number of times you eat there. Consider taking a sack lunch to work instead of eating out. Not only will this save time and money, but it also gives you control over the calories and fat which you consume.

Restaurants can be just as damaging to your "eating right" plan as fast food places. Buffets and "all you can eat for just one price" establishments can cause a major set-back in your program. So limit the number of times you might do this in a given month.

If you drink alcoholic beverages before dinner, be careful about letting the alcohol affect your judgment when ordering the meal. Where after-dinner cocktails, flavored coffees and elaborate desserts are the norm, be aware of the impact this has on your eating program. Eating out should not cause the complete and total disintegration of your "eating right" program. With a little common sense, motivation and will power, we can make healthy choices and still enjoy the social experience. If you eat out, be smart.

Motivational Forces

Changing our behaviors is difficult. This is especially true with behaviors that allow us the pleasure of eating what we want, when we want and how much we want. Add to this our negative concept of a "diet" and we have a scenario that is simply too demanding for most people.

As with other healthy lifestyle behaviors, the decision to eat right requires commitment and control. We must first be committed to eating right in order to establish the control we need. This requires a long-term perspective to eating right, rather than a short-term commitment to temporary diet fads.

The biggest obstacle we face in adopting a healthy diet is the sense of losing control over an important aspect of our lives. After all, we decide what we like to eat, we decide how much we are going to eat, and we decide when we are going to eat. These are our decisions and we resent being deprived of the power to make them by others who are constantly reminding us of how unhealthy our eating habits are. In fact, we might eat the very things we have been warned against just to prove to ourselves and others that we make these decisions, healthy or otherwise.

The first step in committing to a new and healthier eating plan is to recognize that we are in control. This is our decision, and it is being made to improve our health status. We cannot control hereditary influences which contribute to weight problems, but we can control our food plan and our own behavior.

OUTLINE 65

"EATING RIGHT" BEHAVIORAL CONCEPTS

❦ Follow the guidelines in Outline 61 to calculate the calories you need in a day (normally 1200-2000 calories).

❦ Reduce your caloric intake by 300 calories/day.

❦ Limit fat intake to no more than 30% of daily calories (usually about 35-65 grams).

❦ Eat a variety of foods, using the Basic Food Pyramid (Outline 41). You will probably find that you need to limit meat, milk, eggs and cheese, and increase fruits, vegetables and grains.

❦ Exercise to increase your daily caloric expenditure and increase your basal metabolism. Increase your caloric output (i.e., exercise and activity) by at least 200 calories / day. Examples would include at least 20 minutes of walking, biking or jogging. If you already exercise, it may be necessary to increase your activities.

❦ Use sugar and salt sparingly.

❦ Drink plenty of water.

❦ Consume alcoholic beverages only in moderation, if at all.

❦ Set realistic goals for weight loss. Safe, effective weight loss is a slow process (1 to 2 pounds / week). Plateaus are normal. It is normal to lose weight for a week or two, level off, and then lose again.

OUTLINE 65 cont'd

- Don't get discouraged. "Falling off the wagon" does not mean that you have "failed." Eating right most of the time is better than eating poorly all of the time.

- Don't skip meals . . . it will just make you hungry.

- Avoid snacking. Don't eat between meals and don't eat the "junk" that's normally associated with snacking. Snacking invariably involves eating the wrong kinds of food (high fat, sugar & salt) in place of regular meals of nutritious foods.

- Be mindful of eating. Eating in front of the TV or at your desk can distract you from your "eating right" commitment.

- Eat slowly and enjoy eating. Be conscious of how good your food tastes.

- Hot foods and foods requiring utensils will slow your eating and allow you to enjoy the eating experience.

- Don't eat late at night (after 9 p.m.). Most of those calories are not burned, but stored as fat.

- Commit to change. You are changing your eating habits for a longer, healthier life.

Once we acknowledge this, the next logical step is to express this decision openly. By making our commitments public, we encourage the support of family and friends. (It is a particular irony of human behavior that we are quick to support the good efforts of others to change, even though we are unwilling to make the same changes ourselves).

The next item on our weight reduction agenda is to decide upon the goals and objectives for our efforts (e.g., Do you wish to lose 10 pounds? 50?). Our goal should be broken into short, easily attainable objectives on a daily or weekly basis. And finally, it is important to reward ourselves for even small gains on a regular basis. It's OK to depart from your plan on special occasions. But be careful that this does not lead to increasing the number of special occasions.

Special Diets

It is sometimes necessary for people with special health problems to conform to certain dietary restrictions. For example, people with high blood pressure or heart diseases may need to be on a "salt-restricted" diet. Diabetics must monitor their sugar and fat intake. In these cases, special diets should be prescribed by your physician.

Mark Twain once said that "the only way to keep your health is to eat what you don't want, drink what you don't like and do what you'd rather not." This advice works well if your goal is to elicit laughter, but not if your goal is to lose weight. The key to a long and healthy life need not be a life of deprivation, but it does involve common sense, moderation, and creative adaptations. This can include rethinking our lifestyles and even changing our tastes if they involve risky behaviors. It is important for each of us to do what we are capable of doing, and to celebrate our opportunities to make healthy lifestyle choices!

OUTLINE 66

SOURCES OF INFORMATION ABOUT HEALTHY COOKING AND EATING

Check with your local bookstore for these books. Be sure to ask for the latest edition.

❦ ALL NEW COOK BOOK FOR DIABETICS AND THEIR FAMILIES
  Research Nutritionists, School of Medicine, University of Alabama at Birmingham, Birmingham, AL

❦ AMERICAN HEART ASSOCIATION COOK BOOK
  American Heart Association, Ballantine Books, New York

❦ ANNETTE'S EASY COOKIN'
  Annette Adkins, Muskogee, OK

❦ CHOICES FOR A HEALTHY HEART
  J.C. Piscatella, Workman Publishing Co, Inc., New York City

❦ CONTROLLING CHOLESTEROL
  K. Cooper, Bantam Books

OUTLINE 66 cont'd

❦ COOKING A LA HEART
L. Hochfeld and B. Eykyn, Appletree Press, MN

❦ DELICIOUSLY SIMPLE
Harriet Roth, New American Library, New York City

❦ EASY GOURMET TO LOWER YOUR FAT THERMOSTAT
H. Gifford, Vitality House International, Inc., Provo, UT

❦ EAT RIGHT THE EASY WAY
J.S. Blake, Prentice-Hall, New York City

❦ EATER'S CHOICE
R. Goor, Houghton Mifflin Co., Boston, MA

❦ FAMILY COOK BOOK, Vol. 2
American Diabetes Association, Prentice-Hall, New York City

❦ JANE BRODY'S GOOD FOOD BOOK
J. Brody, Bantam Books, New York City

❦ LIVING LEAN AND LOVING IT
Eve Lowry, R.D., C.V. Mosby

❦ MEDITERRANEAN SPECIALTIES FOR HEALTHY EATING
Edward Matzaganian, Mancorp Publishing, Inc. Tampa, FL

❦ SEAFOOD — A COLLECTION OF HEART HEALTHY RECIPES
J. Harsila and E. Hansen, Bookcrafters, Chelsea, MI

❦ THE AMERICAN HEART ASSOCIATION COOKBOOK
R. Eshleman and M. Winston, Random House, Inc., New York City

❦ THE FAT GRAM COUNTER
J. Zimmer, Miller Press, Berkley Books, New York City

❦ THE LIVING HEART BRAND NAME SHOPPER'S GUIDE
Michael, E. DeBakey, M.D., et. al., Mastermedia Ltd., New York City

OUTLINE 66 cont'd

❧ THE NEW AMERICAN DIET
S. Connor and W. Connor, Simon & Schuster, Inc., New York City

❧ THE NEW AMERICAN DIET SYSTEM
S. Connor and W. Connor, Simon & Schuster, Inc., New York City

❧ THE NEW DIABETIC COOKBOOK
Mable Cavaiani, R.D., Contemprorary Books, Chicago, IL

❧ THE NEW LAURELS KITCHEN
L. Robertson, C. Flinders and B. Ruppenthal, Ten Speed Press,
Berkley, CA

19. EXERCISE

"No need to give up the race just because you
joggle when you jog."

— Wendell's Observation, John Peers

Exercise may not be a panacea, but it is an essential component of
all realistic health programs. In a recent Options for Health Tip
released by Scott and White Hospital and clinics in Temple, Texas,
exercise was described in the following way:

> It's been suggested that exercise is the closest
> thing we have to an anti-aging pill.
> Regular exercise can help you feel less stressed;
> help you get down to and maintain an ideal
> weight; help you strengthen your bones; help you
> improve your concentration and creative thinking;
> help you reduce the risk of heart disease, diabetes
> and some cancers; help you keep your digestive
> system in good working order; and help you look
> and feel great.

The overall benefits of exercise to the human body are based on
the philosophy, "Use it or Lose it". Sedentary people will deteriorate
at a faster rate than active people. Moreover, the decline of inactivity
can involve many body functions and systems. Conversely, exercise
may slow the degeneration process in some or all of these systems.

Unfortunately, our lifestyles seem to promote more of a sedentary
existence than an active one. Consider a typical day: 8 hours of work
(longer where a half hour to 1 hour round trip is involved); 7 to 8 hours
sleep, and the remaining time watching TV or equally passive activity. In a schedule of this type there is little time devoted to physical
activity.

Most surveys bear this out. Only about 10% of Americans exercise
for 30 minutes or more daily and only about 20% exercise 30 minutes
or more at least 5 times each week. More than 25% of Americans over
age 18 report no leisure time physical activity, and about 40% over the
age of 65 report that they lead a sedentary lifestyle.

OUTLINE 67

EXAMPLES OF WAYS OF INCREASING DAILY PHYSICAL ACTIVITY

🌱 Get up and move around.

🌱 Use the stairs whenever possible (to go both up and down) instead of elevators or escalators.

🌱 Park farther away from buildings and walk.

🌱 If you use public transportation, get off a few blocks early and walk to your building.

🌱 Take exercise breaks, stretch, walk around, give your mind and body a break.

🌱 Move about instead of snacking.

🌱 Park farther from the office or supermarket door to increase walking distance.

🌱 Instead of watching TV in the evenings, take a walk.

🌱 Playing golf? Carry clubs or use a pull cart instead of riding.

🌱 Put on fast paced music and do some "aerobic" house cleaning.

About half of our youth do not participate in appropriate physical activities. This is no surprise when you consider how many chubby children you see on a daily basis. And why shouldn't they be over-weight? Their parents usually are. Our children grow up in homes where healthy lifestyles are simply not a priority. But what about the schools? Do they help to undo our fad for flab? Well, fewer than 36% of elementary and secondary schools offer daily physical education classes and less than 50% of the available classes encourage long term fitness patterns. This is not a criticism of our schools. The curricula is also a reflection of our culture. And as a culture, we are far more concerned about having a winning football season this year than we are about heart diseases that these young people may face 30 years from now.

CASE STUDY

LESSONS FROM REAL LIFE – JAMES

James is a 56 year old male who came to the Wellness Center for an exercise tolerance test (treadmill) and a physical examination. His blood pressure was 150/94 and he was 30 pounds overweight. His treadmill test did not indicate any sign of disease, and his lifestyle prescription consisted of aerobic exercise, reduced caloric intake (diet) and no salt.

James is an account executive (stock broker) and confessed that his schedule was too hectic to allow time for exercise. He was able to make the recommended dietary changes, but complained that he could not find the right type of aerobic exercise, nor the time to do it. He tried walking, swimming at the "Y," and even enrolled in an aerobics class, but was "unable" to fit any of these into his busy schedule.

After several consultations with James about his time management and his priorities, it was recommended that he try the stationary bicycle. Since James spends the first thirty minutes of each day watching the stock market reports on TV, he now rides his bike while watching those reports.

Since starting this routine, James has lost 30 pounds and his blood pressure is 134/84. More importantly, he reports that he feels much better, he is more energetic throughout the day and he believes he gets more work done.

HOW ABOUT YOU?

Are there times during the day when you could combine exercise with other daily activities?

A POINT TO PONDER:

There's always a parking space . . .
for the person who is willing to walk!

Exercise Versus Physical Activity

For the purposes of this book we will make a distinction between exercise and physical activity. Exercise is accomplished for a physiological purpose (walking for cardiovascular endurance, stretching for improved flexibility, deep breathing for relaxation and strength training for improved strength and muscle tone).

Physical activity is undertaken for no particular reason other than its own benefits (e.g., enjoyment). Examples may include back-yard badminton, shooting baskets with the kids or grandchildren, golf and gardening. Defined in this manner, many low-level daily activities can be considered examples of physical activity. Sometimes the advantages of physical activity are overlooked.

Increasing our levels of daily physical activity is one way to alter our sedentary habits. In addition, increasing physical activity can generally move in the direction of a regular exercise routine. As a general guideline, physical activity should be undertaken every day, while the frequency of exercise may vary depending upon your exercise goals. There are certain terms worth knowing which are associated with activity and exercise.

Frequency refers to how often you exercise or are active (e.g., once a day, three times per week).

Intensity refers to how hard you exercise or are active. When speaking of cardiovascular exercise, intensity may be determined by target heart rate (in beats per minute that the heart pulses during the sustained portion of the exercise session). In strength training, intensity is measured by the amount of weight or resistance being lifted or moved.

Duration refers to how long you exercise or are active. In aerobic (cardiovascular) exercise, a minimum of 20 minutes at moderate intensity is usually sufficient to obtain desired results. Duration is usually determined by intensity. Moderate intensity exercises require a minimum of 20 minutes, while lower intensity exercises may require at least 40 minutes to gain the same benefit.

The type of exercise or activity is determined by your goals. If the goal is cardiovascular endurance, aerobic exercise is the recommended type. If the goal is stress relief, relaxation exercises may be appropriate. Aerobic exercise has become a popular topic in health discussions. "Aerobic" means "with oxygen." Literally, the term means that the heart and lungs are involved in supplying adequate oxygen to the muscles doing the work. Appropriately designed aerobic exercises should allow your body to keep up with its oxygen demands. These exercises should not be too intense or too fast-paced to cause dangerous oxygen demands. Examples of aerobic exercises include walking, swimming, running, cross country skiing, bicycling, stair climbing and aerobic dance. Exercise that is too intense or too hard is called anaerobic (e.g., sprinting). If you are exercising at such an intensity that you become breathless, you are doing an anaerobic exercise, which can actually be counter-productive.

Exercise Goals

Exercise can also be categorized according to how vigorous it is and how it relates to physical conditioning (see Outline 68). While some types may have more social appeal, they may offer fewer health benefits. So, it is important to make exercise decisions based on your exercise goals.

OUTLINE 68

TYPES OF EXERCISE AND THEIR IMPACT ON PHYSICAL CONDITIONING

Type A

These exercises are naturally vigorous. They should be done for at least 20 to 30 minutes 3 or 4 times each week in order to condition heart and lungs, burn off extra calories, and provide other health benefits.

Aerobic dance	Jumping rope
Basketball (full court)	Rowing
Bicycling	Running
Cycling	Skiing (cross country)
Hiking (uphill)	Swimming
Ice hockey	Walking (brisk)
Jogging	

OUTLINE 68 cont'd

Type B

These activities are moderately vigorous, but can be excellent conditioners. When done briskly, or for longer periods, they can provide similar benefits to those listed in Type A.

Basketball (half court)	Skiing (downhill)
Field hockey	Soccer
Calisthenics	Squash
Handball	Tennis (singles)
Racquetball	Volleyball

Type C

These activities tend not to be as vigorous or as sustained. They can offer benefits in that they tend to be enjoyable, can help to improve coordination and muscle tone, can help to relieve tension, and may help lower risk of heart disease.

Baseball	Golf
Bowling	Softball
Football	Tennis (doubles)

There are different reasons for exercising. But, the basic goals for exercise may be classified into the following categories: Weight control, cardiovascular health, strength, flexibility, relaxation and revitalization.

1. Cardiovascular Health

Cardiovascular (CV) health refers to the efficiency of the heart, lungs and blood vessels to process and deliver oxygen to the muscles, where it can be used for work (e.g., exercise). People who become tired after walking up one flight of stairs do not have good CV health (or more simply, they are not in good "shape"). CV health should be a goal of everyone who exercises, and aerobic exercise should be the foundation of every exercise program.

Like other muscles, the heart works better when it gets regular exercise. A lack of exercise contributes to weight and cholesterol problems. You are more likely to have a heart attack if you are inactive, and you are less likely to survive a heart attack if you do have one.

A regular program of aerobic exercise can help to insure a healthy heart and a quality life. Types of aerobic exercise:

❦ Basketball	❦ Running
❦ Cycling	❦ Soccer
❦ Dance (aerobic)	❦ Swimming
❦ Jogging	❦ Tennis
❦ Racquetball	❦ Walking (brisk)

Exercise tips for improved CV health include the following:

❦ Exercise that raises your pulse rate, makes you breathe harder and perspire;

❦ 3 workouts each week;

❦ 20 minutes each workout;

❦ The best programs are those that condition your heart and lungs for 30-60 minutes 3-4 times each week.

❦ Be sure to check with your doctor before beginning any exercise program.

The exercise of choice for most individuals is walking, since it is easy to do, requires little or no equipment (a good pair of shoes) and no special facility. The disadvantage of walking is that it is a low intensity exercise. So, you must walk for a longer period of time (e.g., 40 minutes) to derive the same benefits as a shorter routine (20 minutes) of a higher intensity aerobic exercise.

Walking is not without its problems. Some people have joint pain (e.g., knee, hip) which makes walking uncomfortable, or they have a health problem (e.g., disease, past injury) that precludes walking. These people need an aerobic exercise that does not subject the body to the forces of gravity and pounding the pavement.

The most efficient form of weightless exercise is swimming.

People who swim do not encounter the orthopedic problems associated with walking or running. The problem, of course, is that one must have access to a pool and know how to swim. Some types of water exercise (e.g., water aerobics and power walking) are very effective, even for nonswimmers.

CASE STUDY

LESSONS FROM REAL LIFE — FAT RIPPLES

As a health professional, one of the authors (MM) has taught hundreds of students how to measure body fat, and has conducted weight control clinics for thousands of people. The author explains during the course of these presentations that the only true test of body fat is to cut all of the fat off the body and weigh it (e.g., an impractical and painful option ... but may have some merit for a horror movie). Other methods include hydrostatic (underwater) weight measurements, body impedance (resistance to low levels of electricity) tests, infrared light tests and skin fold measurements.

The simplest and least expensive method is to stand nude in front of full-length mirror, jump up and down, and if something shakes that shouldn't ... you have fat that you do not need. While this seems humorous, the concept is sincere. How we perceive our body "image" determines to a great extent our willingness to make changes. Depending upon this image, we may engage in either healthy or unhealthy behaviors. For example, people with anorexia nervosa will do everything in their power to lose weight even when they are underweight.

In reality, scientific instruments and measurements are not required to indicate unnecessary fat. You will usually know if you need to lose weight. If you feel comfortable with your weight, don't worry about being a few pounds above ideal weight. Conversely, if you know you are overweight, don't dupe yourself into believing that you are content. Consider the people you know who look younger than their age, and those who look older. The distinction often involves weight.

HOW ABOUT YOU?

When is the last time you stood nude in front of a mirror? Don't avoid self-reflection ... you can achieve a more desirable image if you like.

Another type of weightless exercise is stationary bicycling. Bicycling on the street presents the problems of traffic, weather, dogs and inconsistent intensity from riding up and down hills. Stationary bicycling can be done at home, anytime, in any weather. However, there is a substantial cost for the bicycle.

Without a doubt, the most effective type of aerobic exercise to improve CV health is the one that you will actually do. If you do not do the exercise, it is of no benefit. The type of exercise that is right for one person may not be right for another. Choose activities that are right for you.

2. Fat Metabolism

If our goal is to lose fat, it may be to our advantage to exercise after we first arise in the morning and while the stomach is empty. Research indicates that exercising after a 12 hour fast will burn twice the number of fat calories. This does not mean that we can burn twice the number of total calories, but rather that more of the calories burned will come from fat stores in the body. It is also important to realize that skipping breakfast and exercising later in the day will not provide the same outcome.

3. Flexibility

Flexibility is an important and often overlooked component of fitness. The term refers to the suppleness of the muscles and connective tissues and the range of motion around the joints. If you can sit on the floor with your legs straight and only touch your knees . . . you are not very flexible. If you can touch your toes, you are more flexible.

People who wake up in the morning, yawn and stretch their hands over their head are practicing a flexibility exercise. Unfortunately, that may be the extent of their stretching exercises. Flexibility exercises are important for all of the major joints and connective tissues of the body. Of these, none is more important than the low back and hamstrings (back of the legs).

Low back pain and weakness is a common ailment, especially among older persons. Many of these problems can be alleviated or improved by good low back and hamstring flexibility, coupled with good abdominal strength.

Stretching or flexibility exercises are essential to a good fitness regimen. But, just as in all forms of exercise, doing them wrong can

---

LESSONS FROM REAL LIFE — DAN

Dan is a 62 year old male who began cardiac rehabilitation after suffering a myocardial infarction (i.e., MI, or heart attack) and undergoing triple by-pass surgery. Initially, his exercise program consisted of very light aerobics (walking a treadmill at 2.8 mph, 0% grade for 5-10 minutes, three days per week).

After a few weeks of gradually increasing aerobic work, his physician approved some light strength training. Dan was only able to raise 0.25 pound dumbbells over his head three times. He was very worried because he had been told not to lift any weights, especially over his head.

After several weeks of aerobic and strength training approved by his physician, Dan was able to accomplish several kinds of strength exercises (shoulder press, bench press, lattisimus pull-downs and bicep/tricep curls). He still used light weights, but he was able to accomplish several repetitions of each exercise. Not only did Dan's exercise capacity ("shape") increase, but his confidence and physical stamina also improved.

The moral of the story is that you are never too old or out-of-shape to begin strength training . . . especially when coupled with a sound aerobic program. Not only can you "teach an old dog new tricks," but the "old dog" can benefit significantly.

HOW ABOUT YOU?

Don't wait until you have a heart attack to remind you of a need for exercise.

---

have negative outcomes. Stretching exercises practiced too rapidly (ballistic) and by "bouncing" (dynamic) can cause damage to the muscles and connective tissue. Flexibility exercises should always be accomplished slowly, statically, and with adequate oxygen (deep breathing). Done properly, stretching exercises not only improve flexibility, but are also a great relaxation exercise.

The Low Back / Hamstring Stretch is accomplished by lying on the back with knees bent, feet 12 to 18 inches from the buttocks (same basic position as the cruncher). Make sure the lower back is supported by the floor by tilting the pelvis (hips) back and downward. This position is also known as the pelvic tilt. Lie in this position for a minute or two while breathing slowly and deeply from the diaphragm. Grasp one leg (behind the knee joint) and pull that leg slowly towards the chest; hold and breathe. Make sure that the lower back is firmly supported by the floor (good pelvic tilt position) during this exercise. Return that leg to the original position and repeat the exercise with the other leg. Do this two or three times with each leg; 1-2 minutes per leg. Each time the exercise is accomplished, the legs should be pulled a little closer to the chest. Do this exercise 2 or 3 times per day (e.g., morning and night or before and after exercise or physical activity).

4. Relaxation

In our stress-filled society, people need to make time for relaxation, exercise and rejuvenation activities. There are two basic ways to physiologically relax a muscle. One is to contract it; then relax it. The other is to stretch the muscle slowly, then relax it. Good breathing technique also contributes to muscle relaxation.

Proper breathing includes slow, deep, diaphragmic breathing. The diaphragm is the mechanism by which breathing occurs. When breathing properly, the diaphragm contracts, creating a vacuum in the lungs, air rushes in and the chest and abdomen expand. When it relaxes, the lungs collapse, pushing air out and the chest and abdomen return to their normal position. Proper breathing differs drastically from "macho" breathing (i.e., the abdomen is held in, chest puffed out and shoulder and arm muscles contracted constantly). During relaxation exercises, inhalation should last 3-4 seconds and exhalation should take 4-8 seconds.

Most types of exercise contribute to relaxation, since exercise causes muscles to contract, stretch and relax. Appropriate exercises require deep breathing and will burn some of the energy and chemicals produced in response to stress.

Many forms of exercise also provide for mental and emotional breaks from life's daily "grind." Some activities are better than others in providing this stress break. Walking with a friend or spouse may provide adequate exercise and an opportunity to talk and relax. Playing a fast game of singles tennis is good exercise, but if competition becomes too important, mental and emotional relaxation may not occur.

CASE STUDY

LESSONS FROM REAL LIFE — DOROTHY

Dorothy is a 61 year old female who complained of low back pain, especially at night. She was in generally good physical condition, walked 1-2 miles per day, gardened and was at her ideal body weight. She was given a prescription of low back and abdominal strengthening exercises. Her prescription also included training in proper lifting and bending techniques that greatly improved her posture while gardening.

She began to practice these exercises at night while watching the news. She also did the exercises before and after she walked or gardened. She reported later that her back pain had all but disappeared and that she so enjoyed the quiet time (relaxation and deep breathing) that she now turned off the news and played relaxing music while she did her back exercises.

HOW ABOUT YOU?

Do you sometimes have low back pain? Give some thought to exercise as a means for helping this problem. Notice your posture, and how you lift.

---

5. Strength

Most of us consider ourselves to be strong enough to accomplish the tasks of daily living with relative ease. But we should still try to improve our strength. Strength exercises improve muscle tone, help burn calories (although not as efficiently as aerobics) and help reduce intramuscular fat (the fat inside the muscles).

There are various forms of strength exercises. Most common are calisthenics (i.e., those that use the body's weight as the resistance), such as a push up.

One strength exercise that everyone should do is a sit up or "cruncher," which helps to strengthen abdominal muscles. Strong abdominal muscles help alleviate low back pain and improve posture. However, it is important to note that more damage than good can be derived by doing a sit up improperly.

The cruncher is accomplished by lying on your back with the knees bent and the feet flat on the floor, approximately 12-18 inches from the buttocks. Slowly raise the head, neck and shoulder blades off the floor.

Do not put the hands behind the head and pull on the neck and do not try to sit all the way up. Do only as many as are comfortable. Gradually increase the number over a period of time until 40 or 50 can be accomplished without too much difficulty.

The most common forms of strength training involve the use of weights or machines. Free weights (dumbbells and barbells) provide weight or resistance, while machines utilize weight stacks, gears, pulleys, cables and/or hydraulics to provide the resistance.

The advantage of machines is that they are relatively easy and safe to use. The disadvantage is that they can be very expensive. In fact, most people opt to join a fitness center to have access to these machines.

While free weights may be more difficult to use, they can be relatively inexpensive. A set of adjustable (variable weight) dumbbells at a local discount house may cost less than $50. Most come with a set of instructions for safe and effective use. The key is to use a weight that is light enough to lift comfortably. Gradually increase the amount of weight or the number of repetitions of the exercise as strength increases.

6. Weight Control

In the broadest sense, weight control involves a desire or need to gain, lose or maintain a particular weight status. And, every effective weight loss plan includes exercise. Since aerobic exercise increases metabolism (the rate at which the body burns energy or calories) and helps burn fat, aerobic exercises should be included in any weight control program.

Whatever the specific exercise goals, every program should include some form of each of the basic exercises; aerobics (cardiovascular and weight control), strength, flexibility and relaxation. The foundation of every good exercise program is aerobics, but the other forms should not be overlooked.

Benefits of Exercise

Regular exercise leads to a higher state of physical fitness. Fitness has several synonyms (e.g., "shape"). Yet, physical fitness actually refers to the ability of the body to accomplish work or exercise. This is known as physical work capacity (PWC). Work can include carrying or lifting, climbing stairs, riding bikes or any number of activities. The President's Council on Physical Fitness and Sports defines fitness as an "ability to accomplish life's daily tasks and still have enough energy for emergency expenditures."

Physical fitness leads to many mental, physical and emotional benefits. These widely accepted benefits were first delineated by Dr. Sam Fox, a well-known cardiologist, in the late 1950s. He presented this comprehensive list of potential benefits of exercise by prefacing with the statement: "Physical fitness may improve these facets of life." The emphasis here is on the term "may." The potential benefits of increased exercise and activity are summarized in Outline 69. In general, exercise and improved physical fitness can:

- ❦ Help prevent heart disease

- ❦ Help you to relax and manage stress

- ❦ Help control weight

- ❦ Allow you to do more work or exercise

- ❦ HELP YOU LIVE LONGER

> *In other words, exercise makes you look better, feel better and live longer.*

It is important to differentiate between physical fitness and athletic skills. Health-related fitness places an emphasis on cardiovascular endurance, muscle strength and endurance, flexibility and body composition. Athletic-related fitness tends to emphasize power, speed, balance, agility, reaction time and coordination.

Fitness Slows Degeneration

Virtually all of our body systems begin to deteriorate or diminish with age. Heart and lung efficiency decrease, while resting heart rate and blood pressure increase. Flexibility, strength and endurance decrease. Because metabolism decreases, body fat generally increases.

OUTLINE 69

POTENTIAL BENEFITS OF EXERCISE

Increases / Improvements in:

- Ability to Control Appetite
- Ability to Control Weight
- Ability to Cope with Stress
- Ability to Maintain Idea Weight
- Ability to Work
- Appearance (e.g., muscle toning)
- Arterial Oxygen Content
- Calcium Content of Bone Structure
- Capacity for Leisure Productivity
- Capacity for Physical Work
- Cardiac Stroke Volume
- Chances for Surviving a Heart Attack
- Chest Expansion
- Coronary Collateral Vascularization
- Diastolic Portion of Pulse Cycle
- Efficiency of Capillaries and Arteries
- Efficiency of the Peripheral Blood Return
- Energy Levels
- Fitness of Bones and Muscles
- Fitness of Heart and Lungs
- Heart and Lung Efficiency
- Heart Fitness
- Libido (i.e., Sex Drive)
- Life Outlook
- Muscle Strength
- Myocardial Efficiency
- Oxygen Consumption
- Red Cell Mass to Blood Volume Ratio
- Relaxation and Sleeping
- Renal Plasma Flow
- Resistance to Anxiety
- Resistance to Fatigue
- Resistance to Stress
- Sexual Ability
- Blood Vessels Capacity (including heart arteries)
- Stamina for Physical Activities
- Tolerance to Emotional Stress
- Total Body Muscle
- Zest for Living

Decreases / Reductions in:

- Anxiety
- Blood Pressure
- Body Calcium Loss
- Constipation
- Depression
- Gastric Secretions
- Heart Arrhythmias
- Heart Attach Risk
- Heart Rate
- Heart Size
- Irritability of Heart Muscle
- Nervous Reflexes
- Platelet Stickiness
- Psychological Depressions
- Rate of Development of Degenerative Joint Disease
- Reaction Time
- Risk for Sudden Death due to Heart Attacks
- Serum Cholesterol
- Serum Triglycerides
- Tenseness
- Total Body Fat
- Peripheral Vascular Resistance

Regular exercise and physical activity can help reverse or stabilize these trends. Exercise, when coupled with proper diet, stress management techniques and wise use of medications and other substances provides an effective "formula" for increasing the quantity and quality of your life.

CASE STUDY

LESSONS FROM REAL LIFE – EXERCISE & LIBIDO

During a class consideration of the benefits of exercise, participants discussed in great detail such factors as heart and circulatory benefits. The discussion eventually turned to libido. Class members were asked how libido could be enhanced by fitness. The usual answers included improved muscle tone, enhanced self-concept and increased zest for living. From the back of the room, a quiet, shy young lady (who had not previously contributed to the discussion) raised her hand. The instructor, anxious to encourage her participation, happily called on her. She responded, "I think it's because you sweat less."

Well after all, there are many different kinds of benefits to be derived from exercise!

HOW ABOUT YOU?

Sexual relations are a major topic in nearly all of the women's magazines at the supermarket, just as they are on most of the talk shows. Our sex drive is affected by our overall health and can be improved by lifestyle changes that enhance our well-being. How about exercising with your mate?

Getting Started

Starting an exercise program can be very difficult, especially for those people who may have been sedentary for many years. But, take heart. Many adults do not begin exercise until they are older, yet they still reap the benefits of physical fitness lifestyle changes.

The first step towards an active life is to check with your physician. A complete physical examination and exercise tolerance test can determine if you may have problems with certain types of exercise.

The second step is to consider some easy ways to increase simple physical activity that are compatible with your own individual daily routines, for example, standing in place and bending at the waist for the first two minutes of a TV program.

OUTLINE 70

SEE A DOCTOR FIRST IF . . .

❦ You are 40+ in age and not accustomed to regular exercise.

❦ You have had a heart attack in the past.

❦ You have had pain or pressure in the chest, neck, shoulder or arm after activity.

❦ You have experienced shortness of breath after mild activity or exertion.

❦ You have bone or joint problems.

❦ You have a medical condition that requires special attention (e.g., diabetes).

❦ You have a history of high blood pressure, or don't know what your blood pressure reading is.

❦ You have a family history of heart disease.

❦ You have had spells of fainting or lightheadeness.

Most people derive substantial benefits from a simple walking program, but start slowly if this is your decision. Walk a distance and at a pace that is comfortable for you. Gradually increase the distance and pace until you are walking 40 to 60 minutes per day at a brisk pace. A walking program, supplemented by strength, flexibility, and relaxation exercises can be an integral part of any life extension program.

Exercise Classes

Classes offer several advantages. First, the social aspect of exercising with friends or persons your own age can be a distinct advantage over exercising alone. Classes can provide a change of pace from walking or other more monotonous types of exercise. Classes generally are conducted indoors, which is an advantage during the hot and cold seasons.

When selecting a class, make sure the instructor is qualified and competent. Do not hesitate to ask if the instructor is certified (and by whom) and talk to people who have attended the classes before. Make sure the intensity of the exercises being taught is right for you. And, see if people your own age are in the class.

CASE STUDY

LESSONS FROM REAL LIFE – PARK BENCH PHILOSOPHY

A cartoon showed two older men sitting on a park bench. One said to the other, "The older I get, the faster time goes by." The other responded, "That's because when you're over the hill, you pick up speed".

Imagine life as a giant hill. From the time we are born until our mid 30s or early 40s, the efficiency of our bodies improves. Once we reach our peak physiological age (35-45), our body systems begin to degenerate. The keys to this degeneration rate are the lifestyle choices we make throughout our lives. If we choose to smoke, eat poorly and live a sedentary existence, the "downhill slide" can be very steep and short (early death). If we make the right lifestyle choices (e.g., exercise, good nutrition, wise use of substances, proper stress management) the "downhill slide" may be reduced to a pleasurable "coasting."

HOW ABOUT YOU?

Where are you on the "hill"? Are you "sliding" faster than you like? You can have significant control over the rate if you are willing to make appropriate lifestyle choices.

Fitness Centers

Some of the same advantages and disadvantages of exercise apply to fitness centers. Visit the center before joining. Beware of "buy now or lose the discount" types of sales approaches! Once you join a center, do not hesitate to ask instructors for help. That is what they are paid to do. Finally, remember that the vast majority of people who join fitness centers stop attending after 2 to 3 months. You must make a commitment to it if you are to realize the benefits.

Home Exercise Equipment

The most common types of home exercise equipment are treadmills and stationary bicycles. Both are good for aerobic conditioning. When buying a treadmill, look for one that has adjustable speed and grade (hill). As your aerobic conditioning improves, the speed and grade can be adjusted to increase the intensity of your fitness activities.

A bicycle should have an adjustable tension mechanism and a comfortable seat. As your fitness improves, the tension can be increased to provide adequate intensity. An uncomfortable seat has foiled many a splendid exercise program.

If there's a piece of equipment already sitting in the attic or garage gathering dust, it's safe to assume the new equipment being considered will do the same. Buying the equipment doesn't do the trick. You have to use it.

CASE STUDY

LESSONS FROM REAL LIFE — JANE

Jane is a 45 year old female. She is a paraplegic. She has a very demanding job and because of her disability spends more time at her work than most people. Getting dressed in the morning is a challenge. But she still finds time for regular exercise. She is very conscious of her nutritional habits and she practices yoga and imagery on a daily basis. Odds are she will not live as long as "normal" people, but she says she's going to make the most of her life and enjoy the time she has. She does not have as much physical potential as most people, but she works to be as healthy as she can be.

HOW ABOUT YOU?

When you hear people complain and make excuses about the difficulties involved in adopting healthier lifestyles ... think about Jane! What about your excuses?

Overcoming the Obstacles to Exercise

Over the years, we Americans have invented every conceivable excuse for not exercising. Some of these actually involve valid reasons. Yet, they are only obstacles if we allow them to be! Outline 71 summarizes the "Big 8" excuses along with some thoughts for overcoming them.

OUTLINE 71

THE "BIG 8" EXCUSES FOR NOT EXERCISING AND SOME THOUGHTS FOR OVERCOMING THEM

1. "I can't afford equipment."

The only equipment required is a good pair of shoes. There's probably an appropriate pair of athletic shoes in the closet right now (used for SHOW, not GO!).

2. "I've got too many health problems."

Most physicians recommend exercise as a part of the treatment program for many of their patients. Diabetes, osteoporosis, hypertension, arthritis, and heart disease can be improved with regular exercise. If you do have health problems, your physician's approval is essential prior to beginning an exercise program. The idea is not to avoid exercise, but to identify a healthy exercise program designed to fit your needs.

3. "I've tried exercise before and just can't stick with it."

Find the type of exercise that's right for you, even if you have to try several. Find a friend to exercise with. Join a fitness center or exercise class. Above all, give exercise a chance to become an integral part of your life. When people begin to derive the benefits from exercise, they're more likely to adhere to a regular program.

4. "I'm too out of shape."

Then you really do need exercise. After all, that is what this is really all about . . . isn't it? Start slowly and gradually increase the duration and intensity of exercise. Develop realistic expectations for your efforts.

OUTLINE 71 cont'd

5. "I can't seem to get started."

Set a time to start and stick to it. Get up right now and walk around the block. See, that wasn't so hard. Get up thirty minutes early tomorrow and go for a walk. Take an exercise break at lunch. Take a walk in the evening. Park your car a bit farther from your destinations. That's how easy it is to start. Establish a routine (We humans are creatures of habit!) and make it as much a part of your life as eating, sleeping and watching TV.

6. "I don't feel like it."

That's exactly the time to exercise. When your energy is depleted from a stressful day, an exercise break recharges your batteries. Caution: If you have fever or are sick, don't exercise. But if it's just a case of low motivation, exercise can be just the medicine. In fact, exercise can become one of your most effective "coping" tools for a hectic life.

7. "I don't like to sweat."

Some people sweat more than others. Sweat is nothing more than your body's cooling system at work. Your body is washing away many of the toxins and chemicals produced in response to stress. Milder forms of exercise, like walking, won't produce as much sweat as more intense exercises. Be prepared to deal with sweat after you exercise by showering or toweling off (There is nothing quite like a hot shower or bath after exercising! Allow it to be part of the "reward" of your new exercise and health program.).

8. "I don't have the time."

The best (weakest) excuse of all. It's not a question of time. It's a question of priorities. Make exercise a priority. If the President of the United States has time for exercise, you can probably fit it into your "busy" schedule. Get up earlier or go to bed later Substitute exercise for TV time or some of the lunch hour. Make the time.

Exercise is only one component of a healthy lifestyle that can extend your life, improve your quality of life and offset some of the negative consequences of aging. But, for exercise or any other components to be effective, they must be practiced. Health must become a priority in our lives. We must become responsible for our own well-being. There are really no excuses. There are positive or negative outcomes . . . depending upon the choices we make.

OUTLINE 72

EXERCISE BASICS

General Guidelines

- Find something that is fun and that you will enjoy doing.
- Set goals and objectives and work to accomplish them. However, these should be realistic. Don't expect miracles the first week.
- Exercise at an even pace. You should be able to talk at the same time.
- Exercising is NOT a contest! So, don't make it into one!
- Avoid the "no pain, no gain" stupidity! Exercise does NOT have to hurt to be effective. You can expect to become tired, but don't overdo. Build up your tolerance over time. Your sessions should feel good and leave your relaxed . . . not "wiped out."
- Try to work out at least every other day.
- Don't quit!

Be Attentive to Signs of Injury or Damage

Pain is a sign of damage. Don't ignore it. Minor muscle and joint injuries can usually be treated effectively. Don't ignore signs of a heart problem (e.g., chest pain that radiates into the arms or shoulders, lightheadedness, cold sweats, fainting).

Bicycle Tips

- Always wear a helmet.
- Avoid busy streets.
- Use reflectors and lights.

OUTLINE 72 cont'd

Clothing

☙ Wear clothes and shoes which are comfortable and appropriate for the type of exercise which you have planned.

☙ Choose loose-fitting clothes (cotton or natural fibers) that allow your skin to breathe.

☙ Wear bright-colored clothing or reflective markers if you are walking after dark.

Eating and Exercise

Avoid eating 2 hours before or about 20 minutes after exercise. Your digestive system must compete with the blood supply that muscles demand during exercise.

Equipment

Use appropriate equipment to protect your eyes, limbs, hands, feet, etc.

Exercise Partners

Some people prefer to exercise alone. For others, exercise can be a fun social activity when others share in the experience and encourage them to persist. Exercise partners should be able to keep the same schedule and pace as yours.

Increase Activity Levels Gradually over Time

☙ Warm up (i.e., limber up) before exercising.

☙ Don't push yourself too quickly.

☙ Build up slowly to your target zone over time.

☙ Begin slowly, then increase your exercise time each time until you have worked up to at least 30 minutes each session.

☙ Always cool down after exercise.

Location

Consider locations that will allow you to exercise year-round. Also consider safety factors (e.g., traffic).

Pace Yourself

Avoid pushing yourself too hard when you begin. Reduce your pace if it takes longer than 15 minutes for you to feel normal after exercise. As a

OUTLINE 72 cont'd

general rule, you should be able to comfortably keep up a conversation while exercising if your pace is appropriate.

Runner's Checklist

❦ Check with your doctor before beginning.

❦ Choose a convenient time and place to run (e.g., consider safety).

❦ Select proper shoes and clothing.

❦ Always warm up before a running session.

❦ Try to reach at least 50% of your maximum heart rate during your run.

❦ Run regularly (e.g., at least 3 times per week).

❦ As you get into shape, progressively increase the time spent in your target heart rate (up to 60 minutes per exercise session).

❦ Cool down after each run.

❦ Enjoy the benefits (e.g., feeling and looking better)!

Shoes

Shoes are an important consideration. The force of feet hitting the ground can cause problems for joints, muscles, ligaments and the back. Exercise shoes should have thick, flexible soles that cushion the feet and absorb the shock of running or walking. Hiking, walking or jogging shoes are best. Tennis shoes are less desirable because they are designed to allow side-to-side movements during athletic activities. Thus, they tend not to provide ample support for walking and running.

Desirable shoe characteristics:

❦ Arch support.

❦ Firm support behind the heel to prevent slipping.

❦ Good fit (allow for ample width for toes, and about 1/4 -inch between the longest toe and the front of the shoe).

❦ Shoe fabric that allows the feet to breathe (e.g., leather, fabric).

❦ Soles that cushion the feet (rubber or crepe).

❦ Slightly elevated heel.

Surfaces

Landing on your heels, rather than the balls of your feet, can minimize strain and injury on your feet and lower legs. Injuries are more likely to

OUTLINE 72 cont'd

occur on hard or uneven surfaces (e.g., cement, pavement, rough fields). Soft, even surfaces are easier on feet and joints.

Target Heart Rate

Exercise should increase your heart rate to a certain "target" level if your are to receive maximum benefits from your efforts.

In general, your Target Heart Rate (THR) should be within 50-75% of your Maximum Heart Rate (MHR). An estimate of your MHR can be determined by subtracting your age from 220. So, if you are 40, your MHR would be 180 (i.e., 220 - 40 = 180). Your THR would be 50-75% of this, so it would be 90-135.

In one research project two groups of people were studied regarding THR. Group 1 participants were given a treadmill test in order to determine their exact THR. They were then taught how to determine THR during exercise and instructed to exercise at the THR that had been identified for them. Group 2 participants were given estimated THRs based on formulas, such as the one above. This group was also taught how to estimate their THR during exercise and instructed to exercise at the estimated THR. Group 3 participants were simply told to "go out and exercise at a pace you think is right for you." The results indicated that all three groups were within 5 beats (+ or -) per minute of their THR.

There are a number of methods for estimating THR. Regardless of how it is calculated, THR is only a guide. Listen to your body! If you think that you are exercising at an appropriate intensity level, then you probably are.

Time of Day

Give some thought to the time of day that you would like to exercise. Do you have more energy at certain times of the day? Some people prefer to start the day with exercise as a means of preparing themselves for the day ahead. Others prefer to de-stress themselves from their day with exercise after they come home. Choose the best time for you.

Traffic

❧ Face oncoming traffic.

❧ Never assume that drivers have seen you.

❧ Watch for traffic while exercising.

❧ Wear reflective clothing.

OUTLINE 72 cont'd

Warm Up

Identify appropriate warm up exercises before strenuous exercise sessions. The warm up serves to limber up muscles and prepare the body for more strenuous exercise.

Weather

Winter (Cold Weather) Exercise

❦ Clothing

Wear multiple layers, rather than one heavy layer, since layers of clothing will help to avoid cold and wind. Wear one layer less than you would wear if you were going to be outside, but not exercising.   Protect all skin areas.   Use a wool cap, mittens and face mask when it is really cold. Protect your hands (e.g., gloves, mittens). Wear a hat (up to 40% of your body heat is lost through your neck and head). Cottons, wools and nylons allow sweat to evaporate while providing warmth.

❦ On Rainy, Icy or Snowy days

Be aware of reduced visibility (i.e., both yours and those around you, such as drivers).   Be aware of slippery surfaces.

Summer (Hot, Humid Weather) Exercise

❦ Clothing

Wear porous materials that allow sweat to evaporate and heat to escape. Wear minimal, light, loose-fitting clothing. Avoid rubberized or plastic clothing, sweatshirts, sweat pants. This type of clothing does NOT increase weight loss, but can predispose you to heatstroke.

❦ Drink Ample Fluids (especially water)

Exercise in the heat can cause excessive fluid loss, so it is important to drink ample water (before, during and after each exercise session).   It is not really necessary to take extra salt, since the average American diet has 10 times the amount of salt actually needed by the body. Also, a well-conditioned body will tend to conserve salt, so that most sweat is water.

❦ Pace

Pace yourself more carefully. You may need to cut back when the heat is excessive. Slow your pace if the temperature is above 70 degrees, and be alert to signs of heat injury and dehydration. Watch out for

OUTLINE 72 cont'd

   signs of heat stroke (e.g., dizziness, weakness, lightheadedness, excessive tiredness, reduction in sweating, increased body temperature).

❦ Sun Protection

   Use sunscreens and sunvisors.

❦ Timing

   Exercise during times of the day when it is cooler and less humid (e.g., early morning or evening). Avoid running at times when the air temperature is above 80 degrees.

CASE STUDY

LESSONS FROM REAL LIFE – PHIL

Phil is a 68 year old retired insurance claims adjuster. Two years ago he and his wife sold their home in Michigan and bought a townhouse in South Florida. Phil had always been involved with a moderate exercise program (e.g., walking, biking, a morning routine, etc.). His exercising behaviors were not of a formal or fixed nature, but could be described as casual and reasonably regular.

Except for an episode with kidney stones 8 years prior, he had always been in good health. Since moving to Florida, however, Phil adopted a sedentary lifestyle. He stopped exercising completely within his first year in Florida and added 40 pounds to his already stocky frame.

Recently, he experienced mild to moderate pain in his right shoulder which radiated down his arm. He also began to complain of shortness of breath and discomfort when he breathed deeply. His doctor diagnosed a mild case of angina. He was instructed to lose 20 pounds and to exercise at least 3 times each week (for at least 20 minutes each time). The doctor prescribed digitalis for the angina, but told Phil that the rest of his recovery would be up to him.

Phil vowed to his wife that he would start his exercise program as soon as possible. Yet, every day that she suggested that they walk or go for a bike ride, he provided an excuse not to participate. "Well, not today. My knee bothered me last night and I do not want to aggravate it," or, "Maybe tomorrow. It is too hot today."

Phil's wife eventually stopped asking him to exercise, and has now started an exercise program of her own with her friends who walk on a daily basis.

HOW ABOUT YOU?

Are you having signs and symptoms that indicate the hazards of a sedentary lifestyle? Have you really thought about how much exercise you are getting each week? Do you really want to wait until you have heart or other symptoms before you change your lifestyle?

20. LEISURE AND RECREATION

"Learn to create, not compete."

— Robert Anthony

It is a sad commentary on our society that our primary leisure pastimes are spectator events. Racing, baseball, football and basketball, whether watching in person or on TV, consume more leisure dollars and time than any other leisure activity. Moreover, many of our major recreational "activities" revolve around eating, watching TV and going to the movies. Maybe our definition of "activity" needs reworking.

Culturally, our definition of leisure is "free time" (i.e., activities that are not associated with work or duty). If leisure really is freedom from such demands, the first test of a genuine leisure activity is to ask the question, "Am I truly free from the demands of work or duty when I am involved in this activity?" All too often we bring work or other responsibilities home, on vacation or even when we are supposed to be playing.

Historically, "leisure" was synonymous with school or learning. Only the leisure (upper) class had time for learning, reading and the arts. Today, most people "work to play." We spend our energy at work earning the time and money to pursue leisure activities. Then, we find ourselves in the "rut" of always thinking about the demands placed upon us by others. Suddenly, we discover our life is our job. This is not to suggest that we indulge in our fantasy and quit work just so we can play. But, we do need to keep our priorities straight and to introduce some balance in our lives. There must be time for work, but there should also a time for leisure! Recreation is the refreshment of the body and mind. It should represent a departure from the demands and stress of our obligations, and then it will contribute to a healthier lifestyle.

For most of us, unfortunately, recreation is synonymous with competition. We often "play" certain sports (e.g., golf, tennis, racquetball or softball), but drown the spirit of play in competition. Young people are conditioned early in life to believe that competition is "healthy." Coaches and parents alike insist, "Competition is good for them. It builds character!" Perhaps, but it also destroys our ability to enjoy leisure activities for their inherent value. And, in the extreme, our obsession with winning becomes a justification for abusive treatment of young athletes.

Competition is not a necessary ingredient of recreation. There is a time and place for competition and a time and place for play. Our "play" activities lose their recreational value (and become an extension of our obligations and stress) when the demands of competition suppress the true spirit of play.

CASE STUDY

LESSONS FROM REAL LIFE — WILLIAM

William was a 58-year old male who was regularly given a fitness evaluation. He had slightly elevated blood pressure (148 / 94), was seven pounds overweight, but had a normal treadmill test. He professed to be a regular exerciser; playing racquetball 3 times per week. It was suggested that he might want to find a milder form of exercise, such as walking. William was a highly successful professional and very competitive, a quality which he displayed on the racquetball court.

One day he left the racquetball court red-faced and breathing very hard. He was very angry because he had lost the match. One of the authors (MM) told him that the competitive nature of this sport was not doing much for his health. He ignored the warning and continued his regular matches.

A few months later, William was playing a vigorous game of racquetball, when he collapsed and died from a heart attack. Racquetball didn't kill him. There can be little doubt that his competitive nature and the excessively high intensity of his exercises contributed to his death.

One important lesson to be learned here is that a normal treadmill test does not necessarily indicate the absence of heart disease. Treadmill tests are only about 80% accurate in predicting heart disease in males (less in females).

HOW ABOUT YOU?

Do you really play, or are your leisure activities yet one more extension of stresses in your life? Are you "playing" yourself to death?

The Concept of Play

Play is a diversion. It is frolic. By its very nature it should imply fun and humor. Play is expressive and should elicit creativity. If it is not characterized by fun, humor, creativity and expressiveness . . . it is probably not truly play. Play and leisure should also serve to re-create, refresh and revitalize the human "being" in us.

We "play" sports. But, are these activities really creative and expressive? Fun? Do you play golf, but then become frustrated and angry if you make bad shots or miss putts? How often are these weekend golf matches really business meetings in disguise?

One of the authors (GH) used to referee league basketball games in Oklahoma City. The players (young to middle aged "adult" men) were frequently abusive to each other, and certainly to the referees. Many of these players were overweight and out of shape. Many came to the games inebriated, perhaps to bolster their courage and performance or perhaps to dull the pain. They were clumsy. Every missed shot or foul elicited a heated response as they attempted to recapture the vigor and flexibility they had "enjoyed" while in high school. There seemed to be very little true enjoyment in this activity, as they pushed themselves to potentially hazardous levels of physical and emotional demand.

Does this really sound like "play?" Certainly, sports and competition have their place in our lives, but they are no substitute for play. A healthy lifestyle, then, is one in which recreation and play both complement and separate us from our work and routine obligations. There are many recreational activities that provide opportunities for fun and relaxation. Reading, arts and crafts, puzzles, walking, listening to music, hiking and backpacking are just a few. "Life time sports" (e.g., tennis, golf, racquetball, and skiing) are viable recreational sports, IF pursued in the spirit of play (i.e., for the mere enjoyment of the activity). If, however, you are not refreshed (mentally and spiritually) as a result, maybe there's something wrong with your concept of leisure.

Travel and vacationing are major leisure pursuits in our society. A vacation affords the opportunity to visit new places, revisit old favorites, see friends, meet new people and generally revitalize the spirit. But all too often our vacations are as stressful as the environments we left behind.

One way to insure that a vacation is recreation is to plan the trip well in advance. Investigate travel arrangements (driving, flying, bus or train). Call ahead for lodging accommodations that are suitable for the trip. For example, staying in a very expensive hotel may not be prudent if you plan to spend all of your time on the beach or seeing the sites. Save enough money for the trip so that you are not overwhelmed with credit card bills when you return home (another stress!), or search for inexpensive vacations, (e.g., hiking or bicycling close to home, or a week-end in a state park).

Traveling itself can be stressful. Allow sufficient time when driving for frequent stops and rest time. When flying, make sure to arrive at the airport in plenty of time to check baggage and make it to the departure gate without having to rush. Bring leisure items along (e.g., a book you've been wanting to read), so that the "dead" time in the airport and on the plane allows you to engage in something that

CASE STUDY

THE COUPLE AND THE SNAKE

Once upon a time there was a man and a woman who lived alone together in a beautiful place. One day they were playing and frolicking and generally having fun. Along came a snake who said, "Whatcha doin'?" The man replied, "We're playing." To which the snake inquired, "Who's winning?" The woman asked, "What's winning?" The snake countered, "You know . . . winning. Who has the highest score?" The man asked, "What is score?" The snake replied, "When you play, there are certain rules. The one who has the highest score, wins the prize." The woman asked, "What's the prize?" The snake said, "The prize can be anything. Take for instance, this apple. It could be the prize."

Obviously, this is an adaptation of a very old and well-known story. But the message is that you do not have to have rules, scores, winning and prizes in order to play. And, very often the "prize" is not worth the effort required to get it! Get it?

HOW ABOUT YOU?

Give this one some thought the next time you are sitting at a little league ball game! The parents (i.e., the role models for the kids!) are usually far more frustrated with errors than the kids. The kids would be much better off if nobody was keeping score! And what about us. Do we play for "prizes?" Are you really enjoying your leisure activities, or just telling yourself that you do?

represents fun. Or just allow yourself the freedom to relax at a time when no demands are being placed on you.

When travelling it is helpful to allow sufficient time at our destination to enjoy the sights and the people. Allow time for walks or other forms of exercise while on vacation. Plan ahead for unexpected problems (e.g., car problems, lost credit cards, lost keys). Get plenty of sleep. Eat right and don't over indulge. If you are crossing time zones, give some thought to the impact this may have on you (especially in terms of eating, sleeping, taking medications, etc.). Your travel agent may be able to provide information about how to prepare for this.

Above all, do not call the office, think about or discuss work while on vacation. It is easier said than done, of course, but after all . . . what is the point of going on vacation if you are going to "take your work with you?"

Give some thought to creating opportunities when you can leave your watch at home. Avoid keeping yourself on a schedule at times when it is truly unnecessary. Go on a one-day outing on a Saturday when there is no other agenda. Create the agenda as you go!

We live in an age when everyone wants a car phone and a pager on their belt. These are our contemporary images of achievement and importance. Yet, they are also the devices that keep us tethered to our work. In such cases, we are always available, no matter where we are. There was a time when a car offered us a respite from our work and responsibilities. Driving was a time to reflect and relax. Now it has become an extension of the workplace and we allow ourselves virtually no time away from the demands which are placed upon us. Perhaps we have made ourselves too accessible!

Becoming More Playful

After all, we are born playful and we can remain so as adults. Children laugh and enjoy most situations. But we slowly lose the art of playfulness over time as we are transformed into adulthood. Competition becomes the "rule" of every leisure activity and winning becomes the objective. We condition ourselves to believe that we cannot have "fun" unless we win. In truth, it is far more likely that we cannot "win" unless we have fun!

Becoming playful all over again requires some planning. Think, remember, discover and rediscover what fun and enjoyment there is in life. Recapture the playful spirit that we "boxed away" in the recesses of our mind as we "matured." Learn to see the humor in all of life's situations. Tell yourself that you are a positive person. Associate with positive people who enjoy laughter and play. Explore your creativity. If you have always wanted to paint but were "too busy" to do so, start painting or drawing this week. If you like to play the piano, play more often. There is time in everyone's life to indulge one's fantasy at least to some minimal extent, perhaps half an hour each week.

As we have continuously suggested, increasing the quality and quantity of our lifespan requires that we must take charge of our own lives, attitudes and behaviors. No one else can move us in a direction of healthful living. Learning to play and enjoy life is an essential element of any healthy living formula.

CASE STUDY

LESSONS FROM REAL LIFE — JOYCE

Joyce had attended many wellness education classes. These included courses which addressed time management, stress management, quality leisure and others. She always seemed to be looking for "the answer" or "the key."

The general theme of any wellness life style class is that wellness is your responsibility.

Joyce attended a workshop given by one of the authors (MM) entitled, "Laugh and Live Long: The Role of Laughter and Positive Attitude in Health." After the workshop, evaluation forms were distributed to all participants. At the bottom of the form they were invited to provide additional comments. Joyce's evaluation of the workshop was "fair" and at the bottom she wrote, "Thanks for trying to help."

Joyce never learned that attending classes, reading self-help books, watching videos are all useless unless you put into practice what you have learned!

All healing involves self-healing. All learning is self-learning (i.e., teachers do not "learn" you!).

You are the only person who can make you well.

HOW ABOUT YOU?

Are you waiting for someone else to save you? We need the support of others, but our lifestyle choices must begin with us.

21. STRESS

"The world has become so tense and nervous it has
been years since I've seen anyone asleep in church
— and that is a bad situation."

— Norman Vincent Peale

Stress has been called "the ailment" of modern society. It often
seems as if stress is interwined in everything we do. Life is more fast-
paced today than it was two or three decades ago. Many authorities
argue that death and disease are directly related to stress and our
inability to cope with stress. Heart disease, high blood pressure,
stroke, suicides, homicides, drug problems and accidents have all
been associated with the way in which we respond to stress. Some
authorities even claim that the development of certain cancers may
be affected by our ability to cope with stress (e.g., stress lowers our
normal immune response and lowers our resistance to disease,
including cancers).

Dr. Hans Selye, generally considered the father of the study of
stress, wrote several important books and papers on the human
response to stress. In *Stress Without Distress,* he delineates what
happens to the human body when presented with a stressful stimulus, a reaction which he termed the General Adaptation Syndrome
(GAS).

While Dr. Selye's research was primarily concerned with the ability of the body to fight disease, his theories may also serve as a basis
for the study of the stress syndrome in a larger sense. According to
Selye, the "fight or flight" response, for example, occurs whenever we
are threatened in some way. However, the human brain does not differentiate between an intense stress (i.e., the "saber toothed tigers" in
our lives) versus less intense stresses (i.e., the "little things" that
occur each day). So, having a flat tire, being late to work, finding that
our secretary is out of the office due to illness and failed to finish that
important report (due today!), or a spouse who forgot to pick up the
children at the day care are all interpreted physiologically as if there
was a "saber toothed tiger" on our doorstep.

The major difference between contemporary man and a cave man
is that the cave man used a great deal of energy in order to fight the

tiger or flee from it. We may go home after a stressful day, "kick back" in our recliner, watch the news and a plethora of mindless sitcoms on TV and drink a 'light' beer (because, after all, 'light' beers are more healthy) in an effort to reduce stress levels. Unfortunately, if Selye is correct, these "coping" strategies offer few health benefits.

Small stresses, of course, occur everyday. However, the cumulative effect of these incidents can be as significant as a single great stress, but we tend to focus on the "big" stresses. Experiencing a major stress (for example, a disease), results in an attempt to adapt to it. However, this coping process is non-specific (i.e., we may adjust to the stimulus or stress in a variety of ways, rather than a specific way every time). If we reach a point at which we can no longer adapt to the stimulus, exhaustion occurs. So, the general adaptation syndrome predicts excessive wear and tear on the body through years of constantly attempting to adapt. The inability to successfully manage stress in our daily lives can also accelerate degeneration processes in the human body. This in turn can lead to health problems that result from wear and tear (e.g., heart disease, cancer, stroke and suicide).

Most people consider the word "stress" as having a negative connotation. It is interesting to note, however, that Selye did not apply a negative connotation to it. Rather, he differentiated between eustress or good stress, and distress or bad stress (see Outline 73). Eustress can bring out the best in us (e.g., peak performances and emotions, joy, excitement, exhilaration and happiness).

In this context, distress from a lack of stimulus can result in inactivity due to poor motivation, anger, frustration and boredom. Distress from too much stimulus can elicit anxiety, tension, anger and frustration. The healthiest adaptation then is a proper balance between eustress and distress.

OUTLINE 73

SUMMARY OF STRESS, EUSTRESS AND DISTRESS

UNDERSTRESSED ZONE

Dissatisfaction

Bored

Easily Fatigued

Frustrated

DESIRABLE STRESS ZONE

Good Self-Esteem

Ability to Change

Egffective Problem-Solving Skills

Creativity

Self-Motivated

OVERSTRESSED ZONE

Tiredness

Illness

Low Self-Esteem

Extreme Tension

Irrational Behavior

Performance Level — High / Low

Stimulus Quantity/Intensity — High

CASE STUDY

LESSONS FROM REAL LIFE — KARL

Karl is a 21-year old male. He is a varsity wrestler on a nationally ranked college team. Although he was considered to be one of the top wrestlers in the country at his weight, he began his senior year with two losses and a narrow victory over a lesser opponent.

Karl became so nervous before matches that he would vomit and "get the shakes." During a series of stress management sessions, he was able to understand his acute distress syndrome. He learned relaxation techniques (e.g., progressive relaxation, imagery and visualization). More importantly, he learned to deal with the unrealistic expectations and irrational beliefs that he had placed on himself. Eventually, he was able to move from the distress side of the curve toward a eustress position.

Karl practiced his stress management techniques everyday and they became a part of his pre-match routine. He finished the season at "peak performance." And while he did not win the national championship, he finished much higher than predicted.

HOW ABOUT YOU?

Are your performance levels where you would like them to be? Does anxiety and stress interfere with your ability to participate in meaningful life activities? Give some thought to stress reduction techniques.

The Signs and Symptoms of Stress

As we have seen, our response to stress can include many different physiological reactions. When we encounter a stressful situation, our body responds instantly. The central nervous and endocrine systems prepare the body for action (e.g., adrenalin, glucose and cholesterol are produced and released). This is known as the Fight or Flight Syndrome, referred to above. Our responses to stress are often over-reactions to the world around us. The "fight or flight" response is also better understood when we realize that anger is the emotion of fight and fear is the emotion of flight.

The acute signs of stress (and the "fight or flight" response) include increased heart rate, elevated blood pressure and sharpening of the senses. Blood moves from the extremities (hands and feet) in order to prevent excessive bleeding and pools in the central cavity of the body to protect the vital organs. Digestion slows and respiration becomes rapid and shallow. The result is a variety of symptoms which may or may not be obvious (see Outline 74). We may experience some, all or none of these signs at different times. Any of these symptoms indicate a need to identify the causes of stress, as well as effective stress management strategies.

OUTLINE 74

THE SIGNS AND SYMPTOMS OF STRESS

Acute Stress

- Acid indigestion
- Belching
- Chest pain
- Cold hands or feet
- Constipation
- Diarrhea
- Drowsiness
- Face feels hot
- Finger biting
- Flustered face
- Gas (e.g., stomach or intestines)
- Heart palpitations
- High blood pressure

- Jaw clenching
- Loss of appetite
- Need to urinate
- Nervous tics (twitching)
- Oily skin
- Overeating
- Shallow, rapid breathing
- Sharpened senses (e.g., sensitivity to noise and light)
- Shortness of breath
- Sleeplessness
- Sweaty palms
- Increase heart rate

Chronic Stress and Burnout

- Anger or resentment
- Anxiety or tension
- Change in activity patterns
- Change in eating habits
- Digestive problems (chronic)
- Feeling tired or exhausted most of time
- Feelings of failure
- Feelings of worry
- Feelings of helplessness
- High resistance to going to work every day

- Guilt
- Sleep disturbances
- Irritability
- Isolation or withdrawal
- Marital or family conflicts
- Negativism
- Poor job performance
- Psychosomatic illness
- Resistance to change

The emotional effects of stress are also numerous and emotions themselves can be stressful. The stress-emotion cycle can be an ever-tightening spiral. The emotional responses to distress include anger, frustration, anxiety, worry, guilt, helplessness and sadness. Eustress can elicit joy, excitement, exhilaration and happiness.

Two common emotional responses to stress are worry and guilt. These are typically regarded as "wasted" emotions because there is usually little we can do about the situations that caused them. Guilt is an emotional response to something that has already happened. We cannot undo the past, but we can learn from our mistakes. Worry is an emotional reaction to something that has not yet happened and may never happen! While we cannot usually control the future, we can prepare for possible events and learn to control our emotions. People who worry a great deal often lack a plan to deal with situations and possible outcomes.

The long term effects of stress vary from one individual to another. They depend upon exposures to both eustress and distress as well as our coping strategies. Whatever the particular factors, they are very real and in some cases may be a consequence of contemporary society pressures. A few decades ago, for example, "chronic stress syndrome" was unknown. Today, it is commonplace.

For years, the term "burnout" was a syndrome confined to people in the "helping" professions (e.g., counseling, teaching and health care), i.e., those who devote their time and energy to helping others, but then begin to feel a sense of failure if they are unable to make a "difference" in the lives of their clients or patients. Today, many people suffer from these same symptoms, regardless of whether or not they are in a helping profession. Chronic stress syndrome then is the result of long-term distress and our inability to successfully manage or cope with that stress. Helplessness, failure, frustration, anger and resentment are feelings that occur when we are not able to keep up with the demands of modern society. These reactions can manifest themselves as physical symptoms (e.g., headaches, sleep disorders and digestive problems). When this occurs it is important to identify the causes and then to learn to deal with them in healthy ways.

Causes of Stress

Selye's work on stress paved the way for an understanding of the adaptation response process. Most stress today is caused by people (e.g., family, co-workers, self). Since each of us contributes to the stresses in our lives, we can also learn to successfully manage these stresses.

CASE STUDY

LESSONS FROM REAL LIFE — COACHING

Coaching a team can have valuable applications to daily life. When you see your team begin to make a few mistakes and the players are becoming frustrated with themselves or the officials, you know that they are going to continue to perform poorly. This is the point at which good coaches call a "time-out" and help them to re-focus on the tasks at hand.

HOW ABOUT YOU?

Do you call "time out" when the stresses in your life are getting the best of you? Can you take a "mental health day" off from work, regroup and re-focus on the important tasks in life? Seek to identify the causes of stress in your life.

People, relationships and communication contribute to the eustress and distress in daily life. Associating with positive people, good relationships with significant others and effective communication with others can have a positive impact on our health and well-being. Associations with negative people, poor relationships with others, and poor communication contribute to distress.

Work is perhaps the primary source of stress for most people. In many cases it is not so much the job, per se, as it is the relationships between people on the job that is the problem. In other cases there is a poor "fit" between the personality of the individual and the characteristics of the job. Studies conducted by one of the authors (GH) clearly indicates that a lack of fit between personality and work environment characteristics contribute to job dissatisfaction.

According to our traditional work ethic, the function of work is to provide financial security. We don't have to like our job, we simply have to tolerate it. Yet, this view overlooks the opportunities for individuals to find meaningful jobs and careers. Unfortunately, many people stay with jobs that they dislike for various reasons. Too often these work situations become a source of frustration and stress.

Self-responsibility is a theme that is repeated throughout this book. Each of us is responsible for our own health and well-being. Each of us makes career choices. If changing jobs is not a realistic alternative, then it becomes even more important to learn to effectively deal with job stress.

Poor health can also be a source of distress. Stress may cause poor health, which causes more stress, and so on. A key element in increasing our quality and quantity of life is learning to be optimally healthy (i.e., being as well as we can be within the limitations of body, genetic make-up and present state of health). Stress management cannot cure cancer or heart disease, or find you another job, but it can help to improve your quality and quantity of life (especially when combined with other positive health practices).

Time is one of the common factors in stress. Most of us feel that we do not have enough time in our lives to complete the tasks that are important to us. After all, we have a finite time on this earth and we cannot accomplish everything we have planned for. Perhaps the key for dealing with this source of stress is one of prioritizing the "right" and important things and learning to let go of the rest.

The ABCs of Stress

When you show Pavlov's dog a bone, he slobbers on your shoe. That is known as a stimulus-response sequence. (Actually, the experiment was done with meat powder and a bell, but the dog still salivated.) Animals can be conditioned to respond in particular ways when presented with a specific stimulus.

Humans can also be conditioned, but our responses to the environment are more complex than the example above. When we are presented with a stimulus, we attach a value to that stimulus based on our experiences, morals and beliefs. So, we respond or behave to the value which we place on the stimulus. The following model may help to explain:

A ➡	**B** ➡	**C**
Stimulus	*Attitudes*	*Response*
Stressors	Values	Behaviors
Situations	Beliefs	Emotions
Events	Morals	Experiences

The stressors in A can be virtually anything (e.g., a belligerent salesperson, a dead car battery or a deadline at work). But, it is how we interpret the event that determines how we react.

A stressor can also be a poor performance of some kind. We often have unrealistic expectations of ourselves, and when we fail to live up to them we become angry and frustrated. This can contribute to more poor performances. Poor performance (A) coupled with an irrational belief (B) results in a negative response (C). Negative emotions can cause more poor performances, and so a stress cycle begins. Actors and musicians offer an example of this type of problem. They are conditioned to strive for the "perfect performance" even in rehearsals. Performance anxiety involves a threat to self-esteem (i.e., a fear of being rejected by the audience). The training of young musicians and actors should include realistic performance objectives. A 20 year old tenor cannot realistically expect to sound like Placido Domingo. Mistakes are tolerated and even expected in the live performances of younger performers.

Our educational system also conditions students to have unrealistic expectations. We place so much emphasis on grades that students are conditioned to compete for grades as a measure of self-worth. Unfortunately, learning for its own sake is not valued. This results in a stressful educational system characterized by a fear of learning efforts (i.e., because "failure" is a threat to self-esteem). These stressors are particularly intense during adolescence when self-esteem is already fragile.

Some people experience more stress than others. The concept of stress personalities was first described by Friedman and Rosenman in which they differentiated Type A (stressed) and Type B (nonstressed) personalities. Outline 75 summarizes characteristics of the Type A personality. We all know people (perhaps ourselves!) who exhibit Type A characteristics. The question of interest is whether or not a Type A individual can become a Type B person.

Not all Type A people display all of these behavior characteristics. They may demonstrate these traits only in certain situations. It is important to recognize unhealthy characteristics, as well as the situations that cause us to react in negative ways. By doing so, we can learn to modify behaviors which are counterproductive or unhealthy. Successful stress management strategies can help to modify Type A personality outcomes.

OUTLINE 75

CHARACTERISTICS ASSOCIATED WITH THE TYPE A PERSONALITY

☙ Walking, talking and eating rapidly

☙ Hurrying the ends of sentences

☙ Feeling impatient with the rate at which most things take place

☙ Feeling guilty about relaxing or doing "nothing"

☙ Scheduling more and more in less and less time

☙ Spending so much time acquiring things that there is no time left to enjoy them

☙ Thinking about work even on vacation

☙ Never seeming to have enough time to get things done

☙ Unable to pay attention; preoccupation with other things

☙ "Polyphasic" thought or performance (doing or thinking about more than one thing at a time)

☙ Believing that success is due to the ability to get things done quickly, and thus being afraid to stop doing everything faster and faster

---

While much attention has been given to the potentially adverse effects of Type A personalities, recent studies have added a Type C personality to the list. Type C people are passive to the point of allowing others to "walk all over them." They feel the same frustrations, anger and resentment as Type A people, but they tend to keep it to themselves.

If Type A is aggressive to the point of being unhealthy and Type C is passive to the point of being unhealthy, then Type B refers to assertive people who are able to express their desires and participate in life activities as desired without abusing the rights of others.

Stress Remedies

Obviously, the best stress management strategy is to eliminate our stressors. Since this is not always practical, the best alternative is to learn to manage stress in a way that enables us to achieve the highest quality of life possible. There are a variety of strategies which

---

CASE STUDY

LESSONS FROM REAL LIFE — THE BEAKERS OF LIFE

Imagine the time you have available for all of your daily activities could be measured like a fluid and poured into beakers:

Each beaker in this simple analogy represents aspects of our lives to which we choose to devote time.

Into our "beakers of life" we pour an amount of fluid which represents the time that we devote to each beaker. The goal is to try to balance your beakers so that you have a meaningful amount of time available for each.

When we overfill our "beakers of life," or if we balance them in ways that are frustrating, we increase stress and anxieties for ourselves.

We've all known people who pour so much fluid (i.e., devote so much time) in their work beaker, that they have no time for anyone or anything else. These are "workaholics."

HOW ABOUT YOU

How full are your beakers?

---

we can use to manage stress (Outline 76 summarizes the top five best stress relievers).

Chemicals and Medications in Stress Management

As a culture, we Americans believe in the notion that reality is for people who cannot handle drugs. Our society uses, misuses and abuses chemicals and medications more than any other culture in the world, especially for the purposes of relieving stress. In fact, most chemicals are not healthy stress management alternatives, especially since the body produces its own chemicals to combat stress. Adding more drugs to this vat often causes more harm than good. This is not to suggest that drugs prescribed by physicians for legitimate stress reactions are inappropriate. Rather, it does suggest that as a drug-oriented culture we rely on them even when healthier alternatives are often available.

OUTLINE 76

THE TOP FIVE STRESS RELIEVERS

These are the five remedies that more people seem to be able to practice successfully than all the other strategies combined.

❧ **Sleep**

The body must have adequate rest to re-energize and refresh.

❧ **Nutrition**

You are what you eat. There is a price to pay for over-consumption of unhealthy substances (e.g., caffeine, alcohol).

❧ **Play / Humor / Positive Attitude**

Developing a positive outlook on life can be a significant coping strategy for stress.

❧ **Relaxation / Deep Breathing**

Everyone needs time to relax and escape from stressors.

❧ **Exercise**

It may not be a panacea, but it's the closest thing to a "magic bullet" that we have.

Of the many chemicals we use for stress relief, none are more popular than alcohol and nicotine. At the end of a hard day, for example, many of us may relax with a cocktail. And, while alcohol in moderation (i.e., no more than one drink per day) may be good for the cardiovascular system, using alcohol to cope with the daily stresses of life is rarely a healthy alternative.

Ironically, a problem with alcohol is that it is effective in relieving stress for people in some situations. But the hazards of alcohol occur with repeated use. For example, many performers have discovered that moderate alcohol consumption can prevent performance anxiety (i.e., "stage fright"). However, this is a risky practice, since they must eventually take more and more to achieve the same effect. And indeed, many performers eventually become alcoholics.

Like alcohol, nicotine is not a healthy stress reliever. In fact, nicotine is a stimulant which produces effects on the body similar to the stress it is supposed to aleviate (e.g., elevation of blood pressure and heart rate. In fact, it compounds stress and contributes to the formation of a stress cycle.

The use of tobacco products for relaxation is probably due to a learning phenomenon known as classical conditioning (It's a Pavlov's dog type of situation). A smoker may say, "I'm going to sit down, have a cigarette and relax!" This sequence becomes "conditioned" (or learned). The stimulus or cue to "relax" is the cigarette. But, the cigarette is NOT actually causing a relaxed state . . . the smoker is! You could accomplish the same purpose with a pencil or empty pipe in your mouth!

Caffeine is another stimulant which we consume in large quantities, particularly when we are attempting to relax. Unfortunately, it is possible to develop a physical dependency for caffeine if large amounts are consumed over time. In fact, when our craving for caffeine is not replenished, we experience withdrawal symptoms. This withdrawal is "satisfied" (i.e., a type of stress relief) by the consumption of more caffeine. We mislead ourselves into believing that caffeine helps us to relax, when in fact, we are merely completing a drug-dependency cycle.

People often use both tobacco and caffeine products in social settings. So, they may relax because of the people with whom they are interacting. We are easily misled into believing that the drug is relaxing, when in fact, it is the social interaction that lowers our stress levels. Consequently, efforts to reduce drug use must take into account the social contexts in which these substances are being used.

In addition to the popular stress relievers, there are literally thousands of other drugs available to us that are used for dealing with stress. It is not our intent to imply that all medications are unhealthy or that doctors are wrong for prescribing them. Yet, the use of drugs to alleviate stress only deals with the symptoms (i.e., stress) and not the cause (i.e., the stressors). We often demand prescription medications from our doctors because this is easier than changing our lifestyles . . . even when we are aware that our lifestyles are the greater threat to health. For example, exercise can be more effective than drugs in relieving the symptoms of muscle tension, and it is healthier and less expensive than the use of drugs. However, exercise requires a time and energy commitment that most of us simply are not willing to make.

Of all the chemicals we take to cope with stress, vitamins are probably the most valid. Both, vitamins and minerals are more likely to be depleted during times of stress (especially vitamins C and B complex). And, there is some evidence that vitamins may be able to protect the body in various other ways. On the other hand, there is little evidence to support taking excessive doses of vitamins. In fact, some vitamins (especially A, D and K) are toxic when taken in large doses. One multivitamin/mineral tablet per day is sufficient to "treat" stress.

As a simple test of whether vitamins will work for you in this context, select a reputable vitamin / mineral product (ask your pharmacist to recommend one if you are uncertain) and take it as directed for several weeks. If you feel better as time progresses, then perhaps you were vitamin deficient. However, it is important to note that fatigue can be due to many lifestyle factors. So, one should also consider other aspects of our lifestyle that could contribute to fatigue. Also, remember that vitamins are not energy producing substances (i.e., they cannot "give" you energy). Although they are involved in the energy production cycle in the body and are required in order for the body to produce energy, they do not produce energy, per se. This may also explain why vitamin-deficient individuals often claim to feel more energized after a few weeks of supplementation.

Advertisers and promoters are aware of our preoccupation with vitamins and minerals as "magic bullets" for virtually every human ill. There is no end to the hype about these products, the availability of "new" products (i.e., old products with new names) or shelves lined with "stress tab" products at every conceivable retail outlet.

Although the concept has some merit, "stress" vitamins are usually just multivitamin products with extra C and B complex. You will tend to pay extra for the privilege of having "stress" printed on the label. In fact, any multivitamin product is as good as the higher priced "stress tabs" or "super potency" brands. Here again learning to read labels can save you money! But, if you are uncertain, ask your pharmacist for recommendations.

Nutritional Remedies

The adaptive processes of the body are affected by what we eat and drink. Unfortunately, we often neglect to consider the impact of even simple dietary changes on our stress levels. For example, reducing caffeine intake is an obvious and simple way to reduce one type of drug-induced stress.

There are other interesting ties between stress and nutrition. For example, many people increase their food intake in response to stress, while others reduce their food intake in response to stress. Such changes in food consumption as a stress reaction can pose significant health risks. In the extreme, binge eating and purging (e.g., bulimia) as well as anorexia due to anxiety or depression can be very dangerous.

Psychological Remedies

When stress becomes unbearable, professional counseling may be in order. Stress can also involve situations in which normal people are unsuccessfully attempting to cope with normal problems. Mental health professionals are trained to identify your stressors and ways to cope with them in healthy ways.

On the other hand, there are several psychological techniques that can be learned with or without the aid of professional help. One of these is assertiveness (i.e., seeking what you want without aggression). Passive people may suffer stress if they feel that they have failed to achieve or receive valued things, or if they feel "victimized" by others. Aggressive people often "get their own way" at the cost of friendships, relationships and marriages. Assertiveness teaches individuals to express themselves and to resist being exploited by others. "I just couldn't say no" is a common expression of a non-assertive person.

Other reactions to stress may involve misperceptions, and in the extreme, irrational beliefs. In such cases, a key element in effective stress management is an analysis of our beliefs about certain situations. This may serve as a basis for changing irrational thoughts into rational thoughts and can be a very effective stress management tool. Some of our irrational beliefs include the following:

1. **"I must have love and approval from all family, friends and peers."**

First, of course, it is impossible to please all the people all the time. Secondly, since none of us is perfect, criticism from those who love us may represent a more accurate perception of events than those we impose on them. In such cases, a healthy give and take may offer the most adaptive approach to reducing this type of stress.

2. **"I must be perfect and unfailing in all that I do."**

People are not perfect. People make mistakes. You are not perfect and you, too, make mistakes. People who believe that they must never fail, create failure because they cannot be perfect. Low self-esteem, emotional paralysis, guilt and worry are results of the "perfectionist" irrational belief. Accept your mistakes, learn from them and move on. All that you can ask of yourself and others is to do your best.

3. "Other people and events are the cause of my unhappiness."

Each of us creates our own stress and unhappiness in the ways in which we perceive and respond to the world around us. Accordingly, each of us can change the ways in which we choose to relieve that stress. We have little or no control over others. We have a great deal of control over our own thoughts and actions. No one can make us unhappy unless we allow them to.

4. "Life owes me something."

Many people go through life believing that they can do only the "minimum required" and that life or other people will take care of them. While we cannot control the circumstances of life, we can control much about the way we respond to such circumstances. We must learn to like ourselves and exercise self-control over situations and relationships. Life does not owe us . . . but it does offer many opportunities.

CASE STUDY

LESSONS FROM REAL LIFE — BILL

Bill is a licensed psychologist. He refers to himself as a "rent-a-friend." Bill is very good at what he does and boasts a very lucrative practice. But, he will be the first to tell you that many of the people he sees don't need a "shrink" as much as they just need an objective, sympathetic ear to hear their problems. Bill says that people need good friends to hear their problems. Friends who will not be judgmental. Friends who can be used as "sounding boards" and help analyze alternatives to certain stressful situations. The main objective of most counseling is to teach people to make their own decisions about situations. They just need encouragement in arriving at that decision.

HOW ABOUT YOU?

Do you have friends or family with whom you can share concerns and frustrations without fear of their being judgmental? Can you let them be a listener when you need one?

Self-Help

A great deal has been written about self-help and a sampling of self-help techniques are briefly described below. As you will note, there can be considerable overlap between the various approaches.

Autogenic Training is a systematic program in which you learn to control your autonomic responses to stress, then immediately employ techniques to alter them. Muscle tension, heart palpitations, headaches, cold hands and feet and high blood pressure are a few of the autonomic responses to stress that we can control with autogenic training. The basic tools of autogenic training are deep breathing, internal focus and control of emotions.

Biofeedback uses instruments and devices to detect the signs and symptoms of stress. Once these signs are measured, the same devices can help determine the effectiveness of the relaxation efforts. Several types of devices can be used as biofeedback instruments (e.g., a lie detector is a type of biofeedback machine). They are all designed to help you "listen" to your body and become aware of the signs and symptoms of stress.

Body Awareness has been labeled many things. It has its scientific foundations in biofeedback and autogenic training. Basically, body awareness is "getting in tune with your body" and learning how you react to stressful situations. Learn your signs and symptoms of stress. Learn how to identify symptoms early and correct the situations involved, your perception of the situations and your response to the situations.

Deep Breathing is an effective relaxation technique. When you are "stressed out" your breathing tends to become rapid and shallow. Taking a few moments to breathe deeply can provide some immediate stress relief.

Electroencephalogram (EEG) training is sometimes referred to as alpha training. EEG machines measure brain activity which is associated with stress. EEG training is designed to teach you how to achieve a relaxed mental state.

Electromyography measures small amounts of muscle tension and is similar to biofeedback. Electrodes are usually attached to the forehead or neck (sites where stress-related muscle tension may be apparent). When your muscles become tense due to stress, the machine emits a sound or graphs the response.

Galvanic Skin Response (GSR) instruments measure skin conductivity. Anxiety can cause your skin to become clammy or sweaty. GSR machines can detect this moisture.

Imagery and Visualization are similar to meditation. Begin by relaxing your body and breathing deeply. Imagery is imagination using all of the senses (e.g., touching, smelling, seeing, hearing and feeling). For example, imagine a deserted beach that is calm and beautiful. Use all of your senses to experience being on that beach. Visualization emphasizes the visual aspect of imagery. Since most people are visually stimulated, visualization can be an effective means of imagery. Visualization is also used in performance situations, such as sports. The athlete visualizes himself accomplishing the task in an appropriate manner (i.e., a "peak performance").

Meditation originated in Far Eastern religions, but it has been adopted in very positive ways by people in our culture. Meditation begins with a relaxed body and deep breathing. By mentally focusing and thinking peaceful and relaxing thoughts, your body and mind can relax.

Progressive Relaxation involves systematically relaxing all the muscles of the body. By alternately contracting and relaxing each muscle group, breathing deeply and telling yourself to relax, you can learn to relax your entire body. An alternate approach is to focus attention on each muscle group and tell yourself to relax. Either way, taking the time to consciously relax the muscles is a viable stress management tool.

Self-Hypnosis is similar to meditation in that you become very relaxed and internally focused. Self-hypnosis often uses an external stimulus (e.g., a pendulum) to induce the relaxed state of mind. While in this state, your mind can focus uncritically on problems or situations and explore alternative solutions to those problems.

Temperature Training is one of the most widely used methods of biofeedback because of its simplicity. It is based on the idea that peripheral circulation (e.g., hands and feet) is reduced when you are stressed and so the skin temperature in your hands and feet will be reduced. Learning to relax increases the temperature in your hands and feet. Many of the "gadgets" on the market (e.g., Biodots (TM) and the plastic stress business card) use a substance that changes color with different temperatures.

Thought Stopping is a form of reversing irrational beliefs. It is simpler than the rational-emotive therapy techniques used by professional counselors, but its results can be just as effective.

CASE STUDY

LESSONS FROM REAL LIFE — THOUGHT STOPPING

Harvey suffers from stress brought on by irrational beliefs. After analyzing those beliefs, he became aware they were irrational and attempted to address them. But, he continued to be unable to control his feelings and emotions when the same stressful situations presented themselves. And so, he sought help from a professional counselor.

Therapist: Pretend you are getting into one of those stressful situations. Tell me how you tell yourself to stop your thoughts.

Harvey: I just tell myself to stop, but it doesn't always work.

Therapist: What if you were in the house and you saw your child run into the street in front of an on-coming car. How would you tell him to stop?

Harvey: I'd run out the front door and scream "STOP!"

HOW ABOUT YOU?

Are there times when you need to shout "STOP!"? Sometimes we have to treat ourselves like a child playing in the street in order to get the point.

Time Management is a widely used and effective stress management strategy. Most of us feel that we do not have enough time to accomplish everything we would like to. It is true that we rarely have enough time to accomplish everything. But, we can accomplish many of the important things in life. The secret is to learn what is important in life and focus on those (i.e., learning to prioritize).

The basic components of effective time management are planning, prioritizing and controlling. A key theory in time management is that "effective" time management is more important than "efficient" time management. Effectiveness implies getting the right things done at the right time, while efficiency refers to doing as many things as possible in a short amount of time.

Planning is not as simple as it sounds. It requires us to plan our life's goals. Knowing what you want out of life is essential to the planning process. Establishing life goals takes time. Common life goals can include:

- Close friends
- Financial security
- Health
- Meaningful relationships with others (e.g., family, friends, co-workers)

- Professional success or achievement
- Travel
- Strong family ties

These may not be exactly congruent with your life goals, but they do seem to represent goals witnessed by one of the authors (MM) over the years in working with people. Once our goals have been identified, the next step is to formulate objectives or steps by which we can achieve meaningful goals.

Translating goals into workable daily or weekly objectives is the next step. It is important to accomplish target items on your agenda on a regular basis that help you move toward your life's goals. These little successes along the way provide direction and motivation and allow you to reassess your planning and prioritizing as you go. For example, if health is a lifetime goal, you should accomplish at least one target every day that moves you closer to that goal (e.g., exercise, good nutrition, relaxation). Reading a self-help book about health may be a monthly objective. Having a complete physical examination could be a yearly objective.

Take time to list your life's goals. Analyze your present time and energy expenditure toward those goals. You may find that you spend too much time and energy on the job and too little on health and family. Readjusting your priorities may not be entirely within your control. We have to spend a certain number of hours per week at work or attending to other responsibilities. Still, this analysis may help you to identify potential areas of change.

A basic philosophy of effective time management is learning to control your life. This is also the foundation of life extension and enhancing our quality of life. You are responsible for your health, your well-being . . . and your time!

There are many sources of job stress (e.g., ineffective bureaucracies, incompetent bosses, relationship problems with colleagues or a misunderstanding regarding your assignments at work). Whatever the reason, it is important for us to periodically analyze job stress to identify the causes. Once the true problems have been identified, focus on solving those problems which are within your control. Learn to accept those things over which you have no control and learn to cope with them more effectively.

Physical Remedies

Some self-help strategies can also be classified as physical remedies (e.g., relaxation, deep breathing and autogenics), since they help calm the body and the mind. But of all the physical self-help remedies available, none is more effective than exercise.

The result of the fight or flight syndrome is the mass production of chemicals in the body designed to prepare the body for action. If not utilized in some way, this energy and the resultant chemicals are processed slowly in the body or stored. Exercise provides a means by which the body can effectively process these reserves (e.g., by burning off the excess) and provides a mental break from the stresses of the day. So, regular exercise should be a part of every stress management program.

Experiment with different types of exercises and different environments to determine the best stress relief strategies for you (e.g., some people prefer exercising alone, while others prefer to exercise with other people). Remember that exercise can also be a stressor. Too much or the wrong type can be harmful and elicit bodily responses that are similar to other types of stress reactions.

Combination Approaches: Physical and Mental

Combination strategies address both physical and mental stress. In addition to deep breathing, autogenics and exercise, the list can also include body massage, which helps to relax muscles and allow the mind to defocus and enjoy life; foot massage, which can be self-administered with some of the same benefits of body massage. (A formalized version of foot massage is known as reflexology, which is a type of legitimized folk medicine); and finally, stretching coupled with deep breathing, which can provide a quick and easy means of stress management.

OUTLINE 77

SUMMARY OF USES FOR VARIOUS
STRESS REDUCTION TECHNIQUES

Problem	Most Effective Techniques	Other Helpful Techniques
ANGER IRRITABILITY RESENTMENT HOSTILITY	❦ Assertiveness Training ❦ Breathing ❦ Refuting Irrational Ideas ❦ Talk to a friend or other person with whom you feel that you can confide	❦ Autogenics ❦ Biofeedback ❦ Exercise ❦ Medication ❦ Nutrition
ANXIETY associated with specific situations (e.g., tests, deadlines, interviews, etc.)	❦ Breathing ❦ Coping Skills Training ❦ Progressive Relaxation ❦ Rehearsal (i.e., of appropriate responses to stressors) ❦ Role Playing ❦ Thought Stopping	❦ Imagery ❦ Meditation ❦ Refuting Irrational Ideas ❦ Self-Hypnosis ❦ Time Management
ANXIETY in personal relationships (e.g., spouse, parents, children, etc.)	❦ Assertiveness Training ❦ Breathing ❦ Progressive Relaxation ❦ Role Playing Exercises	❦ Self-Hypnosis

OUTLINE 77 cont'd

ANXIETY in general, regardless of the situations or people involved.	❧ Biofeedback ❧ Breathing ❧ Meditation ❧ Exercise ❧ Progressive Relaxation ❧ Imagery ❧ Refuting Irrational Ideas ❧ Thought Stopping ❧ Rehearsal (i.e., of appropriate responses to stressors) ❧ Role Playing	❧ Autogenics ❧ Coping Skills Training
DEPRESSION **HOPELESSNESS** **POWERLESSNESS** **POOR SELF-ESTEEM**	❧ Assertiveness Training ❧ Meditation ❧ Refuting Irrational Ideas ❧ Thought Stopping	❧ Breathing ❧ Exercise ❧ Nutrition ❧ Progressive Relaxation
FATIGUE (chronic)	❧ Breathing ❧ Exercise ❧ Self-Hypnosis ❧ Time Management	❧ Autogenics ❧ Nutrition ❧ Progressive Relaxation

OUTLINE 77 cont'd

FEARS **PHOBIAS**	❧ Coping Skills Training ❧ Progressive Relaxation ❧ Thought Stopping	❧ Biofeedback
HEADACHES **NECKACHES** **BACKACHES**	❧ Biofeedback ❧ Exercise (Flexibility and Strength) ❧ Imagery ❧ Massage ❧ Progressive Relaxation ❧ Self-Hypnosis	❧ Autogenics ❧ Nutrition
HIGH BLOOD PRESSURE	❧ Autogenics ❧ Biofeedback ❧ Nutrition ❧ Progressive Relaxation	❧ Combination of Techniques ❧ Exercise ❧ Meditation
INDIGESTION **IRRITABLE BOWEL** **ULCERS** **CHRONIC** **CONSTIPATION**	❧ Autogenics ❧ Nutrition ❧ Progressive Relaxation ❧ Self-Hypnosis	❧ Biofeedback ❧ Combination of Techniques ❧ Exercise

OUTLINE 77 cont'd

INSOMNIA SLEEPING PROBLEMS	❦ Deep Breathing	❦ Autogenics
	❦ Imagery	❦ Biofeedback
	❦ Progressive Relaxation	❦ Exercise
	❦ Thought Stopping	❦ Nutrition
	❦ Self-Hypnosis	
JOB STRESS	❦ Combination Techniques	❦ Assertiveness Training
	❦ Job Stress Management	
		❦ Time Management
MUSCLE SPASMS TICS TREMORS	❦ Biofeedback	❦ Exercise
	❦ Progressive Relaxation	❦ Imagery
	❦ Self-Hypnosis	
MUSCULAR TENSION	❦ Autogenics	❦ Combination of Techniques
	❦ Biofeedback	
		❦ Imagery
	❦ Breathing	
		❦ Self-Hypnosis
	❦ Exercise	
	❦ Progressive Relaxation	

```
┌─────────────────────────────────────────────────────────────┐
│                    ████████████████████████                   │
│                    █ OUTLINE 77 cont'd █                       │
│                    ████████████████████████                   │
│  ─────────────────────────────────────────────────────────   │
│                                                               │
│  OBESITY              ❦ Exercise                              │
│                                                               │
│                       ❦ Nutrition                             │
│  ─────────────────────────────────────────────────────────   │
│                                                               │
│  OBSESSIONS,          ❦ Meditation          ❦ Breathing       │
│  UNWANTED                                                     │
│  THOUGHTS             ❦ Thought Stopping                      │
│  ─────────────────────────────────────────────────────────   │
│                                                               │
│  PHYSICAL WEAKNESS    ❦ Exercise                              │
│                                                               │
└─────────────────────────────────────────────────────────────┘
```

Play, Humor and Positive Attitude

The benefits of play, humor and positive attitude are not merely restricted to leisure time activities. They must be learned and practiced daily in order to serve as an antidote for the stressors which we encounter in our "civilized" world.

Can you learn to be positive? This has become a common question in our society and is the focus for a great many self-help books. If you believe that your attitudes and behaviors are based on previous experiences, beliefs and thoughts, then you must also believe that they can be changed. Perhaps the best known example of this concept is personified by Ebenezer Scrooge in Dickens' *A Christmas Carol*. Although the story is one of fiction, the moral is not. We can change our attitudes and behaviors. Unfortunately, we often change only as a form of crisis intervention. For example, many people quit smoking only after they have a heart attack! It seems irrational to wait until we are visited by ghosts or have a heart attack in order to be compelled to adopt more healthy behaviors and lifestyles.

Our discussion about stress management is not offered as an ending, but as a beginning. If you feel like stress is winning the battle and you are not operating at peak performance levels, you should consider other coping strategies. The wear and tear of stress on your life can be avoided. Take control to discover a less stressful and more meaningful and stimulating life.

CASE STUDY

LESSONS FROM REAL LIFE — A BUMPER STICKER

Bumper stickers are ubiquitous. So much so, that we sometimes fail to appreciate their messages. One which has been around for a while reads:

"Life is a bitch ... and then you die"

There are two ways to interpret that statement:

Negative: Life is tough and full of problems and the only end to those problems is death. This is a view of life characterized by unhealthy coping strategies (e.g., drugs, unhealthy lifestyle behaviors).

Positive: Life is a challenge, full of obstacles to be overcome, mountains to be climbed ... and peak experiences to be achieved or experienced. From a perspective of holistic health and most religions, death is the final stage of a meaningful life and a transition to an even greater experience. In this interpretation we should give far more attention to our quality of living.

While it is not a great bumper sticker (as far as bumper stickers go), there is a lesson that can be learned by viewing it in a proper perspective.

22. SOILING OUR OWN NESTS — PEOPLE, ENVIRONMENTS AND HEALTH

"The future is purchased by the present."

—Samuel Johnson

It might seem odd to include a chapter regarding the environment in a book on health. Yet, this is a book about achieving and maintaining health in the fullest sense of the term. Taking steps to insure good health involves not only those decisions that directly impact our own health, but also the health of those around us and even the health of entire nations. Health-related events that occur half-way around the world may also affect us one way or another (e.g., the AIDS virus). We are all inter-connected in varied and complex ways and no book on health would be complete without considering these connections.

Human Ecology

Let us start by considering the term ecology which comes from a Greek word *oikos* meaning "house" or a place to live. The study of ecology literally is a study of organisms (including people) at home, how we interact with others (e.g., people, animals, nature and our planet) and the impact we have on our environments, and ultimately, on ourselves. This includes a consideration of the degree to which we are guilty of "soiling our own nest." There is now little doubt that we have set many destructive, anti-health initiatives in motion, and we must also consider how those forces can be reversed.

Human beings are the most intelligent, the most arrogant and the most selfish of all life forms on Earth. The great paradox of our wisdom is our failure to appreciate the damage of our actions on our future. We have created many of our own health problems (e.g., diseases and injury) in the pursuit of personal gains. We willingly sacrifice long term health in order to acquire short term benefits. Industry pollutes the air and waters; large cities now seek rural communities where they can dump their garbage (without regard for these communities); the auto and oil industries resist developing more efficient engines that might reduce our consumption of natural resources; and the average man or woman has little remorse about dumping trash from a moving car onto the streets and highways, as if the Earth has unlimited resources to clean up after us. We destroy natural resources on a daily basis (e.g., animals, forests) with virtually no regard for life or nature beyond potential profit margins or the value of hanging a stuffed head on a wall. Indeed, if there were only one deer left on the planet, there would be literally thousands of hunters who would be proud to exclaim, "I'm the one who shot it!"

Our Ecological Ignorance

> "We abuse land because we regard it as a commodity belonging to us. When we see land as a community to which we belong, we may begin to use it with love and respect."
>
> — Aldo Leopold

We seek to conquer and control the environments in which we live as callously and casually as we set the thermostats in our homes and automobiles. We air-condition our homes, cars and work environments, then boast that we have "mastered" our environments. In fact, we have done nothing of the kind.

Nature can (and is) responding with a vengeance to the damage we have inflicted upon our planet. The impact of pollution and over-population has only begun to be realized in the form of cancers, respiratory diseases, famine, epidemics and myriad other problems at all levels of the human spectrum.

Our dilemma is one of making difficult comparisons. How do we compare the value of a healthy atmosphere with the value we place on polluting the air to make paper? Industries argue that it is too expensive to develop pollution control systems that would completely eliminate wastes. In response, federal regulations dictate the levels at which industry is allowed to "gunk up" the air we breathe!

Until recently, there really was little need for these concerns. Environmental damage was small and nature was indeed able to "clean up." However, modern industrial processes and expanding populations have increased environmental damage, so that nature is progressively less able to keep up. This dilemma involves two distinct views of the "value" of nature. The first is called the *instrumental* view. Accordingly, we evaluate nature in terms of what nature can do for us (e.g., life support, esthetics, material gains, recreational value, profits). The second view is called the *intrinsic* value of nature, which suggests that nature has inherent value. To better appreciate this difference we may ask, "Does a tree have value merely because it is a tree (intrinsic value), or does a tree have value only in terms of how many toothpicks we can make from it (instrumental value)? Clearly our perspective throughout history has been an instrumental one.

Environments and Health

Our future health will increasingly depend upon how we choose to care for our planet. Basic levels of concern for the preservation of the environment include:

- ❧ Insure the elements of basic survival.

- ❧ Prevent disease and poisoning.

- ❧ Maintain an environment that is suited to an efficient human existence.

- ❧ Preserve human comfort and the enjoyment of life.

Our acceptance of a moral responsibility for nature must somehow keep pace with our technological, industrial and recreational capacity to destroy it.

Populations

Societies are reluctant to address population controls because of the complex ethical questions involved. For example, Americans are almost evenly divided on the abortion issue. And more recently, this debate has been characterized by increasing violence. How ironic that people who are protesting what they consider to be murder . . . are expressing their protests with murder!

Human Populations versus Natural Populations

Despite the popular myth promoted by hunters, natural populations do NOT require human interventions. Natural species tend to establish a population balance with their environments relative to available food supplies and other natural resources.

OUTLINE 78

HUMAN ECOLOGY: CONCEPTS FOR CONSIDERATION

❧ The optimum for a quality existence is always less than the maximum quantity that can be sustained.

By the time we reach the maximum population that the Earth is capable of sustaining, or the maximum level of garbage that we can conceivably dump on ourselves, we will have already compromised our health. The Earth can support more warm bodies sustained as so many domestic animals in a polluted feed lot, than it can support quality human beings who exercise the right of a pollution-free environment, a reasonable change for personal liberty and a variety of options for the pursuit of happiness.

—Eugene Odom

❧ It is not energy itself that is limiting, but the pollution consequences of exploiting energy. Pollution may well be the most limiting factor for our continued existence.

❧ The more we demand from nature, the fewer resources nature has for self-maintenance.

❧ Up to now we have generally acted as a parasite on our environments. We take what we want with little regard for the welfare of our planet.

❧ Restrictions on the use of our natural resources are the only practical means for avoiding overpopulation and the over-exploitation of resources.

❧ Technology alone cannot solve our population and pollution problems. Instead, solutions will require moral, economic and legal constraints that are the product of public awareness.

In humans, however, the same principle does not hold true. Our population levels and birth control rates are more the product of cultural values and norms than they are available resources. Among industrialized nations, birth and growth rates are declining. While this may seem a positive development, it actually creates a different type of problem. Birth and population rates are declining more rapidly among affluent and more highly educated groups than among less affluent and less educated groups. If this trend continues, the middle and upper classes will bear an increasing burden for the care of the underprivileged. This is not an issue of bias, but rather an economic realization that eventually fewer and fewer people will be required to support more of those who will need assistance. The social problems that accompany this trend (e.g., housing, crime, education, low self-esteem, health) could become worse.

Human Options

Given these circumstances two options may be considered. We can, of course, do nothing (i.e., allow unrestricted population growth until our demands on resources, such as food, water and space exceed the supplies which we have available). Unfortunately, this option will result in increasing diseases, deaths and suffering until the population size realigns with the available resources (a scenario which is already present in some communities in the world).

An alternate approach is the adoption of responsible population controls to maintain populations below critical levels. This requires a balance between science, technology and ethics.

Maximum versus Optimum Populations

The population levels which the Earth can sustain can be categorized in two ways. The first is called the *maximum population*, which reflects the physical capacity of the Earth to support people. It refers to the maximum number of people who could exist on Earth without exhausting needed resources. This scenario does not include the concept of quality of life, but only the largest number of people that the earth can support (much like a farmer who continues to add cattle to a pasture without concern for the health or living status of his livestock). This maximum level is limited only by such factors as land area, availability of resources, technology, food production, waste accumulation and disposal.

A second way of categorizing population limits involves an *optimal population* concept in which quantity and quality are taken into account. Whatever the number in making such a determination it is clear that this level is smaller than the maximum population level. Yet, the ethical issues involved are not so clear.

Certain of the ethical issues involve conflicts between individual "rights" versus the collective "rights" of societies. Even the notion that population controls might be necessary is the object of heated controversy. Many people argue against the view that a society has a responsibility or even a right to regulate its population size (i.e., a conflict between individual versus collective freedoms), a practice that we associate with totalitarian societies (e.g., the Peoples Republic of China).

Even if we could agree with the optimal population argument, we would still debate the two approaches for population control: (1) increase in death rates (e.g., withholding medical care from certain individuals who could actually be saved), and (2) birth control. Of the two alternatives, birth control is really the only humane and acceptable alternative. Yet, even with this option the courses of action are controversial.

Pollution

> "A planet cannot, any more than a country, survive half slave, half free, half engulfed in misery, half careening along toward the supposed joys of almost unlimited consumption. Neither our ecology nor our morality could survive such contrasts."
>
> —Lester Pearson

Pollution has been defined as an undesirable change in the characteristics of our air, land and water that may harm humans or other desirable species, our industrial processes, living conditions, and cultural assets; or that may waste or deteriorate natural resources.

Pollution consists of the leftovers of the things we make, use and throw away. It has become of increasing concern because of increasing populations (more people use more resources, producing more leftovers). While there are some sources of natural pollution (e.g., volcanoes), the bulk of pollution is the product of human activities.

Different people define pollution in different ways in order to fit their own specific needs. For example, an industry may pump a considerable volume of unhealthy residue into the air, but successfully convince the public and regulatory agencies that they are not actually "polluting," or that this is a small price to pay for the economic benefits. Consequently, they are not required to clean up a clear source of industrial waste.

For the most part, and in favor of economic gains, we have adopted an essentially crisis intervention approach to dealing with pollution. That is, we accept the inevitability of pollution until a crisis occurs (e.g., a multi-million gallon oil spill which threatens the environment). The trouble with the "crisis intervention" orientation is that by the time real problems emerge, considerable damage may already have occured. In all likelihood it will take years to undo the damage the earth has already sustained (if that is actually possible), and to prevent future damage. Unfortunately, when the last member of an animal species is destroyed . . . it is too late to respond to the "crisis."

The potential costs of pollution include:

❦ Loss of resources

❦ Costs of pollution control

❦ Costs in human health

Pollution may become one of the most significant threats for the future of mankind. The impact of pollution can involve damage to property, health, and quality of life. There is a strong relationship between pollution and the development of respiratory diseases and cancer, for example. Conversely, reductions in air pollution could save billions of dollars annually in medical care, work hours lost and sick leave. This does not include the costs of human misery, disability, or death.

```
CASE STUDY
```

TRAGEDY OF THE COMMONS

Picture a pasture open to all. It is to be expected that each herdsman will try to keep as many cattle as possible on the commons. Such an arrangement may work reasonably satisfactorily for centuries because tribal wars, poaching and disease keep the numbers of both man and beast well below the carrying capacity of the land. Finally, however, comes the day of reckoning; that is, the day when the long-desired goal of social stability becomes a reality. At this point, the inherent logic of the commons remorselessly generates tragedy. As a rational being, each herdsman seeks to maximize his gain. Explicitly or implicitly, more or less consciously, he asks, "What is the utility to me of adding one more animal to my herd.?" This utility has one negative and one positive component. The positive component is a function of the increment of one animal. Since the herdsman receives all the proceeds from the sale of the additional animal, the positive utility is nearly +1.

The negative component is a function of the additional overgrazing created by one or more animals. Since, however, the effects of overgrazing are shared by all the herdsmen, the negative utility for any particular decision-making herdsman is only a fraction of -1.

Adding together the component partial utilities, the rational herdsman concludes that the only sensible course for him to pursue is to add another animal to his herd. And another, and another . . . .

But this is the conclusion reached by each and every rational herdsman sharing a commons. Therein is the tragedy. Each man is locked into a system that compels him to increase his herd without limit - - in a world that is limited.

Ruin is the destination toward which all men rush, each pursuing his own interests in a society that believes in the freedom of the commons. Freedom in a commons brings ruin to all.

—William Forster Lloyd

This anecdote was popularized in an article entitled "The Tragedy of the Commons," by Garrett Hardin. It is considered a classic example for students of public health, but should be required reading for everyone. In reality, we all live out the tragedy of the commons every day of our lives. The "commons" include our oceans, lands, air and a great many other things which we take for granted. And, the tragedies are our losses of health and resources.

To date, our efforts to control industrial pollution have not been very successful. When questioned about their initiatives, the typical response is: "We are only pumping a small amount of pollution into the air that is well below the limits prescribed by the Environmental Protection Agency. Redesigning our manufacturing processes to eliminate pollution would be cost prohibitive and we would have to eliminate jobs."

Unfortunately, all producers of pollution are making the same argument. The collective outcome of all manufacturers pumping just "a little" pollution into the air . . . is a lot of pollution in the air!

The average person also seems to be equally insensitive to these issues. When the catalytic converter was first required on automobiles, for example, the response of many people was to disconnect this anti-pollution device. Now we know that catalytic converters have reduced air pollution in most major communities. Still, it is not as effective as it could be as a result of the numbers of people who have excused themselves from this "inconvenience."

Hardin suggests that technical solutions are inadequate to solve the pollution problem, since they only involve the ways in which science can solve our problems for us. This creates a dependency on science and a lack of self-responsibility in our society. Technological and scientific solutions cannot change human values or morality. Even when technology provides alternatives, people must choose to accept them (e.g., the catalytic converter).

In our high-tech society, we hear daily pleas for technical solutions so that we do not have to be inconvenienced with changing our beliefs or lifestyles. While it is common to see protesters carrying signs at the Centers for Disease Control and FDA demanding new treatments for AIDS, we never see signs promoting healthy lifestyles.

According to Hardin:

> The owner of a factory on the bank of a stream - - whose property extends to the middle of the stream - - often has difficulty seeing why it is not his natural right to muddy the waters flowing past his door.

> The individual benefits as an individual from his ability to deny the truth, even though society as a whole, of which he is a part, suffers.

The problem involves a conflict of freedoms and our inability to define the "common good." Ours is a free society and we resent any restrictions of our freedoms. Yet, sometimes we must limit our individual freedoms in order to preserve our society (e.g., What would our lives be like without laws, police, etc.?). How do we balance the freedom of individuals to destroy the environment (e.g., for profit or recreation) with the need of societies to protect it? Consider recent laws and social policies which limit the freedom of smokers to endanger the health of those around them.

Even the concept of the "common good" is a quagmire of confusion. According to Hardin:

> To one person it is wilderness, to another it is ski lodges for the multitudes.

> To one person it is estuaries to nourish ducks for hunters to shoot; to another person it is factory land.

Our laws cannot force people to comply with reason. Laws, like our values and priorities, are culturally defined and conceived. If we do not truly value our environments, it is doubtful that the imposition of laws will protect them. There are many hunters who knowingly and willingly kill animals out of season or under questionable circumstances. One tragic example that may serve to make the point involves the mother of twin babies who was shot and killed by deer hunters as she stood in her own back yard in a residential neighborhood in Maine in 1988. She had gone out into the backyard to caution the hunters about shooting so close to her home and young children. The hunters knew that houses were nearby. They had parked in this residential area in order to hunt. The unfortunate victim of this senseless accident made the mistake of wearing white gloves, which apparently the hunters mistook for the tail of a deer. So, this young mother was shot and killed by an "experienced hunter."

According to an article which appeared in the October 1988 issue of Good Housekeeping, there were no major obstructions between the hunter and his victim. In published reports he is reported as feeling "sorry," but NOT "neglectful" or "negligent." Apparently, , we are supposed to believe that an experienced hunter armed with a high powered rifle with a telescope, and clearly shooting in an area where homes and people were present, was unable to discern between a tall, young woman and a game animal. Incidentally, no evidence of a deer was found (e.g., there were no tracks or droppings).

And what of the attitude of the community in which this tragedy occurred? According to the article, there was a "strong and vocal minority who sympathized with the hunter" and who also seemed, "either insensitively or callously to blame" the victim "for her own death because of her actions (e.g., going out in her backyard to caution the hunters) and attire (i.e., wearing white gloves and not wearing bright orange)." Many felt that the woman was as much to blame as the hunter. Apparently, a grand jury felt the same way. It was just an accident, so he was free to go . . . and hunt again. She is still dead.

The point here is not a criticism of the hunter. Rather, it is really an effort to question our traditions. At what point do we truly begin to take responsibility for our actions? Perhaps never. We are quick to say, "I'm sorry," as if that should be sufficient:

- Oops . . . so sorry . . . I didn't realize that any one was drinking this water!

- Oops . . . so sorry . . . I didn't realize that any one was breathing that air!

- Oops . . . so sorry . . . I thought there was still one of those critters left!

- Oops . . . so sorry . . . I didn't think anyone needed that tree!

- Oops . . . so sorry . . . I thought it was a deer!

Even when laws are enacted to control such circumstances, problems exist. Laws tend to generate bureaucracies to monitor and administer them. Invariably, we face the problem of *quis custodiet ipsos custodes*? (i.e., "Who shall watch the watchers themselves?") Give that one some thought at the next election!

Hardin also believes that it is a mistake to believe that human actions can be controlled by appeals to conscience:

> People vary. Confronted with appeals to limit certain activities, some will respond, and others will not. The population example is of interest. Those who do not agree to limit family size will continue to produce children, who will likely adopt the attitudes of their parents. Eventually, the number of people who refuse to adopt limited family sizes will outnumber those who do.

It is unlikely that we will ever have universal agreement regarding environmental issues. Yet, it is clear that our future health will depend upon how we choose to care for our environments and ourselves. Ultimately, we must question our freedom to destroy our environments and our resources. Perhaps, the dilemma is best summarized in the following humorous way:

> Men and nations will act rationally when all other possibilities have been exhausted.
>
> — Katz's Law, John Peers

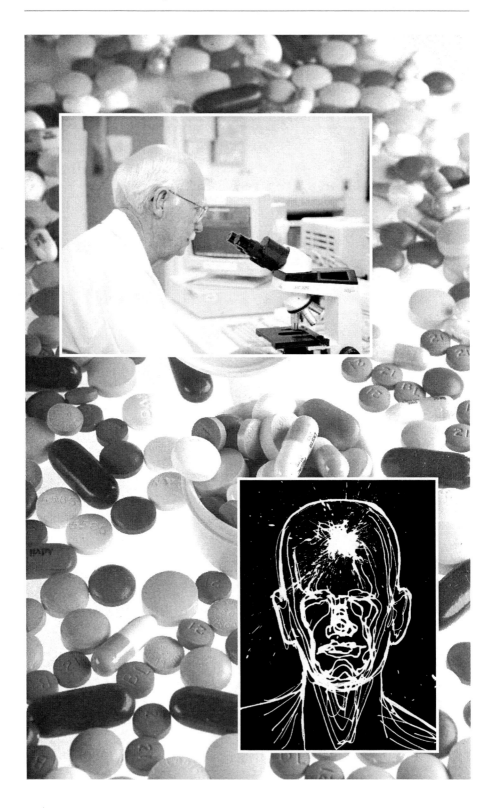

SECTION FOUR

Drugs and Health

23. WHAT IS A DRUG?

"A drug is a substance which, when injected into
rats, will produce a scientific report."

— Danowski's Law, John Peers

The terms *drug, medicine,* and *medication* are commonly used to
mean the same thing, even though there can be confusion about them.
The term *drug* comes from the Middle English, drogge, and literally
means "a substance used as a medicine." It is also defined as "any
substance used as a medicine or in the preparation of medicines" and
as "any chemical agent that affects living processes." The legal definitions of a drug include:

- ❦ Articles recognized in official drug listings of the United
States;

- ❦ Articles intended for use in the diagnosis, cure, mitigation,
treatment or prevention of diseases in man or animals;

- ❦ Articles (other than food) intended to affect the structure or
any function of the body of man or other animals; and

- ❦ Articles intended for use as a component of any of the above.

The legal definition of a drug takes into account not only what it
contains, but also its intended uses. This is a very important consideration. Disreputable manufacturers and advertisers frequently promote their products as "natural" substances or "foods," even though
they are being promoted for the treatment or cure of diseases or health
problems. In such cases, the law is being circumvented by claiming
that such "natural" products are not "drugs."

A recent example of this subterfuge involved the claim that cereals served to prevent heart problems and certain types of cancer. The
FDA ruled however that if cereals are promoted to be "effective" for
the prevention of heart conditions and cancer, then they must prove
their claims. In essence, since these companies were promoting their
products for a drug purpose, they had to conform to the same testing
guidelines required of any drug product, or stop making such claims.

While this action on the part of the FDA may seem ridiculous to some, it is really quite appropriate. Federal laws require that drug products must be proven to be safe and effective for their stated claims. The FDA is not opposed to the advertisement of cereals for the prevention of heart disease and cancer, but they do require that advertisements must be truthful. While fiber has been shown to help prevent heart problems and certain cancers, the cereal products that contain fiber have not. Moreover, cereal companies may not use the studies of other products for their own monetary gain. Nor can they excuse themselves from drug testing if they are going to promote their cereals for a drug purpose. This same requirement applies to any products promoted for a drug purpose.

In other recent examples, herbal and health food promoters criticized the FDA because vitamin products were forced to conform to federal labeling guidelines. Again, the FDA did not prohibit sale of these products, it only demanded truthful labeling. Manufacturers and promoters are not allowed to make claims that are unsubstantiated. Freedom of speech does not allow for a freedom to deceive. Herbal and health food promoters can make any claims they want on their labels ... as long as their claims are truthful.

A drug is *any* product which is promoted for a drug purpose regardless of what it contains. If a capsule contains dirt and is promoted for the prevention or treatment of a health problem, its manufacturer must prove their claims. In this way, the FDA attempts to protect us.

Newspapers and the media use the term "drug" to designate illegal substances because it contains fewer letters than "medication" or "medicine." Space is usually limited when writing headlines and the term drug requires less space. Since illegal and problem drugs are popular headline news items, the term is often used to designate illegal substances and situations.

The term *medicine* comes from the Latin term, medicina, which means "medicine" or "any substance used in treating disease or for healing. The term *medication* comes from the Latin term, medicatio, which means "to heal" and refers to "any product which contains a medicine." The term *medicament* is not commonly used, but is similar to these other terms. It comes from the Latin term, medicamentum, which means a "remedy" and refers to "a medicinal substance."

The similarity of terms and the different meanings which people use can contribute to communication problems. For example, consider the term dope. People often say to their doctor, nurse or pharmacist, "I don't want any 'dope'!" Yet, "dope" is actually a slang term which has no universal meaning. In such cases they may be referring to drugs that sedate them or reduce their mental competence in some way. There are, of course, many drugs which have a "doping" effect, including many nonprescription products (see Outline 79).

OUTLINE 79

EXAMPLE DRUG CATEGORIES THAT CAN CAUSE SEDATION OR REDUCED MENTAL ALERTNESS

- Allergy products
- Antianxiety products
- Antidepressants
- Antihistamines
- Blood pressure medications
- Cold and flu products
- Cough products
- Diarrhea products
- Dizziness, nausea, vomiting

- Epileptic medications
- Muscle relaxants
- Narcotics
- Pain medications
- Parkinson drugs
- Sleep products
- Stomach and intestinal products
- Tranquilizers
- Ulcer products

Outline 80 summarizes a study done by one of the authors (GH) in which consumers were asked to select the definition which they thought best defined the terms "drug," "medicine," "medication," and "dope." The results are quite revealing.

Having a common language base is important for effective communication between people. Health professionals sometimes forget this and use jargon which the consumer does not understand. The same terms may have different meanings to consumers and health professionals, which results in misunderstandings and incorrect messages.

OUTLINE 80

CONSUMER INTERPRETATON OF DRUG-RELATED TERMS

Response	Percent of people who selected each response for these terms.		
	"Drug"	"Medicine"	"Medication"
❦ A substance prescribed by a doctor (including nonprescription products)	12	22	15
❦ A substance which requires a doctor's prescription.	12	5	7
❦ An illegal substance used for recreation, pleasure, or for a nonmedical purpose.	9	——	>1
❦ Any substance used in preventing, diagnosing or treating a disease or health problem or some kind.	34	70	74
❦ Any substance which alters normal body function.	33	3	3

Response	Percent of consumers selecting each response as a definition for the term "Dope"
❦ A substance that will cause you to behave differently than you would normally.	8
❦ A substance which interferes with your ability to think clearly or normally.	13
❦ A substance which makes you sleepy or tired.	3
❦ An illegal substance used for recreation, pleasure, or for a nonmedical purpose.	63
❦ Any substance which can cause addiction.	13

The Generic Versus Brand Name Controversy

Among the various drug-related issues that are confusing to the general public is the difference between generic and brand name drugs. It is easy to understand the confusion since drugs are assigned several names by the time they are made available for purchase. The best way to understand how names are assigned to a particular drug product is to consider the sequence of relevant events once a drug is discovered.

Once researchers identify a new chemical with medicinal potential, it is assigned a chemical name. This name is a reflection of the chemical structure of the drug, but may be long and cumbersome. For example, the chemical name of acetaminophen (a common nonprescription pain reliever) is N-acetyl-p-aminophenol! Actually, several chemical names may be assigned, since there are several chemical naming systems.

So, for example, other chemical names of acetaminophen include *4'-hydroxyacetanilide, p-hydroxyacetanilide, p-acetamidophenol* and *paracetamol*. While these names are meaningful to medicinal chemists, they are awkward for everyone else, including health scientists.

For this reason while the drug is undergoing continued investigation, it is assigned a more convenient code designation that typically takes one of two forms: (1) A letter and number combination (e.g., GH 123); or (2) A letter combination (e.g., ABC). A code designation is a more convenient "label" than a chemical name and is discarded once an official name has been assigned to the drug. Code designations are not very descriptive, and their use is discouraged outside of the research institution.

A more concise nonproprietory or generic name is eventually assigned to a drug product if it appears to have market potential. This may reflect the chemical structure of the drug, or it may be similar to other drugs in a given class of drugs (e.g., notice the similarity of the generic names of these common nonprescription antihist*amines:* diphenhydr*amine,* pyril*amine,* chlorphenir*amine,* bromphenir*amine).* The generic name for a drug is not protected by a patent and is not owned by anyone. These names are assigned by a formal process involving the research institution and the United States Adopted Names (USAN) Council, which is the agency responsible for the selection of appropriate nonproprietary names for U.S. drugs. The USAN is an expert committee which is jointly sponsored by the American

Medical Association (AMA), the U. S. Pharmacopeial Convention, and the American Pharmaceutical Association (APhA). Even though a drug may eventually have different brand (or trade) names, the generic name remains the same. This provides for consistency and ease of evaluation of the many products in which the drug may be included.

The *brand name* or *trade name* of a drug is the legal possession of its owner. If a generic drug is manufactured by more than one company, each company may assign a different brand name to the drug, but the generic name remains the same. Brand names tend to be brief, clever and easy to remember. They are designed to facilitate sales, and can be deceptive if the name selected is similar to other products already on the market. For example, *Anacin-3* is a nonprescription product containing only acetaminophen, while *Tylenol #3* is a prescription product that contains codeine in addition to acetaminophen; *Retin-A*, is a prescription product used to eliminate wrinkles in the skin, while *Retinyl Palmitate-A* is a nonprescription product unlike its prescription sound-alike. Brand names rarely provide accurate information about the chemical or pharmacological properties of the product.

There are two questions commonly asked about generics: (1) Are generics just as effective as their brand name counterparts?; and (2) Do generics always cost less?

The answer to both questions is NO! Despite the rhetoric to the contrary found in many self-help books, generics are not always equivalent to brand products, nor do they always cost less.

Many studies have shown, for example, that generics and brand-name products may differ in their biological effects. Even the FDA allows for a 20% difference (plus or minus) in activity from the standards established by the original brand name product, and this can represent a sizable and perceptible difference in the way a patient reacts. Of course, there are many products for which there is no real difference, and therapeutic outcomes are not affected.

In reality, the conflict is not between a brand name drug and its generic equivalent. Rather, every drug product should be judged on its own merit. Two different brand name products can differ from one another, as can two different generic products. So, it is really a matter of comparing one product with another, regardless of whether the products involved are brand name or generic.

Similarly, the decision to switch from brand to generic should consider the condition which is being treated. Drugs used in serious serious health conditions (e.g., heart disease, epilepsy, diabetes, asthma) involve careful consideration, since differences in drug activity can actually threaten one's health in such circumstances. For antibiotics, pain medications, cold and allergy products, the differences between products will not usually impact overall health and safety.

In any event, it is always best to discuss these options with your doctor, nurse and pharmacist. In this way, your doctor will know about the switch in case your health problem becomes worse or new side effects appear.

It is also worth mentioning that doctors have been criticized by many naive health writers because of their reluctance to prescribe generics. Yet, it is important to realize that doctors prescribe drugs with which they have experience and which have proven to be effective for their patients. For many prescribers this is not really a generic versus brand name issue. Rather, it is simply a matter of prescribing familiar products which have proven successful in the past. Changes involve the use of new products that are less familiar to the prescriber. So, the issue is not really a reluctance to prescribe less expensive drugs, as much as it is a familiarity with drugs which they trust.

The cost issue is equally deceptive. It is ironic to note that several popular books (usually written by nonpharmacists) insist that generics are always cheaper. This is simply not true. Generics may, or may not, be cheaper. For example, some pharmacies may average the cost of all penicillin products and charge the same price regardless which product is selected. In such cases, the consumer does not save money by buying a generic, but the pharmacy makes more money on the sale.

The generic savings issue has another interesting ramification. We demand new drug products. For example, we desperately need cures for AIDS, cancers, heart disease and many other ailments. New drug products come from the major research and development (R & D) companies, not from the generic companies. Consequently, as more and more consumers switch to generics, less financial support is provided for the R & D companies to identify and develop new drug products. In turn, the cost of new drugs increases to offset these research and promotion costs. It is a "catch-22" situation. How do we deal with the rapidly increasing costs of health care (including medications) while providing support for research and development?

24. HOW DRUGS WORK

"The common use of the word "miracle" in referring to the effect of a new drug reveals that men still find it easier to believe in mysterious forces than to trust in rational processes."

— Rene Dubos

Even though drugs are used for different purposes, there are many similarities about how they work. Understanding these basic drug concepts helps us to appreciate their effects, how they cause problems and why they must be used carefully.

Drugs work by causing an alteration in normal body function (see Outline 81). The activity of a drug can mimic or enhance a normal body function, or it can inhibit or disrupt a normal body function. Very often the desirable activities of a drug also cause undesirable side effects. For example, an antihistamine may dry a runny nose. However, the same drug action that dries the nose will also dry the eyes and throat. We tend to think of drug activity in terms of the purpose for which we use it, but we often overlook its potential for adverse drug reactions.

The Receptor Theory

One of the most widely accepted explanations of drug activity is called the receptor theory. Basically, this theory suggests that a drug molecule has a certain shape and chemical structure that allows it to "plug" into certain receptors in the body. It is much the same idea as plugging a lamp into a wall outlet. The 220 volt outlet of a clothes dryer cannot be plugged into a normal 110 volt outlet. Similarly, some receptors in the body will allow a given drug molecule to "plug in," while others will not.

This theory is important because it explains why drugs with similar physical or chemical characteristics result in similar effects in the body. For example, it explains why "natural" vitamins offer no therapeutic advantage over synthetic ones (despite claims by vitamin and health food salesmen). It does not matter to your body whether a vitamin is natural or synthetic as long as it has the proper chemical and physical characteristics to "plug" into the appropriate receptor.

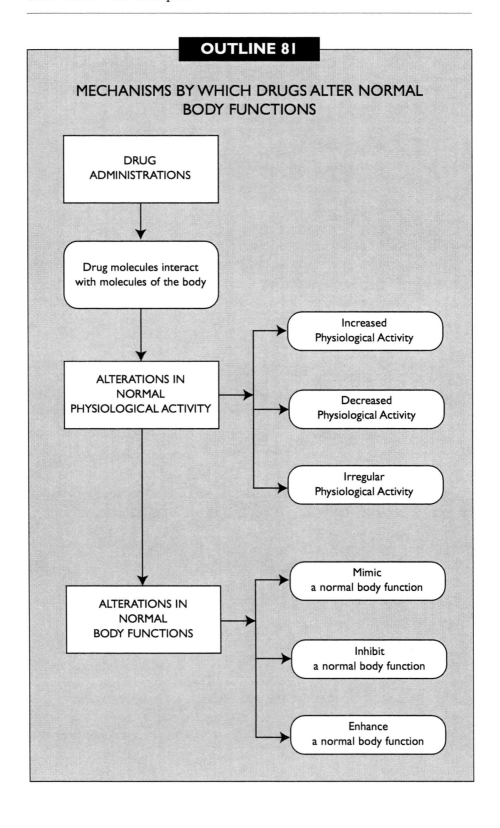

OUTLINE 81

MECHANISMS BY WHICH DRUGS ALTER NORMAL BODY FUNCTIONS

DRUG ADMINISTRATIONS

Drug molecules interact with molecules of the body

ALTERATIONS IN NORMAL PHYSIOLOGICAL ACTIVITY

Increased Physiological Activity

Decreased Physiological Activity

Irregular Physiological Activity

ALTERATIONS IN NORMAL BODY FUNCTIONS

Mimic a normal body function

Inhibit a normal body function

Enhance a normal body function

Additionally, this theory helps to explain why adverse effects occur. In an overly simplistic way the following scheme can be proposed:

Drug A + Receptor A = Desired Effects

Drug A + Receptor B = Side Effects

Once a drug is taken, it is distributed throughout the body and, it will plug into any receptor that will accept it. In the scheme above, Drug A is taken to achieve a certain therapeutic benefit. When Drug A plugs into Receptor A, the desired outcome occurs. However, Drug A is also able to plug into Receptor B. When this happens, side effects occur. Virtually all drugs produce both desirable and undesirable effects.

With antihistamines, drying a runny nose is the desirable outcome. However, this drying effect is not restricted to just the nasal tissues. It also affects the eyes, mouth and throat, and can cause blurring of vision and drowsiness. With this in mind, driving a car after taking an antihistamine can be risky. In fact, studies have shown that nonprescription sleep medications can impair your coordination and reaction time the next morning. So, proper planning is necessary to account for the side effects that can occur.

A Sequence of Drug Action

Outline 82 summarizes the steps that occur after you take a drug. The exact sequence can vary depending upon the drug involved and the route of administration. Before a drug can achieve its desired effects, it must first be administered in some way. Even though there are many routes of administration, they can all be classified as: (1) enteral (oral or rectal); (2) parenteral (injections), or (3) topical (applied to the skin). Once the drug has been administered, it is absorbed into the bloodstream, then distributed throughout the body. Some of the drug molecules are carried to the liver and other sites in the body where metabolism begins (i.e., the process by which the body alters the drug molecule so that it can be more easily eliminated). As they are carried throughout the body, some drug molecules reach the desired sites of action and drug activity occurs. Eventually, the drug is excreted.

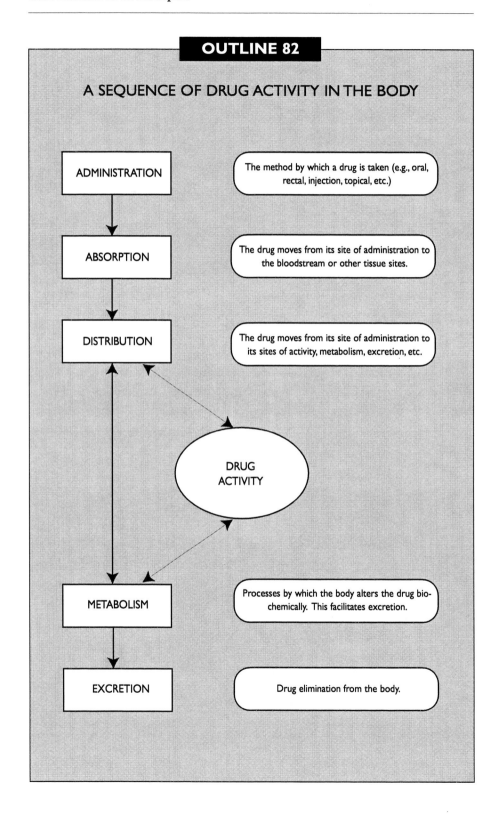

OUTLINE 82

A SEQUENCE OF DRUG ACTIVITY IN THE BODY

ADMINISTRATION — The method by which a drug is taken (e.g., oral, rectal, injection, topical, etc.)

ABSORPTION — The drug moves from its site of administration to the bloodstream or other tissue sites.

DISTRIBUTION — The drug moves from its site of administration to its sites of activity, metabolism, excretion, etc.

DRUG ACTIVITY

METABOLISM — Processes by which the body alters the drug biochemically. This facilitates excretion.

EXCRETION — Drug elimination from the body.

It is helpful to realize that your body does not "know" that you are taking a drug for a beneficial purpose. Your body "perceives" all drugs to be a foreign substance. So, it tries to eliminate the drug as quickly as possible. Drug research determines how the body attempts to rid the drug (e.g., metabolism and excretion) and how long this process normally takes. Dosing instructions reflect these studies (which is why you should always take mediations as directed).

25. DRUG INTERACTIONS

> "Faith in the magic power of drugs is not new. In
> the past, as today, it contributed to give medicine
> the authority of priesthood and to re-create the
> glamour of ancient mysteries."
>
> — Rene Dubos

Physicians often prescribe more than one drug to treat medical problems, and consumers often use multiple OTC drug products or mix OTC products with prescription products. Under such circumstances, drugs can interact with each other and with certain foods. These examples of multiple drug use are referred to as *polypharmacy*.

Polypharmacy can be beneficial when conditions require the use of multiple drugs. However, the potential for drug interaction problems can also be present in such cases. While many drug interactions are known (e.g., the interaction between alcohol and barbiturates), many others are not. Very often, drug interactions are not discovered until they happen in a patient. Moreover, the possible number of such interactions is infinite since there are as many as 600,000 OTC products and another 400,000 prescription drugs. With possibly a million drug products available to us, it is virtually impossible to identify all possible drug interactions.

Of course, the more medications you take, the greater the chance for a drug interaction to occur. So, it is important to ask your doctor, nurse or pharmacist about drug interactions whenever you take any drug product (prescription or OTC) for the first time. Also, make sure that your health professionals have complete records of all prescription and OTC products that you are taking.

Drug / Drug Interactions

The effect of one drug on another is the most common type of drug interaction problem. Outline 83 summarizes the possible outcomes of mixing two drugs. Basically, the activity or effects of a drug (including adverse drug reactions and toxicity) can be increased, decreased or not affected when mixed with another drug. As you might imagine, the possible outcomes become much more complex each time another drug is added to the mixture.

OUTLINE 83

THE POSSIBLE OUTCOMES OF MIXING TWO DRUGS

		DRUG A		
		Increased Activity	**No Effect**	**Decreased Activity**
DRUG B	**Increased Activity**	Increased effects of both drugs (including side effects or toxicity)	Increased effects of DRUG B and NO effect on DRUG A	Increased effects of DRUG B and decreased effects of DRUG A
	No Effect	Increased effects of DRUG A and NO effect on DRUG B	NO effect on either drug	Decreased effects of DRUG A and NO effects on DRUG B
	Decreased Activity	Increased effects of DRUG A and decreased effects of DRUG B	Decreased effects of DRUG B and NO effect on DRUG A	Decreased effects of both drugs

There are many mechanisms by which these interactions can occur. A drug can impact any of the steps listed in Outline 82, (increase or decrease the absorption, distribution, metabolism or excretion of another drug). For example, antacids tend to interfere with the absorption of other drugs. Cimetidine can interfere with the normal metabolism of some drugs. Aspirin is highly bound to proteins in the blood. When taken with another drug that is highly protein bound (e.g., Coumadin, which is a blood thinner), aspirin and Coumadin compete for these blood protein binding sites. This causes more of both drugs to be available to exert their actions. As a result, excessive bleeding is a risk. Some drugs change the chemistry of the urine, so that other drugs are excreted more or less quickly than normal.

There are references available which summarize many of the known drug interactions. The outcome of mixing drugs can also depend upon factors such as the amount of drug being taken, patient characteristics (e.g., age, gender and weight) and the diseases being treated. So, health professionals make a determination of the risk based on the nature of the drug interactions involved and the health status of the patient.

Drug/Food Interactions

Foods can interact with drugs just as drugs can, even though we may not consider foods as a potential drug interaction problem. A book written by one of the authors (GH), *Food and Drug Interactions — A Health Care Professional's Guide,* summarizes many of the known food and drug interactions.

Food/drug interactions can be even more difficult to predict than drug/drug interactions. Interactions between foods and drugs can depend heavily upon the amount of food being consumed. Therefore, some interactions may occur only rarely (e.g., with fad diets).

Other food and drug interactions are well known. For example, a category of drugs known as Monoamine Oxidase Inhibitors (MAOIs) can combine with alcoholic beverages and aged foods (e.g., cheeses) to cause a very dangerous reaction. The MAOIs are not used very often in contemporary medical practice, so this risk is much lower today than it has been in the past.

The most common "food" item involved in drug/food interactions is alcohol. Alcohol is most correctly viewed as a drug, but it is consumed in our culture as a food (which is part of the problem). Alcohol is a depressant drug. When mixed with any other drugs that are sedating, the outcome can be risky. Always check with a health professional before drinking an alcoholic beverage while taking any drug.

Vitamins are an odd category of products since they can be involved in either drug/drug interactions or drug/food interactions.

Vitamins can be categorized as "foods" or "drugs" depending upon the product being taken and the purpose for which it is being taken. Prescription vitamin products usually contain high doses of vitamins and minerals and are used for a drug purpose. Vitamins available without a prescription are intended to be used as dietary supplements (i.e., as a "food") and not as a "drug." Interactions can also occur between drugs and vitamins consumed in foods.

Finally, there are many foods which change the normal chemistry of the urine. For example, some drugs can make the urine more acidic or more alkaline. These changes can cause some drugs to be excreted more or less quickly than normal.

As with drug/drug interactions, it is important to check with a health professional about any foods you should avoid while taking medications.

Drug/Behavior Interactions

This category of drug interactions is the least considered of all, and refers to behaviors which should be avoided while taking drug products. For example, many pain medications cause sedation and can slow your reflexes. So, you should avoid driving while taking this kind of medication. As indicated above, always check with a health professional about activities to avoid while taking medications.

26. DRUG DOSING

"Drugs cannot be effective in the long run until
steps have been taken to correct the physiological
and social conditions originally responsible for the
disease that is to be treated."

— Rene Dubos

Drugs must be taken at the right time intervals and in appropriate ways in order to provide maximum benefits with fewest adverse effects. If drugs are taken too often, adverse effects may become more severe. If doses are not taken often enough, the condition being treated can become worse.

Some medications are taken only when needed, so that a single dose is effective. This is common with OTC products. For example, OTC eye drops may relieve redness with only one application unless a more serious eye problem exists. Other products must be taken on a regular schedule in order to be effective. Most prescription drugs are utilized in this way. For example, when using antibiotics it is important to take them on a regular schedule for the full period prescribed by the doctor to insure that the infection is eliminated. Otherwise, you may not get well.

Since each of us is different and can vary in our response to a particular medication, doses of medications must often be individualized. The dose must be large enough to achieve a desired therapeutic effect without causing too many adverse effects. This may depend upon the amount of side effects that you are willing to tolerate. Side effects tend to be mild and predictable with OTC products. Even so, some side effects are more tolerable than others.

Very often the dose selected is a compromise between an effective dose and a dose that produces intolerable adverse effects. Ordinarily, health professionals prescribe a dose that is appropriate for your age, weight and particular situation. This can be altered once it is known how you will react to the drug. Your tolerance for a medication is always unpredictable and is only known after therapy begins.

To appreciate why many drugs must be taken on a regular time schedule, it is again necessary to consider what happens to a drug after it is taken (see Outline 84). Drugs are usually absorbed into the

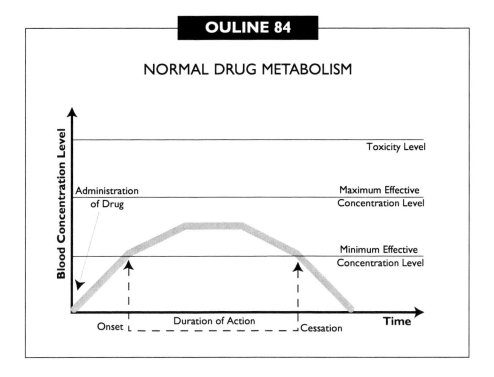

OULINE 84

NORMAL DRUG METABOLISM

bloodstream once they have been administered. Blood is the means by which oxygen, nutrients and other substances are transported to the various tissues and organs of the body. This is also the way in which drug molecules are transported throughout the body. The amount of the drug in the bloodstream is an indicator of the drug's activity. Greater drug activity normally occurs when there is a higher concentration of the drug in the blood stream. Less drug activity occurs with lower blood concentration levels.

After a drug is taken it usually takes a while before any effects are noticed. This is because it takes time for a sufficient quantity of drug to appear in the bloodstream. In time the body begins to metabolize the drug and excrete it, so that the blood concentration level drops.

Drug activity is not observed until the blood concentration level reaches the *minimum effective concentration level*. This is the level at which enough drug is in the body to result in drug effects. The *maximum effective concentration level* is the level at which maximum therapeutic benefits occur. Going beyond this level offers no additional benefits, but can result in more significant side effects. Additional dosing may cause the drug concentration to reach a *toxicity level* at which serious adverse drug effects occur.

The time required to reach the minimum effective concentration level is called the *onset of action time* or simply, *onset time*. The time period during which drug effects occur is called the *duration of action time*. This period ends once the blood concentration drops to the minimum effective concentration level.

Dosing schedules (for both prescription and nonprescription drugs) are used to reach the maximum effective concentration level without reaching the toxicity level. The range between the maximum effective concentration level and the toxicity level is called the *safety range* or *safety margin* and represents a safety buffer for therapy. This range can be relatively wide or relatively narrow depending upon the drug involved. For most OTC products the safety range is relatively wide. For prescription drugs it can be either wide or narrow. Narrow safety ranges can be a problem, since the maximum effective concentration level may be difficult to achieve without overshooting to the toxicity level.

Toxicity levels can also occur if you take too much of a medication. Americans tend to believe in the "More is Better Principle." This is a drug-taking philosophy that says, "If one tablet will do me some good . . . just think what several tablets will do!" People often ask pharmacists, "If I take 2 or 3 of these OTC tablets, wouldn't that be like taking a prescription drug?" Sometimes, perhaps, but it is a bad idea! OTC products are formulated to give you effective blood levels of the drug. There is no rational reason to exceed the dosage instructions on product labels. Doing so will not usually offer therapeutic benefits, but may greatly increase your risk for adverse effects or even toxicity. So, do not increase dosages without first checking with a pharmacist, nurse or physician.

Dosage schedules are designed to maintain effective drug levels over extended time periods. Outline 85 illustrates this concept. Each dose is taken often enough to prevent the drug from dropping below the minimum effective concentration level. This model illustrates the importance of taking medications on a regular schedule. If doses are taken too late (see Outline 86) the drug concentration will drop so low that it is no longer effective (i.e., below the minimum effective concentration level). If doses are taken too soon (see Outline 87), the concentration level will increase, resulting in side effects or toxicity.

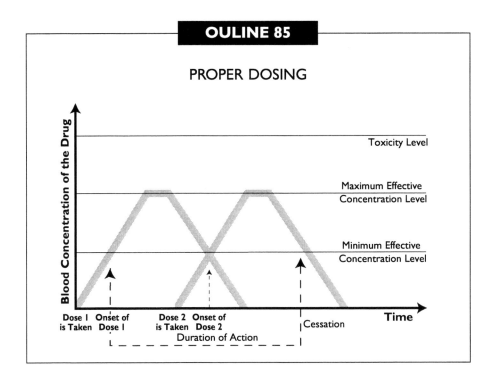

OULINE 85

PROPER DOSING

Blood Concentration of the Drug

Toxicity Level

Maximum Effective
Concentration Level

Minimum Effective
Concentration Level

Time

Dose 1   Onset of   Dose 2   Onset of
is Taken   Dose 1   is Taken   Dose 2   Cessation

Duration of Action

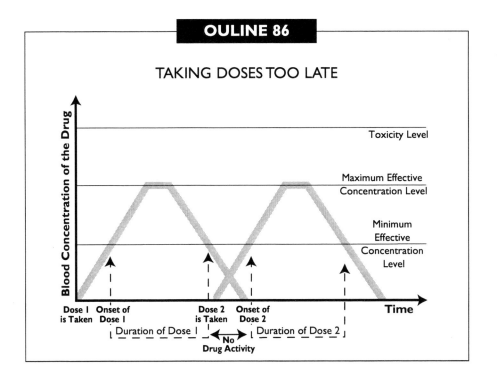

OULINE 86

TAKING DOSES TOO LATE

Blood Concentration of the Drug

Toxicity Level

Maximum Effective
Concentration Level

Minimum
Effective
Concentration
Level

Time

Dose 1   Onset of   Dose 2   Onset of
is Taken   Dose 1   is Taken   Dose 2

Duration of Dose 1   Duration of Dose 2

No
Drug Activity

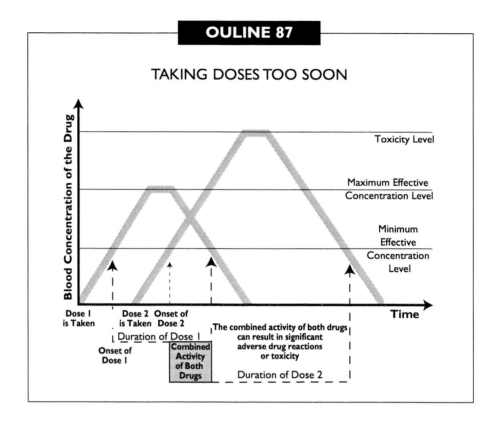

Common Label Instructions

The instructions provided on both OTC and prescription drug products seem quite simple. Yet, research by the authors indicates that even simple instructions are often misunderstood. For example, the instruction, "Take one tablet three times daily," has been interpreted in 20 different ways. As much as 6% of all consumers will not take the correct number of doses per day as indicated by simple label instructions. Finally, national studies have repeatedly shown that people take 50% of all medications incorrectly (i.e., both prescription and nonprescription drug products) regardless of the instructions used.

Outline 88 summarizes some common label instructions and what they usually mean. Variations can occur depending upon the actual medication involved. It is important to always ask your doctor, nurse or pharmacist exactly how your medications should be taken. Also find out what to do if you forget to take a dose.

OUTLINE 88

INTERPRETATION OF COMMON DRUG LABEL INSTRUCTIONS

Instruction	*Correct Interpretation (and comments)*
❦ Take 1 tablet daily.	It depends upon the medication being taken. Some medications should be taken in the morning while others are best taken in the evening. With some medications it really doesn't matter. Always check with a doctor, nurse or pharmacist about the best time to take medication.
❦ Take 1 tablet twice daily.	Take a tablet every 12 hours (unless advised otherwise by a health professional).
❦ Take 1 tablet every 12 hours.	Take a dose every 12 hours.
❦ Take 2 tablets daily.	Take 1 tablet every 12 hours (unless advised otherwise by a health professional).
❦ Take 1 tablet 3 times daily.	Take a tablet every 8 hours (unless advised otherwise by a health professional). For example, it may be taken with meals. However, meals are not normally spaced evenly apart (e.g., every 8 hours). The times span between breakfast and lunch may only be 2 to 4 hours. Taking medications this close together can result in adverse drug effects. The time span between supper and breakfast can be 10 to 14 hours. This may allow drug levels to drop to such low levels that the drug will stop working before another dose is taken.
❦ Take 1 tablet every 8 hours.	Take a dose every 8 hours.
❦ Take 3 tablets daily.	Take a dose every 8 hours (unless advised otherwise by a health professional).
❦ Take 1 tablet 4 times a day.	Take a dose every 6 hours (unless advised otherwise by a health professional).
❦ Take 1 tablet every 6 hours.	Take 1 tablet every 6 hours.
❦ Take 4 tablets daily	Take 1 tablet every 6 hours (unless advised otherwise by a health professional).

OUTLINE 89

GENERAL GUIDELINES FOR TAKING YOUR MEDICATIONS

❧ Take all medications exactly as directed by labeling or by a health professional.

❧ Doses must sometimes be individualized.
Package labeling on OTC products provides a normal, average dose that is appropriate for most individuals. If adverse effects are intolerable, or if the product does not seem to work, consult with a physician, nurse or pharmacist before changing the dose. Prescription dosing often requires a compromise between an effective dose and a dose that results in intolerable adverse effects. OTC products usually have a wide safety margin, so that this consideration is a minor one. It can become a significant problem if a dose is increased without first checking with a health professional.

❧ Doses should be large enough to achieve a desired therapeutic effect with minimal adverse effects.

❧ Your tolerance for a drug is unpredictable and is only known after you begin taking it.

❧ Children and elderly are much more susceptible to drug effects. Dosage alterations are often necessary with these individuals.

Long-Acting Products

There are many products on the market that are designed to provide drug effects over longer time periods. This is done so that you do not have to take as many doses. The fewer doses required each day, the easier it is to remember to take them.

There are actually several ways in which manufacturers can accomplish this. For various reasons many of these products do not work as perfectly as advertisements would have us believe. Even so, their duration of action is usually longer than standard product formulations.

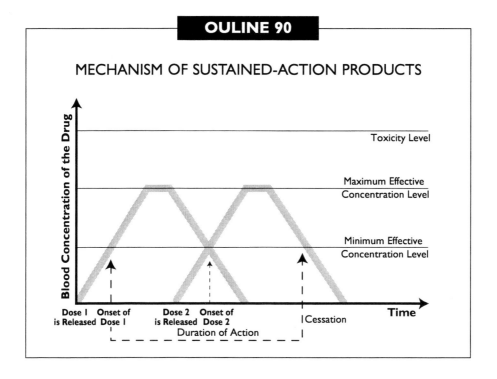

Slow Erosion Core Tablets

This type of product consists of a waxy substance which contains the drug within it. It dissolves slowly, and releases the drug as it dissolves. It usually has a slow onset of action, which can be undesirable if a faster onset of drug activity is needed.

Slow erosion core dissolves slowly

Tablet-Within-A-Tablet Design

This product involves a tablet within a tablet. The outer coat dissolves quickly so that an initial dose of the drug is released immediately. The inner core (the "erosion" core) is usually a waxy substance that erodes slowly. As it erodes, it slowly release the drug contained within it.

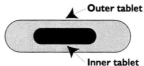

Laminated Tablets

These tablets involve two layers pressed together. One layer dissolves quickly, so that an initial dose of the drug is released immediately. The second layer is an erosion core that dissolves slowly. As it dissolves, it releases the drug contained within it.

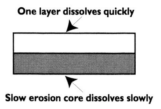

Pellets Within A Capsule or Tablet Design

Each of the little coated beads contains some of the drug. The beads are coated with a wax coating of varying thicknesses. As this wax coating dissolves, the drug is released. Beads with a thinner coating release the drug more quickly, while those with a thicker coating release the drug later.

Don't Crush These Tablets!

In order to make swallowing easier, people sometimes crush tablets, break them into halves or break capsules open to obtain the contents. Yet, there are many products for which this can be inappropriate or even dangerous.

Bad Tasting Medicines

Some medications taste quite bad. They may be coated with special coatings to mask the taste. If these products are broken or crushed they can truly become a "bitter pill to swallow."

Long-Acting Products ("sustained action", "timed-release", etc.)

Most long-acting tablets contain much more than an average normal dose. The sustained-action mechanism of the product allows the dose to be released over a period of time. Breaking or crushing these products may allow the entire contents of the product to be released into the body at one time

Drugs That Irritate Mucus Membranes (e.g, mouth, throat, etc.)

Some drug ingredients can irritate the mouth, throat and other areas. These products are coated to protect these delicate tissues. Breaking, chewing, or crushing these tablets will release the drug, resulting in irritation.

Enteric Coated Products

The special coating on these products prevents the drug from being released in the stomach. Instead, it is released in the intestines. Enteric coatings are often used on drugs which are irritating to the stomach. Breaking, chewing, or crushing the product will release the drug into the stomach so that the enteric protection is lost.

Liquid-Filled Products

Drugs are sometimes dissolved in a liquid and then placed in a gelatin capsule or tablet. This is done to insure that the drug is released in the stomach and not the mouth. If these products are broken, chewed or crushed, the drug will be released in the mouth.

Sublingual Tablets

These products are specially formulated to dissolve when placed under the tongue. Crushing, chewing or breaking the tablet interferes with the intended route of administration.

* * * * * *

Most nonprescription products will indicate on the package labeling if they are long-acting, enteric coated, etc. Pharmacists should inform you if a prescription medication has a special coating. If you have any doubts, ask a doctor, nurse or pharmacist.

Most products which are designed to be broken into halves will have a score line on them. Products which do not have a score line should not be broken, chewed or crushed without first consulting a health professional. Outline 91 summarizes a simple method for breaking tablets into halves.

OUTLINE 91

GUIDELINES FOR BREAKING TABLETS INTO HALVES

❦ **Never use a knife, or scissors, or hammer to break or cut tablets into halves.**

This will likely destroy too much tablet contents, so that less drug is taken than the doctor intended.

❦ **Some tablets have a line indented into them (the "score").**

These are products which can safely be broken into halves. The manufacturer includes the score line to weaken the tablet and facilitate breaking.

❦ **If a tablet does not have a "score" line in it, check with a health professional to see if it is permissible to break the tablet.**

Tablets without a score line are NOT usually intended to be broken.

❦ **A simple method for breaking tablets into halves (see illustration below):**

1. Place the tablet on a hard surface with the score line pointing toward you.
2. Place your fingers as indicated below.
3. Press down firmly and the tablet should break fairly evenly along the score line.

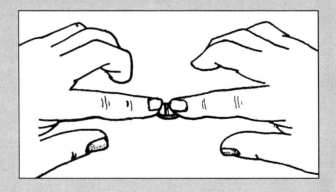

27. ADVERSE DRUG REACTIONS

"These pills can't be habit-forming, I've been taking them for years!"

—Shalit's Drugstore Observation, John Peers

Adverse effects are a major concern of drug therapy. Ironically,
we sometimes depend upon side effects as "proof" that a drug is actually working. For example, a narcotic pain medication may cause you
to feel drowsy and can create a feeling of euphoria (an increased sense
of well-being). We may depend more on these side effects as signs that
the medication is working than upon the relief of pain.

To varying degrees, we like to have tangible proof that our medications are working, but this can be misleading since the adverse
effects of drugs are often unrelated to the reasons for taking them.
Sometimes, in fact, we can become so preoccupied with side effects
that we fail to evaluate the drug in terms of how effectively it actually worked.

It is reasonable to anticipate that drugs in the future will have
fewer side effects. Consequently, if we continue to depend upon side
effects as a sign that our medications are working, we may falsely
conclude that the drug is not working. As a result, we may be tempted to increase the dose (and the chance for adverse drug effects), or to
stop taking the drug altogether.

Classification of Adverse Drug Effects

Adverse drug effects can result in many types of problems. These
reactions can affect virtually any cell, tissue, organ or organ system.
Many adverse effects are predictable once the pharmacology of the
drug is understood. Other adverse effects may be related to the dose,
duration of therapy or to patient sensitivity. Some of these factors are
difficult to predict.

Classification of adverse effects is difficult because there is no general agreement regarding drug reaction terminology. In fact, definitions for the terms which have been in use over the past few decades
seem to vary from reference to reference and even from one edition to
the next in the same reference.

In a very broad sense only two types of drug effects are observed: (1) desirable drug effects; and (2) undesirable drug effects. Usually, both types occur when a drug is taken. Outline 92 lists an example of a classification scheme for drug reactions. In order to appreciate the scheme, a consideration of the terms is helpful. In casual conversation many of these terms are used interchangeably, even though this is technically incorrect.

OUTLINE 92

CLASSIFICATION OF ADVERSE DRUG EFFECTS

Drug Reactions

❦ Adverse Drug Reactions (ADRs)
- Extension Effects
- Hypersensitivity (Allergies)
  - ◊ Anaphylaxis
  - ◊ Atopic Allergies
  - ◊ Delayed Reaction Allergies
  - ◊ Serum Sickness
- Idiosyncrasy
  - ◊ Hyperresponse (Overresponse or Abnormal Susceptibility)
  - ◊ Underresponse (Abnormal Tolerance)
  - ◊ Paradoxical Reaction
  - ◊ Miscellaneous

❦ Iatrogenesis
- Blood Disorders
- Dermatological (Skin) Effects
- Hepatic (Liver) Toxicity
- Renal (Kidney) Damage
- Teratogenic Effects (Birth Defects)

❦ Side Effects

Cumulation Effects

Tolerance

❦ Cross Tolerance

❦ Tachyphylaxis

Adverse Drug Effects refers to all undesirable reactions experienced while you are on therapy. It can include reactions that occur while you are on drug therapy, even though the drug may not have caused it.

Drug Reaction is an adverse effect which is definitely known to be caused by a drug. It also includes problems associated with drug administration (e.g., taking the wrong drug, the wrong dosage, or taking the drug at the wrong time). Drug reactions are not necessarily harmful and some serve useful purposes. For example, high doses of aspirin may result in ringing in the ears. Physicians sometimes use this as an indicator to tell them when a maximum dose level has been reached. In this manner, drug reactions may alert your doctor to drug toxicity or other problems.

Adverse drug reactions (ADRs) are undesirable, unintended and occur with an appropriately given drug at normal doses. Some authorities have included all adverse drug effects under this heading. However, the literature tends to reserve this term for reactions which are unusual, unexpected, and intolerable to the patient (e.g., hallucinations due to antihistamines). To properly apply this term it is necessary to establish that the drug actually caused the observed reaction. The fact that unusual symptoms occur while on drug therapy does not necessarily mean that the drug was responsible.

Extension effects are similar to those for which the drug was prescribed. However, they differ in the extent and degree of the effect produced. For example, a drug which is toxic to tumors is likely to be toxic to other tissues as well. Extension effects may occur for a number of reasons (e.g., idiosyncracy, hypersensitivity, overdosage, accumulation, a narrow range of safety between the maximum therapeutic level and the toxicity level).

Allergy (or hypersensitivity) is a commonly used term. People tend to refer to any undesirable drug reaction (including side effects) as an "allergy." Yet, the term allergy actually refers to a specific type of reaction. Allergy responses involve a reaction by the immune system and are usually unrelated to dosage or the normal pharmacology of the drug involved.

The human body has the ability to develop immunity against certain invading agents (e.g., drugs, viruses, bacteria, pollens). The terms "antigen" or "allergen" refer to any of these invading agents that can cause an immune response. Once exposed to an antigen, the body produces substances called "antibodies" that are capable of reacting with the antigen and destroying it. Unfortunately, this reaction between antigens and antibodies results in tissue injury, inflammation, and allergy symptoms (e.g., itching, rash, redness, shortness of breath, cardiovascular and respiratory arrest). The nature of the allergy response is somewhat puzzling from a biological perspective, since it usually causes far more damage to the person than to the antigen. It is also puzzling why some people are more affected by allergies than others (it is sometimes attributed to inheriting an abnormal immune system). A complete listing of all the different types of allergies is beyond the scope of the present discussion. However, a consideration of a few special types of allergies to drugs is appropriate:

1. *Anaphylaxis* is a sudden short-term allergic reaction that is widespread throughout the body. The reaction occurs close to blood cells and blood vessel tissues, and therefore involves the circulatory system. The cell and tissue damage that results in anaphylaxis release a number of substances into the bloodstream (e.g., histamine) which can cause severe circulatory collapse and respiratory difficulty. Anaphylaxis is not always fatal, but it is always serious. For example, some people have anaphylactic reactions to penicillin or bee stings.

2. *Serum sickness* is similar to anaphylaxis except that it develops over a period of time (e.g.,1 to 2 weeks). Because the process occurs slowly, the body is better able to adjust to it and medical intervention can more easily address problems as they arise. Symptoms may include fever, swollen lymph glands and joints, and skin reactions.

3. *Delayed reaction allergy* occurs when you are first exposed to a particular antigen (e.g., poison ivy, a drug, etc.). After this initial exposure, your body develops specialized cells which are capable of reacting with the antigen. A second exposure results in a delayed reaction. Symptoms may not appear for a day or two.

Idiosyncrasy (or *meta-reaction*) refers to an unexpected, abnormal or peculiar response to a drug that is different from the usual effects, and one that cannot be attributed to one of the other classes of adverse drug reactions. These tend to occur in a relatively small percentage of people who take the drug. As drug knowledge increases, many idiosyncratic reactions are actually found to be genetic problems which result in abnormal reactivity to drugs. This term is somewhat of a catch-all category. Like allergies, idiosyncratic reactions are not considered to be related to dose or normal pharmacology of the drug involved. These reactions occur unpredictably and only in a small number of patients who seem susceptible to them. They are thought to occur because the patient has some type of genetic deficiency which results in an abnormal metabolism of the drug. Four categories of idiosyncratic reactions have been proposed: (1) hyperresponse; (2) underresponse; (3) paradoxical reactions; and (4) a miscellaneous category

Hyperresponse (also called overresponse, abnormal susceptibility, hyperreactive response, hypersusceptibility or drug intolerance) refers to a reaction in which the effects of the drug are exaggerated and occur at lower doses than normal. For example, a dose of a tranquilizer that causes most people to become calm may cause a hyperresponder to become heavily sedated.

Underresponse (also called abnormal tolerance or hyporeactive response) refers to a situation in which a larger dose of the drug must be given in order to achieve the desired therapeutic response. In this case the individual is able to "tolerate" the drug much better than most people.

Paradoxical reactions involve responses which are opposite of the anticipated response. For example, some individuals may become extremely restless or even agitated when given certain tranquilizers. Another example involves overactive (hyperkinetic) children, who are given amphetamines to calm them down. In adults amphetamines act as powerful stimulants, but in children they may have just the opposite effect. Some groups of people are more likely to experience paradoxical reactions (e.g., children and elderly).

The fourth category of idiosyncratic reactions is a catch-all category which has no official name. It includes any unpredictable and unexplainable reactions which do not fit into one of the other categories of drug reactions.

Iatrogenesis is an unintentional outcome of therapy (i.e., professional therapy or self-care practices). By definition, iatrogenesis can also include the impact that a doctor's words or actions have on you. However, the term is usually reserved for more serious problems which arise as a consequence of drug use or therapy (e.g., surgery).

Side effects are undesirable and often unavoidable extensions of the pharmacologic effects of the drug. However, the term refers to effects that are pharmacologically different from the desired drug effects. For example, an antihistamine taken to dry a runny nose may also cause drowsiness. Drowsiness is a side effect. Side effects occur because drugs are capable of producing more than one kind of effect in the body. Many people inaccurately use the term "side effect" to refer to any undesirable drug reaction. Side effects tend to be predictable and minor. We can often tolerate them or adjust to them until therapy is discontinued.

Cumulation is not a drug reaction, per se. It occurs when the body fails to metabolize and excrete one dose of a drug as quickly as normal. Toxicity can occur if the dosage is not adjusted, since the drug will continue to accumulate with each successive dose.

Tolerance is a situation in which the individual must take more of the drug to achieve an effect that was previously achieved with smaller doses. This phenomenon is not well understood in all cases. In some cases the body develops an increased ability to inactivate or eliminate a drug before it has a chance to work. For example, some drugs stimulate the liver to increase production of the enzymes used to metabolize the drug. Tolerance develops for some drugs more than others. It may also develop for certain effects of a drug, but not for others. This is because different drug effects operate by different mechanisms. In any case, tolerance is not necessarily a problem. People may develop tolerance for side effects, even though the drug is still able to achieve its desired effects. For example, an individual may develop tolerance for the sedation caused by antihistamines, even though the antihistamine remains effective for treating allergy symptoms. Dosage increases are sometimes required if the desired effects are affected.

Cross tolerance refers to tolerance that occurs between chemically related drugs. For example, individuals who develop tolerance to alcohol may also exhibit tolerance for other central nervous system depressants (e.g., tranquilizers, sleeping pills, muscle relaxants, etc.).

Tachyphylaxis refers to a type of tolerance which develops very rapidly (e.g., after taking only a few doses).

Causes of Adverse Effects

Thousands of Americans are admitted each year to hospitals as a result of adverse drug reactions to both prescription and nonprescription drug products. The manner in which a drug is prescribed or used can result in the development of adverse drug reactions. We may misdiagnose our condition, select the wrong drug product for our needs or misuse the product which we have selected.

Doctors may overprescribe medications. In fact, many health professionals feel that prescriptions are being given well out of proportion to their actual needs. For example, some diseases are not positively affected by drug therapy, and the tendency to overprescribe may predispose us to unnecessary adverse effects.

The incidence and severity of adverse drug effects increases with larger or excessive doses. However, even when you are taking the correct dose of an appropriate drug, adverse effects can still occur.

Some adverse drug effects mimic or cause the symptoms of illnesses. When this happens, one is tempted to take even more drugs instead of simply removing the problem drug. A common example of this type of reaction involves the use of nasal sprays or drops to treat nasal congestion. When these products are used for more than three or four consecutive days, a drug reaction known as "rebound phenomenon" (*rhinitis medicamentosa*) may develop. The primary symptom of this adverse drug effect is nasal congestion! You may continue to use the drug to treat a problem that the drug is actually causing! Sometimes this condition can become so severe that physician intervention is required.

This type of problem occurs because drugs may alter delicate and sophisticated mechanisms that are necessary for normal body functioning. Drugs can affect healthy organs in negative ways or further impair diseased organs. Also, each of us may vary in our susceptibility to adverse drug effects.

As we have already described, multiple drug use (polypharmacy) creates special diagnostic problems with regard to adverse drug effects. To begin with, one drug can react with another. Also, it can be difficult to determine if a single drug is responsible for the adverse effect or if multiple drugs are causing them. Adverse effects can even occur after a drug has been discontinued. The decision to use a drug should consider the risks and benefits of therapy, which drug to select or whether a drug is actually indicated at all. The term "risk" as used here is a relative term. Risks are not necessarily serious. Rather, a "risk" exists anytime an effect of the drug can interfere with normal activities. The major problem with nonprescription drug products is that we tend not to view them as "drugs" at all. Therefore, their risk potentials tend to be ignored.

Some conditions may dictate that a particular medication must be used regardless of its potential for risks. In such cases we must make lifestyle adjustments in order to accommodate the drug.

In actuality, almost all drugs require some lifestyle adaptations.

Even nonprescription drug products usually involve minor alterations in lifestyle to accommodate the drug or the condition being treated. For example, in order to take a tablet two or three times a day . . . you must remember to take the doses.

There are no specific tests for a diagnosis of adverse drug effects. Health professionals rely upon a description of the symptoms and your drug history. Even this information may be insufficient to rule out all possible causes. There are many factors to be considered in addition to the basic properties of the drug. Some people simply cannot tolerate some drugs. Other factors include gender, weight, environmental exposures, ethnic background, and so on. In fact, any reaction is possible when the right patient is given the right drug. Other factors to consider include how and when the medication was taken, what other medications were taken during the same period and whether the symptom is actually an adverse drug effect or a symptom of some disease. Finally, adverse drug effects can occur if the drug has been stored improperly in the home.

One of the more recent categories of concern regarding possible causes of adverse drug reactions is an informational one. For example, studies indicate that many patients are inadequately informed about medicines in general, potential food and drug interactions, timing of doses, how long to take medications, correct dosages, proper use of medications, or even why the medication is actually being taken.

Other studies indicate that people may not interpret prescription or nonprescription labels correctly. About one-third of prescriptions are misused in a way that poses a serious health threat; 50% of people with high blood pressure stop their therapy within a year; about 75% of diabetics do not take their insulin injections within 30 minutes of the scheduled time; and one-fourth of epileptic patients take their medications incorrectly. About 40% of patients skip doses occasionally, half make mistakes in the timing of doses, about 10% take doses that are too high, and significant numbers simply change their doses. The family members of hospitalized patients have been known to change the drip rates on IVs because "He seems so much better today, that I just decided, let's give him more of that stuff!"

Problems arise because we may forget 50% of the instructions given to us by doctors. Even when the health problem is serious (e.g., heart attack), we frequently forget important information within a few weeks.

Approximately 39% of medicine-related hospital admissions

resulted from drug noncompliance. Often, people make their problems worse by not taking medications properly (or not taking them at all). As much as 9% of prescriptions are never filled, and since people are not always willing to admit this, this number is probably higher. Our unwillingness to admit to this problem is nothing new. Hippocrates complained 2400 years ago that "patients often lie when they state they have taken certain medications." At least more people seem willing to admit these days that they are not having their prescriptions filled. The important point to be made here is that we cannot benefit from medications that we choose not to take. This is not exactly an adverse drug reaction, but it would allow your health problem to become worse.

The Incidence of Adverse Effects

The exact incidence of adverse effects is not known, since there are no generally accepted guidelines for identifying an adverse drug effect. Rather, identification is typically based primarily on the judgment of the health professional involved. This lack of guidelines has made it very difficult to establish a direct link between a given drug and specific outcomes. A drug history and the appearance of unusual symptoms may or may not indicate adverse drug effects.

It is currently estimated that more than one-half of the U.S. population receives at least one prescription per year. The average medication user obtains about 8 prescriptions per year. The average doctor writes about 8,000 prescriptions per year and about 67% of all office visits to a physician will result in a prescription. Currently, more than 2 billion prescriptions are dispensed annually. So, our potential for adverse reactions is significant.

In 1986 the FDA received almost 54,000 reports of adverse drug reactions. This included 1,347 deaths and 4,481 hospitalizations. It is estimated that 20% of us experience adverse drug reactions. It appears that as many as 5% of hospital admissions are due to adverse drug reactions (and perhaps as high as 17% among elderly). It is not known how large this number really is, but some estimates suggest that it may be 500,000 hospital admissions annually. The projected costs of adverse drug reactions is quite high. For example, hospital admissions for such reactions alone may account for $3 billion in health care costs annually. This latter figure is an important one in a day and age of staggering health care costs, because it is largely preventable! Moreover, these figures do not include lost time from work, lost productivity, and other costs that directly affect patients and their families; nor does it reflect increases in insurance premiums and other costs that affect us indirectly. Think about how this money could be better spent if adverse drug reaction problems were largely prevented. However, the problem is not restricted to patient behaviors, since 28% of patients experience adverse drug reactions while hospitalized. Some of these, of course, are unavoidable consequences of using powerful drugs to treat serious diseases.

Elderly are a great concern for adverse drug reactions, since they tend to use more medications that younger age groups. In 1985 for example, it was estimated that adverse drug reactions resulted in 243,000 hospitalizations for the elderly. These numbers are even more striking considering that the elderly account for only about 17% of the population (depending upon how you choose to define "elderly"), yet they account for 39% of all hospitalizations and 51% of fatal drug reactions. Furthermore, drug use results in 32,000 hip fractures from falls each year, and is responsible for serious mental impairments. The price tag for all of these problems has been estimated to be as much as $7 billion annually.

Among the elderly as many as 50% of all prescriptions fail to produce desired results because they are used inappropriately, while 20% of all hospital admissions and 23% of nursing home admissions are related to the incorrect use of prescription medications. And, as many as 90% of patients may make errors in administering their medications.

It is also interesting to note that adverse drug reactions are sometimes reported by patients, when in actuality, no adverse reactions have taken place! This may also be due to a lack of uniform criteria for identifying adverse drug reactions. Certainly, most people lack information and understanding about adverse drug reactions. They frequently misuse terms and may refuse therapy based upon their misunderstanding. For example, people sometimes insist that they are "allergic" to a narcotic pain reliever because the drug causes nausea. Subsequently, they may refuse to take narcotic pain medications even when they are needed because of this "allergy." In this example, nausea is a side effect of therapy, but it is not an allergy. Because we are aware that we should not take medications to which we are allergic, our misuse of terms can actually cause us to make inappropriate decisions.

Factors Which Affect Drugs in the Body

There are many possible factors which can affect drug activity in the body. These and other factors must often be considered in order to determine appropriate dosing regimens. They may also explain why therapy sometimes fails to achieve desired results.

Administration Route

The route of administration can affect drug outcomes. To begin with, drugs are absorbed more effectively from some sites than others. For example, insulin cannot be taken orally since stomach acids destroy it. Some drugs cannot be absorbed through the skin, while others can. Drugs may work more quickly from some administration sites than others. For example, consider the onset time for these common administration sites:

Oral	30-60 minutes
Rectal	30-60 minutes
Injection into the muscle (IM)	10-20 minutes
Injection into a vein (IV)	Immediate

The onset times for oral medications may be much faster if the drug is taken on an empty stomach; or much slower if taken on a full stomach.

Administration Time

The time of day that a medication is taken can be important. Some drugs should be taken in the morning, or at other specific times of the day. For example, diuretics ("water pills") are usually taken in the morning (e.g., before 10 AM) in order to avoid the need to urinate during the night when it would interfere with sleep. It is usually best to take drugs that cause sedation at bedtime, so that they are less likely to interfere with normal daily activities. Always check with a doctor, nurse or pharmacist regarding how medications should be taken.

Age

Children and elderly tend to be more susceptible to the effects of drugs than other age groups. Dosage adjustments are often necessary in these groups.

Body Temperature

Body temperature is important for normal body functioning. In turn, drug activity can be affected by body temperatures. For example, higher body temperatures can sometimes result in increased metabolic rates, while cold temperatures can result in a lower metabolism. Changes in body temperature can also impact the distribution and excretion of drugs.

Circadian Rhythms

The term circadian comes from the Latin phrase *circa dias*, which means "about a day." It refers to fluctuations in body temperature, hormone levels and other body functions that occur throughout the day. Scientific interest in circadian rhythms is not new. However, the actual significance of these natural cycles is not well understood. These fluctuations occur in a rhythmic pattern that recycle approximately every 24 hours. Similar patterns have been observed in plants and other animals. It seems possible that two effects may occur regarding drug therapy: (1) Circadian rhythms may influence how well a drug can be handled by the body. For example, if the drug is taken at a time when the body's normal functioning levels are low, then it may not handle the drug as effectively. (2) The drug can affect your normal rhythm patterns. If so, you may be more likely to experience adverse drug effects.

Disease

Diseases or health problems can affect drug responses in the body. For example, liver conditions can affect the ability of the body to metabolize a drug, while kidney problems can interfere with the ability of the body to excrete the drug. The impact of health problems and physical status can vary considerably from individual to individual. Thus, each patient must be evaluated on an individual basis.

Environmental Factors

Environmental temperature extremes, changes in oxygen levels (e.g., high altitudes versus lower altitudes), exposure to micro-organisms and pollution are examples of environmental exposures. Since environmental factors can affect normal functioning of the body, they can also impact drug activity.

Fat Concentration in the Body

Some drugs are more highly stored in fat tissue. While stored, they do not exert their effects, nor are they available for distribution, metabolism, excretion or other biological processes. For example, consider Patient A (very thin) and Patient B (much body fat). If both are given a drug that is highly bound to fat, it is likely that Patient A will experience much more drug action than Patient B. Doctors sometimes give larger doses to heavy patients in order to saturate the fat binding sites in the body. This leaves more drug free to exert its effects. Some drugs are released slowly from fat binding sites as free drug in the bloodstream is eliminated from the body. In such a case the drug effects may be prolonged in individuals with greater body fat.

Gender

Females are more susceptible to the effects of some drugs than males for a number of possible reasons. Women tend to be smaller than men. Thus, on a weight basis, women may require smaller doses. Women tend to have higher percentages of fat tissue than men (e.g., breasts, and tissues that give women their smooth, curved appearances). It is sometimes necessary to alter the dosage for drugs that are more highly bound to fat tissues. However, the actual incidence of these differences appears to be very small.

The one gender factor that is a significant concern regarding drug use is pregnancy. Many drugs can cause birth defects if given at certain times during pregnancy. Teratogenicity is the term applied to the ability of drugs to cause birth defects. For many drugs it is simply not known whether or not birth defects will occur. Rather than take chances, medications should be avoided during pregnancy if at all possible.

Genetic Factors

Genetic differences may be involved in variations in drug response. For example, many idiosyncratic and allergy reactions are thought to be due to the genetic differences between people.

Nutritional State

Your nutritional state can have a significant bearing upon your overall health. In turn, this affects how well your body systems are able to function. For example, your nutritional state can contribute to the amount of enzymes you have available for metabolism. It can significantly affect blood chemistry. A poor nutritional state can deprive you of components needed for normal functioning. Fad diets (e.g., high protein diets) often result in serious health problems. These occur because the body must have a balance of fats, sugars and proteins. Since fats and sugars are lacking in high protein diets, the body will begin to break down proteins in order to synthesize the sugars and fats it needs. The by-products of this protein metabolism can result in dangerous alterations in normal blood chemistry. Death can occur if this problem is not resolved. Problems involving starvation include anorexia nervosa or bulimia.

Weight

Drug dosing is often based upon the weight of the individual. As an example of this concept, consider the following example:

> Patient A weighs 100 lbs, while Patient B weighs 200 lbs. Each is given a dose of 200 mg of a certain drug:
>
> For Patient A: 200 mg drug / 100 lbs = 2 mg / lb
>
> For Patient B: 200 mg drug / 200 lbs = 1 mg / lb

Thus, Patient A is receiving a much higher concentration of drug per pound of body weight than is Patient B.

The dosing of many drugs is much more complicated than this simple example. It is important not to extrapolate this concept to all drugs, since not all drug doses are based on weight. Always check with a health professional before altering doses of drugs.

CASE STUDY

DR. ROSE' S NOSE KNOWS

Dr. Rose was a resident physician for Uptown Hospital. He awakened one night with a stuffy nose from a head cold. Without turning on the light, he went to his dresser and reached for the nasal spray which he knew was there. He inhaled 2 sprays in each nostril. In a very short time, he felt quite ill.

He turned on the light and discovered that instead of the nasal decongestant that he thought he had taken, he had actually inhaled a potent narcotic pain reliever that is taken by nasal spray. The normal dose of pain reliever is only 1-2 sprays. Many patients do not tolerate 2 sprays because of the distressing side effects that can occur.

Dr. Rose was miserable for several hours and no longer takes his medications in the dark!

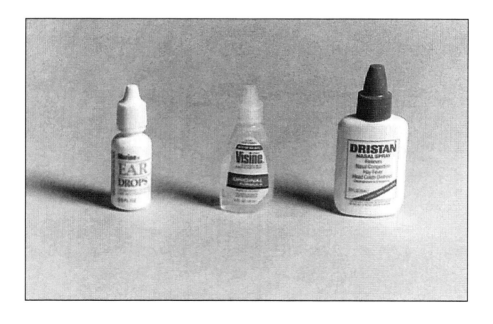

28. SMOKING

"It is now proved beyond doubt that smoking is one
of the leading causes of statistics."

— Knebel's Law — John Peers

Tobacco use is a major health problem in America. In fact, smoking is considered to be the greatest preventable cause of death in the U.S. today. Each year 450,000 Americans (the approximate population of the entire state of Wyoming) will die prematurely because they smoke. This is an average of more than 1,200 deaths each day. The annual costs of smoking in terms of deaths and disease are greater than that from all other diseases combined. The monetary costs to the U.S. economy from illness and premature death due to smoking has been estimated to be greater than $68 billion per year. (Our politicians should think about this the next time they discuss the health care cost issue!)

Approximately 28% of men and 24% of women are smokers. Statistically, smoking is more common among people with only a high school education or less, than those who are college educated. The World Health Organization reports that as many as 35% of women in wealthy nations smoke, compared to less than 10% in less wealthy nations.

Women smokers who use birth control pills are 39 times more likely to have a heart attack and 22 times more likely to have a stroke than women who use neither birth control pills or tobacco products. If you smoke you are four times more likely to die of a sudden heart problem and twice as likely to have a heart attack. Smokers are less likely to survive a heart attack if they have one and are more likely to die within one hour of the attack.

In addition to these sobering facts, smoking is clearly associated with a variety of health problems (e.g., cancer, heart disease, respiratory problems, sleeping problems, anxiety, depression, irritability, decreased fertility and increased rates of spontaneous abortion), and children born to women who smoked during pregnancy tend to have reduced birth weights. The supreme irony in all of this is that smoking is the most obvious preventable cause of death and disease in the United States.

Tobacco (Nicotiana tabacum) is a product of the New World. Historical evidence suggests that tobacco may have been cultivated in North and South America as early as 5000 B.C. Following the explorations by Columbus of the New World, tobacco products were introduced to Europe. The popularity of tobacco spread quickly and compulsive use was soon documented in virtually every society.

The number of smokers over the past 25 years (since the Surgeon General's first warning about the health consequences of smoking) has decreased and there are now reported to be approximately 40 million ex-smokers in the U.S. However, other statistics are less encouraging. For example, the number of adults who smoke heavily (i.e., 25 or more cigarettes each day) has actually increased. Also, the number of young people and women who smoke has increased. Quitting becomes more difficult over time and the withdrawal symptoms (see Outline 93) are more intense in individuals who smoke heavily.

OUTLINE 93

SIGNS AND SYMPTOMS ASSOCIATED WITH NICOTINE WITHDRAWAL

- Anxiety
- Cognitive impairment
- Craving for tobacco
- Difficulty concentrating
- Drowsiness
- Frustration
- Headache
- Hostility
- Restlessness

- Impatience
- Increased appetite
- Insomnia
- Irritability
- Light headedness
- Palpitations
- Psychomotor performance impairment

Outline 94 summarizes success rates for quitting, which increase with each attempt to stop. So, while only about 17% may succeed on their first attempt, the success rate increases to about 39% by the seventh attempt. At least one study has suggested that having a heart

OUTLINE 94

SUCCESS RATES FOR SMOKERS WHO ATTEMPT TO QUIT

By Attempt

Attempt	Succeed (%)	Fail (%)	Total Quitters (cumulative) (%)
1st try	17.2	82.8	17.2
2nd try	5.3	53.7	22.5
3rd try	4.8	38.1	27.3
4th - 6th try	4.8	26.6	32.1
7+ tries	6.6	1.3	38.7

By Methods

	Quit Rate (%) at 6 Months	Quit Rate (%) at 1 year
Acupuncture	18	27
Behavior modification programs	38 - 46	27 - 30
Educational programs	36	25
Group therapy	24	39
Hypnosis	25	38
Nicotine gum + Behavior modification or group therapy	35	29
Self-help literature	17	18

attack is the single most likely factor to cause a person to stop smoking – a sad commentary about what it takes to change this behavior.

Despite a desire to do so, people report difficulty quitting, which is usually attributed to *addiction*. Smoking is also associated with *recidivism* (an inability to refrain from smoking after a period of abstinence). Relapses are common and are probably influenced by the billions of dollars spent each year on the advertising and promotion of tobacco products.

Nicotine and Adverse Effects of Smoking

Nicotine is the primary chemical substance in tobacco. It is colorless but turns brown and acquires its characteristic odor when exposed to air. Its effects on the body are complex and not always predictable. For example, nicotine is associated with both stimulant and depressant effects. It is known to be rapidly absorbed into the bloodstream and reaches the brain within 8 seconds of inhalation. This prompt action is thought to explain the "rush" which smokers may experience soon after they begin to smoke and why their craving is quickly satisfied.

Nicotine and tobacco products are associated with a variety of adverse effects (see Outline 95). The risks are directly related to the number of cigarettes smoked per day. It is estimated, for example, that life expectancy is reduced by 5.5 minutes for every cigarette smoked. Male smokers (2 packs/day) have twice the death rate of nonsmokers. Women smokers who also take birth control pills are several times more likely to die from heart disease as compared with nonsmokers.

OUTLINE 95

NEGATIVE EFFECTS OF TOBACCO PRODUCTS

Increases in

- Angina pectoris (chest pain due to insufficient oxygen supply to the heart)
- Atherosclerosis
- Bad breath
- Blood clots
- Blood pressure
- Blood vessels damage
- Carbon monoxide in the blood

OUTLINE 95 cont'd

❦ Cholesterol deposits

❦ Chronic Obstructive Pulmonary Disease (COPD)

❦ Constriction of blood vessels.

❦ Costs (e.g., disease, death, time lost from work, health care costs)

❦ Heart attacks

❦ Heart damage

❦ Heart rate

❦ Heart rhythm disturbances

❦ LDLs (low-density lipoproteins, or the "unhealthy" blood lipids)

❦ Lung diseases (including cancer, bronchitis, and emphysema)

❦ Metabolic demands of the heart

❦ Motel room costs (i.e., smoking rooms are more difficult to clean)

❦ Oxygen demand by heart muscle

❦ "Silent" heart attacks

❦ Spasms of heart blood vessels

❦ Sudden deaths due to heart attacks

❦ Tobacco odor on clothes, furniture, carpets

Decreases in

❦ Ability of the blood to transport oxygen

❦ Ability of the lungs to clear accumulated debris and fluids

❦ Blood flow in blood vessels

❦ Blood flow to the heart

❦ Blood flow to kidneys

❦ Blood oxygen levels

❦ HDLs (high-density lipoproteins, or the "healthy" blood lipids)

❦ Immune function

❦ Normal enzymes function in the lungs

❦ Oxygen supply to the heart

❦ Protective mechanisms of the body (can result in increased risk of damage from environmental carcinogens, e.g., asbestos)

❦ Respiratory function

OUTLINE 95 cont'd

Cancers

- Bladder
- Breast
- Cervix
- Esophagus
- Kidney
- Larynx
- Lip

- Liver
- Lung
- Mouth
- Nose
- Oral
- Pancreas
- Pharynx

- Prostate
- Skin
- Stomach
- Throat
- Tongue
- Trachea
- Uterus

Other health problems made worse by tobacco use

- Allergies
- Angina Pectoris
- Circulatory Disease
- Diabetes

- High Blood Pressure
- Lung Disease
- Stomach and Intestinal Problems

Adverse effects of smokeless tobacco products

- Bad breath
- Cancer of the oral cavity
- Decreased ability to smell
- Decreased ability to taste
- Dependency (psychological and physiological)
- Discolored teeth
- Excessive wearing of tooth surfaces

- Gum irritation and other problems
- Lesions of the oral mucosa (e.g., leukoplakia)
- Slow healing of mouth cuts and lesions
- Tooth loss
- Toxicity of the fetus in pregnancy
- Toxicity of newborn infants

In addition to the harmful chemicals found in smoke and tobacco products (see Outline 96), the high temperature of inhaled smoke or pipestems can cause damage to the tissues of the lips and mouth. In turn, this damage can eventually result in cancer.

OUTLINE 96

HARMFUL CHEMICALS IN TOBACCO SMOKE

In addition to nicotine, there are at least 4,000 other harmful chemicals in tobacco smoke, including:

❧ Acetaldehyde	❧ Creols	❧ Nitrogen oxides
❧ Acrolein	❧ Cyanides	❧ Nitrosamines
❧ Alcohols	❧ Formaldehyds	❧ Particulate matter
❧ Aldehydes	❧ Hydrocarbons	❧ Radioactive compounds
❧ Ammonia	❧ Ketones	❧ Sulfur-containing compounds
❧ Carbon monoxide	❧ Metal ions	❧ Tar

Passive (Involuntary or Secondary) Smoke

In recent years health authorities have become concerned about involuntary exposure to smoke, which is an unavoidable risk to nonsmokers when smokers are nearby. The U.S. Environmental Protection Agency considers environmental tobacco smoke to be one of the most harmful indoor air pollutants. This is hardly surprising when you consider the 4,000 lung cancer deaths which occur each year due to involuntary smoke inhalation (it represents about 3% of the annual lung cancer death toll). Nonsmokers married to heavy smokers have 2 to 3 times the risk of lung cancer as compared to people married to nonsmokers. And, even these figures are small compared to the 50,000 deaths that occur each year as a result of exposure to passive smoke.

Even if you don't sit next to a smoker at work, you can still be at risk from smoke in building air. Separation of smokers from nonsmokers in the same environmental space reduces the risk of tobacco exposure, but does not eliminate it entirely. In fact, some efforts to separate smokers from nonsmokers is a bit absurd (e.g., your desk is nonsmoking, but the desk next to you is not; your table at the restaurant is nonsmoking, but the table next to you is not). In all too many public places, the "no smoking policy" consists of placing "no smoking" signs randomly about the room.

Passive smoke increases the risk for children to develop:

- ❦ Bronchitis
- ❦ Ear infections
- ❦ Chronic coughs
- ❦ Impaired lung functioning
- ❦ Colds
- ❦ Pneumonia

Not surprisingly, the children of smoking parents are more likely to develop respiratory diseases, have a higher incidence of hospitalizations (e.g., due to bronchitis and pneumonia) during their first year of life, experience more frequent coughs and phlegm and have more chronic ear infections.

Smoking and Your Children

Each day 3000 young people become regular smokers. This is more than the population of Stigler, Oklahoma, home town of two of the authors (GH and MM). During the lifetimes of these 3,000 new smokers, 30 will be murdered, 60 will die in traffic accidents and 750 will be killed by a smoking-related disease. Smoking rates had actually declined among high school seniors by the late 1970s. However, during the past 15 years these rates have begun to slowly climb again. Moreover, the age at which young people begin smoking has declined, especially for females, and about 90% of smokers are regular users by the time they are 21. The age at which young people begin smoking is important. The earlier smoking begins, the more difficult it is to

CASE STUDY

LESSONS FROM REAL LIFE — LARRY

Larry is a 44 year old male in relatively good health, except for the fact that he dips snuff (powdered tobacco). He averages 1 can of snuff per day. He has a "dip" in his mouth most of his waking hours. Larry often wakes up in the middle of the night "needing a dip." He puts some snuff in his mouth and goes back to bed.

HOW ABOUT YOU?
Is this really the kind of lifestyle that you want?

give up in adulthood. Additionally, starting early usually means heavy use by adulthood, and the likelihood of smoking-related diseases during adulthood is much greater.

Children often become aware of tobacco use behaviors very early in life. If their parents smoke, they are exposed early to the behaviors and products associated with tobacco use. They may be allowed to handle these materials ("Get my cigarettes for me, O.K.?"). Eventually, they may imitate tobacco use behaviors as a part of trying out "adult" behaviors. Since tobacco use is "acceptable" in our society, children learn early to accept it as well.

Teens typically face the pressure to smoke after the age of 12, when they begin to identify strongly with peers. They are also more likely to rebel against adult authority, take more risks and engage in behaviors which they perceive to be "adult."

Teens who smoke are more likely to have friends who smoke. And, teens report that pressure from their friends is often the reason that they started to use tobacco products. However, this does not mean that peer pressure is the actual cause of teen smoking. The family is a major influence on teen behaviors and attitudes long before peer pressure enters the picture. Teens are more likely to smoke when they come from a family in which a parent, older brother or sister also smokes.

Another influence of concern is tobacco advertising. Despite their protests of "innocence," it is reasonable to assume that tobacco advertising is associated with tobacco use by teens. Despite their claims that advertising is not a factor in smoking behaviors, the tobacco industry continues to invest heavily in advertising and promotion of their products.

Limiting smoking-related influences is not easy, since the messages that promote smoking are everywhere. Even so, there are steps that one can take to change the prevailing winds of smoke.

- Don't use tobacco products in the home.

- Don't smoke in front of your children.

- Don't keep tobacco products around for children to see and handle.

- Support school and community efforts to reduce tobacco use.

- Support efforts to create smoke-free environments at work and other public places.

Nicotine Dependence and Withdrawal

A 1987 Surgeon General's report ("Health Consequences of Smoking: Nicotine Addiction") helped to promote public opinion that nicotine addiction is the major cause of chemical dependence in America. There is little doubt that nicotine is one of the most widely used psychoactive drugs in the world. Furthermore, according to many health authorities the psychological and behavioral aspects of nicotine meet the criteria for drug dependence (see Outline 97).

OUTLINE 97

CRITERIA FOR CHEMICAL DEPENDENCE

❦ Compulsive use

   (i.e., a craving for continued use)

❦ Drug-reinforced behavior

❦ Physical dependence

❦ Pleasant effects (euphoria)

❦ Psychoactive effects

❦ Recurrent drug cravings

❦ Relapse following abstinence

❦ Stereotypical behavioral patterns

❦ Tolerance with continued use

❦ Use of the substance

   despite harmful effects

❦ Withdrawal symptoms

   (psychological and physical)

Evidence regarding dependency is based upon observations that smoking and intravenous administration of nicotine result in similar effects:

> ❦ Only tobacco that contains nicotine is accepted by users (i.e., products from which the nicotine has been removed is not acceptable);
>
> ❦ Tobacco use reflects elimination rates from the body; deprivation results in nicotine-seeking behavior; and
>
> ❦ Many successful smoking cessation programs include the use of nicotine-containing products as a smoking substitute.

Even though a "withdrawal syndrome" is reported during abstention, the types and severity of symptoms which people experience varies considerably, and can range from mild discomfort to incapacitation. The onset of withdrawal symptoms tends to occur quickly after deprivation and reaches peak levels within 24 to 48 hours. Symptoms then subside over a period of two weeks. The craving for tobacco products may decline in a matter of weeks or persist for years.

Part of the cigarette habit is a reflection of learned behaviors. For example, nicotine is a stimulant, yet, people often smoke to "relax." The act of lighting a cigarette becomes a cue for relaxing, even though the drug is incapable of producing this effect. This observation suggests that tobacco use involves a strong psychological dependence in addition to physical dependence, which can result in disturbing symptoms when a drug that has served as a coping mechanism for the individual is removed. The fact that the withdrawal experience can vary significantly from person to person raises questions about addiction as the only problem to overcome. Obviously, the use of tobacco products involves varying degrees of both physical and psychological dependence.

It is interesting to note that people may use "addiction" as an excuse for not quitting, since addiction is seen as something that is beyond our control. However, interpreting smoking as a psychological problem suggests that people could quit . . . if they would commit to it. Unfortunately, the psychological view is less comfortable to smokers, since it places responsibility for smoking (and quitting) squarely on the shoulders of the smoker. The physical view is perceived to be beyond the realm of individual control, which provides a more comfortable rationale.

Actually, it would be best if the term "addiction" was eliminated from the health jargon. Instead, the terms psychological dependence and physical dependence are much more accurate descriptors, encourage more honest and precise patient assessments and allow for more effective treatment regimens.

Drug Interactions

Tobacco products can result in a variety of drug-drug interactions (see Outline 98). Because of the large number of chemicals that occur in these products, it is difficult to determine exactly which chemicals are involved. The physiological consequences of tobacco use are myriad and complex, so that the potential for drug interactions is a significant concern.

OUTLINE 98

DRUG-DRUG INTERACTIONS: TOBACCO PRODUCTS DECREASE THE EFFECTIVENESS OF THE FOLLOWING DRUGS

Category	Examples
❦ Anti-anxiety	❦ Benzodiazepines (e.g., Valium, Librium, Xanax, Halcion)
❦ Anticoagulants ("blood thinners")	❦ heparin ❦ warfarin
❦ Anti-depressants	❦ Phenothiazines (e.g., Thorazine) ❦ Tricyclics (e.g., Elavil)
❦ Asthma medications	❦ Theophylline (e.g., TheoDur, Sustaire, Elixophyllin)
❦ Diabetic medications	❦ Insulin
❦ Diuretics ("water pills")	❦ furosemide (e.g., Lasix) ❦ hydrochlorothiazide (e.g., Hydrodiuril)
❦ Heart medications	❦ beta blockers (e.g. Inderal, Visken) ❦ calcium channel blockers
❦ Hormones	❦ estrogen (e.g., Premarin)
❦ Pain medications	❦ acetaminophen ❦ naproxn (e.g., Aleve) ❦ aspirin ❦ pentazocine (e.g., Talwin) ❦ ibuprofen (e.g., Motrin) ❦ propoxyphene (e.g., Darvon) ❦ morphine
❦ Ulcer medications	❦ H2 Blockers (e.g., Tagamet, Axid, Zantac)

Alternatives to Smoking

Smokers may believe that changing to some other tobacco product reduces the risks associated with smoking. Yet, in most cases this decision simply involves exchanging one set of problems for others.

Pipe smoking, for example, may be even more dangerous than cigarettes. Pipe smokers may actually inhale more undesirable substances than cigarette smokers and pipes may hold a larger volume of tobacco which smolders for long periods.

People sometimes make a "good faith" effort to reduce their tobacco use by turning to low tar products. Unfortunately, they are probably fooling themselves. And in fact, they may be exposing themselves to even greater harm. Because less nicotine is being delivered with each inhalation, the smoker may inhale more deeply, or may increase the number of cigarettes being smoked in order to satisfy the craving. Tar and nicotine are not the only harmful chemicals in tobacco products. Increasing the number of cigarettes smoked may deliver the same amount of tar and nicotine, but exposes the individual to even larger amounts of the other harmful chemicals in cigarettes.

Smokeless tobacco products are also associated with significant health risks (see Outline 95). In particular, use of these products (e.g., snuff and chewing tobacco) increases the risk for oral cancers.

The inescapable reality is this: NO tobacco products are safe!

Tobacco Cessation Programs

Over the years, people have tried to quit their tobacco habit using a variety of techniques. Their "addiction" is only part of the problem in such efforts. There are also behaviors associated with tobacco use which become an integral part of the tobacco use lifestyle. So the key to ceasing tobacco use is to change the behaviors and withdraw from the drug.

"Kicking the habit" can be a difficult task. It may be necessary to make numerous attempts. And, many tobacco users find that they never completely lose the desire. Yet, it is worth the effort when the health benefits for self and significant others are considered, not to mention the economic benefits, which can be considerable.

OUTLINE 99

TIPS FOR HELPING YOU TO "KICK THE HABIT"

Analyze Your Behavior Patterns

- When do you use the drug?
- How do you feel when you use it?
- Make a list of the reasons that you want to quit (Put it where you will see it often).
- Calculate the money you would save by not smoking (use it to purchase a "reward").
- Deprogram yourself: close your eyes, take 10 breaths, and think, "calm."

Create Barriers

- Wrap your cigarettes in aluminum foil. This serves to interrupt the behavior in order to get to them.
- Get rid of your smoking accessories . . . they're your reminders to smoke (e.g., ashtrays, unopened cigarette packs, matches, lighters, etc.). Stay busy and ignore the reminders. Doodle with paperweights, pencils, toothpicks, coins as a substitute for these old accessories.
- Engage in activities that interfere with tobacco use. (e.g., gardening, washing the car, rake leaves, ride a bike, give yourself a manicure, wash your hands, take a shower, meditate).
- Identify and avoid "triggers" that you normally associate with tobacco use.

Gradually Reduce the Amount of Drug Being Used

- Decide on a date to stop smoking . . . and stick to it! Most successful stoppers are successful because they stopped instantly. Coordinate the quit date with some positive life event.

Behavior and Activity Substitutes

- Identify substitute behaviors that you can do when you have the urge to use tobacco products:

Brush your teeth (after meals)   Give yourself a manicure

OUTLINE 99 cont'd

deep breathing	go for a walk
doodle	jog
drink a glass of water	meditate
exercise	play solitaire
fiddle with something	rake leaves
(e.g., pencil, paper clip, marble,	reading
worry beads)	ride a bike
gardening	take a shower
get involved in a hobby (e.g., needlecraft)	wash the car
get up and move around	wash your hands

❧ Become more active.

This will help you to relax. Organize activities with colleagues. Exercise and activity help to boost energy levels.

❧ Change your routine. Avoid going past the places where you normally purchase tobacco products. Visit different places at lunch. The habits of one part of your daily routine reinforce the habits of others. Break the cycles. People often do not realize the degree to which smoking becomes a part of their daily routines. Pay attention to these associations. Change behaviors and routines.

❧ Accentuate pleasure and relaxation. Avoid negative feelings. Substitute other activities. Consider alternate coping strategies (e.g., group therapy, counseling).

❧ Avoid alcohol (it can weaken your determination to quit).

❧ Avoid other people who smoke.

❧ Avoid smoking environments. Go to places which you do NOT associate with tobacco use (e.g., libraries, museums, movies, stores). Sit in nonsmoking sections of restaurants, public buildings and transportation.

❧ Exercise

❧ Keep your hands busy.

❧ Listen to music (sing along, dance, get involved).

❧ Talk to yourself: "This urge will pass in a few minutes!"

❧ Relaxation Techniques:

Breathing Exercise

Take a long deep breath, count to ten, then release it. Repeat this five times. See how relaxed you feel.

OUTLINE 99 cont'd

Relaxed Concentration

Allow about 20 minutes twice a day. Close your eyes, relax your muscles, concentrate on a key word (e.g., "calm"). Notice how you can condition yourself to relax.

🐛 Take advantage of social support. Call on friends, family or others to be a support for you during the time that you are trying to quit. Let people know that you have stopped.

🐛 "Out damned thought!" Snap your fingers and command yourself to get rid of thought about tobacco use. Think about clean air and good health.

🐛 If you are driving, stop the car and walk around just a bit.

Oral Substitutes

🐛 Identify alternative items that you could put in your mouth instead of tobacco:

candy (sugar free)

fruits

gum (sugar free)

mints

vegetables

toothpicks (flavored)

Make sure the alternative is healthy one (e.g., non-fat, low-calorie). These might include flavored toothpicks, sugar-free gum or mints, fresh fruits or vegetables.

🐛 Drink lots of water. Keep a glass of water at hand while you work. Sip it on a regular basis.

🐛 Monitor your diet. People do NOT necessarily gain weight when they quit. If this is a concern for you, monitor your diet. You may need to change your dietary habits. However, weight gain is a poor excuse to smoke.

🐛 Change other habits in addition to smoking (e.g., give up coffee for a while if you tend to smoke while drinking coffee; move away from the table if you tend to smoke after meals at the table; brush your teeth after meals).

🐛 Chew gum

🐛 Eat fruit or raw vegetables (e.g., carrots, celery).

🐛 Suck on a piece of sugar-free candy.

OUTLINE 99 cont'd

Measuring Progress

🐾 It's "OK" to experience the signs that you are "kicking the habit" (e.g., dizziness, irritability, headaches, sore throats, etc.). Don't worry! These reactions are nor mal and will eventually go away. Think of them as signs of progress.

🐾 Reward yourself. Use the money you're saving to treat yourself to something special every now and then (e.g., new clothes, a trip, dinner at a nice restaurant).

🐾 Avoid "crisis intervention" with "just one cigarette." People tend to use cigarettes at a time when they want to relax. When the daily routine becomes stressful, they are conditioned to automatically reach for a cigarette. It's easy to believe the "perhaps just one . . ." myth. One cigarette leads to another, and another, and another. Go for a walk instead. Consider alternate coping strategies (e.g., support groups, counseling).

🐾 One day at a time. Each day without tobacco products reinforces your new good health habit.

🐾 Take advantage of social acceptance. Perceptions of smokers have changed. Involvement in healthy activities and hobbies has a much higher social value.

🐾 Avoid "failure" branding. If you have a setback, do not give up altogether. A mistake doesn't warrant the "abuse" of returning to bad habits. Just keep trying.

🐾 Encourage yourself: "I am in charge! I don't have to give in!"

🐾 Positive reinforcement: tell yourself what you've accomplished and that you don't want to be a tobacco user.

🐾 Reward yourself for not smoking (e.g., buy a record, sleep in late).

Kicking the habit — dealing with failures

🐾 "Cold turkey" is difficult (Give yourself permission to continue trying).

🐾 Acknowledge your setbacks. OK, you gave in. Don't give up. Research indicates that the more times you "quit," the more likely you are to eventually be successful.

🐾 Avoid Guilt. No point "kicking" yourself. A setback does not mean that you can't stop. Continue to tell yourself that you are quitting. Continue to reinforce nonsmoking behaviors.

🐾 Identify and avoid triggers that caused your setback.

🐾 Identify Successful Coping Skills

🐾 Contract with yourself. Write and sign a contract with yourself to become a non smoker. It will help to reinforce your decision. If possible, share this with others.

OUTLINE 100

IMMEDIATE BENEFITS OF "KICKING THE HABIT"

Increased / Improved	Decreased / Reduced:
❦ Ability to Perform Physical Work	❦ Ashtrays to empty
❦ Breath Odor	❦ Burn holes around the house
❦ Breathing	❦ Carbon monoxide levels
❦ Employment Opportunities	❦ Grocery bills
❦ Energy levels	❦ Heart rate
❦ Extra time	❦ Insurance premiums
❦ Heart and circulation functioning	❦ Insurance risk
❦ Lung functioning	❦ Passive smoke to those around you
❦ Money savings	❦ Perspiration
❦ Odor-free environments	❦ Risk of death by fire (by 50%)
❦ Sense of smell	❦ Sleep requirements
❦ Sense of taste	❦ Social pressures
❦ Tolerance for exercise	❦ Tobacco stains (e.g., teeth and fingers)

Sometimes professional help is needed. There are mental health professionals available (e.g., psychologists, counselors) and programs which address smoking cessation. Even so, the ultimate outcome must be a product of your determination and commitment.

Nicotine patches and gum have proven successful for some people, even though this means that they are still using the drug. Just remember: the idea is to eventually quit, rather then merely switching to another form of nicotine.

OUTLINE 101

AVOIDING WEIGHT GAIN WHEN YOU STOP SMOKING

The After Dinner Smoke Routine

Many people get into the habit of having a smoke after dinner. They may even rush through dinner to reach this part of their culinary ritual. When they stop smoking, these individuals may eat more, spend more time at the table, or add high-caloric deserts to their normal meal.

- Slow Down while Eating
- Cut your food into smaller pieces. This gives you more food to chew.
- Put your fork down between each mouthful. Then completely chew and swallow before refilling your fork.
- Sip ice water frequently during the meal.
- Extend the time between bites.
- Slow down and enjoy the meal (e.g., the taste and texture of the meal).
- Avoid Second Helpings
- Eat low-calorie fruits or more simple desserts (e.g., plain cake, cookies) instead of rich desserts.
- Get up from the table as soon as you are finished. Don't linger at the table and be tempted by the availability of second helpings.
- Serve beverages in another area in order to move away from the table.
- Brush teeth or eat an artificially sweetened mint immediately after dinner as a signal that the meal is "finished."
- If coffee is part of the routine, switch to another beverage.

Oral Cravings

Tobacco users often have a craving to have something in their mouth. This can result in frequent nibbling, especially sweets.

- Carry sugarless gum and artificially sweetened mints to use as substitutes.
- Give your hands something to do, rather than reaching for food (e.g., crafts, home repairs, gardening, working crossword puzzles, etc.).

OUTLINE 101 cont'd

❦ Opt for snacks that require some "work" (e.g., nuts or seeds that must be cracked; fruits that must be peeled). This will tend to reduce the total amount you consume.

The Evening Snack as a Replacement for Tobacco Products

❦ Opt for low-calorie snacks (e.g., raw vegetables, fruits). These might be served with low-calorie cottage cheese or other dips.

❦ Opt for plain crackers, bread sticks, pretzels, unbuttered popcorn or dry cereals; just watch out for how much you eat.

❦ Reduce visibility/availability of high-calorie snacks. Place them in storage areas where they require more effort to obtain, and where they are not so readily visible.

❦ Delay the snack for a predetermined time when you feel the urge. By reinforcing this delay, you can reduce your tendency to automatically reach for snacks.

❦ Substitute other activities for the snack. Control your impulse to eat just for the sake of eating. We often snack when we are not really even hungry!

❦ Portion snacks. Resist snack offers when visiting other households.

❦ Delay the evening meal. By moving dinner to a later time, you may reduce the desire for a snack closer to bedtime.

Social Situations that Encourage Eating and Tobacco Use

Coffee breaks, cocktail parties, sporting events, and other situations can become "triggers" that encourage eating and tobacco use behaviors.

❦ Break the coffee break routine:

❦ Take walks, read or engage in some other activity.

❦ Avoid foods and beverages which encourage tobacco use behaviors. We tend to associate coffee drinking with tobacco use. So, substitute a "neutral" food or beverage in the place of coffee (e.g., milk, fruits, vegetables, juices, diet drinks).

❦ Be an active participant in sporting and social events, rather than a mere passive observer. Observers are more likely to eat or use tobacco products to "keep busy" during periods of inactivity.

OUTLINE 102

EXAMPLES OF SELF-HELP SMOKING CESSATION GUIDES

- ❦ Self-Testing Kit
  National Clearing House for Smoking and Health
  (404) 441-5556

- ❦ You've Kicked the Smoking Habit
  National Cancer Institute
  (800) 4-CANCER

- ❦ I Quit Kit
  American Cancer Society
  (404) 320-3333

- ❦ Freedom From Smoking in 20 Days
  American Lung Association
  (212) 315-8700

- ❦ The Joy of Quitting
  by Burton and Wohls
  At your local library or bookstore

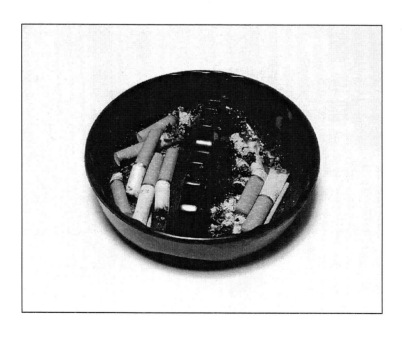

CASE STUDY

LESSONS FROM REAL LIFE — HERSHEL

Hershel is a 46 year old postal office supervisor. He is married with three grown children and six grandchildren. Hershel was a star athlete in high school. Although he still loves athletics, he now leads a sedentary lifestyle, except for one time each month when the whole family gets together for a softball game.

Hershel's medical plan enables him to have a physical exam each year. He was previously diagnosed with high blood pressure, which is under reasonably good control (as long as he remembers to take his medications).

Hershel smokes 2 to 3 packs of cigarettes each day and knows he should stop. He has attempted to go "cold turkey" on a number of occasions, but has more or less given up and switched to a "low tar" brand of cigarettes.

Hershel collapsed one day while running after a grounder at one of the family softball games. Fortunately, his daughter had been trained in cardiopulmonary rescusitation (CPR) and was able to administer emergency treatment until an ambulance could reach the scene.

After a series of tests, Hershel was diagnosed with cardiac insufficiency, and instructed to follow a strict recovery program. More recently he has once again begun to smoke and is not following his exercise program.

It is very possible that his next heart episode . . . could be his last!

HOW ABOUT YOU?

Are you still smoking despite your awareness that it poses a serious health risk? Is smoking really worth risking your longevity? There will never be a better time (next week, tomorrow...) to make a commitment to stop than now — this instant!

29. CAFFEINE

"Are you a part of the problem, or a part of the solution?"

— Robert Anthony

The use of caffeine as a stimulant is as old as recorded history. Found in plants and distributed throughout the world, scholars believe that even primitive man made beverages that contained caffeine. One legend credits the discovery of the merits of caffeine to a Middle Eastern convent. Shepherds noticed that goats frisked about all night long instead of sleeping after eating the berries of coffee plants. Convent officials recognized the potential benefits to those who were to endure long nights of prayer and instructed the shepherds to gather the berries so that they could be brewed into a beverage.

Contemporary man is equally enamored with the qualities of caffeine (the shepherds have been replaced by Juan Valdez and his mule). Its popularity is based on the belief that caffeine can offset drowsiness, elevate mood, relieve fatigue and increase our capacity for work.

Surveys suggest that about 80% of the people in the world consume caffeine on a regular basis. In the U.S., each of us consumes about 200 mg daily. Unlike most problem drugs, caffeine does not typically produce intense feeling of euphoria (an exaggerated sense of well-being), but it can result in some feelings of well-being. It also may result in negative feelings (e.g., impatience, restlessness, anxiety) in people who do not use it regularly. Caffeine dependence can occur after daily consumption of more than 400 mg for one or two weeks.

Outline 103 summarizes some of the biological activities of caffeine. There is good evidence to suggest that it can increase one's capacity for sustained intellectual effort and decrease reaction time. Thus, people engaged in typing tasks, for example, may work faster and with fewer errors. Caffeine may also improve your capacity for muscular work. For example, it has been found to improve the racing performance of cross-country skiers, especially at high altitudes. However, recently acquired skills involving delicate muscle coordina-

OUTLINE 103

BIOLOGICAL EFFECTS OF CAFFEINE

Central Nervous System (CNS)

🐜 Anxiety

🐜 Clearer and more rapid flow of thought

🐜 Excitement

🐜 Headache

🐜 Inability to sleep

🐜 Lghtheadedness

🐜 Muscle tremors

🐜 Nervousness

🐜 Relief of drowsiness and fatigue

🐜 Restlessness

🐜 Ringing in the ears

🐜 Tremors

Heart

🐜 Increased heart rates

🐜 Increase in blood pressure

🐜 Irregular heart beat

🐜 Palpitations (beating sensation in the chest)

Kidneys

🐜 Increased urination (loss of water and electrolytes)

Lungs

🐜 Relaxation of lung passages (promotes ease of breathing)

Stomach and Intestines

🐜 Diarrhea

🐜 Increased output of stomach acid

🐜 Nausea/vomiting

🐜 Stomach irritation

🐜 Stomach pain

tion and accurate timing (e.g., piano playing) may not be improved by caffeine and can even be affected in negative ways. Also, math skills may be impaired. So, while caffeine may enhance certain types of mental functioning (e.g., typing skills), it should not be viewed as a panacea for solving mental alertness problems in general. Moreover, any "benefits" from the use of caffeine may actually be due to alleviation of caffeine withdrawal rather than from the drug itself.

One commonly recognized side-effect of caffeine is increased frequency of urination. Studies indicate, for example, that caffeine and related drugs increase the production of urine and the loss of both water and electrolytes. Caffeine also stimulates the output of stomach acid and enzymes which irritate the stomach. Moreover, the potential for stomach irritation is not due solely to caffeine. In fact, decaffeinated coffee is only slightly better on your stomach than regular coffee. So, if you are having "tummy problems," you are well-advised to give up coffee altogether.

Caffeine is found in many OTC products, as well as many popular beverages and foods. It is also used as a stimulant to offset the sedative effects of antihistamines, but does nothing for colds, per se. Some aspirin products include caffeine to enhance pain relief, although its effectiveness in this regard is questionable. Caffeine may offer some additional benefits for certain types of headaches and pain (e.g., migraine). However, here again its effectiveness is quite limited. And finally, the amount of caffeine in many OTC products is too low to provide any real benefits even if such an effect could be established.

Caffeine is included in some weight control products to curb appetite and is also added to both weight control and menstrual products for its mild diuretic activity. However, the use of caffeine to reduce appetite is questionable at best. Eating a balanced diet and adopting an appropriate exercise routine is a much more effective, healthy and sensible way to lose weight. And, the effectiveness of caffeine as a diuretic is also limited as compared to prescription diuretics. With regard to PMS and menstral discomfort, the naprosyn (e.g., Aleve), ibuprofen (Motrin IB) and even aspirin products will provide far more relief. If higher dosages than those found on OTC product labels are needed to produce a particular effect, patients are strongly advised to check with their doctor or pharmacist about effective, but safe, dosages.

Finally, caffeine is included in stimulant products to offset fatigue, and supposedly, to improve mental alertness. Although caffeine can reduce drowsiness and fatigue and may promote a more rapid and clear flow of thought, it should not be used to prevent or offset normal sleep, since this would have a disruptive impact on general health and energy levels. Unfortunately, this is one of its most common uses.

OUTLINE 104

WARNINGS AND PRECAUTIONS ABOUT CAFFEINE CONSUMPTION

❦ **Oral contraceptives ("birth control pills") and cimetidine (Tagamet) can interfere with the metabolism of caffeine in the body.**
This can result in increased effects of caffeine in the body, including side effects.

❦ **Smoking**
Can increase elimination of caffeine from the body.   If the individual suddenly stops smoking without also changing heavy caffeine consumption habits, increased side effects can occur.

❦ **Pregnancy**
Safety during pregnancy has not been established. Pregnant women are advised to minimize caffeine intake, or avoid it all together.
There have been some weak correlations in studies between caffeine intake and low birth weight, premature deliveries, etc.

❦ **Breastfeeding**
Caffeine is excreted in breast milk.

❦ **Diabetics**
Caffeine use can result in higher blood sugar levels. This can be a particular problem for diabetics.

❦ **Anxiety Neurosis**
Large doses of caffeine may produce symptoms which mimic a condition known as anxiety neurosis (e.g., tremors, muscle twitching, sensory disturbances (e.g., vision, hearing, etc.), irritability, flushing, palpitations, irregular heart beats, rapid breathing, stomach disturbances, increased urination).

❦ **Withdrawal**
Can occur if the individual suddenly stops consuming caffeine after regular, continued use (e.g., 500 mg or more per day for an extended time period). It is likely to occur in heavy coffee drinkers who suddenly stop drinking coffee, or who suddenly switch to decaffeinated

---

OUTLINE 104 cont'd

products. Symptoms include headache, anxiety and muscle tension. Symptoms will usually start 12 to 18 hours after the last caffeine ingestion.

❦ Death has occurred with oral doses of 5 grams (5000 mg) or more.

❦ Check with your doctor, nurse or pharmacist before taking if:
You are allergic to caffeine.
You have any of the following conditions:
-heart problems
-kidney problems
-depression or other psychological disturbances
-pregnancy

Many people, for example, use caffeine in an effort to stay up all night (e.g., studying for examinations or driving late at night). Use in this manner can result in more problems than benefits, both because of the loss of normal sleep and as a result of adverse effects of the drug.

Consumption of 250 mg over time can result in a variety of symptoms (e.g., restlessness, nervousness, excitement, insomnia, muscle twitching, rambling flow of thought). Moreover, this can also result in problems involving the heart, stomach, intestines and can aggravate panic disorder. While caffeine does not pose the health threats of smoking or alcohol, it is clear that most Americans consume far more of this drug than they should. Ultimately, heavy caffeine users might question why continue to consume a substance in large quantities that will cause an increase in stress levels?

Caffeine withdrawal is not a particularly serious health problem, but it does serve to reinforce consumption behaviors. The most common withdrawal symptom is headache, but fatigue, lethargy and anxiety are also reported. These symptoms can appear within 12 to 24 hours after the last dose of caffeine. So, for example, if you drink a coke at 5 p.m., you may begin to experience withdrawal by the next morning. However, this is no problem, since we usually begin the day with a cup of coffee.

OUTLINE 105

CAFFEINE CONTENT OF SOME COMMON BEVERAGES

Beverage	Caffeine Content (mg/100 ml)
Carbonated Beverages	
Diet Mr. Pibb	16
Mello Yello	15
Mountain Dew	13
Diet Mountain Dew	13
Coca Cola	13
Diet Coca Cola	13
Cherry Coke	13
Diet Cherry Coke	13
Tab	13
Dr. Pepper	11
Diet Dr. Pepper	11
Mr. Pibb	11
Cherry Pepsi	11
Pepsi-Cola	10
Diet Pepsi-Cola	10
Pepsi Lite	10
Diet Cherry Pepsi	10
RC Cola	9
Diet RC	9
Coffee	
Drip	97
Percolated	73
Instant	44
Decaffeinated Coffee:	
Nescafe	3.30 - 5.60
Infused	1.00 - 3.00
Sanka	1.80
Instant	0.50 - 1.50
Decaf	0.90
Tea (bagged):	
Black (5 minute brew)	33
Black (1 minute brew)	20
Tea (loose):	
Black (5 minute brew)	29
Green (5 minute brew)	25
Green (Japan, 5 minute brew)	15
Other:	
Cocoa	6
Chocolate Milk	2

REFERENCES - CAFFEINE

1. *Caffeine Content of Some Common Beverages.* Pharmacy Times, (November, 1989), p. 106.

2. *Facts And Comparisons.* Facts and Comparisons, Inc., St. Louis, MO, (April 1995).

3. Jaffe, Jerome H. *Drug Addiction and Drug Abuse.* Goodman And Gillman's — The Pharmacological Basis of Therapeutics 8th ed., Pergamon Press, New York, (1990).

4. Rall, Theodore W. *Drugs Used in the Treatment of Asthma* Goodman And Gillman's — The Pharmacological Basis of Therapeutics 8th ed., Pergamon Press, New York, (1990).

5. Rang, H.P. and Dale, M.M. *Pharmacology.* Churchill Livingstone, NY, (1987).

30. ALCOHOL

"If you think that something outside of yourself is
the cause of your problem, you will look outside of
yourself for the answer."

— Robert Anthony

Alcohol is considered to be the oldest "medicine" in existence.
And, its continuing popularity among Americans today is apparent.
At any given time, more than half of the U.S. population over the age
of 12 are current users of alcohol, and more than 85% will have consumed alcohol at some time. Alcohol is often used in our society as a
food substance, but perhaps even more often as a coping mechanism
to reduce the pressures and pains of our daily lives.

Despite the variety of alcoholic products available for purchase,
there is only one drinkable form of alcohol, ethyl alcohol or ethanol,
which is the "alcohol" found in all alcoholic beverages. The historical
origins of alcohol are not really known. Since the fermentation
process can occur naturally whenever fruits or honey are exposed to a
warm atmosphere, it is probable that ancient man accidentally discovered the process. Whatever the origins, humans discovered that
they liked its effects, and how to make it whenever they wanted more.
Alcohol has been used as a part of religious rituals and as a medication throughout history and is probably the oldest and most widely
used drug in the history of mankind. Early writings refer to fer-
mented beverages as medicine agents. The Arabs introduced distilla-
tion techniques to Europe during the Middle Ages. Distilled alcoholic
beverages became popular as the "elixir of life" and have been promoted as a therapeutic agent for nearly every disease condition at
some point during the course of history, even though its true medical
value is extremely limited.

The use of alcohol as a medicinal agent has been popularized on
television, and appears frequently in Western movies as an anesthetic when bullets need to be removed. Actually, ethanol is a dangerous
anesthetic, since doses large enough to cause anesthesia are likely to
result in respiratory arrest. Alcohol does increase pain tolerance and
produces an exaggerated sense of well-being (euphoria), which would
explain its popularity, and its use as an anesthetic.

OUTLINE 106

EFFECTS OF ALCOHOL

Body Temperature

❦ Decreased temperature regulation ability of the body
❦ Feeling of warmth (although body temperature actually decreases)
❦ Increased sweating causes body temperature to decline
❦ Increased risk of harm when exposed to cold environmental temperatures

Central Nervous System (CNS)

Acute Use

Decreases in:

❦ Ability to concentrate
❦ Ability to discriminate
❦ Central Nervous System (CNS) functions
❦ Insight
❦ Memory
❦ Normal inhibitions
❦ Organized thinking
❦ Restraint
❦ Self-control
❦ Sound judgment

Increases in:

❦ Emotional outbursts
❦ Feelings of confidence
❦ Mood swings (may become wide and uncontrolled)
❦ Social aggressiveness
❦ Unrestricted speech

Chronic Use

❦ Brain damage
❦ Memory loss
❦ Psychoses

❦ Seizures
❦ Sleep disturbances

Gastrointestinal

❦ Constipation or diarrhea
❦ Increase output of stomach enzymes

❦ Increased ulcer risk
❦ Irritation of stomach and intestines

OUTLINE 106 cont'd

Heart and Circulation

Acute Use

- Flushing
- Vasodilation
- Increased risk of angina and ECG changes in patients with heart problems.

Chronic Use

- Increased risk of heart disease
- Increased risk of high blood pressure

Lipoproteins

Moderate Consumption

- Decreased heart disease
- Increases in HDL levels
- Decreased LDL levels

Respiration

Moderate Consumption

- Increased or decreased respiration

Heavy Consumption

- Dangerous or lethal respiratory depression

Sexual Functioning

Acute

- Decreased inhibitions and restraint can encourage sexual behaviors
- Decreased ability to perform sexually
- Decreased sexual responsiveness

Chronic

- Atrophy of testicles
- Development of breast tissue in males
- Impotence
- Sterility

Skeletal Muscle

Moderate Consumption

- Decreased feelings of fatigue
- Increased work capacity

Heavy Consumption

- Decreased work capacity (due to CNS depression)
- Muscle damage

OUTLINE 106 cont'd

Sleep

Acute
- Decreased quality of sleep
- Increased feeling of fatigue (after sleep)
- Increased risk of sleep apnea
- Increase in wakeful periods
- Increased time spend in deep sleep
- Longer time required to get to sleep
- Longer time to reach REM (dream phase) sleep

Chronic
- Erratic sleep
- Increased incidence of awakenings

Miscellaneous
- Birth defects
- Liver damage
- Pancreatitis
- Throat lesions

Regarding side effects, we are all aware that alcohol can cause thought processes to occur in a jumbled and disorganized pattern. Typically, the first mental processes to be affected with increased consumption are those that depend upon training and previous experiences, and which contribute to sobriety and self-restraint. Memory (especially short term memory), concentration and insight are affected next. Confidence may be increased, but this may actually represent the loss of sound judgment. As consumption increases, personality changes occur and the individual may become expansive and vivacious; speech may also become slurred, but sometimes eloquent and occasionally brilliant. Finally, there may be uncontrolled mood swings, emotional outbreaks, and disturbances of the senses. Generally speaking, alcohol impairs both mental and physical abilities.

Even though alcohol is a depressant drug, it is often perceived to be a "stimulant" because it can reduce certain inhibitions and feelings of fatigue while engaging in strenuous activities. People may report that drinking before engaging in strenuous activities increases their energy level. As a matter of fact, the total amount of work which people can accomplish does sometimes increase while under the influence of alcohol. However, this is an unpredictable outcome, since work quality may also decrease, and in the long run alcohol can actually damage muscles.

The effects of alcohol are related to the rate and amount consumed, which determines the concentration of alcohol in the bloodstream. Most people are familiar with the use of instruments (e.g., Breathalizer, Intoxilizer) used by law enforcement officers to estimate the amount of alcohol in the breath. The alcohol concentration in the breath is then multiplied by a constant (e.g., 2100) in order to estimate the blood/alcohol concentration. These instruments are controversial, since the blood to breath ratio of alcohol is not constant. And in fact, studies have indicated that the blood/breath ratios can range from 1117:1 to 7289:1. Thus, the use of a constant such as 2100 to determine blood/alcohol levels may be considerably inaccurate. Furthermore, a variety of factors may impact blood/breath ratios (e.g., body temperature, variations in breathing techniques, underlying disease states).

Alcohol is often viewed as a ready source of energy since it is absorbed quickly from the stomach and intestines, and requires no previous digestion. However, it is also an "empty" source of calories, since it can supply a considerable amount of our daily calorie requirements, but few of the nutrients needed by our body for normal functioning. Moreover, people who drink heavily may begin to neglect other foods that would normally balance their diets, and often develop dietary deficiencies. Drinking can also contribute to weight gain (e.g., "beer belly").

Foods such as milk, fats and meat tend to slow the absorption of alcohol from the stomach and intestines. And, alcohol in more diluted beverages (e.g., 10% or less in highballs) is absorbed more slowly than in more concentrated drinks (e.g., Martinis and Manhattans). Carbonation can also increase alcohol absorption.

Alcohol is a significant irritant of the gastrointestinal tract and can result in a variety of inflammatory and bleeding lesions of the stomach and esophagus. The likelihood of such effects is related to the concentration and amount of beverages consumed and also to the use of anti-inflammatory drugs (e.g., aspirin, ibuprofen and related drugs). Alcohol stimulates the intestines, so that some people experience diarrhea after chronic use. They may also complain of "irritable bowel and stomach" problems, including abdominal pain, diarrhea, intestinal gas and other symptoms.

Alcohol is metabolized by the body at a fairly constant rate. For most people, the amount of alcohol lost per hour is approximately equivalent to that contained in a 12-ounce beer or 1 ounce of whisky. It is metabolized to acetaldehyde and eventually to acetate. Under normal circumstances this transformation occurs quickly. However, acetaldehyde can accumulate when large amounts of alcohol have been consumed. The result is "hangover" (e.g., headache, stomach irritation, nausea/vomiting, dizziness).

Many people drink alcohol to keep warm at outdoor events or during other activities when it is cold. However, this is not an effective way to keep warm. In fact, alcohol can interfere with the ability of the body to maintain a normal temperature, since alcohol dilates blood vessels in the skin of the face and arms. When this happens, body heat is actually lost through the skin. As this heat is being lost, nerve endings in the skin feel the heat as it leaves the body. This causes the individual to feel "warmer" even though heat is actually being lost.

Many people also believe that alcohol aids in sexual activities ("candy is dandy but liquor is quicker"). This, too, is a popular myth. Alcohol may reduce sexual inhibitions, but lowering inhibitions is not the same as stimulating sexual urges or enhancing performance. In fact, alcohol can actually interfere with your ability to perform sexually.

Despite the media attention given to popularized illegal drugs (e.g., marijuana, cocaine, etc.), alcohol has always been the number one abused substance in America. The social and economic costs of alcoholism and heavy drinking is estimated to be in the billions of dollars each year. These figures represent the costs of deaths, illnesses, days lost from work, accidents, disruption of family life, mental illnesses, suicides, and so on. Also, despite the popularized notion that American youths constitute the primary group of drug abusers, the largest group of drug abusers are young and middle aged adult users of alcohol.

With chronic use of alcohol, many health problems can occur. These include nerve damage, brain damage, memory loss, sleep disturbances, mental disorders, nutritional and vitamin deficiencies, liver damage, heart damage and stomach ulcers. And, much of this damage can become permanent with repeated abuse. Heavy drinkers appear to have shorter life spans than abstainers, although there is little evidence that light or moderate drinking is a serious health threat.

The amount of alcohol contained in the miscellaneous beverages available for purchase can vary significantly. Outline 107 summarizes average alcohol levels for many popular beverages. Alcohol content is normally expressed as "proof points." "Proof" refers to the relative alcohol concentration of a beverage. In the U.S., two proof points are equal to 1% alcohol. Therefore, a 100 proof beverage is actually about 50% alcohol.

OUTLINE 107

AVERAGE ALCOHOL CONCENTRATION OF SOME POPULAR ALCOHOLIC BEVERAGES

Beers	2 - 8%
Cordials (e.g. Sloe Gin)	25 - 40%
Spirits	40 - 50%
Brandies	
Gin	
Liqueurs	
Rum	
Vodka	
Whiskies (Rye, Scotch, Bourbon, etc.)	
Vermouth & Aperitif Wines	18%
Wines	8 - 14%
Dessert, Sweet & Cocktail Wines	20%
Muscatel	
Port	
Sherry	

CASE STUDY

LESSONS FROM REAL LIFE — STACEY

Stacey is a 34-year-old construction worker who supervises a roofing crew. His employer considers him to be a top-notch worker and tolerates his occasional absences from work due to hangovers and the like. Stacey is a confirmed beer drinker who usually consumes 3 or 4 cans of beer during the day, since this "helps him deal with the heat and keeps the juices flowing." For the most part, his fellow workers also drink several cans of beer during the day. At the end of the day, Stacey will usually pick up a six pack because this helps him unwind when he gets home. He is a good husband and father to his two kids, and his wife tolerates his drinking because he is a good provider and considerate of his family. She wishes he would cut down, but the one time she mentioned this to Stacey, he became furious and threatened to hit her. She went into the bedroom and found him asleep on the sofa the next morning with no recollection of this episode. Yesterday, Stacey lost his balance as he was descending from the roof and injured his ankle and shoulder. This was his first injury in 17 years of construction work. He told the doctor that he had experienced a dizzy spell which caused him to fall, but he failed to mention that he had two beers in a row just before the incident. The doctor suspected that Stacey had been drinking because of the beer on his breath, but was reluctant to discuss this. He did, however, include this information in the report he filed with the insurance company that handled Stacey's claim. One of the provisions in Stacey's insurance policy is that he is not covered for injuries that are the result of alcohol. Two men in his crew were laid off during the last two months for excessive alcohol consumption. Stacey doesn't know it yet, but he may be the third.

31. HERBS

"Modern man has done many odd things to display his faith in the fundamental goodness of nature. Following in the steps of Rousseau, one hundred million Central Europeans went bontanizing in the hope of discovering among lowly flowers both the soul of the universe and natural remedies for chest troubles. More prosaic 20th Century man tries to re-establish contact with this forgotten biological past in countless country clubs, hunting or ski lodges and beach bungalows, through clambakes in the moonlight and barbecue parties in suburban gardens and picnic groves. Nature cults and practices have sent people in all walks of life tramping barefoot in the morning dew, exposing themselves to discomfort in the wind and sun, drinking ill-tasting plant and animal juices, and imagining that the compost heap in the garden can become a fountain of youth. Whatever his inhibitions and tastes, Western man believes in the natural holiness of seminudism and raw vegetable juice, because these have become for him symbols of unadulterated nature."

— Rene Dubos

Herbalism is alive and well in the U.S., but not necessarily because it is effective. Rather, it remains as a component of our incessant search for the *"magic bullets"* that medical science has somehow missed. We want very much to believe that there are substances with mystical properties that can somehow protect us from the ills, ailments and stresses of modern life. Consider the elderly woman who drank vinegar every day, and explained, "It cleans out all the toxins from your body, you know!" After all, if vinegar can clean out our automatic coffee makers . . . just think what it can do for us! It is also likely that we like having products available to us for our self-care needs.

Herbs have been used for health circumstances with varying degrees of success throughout history. American Indians, as well as settlers of the American West, gathered and used them as medicines. Perhaps it is this folklore mystique that continues to intrigue us.

Many people continue to ask why herbs are not used for medicinal purposes today if they were successful for other groups throughout history. As a matter of fact, drug manufacturers have studied virtually all of the herbs which consumers are likely to encounter. When plant components appear to have medical value, drug manufacturers isolate the active ingredients and study them just as they would any other potential drug product.

Drug companies isolate individual chemicals of interest as a part of their ongoing search for new drug products. Medicinal chemists and pharmacognocists (scientists who specialize in drugs from natural sources, such as plants) identify the chemical structure, then design a way to make the drug synthetically (because it is less expensive to make drugs in the laboratory than to extract them from their natural sources).

By isolating the active components of interest, it is possible to determine the most effective dose with the fewest side effects. Indeed, one of the major dangers of traditional herbal therapy is that natural products typically contain numerous chemicals. Some can be helpful while others may be harmful, especially when used over time.

Medical science has never denied that some herbs have medicinal value. Yet, these natural products are invariably weaker or more dangerous than the synthetic products which are eventually developed.

Sometimes scientists begin with components isolated from herbal sources, then create related chemical substances which are more effective and have fewer side effects. Medicinal chemists do this by taking the original molecule and altering it in various ways to create ingredients which are safer and more effective.

Finally, it is worth noting that drug companies are interested in profits. Almost invariably when medical science demonstrates no interest in an herbal product, it is because it either has too little potential or it is too dangerous. Advertisements often promote herbals as items "overlooked" by medical science. However, they fail to mention that these products have been deliberately rejected by legitimate health authorities because of the problems associated with their use, or because they lack true benefits. In many cases, the medicinal properties of the herbal are far less effective than commercial products which are available.

Give it some thought. You can be assured that herbals that have actual medicinal potential will be developed by the major drug companies. Herbals that are being ignored . . . are being ignored for a reason!

Hyssops Fables

In an effort to help you begin to sort out the conflicting messages about herbs, here's a summary of typical promotional information and scientific information[2] about some of the common products that you are likely to encounter.

Alfalfa

Promoted uses:

❦ arthritis

❦ asthma

❦ diuretic

❦ blood purifier

❦ bladder problems

❦ kidney problems

❦ prevent tooth decay

❦ prostate problems

❦ rebuild decaying teeth

❦ source of carotene (Vitamin A)

❦ source of natural fluoride

❦ stomach problems

What medical science knows:

❦ Research has failed to demonstrate that alfalfa is effective as a diuretic, or in the treatment of inflammations, diabetes, asthma, ulcers, or in reducing cholesterol levels.

❦ It does contain natural sources of protein, calcium, trace minerals, carotene, Vitamin E, Vitamin K and numerous water-soluble vitamins.

❦ There is no evidence to support its claim regarding dental health.

❦ Human and animal studies indicate that this agent may result in a disease similar to Systemic Lupus Erythematosus, blood problems, changes in immune system functioning, and has resulted in cases of Systemic Lupus in at least 2 patients.

Aloe

Promoted uses:

❦ a "great healing agent"

❦ cleans out the colon

❦ hemorrhoids

❦ laxative

❦ skin sores

What medical science knows:

❦ Has been used for centuries as a drastic laxative, because it irritates the large intestine. Therefore it must be used with caution as a laxative.

❦ Research has failed to show sufficient evidence that it is useful in the treatment of skin problems (e.g., minor burns and cuts), or for vaginal irritations. Some evidence does exist for its use in promoting wound healing. However, there have been conflicting reports. Minor skin irritations have been reported with topical use.

❧ Internal use can result in severe abdominal cramping and it should not be used in pregnant women and children.

Angelica

Promoted uses:

❧ discourages alcohol consumption

❧ gas

❧ heart disease

❧ heartburn

❧ lung disease

❧ strengthens the heart

❧ stomach troubles

What medical science knows:

❧ According to legend, this herb was revealed to humans by an angel as a cure for the plague (hence its name).

❧ Its preparations have some activities which affect the heart, smooth muscle, metabolism and have some anti-infective properties.

❧ It is generally considered to be safe for consumption as a natural seasoning and flavoring. Topical applications can result in sensitivity reactions to light.

❧ Animal studies indicate that it may cause skin changes, including cancers.

Anise

Promoted uses:

❧ fermentation and gas in the stomach and bowels

❧ respiratory problems

What medical science knows:

❧ No significant medicinal properties have been identified by research, even though it continues to be used for intestinal and respiratory problems in folk medicine.

❧ It is commonly used as a fragrance and spice and appears to be safe for these purposes.

Barberry Bark

Promoted uses:

- bad breath
- digestive problems
- kidney problems
- liver problems
- promotes bile secretion
- skin problems
- sore throat
- rheumatism

What medical science knows:

- Dates back to the Middle Ages.
- It does appear to have anti-infective properties and may be effective in the treatment of diarrhea associated with cholera. However, it has not been shown to be effective in non-cholera diarrhea.
- Toxicity can result in stupor, daze, diarrhea and kidney inflammation.
- Although it has been around a long time, its actual medical value is minor at best, even among herbalists.

Bayberry

Promoted uses:

- gargle for sore throat
- improved circulation
- tones all tissues
- topically to prevent varicose veins

What medical science knows:

- It is best known for its berries, from which a wax is derived to make fragrant bayberry candles.
- Its astringent properties probably explain its use for wound healing.
- The plant has a high tannin content and should not be taken internally. Oral use can cause stomach irritation and vomiting.
- Skin research in animals resulted in tumor formation.
- There is little clinical evidence to suggest that it has any rational potential for the treatment of any disease.

Bee Pollen

Promoted uses:

- acne
- aging
- allergies
- digestive upsets
- disease-fighting

- fatigue
- healing & rejuvenating
- maintenance of good health
- prostate disease

- sexual problems
- sore throats
- total nutrient
- a host of other problems

What medical science knows:

- Consists of plant pollens combined with plant nectar and bee saliva.
- The use of bee pollens increased during the 1970s because of testimonials by athletes that this product was able to improve their their stamina and athletic performances.
- These products contain mixtures of pollens from diverse types of plants, and these vary from one geographic region to another.
- Studies have failed to demonstrate the claims of its promoters.
- Allergic reactions can be a serious adverse reaction with this product, so it must be taken with caution by people who have a history of serious allergic reactions.
- In the long run, it is an expensive source of carbohydrates and trace nutrients.

Bergamot

Promoted uses:

- calming

- soothing to the system

What medical science knows:

- The bergamot is a small tree of Asia which is cultivated extensively on the southern coasts of Italy.
- Oil from the tree is used as a citrus flavor and is often added to perfumes and cosmetics.
- It appears to have no significant medicinal value.
- It contains some components which can result in skin rashes and damage when exposed to the sun or other sources of UV radiation (i.e., photosensitivity).

Black Cohosh

Promoted uses:

- a natural estrogen source (without cancer causing properties)
- regulate menstrual flow
- insect repellent
- menstrual cramps
- stomach problems
- rheumatism
- snakebites (Native Americans)

What medical science knows:

- This open woods plant has been used for a variety of medicinal purposes and does appear to have some effect on certain reproductive hormones and the endocrine system.
- Some of its components have been shown in animal studies to lower blood pressure and dilate blood vessels.
- It may also have some anti-infective properties.
- Oral use of some components can result in nausea and vomiting because of the high tannin content.
- Large doses can result in miscarriage.
- Future research may identify ingredients which could be utilized for the treatment of menopause symptoms.
- Must be used with caution by people who are taking medications for high blood pressure.

Bloodroot

Promoted uses:

- breast tumors
- colds
- coughs
- dental anesthetic
- digestive stimulant
- expectorant
- heart stimulant
- nasal polyps
- rheumatism
- skin cancers
- to cause nausea (e.g., for poisonings)
- warts

What medical science knows:

- The numerous promoted uses for this product have prompted considerable research.
- Some anti-infective properties have been observed, as well as effects on the heart.

🐛 Toothpastes are commercially available with bloodroot components to reduce plaque formation. Even so, it is not recognized as being safe and effective by drug reviews.

🐛 Cancer research continues.

🐛 Even though it is an old-time remedy which continues to be used, it is not recommended that it be taken orally. Oral toxicity is considered to be low, but safety concerns still exist. Large doses can result in nausea, vomiting, CNS depression, lowered blood pressure, shock and coma.

Blue Cohosh

Promoted uses:

🐛 regulates menstruation   🐛 suppressed menstruation

What medical science knows:

🐛 Has been used extensively in folk medicine throughout U.S. history.

🐛 Components of this plant have activities that increase blood pressure, stimulate the uterus and constrict blood vessels of the heart. It may also have contraceptive and anti-infective properties.

🐛 Even though the plant may prove to have some medicinal value (i.e., as a result of future research), its effects are unpredictable and it can result in serious toxicity problems.

Boldo Leaf

Promoted uses:

🐛 diuretic   🐛 liver problems   🐛 stimulates bile secretion
🐛 gallstones   🐛 stimulates digestion

What medical science knows:

🐛 Boldo leaves have been used by South American natives for liver disease and gallstones.

🐛 Folk medicine has used the plant for a variety of health problems and an extract is used as a flavoring alcoholic beverages.

🐛 It does appear to have diuretic properties, as well as a stimulation of bile flow.

❦ In toxic doses (animal studies) it stimulates the central nervous system (e.g., exaggerated reflexes, disturbances of coordination, convulsions). Large doses cause paralysis and death due to respiratory arrest.

Boneset

Promoted uses:

❦ as a tonic

❦ colds

❦ flu

❦ laxative

What medical science knows:

❦ Used as a charm and medicinal remedy for centuries by North American Indians.

❦ The name was derived from its use in the treatment of breakbone fever, a term used to describe the high fever associated with influenza.

❦ The plant appears to have diuretic and laxative properties.

❦ Some extracts have been shown to have weak anti-inflammatory and anti-fever properties. However, these properties are weak compared to commercially available products.

❦ Other components of the plant have been shown to have some anti-cancer activity, enhancement of blood coagulation and protective effects on the liver.

❦ Despite its seeming potential, health authorities question the safety of this plant. Large amounts cause diarrhea, and there is a distinct possibility that long-term use could damage the liver, rather than protect it.

Borage

Promoted uses:

❦ bronchitis

❦ colds

❦ diuretic

❦ fever

❦ induce sweating

❦ lung problems

❦ rheumatism

❦ skin and mucous membrane problems

❦ increase flow of breast milk

What medical science knows:

❦ It has been an official part of European herbal medicine for centuries, and has been an official drug in Germany, Spain, Portugal, Romania, Venezuela and Mexico.

❦ It is used as a food (e.g., the leaves are soaked in vinegar and eaten like spinach as hors d'oeuvres).

❦ Despite its promoted medicinal uses, the plant actually has no true medicinal activity. The tannin content might result in some constipation. Other components may have some expectorant and diuretic activities, even though these have not proven to be significant.

❦ Borage teas may offer some soothing effects, like many other teas. However, it appears to be associated with neither significant toxicity or medicinal value.

Buchu

Promoted uses:

❦ bladder problems

❦ diuretic

❦ kidney problems

❦ painful urination

What medical science knows:

❦ This south African plant is the source of medicinal products which have been available for some time. Early U.S. patent medicines touted its virtues for the management of a variety of health problems. The drug was included in the National Formulary of the U.S. as a diuretic and antiseptic. However, it has been abandoned as an official product in favor of more effective diuretics and anti-infectives. It remains a popular item in herbal preparations.

❦ Clinical reviews of buchu as a diuretic ingredient in OTC menstrual products have failed to demonstrate effectiveness. The actual diuretic activity is certainly no greater than that of coffee or tea.

❦ It has not been shown to be clinically effective as an anti-infective ingredient.

❦ Casual use has not been shown to be harmful.

Burdock

Promoted uses:

- arthritis
- blood purifier and cleanser
- cancer
- diuretic
- induce sweating
- skin problems (boils, acne, eczema, warts)
- stimulate bile flow
- remove "toxins" from the body

What medical science knows:

- This plant has been known since the Middle Ages in Europe, but grows in North America as well.
- Historically, it has been a popular item in herbal medicine, but appears to have little medicinal activity and is not considered to be of value in the treatment of any human disease.
- One of its components may have some potential in blocking cell mutations and chromosome aberrations. More research is required to explore this potential.
- It has lost popularity even among herbalists and is used only occasionally in homeopathy. Even so, it continues to be found in natural food stores.
- Toxicity is unlikely, since the plant lacks significant biological activity. However, 2 cases of burdock poisoning have been reported. It is thought that the toxicity actually occurred because of contaminants on the plant and not because of activities of the plant itself (the poisoning was traced to an active component not normally found in burdock).

Calendula

Promoted uses:

- anti-inflammatory
- cancers
- cuts and wounds
- fever
- painful menstruation

What medical science knows:

- This plant is found world-wide, but is believed to have originated in Egypt.
- Not many human studies have been conducted, but the plant does appear to have some potential medicinal value. It appears to promote

wound healing, has anti-inflammatory properties, anti-infective properties and may stimulate the immune system. Some European studies suggest that it may have some value in the treatment of some digestive disorders (e.g., ulcers, inflammatory bowel problems), and in the treatment of certain dental problems. Yet, its real value as a medicinal agent remains unclear. Its true medicinal value is questionable at present and it is not recommended for the treatment of any particular disease based on studies to date.

❦ Fortunately, it has a low potential for adverse reactions. Some allergic reactions have been reported.

Capsicum

Promoted uses:
❦ bleeding

❦ blood pressure

❦ circulation

❦ general "cleansing" of the body

❦ promotes elasticity of blood vessels

❦ promotes general healing

What medical science knows:
❦ Capsicum was first described in the 1400s by a physician who traveled with Columbus to the West Indies.

❦ The name (from Latin, "capsa," meaning "box") refers to the box-like fruit.

❦ It is quite popular as a spice worldwide.

❦ It is a powerful irritant and can product a sensation of warmth or burning depending upon the concentration used.

❦ Topical preparations are used to mask the pain associated with other conditions (e.g., nerve pains, post-mastectomy surgery).

❦ At least one product is available which is sprinkled into socks or massaged on the feet to provide a sensation of warmth during cold weather.

❦ The major adverse effect involves irritation of skin and mucous membranes.

❦ Capsicum is included in some self-defense sprays because of its extreme irritating effects.

Cascara Sagrada

Promoted uses:

- constipation
- gallstones
- hemorrhoids
- digestive stimulant

What medical science knows:

- This product is a stimulant laxative. Stimulant laxatives should never be used as a first option for the self-care of constipation or any other problem. Promoters conveniently neglect to mention that stimulant laxatives are addicting (i.e., they result in a physical dependency, so that you must eventually take the laxative in order to have a bowel movement); nor do they mention that the stimulant laxatives can cause significant abdominal pain and cramping.

- These products should never be used to treat gallstones, nor should they be used in the presence of hemorrhoids unless you have first consulted a physician.

Catnip

Promoted uses:

- as a hallucinogen
- "cleans out" mucus in the body
- colds
- delayed menstruation
- digestive aid
- hives
- lung problems
- nervous conditions
- quiet the nervous system
- stomach problems (e.g., gas, cramping)
- swelling

What medical science knows:

- This product is known for its ability to produce "euphoria" in some cats. The "catnip response" is well documented and consists of 6 phases, each lasting about 10 minutes. These stages include stretching, animation, euphoria and sexual stimulation. The response is consistent between cats, but not all cats react to it. Some people, apparently not wanting to miss out on this fun, have described a happy intoxication similar to what is perceived to be the experience of the intoxicated cat. At least four cases of catnip abuse have been reported in individuals who were using it in a manner similar to marijuana. They reported mood elevations, euphoria, giddiness and feeling of unreality. The validity of these reactions is questionable, and it is suspected that the human response to catnip may be related to the user's expectations.

❦ A pleasing tea can be brewed from the leaves.

❦ Adverse reactions due to catnip can include headache, malaise, nausea and vomiting, although serious toxicities have not been reported.

❦ Catnip tea is consumed as a mild beverage.

❦ There is little evidence of any real therapeutic benefits. Ultimately, your cat is much more likely to benefit from it than you are.

Celery

Promoted uses:

❦ aphrodisiac
❦ arthritis
❦ digestive aid
❦ diuretic

❦ headaches
❦ intestinal gas
  (stomach or intestines)

❦ nervousness
❦ rheumatism
❦ urinary incontinence

What medical science knows:

❦ Yes, that rather unassuming resident of your grocer's produce shelf has a rich history that ranks it among the other herbal marvels of our time. It originated as a wild plant in the salt marshes around the Mediterranean Sea. The Greeks used it to make wine around 450 B.C. and it was used as an award for the early athletic games (much as laurel leaves or olive branches) have been used. Over time it has been used both as a food and as a medicine.

❦ By the late 1800s celery tonics and elixirs were readily available, often containing significant amounts of alcohol (which, no doubt, contributed to their popularity).

❦ Actual research indicates that its components can lower blood pressure, have antifungal properties and can lower blood sugar.

❦ Celery is high in mineral (especially sodium and chlorine), but it is a poor source of vitamins.

❦ Adverse effects are unlikely, although allergic reactions have occurred to people who cultivate or process it. And, it may develop carcinogens as it decomposes following exposure to sunlight.

❦ Its true medicinal value is relatively worthless, but it makes a worthy snack.

Chamomile

Promoted uses:

❦ digestive problems   ❦ menstrual cramps   ❦ sedative

❦ nervous stomach   ❦ rheumatism   ❦ worms

What medical science knows:

❦ This plant has been around since the days of the Romans as a medicinal entity.

❦ It has been shown to reduce inflammation, reduce fever, promote wound healing, prevent ulcer formation and have an antispasmodic effect on the intestines. It has been used as a hair tint and conditioner and as a flavor for cigarettes.

❦ The true medicinal benefits are much less than those of commercially available medicines.

❦ Adverse reactions primarily involve allergic reactions of various kinds.

Chickweed

Promoted uses:

❦ blood purifier   ❦ rheumatism   ❦ sores

❦ psoriasis   ❦ source of vitamins and   ❦ to dissolve plaque

❦ rashes   minerals (e.g., vitamin C,   on blood vessels

❦ removal of "toxins"   calcium, magnesium,

   from the body   potassium)

What medical science knows:

❦ Parts of it are edible and have been used as salad greens.

❦ Despite the glowing medical recommendations by many of its promoters, most of the legitimate attention given to this plant has involved trying to get rid of it as an unwanted weed.

❦ Research does not indicate that it has any significant medicinal value, and its vitamin and mineral content is too low to be of merit.

❦ Taking large amounts can result in nitrate toxicity (e.g., paralysis), although its toxicity potential is quite limited.

Coltsfoot

Promoted uses:

- asthma
- bronchitis
- coughing
- lung problems
- lung problems
- phlegm in the chest
- sore throats
- to soothe mucous membranes
- wheezing

What medical science knows:

- Research has identified a Platelet Activating Factor (PAF) and an agent that acts as both a heart and respiratory stimulant.
- The plant is not associated with acute toxicity, but it has the potential to cause allergic reactions, liver damage, increased blood pressure, and may pose a risk for cancer if used over time.

Damiana

Promoted uses:

- bed wetting
- headaches
- hot flashes
- impotence
- infertility (male or female)
- menopause
- to strengthen reproductive organs

What medical science knows:

- This plant is found in both North and South America. The scientific literature dealing with it dates back for at least 100 years. The Aztecs used is as an aphrodisiac and contemporary users tout its value value in producing a legal herbal "high."
- There is no scientific evidence to support either aphrodisiac or hallucinogenic properties.
- It may contain caffeine, which would explain its activity for certain types of headaches (e.g., migraine or vascular types of headaches, although more potent medications are commercially available).
- It is a plant which has received much attention. However, it appears to have no real medicinal value or significant adverse effects.

Dandelion

Promoted uses:

❦ blood pressure

❦ "detoxify" liver poisons

❦ diabetes

❦ laxative

❦ skin problems

❦ stimulate appetite

❦ stimulate bile flow

What medical science knows:

❦ The term "dent-de-lion" means "lion's tooth" in French and refers to the toothed appearance of some leaves. It is mentioned by Arab physicians as early as the 10th Century.

❦ It has been used as a beverage as well as a medicinal agent, including a coffee-like beverage touted to lack the stimulant properties of coffee.

❦ Clinical research indicates that the plant does have potential in the treatment of colitis, colon pain, diarrhea, constipation, as a diuretic and weight reduction. Even so, it is not presently considered to have any significant medicinal value, even though its use persists in herbal medicine.

❦ The most significant hazard with its use involves the potential for allergy reactions.

❦ As it stands, it presently remains a common weed that is more of a nuisance than a medical miracle.

Dong Quai

Promoted uses:

❦ allergies

❦ anemia

❦ blood purifier

❦ constipation

❦ female "troubles"

❦ high blood pressure

❦ menstrual problems

❦ maintain balance of
  female hormones

❦ ulcers

❦ Vitamin E deficiency

❦ symptoms

What medical science knows:

❦ This is a common herb of the Orient which has been used to treat a variety of health problems.

❦ Scientific research indicates that the plant could potentially dilate blood vessels, have antispasmodic effects, act as a central nervous system stimulant, and may suppress the immune system.

❧ Despite any potential benefits, some components of the plant are potentially hazardous when taken orally.

❧ Skin reactions (e.g., reactions to light, depigmentation, psoriasis) and a risk for cancer are associated with some of its components. Thus, its potential hazards clearly outweigh any potential benefits.

Echinacea

Promoted uses:

❧ anti-infective

❧ blood purifier

❧ dizziness

❧ gland infections and ailments

❧ lymph gland problems

❧ rattlesnake bites

❧ stimulate the immune system

❧ strep throat

❧ to clean the "morbid matter" from the stomach

❧ to expel "poisons and toxins" from the body

❧ wound healing

What medical science knows:

❧ This plant was used as a medicinal agent by American Indians and settlers, and continues to be used for a variety of purposes.

❧ Clinical research has confirmed that it does have medicinal activity regarding wound healing and as a stimulant of the immune system.

❧ Its potential as a medicinal agent has not been established and more studies are in progress.

❧ Not much is known about its toxicity, although it does not appear to be associated with problems.

Elder

Promoted uses:

❧ astringent

❧ cancer

❧ colds

❧ diuretic

❧ flu

❧ laxative

What medical science knows:

❧ Elder has been used in folk medicine for centuries.

❧ Research confirms that it does have diuretic and laxative properties.

❦ It contains cyanide which has caused some concern about adverse effects. Some individuals have had significant adverse reactions (e.g., nausea, vomiting, weakness, dizziness, numbness and stupor), although these cases were not known to be due to cyanide.

❦ Ironically, the plant is considered to be edible if prepared properly.

❦ Although the plant is used medicinally, it is not considered to have significant medicinal value. To be sure, its use in the treatment of colds and flu would be a waste of effort considering its lack of pharmacological properties.

Eyebright

Promoted uses:

❦ eye infections   ❦ inflammations   ❦ weak eyesight

What medical science knows:

❦ The flowers of this plant have the appearance of bloodshot eyes, which is thought to explain its use since antiquity to treat eye problems.

❦ Even though there have been no well-controlled studies in humans, chemical analysis of the drug does not indicate that it has any significant medicinal potential.

❦ No significant adverse effects are associated with this plant. However, it is never a good idea to apply nonsterile herbal solutions into the eyes.

Fennel Seed

Promoted uses:

❦ acid stomach
❦ antidote for poisons
(e.g., herbs, mushrooms, snake bites)
❦ cramps and spasms

❦ eyewash
❦ gas
❦ gout
❦ indigestion

❦ inflammation of the stomach and intestines
❦ liver "cleanser"
❦ obesity
❦ stimulate lactation

What medical science knows:

❦ Greek legends tell that man received knowledge from Mount Olympus as a fiery coal enclosed in a stalk of fennel. The herb was known to many ancient cultures (e.g., Chinese, Indians, Egyptians, Greek).

❦ Studies indicate that it does have medicinal properties (e.g., estrogen-like activity), which has stimulated research of this plant.

❦ It appears that its potential hazards outweigh any benefits. Animal and human studies indicate a potential for liver damage, nausea, vomiting, seizures, fluid accumulations in the lungs, allergic reactions, sensitivity to light, and tumor development.

Fenugreek

Promoted uses:

❦ allergies   ❦ intestinal inflammation   ❦ sore throat

❦ coughs   ❦ lung problems   ❦ stimulate digestion

❦ emphysema   ❦ problems involving   ❦ ulcers

❦ headaches   mucous membranes

❦ migraines

What medical science knows:

❦ This plant is found in Europe and Asia. Its seeds are used to flavor maple syrup substitutes, and it has been promoted for numerous medicinal purposes.

❦ Animal studies indicate that it has the potential to lower cholesterol and blood sugar levels. It also appears to have some ability to stimulate the uterus and inhibit cancers, although it has not been studied for these purposes.

❦ Adverse effects are unlikely in the normal doses used for food and medicinal purposes. However, large doses could have a negative effect on blood sugar levels.

Feverfew

Promoted uses:

❦ arthritis   ❦ migraines   ❦ restore normal liver function

What medical science knows:

❦ This plant has been extensively studied and does appear to offer some benefit to migraine patients. Historically, it has been promoted for conditions which respond to aspirin therapy (e.g., fever, rheumatism, headaches).

❦ It does not appear to be beneficial in the treatment of arthritis and related diseases.

❦ Adverse effects appear to be mild. However, long term studies have not been conducted. The most common side effects have been inflammation of the mouth and tongue, swelling of the lip and loss of taste.

❦ It should not be used by pregnant women.

Garlic

Promoted uses:

❦ blood clots

❦ deafness

❦ earaches

❦ intestinal gas

❦ "natural" antibiotic

❦ leprosy

❦ scurvy

❦ to "detoxify and rejuvenate everything in the body"

What medical science knows:

❦ Garlic was used as a medium of exchange in ancient Egypt and is even mentioned on Cheops pyramid. (Well after all . . . if you can't trust your mummy . . . who can you trust!)

❦ It contains numerous vitamins, minerals and trace elements. However, most of these are found in very small amounts (Its use would certainly be less cost-effective than commercially available vitamin and mineral products).

❦ Garlic has received attention in the scientific literature for its potential role in treating atherosclerosis and high blood pressure. It appears to be able to lower cholesterol, LDL and triglyceride levels, while raising HDL levels. At least one study indicates that tablets which contain dried garlic may not offer this advantage. It may have some potential in treating diarrhea and other intestinal disorders. Other studies have indicated that it can have a positive impact on blood sugar levels.

❦ It has been used for its anti-infective properties for centuries, to disinfect wounds and even to treat tuberculosis, although its potential for this latter use is questionable. Interestingly, it has antimicrobial activity equal to about 1% of that of penicillin. It has some antifungal properties, but these appear to be too weak to be of significant value for the treatment of systemic infections. Despite the claims made for it, it is not comparable in effectiveness to commercially available antibiotics.

❦ Garlic has also been of interest as an anti-cancer agent. It contains the trace elements germanium and selenium, which may improve immunity and normal cell functioning.

❦ While garlic used as a food is not associated with adverse effects, the long term consequences of its use as a medicine is not known. It has been associated with burning (mouth, esophagus, stomach), nausea, sweating, lightheadedness, and asthma.

❦ Garlic is available in a variety of forms, including "deodorized" products. However, many of the medicinal properties are contained in the components which have the odor. Thus, the therapeutic value of deodorized garlic is questionable.

Gentian Root

Promoted uses:

❦ arthritis	❦ colds	❦ fever
❦ appetite (stimulation)	❦ digestion (improves)	❦ jaundice
❦ "benefits" the female organs	❦ digestive problems (heartburn, vomiting, stomach aches, diarrhea)	❦ liver problems
❦ circulation (improves)		❦ skin wounds
		❦ sore throat

What medical science knows:

❦ Gentian plants have been used for centuries for medicinal purposes.

❦ Gentian has a bitter taste. Bitter substances taken before eating are thought to improve the appetite and aid digestion by stimulating the flow of stomach fluids and bile. However, gentian is usually dissolved in alcohol before it is taken, and alcohol has a similar effect on the digestive system. Thus, benefits may be due to alcohol as much as to gentian.

❦ At least one component appears to have some anti-inflammatory activity.

❦ Gentian preparations can cause stomach irritation, nausea, vomiting, and should avoided by people with high blood pressure and pregnant women.

❦ Aside from some possible effects on appetite and digestion, none of the other medicinal benefits of this plant have been substantiated in humans.

Ginger

Promoted uses:
- "cleanse" kidney and bowels
- digestive aid
- digestive distress
- diuretic
- nausea
- sore throats
- stimulant
- stimulate circulatory system

What medical science knows:
- Ginger has been an important herb in Oriental and Indian medicine. In addition to its promoted medical uses, it has also been used as a pesticide (aphids, fungal spores).
- Research has indicated some activity on the heart, some anti-infective activity, and a possible effect on cancer cells. However, the true value of these activities requires further research.
- Studies have demonstrated that it can prevent motion sickness and possibly morning sickness in pregnant women (although it has little impact on nausea once it develops).
- Its use does not appear to be associated with serious adverse effects. Even so, there is a concern that large doses could cause depression of the central nervous system and irregular heart rhythms. Its potential to cause cancer is unknown at this time. The safety of taking large amounts by pregnant women is also unknown.

Ginseng

Promoted uses:
- atherosclerosis
- bleeding disorders
- blood disorders
- cancer
- colitis
- diabetes
- neurosis
- radiation sickness
- "resistance" against stress (mental and physical)
- senility
- to improve mental and physical functioning
- slow the aging process
- weakness

What medical science knows:
- Gensing is possibly the most widely utilized herbal medicine. Various forms have been used for more than 2000 years. The man-shape of the root has led to a belief that it can be used to strengthen any part of the body.

❧ Animal studies have indicated that it can prolong swimming time, prevent stress-induced ulcers and stimulate the immune system. However, results vary depending upon the animal used for study.

❧ There is significant evidence to suggest that some of its components have central nervous system activities (depressant, anti-seizure, pain relief, antipsychotic), protect against the development of stress ulcers, lower blood sugar levels, accelerate some cellular activities, decrease cholesterol and triglyceride levels and enhance the normal function of the adrenal gland (for "anti-stress" activity).

❧ It appears to be quite safe, even though some adverse effects have been reported. The most common side effects have been nervousness, excitation, and irritability (with long term use). Other reports have mentioned diarrhea, skin reactions, sleeplessness, increased blood pressure, and an estrogen-like effect in women (breast nodes and vaginal bleeding). Diabetics should use it with caution because of reports that it can lower blood sugar levels. It has been associated with a "Ginseng Abuse Syndrome" (e.g., feelings of stimulation, well being, increased motor and mental efficiency).

❧ It remains a popular herb which is promoted for its "anti-stress" effects. Research has demonstrated an "adaptogenic effect" (i.e., an increased physical and mental capacity for work), but an appropriate dose and duration of use has not been clarified.

Golden Seal

Promoted uses:

❧ antispasmodic
❧ bladder infections
❧ bronchitis
❧ canker sores
❧ colds
❧ coughs

❧ earaches
❧ eye wash
❧ inflammations
❧ menstrual disorders
❧ mouth sores
❧ mucous membrane problems

❧ muscle pain
❧ nasal problems
❧ rheumatism
❧ sciatica pain
❧ ulcers

What medical science knows:

❧ This plant was introduced to American settlers by Indians, who used it as a dye and medicine.

❧ Today, some of its components are used in sterile eye washes. However, there is little evidence that these are actually effective.

- Large doses can be toxic. Adverse effects include exaggerated reflexes, increased blood pressure, convulsions, respiratory distress, nausea, vomiting, diarrhea, numbness of the fingers, irritations of the mouth and throat, constriction of certain blood vessels, increases in heart activity and dilated pupils. Small doses are probably harmless.
- Although many of its components have some pharmacological activities, they are weak and ineffective as compared to commercially available products.

Gota Kola

Promoted uses:

- abscesses
- aphrodisiac
- fever
- high blood pressure
- improve memory
- increase learning ability

- jaundice
- leprosy
- mental problems
- nerve tonic
- nervous disorders

- rheumatism
- skin problems
- stimulate circulation to the brain
- ulcers

What medical science knows:

- The plant is popular among elephants, which has probably given rise to its association with memory and long life.
- Certain components of the plant appear to have pharmacologic properties, including wound healing, anti-inflammatory properties, as a treatment for psoriasis and some liver disorders.
- Its toxicity potential is low, but it has been associated with allergy reactions.
- No clinical evidence exists to support its potential benefits on memory and mental functioning.

Hawthorne

Promoted uses:

- angina pectoris
- antispasmodic
- blood pressure problems (high or low)

- insomnia
- sedative
- strengthen and regulate the heart

- stress

What medical science knows:

❦ This plant is very ancient, but has only been popular since the late 1800s.

❦ Research indicates that components of the plant can dilate blood vessels (especially heart vessels), which can reduce work load on the heart. In higher doses it results in depression of the central nervous system, sedation and can result in lowered blood pressure.

❦ Adverse effects are unlikely.

Hibiscus

Promoted uses:

❦ cancer

❦ diuretic

❦ emollient

❦ heart problems

❦ laxative

❦ nerve problems

❦ stimulate intestines

❦ stimulate kidneys

What medical science knows:

❦ This ancient plant originated in Africa, but is now more widely available. It has been used in sachets, perfumes, as a jute substitute in ropes and in various food preparations.

❦ It is generally considered to be nontoxic, although death has occurred in animal studies.

❦ Research indicates that it is not effective as a laxative or as a sedative.

❦ It is a popular plant which imparts a pleasant taste to teas and other beverages.

❦ In normal concentrations it has no significant medicinal benefits.

Hops

Promoted uses:

❦ bladder inflammation

❦ cancer

❦ decreased desire for alcohol

❦ diuretic

❦ insomnia

❦ intestinal cramps

❦ liver tonic

❦ menstrual problems

❦ sedative

❦ tuberculosis

What medical science knows:

❦ The social value of hops is in the production of beer.

❦ Research indicates that components of hops have some antimicrobial activity. It has some properties related to marijuana, so that smoking has been associated with mild sedation.

❦ Allergic reactions appear to be the most significant adverse affect associated with its use.

❦ Even though hops are promoted by many herbal enthusiasts for a variety of medicinal purposes, there appears to be little, if any, true medical value. There is no evidence of estrogen-like or hormonal activity and the use of this herb for "female disorders" is not justified.

Horehound

Promoted uses:

❦ coughs   ❦ sore throats

What medical science knows:

❦ Horehound is a member of the mint family and has long been used as a cold treatment. It is primarily used today as a flavoring agent (e.g., liqueurs, candies, cough drops).

❦ It is associated with expectorant activity and may increase bronchial secretions, which would explain its use in colds.

❦ Although it has been widely used in herbal remedies, and is well known, it has not been the object of a great deal of scientific literature. It is unlikely that its true therapeutic benefits are significant.

Horsetail

Promoted uses:

❦ bladder problems   ❦ kidney problems   ❦ split ends in hair

❦ bleeding   ❦ nasal disorders   ❦ throat disorders

❦ diuretic   ❦ promotes strong   ❦ promotes healing of

❦ ear disorders   fingernails and hair   broken bones

❦ eye disorders   ❦ source of minerals   ❦ stimulates wound healing

❦ gland problems   (e.g., silica)   ❦ tuberculosis

What medical science knows:

❦ In addition to its promoted medical uses, this fern has been used as a metal polisher and as a component of cosmetics.

❦ It causes significant adverse effects in both animals and humans (muscle weakness, weight loss, abnormal pulse rates, fever, cold hands and feet, difficulty walking, and seborrhea).

❦ It contains sufficient nicotine to account for at least some of its pharmacologic and toxic effects.

❦ There is no evidence to justify its use in the treatment of the medical problems for which it is promoted as an herbal remedy.

Hyssop

Promoted uses:

❦ asthma

❦ blood "regulator"

❦ colds

❦ expectorant

❦ eye troubles

❦ hoarseness

❦ sore throats

❦ stomach and bowel problems

❦ wounds

What medical science knows:

❦ Although "hyssop" is mentioned in the Bible, there is actually little evidence to suggest that this was actually the plant to which biblical writers referred.

❦ In addition to the medical problems for which it has been promoted, it has also been used in perfumes and to flavor liqueurs.

❦ Hyssop is a member of the mint family which would explain its use for sore throats and as an expectorant.

❦ It appears to be harmless, even though its true medicinal benefits are questionable.

Juniper Berries

Promoted uses:

❦ arthritis

❦ bronchitis

❦ diuretic

❦ intestinal gas

❦ kidney ailments

❦ removal of "waste products" from the bloodstream to prevent disease

What medical science knows:

☙ Juniper products appear to have far more value as flavoring agents (e.g., foods, alcoholic beverages such as gin) and in the manufacture of perfumes and cosmetics, than they do as medicinal agents.

☙ These products do have some diuretic activity, increase tone of the uterus and have some antimicrobial activity.

☙ Adverse effects include allergic reactions, convulsions, kidney damage (diuretic actions are due to kidney irritation), diarrhea and stomach irritation.

☙ There is little justification for use for medicinal purposes. The potential risks far outweigh any potential benefits. Use should be avoided by elderly, people with kidney problems and pregnant women.

Kava Kava

Promoted uses:

☙ aphrodisiac ☙ inflammations of the uterus ☙ to promote deep and
☙ colds ☙ nervousness restful sleep
☙ headaches ☙ rheumatism ☙ venereal disease
☙ sedative ☙ wound healing

What medical science knows:

☙ This South Pacific plant is used most commonly to prepare a beverage to induce relaxation. Kava drink has been compared to our alcoholic drinks and is used socially to promote a relaxed and pleasant atmosphere.

☙ Clinical studies indicate that in man kava produces mild euphoria, feelings of happiness, more fluent and lively speech and increased awareness of sounds. Higher doses are associated with muscle weakness, visual and hearing changes and sleep. It appears to have pharmacologically active components which can cause depression of the central nervous system.

☙ Chronic ingestion is associated with skin discoloration and "kawaism" (dry, flaking, discolored skin; and red eyes).

☙ Its usefulness as a folk remedy for other purposes is questionable.

Lavender

Promoted uses:

- a general tonic
- acne
- antispasmodic
- diabetes
- diuretic
- intestinal gas
- lower blood sugar
  levels
- migraines
- relaxation
- rheumatism

What medical science knows:

- Lavender has been used in folk medicine for quite some time.
- Research indicates that it results in central nervous system depression and lowers blood sugar.
- Adverse effects appear to be unlikely as it is normally used.
- Despite its longstanding use, it appears to lack true therapeutic benefits.

Licorice Root

Promoted uses:

- increase general
  vitality
- laxative
- strengthen heart and
  circulatory system
- throat muscle injury
- throat problems

What medical science knows:

- Licorice can be traced to Roman and Chinese cultures where it was viewed as a drug which could exert a godly influence on the body and lengthen life. Today, it is used primarily as a flavoring agent and is widely used as a candy and flavor.
- The pharmacologic properties of licorice components include anti-ulcer, antibacterial and anti-inflammatory activity.
- Adverse effects are well-documented and include swelling, increased blood pressure, low potassium levels, lethargy, weakness, dulled reflexes and quadriplegia. Its potential medicinal uses pose far more risks than benefits as compared to commercially available products. High doses can result in significant electrolyte disturbances and other serious side effects.
- People with kidney, liver and heart disease should avoid these products.

Ma Huang

Promoted uses:

❦ "clears" the respiratory
system

❦ colds

❦ coughs

❦ fever

❦ keeps the eyes "bright"

What medical science knows:

❦ It is believed that these plants were used 5,000 years ago by the Chinese to treat asthma. It has been used throughout history by many cultures to treat a variety of respiratory conditions.

❦ The plant contains a number of natural decongestants that are used commercially today (e.g., ephedrine, pseudoephedrine). Decongestants are central nervous system stimulants. They stimulate the heart, increase blood pressure and heart rate, dilate the bronchioles, stimulate contraction of the uterus and have diuretic properties.

❦ Most of these plants have a high tannin content and can cause constipation.

❦ Adverse effects can include nervousness, headache, insomnia, dizziness, palpitations, skin flushing, tingling, vomiting, skin reactions and changes in blood sugar levels.

❦ Although the risk is considered to be small, some components of these plants can cause cancer formation.

❦ Many species of the plant (e.g., most of the ones found in North America) do not contain the components with pharmacological properties.

Mandrake

Promoted uses:

❦ bowel regulation

❦ cancer

❦ laxative

❦ liver problems

❦ snake bite antidote

❦ warts

❦ worms

What medical science knows:

❦ Also known as podophyllum, it has been used by American Indians and colonists as a poison, as well as a medicinal agent.

❦ While it does have some medicinal properties, it is far too dangerous to be used as a herbal remedy. It is far too harsh for use as a laxative and can even cause death when taken orally. Birth defects and fetal deaths have occurred when it was given to pregnant women.

❦ You are well advised to just leave this one alone!

Melaleuca

Promoted uses:

❦ acne   ❦ cold sores   ❦ skin ailments

❦ as a douche   ❦ cuts   ❦ sunburns

❦ boils   ❦ joint pains   ❦ topical antiseptic

❦ burns   ❦ muscle pains

What medical science knows:

❦ The plant is also known as the Australian Tea Tree. It is found naturally in regions of New South Wales (Australia), especially in swampy lowlands.

❦ It has a noteworthy folklore history. It was first described in detail by crew members of Captain James Cook's expeditions in the late 1700s. It became popular as a result of its use for skin problems. Extracts from the plant were used as an antiseptic during World War II before more effective products were developed.

❦ Few studies have been conducted to assess the merits of this herb. Antiseptic properties were noted by dentists 60 years ago, and a mixture of melaleuca and isopropyl alcohol have been used as a vaginal douche for the treatment of a number of vaginal infections (e.g., trichomonas, candidiasis). Oral capsules have been used in the treatment of certain types of bladder infections, although this therapy was not particularly effective as compared to other anti- infectives. Melaleuca preparations have been used to treat a variety of skin and foot problems (e.g., athlete's foot, corns). Even so, the activity of this herb as an antimicrobial is considered to be only marginally effective.

❦ The toxicity potential is low. Some skin and vaginal irritations have occurred.

❦ Despite the benefits which are being promoted by some herbalists and pro motional programs, this herb appears to offer limited benefits as compared to commercially available products.

Milk Thistle

Promoted uses:

- bleeding
- bronchitis
- gall stones
- jaundice
- liver disorders
- liver "detoxifier"
- peritonitis
- varicose veins

What medical science knows:

- The plant does appear to have a liver protecting effect. It is currently under investigation for use in certain types of mushroom poisoning and for the treatment of cirrhosis. Apparently, some components of the plant are able to protect liver cells from damage due to biological and chemical injury.

Mullein

Promoted uses:

- asthma
- burns
- bruises
- colds
- croup
- coughs
- earaches
- gout
- hemorrhoids
- promotes free breathing
- respiratory ailments
- skin softener and protectant
- source of minerals (e.g., iron, magnesium, potassium)
- "strengthens" sinuses
- swollen joints
- tuberculosis

What medical science knows:

- This plant has enjoyed a popular history as an herbal medicinal.
- Some of the components of the plant have a demulcent (soothing) effect, but beyond that it appears to offer few medicinal benefits. Certainly, the advantages touted for it are more the product of hype than fact.
- It does not appear to be associated with significant adverse reactions.

Nettles

Promoted uses:

- antispasmodic
- asthma
- colds
- dandruff
- diuretic
- expectorant
- fever
- kidney troubles
- rheumatism
- to restore natural hair color
- to stimulate hair growth (applied topically to scalp)

What medical science knows:

- This plant is known for its stinging properties, but has also been used medicinally.
- It has been used as a cooked pot herb in salads.
- The primary adverse effect is stinging of the skin.
- Despite the variety of uses which have been promoted, the ability of this plant to irritate the skin far exceeds any medicinal value. None of the medicinal benefits listed above are substantiated by scientific research.

Parsley

Promoted uses:

- anemia
- antimicrobial
- aphrodisiac
- arthritis
- bruises
- cancer
- colic
- diuretic
- dysentery
- gallstones
- high blood pressure
- insect bites
- intestinal gas
- iron supplement
- kidney ailments
- kidney stones
- lice and other skin parasites
- liver ailments
- problems of the spleen
- prostate problems
- regulate menstrual flow
- stimulate hair growth (topical)
- to cause abortions
- tonic for blood vessels
- expectorant

What medical science knows:

- Parsley leaves and roots are popular as condiments and garnish around the world. It is the major ingredient in a national Lebanon dish called Tabbouleh.
- Parsley is a good natural source of a number of vitamins and minerals, including calcium, iron, carotene, Vitamins C and A.

❦ It contains some hallucinogens and was used as a substitute for marijuana during the 1960s.

❦ It has been used in a Russian preparation to stimulate uterine contractions during labor. However, its safety and effectiveness for this purpose have not been established.

❦ It may have some slight antimicrobial activity, but it is not known to what extent it is actually effective. To be sure, its activity is far less than commercially available products.

❦ Adverse effects are rare. People can be allergic to it, and it should not be taken by pregnant women. Other side effects have included headache, giddiness, loss of balance, convulsions and kidney damage.

Passion Flower

Promoted uses:

❦ attention disorder in children
❦ pain
❦ lung problems (e.g., asthma)
❦ burns
❦ nervous exhaustion
❦ excitability in children
❦ hemorrhoids
❦ nervousness in children
❦ "calms" blood pressure
❦ inflammations
❦ deter alcoholism
❦ calm nerves
❦ insomnia
❦ sedation

What medical science knows:

❦ The Passion flower was discovered in 1569 by Spanish explorers in Peru. They saw it as symbolic of the passion of Christ, and thus it represented Christ's approval of their efforts.

❦ The folklore surrounding this plant is ancient, and has been used by homeopaths to treat a variety of problems.

❦ The components of this plant have complex activity on the central nervous system, including both stimulation and depression. Effects include dilation of blood vessels, decreases in blood pressure and some antimicrobial activity.

❦ Its popularity in folk medicine is primarily in its sedative effects.

Pennyroyal

Promoted uses:

- fever
- gout
- induce delayed menstruation
- lung problems
- induce abortions
- toothaches
- skin problems
- stomach pains
- promotes circulation (by promoting perspiration)
- weakness

What medical science knows:

- The oil from this plant can irritate the uterus and stimulate uterine contractions. However, this action is considered to be unpredictable and dangerous.
- Use of the oil and teas made from this plant have long been associated with adverse effects (e.g., abdominal cramps, nausea, vomiting, lethargy, agitation, kidney damage, liver damage, blood disorders, seizures, hallucinations, and lung damage).
- Health authorities consider the plant to be dangerous and emphasize that extracts from it should not be ingested.

Peppermint

Promoted uses:

- bowel problems
- cancers
- colds
- cramps
- headaches
- nausea
- sore throats
- indigestion
- intestinal spasms
- "improvement of the entire system"
- toothaches

What medical science knows:

- Despite the many health uses which have been promoted for it, peppermint is used today primarily as a flavoring agent. Its therapeutic benefits are relatively minor as compared to other commercially available products.
- Peppermint oil is a complex mixture of more than 100 compounds. Menthol is the ingredient present in the highest concentration, and is responsible for some of its biological actions.
- It does have some antimicrobial activity although this has not been shown to be of clinical significance. It also appears to possess minor anti-inflammatory and anti-ulcer activity.

❦ Some people are allergic to some of the components found in peppermint.

❦ Because it can relax the digestive tract, it can worsen the symptoms of hiatal hernia.

Plantain

Promoted uses:

❦ chronic skin problems

❦ colon "cleanser"

❦ cuts and wounds

❦ hemorrhoids

❦ intestinal "lubricant"

❦ removes "putrefactive toxins" from the intestines

❦ skin infections

❦ skin inflammations

What medical science knows:

❦ Plantain is a perennial weed that is distributed worldwide. It grows aggressively, is spread easily, and has long been associated with agriculture.

❦ North American Indians referred to it as "Englishman's foot" because it spread from areas of English settlements.

❦ It is the source of psyllium seed which is used in many commercially available products as a bulk laxative.

❦ It may have some merit in treating irritable bowel syndrome and hemorrhoids.

❦ Its use on skin problems is not scientifically established, although some anecdotal studies have suggested that it may have potential in treating poison ivy.

Psyllium Seed
[see Plantain]

Rosehips

Promoted uses:

❦ arteriosclerosis

❦ infections

❦ source of Vitamin C

❦ stress

What medical science knows:

🐦 Rose hips are a natural source of Vitamin C, which explains why it is a popular item among the natural health enthusiasts. Ironically, much of the Vitamin C is lost during commercial processing, so that "natural vitamin supplements" containing Rose Hips have Vitamin C added artificially. This information is not always included on the label (especially if the promoters want you to believe that it is a "natural" product).

🐦 Actually, one would have to ingest an impractical volume of rose hips in order to obtain benefits as a nutritional supplement. Commercially available vitamin supplements are far more economical.

🐦 The role of Vitamin C in treating or preventing infections or stress-related problems has not been scientifically substantiated.

🐦 Arteriosclerosis is NOT a Vitamin C deficiency disease.

Rosemary

Promoted uses:

🐦 astringent

🐦 colds

🐦 coughs

🐦 intestinal gas

🐦 intestinal problems

🐦 intestinal spasms and cramps

🐦 nervous conditions

🐦 nervous headaches

🐦 prevent baldness

🐦 promote menstrual flow

🐦 stimulate hair growth

🐦 swelling

🐦 tonic

🐦 mouth sores

What medical science knows:

🐦 This plant is native to the Mediterranean, but is now cultivated worldwide. It is widely used as a spice. Folklore suggests that it will only grow in gardens of households where the "mistress" is truly the "master" of the house.

🐦 In addition to its promoted medical uses, it has been used in cosmetic formulations (e.g., hair products).

🐦 The actual medicinal value of this plant is difficult to assess because of a lack of studies in humans. It appears to be an antioxidant, and may have anticancer properties. Even so, there is no indication at present that the plant has any real medicinal value.

🐦 Ingestion of large amounts can be toxic (e.g., irritation of the stomach and intestines, kidney damage), and some people are allergic to it when applied to the skin.

Rue

Promoted uses:

- a "splendid remedy" for many human illnesses
- suppressed menstruation
- "tightness" of the stomach
- dizziness
- headache
- inner ear problems
- insect repellent
- intestinal worms
- sedative
- stiff neck
- stomach troubles
- antispasmodic
- bowel cramps

What medical science knows:

- Rue is a native of Europe, but is now cultivated worldwide. It has been used for centuries for a variety of medical and other purposes.
- Research indicates that components of rue do have an antispasmodic action on the smooth muscles of the digestive and circulatory system. Other components appear to have some antibacterial and antifungal actions.
- Rue can cause kidney and liver damage, violent abdominal pain, vomiting and death. It should never be used by pregnant women.
- Although it continues to be included in herbal remedies, health authorities discourage its use because of its toxicity potential.

Safflower

Promoted uses:

- fever
- induce sweating
- laxative
- prevents and helps eliminate "buildups" of lactic acids in the body

What medical science knows:

- The traditional use of safflower has been for its yellow and red dyes which have been used for centuries to color cosmetics and fabrics. It has been used as a solvent in paints, and the tea has been used for therapeutic purposes.
- As a source of unsaturated fats it has been investigated for its ability to lower cholesterol and blood lipid levels.
- It appears to have limited value as a laxative and to treat fevers.
- There is no indication that it is useful in preventing or treating gout, or in eliminating uric and lactic acids.

Saffron

Promoted uses:

- a "natural" digestive aid
- expectorant
- to promote perspiration
- aphrodisiac
- gout
- to soothe the entire digestive tract
- arthritis
- sedative
- colds
- skin balm

What medical science knows:

- True saffron is native to Asia Minor and southern Europe. It takes about 70,000 flowers to provide 1 pound of true saffron, which can bring $30 / ounce in American markets. The less expensive American saffron is sometimes used to adulterate true saffron.

- Saffron has been used as a flavor and as a dye for cloths.

- Research indicates that some components of saffron may offer some potential in the treatment of some skin problems, for spinal cord injuries, high blood pressure, and may have anticancer activity. A German patent has been granted for a product used to treat premature ejaculation, and an Australian patent has been granted for a product designed to restore hair growth in baldness. (NOTE: The fact that a patent has been granted does NOT mean that the product is actually effective!).

- An unusual property of one of its components is that of increasing the oxygenation of blood. Thus, a commercial product may prove useful in treating conditions such as atherosclerosis. It may also be able to reduce cholesterol and triglyceride levels in the blood.

- There is some epidemiological evidence that the low incidence of heart disease in some parts of Spain may be related to the frequent consumption of saffron.

- The promotion of perspiration is not a cold remedy.

- It is not generally considered to be toxic when ingested as a food. However, some adverse effects have been reported with large amounts.

Sage

Promoted uses:

- as a hair tonic
- excessive sweating
- stomach inflammation
- asthma
- improve heart circulation
- stomach troubles
- astringent
- topical anesthetic
- diarrhea
- poor digestion
- painful menstruation

What medical science knows:

❦ This plant is native to the Mediterranean and grows throughout much of the world. It should not be confused with red sage or the sage brush of the desert.

❦ As a fragrance it has been used to suppress fish odors and is used as a fragrance in soaps and perfumes. It is widely used as a flavoring agent.

❦ Extracts of the plant have been used for a wide range of problems. Research indicates that components of sage do have some properties as anti-oxidants, antimicrobials, and anti-spasmodic effects. Despite its long history of use for the treatment of health problems, there is little evidence that it is actually effective for any of them. Certainly, it appears to offer no particular benefits over other commercially available products.

❦ Side effects and toxicities are rare, but there have been reports of stomach irritation from sage teas and the ingestion of large amounts have caused dry mouth and local irritation.

Sassafras

Promoted uses:

❦ clears toxins from the body

❦ to induce sweating

❦ skin disorders

❦ liver "stimulant"

❦ "purifies" the blood

❦ insect bites and stings

❦ "useful" for the blood system

What medical science knows:

❦ Sassafras is an ancient plant which has been present in Europe, North America, Greenland and Eastern Asia. American Indians used it for the treatment of a variety of ailments. American settlers then exported it to Europe, where it proved to be ineffective.

❦ It has been used as a fragrance in soaps and perfumes, as a soup thickener and as a flavor in Root Beer.

❦ It has been banned in the U.S. by the FDA because of its potential to cause cancer. Yet, it continues to be used by an uninformed public. Ironically, there is at least one report that it has anti-cancer activity. However, animal studies have repeatedly confirmed its potential to cause certain types of cancers. Some of these are similar to certain human cancers.

❦ Research indicates that components of the plant have some antimicrobial properties.

❦ Allergic reactions have been reported in humans, and animal studies have indicated that it can cause loss of coordination in movement, drooping eyelids, sensitivity to touch.

❦ Scientific evidence clearly indicates that this agent has no rational place in human medicine. Long-term consumption can pose a significant health risk. Since there are no documented health benefits from its use, the risks clearly outweigh any possible benefits.

Saw Palmetto Berries

Promoted uses:

❦ diseases of the reproductive system

❦ relieves mucus in the head and nose

❦ diuretic

❦ urinary problems

❦ increase breast size

❦ organs (male and female)

❦ increase sexual vigor

❦ increase sperm production

❦ enlarged prostate

What medical science knows:

❦ Scientific research has indicated that some components of the berries may actually be beneficial in reducing benign (non-cancerous) enlargement of the prostate. However, this is NOT a problem that should be self-diagnosed and self-treated. Only a physician can determine if prostate symptoms are due to a benign problem or to cancer of the prostate.

❦ Adverse effects and toxicity appear to be infrequent.

❦ Studies do not support the reports that these berries are sexual stimulants or aphrodisiacs.

Scullcap

Promoted uses:

❦ "calms and soothes" the entire nervous system

❦ digestive aid

❦ female "weakness"

❦ hangovers

❦ hydrophobia (rabies)

❦ nerve sedative

❦ tranquilizer

What medical science knows:

❦ Grows throughout the U.S. in moist woods. Related species are found elsewhere in the world (e.g., China).

❦ It has been promoted for a variety of problems for centuries. However, even many herbalists have abandoned its use for many of its touted purposes.

❦ Research has indicated that the plant appears to have little ability to depress the central nervous system (i.e., limited potential as a tranquilizer) and has little activity on the circulatory system. Some animal research indicates an ability to reduce blood pressure, although the significance for humans is unknown. Components of the plant have some anti-inflammatory activity and may have some potential as anti-cancer agents. Other components have antibacterial and antifungal activity.

❦ It appears to be associated with a low tendency for toxicity if used in "normal" doses. However, overdoses can result in epileptic-type symptoms (e.g., stupor, confusion, giddiness, twitching of the limbs, irregular pulse).

❦ The present position of health authorities is that the plant has not been demonstrated to offer true medicinal benefits. It continues to be investigated for possible uses.

Senna

Promoted Uses:

❦ a "splendid" laxative

What Medical Science Knows:

❦ Senna has a long history in both Arabic and European medicine as a laxative. The leaves are brewed as a tea for this purpose. Unfortunately, it is almost impossible to control the concentration of the resulting brew and the results can be quite disturbing.

❦ This is a potent laxative which should hardly be described as "splendid!" It belongs to a category which is known as "stimulant laxatives" and is capable of causing laxative dependency (along with other such notables as Exlax).

❦ Do yourself a favor . . . avoid this one. Even if you truly wanted a senna product, there are safer commercial products available at every pharmacy, grocery and convenience store.

❦ Stimulant laxatives should never be selected as a first choice for treating bowel problems, including constipation. Instead, first try a bulk laxative (e.g., psyllium, Metamucil, etc.), which work naturally, are less harsh, less dangerous and do NOT cause laxative dependency.

Slippery Elm

Promoted uses:

- black or bruised eyes
- boils
- "cleans out" the colon
- cold sores
- constipation
- diarrhea
- digestive aid
- eye pain
- hemorrhoids
- kidney problems
- lung "pain"
- "normalizes" bowel
- movements
- sore threats
- urinary tract inflammations

What medical science knows:

- The Slippery Elm grows in moist woods in the U.S. and Canada. Parts of the plant have been used by Indians to treat a variety of health problems.
- It has been used for more than 100 years in folk medicine and continues to find use in products such as throat lozenges and as a demulcent for respiratory irritations.
- Its medicinal potential is questionable, and you are certainly well-advised to not waste your money on it as a digestive aid.

St. John's Wort

Promoted uses:

- a powerful blood "purifier"
- anxiety
- boils
- cancer
- chronic problems of the uterus
- depression
- diuretic
- insomnia
- menstrual irregularities
- stomach irritations
- skin problems
- tumors

What medical science knows:

- This plant was native to Europe, but is now found in the U.S. and Canada. Legend has it that its brightest blooms coincide with the birthday of John the Baptist.
- It has been used as an herbal remedy since the Middle Ages. For some time folk healers lost interest in it, but more recently it has again become of interest to herbalists.
- There is no scientific evidence to support its use in cancer.

- Research indicates that components of this plant do have an astringent action, which would explain how it might be perceived to promote wound healing. It may also have some antibacterial actions.

- Of greatest concern is the finding a component of this plant belongs to a category of compounds known as Monoamine Oxidase Inhibitors (or, MAOIs). MAOIs are associated with some very serious drug / food interactions. These foods include certain alcoholic beverages, aged cheeses and many other foods. The result is a very dangerous, and sometimes fatal, increase in blood pressure.

- AVOID THIS ONE! The risks far outweigh any potential benefits as compared to commercially available medicinal products.

Tansy

Promoted uses:

- antispasmodic
- "very good for heart"
- to induce menstruation
- soothes the bowels
- "strengthens weak veins"
- insect repellent
- worms
- "tones" the system

What medical science knows:

- The name Tansy is thought to be derived from "athanasia," which is the Greek word for immortality. Thus, the herb has been used in embalming!

- Despite its potential for toxicity, it has been used for centuries for a variety of therapeutic purposes. It has also been used as a flavoring agent, and as a green dye in perfumes.

- The toxicity potential of this product is significant. As little as 10 drops of the oil has been fatal, as have teas prepared from this plant. Adverse effects include rapid and feeble pulse, severe stomach irritation, violent spasms, convulsions and death. Skin allergies can occur with topical exposure.

- There is little scientific evidence to support any use of this product as a medicinal product.

- We recommend you avoid this one!

Uva - Ursi

Promoted uses:

- bladder infections
- bladder irritations
- digestive stimulant
- kidney infections
- kidney irritations
- laxative
- to "cleanse and strengthen" the spleen

What medical science knows:

- This is another product that has been around for centuries. The leaves have been smoked, and the berries have been used to prepare liquid vehicles in which other drugs could be given. It has been included in many nonprescription diuretic products.

- Some components of the plant do have mild diuretic activity, stimulate the flow of bile, have mild antimicrobial and astringent effects.

- It is toxic in large doses. Symptoms include ringing of the ears, nausea, vomiting, cyanosis, convulsions, collapse and death. However, serious adverse effects are rare with the use of commercial products because the dose is quite low. It can cause the urine to turn green in color.

- There is no scientific evidence that this plant provides true medicinal benefits.

Valerian

Promoted uses:

- "good" for the circulatory system
- sedative
- promote sleep
- "quiet and calm" the nervous system
- a natural source of the prescription drug Valium

What medical science knows:

- The plant sometimes has a disagreeable odor, although it was used as a fragrance for perfumes in the 1500s. It has been used as a sedative for centuries, and is still popular in many European countries for this purpose. American chiropractors, naturopaths and herbalists sometimes "prescribe" it for their patients.

- Scientific research indicates the components of this plant are able to increase blood flow to the heart, decrease heart rate, blood pressure and oxygen consumption. Its sedative effect is thought to be due to several components of the plant, and not to any single component. It appears to be able to reduce the time required to go to sleep, although larger doses can increase morning drowsiness.

- Adverse effects appear to be low. A decrease in coordination in movement, decreased temperature, muscle relaxation, headaches, excitability, uneasiness and heart disturbances have been reported. It is not known if it can interact in negative ways with other sedative-type drugs, although it does not appear to have an additive effect with alcohol.
- Even though it is generally considered to be safe, there are concerns about long-term use.
- Some herbal promoters have claimed that the prescription drug VALIUM is obtained synthetically from this plant. However, this is NOT true!

Wintergreen

Promoted uses:

- astringent
- bowel obstructions
- muscle aches and pains
- intestinal gas
- colic
- pain relief
- "stimulate" the stomach
- "stimulate" the heart
- "stimulate" respiration

What medical science knows:

- This plant has been used in traditional medicine for years for medicinal purposes and as a flavoring agent.
- Small doses of wintergreen oil stimulate digestion and secretions of the stomach. Large doses cause vomiting and can be fatal. However, there are no deaths reported as a result of ingestion of the plant itself. If ingested over long periods of time, people have experienced ringing in the ears, nausea and vomiting.
- Bowel obstructions should never be treated with self-care because of the risk of intestinal rupture, which can be fatal.
- Even though this plant has some usefulness, there are commercial products available which are are considerably more effective and convenient to purchase. So why bother with the herb?

Witch Hazel

Promoted uses:

- burns
- cancers
- colds
- diarrhea
- eye irritations
- fever
- hemorrhoids
- "restore" circulation
- itching and inflammations
- stiff joints
- tuberculosis

What medical science knows:

- Witch Hazel has a long history of use in the U.S. In Europe, an alcoholic preparation is taken internally to treat varicose veins.
- It is an astringent, which explains its use for hemorrhoids and diarrhea.
- Health authorities do not recommend that Witch Hazel preparations be taken orally. The toxicity potential is not well known, although nausea, vomiting and constipation have been reported. Some of the components could cause liver damage if absorbed in sufficient quantity.
- Some health foods suppliers promote teas which can be brewed from leaves and twigs of the plant, but this is not recommended, since the safety of this practice has not been established.
- One of the components in this plant is known to cause cancer, but it is present in smaller quantities than that found in sassafras.
- There is little scientific evidence to support the many medical benefits which are promoted for this product.

Wood Betony

Promoted uses:

- anxiety
- "cleans impurities" from the blood
- diarrhea
- head and face pain
- headaches
- heartburn
- indigestion
- liver obstructions
- mouth irritations
- spleen obstruction
- stomach cramps
- throat irritations

What medical science knows:

- There are few plants with the history of this one. It has been around since the Roman Empire, where it was promoted as a "cure" for practically every known ailment. During the Middle Ages it was thought to have magical powers. It is used by herbalists today to treat a variety of problems.

❦ It appears that it might offer some meager benefits for the treatment of diarrhea, although there are numerous commercial products which are far more reliable. Apparently it is able to produce a mild lowering of blood pressure, which may account for its use in headaches. However, research does not support this.

❦ Adverse effects are thought to be rare, although it can cause irritation of the stomach and intestines in larger doses.

❦ The available information suggests that it has more potential as an ornamental plant than a medicinal agent.

Woodruff

Promoted uses:

❦ antispasmodic

❦ restlessness

❦ insomnia

❦ diuretic

❦ expectorant

❦ "gravel" and bladder stones

❦ improved wound healing

❦ calmative for nervous conditions

❦ to induce sweating

❦ hysteria

❦ stomach pain

❦ swelling

❦ throat irritations

❦ liver problems

What medical science knows:

❦ In addition to its promoted medicinal uses, the dried herb is used in sachets, perfumes and fragrances. It is used as a flavor in some wines, vermouth, bitters, food and candies.

❦ Components of the plant have been shown to have some anti-inflammatory and antibacterial activity.

❦ It is considered to be generally safe when used in foods or as a flavoring agent. However, one of its components could result in liver damage, growth retardation, atrophy of the testicles and impaired blood clotting if ingested in large quantities.

❦ As used by most herbalists it is probably harmless, but relatively useless in terms of its true medicinal value.

Wormwood

Promoted uses:

- bruises
- sedative
- sprains
- to produce sweating
- tonic
- worms

What medical science knows:

- The name of this plant comes from ancient physicians who used it to treat worms. It was the primary ingredient in absinthe, a toxic liqueur that caused absinthism (characterized by intellectual enfeeblement, hallucinations, psychosis and brain damage). The drink is now outlawed, but was popular until the early 1900s. Some people will try anything, which is why herbs and health fraud are thriving businesses!

- Components of wormwood can be used to treat certain worm infestations. However, these products can also cause convulsions, digestive disorders, thirst, restlessness, vertigo, trembling of the limbs, numbness of the extremities, loss of intellect, delirium, paralysis and death. It's a high price to pay for treating worms!

- The FDA has classified wormwood as an unsafe herb . . . with good reason!

Yarrow

Promoted uses:

- astringent
- fever
- flu
- "healing and soothing" effect on mucous membranes
- shampoos
- sneezing
- tonic
- toothaches

What medical science knows:

- Yarrow is native to Europe and Asia and is now found in North America. Its use in food and medicine is ancient. Folklore has it that it was used by Achilles.

- It has been used as a tea, in salads, as cosmetic cleansers and as a medicine.

- The plant appears to induce sweating, promotes wound healing, causes bleeding to stop when applied to wounds and may have some anti-cancer and anti-inflammatory activities.

- It is generally considered to be safe when used as a food or beverage, although some people have allergic reactions to it.

❦ Although the plant appears to have some medicinal potential, there is insufficient scientific data to indicate appropriate doses. As mentioned earlier, sweating is a folklore treatment for colds and flu. There is no real evidence to support the belief that sweating can impact colds and flu.

Yellow Dock

Promoted uses:

❦ a blood "purifier"

❦ an endurance builder

❦ "cleansing" the lymph system

❦ laxative

❦ skin problems

❦ venereal disease

❦ toothpaste

❦ tonic

❦ "tones" the entire system

What medical science knows:

❦ This one has been used in salads, but some folks find the tart taste to be disagreeable. It has been used for the treatment of a variety of health problems.

❦ Little research has been conducted on this plant. It is known that some of its components can cause both a laxative effect and constipation. And, it may possibly have some anti-cancer activity.

❦ It can be irritating to tissues of the digestive and other systems, causing irritation to the stomach and intestines, kidney damage, diarrhea, nausea and frequent urination. Large amounts eaten by livestock have resulted in deaths. Some people are allergic to it when applied to the skin.

❦ It would appear that the few potential benefits of this plant (i.e., a laxative effect) are minor compared to the potential problems which it can cause. Commercial laxatives are available which have more predictable results, and which are much safer.

Yerba Santa

Promoted uses:

❦ asthma

❦ bruises

❦ bronchial congestion

❦ chest conditions

❦ colds

❦ coughs

❦ expectorant

❦ fever

❦ nasal discharge

❦ rheumatism

❦ tuberculosis

What Medical Science Knows:

❦ The name of yerba santa means "holy weed" and was given by Spanish priests who learned of its medicinal potential from American Indians. A tea from this plant has been used in the treatment of numerous health problems. It has also been used as a flavor in foods and beverages.

❦ Components of the plant do appear to have an expectorant action, although the true value of expectorants is controversial. It is unlikely that it is able to offer any significant benefits for nasal drainage, per se, and there is no evidence that the plant offers any benefits for problems such as rheumatism.

Yucca Root

Promoted uses:

❦ arthritis	❦ high blood pressure	❦ migraines
❦ colitis	❦ joint inflammations	❦ rheumatism

What medical science knows:

❦ All of the various species of yucca plants depend upon Yucca moths for pollination. These plants provided American Indians with the materials needed for making ropes, sandals, and cloth. It has been used in the making of soap. Both Indians and California settlers used it for food, and the Indians used it to make a beverage for high rituals. Today it is used as a foaming agent in carbonated beverages, as a flavor and in drug synthesis.

❦ Contemporary medical research has indicated that components of yucca may have anti-cancer activity, be useful in the treatment of arthritis, lower blood pressure and cholesterol levels and reduce the frequency of migraine headaches.

❦ Taking these products orally does not appear to be toxic to humans. However, little is actually known about the potential toxicity of this plant, especially in long-term use.

REFERENCES - HERBS

1. *A Useful Guide to Herbal Health Care.* Health Center for Better Living, Inc., Naples, FL. (1995).

2. *The Lawrence Review Of Natural Products,* Facts and Comparisons, St. Louis, (1995).

32. BIOTECHNOLOGY — BETTER LIVING THROUGH HIGH-TECH SCIENCE

> "It is easier for the scientific mind to unleash natural forces than for the human soul to exercise wisdom and generosity in the use of power."
>
> — Rene Dubos

The future of professional medical care looks promising. Because of biotechnology, it is reasonably clear that there will be major advances in the prevention, diagnosis and treatment of many diseases. It is less certain that biotechnology will somehow offer an antidote for aging. New technological advances will likely increase the average age to which people can expect to live (e.g., by better control of certain diseases), but it is not known at present if biotechnology can increase the absolute age to which people can expect to live. This is because aging may not be altered by eliminating certain diseases (e.g., heart disease, cancers), or by somehow "switching off" a certain aging gene that would allow us to live forever.

We tend to live unhealthy lifestyles despite the attention being given to exercise and diet in the media. We are damaging the Earth and our natural resources at an alarming rate, and with an almost total disregard for the impact of this folly on our health. No doubt there are limits to the ability of biotechnology to completely reverse the impact of generations of unhealthy and destructive living. The real potential of biotechnology may occur by combining technology with the adoption of more healthy lifestyles.

In any case, biotechnology merits discussion in a health book because of the potential it offers for solving many health problems. In fact, most authorities are convinced that biotechnology will become the basis for scientific and technological advances in medicine for the next century.

Biotechnology uses living organisms (or parts of organisms) to make new products, modify existing ones, or to improve plants or animals. It has already provided new products and new ways of producing drug products. And when a needed drug is relatively unavailable from other sources or may cause serious adverse reactions (e.g., allergies) then biotechnology is a particularly attractive alternative. For example, many products formerly obtained from human blood sources are now being developed using biotechnology techniques because of concerns about Hepatitis B and HIV infections.

Actually, biotechnology dates back thousands of years. It has been used throughout history in food production (leavening bread, making cheese and yogurt and fermenting wine). Farmers used biotechnology for centuries to modify plants and animals through selective breeding processes in order to produce more desirable offspring, and more recently to alter their crops or livestock by gene modification. These advances could have a significant impact on the quality and quantity of the world's food supply in the future.

It may also be possible to create plants that can better withstand environmental extremes (e.g., temperature extremes) pests and diseases. Gene changes could reduce the need for chemical pesticides. Some of these new crops may serve as new energy resources, which would help to reduce our dependency upon petroleum imports, and improve the environment. Animals can be bred that are more resistant to diseases and stress. The development of safer and more effective vaccines could prevent livestock diseases, thus reducing the need for antibiotics and other drugs.

Certainly, agricultural biotechnology can benefit society by providing a higher quality food supply, reducing environmental damage, and by providing a means for the development of new drug products.

But perhaps the most intriguing biotechnology advances are those being explored to address various health problems. During the past two decades, for example, scientists have been particularly interested in learning how to modify genes in order to treat diseases. In fact, farm animals and plants are being genetically modified to produce new drug products. For example, researchers have genetically modified animals so that they produce drugs in their milk. One company has developed pigs that produce human blood cells. If this process proves to be safe and effective, it could provide a readily available human blood substitute. The advantages of this approach would be reduced costs for blood products, a reduced risk of contamination by infectious agents (e.g., HIV), and elimination of blood typing and cross matching.

Biotechnology offers a number of advantages as compared to traditional methods of drug manufacturing. It provides an alternative method of producing highly purified drug products. It allows for the production of medicinal agents that were previously unavailable, or only available in small quantities. Finally, it has allowed scientists to better understand some diseases. Nevertheless, biotechnology is still not viewed as a replacement for traditional medicine. Instead, current research efforts are attempting to combine biotechnology products with traditional therapies.

The Ocean: A New Biotechnology Frontier

During the 1970s scientists learned that ocean coral contained compounds with medicinal qualities (e.g., prostaglandin-like substances). This was the first observation that the ocean might be a source of potential drug products. The interest in prostaglandins stemmed from their use as muscle relaxants and heart drugs, but their natural supply is limited. This ocean discovery provided the potential for a new supply.

Some marine animals may also represent a source of anti-inflammatory agents. In fact, scientists have isolated more than 30 different substances from about 200 species of animals. Many of these potential drug agents are more powerful than anti-inflammatory drugs which are currently available. Finally, new microorganisms have been identified from sediments taken from the sea floor, resulting in the development of two new antibiotics.

The Push for Biotechnology

Some people predict that biomedical science will advance more in the next 10 years than it has in the past 100. This should come as no surprise, since it was estimated that in 1979 more than 80% of all of the scientists who have ever lived . . . were still living! Much of this scientific focus involves medicine. Obviously, there are compelling reasons for this interest.

As more and more Americans expect to reach old age, the diseases associated with aging receive more attention. Our health concerns have shifted from surviving *to* old age to surviving *through* old age. In many ways this represents a shift of concern from our quantity to our quality of life.

There are currently no cures for many of the diseases that we now fear most (e.g., cancers, arthritis, Alzheimer's, AIDS), which has prompted considerable scientific attention in the search for new preventive and therapeutic agents.

There is little doubt that biotechnology will eventually result in an explosion of new therapies. While most of these will only be available through physicians, self-care products will continue to emerge as they have in the past (e.g., home test kits).

It may be possible to design specific biotechnology products which can destroy cancer cells, prevent cancers formation or prevent them from spreading. Some products may be able to inhibit tumor growth or alter genes that are responsible for cancer growth.

Biotechnology may provide for a greater understanding of cancer as a disease. At least some cancers occur because certain genes malfunction. Scientists are beginning to discover how these genes are activated, which proteins they affect, the nature of the message which they transmit and how to inactivate them. Other genes appear to be able to prevent cancer formation and growth. These genes are known as Tumor Supressor Genes. Understanding how these genes operate may provide valuable information regarding cancers and how to treat or prevent them.

Yet, as wonderful as these prospects seem, problems still exist in the advance of biotechnology. Some techniques are quite expensive and produce no cures (e.g., one current treatment procedure costs $60,000 / year as long as it is used). Many of the emerging biotechnology products have significant adverse effects, which science must learn to control before these drugs are made available to the public. These economic and safety concerns continue to represent significant barriers for many biotechnology products.

In the last decade geriatric medicine has become a major focus of investigation for the health care industry for a number of reasons. Although only 12% of the U.S. population is over the age of 65, more than 40% of hospital admissions involve older people and 40% of our health care dollars are spent on this population. If present trends continue, the number of elderly will double by the year 2000, and will account for 75% of health care dollars by the year 2030. Currently, Americans over 85 represent the fastest growing segment of the population. By the year 2040, 50% of Americans are expected to survive to age 85. Biotechnology offers the hope of reducing health care costs by decreasing our reliance upon expensive hospital and other medical resources. Of course there is the continuing hope that biotechnology can somehow unlock the mystery of the aging process.

With all of these developments, however, there are still concerns. We need to be careful not to be seduced by the glamour of biotechnology or tempted to use it far in excess of what is appropriate or beneficial. This outcome could result in even greater health care costs than we currently have. Some of these products are already being promoted for conditions for which they have not been proven to be either safe or effective.

It is estimated that there will be a 15-fold growth in the sales and use of biotechnology products during the next five years. For this reason alone it is important to learn more about the benefits and limitations of these products so that we avoid doing more harm than good.

Biotechnology Basics

All of the information required by nature to create an organism is encoded in biological units called nucleotides. These four units are:

- Adenine (A)
- Cytosine (C)
- Thymine (T)
- Guanine (G)

These 4 compounds are bound together in certain patterns in DNA units called genes. Scientists have learned how cells "read" the information in genes to make proteins, amino acids and the other substances which our bodies need. The order of A, T, C and G units in a gene determines the number and kind of proteins, carbohydrates and fats produced by the body.

Recombinant Proteins

In the 1970s, molecular biologists discovered how to isolate particular genes and move them from one organism to another. For example, a gene can be removed from a person and transplanted into a bacteria. The bacteria is then used as a "factory" to manufacture a desired protein. This is called *genetic engineering*, and the protein made in this way is called a *recombinant protein* because it is made by recombining DNA from two sources. The advantage of this process is that it can be used to produce larger quantities of the protein for research or for drugs.

There are problems associated with this approach that are not associated with other drug products. Most of these products cannot be taken orally, there may be a limited time during which they can be used effectively as a therapeutic agent and they can be quite expensive to produce.

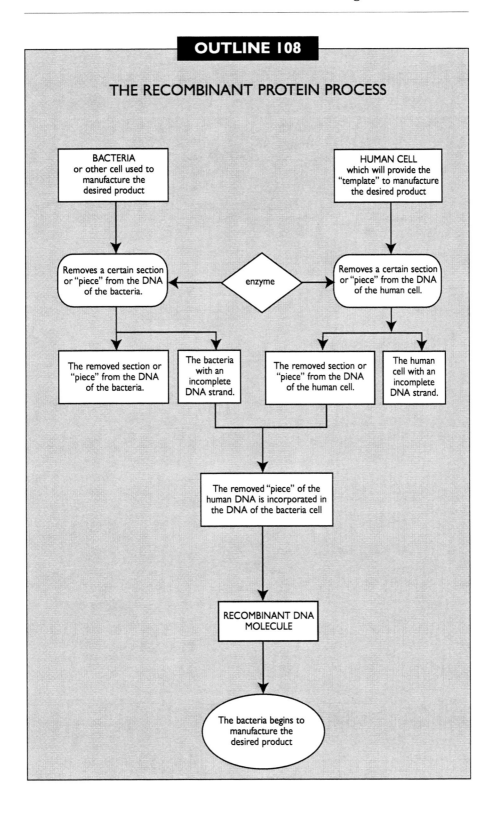

Another application of recombinant protein processes involves the use of computers. Synthetic chemistry is being used in conjunction with computer-assisted modeling of molecular interactions. By using all of these technologies, scientists are able to design and synthesize relatively small chemical entities. Many of these can be used for highly specific therapeutic applications. This is because they can be designed to bind to specific receptors in the body, or can alter the activity of certain enzymes. They can even be designed to regulate certain gene functions.

Monoclonal Antibodies

Outline 109 summarizes how monoclonal antibodies are made. This technology allows for the production of large quantities of certain types of antibodies. This ability to create larger volumes of these specific substances has yielded a new source of agents for the diagnoses and treatment of diseases.

Monoclonal antibodies are the largest category of biotechnology products currently in development. Major areas of research include drugs to prevent the rejection of organ transplants, cancer drugs and diagnostic agents (e.g., heart and cancer diseases). Their use is also being explored in diseases in which the immune system is not working properly. The diagnosis and treatment of cancers has become an exciting arena because of advances in molecular biology and the identification of markers on the surfaces of immune and cancer cells. Monoclonal antibodies appear to be able to guide cancer drugs directly to the tumor cell.

Some monoclonal antibodies can convert inactive forms of a drug into its active form at the tumor site. Radioactive drugs can be attached to a monoclonal antibody that is specifically attracted to cancer cells. In this way the radioactive agent is carried directly to the cell that needs to be killed, or it can be used for location and identification of tumors. Very small tumors can be detected using this approach.

Many diagnostic agents and kits (including home test kits) utilize monoclonal antibodies. This trend will likely continue. They have been used to identify tumors, blood clots, damaged heart tissues, infectious agents and pregnancy. New diagnostic kits will eventually be available as self-test kits.

The majority of monoclonal antibodies are being investigated as anticancer agents (lung, ovary, colon, rectal, pancreas, breast, melanoma). Others are being designed for conditions in which the immune

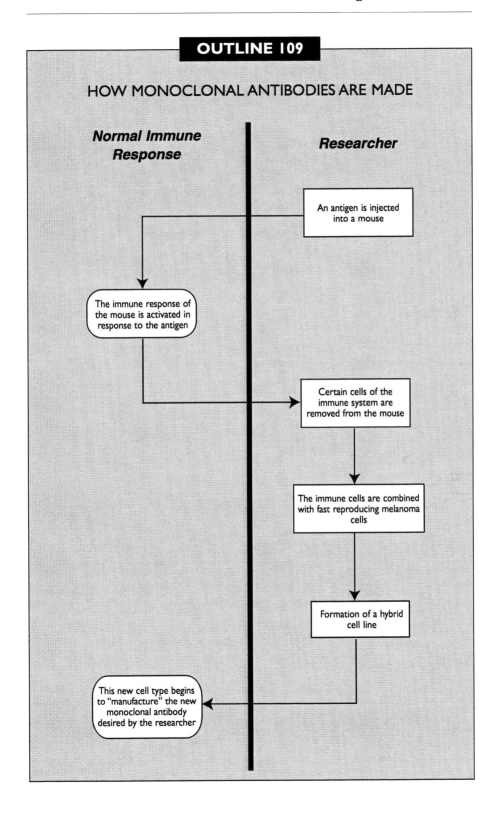

OUTLINE 109

HOW MONOCLONAL ANTIBODIES ARE MADE

Normal Immune Response

Researcher

An antigen is injected into a mouse

The immune response of the mouse is activated in response to the antigen

Certain cells of the immune system are removed from the mouse

The immune cells are combined with fast reproducing melanoma cells

Formation of a hybrid cell line

This new cell type begins to "manufacture" the new monoclonal antibody desired by the researcher system is involved. Since they are able to inhibit clot formation, they have been used in heart patients to block the occurrence of arterial strokes and minimize the damage of heart conditions (e.g., heart attacks). Some monoclonal antibodies target certain cells in the body. This provides them with the potential to target therapy for certain diseases. For example, cytokines (important mediators of disease) may be blocked with specific monoclonal antibodies.

Genetic Engineering (Gene Manipulation)

Genetic engineering is allowing scientists to learn more about the nature of cancer, atherosclerosis, and other diseases. For example, a gene was discovered that is associated with cystic fibrosis. Identification of this gene may allow for a greater understanding of the disease and for the formulation of new ways to treat and prevent this condition.

Other research involves the central nervous system. Substances produced by the brain that affect pain, emotions, appetite, sexuality, mood, desire, motivation and other aspects of behavior are subjects of study. Biotechnology may provide for a greater understanding and therapy for mental illnesses, addictions, emotional and behavioral problems.

Never before in history has medical science had the knowledge and technology to detect and replace defective genes, manipulate complex human cells or identify defects in chromosomes. Scientists are now able to locate specific sites on chromosomes which are responsible for diseases. Even so, the exact relationship between defective genes and the ways in which a disease manifests itself is not always clear.

Genotyping is a genetic engineering processes which may help physicians to identify patients who are more likely to develop serious forms of a disease. For example, rheumatoid arthritis is a crippling disease that can reduce life expectancy by a decade or more in its most severe forms. Aggressive therapy with anti-inflammatory and immunosuppressive drugs can be quite beneficial. However, these drugs can have serious side effects over time. Physicians are often reluctant to prescribe them until the disease has reached advanced stages. In such cases, treatment may be too late to offer much help. If physicians could identify patients who are more likely to develop aggressive forms of the disease, they could select appropriate treatments earlier in its course.

Researchers are genotyping patients, then following them over a period of time to study how well the genotyping predicts the course of the disease. Even though many questions remain to be answered, this process holds great promise for identifying patients who are at high risk.

Gene therapy involves replacing a defective gene with a normal one. This is accomplished by inserting a normal gene into cells with defective genes in order to correct cell function. It may also be possible to provide cells with new functions or properties that they ordinarily would not have. Despite its highly controversial nature, gene therapy may prove to be quite beneficial for people with certain diseases. Problems remain because each disease is different and demands a different strategy. Health scientists are likely to proceed cautiously to insure that the sensationalistic quality of this type of therapy does not outpace established facts.

Currently, gene therapy is being tested in brain cancer to see if it is possible to make tumor cells more susceptible to drug therapy. Viruses are being used to transfer a gene containing a needed enzyme. The enzyme causes brain cancer cells to become susceptible to the cancer drug, ganciclovir. The drug destroys the tumor cells and the viruses which transferred the gene. Normal brain cells do not take up the virus and are not affected by the drug.

Researchers at the University of Pittsburgh have been working with bone marrow cell extracts in an attempt to find a cure for Gaucher's Disease. This is a rare inherited disease characterized by a defective gene. The gene is normally responsible for producing an enzyme needed by the brain to break down certain substances. Preliminary findings indicate that it may be possible to replace the defective gene.

Both animal and human studies indicate that gene replacement therapy may also prove beneficial in the treatment of cystic fibrosis. In the human trials, cystic fibrosis patients are infected with common cold viruses that have been genetically altered. The virus carries a normal gene to replace a defective gene inherited by these patients. As the virus invades the lungs, it spreads the new genetic materials. It is still not known if the process can result in permanent improvements or whether therapy will fail if the patient is immune to the virus being used to carry the new gene.

Some people inherit a defective gene that results in high cholesterol levels (familial hypercholesterolemia). Some studies indicate that it may be possible to improve the patient's problem by replacing the defective gene. Here too, however, it is not yet known whether the results are permanent.

Gene repair techniques involve efforts to repair defective genes. If successful, this would truly represent a therapeutic revolution by allowing physicians to not only manage diseases, but to cure them by repairing defective genes.

Gene modification involves alteration of a natural substance in some way to produce new biological agents (e.g., new drugs). Presently, new medicinals are being investigated to treat infections (e.g., bacteria, fungi, viruses), heart and other problems. Gene manipulation techniques can be used to improve natural products. The activity of a natural substance usually reflects its function in the body. Gene modification could alter the activity of natural substances so that they are stronger, have more specific actions, or have fewer adverse effects.

Gene transfer represents still another genetic engineering technique and is the most controversial example of biotechnology. For example, gene transfer could involve the insertion of new genes into human embryos in an effort to produce a more "perfect" or "desirable" baby. This is forbidden in conventional science and will likely remain so because of ethical concerns and the potential for misuse. Moreover, such experimentation could permanently alter the human gene pool in unpredictable and possibly hazardous ways. Still, if used responsibly, gene transfer techniques might eventually be used to repair genes in a defective embryo or in patients with certain diseases.

Categories of Medicinal Agents

Anti-inflammatory agents are of interest because inflammation is associated with many diseases, injuries and even therapies (e.g., surgery). Reduction of inflammation could serve to reduce tissue damage. Scientists are always searching for new anti-inflammatory drugs.

Cytokines are substances which are involved in communication between cells, especially cells in the immune system. They affect or modify the immune response in various ways. They are produced and released by white blood cells and occasionally by some other cell types. All cytokines act as communicators within the immune system, although some have effects on other body systems as well (i.e., they communicate signals between immune cells or from immune cell to target cells of the body). So, these agents are highly specialized hormones which are responsible for much of the coordination and function of the immune system. Some are able to modify biological responses. Research indicates that there may be more than 100 potential medicinal agents of this type. They are presently associated with intensive investigation largely because recombinant DNA technology has made them readily available.

Cytokines can activate or boost a compromised immune system (e.g., to fight infection or autoimmunity problems); or suppress an immune system which has been activated by infection or autoimmunity. Extreme suppression of the nervous system can result in the development of opportunistic infections and certain cancers. Opportunistic infections may not be easily treated and are often associated with complications.

Some factors which contribute to immune system depression include certain drugs (e.g., chemotherapy, bone marrow suppression, organ transplant rejection agents) which can result in bone marrow disorders that produce low white blood cell counts (e.g., leukopenia, neutropenia) or of all cellular elements (e.g., aplastic anemia). Other factors include viruses (e.g., HIV), nutritional deficiencies, trauma (e.g., severe burns), psychological stress. All of these factors can suppress the immune system and predispose us to certain infections.

Colony stimulating factors (CSFs) are a group of agents presently under investigation for their ability to assist in the growth, development and differentiation of immune cells that have been suppressed by disease, drug therapy or other possible causes. These agents are being investigated for potential use in preventing adverse drug reactions due to cancer drugs (e.g., decreased bone marrow function), treatment of AIDS and related problems, and other diseases which result in bone marrow failures.

Enzymes and regulators of enzyme activities are also of considerable interest for several reasons. Enzymes are substances which accelerate normal biological processes that might not occur without them. Enzymes and enzyme inhibitors can facilitate or inhibit normal bodily functions, as well as disease. They may be used to treat diseases which are characterized by enzyme deficiencies, can correct metabolic problems and can remove pathological metabolites which accumulate during certain diseases.

Growth factors are indirectly responsible for the production of wound healing components in the body that may prove beneficial in the healing process. These agents are now being produced in large quantities by recombinant DNA technology, and may be the next major breakthrough in the care of chronic wounds that are difficult to heal.

One proposed use is to create a large volume of white blood cells. These could then be given to patients to improve their defense against suppression of the immune system for whatever reason. Historically, neutropenia has been the major limiting toxicity associated with chemotherapy, but apparently this can be managed with growth factors.

Hematopoietic growth factors are agents that stimulate the production of red and white blood cells.

Hormones and hormone-like growth factors, chemical messengers in the body, represent another category of medicinals which are of considerable interest to researchers. They are one of the means by which certain body cells and tissues communicate with other cells and tissues. Hormone deficiencies or defects exist in many diseases.

Immune system modifiers. The cells of the immune system communicate with each other through messenger proteins called lymphocytes. There are a number of different types of these cells, some of which have been genetically engineered to produce potentially useful therapeutic agents.

Site directors and carrier proteins transport substances to their intended sites of action. They can extend the period of activity of the therapeutic agent. They are sometimes developed along with the agents they are supposed to carry and administered together. Site-directed delivery of immunotoxic substances is a highly selective therapy. Much of this effort has been used in cancer therapy. Here a cancer drug is linked to a monoclonal antibody (MA) that is highly attracted to a specific type of tumor. The drug is released from the MA carrier and attacks the cancer cell. In an alternative but similar manner, monoclonal antibodies are attached to enzymes which are used to convert an inactive prodrug to an active cancer drug. The monoclonal antibodies deliver the enzyme to the cancer tissues where they are needed, so that cancer drug activity occurs only in the vicinity of the tumor cells. Other monoclonal antibodies have been used to interfere with folic acid metabolism, which is required for cell growth of cancer cells.

Targeting mediators of cancer cell development is also being investigated to address oncogenes (cells which are thought to cause cancer once they are activated in some way). The normal, non-cancerous cell is called a protooncogene, which normally performs some essential cell function until it is changed and becomes an oncogene. Protooncogenes can change to oncogenes because of rare genetic events, viruses, radiation (including sunlight), chemical exposures, and sometimes by long term drug therapy. Oncogenes are being targeted for cancer chemotherapy. Monoclonal antibodies generated against oncogenes can inhibit the growth of the tumors caused by these oncogenes.

Tissue repair agents are involved in tissue repair and regeneration, and wound healing. It has been shown that some of these can be produced by recombinant techniques.

Tumor suppressing genes (Anti-Oncogenes) are associated with the suppression of cancers. There are an increasing variety of human cancers which are clearly associated with specific chromosomal defects. It is theoretically possible to repair the defective gene and block the cancer. This should also allow cancer cells to return to their normal status even after disease has occurred.

Vaccines consist of parts of killed or inactivated organisms. When injected, our bodies develop immunity to the organism (i.e., the immune system develops antibodies against the invading organism). Genetic engineering provides a means for producing specific vaccines in larger quantities. Recombinant vaccines for the prevention of hepatitis B and the flu is already available. Further research is underway regarding vaccines for HIV, certain parasitic diseases and certain types of cancer.

Specific Agents

Many biotechnology agents are quite novel and can be designed for specific functions previously unavailable. This may be increasingly important as medicine changes from the search for cures to a greater focus on prevention.

Most medications currently available are not specific in their actions. Biotechnology will allow for the development of drugs with specific activities, designed for specific health problems. Other agents can be designed for specific preventive purposes. Outline 110 summarizes many of the agents of interest in this regard at the present. A few of the more important ones are discussed in greater detail below.

AIDS vaccine is a product of considerable interest, but presents a number of problems. HIV mutates quickly, even within the same individual. Vaccines are typically ineffective because the virus changes too quickly to be affected by them. Antibodies produced naturally by the patient's immune system are similarly ineffective, since they are produced too slowly to act before the virus changes. Nevertheless, biotechnology continues to search for the development of successful vaccines and therapies.

Alpha-antitrypsin gene is involved in the development of congenital emphysema (i.e., when alpha-antitrypsin enzyme is lacking). If appropriate levels could be re-established permanently, a cure for the disease would be available. Patients are currently being treated with a recombinant enzyme inhibitor, but this requires continuous therapy. The gene transfer approach would insert the gene for alpha-antitrypsin into the patient's liver, thereby offering a durable outcome. Animal studies indicate that this procedure is feasable and that these genetically engineered cells make and secrete alpha-antitrypsin.

AntiSense RNA can "turn off" genes that can result in the formation of disease (e.g., cancer cells). Theoretically, antisense RNA may be used to block the growth and development of certain cancer cells. A portion of the gene of the cancer cell is recognized by the antisense RNA. So, it blocks the cancer cell, but not normal cells. This represents a therapeutic agent which is capable of identifying and killing cancer cells. At present, however, these substances are unstable and it is not known exactly when they should be given, since high and extended doses can produce side effects and toxicities.

DNAse is a recombinant enzyme which degrades DNA. It is being investigated for the prevention of cystic fibrosis, pneumonia, bronchitis, and emphysema. In all of these conditions, extracellular DNA is deposited in mucus secretions which normally occur in the digestive and respiratory tracts. As a result, these secretions thicken. The DNA comes from dying inflammatory cells which fight infections. DNAse breaks down the accumulating DNA and thins the infected mucus. Infections are less likely to occur, or are less likely to become serious as a result of this treatment.

Erythropoietin (EPO) is a substance normally released by the kidneys to stimulate erythrocyte (red blood cell) production. It is currently available commercially as a recombinant product. Stimulation of red blood cells increases the ability of the blood to carry oxygen and helps to prevent other problems associated with this blood component (e.g., clumping or destruction of red blood cells). It is approved for use in the terminal stages of certain kidney diseases and for certain types of anemias. In the future, it is likely to be approved for anemias due to a variety of other causes.

Factor VIIa can impact the overall clotting process, by passing the use of the other factors. The existence of Factor VIIa has been known for some time. However, it has not been possible to produce this protein in sufficient quantities in the past to use for therapy. As a result of the newer recombinant biotechnologies, this is now possible. Clinical trials presently underway indicate that Factor VIIa may offer a valuable option regarding therapy for hemophilia patients. Hemophilias are generally caused by a defect in the protein factors involved in the clotting process (e.g., Factor VIII for Type-A hemophilia and Factor IX for Type-B hemophilia). Historically, these types of hemophilia have been treated by replacing these missing protein factors.

Hepatitis B vaccine (HBV) is of interest because Hepatitis B can cause liver disease and has become a major health concern around the world. The cloning of a HBV antigen provided a new approach for the active immunization of this problem. Prior to biotechnology advances researchers isolated a protein from the surface of a virus obtained from infected individuals. By injecting this protein into noninfected individuals, they were able to produce an antibody which protected them from infection. The problem with this approach is that it required purification of a protein from infected blood. Also, there was an insufficient supply of vaccine for the millions of people infected around the world. Genetic engineering has enabled the development of sufficient quantities of vaccine to address the worldwide HBV problem. Similar strategies are underway to address other forms of hepatitis, as well as herpes viruses.

Human growth hormone (HGH) may be useful in treating certain forms of arthritis. Studies sponsored by the National Institutes on Aging are examining the impact of HGH on the aging process. Specifically, they are analyzing whether this therapy can safely improve such qualities as strength, mobility, balance and endurance. Prior studies have already suggested that therapy with HGH resulted in increases in lean body mass, decreases in body fat and decreased skin aging, thereby possibly slowing the degeneration of muscle, skin and other organs. HGH therapy might also be helpful in preventing the types of atrophy that may occur when older people are required to restrict their activities following surgery. Again, however, the major problem with HGH therapy has been its side effects (e.g., fluid retention), which may pose a major problem for many older Americans with heart conditions and diabetes. The studies which are being proposed will explore the possibility of using smaller doses to reduce these side effects.

Interferons (INFs) are chemicals produced by a variety of cells in the immune system which provide a natural defense against certain diseases (e.g., infections, cancers). Some of these agents are presently available as a result of recombinant technology. Many others are currently being investigated. Some INFs are proteins produced in response to viral infections. They bind to the surface of cells and may change the characteristics of the cell's proteins so that they are more resistant to viral invasion. In laboratory research, INFs have been shown to prevent viral infections. All of the interferons (alpha, beta, gamma) modify immune functions and have antiviral properties. Yet they can be quite different in their other characteristics. Side effects from the interferons are similar and include a flu-like syndrome, elevated liver enzymes, some reversible blood problems, effects on the nervous system and changes in blood lipid levels.

Interleukins (ILs) are involved in the inflammation process and may be tied up by the injection of receptors which are specific for them. This property would serve to inhibit their actions in the inflammatory process.

Tissue plasminogen activator (TPA) is involved in preventing blood clots. It is now possible to produce quantities of TPA which could not be easily achieved by isolating the enzyme from human plasma. TPA is usually effective in dissolving small clots formed in the vascular system in response to injury before they become too large to handle. A more aggressive response might serve to dissolve still larger clots, but of course, it also might produce more harmful side effects. Since no superior agent for use in dissolving blood clots has emerged to date, TPA is still being studied, although TPA is considerably more expensive than other blood clotting agents already available (e.g., Streptokinase, Eminase).

Viral vaccines are being created to treat all strains of a particular virus. Similarly, it may be possible to create vaccines composed of multiple antigens. This would cause the body to produce antibodies to several infectious organisms at the same time.

OUTLINE 110

BIOTECH AGENTS AND THEIR POSSIBLE APPLICATIONS

Agent	*Application*
Adenosine Deaminase (ADA) Gene	❦ Severe Combined Immunodeficiency Syndrome (SCIDS)
AIDS Vaccine	❦ AIDS
Alkaline Phosphatase	❦ Site specific carrier drug
Alpha-Antitrypsin Gene	❦ Emphysema (congenital)
AntiSense RNA	❦ Cancer
Anti-TNF Alpha	❦ Septic shock
Anaritide	❦ Heart and blood vessel problems
Auriculin	❦ Heart and blood vessel problems
Bone Repair Agents	❦ Stimulate bone and cartilage formation in the treatment of dental, orthopedic and surgical problems
Carboxypeptidases	❦ Site specific carrier drug
Cytosine Deaminase	❦ Site specific carrier drug
DNAse	❦ Bronchitis ❦ Emphysema ❦ Cystic fibrosis ❦ Pneumonia
Epidermal Growth Factor	❦ Corneal tissue repair following eye injury surgery ❦ Stimulate growth of skin cells ❦ Wound healing
erb B2 Oncogene	❦ Breast cancer
Erythropoietin	❦ Anemia ❦ Kidney disease
Factors VIIa and VIII	❦ Hemophilia
Fibroblast Growth Factor	❦ Burns ❦ Ulceration ❦ Encourage blood vessel formation ❦ Wound healing
Fibronectin	❦ Tissue reconstruction
Gene Therapy	❦ Brain cancer ❦ High cholesterol (hereditary)

OUTLINE 110 cont'd

	❦ Cystic fibrosis	❦ Melanoma
	❦ Gaucher's Disease	
Genotyping	❦ Rheumatoid Arthritis	
Granulocyte Colony Stimulating Factor (G-CSF)	❦ Blood disorders during cancer therapy	
Granulocyte-Macrophage Colony Stimulating Factor (GM-CSF)	❦ Bone marrow transplants	
Hepatitis B Vaccine (HBV)	❦ Hepatitis B	
Human Growth Hormone	❦ Anti-aging (slow down degeneration of muscle, skin and other organs as a result of aging)	❦ Complications of surgery (e.g., atrophy from inactivity) ❦ Dwarfism ❦ Osteoporosis
Human Tissue Plasminogen Activator	❦ Heart attacks	❦ Pulmonary embolism
IgM Monoclonal	❦ Prevent organ transplant rejections (e.g., heart and liver)	
Insulin (human)	❦ Diabetes	
Insulin-like Growth Factors (IGF-1 and 2)	❦ Bone fractures	❦ Tissue repair
Interferon Alpha	❦ Genital warts ❦ Hairy Cell Leukemia	❦ Hepatitis ❦ Kaposi's Sarcoma (AIDS-related)
Interferon Beta	❦ AIDS ❦ Cancer ❦ High cholesterol levels	❦ Multiple Sclerosis ❦ viral infections (e.g., hepatitis B, HIV, respiratory viruses)
Interferon Gamma	❦ Chronic Granulomatous Disease	
Interleukin-1	❦ Burns	❦ Wounds
Interleukin-2	❦ Cancer (e.g., kidney)	
Interleukin-3	❦ Bone marrow failure after chemotherapy	

OUTLINE 110 cont'd

Interleukin-4	❧ Allergies ❧ Cancer
Interleukin-6	❧ Stimulation of the immune system
Interleukin Receptors	❧ Inflammation
Macrophage Colony Stimulating Factor (M-CSF)	❧ High cholesterol
Nerve Growth Factor (NGF)	❧ Alzheimer's Disease ❧ Tissue damage ❧ Nerve Damage
OKT-3 Monoclonal Antibody	❧ Prevent kidney transplant rejection
PEG Derivatives	❧ To formulate enzymes in order to treat diseases with gene replacement therapy
PEG-Asparginase (PEG-ASP)	❧ Leukemia
PEG-Adenosine Deaminase (PEG-ADA)	❧ Severe Combined Immunodeficiency Syndrome (SCIDS)
Penicillin-V Amidase	❧ Site specific carrier drug
Platelet-Derived Growth Factor (PDGF)	❧ Stimulate connective tissue cells ❧ Tissue healing (after surgery)
Prourokinase	❧ Heart attacks
Stem Cell Factor	❧ Blood disorders (e.g., neutropenia)
Superoxide Dismutase (SOD)	❧ Inflammation
Thymosin-alpha-1	❧ Hepatitis B ❧ Influenza
Tissue Plasminogen Activator (TPA)	❧ Prevent blood clots
Transforming Growth Factor (TGF)	❧ Tissue healing
Tumor-Infiltrating Lymphocytes	❧ Cancer

OUTLINE 110 cont'd

Tumor Necrosis Factor (TNF)	❦ Cancer	
Vaccines	❦ Cancer ❦ Hemophilus influenzae ❦ Hepatitis B	❦ HIV ❦ Parasitic diseases

---

REFERENCES – BIOTECHNOLOGY

1. "A Culture System for B-Lymphoid Cell Progenitors." *Pharmaceutical Biotechnology Monitor*, Vol. 2, No. 4, (December, 1992), pp. 13 ff.

2. "A New Option in the Treatment of Hemophilia: Factor VIIa." *Pharmaceutical Biotechnology Monitor*, Vol. 1, No. 3, (October, 1991), pp. 5-6.

3. "A Radioactive Biopharmaceutical for the Detection of Colorectal and Ovarian Cancer. *Pharmaceutical Biotechnology Monitor*, Vol. 1, No. 4, (December, 1991), p. 12.

4. Abramson, Hanley. "Basic Techniques in Recombinant DNA Technology." *Pharmacy Practice News*, (March, 1992).

5. "Adoptive Immunotherapy for Cancer: IL-2." *Pharmaceutical Biotechnology Monitor*, Vol. 1, No. 3, (October, 1991), p. 6.

6. Aitken, ML; et al. "Recombinant Human DNAse Inhalation in Normal Subjects and Patients with Cystic Fibrosis. A Phase 1 Study." *Pharmaceutical Biotechnology Monitor*, Vol. 2, No. 2, (June, 1992), p. 12.

7. "An Update on Epoetin Therapy." *Pharmaceutical Biotechnology Monitor*, Vol. 1, No. 4, (December, 1991), p. 7.

8. "Anti-B-Cell Monoclonal Antibodies in the Treatment of Severe B-Cell Lymphoproliferative Syndrome Following Bone Marrow and Organ Transplantation." *Pharmaceutical Biotechnology Monitor*, Vol. 1, No. 3, (October, 1991), p. 5.

9. "Balancing the Pharmacy Budget: Breaking Even with Biopharmaceuticals." *Pharmaceutical Biotechnology Monitor*, Vol. 1, No. 3, (October, 1991), pp. 7-9.

10. Ball, JE. "The Clinical Significance of Growth Factors." *Pharmacy Practice News*, (July, 1992).

11. Baron, S; et al. "The Interferons: Mechanisms of Action and Clinical Applications." *Pharmaceutical Biotechnology Monitor*, Vol. 1, No. 4, (December, 1991), pp. 11-12.

12. Barriere, SL; et al. "Biotechnology Products in the Treatment of Serious Infectious Diseases." *Pharmaceutical Biotechnology Monitor*, Vol. 2, No. 4, (December, 1992), pp. 6-7.

13. "Beta Interferon: Trials in Multiple Sclerosis." *Pharmaceutical Biotechnology Monitor*, Vol. 1, No. 3, (October, 1991), p. 5.

14. Beutler, E; et al. "Enzyme Replacement Therapy for Gaucher Disease." *Pharmaceutical Biotechnology Monitor*, Vol. 1, No. 4, (December, 1991), p. 11.

15. Bhatnagar, SK; et al. "Effects of IV Recombinant Tissue-Type Plasminogen Activator Therapy on the Incidence and Associations of Left Ventricular Thrombus in Patients with a First Acute Q Wave Anterior Myocardial Infarction." *Pharmaceutical Biotechnology Monitor*, Vol. 1, No. 4, (December, 1991), p. 11.

16. "Bioequivalence and Bioavailability: Issues that Must be Addressed." *Pharmaceutical Biotechnology Monitor*, Vol. 1, No. 4, (December, 1991), pp. 9-10.

17. "Biopharmaceuticals: Pharmacy's Next Challenge." *Trends — Biotechnology Information for Issues for Pharmacists*, Vol. 1., No. 1, (May, 1991).

18. "Biotechnology: The Promise." *Biotechnology — The New Dimension in Pharmacy Practice — Part 1*. Council of Ohio Colleges of Pharmacy, (1992).

19. Blaese, R. Michael. "Gene Therapy." *Pharmaceutical Biotechnology Monitor*, Vol. 2, No. 4, (December, 1992), pp. 2-4.

20. "Breakthroughs in AIDS Research." *Pharmaceutical Biotechnology Monitor*, Vol. 1, No. 4, (December, 1991), p. 10.

21. Buchner, T; et al. "Recombinant Human Granulocyte-Macrophage Colongy-Stimulating Factor After Chemotherpay in Patients with Acute Myeloid Leukemia at Higher Age or After Relapse." *Pharmaceutical Biotechnology Monitor*, Vol. 1, No. 4, (December, 1991), p. 11.

22. Carlson, RH. "Many Centers Successfully Stopping CSF Rx at Lower Neutrophil Counts." *Pharmacy Practice News*, (June, 1993).

23. Carlson, Robert. "Studies Show Effectiveness of CSFs in Treating AZT-Related Neutropenia, Especially in Children." *Pharmacy Practice News*, (February, 1992), pp. 22, ff.

24. "Comparative Analysis of the In Vivo Radioprotective Effects of Recombinant Granulocyte Colony Stimulating Factor, Recombinant Granylocyte-macrophage CSF, and Their Combination." *Pharmaceutical Biotechnology Monitor*, Vol. 1, No. 3, (October, 1991), p. 11.

25. Comstock, Thomas. "Monoclonal Antibodies: Background and Technology — Part 1." *Pharmaceutical Biotechnology Monitor,* Vol. 1, No. 4, (December, 1991), pp. 2-4.

26. Comstock, Thomas. "Monoclonal Antibodies: Therapeutic Applications — Part 2." *Pharmaceutical Biotechnology Monitor*, Vol. 2, No. 1, (March, 1992), pp. 2-3.

27. Crown, J; et al. "A Phase 1 Trial of Recombinant Human Interleukin-1-beta Alone and in Combination with Myelosuppressive Doses of 5-Fluorouracil in Patients with Gastrointestinal Cancer." *Pharmaceutical Biotechnology Monitor*, Vol. 1, No. 4, (December, 1991), p. 12.

28. Culver, KW. "Applications of Gene Therapy — Part 1: Lymphocyte Gene Therapy." *Pharmacy Practice News*, (March, 1993).

29. "Current Trends in Radioimmunotherapy." *Pharmaceutical Biotechnology Monitor*, Vol. 1, No. 4, (December, 1991), p. 12.

30. deKover, D. "Antibiotic Peptides from Frogs Help Heal Wounds and May Selectively Kill Virus-Infected Cells." *Pharmacy Practice News*, (October, 1992).

31. Drews, Michael R. "Ethical and Legal Issues of the Advanced Reproductive Technologies." *Pharmaceutical Biotechnology Monitor*, Vol. 2, No. 2, (June, 1992), pp. 2-5.

32. Eatherton, Rena. "Biotechnology Applied to Geriatric Medicine." *Pharmaceutical Biotechnology Monitor*, Vol. 1, No. 4, (December, 1991), pp. 5-7.

33. "Effects of Growth Hormones on Aging Studied." *American Pharmacy*, Vol. 33, No. 3, (March, 1993), pp. 16-17.

34. "Effects of Tumor Necrosis Factor on the Proliferation of Leukemic Cells from Children with B-Cell Precursor-Acute Lymphoblastic Leukemia." *Pharmaceutical Biotechnology Monitor*, Vol. 1, No. 3, (October, 1991), p. 10.

35. "Epoetin: Alleviating the Anemia of Cancer." *Pharmaceutical Biotechnology Monitor*, Vol. 2, No. 4, (December, 1992), p. 13.

36. Erlick, Nelson. "Growth Factors and Wound Healing: Identification and Function (Part 1)." *Pharmaceutical Biotechnology Monitor*, Vol. 2, No., 3, (September, 1992), pp. 2-4.

37. Erlick, Nelson. "Growth Factors and Wound Healing: Therapeutics — Part II." *Pharmaceutical Biotechnology Monitor*, Vol. 2, No. 4, (December, 1992), pp. 4-6.

38. "Erythrokinetic Modeling." *Pharmaceutical Biotechnology Monitor*, Vol. 1, No. 4, (December, 1991), p. 8.

39. "Escalating Chemotherapy Doses in Patients with Ovarian Cancer." *Pharmaceutical Biotechnology Monitor*, Vol. 2, No. 3, (September, 1992), pp. 9-10.

40. "Fighting AIDS: Recombinant CD4." *Pharmaceutical Biotechnology Monitor*, Vol. 1, No. 3, (October, 1991), p. 6.

41. "Further Examination of the Effects of Recombinant Cytokines on the Proliferation of Human Megakaryocyte Progenitor Cells." *Pharmaceutical Biotechnology Monitor*, Vol. 1, No. 3, (October, 1991), p. 11.

42. "G-CSF Improved Neutrophil Counts in Small AIDS Trial." *Pharmacy Practice News*, (September, 1992).

43. "Gene-Targeted Immunotherapy in Cancer." *Pharmaceutical Biotechnology Monitor*, Vol. 2, No. 3, (September, 1992), p. 9.

44. "Gene Therapy Research Moving Ahead." *American Pharmacy,* Vol. 33, No. 4, (April, 1993), p. 10.

45. "Genotyping May Change Therapies for Arthritis." *American Pharmacy*, Vol. 33, No. 4, (April, 1993), p. 11.

46. "Getting Information About Biotechnology Products." *American Pharmacy*, Vol. 33, No. 4, ,(April, 1993), pp. 18-19.

47. "GM-CSF Receptors on Nerve Cells." *Pharmaceutical Biotechnology Monitor*, Vol. 2, No. 4, (December, 1992), p. 16.

48. "Growth Factors in Myelodysplasia." *Pharmaceutical Biotechnology Monitor*, Vol. 2, No. 3, (September, 1992), p. 10.

49. Helwick, Caroline. "Most CSF Orders Fulfill Criteria for Use, Yet Costs Dig into Budgets." *Pharmacy Practice News*, (March, 1992).

50. Helwick, Caroline. "Strict Guidelines, Restrictions Help Pharmacists Curb Use of Monoclonal Antibodies for Sepsis." *Pharmacy Practice News*, (March, 1992).

51. Huber, Stephen L. "Colony Stimulating Factors: Clinical Management and.Pharmacoeconomic Issues." *Trends — Biotechnology Information and Issues for Pharmacists*, Vol. 1, No. 3, (January, 1992).

52. Huber, SL. "Reimbursement Issues in Biotechnology." *Pharmacy Practice News*, (November, 1992).

53. "Increased Serum Levels of Granulocyte Colony-Stimulating Factor in Patients with Severe Congenital Neutropenia." *Pharmaceutical Biotechnology Monitor*, Vol. 1, No. 3, (October, 1991), p. 10.

54. "International Conference on Growth Factors in Cancer Therapy." *Pharmaceutical Biotechnology Monitor*, Vol. 2, No. 4, (December, 1992), p. 12.

55. "International Conference on Growth Factors in Cancer Therapy — Part II." *Pharmaceutical Biotechnology Monitor*, Vol. 3, No. 1, (March, 1993), pp. 7 ff.

56. Karlix, JL. "Cytokines: A New Therapeutic Frontier." *Pharmacy Practice News,* (May, 1992).

57. Kessinger, A. "High-Dose Cyclophosphamide, Carmustine, and Etoposide followed by Autologous Peripheral Stem Cell Transplantation for Patients with Relapsed Hodgkins' Disease." *Pharmaceutical Biotechnology Monitor*, Vol. 1, No. 4, (December, 1991), p. 11.

58. Kim, HC; et al. "Purified Factor IX Using Monoclonal Immunoaffinity Technique: Clinical Trials in Hemophilia B and Comparison to Prothrombin Complex Concentrates." *Phar-maceutical Biotechnology Monito*r, Vol. 2, No. 2, (June, 1992), pp. 11-12.

59. Lyman, S; et al. "Biological Activities and Potential Therapeutic Uses of Steel Factor: A New Growth factor Active on Multiple Hematopoietic Lineages." *Pharmaceutical Biotechnology Monitor*, Vol. 2, No. 4, (December, 1992), p. 15.

60. "Managing Epoetin-Related Iron Deficiency with Oral Iron." *Pharmaceutical Biotechnology Monitor*, Vol. 1, No. 4, (December, 1991), pp. 7-8.

61. "Monoclonal Antibodies: The Keys to Disease Detection and Treatment." *Biotechnology — The New Dimension in Pharmacy Practice — Part 1*. Council of Ohio Colleges of Pharmacy, (1992).

62. Montague, Michael J. "Biotechnology and the Future of Medicine." *Pharmacy Practice News*, (January, 1992), pp. 8 ff.

63. Murphy, WJ; et al. "Interleukin-2-Activated Natural Killer Cells can Support Hematopoiesis In Vitro and Promote Marrow Engraftment In Vivo." *Pharmaceutical Biotechnology Monitor*, Vol. 2, No. 4, (December, 1992), p. 15.

64. "New Diagnostics: Cytokine Monitoring." *Pharmaceutical Biotechnology Monitor*, Vol. 1, No. 3, (October, 1991), p. 6.

65. "Novel Approaches to Drug Delivery." *Pharmaceutical Biotechnology Monitor*, Vol. 1, No. 4, (December, 1991), pp. 8-9.

66. O'Connor, TW. "The Biotechnology Price Tag: Its Impact on Pharmacy." *Pharmacy Practice News*, (September, 1992).

67. Parish, DC; et al. "Immunogenicity of Low-Dose Intradermal Recombinant DNA Hepatitis B Vaccine." *Pharmaceutical Biotechnology Monitor*, Vol. 1, No. 4, (December, 1991), p. 11.

68. "Pharmacokinetic Considerations in CSF Administration." *Pharmaceutical Biotechnology Monitor*, Vol. 1, No. 4, (December, 1991), pp. 9-11.

69. "Pioneering a New Pharacologic Frontier: The Ocean." *Pharmaceutical Biotechnology Monitor*, Vol. 2, No. 3, (September, 1992), pp. 6-7.

70. "PIXY321: A New Fusion Protein (GM-CSF+IL-3)." *Pharma-ceutical Biotechnology Monitor*, Vol. 2, No. 4, (December, 1992), pp. 12-13.

71. Prescott, LM. "British and Australian Trials Support the Value of Adjuvant G-CSF in Rx of Various Cancers." *Pharmacy Practice News*, (February, 1993).

72. Prescott, LM. "Interleukin-1 Receptor Antagonist Found Helpful Against Resistant GVHD." *Pharmacy Practice News*, (February, 1993).

73. Prescott, LM. "Second Controlled Trial Supports E5's Ability to Resolve Organ Failure; FDA Reviewing Data." *Pharmacy Practice News*, (June, 1992).

74. Prescott, LM. "SubcutaneousEpoetin Can Correct Anemia without Compromising Dialysis Efficacy." *Pharmacy Practice News*, (April, 1992).

75. Robson, MC; et al. "Platelet-Derived Growth Factor BB for the Treatment of Chronic Pressure Ulcers." *Pharmaceutical Biotechnology Monitor*, Vol. 2, No. 2, (June, 1992), p. 12.

76. Roe, TS; Hall, EL; and Beasley, JG. "Teaching Students about Monoclonal Antibodies Through a Simulated Laboratory Procedure." *American Journal of Pharmacy Education*, Vol. 52, (Fall, 1988), pp. 250-255.

77. Skerett, PJ. "New Investigational Drug for Gram-Negative Sepsis Could Cost Almost $2.3 Billion per Year." *Pharmacy Practice News*, (June, 1992).

78. "The Colony-Stimulating Factors: G-CSF and GM-CSF." *Pharmaceutical Biotechnology Monitor*, Vol. 1, No. 4, (December, 1991), pp. 8-9.

79. "The CSFs: Clinical Uses and Economic Concerns." *Pharmaceutical Biotechnology Monitor*, Vol. 2, No. 4, (December, 1992), pp. 8-9.

80. "The Evolution of Hemodialysis." *Pharmaceutical Biotechnology Monitor*, Vol. 1, No. 4, (December, 1991), p. 7.

81. "The Tools of Genetic Engineering: new Product Development Through Gene Manipulation." *Biotechnology — The New Dimension in Pharmacy Practice — Part 1.* Council of Ohio Colleges of Pharmacy, (1992).

82. "Transforming Growth Factors Beta-1 and Alpha in Chronic Liver Disease: Effects of Interferon Alfa Therapy." *Pharmaceutical Biotechnology Monitor*, Vol. 1, No. 3, (October, 1991), pp. 10-11.

83. "Treatment of Metastatic Renal Cell Carcinoma by Continuous IV Infusion of Recombinant Interleukin-2: A Single-Center Phase II Study." *Pharmaceutical Biotechnology Monitor*, Vol. 2, No. 3, (September, 1992), p. 11.

84. van Haelst, PC; et al. "Administration of Interleukin-2 Results in Increased Plasma Concentration of IL-5 and Eosinophilia in Patients with Cancer." *Pharmaceutical Biotechnology Monitor*, Vol. 1, No. 4, (December, 1991), p. 12.

85. Wadler, S. "The Role of Interferons in the Treatment of Solid Tumors." *Pharmaceutical Biotechnology Monitor*, Vol. 2, No. 4, (December, 1992), p. 15.

86. Weiner, Bruce. "Clinical Applications of Tissue Plasminogen Activator." *Trends — Biotechnology Information and Issues for Pharmacists*, Vol. 1, No. 2, (September, 1991).

87. Zannoni, LW. "Agricultural Biotechnology in the 1990s." *Pharmaceutical Biotechnology Monitor*, Vol. 2, No. 3, (September, 1992), p. 5.

33. THE DRUG APPROVAL PROCESS

"The 19th Century sanitarians believed that health and happiness could be found only through a return to the ways of nature. Modern man, probably no wiser but certainly more conceited, now claims that the royal avenue to the control of disease is through scientific knowledge and medical technology. "Health is purchasable," proclaimed one of the leaders of American medicine. Yet, while the modern American boasts of the scientific management of his body and soul, his expectancy of life past the age of 45 is hardly greater today than it was several decades ago and is shorter than that of many European people of the present generation. He claims the highest standard of living in the world, but 10% of his income must go for medical care and he cannot build hospitals fast enough to accommodate the sick. He is encouraged to believe that money can create drugs for the cure of heart disease, cancer and mental disease, but he makes no worth-while effort to recognize, let alone correct, the mismanagements of his everyday life that contribute to the high incidence of these conditions. He laughs louder than any other people, and the ubiquitous national smile is advertised ad nauseum by every poster or magazine, artist or politician. One may wonder indeed whether the pretense of superior health is not itself rapidly becoming a mental aberration. Is it not a delusion to proclaim the present state of health as the best in the history of the world, at a time when increasing numbers of persons in our society depend on drugs and on doctors for meeting the ordinary problems of everyday life?"

— Rene Dubos

Many people believe that the drug approval process is slow, cumbersome and pointless. Add to this the common belief that the FDA callously prevents the availability of "valuable" drugs. These views have also been popularized in a variety of naive self-help books.

Perhaps, however, an in-depth analysis of our drug approval

process might offer a different perspective. First, it is important to recognize that the FDA is a consumer protection agency. U.S. drug laws require that all drugs marketed in this country must be proven safe and effective for their promoted uses, which is a far cry from the chaos that prevailed before the FDA was created. Even with the FDA regulating the drug industry, rampant health fraud ($100 billion per year) still results in the marketing of unsafe or ineffective products. The FDA attempts to prevent or at least limit the extent to which unsafe or ineffective drug and health products are available to consumers.

The dilemma for the health care industry is that drugs cannot be released until both their potential outcomes (good and bad) have been established. The potential costs and risks to consumers (e.g., health hazards, progression of disease, increased insurance costs) and to the health care industry (e.g., lawsuits, malpractice insurance costs) are too great to allow questionable drugs to be made available to the public.

The Drug Approval Process

The laws which require that drug products must be proven safe and effective for their promoted uses are appropriate. We should allow no less. Yet, it takes time (10 to 12 years) and money (about $360 million) to prove that a drug is safe and effective. Only one drug in a thousand will actually make it from the research laboratories to the drugstore. New drugs are expensive because of the tremendous research and marketing investment made by the major drug companies.

Unfortunately, there are no shortcuts to this outcome. Drug problems (i.e., side effects) may not appear until years after the early drug investigation studies have been completed. Short cuts in the approval process pave the way for disasters.

Despite the negative publicity associated with the FDA, the U.S. is the global leader in the development of new drugs and is the most lucrative pharmaceutical market in the world. Indeed, some of the foreign drug companies with which Americans seem to be so enamored are actually subsidiaries of American drug companies. There are few chemical entities anywhere in the world with which American drug scientists are not familiar.

Even so, an understanding of the drug approval process helps to limit the uninformed and naive criticisms that all too often characterize the media and disreputable self-help books.

There are three basic elements of the new drug approval process:

1. Testing for safety and effectiveness through non clinical and clinical studies (e.g., laboratory, animal and finally human studies);

2. Preparation and submission of prescribed application processes (e.g., the Investigational New Drug Application and the New Drug Application);

3. FDA review of the research information and applications submitted to them.

These basic elements proceed according to certain stages of development:

Discovery

We tend to think of new drugs as unknown entities that are discovered by scientists in laboratories. Yet, new drugs may emerge in many different ways. They can be a new and novel substance never before known. Occasionally, we do inherit a new drug from European markets. Finally, new drugs may represent products that have been previously approved in this country for other purposes. After they are used for a time, we may discover that they have other useful properties.

Preclinical Testing

This phase of research is conducted to acquire basic pharmacologic information about the drug (e.g., how it works in living systems, toxicity). This provides information which allows scientists to begin to evaluate the safety and biological activity of the drug. Toxicity testing is done to indicate adverse effects (including side effects) that may be associated with taking the drug on either a short or long term basis. Toxicity studies also look for the potential of the drug to cause cancer, birth defects, whether or not the drug is secreted in breast milk and other problems. These outcomes are difficult to assess, since it is obviously unethical to actually test these drugs on pregnant women or nursing mothers. Laboratory and animal studies do not always indicate the toxicity potential that may occur in humans.

Only about 1 out of 5 drugs which make it to the animal testing phase will survive this phase of studies.

Investigational New Drug Application (IND)

If the preclinical testing stage of drugs is promising, the drug's sponsor will file an IND application with the FDA. The purpose of this application is to obtain approval for drug testing in humans. The FDA requires that the IND application must contain information about the pharmacological and toxicity properties of the drug based on testing in several species of animals (using the same route of administration that would be used in people). If the IND is approved, then the sponsor must continually update it with information that allows the FDA to periodically reassess the safety of ongoing and upcoming clinical trials. The FDA sets standards for clinical testing to ensure that all studies are accurate and protect human subjects to the maximum possible extent. The reporting of data to the FDA is rigorous and is required after the completion of each phase of clinical testing.

Phase I Clinical Trials

This phase may represent the first use of a new drug in humans. It is a highly exploratory phase. The purpose of this phase is one of safety. These studies consider such things as:

- Onset (how long it takes the drug to work once it is administered)

- Duration (how long a given dose will work)

- Absorption (how well it is absorbed from its site(s) of administration)

- Distribution (where the drug will go in the body)

- Metabolism (how the body changes the drug in its efforts to eliminate it)

- Excretion (the sites in the body from which the drug is eliminated)

Usually fewer than 100 healthy, volunteer test subjects are involved in this effort, which may take up to a year to complete. Approximately 30% of drugs tested in this phase will be eliminated from additional studies.

Phase II Clinical Trials

The focus of this phase is effectiveness. Subjects who participate here consist of people who actually have the disease which the drug is intended to treat. Safety continues to remain a concern, and so, the number of subjects in this phase are less than 500. This phase may require up to five years. Approximately 35% of drugs tested in this phase are eliminated from additional studies.

Phase III Clinical Trials

These studies involve use of the drug under conditions similar to those that would exist if the drug is approved for marketing. The study may involve as many as 3000 people, and can last four years, and approximately 5% of drugs tested in this phase will be eliminated from additional consideration.

New Drug Application (NDA)

This is a formal request to the FDA for approval to market a new drug in the U.S. after completion of Phase I, II and III clinical trials. Literally thousands of pages of data and information are supplied to the FDA to support the safety and effectiveness of the drug. These documents also relate information about the chemistry of the drug, manufacturing and control processes, pharmacology and toxicology, clinical data, proposed labeling and packaging.

The large and complex NDA is assigned to one of nine review divisions of the FDA Center for Drug Evaluation and Research. If approved by the FDA review process, which may take more than two years, the drug may be released to the market. But delays occur because of insufficient FDA funding and staffing, a significant intolerance of errors by the Congress and public, backlog of submissions, prioritizing (new breakthrough drugs are given priority), increasing complexity of submissions and accountability of sponsors and reviewers.

Phase IV Clinical Trials

This phase continues after the FDA approval of an NDA. It is a post-marketing surveillance activity. The intent is to gather additional data regarding safety and effectiveness over time, as well as potential benefits (e.g., quality of life, cost-benefits, cost-effectiveness). The FDA may request these, or the sponsoring agent may conduct it voluntarily.

The FDA drug review process has been refined substantially over the years, and especially in recent years. These changes reflect changing health interests of society (especially regarding drugs for the treatment of AIDS, cancer and other serious serious diseases). The priority is still to protect the public, yet provide for needed drugs as expediently as possible.

Understanding the FDA

As we have said, the Food and Drug Administration (FDA) receives a great deal of criticism. In part, this occurs because we live in a "free" society and we resent organizations and agencies that seem to threaten individual liberties (including self-imposed health threats). As a consumer protection agency, however, the FDA is charged with the responsibility of protecting us, even when we insist that we do not want protection.

There are times when the FDA seems to be a sluggish giant that slowly responds to human needs. And yet, this is usually not the case when the facts are examined in greater detail. To begin with, the FDA is not nearly as large an organization as many people believe it to be. Its slow response is sometimes a reflection of limited human resources to address all of the problems for which it is responsible.

As mentioned previously, U.S. drug laws require that drug manufacturers and promoters must prove their stated claims. It is unfortunate, but nonetheless true, that there are many Americans who are less interested in our health than our pocketbooks. But after all, this is the nature of free enterprise. Health fraud promoters will make any claim in order to sell their products. The FDA attempts to protect you from drug products that are a waste of your money and a threat to your health.

Even "legitimate" drug advertising (e.g., television, radio, magazines) is frequently deceptive and exploits consumer ignorance. Ironically, the major drug manufacturers insist that their efforts are of a high quality and observe self-imposed ethical standards.

When dissatisfied about drug-related issues, we often blame the FDA. It is ironic that we demand the right to make hazardous lifestyle choices, but when something goes wrong, we quickly look for someone to "fix" our problems. If that is not possible . . . we look for someone to blame. The problem is that we have reached a point in human evolution where we simply don't have an effective "fix" for all of our lifestyle follies.

The position of the FDA is one of social responsibility. Drug manufacturers and promoters must prove their claims. They are not allowed to deceive you or to compromise your health merely to increase their profits. Even so, it is not a perfect system. Problems do occur and the process is sometimes slow.

The Plight of Legitimate Drug Manufacturers

The major drug companies who actually identify and develop new drug products are known as Research and Development ("R & D") companies. And to be sure, Americans want new drugs.

The costs of drug development are substantial. Since drug companies recover their research costs only on products that actually make it to the market, these drugs must also pay for research on those drugs that did not make it.

Because we are also concerned about health care costs, there is much support for purchasing generic products. However, this also poses a problem for the R & D companies. Generic companies usually do not conduct expensive research and development, nor are their promotional costs as high (since the R & D companies have already "paved the way" for them). Instead, their promotional costs are relatively low because they can take advantage of the marketing already done by the major R & D companies.

The dilemma for the public is this: If we want new drugs, we must be willing to support the major R & D companies. We cannot have the advantages of generic purchasing and the availability of new products in a free enterprise system as it currently exists.

The OTC Reviews

Even though, as we have seen, Federal laws require that both prescription and OTC drug products must be proven safe and effective, a study in the late 1960s indicated that only 25% of OTC products met the required standards. The FDA decided then that a more comprehensive review was needed. This review began in 1972 and was established to determine the safety, effectiveness and proper labeling for all OTC products. In order to do this, OTC products were divided into 26 categories. Seventeen advisory panels were established to review the OTC products within these 26 categories. Each of these panels included 7 voting members consisting of scientists, physicians, pharmacologists, toxicologists, pharmacists and other technically qualified individuals. The only two conditions for membership were expertise in the category under consideration and the absence of any conflicts of interest.

Each panel also had 3 non-voting members (representing the FDA, consumers and the drug industry). These non-voting members participated fully in all panel discussions, although they were sometimes not allowed to review confidential data submitted to the panels. They presented information to the panels and reported to their respective constituents on all relevant matters.

Panel members were selected by the FDA commissioner. The non-voting members were selected from a list of nominations submitted by relevant organizations. The Consumer Federation of America nominated the consumer liaisons; the Nonprescription Drug Manufacturers Association nominated the industry liaison; and the FDA liaisons were selected from FDA personnel. The Commissioner selected one of the seven voting members to serve as the chairperson.

The responsibility of each panel was to review OTC product ingredients for safety and effectiveness for OTC use. The panels also reviewed labeling claims and recommended appropriate labeling changes.

For nearly a decade the panels reviewed volumes of information and scientific data. Originally, each meeting had a segment which was open to the public, while the remainder of the meetings were closed. However, following the "government in sunshine" legislation, all meetings were open to the public in their entirety.

It was originally anticipated that the Review process would evaluate 200 to 300 ingredients contained in about 200,000 products. However, before completion, the panels reviewed nearly 800 ingredients representing as many as 600,000 products. The results of this effort classified OTC drugs into three possible categories:

Category	Description
1	Generally recognized to be safe and effective for its intended uses.
2	Unsafe or Ineffective for its promoted uses.
3	Insufficient data available to permit classification into Categories 1 or 2

Category assignments were made according to the conditions for which the ingredients were promoted. The panels also considered products which contained combinations of ingredients. Specifically, they considered whether or not a particular combination was rational or not.

Products assigned to Category 2 were required to be withdrawn from the market. Category 3 products could continue to be marketed, but their manufacturers were required to provide additional testing to demonstrate safety and effectiveness. All testing had to be completed with a specific time frame, and eventually, all products had to be assigned to Category 1 or 2. The FDA Reviews are considered to be a continuing process which will extend indefinitely (since new products continue to emerge).

Many ingredients were not found to be safe or effective for their promoted uses. Some were even found to be toxic. Since the Reviews began, many ingredients have been removed from OTC status. And the Reviews have helped to reduce health fraud, although this problem remains a monumental one. The Reviews also resulted in more effective product labeling (even though labeling problems still exist). Whatever criticisms have been leveled against government regulation of the drug industry, it seems clear that the public has been well served by this enterprise.

34. OTCS IN TRANSITION

"Moving fast is not the same as going somewhere."

— Robert Anthony

Rx to OTC Switches

An unanticipated outcome of the OTC Reviews by the FDA (see previous Chapter) for OTC drugs was the recommendation that certain drug products should no longer require a prescription (it was felt that the ingredients involved could be safely and effectively used by consumers without professional assistance).

The results of these changes have been significant. Initially about 40 prescription ingredients were switched from prescription to non-prescription status. Since then, more than 200 products have been approved for the self-care market. In all likelihood, this trend will continue because of a number of cultural factors (e.g., increasing costs of health care and a growing interest in self-care practices). These changes allow us to deal more effectively with common ailments that affect our quality of life.

Another advantage of the switches has been one of increased availability. There are now more than 700,000 retail outlets in the U.S. where OTC products can be purchased (there are only about 70,000 pharmacies). Many of these are 24-hour supermarkets and convenience stores which make product purchases available anytime they are needed.

Increased availability, however, also introduces its own problems. Many health care professionals express concern over the possibility that people may view OTCs callously, which could result in product misuse. For example, people tend to mistakenly believe that OTC products are weaker than prescription products. In fact, some OTC products are actually stronger than their prescription counterparts.

Moreover, in an effort to boost sales, OTC products are sometimes given brand names that sound very much like well-known prescription products. The OTC product may be nothing like the prescription product, even though the names are similar. This is an unethical marketing practice that will likely continue as long as manufacturers find it profitable.

Finally, the pros and cons of self-medicating discussed earlier in this book become important as more and stronger OTC products are made available.

A problem with the initial review process was that there were not consistent guidelines for deciding which drugs should be switched. Each of the FDA OTC Review Panels established its own criteria, so the regulations have lacked consistency.

Many physicians have also expressed concerns with this development. We expect a prescription when we see a doctor, since this serves to "validate" our illness (i.e., If I am given a prescription . . . it means that I really am sick. So . . . I'm justified in taking off from work). If however an OTC product is "prescribed" patients may feel that paying for an office visit is a waste of money. Prescription products have greater placebo value than OTC drugs, even when their actual medical merits are questionable.

Regardless of any other issues involved, it is clear that future opportunities for switches will require the development of uniform criteria and policies. There must be agreement that we can use these products without professional guidance. Labeling must be complete and understandable. Side effects should be minor, predictable and we must be able to adapt to them. Switches are most effective when you can easily monitor the benefits of therapy, and if we are willing to seek professional help when it is indicated.

A Third Class of Drugs

The switch of prescription drugs to OTC status allows more potent drugs to be made available to the public. Some health authorities are concerned that people may not select and use these products appropriately. In response, suggestions have been made to help protect the public from potential harm.

One suggestion is the creation of a third class of drugs (in addition to prescription and OTC). These would be available without a prescription, but only from a pharmacist. In this manner, people would discuss their symptoms with a pharmacist who would help them decide if one of these products would actually be appropriate. The pharmacist would provide additional instructions about proper use of the product.

Many foreign countries have already taken this initiative and it has received considerable support by many professional and consumer groups in this country. This change is opposed by drug manufacturers and the FDA on the grounds that labeling is adequate and that additional professional supervision is unnecessary.

Despite claims that OTC labeling is adequate for safe and effective consumer use, studies clearly indicate that there are problems with OTC labels. It is questionable that some drugs should be switched to OTC status. For example, *Indomethacin* is one of the latest "aspirin" type pain relievers to compete with aspirin, acetaminophen and ibuprofen products. It has long been a concern to health professionals because of its potential to cause stomach irritation, bleeding and ulcers. It is quite effective when used properly, but its potential for harm is equally great if it is misused.

Another drug of concern is Tagamet HB (cimetidine) which has recently received OTC status for the treatment of heartburn (thus, the 'HB'). Consumers are familiar with Tagamet as an ulcer drug. Many health authorities are concerned that consumers may now attempt to self-diagnose and self-medicate ulcers and other digestive problems. This can be dangerous. Tagamet advertising understates the problems that can occur with excessive use over long time periods. Finally, it is unlikely that most consumers are aware of the many prescription and nonprescription drugs with which Tagamet interacts.

Indomethacin and Tagamet are examples of drugs that are ideal candidates for a third category of products.

People who favor this approach point out that a third class would separate these more potent drugs from other products on sale in non-professional outlets. For example, when medications are sold adjacent to tomato juice and cigarettes, people may view them in a more casual, or even careless manner. The restriction of sales serves as a warning that these purchases require careful consideration for appropriate use.

Opponents to this approach do not want products restricted to sale by pharmacists only. They believe that people may opt for professional care, rather than obtaining products from a pharmacist, and they insist that products which have undergone the FDA-OTC review process do not need to be restricted to pharmacies. Finally, of course, the drug manufacturers expect greater profits by avoiding a third class status for their products.

While some of the arguments against a third class of drugs are actually quite weak, it is also clear that the concept has not won widespread approval.

35. AMERICA'S DRUG ABUSE PROBLEM

"You would be surprised at the number of years it
took me to see clearly what some of the problems
were which had to be solved. Looking back, I
think it was more difficult to see what the problems were than to solve them."

— Charles Darwin

Not long ago a drug abuse meeting was held at a high school in an
Oklahoma City suburb in response to an apparent increase in drug
abuse among its youth. A reasonably large crowd attended, consisting largely of high school students and their parents. The speakers
consisted of the anticipated blend of people. There were representa-
tives of the drug abuse counseling clinic that had organized and host-
ed the program (and who, by the way, were seeking clients for their
drug abuse program). There was a local celebrity, who actually knew
very little about drugs, but who was nonetheless engaged to cheer the
community on to greater involvement. And of course, there were
selected victims of drug abuse who provided emotional testimony
regarding the devastation of drugs in their lives. Certainly one could
reason that these kinds of efforts were laudable. Yet, something significant was lacking in the effort.

Perhaps the most glaring flaw involved what might be called a
"WE" versus "THEM" orientation, which is adopted by most adults in
these types of gatherings. Consequently, each speaker addressed the
audience in terms of drug problems among American youths (and
especially teens), and of a need for the "responsible adults" to put a
stop to it. It is worth noting that this is the same approach that is
adopted by governmental officials in dealing with the drug problem.

Statistics were cited regarding the major problem drugs used by
young people and the social costs involved. There was a plea for the
"responsible adults" of the community (the "WEs") to step in and do
something about the "irresponsible youths" (the "THEMs"). This orientation was not only obvious from the words of the speakers, but also
from the manner in which the audience arranged itself for the meeting: Groups of youths sat together in certain areas of the room and
groups of adults in other areas. The atmosphere was one of distrust

and counter-productivity.

Following the general introductory session, audience members were free to attend short seminars on various aspects of drug abuse — all addressing only the drug problems of youth. In one room the police burned marijuana . . . just so parents would know what it smelled like. In other rooms there were discussions about the availability of youth treatment programs.

Similarly, at a drug abuse seminar sponsored by Pharmacists Against Drug Abuse (PADA) there occurred another flaw in our popular approach to the drug problem in our society. The guest speaker was the President of PADA (but ironically, was not a pharmacist!). His presentation consisted of the traditional "scare tactic" approach (i.e., statistics and macabre data) which has been shown to be an ineffective way of dealing with drug education among young people. He eventually asked, "Why do young people use drugs?" He quickly answered, "It is pure and simple peer pressure!"

In reality, there is nothing "pure and simple" about the drug problem in this country, except possibly in the minds of naive guest speakers. Drug use and abuse in our society is a complex sociological phenomenon which is influenced by many factors. The overwhelming flaw of both of these programs was their failure to recognize that the drug abuse problem is not solely a problem of American youths. Rather, it is a problem of all age groups. It was never mentioned at either of these meetings that alcohol is the leading drug of abuse in American culture (as it has always been), or that the majority of abusers are adults! Instead, they focused their attention on the popular "street drugs" (e.g., cocaine, marijuana).

Where do "we" (i.e., the "responsible" adults) suppose that our youth happen to come by their predispositions for a drug problem? Peer pressure has become the convenient, simplistic scapegoat explanation because it relieves adults of the burden of responsibility for drug use in our youth. It shifts the entire blame for drug use on the young, the schools and "pushers" in the restrooms. It is a much more comfortable "solution" for adults when someone else can be held accountable.

Peer pressure may, of course, represent "the straw that breaks the camel's back" as far as initially trying drugs, but in reality adults are guilty of "piling up the straws" for many years before peer pressure becomes a significant factor.

Consider the role that the media plays in this problem. Many of the 1500 advertisements we see each day are for drugs and related products to help modern adults cope with every conceivable stress or discomfort of life. Our children are exposed to this influence at early ages before they are able to discern between reality and fiction. They view cartoons interlaced with drug and vitamin commercials advocated by their favorite "super heroes," cartoon characters and authority figures. At other times they watch commercials for a variety of products designed to offer a reprieve from virtually every pain or distress associated with modern living. The message is clear: Our problems in life cannot be solved alone . . . we need drugs! And when the drug companies cannot create new products to treat old problems, they create new illnesses for old products (e.g., "iron poor blood", the "stubborn cold," "combination skin", etc.).

Beyond these factors, the advertising efforts of Madison Avenue medicine are reinforced in the minds of children by the behaviors of the "responsible" adults in their lives who:

- Consume coffee every morning to "get them going;"

- Use tobacco products, alcohol and other medications to "calm them down" during the day;

- Take sleeping medications in order to sleep at night;

- Insist on diet pills to avoid the discomforts and inconvenience of appropriate diets and exercises.

The majority of children in our society grow up observing the most important people in their lives putting the TV message into actual practice. Moreover, it is "responsible" adults who demand medications from physicians, whether or not they are actually indicated. And physicians frequently comply with these demands, since they do not want to charge their patients for office calls without providing them with "something" tangible to take home! Otherwise, the "responsible" adults become angry with the health care system.

In response to the demands for medication by the adults of our society, antibiotics are handed out like candy for colds and other viral infections even though it is known that antibiotics are ineffective for these conditions. Narcotic pain medications are demanded when aspirin might work just as well. And, a plethora of other medications (both prescription and nonprescription) are used on a daily basis to help adults cope with the stresses and discomforts of life, thereby relieving them of the inconvenience of having to learn to deal with these problems in more healthy ways.

In the midst of all of this "legitimate" drug taking behavior on the part of our "responsible" adults, we look at our youth, shake our heads and say, "We thought we taught you better than that!"

The irony is that we have taught them all too well.

The drug abuse problem among American youth is learned behavior. It is handed down from one generation to the next as a part of the "fabric" of American culture. The particular drugs being used (or misused) may change from year to year, but the problem remains essentially the same: Our drugs are our coping mechanisms. Like adults, our youth have learned to deal with their problems by using whatever drugs are available to them!

Although the solution to drug abuse is complex and multifacetted, we might start by defining some critical terms.

Drug *misuse* refers to the inappropriate use of a drug. It can involve drugs prescribed by doctors or it can involve self-medicating practices. In either case, drug misuse involves wishful thinking and unrealistic therapeutic objectives. For example, people may buy vitamins to "give them energy" even though vitamins are not capable of providing this benefit. Unrealistic expectations and gullibility on the part of our "responsible" adults provides the foundation for the $100 billion health fraud industry in our country.

The term drug *abuse* refers to drug misuse that is associated with social disapproval (although the usual definitions proposed for this term are conveniently designed to identify only certain drugs). Yet, the social disapproval concept is important if we are to truly understand why we willingly tolerate some drugs in our society, but not others.

Drug studies have consistently revealed that alcohol causes much more damage to our society each year than marijuana. Yet alcohol is accepted by our society and marijuana use is not. Alcohol is the drug of a previous generation, while marijuana is a drug of a younger generation. Thus, the social use of marijuana is viewed as drug "abuse" while the social use of alcohol for the same purposes is not.

This is not to suggest that marijuana should be legalized (which would create a new set of problems with which we would need to contend) or that alcohol should be banned. What is needed in both cases is a realistic perspective of American drug use. Little progress is likely to occur as long as this problem exists within an atmosphere in which "responsible" adults ignore their own drug use behaviors, while dictating terms to the "irresponsible" youths.

Adults and youth are guilty of the same offense, but they have different drugs available to them. It is absurd to believe that we can somehow educate or threaten our youth to stop using "their" drugs, when they exist within a culture where drug use is generally accepted and actively promoted by adult role models.

Inherently, there are no "good" or "bad" drugs; it all depends upon how they are used. And, this concept applies to aspirin just as much as it does for cocaine.

The reality of our times is that "responsible" adults prefer to "pop pills" instead of changing their lifestyles. Rather than dealing with stress in healthy ways, we much prefer medications that can numb our feelings of stress and camouflage our discomforts. The use of medications has become the hallmark of the successful, hard-working adult. We live our lives in reckless ways, convinced that if we become ill there will be a "pill" out there somewhere that will take care of the problem and a doctor out there somewhere who will prescribe it.

Our high-tech health care industry, which has brought us so many benefits, has also created a society that is largely unwilling to take responsibility for its own health. Instead, we assign responsibility for our own welfare to other people, or things.

If we truly want to solve America's drug problem, we must not be content with educational programs oriented solely at the young. Instead, the problem demands educational programs designed for all age levels and for the drugs being used by each age group.

There are basically two approaches for dealing with the drug problem. One is called *supply reduction* and the other is called *demand reduction*. Supply reduction is the traditional method of dealing with the problem. It involves more law enforcement, more courts, more attorneys and judges, more jails, and of course, more money. As we have seen, we prefer this approach because it assigns responsibility for the drug problem to someone else.

Demand reduction is more complex, but in the long run, more effective. It involves educating all people regarding responsible drug taking attitudes and behaviors. It also takes advantage of the free enterprise system: If there is no demand for drugs, there will eventually be no supply! Such an educational perspective must address the ways in which adults use prescription and nonprescription drugs, (including the use of tobacco and alcohol products), and the drug-taking messages which we convey to our youth. It must also address social responsibility on the part of the media (e.g., TV and radio commercials) and the messages which are sent into every household on a daily basis that encourage drug use as a coping behavior.

As we have seen, the average American watches more than seven hours of television daily. During that time the typical viewer is exposed to a significant number of socially irresponsible advertisements, high pressure appeals, sitcoms (devoid of morality and intellect) and other programs which sensationalize irresponsible and destructive behaviors. Parents rarely consider the impact that these messages have upon themselves and others. Moreover, they rarely restrict the viewing of their children.

Give it some thought "responsible" adults. Perhaps the solution to the drug problem lies in the words of Pogo:

> *"We have met*
> *the enemy . . . and*
> *he is us!"*

CASE STUDY

LESSONS FROM REAL LIFE — ANGIE

Angie was 8 years old. She had been watching a cartoon show everyday when she came home from school. The cartoon, like many today, was characterized by a discourteous form of humor. It seemed funny when the characters insulted each other for 30 minutes each day.

Angie's friends were also watching the show. So, Angie and her friends began to talk to each other using the same insulting remarks and tones of voice. Except it wasn't funny when they did it to each other.

Angie began to come home in tears each day because of the ways in which she was being treated. Her parents had already noticed that she was insulting her friends. So, they restricted the shows she could watch on television. She could only watch shows which were approved by her parents, and she could only watch TV for a limited time each day.

Angie did not like this new arrangement. She became bored and began reading. She ceased insulting her friends within a few weeks of the new arrangement, and within a year was 2 grade levels ahead of her classmates in reading.

Reading is appropriate "nutrition and exercise" for the mind. Television is the "fat" that clogs up your mental "arteries." This true story reflects the possibilities that can be achieved when parents begin to exercise control over their lives and the lives of their children.

HOW ABOUT YOU?

Do you watch TV with your children in order to interact with them about what they are watching? What about restricting their TV watching? You have the right to screen poorly written shows, emphasize appropriate values, and encourage your children to expand their minds.

Becoming an Informed Consumer

36. INFORMATION YOU SHOULD DISCUSS WITH HEALTH PROFESSIONALS

"If at first you don't succeed, find someone who knows what he's doing."

Kostreski's Theory, John Peers

Making appropriate decisions about your health and treatment starts with accurate information. Yet, for many reasons we often fail to take advantage of the health information resources that are available. Perhaps we don't want to impose on busy health professionals. We may fear that our questions are silly, or we may simply accept the expertise of health professionals without probing for information. Whatever the reason, in all cases it is important to ask questions and to have them answered.

Topics for Discussion

Outline 111 summarizes some of the questions that might be discussed with health professionals regarding your medications and health concerns, but there is only one basic guideline: Every question and every topic is an acceptable one.

The Medication

It is important to learn the names of the medications that you are taking. Try to learn both the brand name and generic name. Keep a list of the medications with you, since this can help if the names are difficult to remember. If you are interested in generics, be sure to ask if the product is available generically and how much you could save by getting a generic product versus the brand name. Not all products are available generically, but in any event you should ask if this is of interest.

Learn what type of medications you are taking, how they work and why you are taking them. It is also important to have realistic expectations of your medications. Drugs may or may not be able to cure your problem, so learn what your medications can and cannot do. You may want to explore other therapy options. For example, are there other types of products that could be taken? How do they compare with the product that has been prescribed?

OUTLINE 111

QUESTIONS WORTH ASKING ABOUT YOUR MEDICATION AND THERAPY

The Medication

❦ What is the name of this medication? (Brandname and Generic)

❦ What's in this stuff? (i.e., What are the ingredients in this product?)

❦ How does this medicine work?

❦ What is this medication supposed to do?

❦ What can the drug do? What are its limitations?

❦ How effective is the medication?

❦ How does this product compare with similar products?

❦ Does this medication have a dependency potential?

❦ Is this medication safe?

❦ Is this medication available in different dosage forms? (e.g., tablets versus liquids)

❦ Is this available as a generic?

Administration Guidelines

❦ How do I take this medication?

❦ How often do I take it?

❦ What times of the day should I (not) take this?

❦ Make sure that you know exactly what the label instructions mean.

❦ Are there other ways to take this medication? (e.g., tablets versus liquids)

❦ How long will I be taking this medication?

Side Effects

❦ What side effects are likely to occur?

❦ What changes in my daily routine will I need to make to accommodate this medication?

❦ What side effects indicate that I should contact my doctor?

❦ Are there other medications or products that can help me cope with my therapy or health problem?

❦ What are the signs of allergy to this medication?

OUTLINE 111, cont'd

Precautions / Warnings

🐦 Be sure to tell your doctor or pharmacist about any other allergies or problems you have had previously to medications.

🐦 What foods or beverages should I avoid while taking this medication?

🐦 What other medications should I avoid while taking this medication? (Rx or OTC)

🐦 What activities should I avoid while taking this medication?

🐦 Can I take this drug if I am (or may become) pregnant?

🐦 Can I take this drug if I am breast feeding?

🐦 Can elderly take this drug safely?

🐦 Is it safe to take this drug for extended time periods? (even years?)

🐦 What lifestyle changes would be helpful while I am taking this drug?

🐦 How often should I have periodic checkups with my doctor?

Storage in the Home

🐦 Where should I store my medications in the home?

🐦 Where should I NOT store my medications in the home?

🐦 Are their special storage instructions for this medication?

🐦 How dangerous is this medication to children? How should I store this to prevent accidental poisoning in children?

Refills

🐦 Did the doctor provide refill instructions on the prescription?

🐦 Am I supposed to have this refilled?

🐦 How many refills am I allowed to have?

Childproof Versus Conventional Containers

🐦 You are entitled to nonchildproof lids if you prefer them. However, don't ignore child safety.

Price Considerations

🐦 How is my prescription price calculated?

🐦 If this is expensive, could I purchase a smaller quantity until I see how well I will tolerate this medication?

OUTLINE III, cont'd

Your Condition or Disease State

☙ Learn as much as you can.

☙ What lifestyle changes might help me adapt to my disease or health problem?

☙ Are there alternatives to drug therapy?

☙ What symptoms indicate that my condition is improving? Getting worse?

Miscellaneous

☙ ASK QUESTIONS!

☙ Find out about other sources of information.

☙ Are there other products and services that would be of help?

☙ Learn as much as you can about health in general.

Safety issues are also valid concerns. Ask what the hazards and side effects of therapy are likely to be. For example, people these days are often concerned about the dependency potential of medications. Although many drugs do not have a dependency potential, others may cause dependency in a very short time.

Many drugs are available in more than one dosage form (e.g., tablets, capsules, liquids). If you prefer some dosage forms over others, don't hesitate to ask about alternatives.

Administration Guidelines

It may seem obvious to say that it is important to know how to take your medication, yet, there is little doubt that many individuals misunderstand drug administration. First, make sure that you understand how often you should take your medications. Are there certain times during the day when they should (or should not) be taken? For example, diuretics ("water pills") are usually taken in the morning. If you take them later during the day, you may miss a great deal of sleep going to the bathroom.

Next, make sure that you understand the label instructions on your medication bottle before you leave the pharmacy. Again, studies indicate that the instructions printed on medication bottles are often misunderstood.

There are alternate methods of taking some medications. For example, the OTC drug Bonine (for motion sickness) can be chewed or swallowed. Also, some tablets can be broken into halves so that they can be swallowed more easily, but there are many other products which cannot be broken, crushed or chewed.

Finally, ask how long therapy is supposed to last. Some health problems (e.g., high blood pressure, arthritis) must be treated for the remainder of your life. Other problems are only treated for a short time before therapy is discontinued. Find out how long you should remain on therapy.

Side Effects

In all cases when drugs are prescribed ask about side effects that may occur, so that you will be properly prepared. For example, many drugs cause sedation. Therefore, driving or engaging in activities that require mental alertness should be avoided! Another example involves drugs that are drying to the eyes. Here it may be necessary to use wetting drops if you wear contact lenses. In any event, health professionals can often help you learn to cope with troublesome side effects.

Obviously, you should also inquire about any side effects that are serious enough to warrant being seen by a physician (e.g., allergy reactions).

Precautions and Warnings

It is always relevant to ask what should be avoided while on therapy (e.g., other drugs, foods, beverages, activities). In addition, doctors and pharmacists should be informed about any special health concerns (e.g., pregnancy, breast feeding) that may be affected by taking medications. Be aware that children and elderly do not always respond the same way to therapy as a young or middle aged adult might. Also, women often have a lower tolerance for medications than men.

Find out if there are lifestyle considerations that may be important in conjunction with drug use. For example, some drugs cause you to sunburn more easily, and this could pose a special risk if you spend a great deal of time outdoors.

Finally, be sure to ask about periodic checkups. Many medications have only minor adverse effects when used for short time periods (e.g., one month), but have potentially serious adverse effects when used for long time periods. Find out whether you need to have laboratory work or physician examinations regularly to prevent any serious problems.

Drug Storage at Home

The storage of drugs at home is not a frequent topic of discussion with health professionals, but it should be! Inappropriate storage can cause drugs to become ineffective or even toxic. Ask your pharmacist to suggest the best place to store medications (e.g., the upper shelves of bedroom or hallway closets, upper drawers of dressers) and what places should be avoided (e.g., bathrooms and kitchens). Some drugs have special storage requirements. For example, most drugs should not be kept in the refrigerator. Yet, liquid antibiotics and suppositories often need to be refrigerated. In considering drug storage sites, don't forget to think about small children who may visit your home.

Refills

This is another topic of infrequent discussion, which is ironic, since it is the reason for a great deal of confusion between pharmacists and their patients. Legally, your doctor must indicate refills on your prescription in order for the pharmacist to refill it. No refill instructions means just that: no refills! Doctors often forget to provide this information, even when they intend for you to have refills.

Consequently, it's a good idea to check your prescription for refill instructions before you leave the doctor's office, so that the doctor or nurse can add this instruction to the prescription if it has been omitted. Make certain that the instructions given to you by your doctor match the instructions provided on your prescription. On most prescriptions, there is a box or blank line next to the word "refills." You can usually find this easily.

Never add this information to a prescription yourself. To do so constitutes prescription forgery and is a violation of federal law.

If refills are indicated, be sure to call the pharmacy two to three days before you are completely out. This will give the pharmacist plenty of time to take care of any problems with your prescriptions before you come in to pick it up. And, by the way, never assume that there are no problems with your prescription. Pharmacists occasionally run out of your medications, or they may need to call your doctor for additional refill authorizations or information. Finally, be aware that federal and state regulations limit the number of refills that you can have and who may authorize them.

Childproof Containers

You have the right to ask for conventional (i.e., nonchildproof) lids, but be sure to ask for them before your prescription is filled. Prescription labels stick very well! Once your pharmacist attaches it to one bottle, it can't be removed and attached to another. So, the only option is to start over. And, of course, this means that it will be a bit longer before your prescription is ready.

Until just recently you were required to ask for conventional containers every time you obtained a new prescription or a refill. Changes in this law now allow you to sign a blanket waiver, so that all of your prescriptions can be dispensed in them.

Believe it or not, the childproof lid law has been a very effective public health measure. The impact of this regulation in reducing the number of accidental poisonings in children under age five has been nothing short of remarkable. Unfortunately, in recent years the incidence of accidental poisonings has once again increased. This is probably because people have never liked the childproof lid law and we are progressively using them less and less. Most folks, though, have never been in an emergency room during an attempt to save the life of a small child who had accidentally taken a medication, while the parents despaired over the experience . . . "We thought he knew better than that!"

Price Considerations

It's appropriate to ask pharmacists how prescription prices are determined. They have nothing to hide. If they do, you should be using another pharmacy. Also, always consider purchase options. For example, if a drug is expensive you may want to purchase only a small amount initially to see if you will be able to tolerate it. Once you take a prescription out of a pharmacy, the pharmacy cannot take it back regardless of the reason that you are returning it. This is a public health law. So, if you purchase the entire prescription, but then cannot take it, you will have lost the purchase price. Purchasing only a small quantity initially may provide you with an opportunity to try the drug before you purchase the full amount.

As indicated earlier, don't assume that buying generically will always save you money. It may, or may not, depending upon how the pharmacy prices medications. If you are interested in saving money by making generic purchases, ask the pharmacist how much money you would save.

Your Condition or Disease State

It is important for you to understand the disease or health problem for which you are being treated, especially as it relates to the medication which you are taking. Ask if lifestyle changes (e.g., diet, exercise, stress reduction) might offer some benefit and circumvent the need for medication. Or there may be nondrug measures which could limit the amount of drug which you are required to take. For example, high blood pressure sometimes responds very well to weight loss, reductions in caffeine intake, diet and exercise. A change in any or all of those factors might reduce the need for drugs.

Understand the symptoms of your disease or health problem. Learn what symptoms indicate the problem is improving, or becoming worse. Also, identify symptoms that indicate a need to contact your doctor.

Miscellaneous Considerations

Ask questions! These may be questions about the problem for which you are presently taking medications, or about other concerns. You should never feel shy about asking questions. Health professionals are most willing to answer them for you.

Identify other sources of information as needed. There are many organizations which address specific health problems (e.g., American Cancer Society, American Heart Association). They usually have a wealth of information, educational materials and support programs. Check it out! You may be amazed at what you can discover by using these resources.

See if there are other products and services which may be of help to you. Pharmacies, hospitals, home health services and other organizations are not all the same. The programs and services which they offer can be quite varied. Some may be of interest to you. Also, larger communities often have a variety of community health programs and support groups. Find out what's going on in your neck of the woods!

37. DOCTORS — JUST WHO ARE THEY ANYWAY?

"But while modern science can boast of so many startling achievements in the health fields, its role has not been so unique and its effectiveness not so complete as is commonly claimed. In reality, the monstrous specter of infection had become but an enfeebled shadow of its former self by the time serums, vaccines and drugs became available to combat microbes. Indeed, many of the most terrifying microbial diseases — leprosy, plague, typhus and the sweating sickness, for example — had all but disappeared from Europe long before the advent of the germ theory. Similarly, the general state of nutrition began to improve . . . even before 1900 in most of Europe and North America. The change became noticeable long before calories, balanced diets and vitamins had become the pride of nutrition experts, the obsession of mothers and a source of large revenues to the manufacturers of colored packages for advertised food products. Clearly, modern medical science has helped to clean up the mess created by urban and industrial civilization. However, by the time laboratory medicine came effectively into the picture, the job had been carried far toward completion by the humanitarians and social reformers of the 19th Century. When the tide is receding from the beach it is easy to have the illusion that one can empty the ocean by removing water with a pail."

— Rene Dubos

The term "doctor" is a confusing one. Most people recognize it as a highly revered title, and as such, tends to be sought after. However, because doctoral degrees can be earned, granted, purchased (for about $3000), and come in many different categories and convey different levels of authority, it is no wonder there is such confusion about them.

Most Americans associate the term "doctor" with the healing professions. However, this is not entirely accurate. The term "doctor" actually comes from a Latin term, *docere*, which means "to teach." So, the original term "doctor" actually meant "a teacher." As used by universities, the title designates an academic title which signifies a high level of competence in a particular discipline, which may have nothing to do with the healing professions.

American universities basically offer two types of doctoral degrees: (1) Academic Doctorates; and (2) Professional Doctorates. The only Academic Doctorate is the Doctor of Philosophy Degree (Ph.D.), which is the highest degree offered by American universities. In theory, it is the more global of the two types of doctorates. It signifies competence in higher order thinking skills, expertise in a given field and is ordinarily associated with a particular emphasis on research skills. The focus of this degree is not only expertise in a given field, but also the discovery of new information as well as the enhancement of knowledge.

Professional doctorates also signify expertise in a given field, and usually, competencies in higher order thinking skills. Yet, in theory the focus of this degree is an emphasis on the application of existing knowledge. There are numerous professional doctorates, including:

- Doctor of Chiropractic (D.C.)
- Doctor of Dental Surgery (D.D.S.)
- Doctor of Medical Dentistry (D.M.D.)
- Doctor of Nursing (D.N.)
- Doctor of Osteopathy (D.O.)
- Doctor of Podiatric Medicine (D.P.M.)
- Doctor of Veterinary Medicine (D.V.M.)
- Doctor of Education (Ed.D.)
- Doctor of Medicine (M.D.)
- Doctor of Optometry (O.D.)
- Doctor of Pharmacy (Pharm. D.)
- Doctor of Psychology (Psych. D.)

There is a great deal of similarity between some professional doctorates and Ph.D.s in the same field (e.g., an Ed.D. versus a Ph.D. in Education, Counseling Psychology, etc.). Both can work as practitioners or researchers. The college hours required for both degrees is often the same, and both often require a major research project for completion. The primary distinction in similar programs is that the Ph.D. usually requires more courses in research and statistics than professional doctorates. Also, the major research project (a dissertation) for Ph.D.s is often more extensive.

Professional degrees in the health fields are designed to train health care practitioners who will apply existing medical information in the care of their patients. Some of these programs can differ significantly from Ph.D. tracts. The issue is not really whether one degree is "better" than another. Rather, the various degree programs simply have a different focus and may emphasize different aspects of learning.

Some newer "doctorates" are controversial. For example, a new "Doctor of Pharmacy" (Pharm.D.) degree is being promoted as the entry level degree for pharmacy practice. The original Pharm.D. held by many clinical pharmacists required two to three additional years of training beyond the Bachelor of Pharmacy degree. The new Pharm.D. requires only one additional year of training. As a matter of comparison:

Degree	Professional Training Required (yrs)
Ph.D. (pharmacy)	6 - 8
Pharm.D. (old)	5 - 6
Pharm.D. (new)	4

Many professional pharmacy organizations now bestow the title of "doctor" upon members for a fee. For example, the National Association of Retail Druggists provides its members with a "P.D." (Pharmacy Doctor) and some state Boards of Pharmacy confer a "D.Ph." (Doctor of Pharmacy) when pharmacists become registered in their states (it replaces the "R.Ph." or "Registered Pharmacist" designation).

Physicians: Allopaths and Osteopaths

Even though the term *physician* is used to refer to all types of health care professionals (e.g., Chiropractic Physicians), this usage is not entirely accurate. Traditionally, the term physician is reserved for two groups of practitioners: (1) Allopaths; and (2) Osteopaths. *Allopathic* medicine uses remedies that produce effects upon the body which are different from those produced by the disease being treated. For example, in order to relieve a fever a drug would be given that reduces the fever. This is just the opposite of *homeopathy*, which utilizes "the law of similars" (i.e., like is cured by like). Accordingly, a fever might be treated with a drug that actually causes fever in a normal person.

The term allopath actually refers to Medical Doctors (M.D.s). However, many M.D.s object to the term, probably not wanting to be associated with any particular orientation to medical practice.

Conversely, *Osteopathic* physicians (D.O.s) readily associate with their designation and promote it almost as a fraternal designation. Osteopathic medicine has tended to be more holistic, asserting that the body is a vital, mechanical organism whose structural and functional integrity are coordinate and interdependent. Thus, a disturbance in one system can produce altered functioning in another system. Since the musculoskeletal system is considered to comprise over 60% of the total body mass, a particular D.O. emphasis was traditionally placed on manipulative therapy.

The distinctions between D.O.s and M.D.s were probably much more clear in the past than they are today. Both require graduation from accredited medical programs, both utilize medicines and surgery, both have medical specialties, and in fact, many D.O.s complete residencies at M.D. training hospitals. There are M.D.s on the faculty of D.O. training programs and there are D.O.s on the faculty of M.D. training programs. In some states, D.O.s and M.D.s take the same state licensing board examination. Thus, contemporary distinctions appear to be more historical than based on real differences in the quality of training.

Osteopathy has traditionally been more concerned with the training of general practitioners than specialists, which is in keeping with their holistic philosophy. Thus, 75% of D.O.s are in general practice, while the opposite is true for M.D.s. In more recent years, M.D. training programs have created a Family Practice specialty to encourage more M.D.s to become general practitioners.

OUTLINE 112

MEDICAL SPECIALTIES AMONG PHYSICIANS

Title	Specialty Area
❦ Allergist	Allergic or immunological problems
❦ Anesthesiologist	Administration of anesthetics and techniques to render patients insensible to pain during surgical and medical procedures.
	[NOTE: Nurse Anesthetists also perform this function under the supervision of anesthesiologists in many hospitals. Nurse Anesthesists are nurse practitioners who have specialized in this branch of medicine]
❦ Cardiologist	heart problems
❦ Dermatologist	skin problems
❦ Family Practitioner	provides comprehensive medical services for members of a family, regardless of age or sex
❦ Flight Surgeon	problems associated with high altitudes, flying, flight personnel and fitness for flight
❦ Forensic Medicine	medical-legal problems, determination of cause of death, court appearances to report their findings
❦ General Practitioners (GPs)	(see Family Practice)
❦ General Surgeon	surgical correction of deformities, injuries, and for the purposes of prevention and improved functioning
❦ Gynecologist	female genital, urinary and rectal organs, pregnancy, and often delivery
❦ Immunologist	allergic or immunological problems
❦ Intern	a resident physician in a hospital, usually in his/her first year of service, who practices medicine under the supervision of hospital staff for a specified length of time following medical school
❦ Internist (Internal Medicine)	nonsurgical treatment of diseases and disorders of the internal organ systems

OUTLINE 112, cont'd

❦ Laryngologist	problems of the throat
❦ Medical Officer	a physician who plans and participates in medical care or research programs in hospital, clinic, or other public medical facilities, providing medical care for eligible persons; these individual may institute programs of preventive health care in county, city or other government or civic divisions, impose quarantines, establishes standards for hospitals, restaurants and other areas of possible danger
❦ Neurologist	nonsurgical treatment of diseases and disorders of the nervous system (brain, spinal cord, nerves, etc.)
❦ Neurosurgeon	surgical treatment of diseases and disorders of the nervous system
❦ Nuclear Medicine	diagnosis and treatment of human disorders using radioisotopes
❦ Obstetrician	care and treatment of women during pregnancy, delivery of the baby and immediately after delivery
❦ Physiatrist	clinical and diagnostic use of physical agents (e.g., heat and cold) and exercises to provide physiotherapy for physical, mental and occupational rehabilitation of patients
❦ Physical Medicine	physical therapy, occupational therapy, physical reconditioning (e.g., heat, water, electricity, exercise, etc.) to restore useful activities to convalescent, disabled or physically handicapped patients
❦ Plastic Surgeon	surgical correction and repair of skin and soft tissues using skin grafts, bone and tissue transplants to restore or repair damaged, lost or deformed parts of the face and body
❦ Police Surgeon	members of a municipal police force who treat injuries and illnesses; civilians while under arrest, examine and report the physical condition of applicants for the police force and keep records of sick personnel
❦ Preventive Medicine (Public Health)	prevention and protection against disease and promotion of maximum health through all appropriate measures (emphasis is on measures involving broad scale action for large groups of people)

OUTLINE 112, cont'd

Proctologist	anus, rectum and colon problems
Psychiatrist	mental, emotional and behavioral disorders
Public Health Medicine	(see Preventive Medicine)
Radiologist	diagnosis and treatment of diseases using X-rays and radioactive substances
Rhinologist	nose problems
Surgeon	the use of operative or manipulative procedures for the treatment of health or medical problems (the term applies irrespective of the field or limitation of practice)
Thoracic Surgeon	problem of organs in the chest cavity
Urologist	genital and urinary organs of both sexes
Ophthalmologist	eye problems
Orthopedics	diseases, injuries and deformities of bones, joints, and locomotor apparatus
Occupational Medicine	illnesses and injuries occurring to employees while on the job or which are related to the job, including fitness-for-duty examinations, personnel health records, care of injured or sick employees while at home [NOTE: Nurses are often employed in industry to function in this capacity]
Otolaryngologist	ear, nose and throat problems
Otologist	ear
Pathologist	nature, cause, development, structural and functional changes caused by diseases; performs autopsies to determine nature and extent of disease, cause of death, and effects of treatment
Pediatrician	diseases and disorders of children
Sports Medicine	diseases, injuries and disorders associated with participation in sporting events

OUTLINE 113

NONPHYSICIAN CLINICAL PRACTITIONERS

Chiropractors (D.C.)

Individuals trained in a system of medicine based on the premise that health is intimately related to the nervous system. Anything that interferes with the normal function of the nervous system will interfere with the health of the individual and his resistance to disease. Chiropractors utilize manual manipulation of various parts of the body in an attempt to reduce interference with normal function of the nervous system. Chiropractors may also employ therapies based on the use of water, heat, light, diet, exercise and rest in the treatment of a given condition. They utilize such diagnostic equipment as X-rays, electrocardiographs, otoscopes, proctoscopes, etc. However, they are not allowed to prescribe drugs or perform surgery.

Dentists (D.D.S. or D.M.D.)

Practitioners who are concerned with diagnosis, treatment and prevention of diseases and disorders of the gums and teeth.

Endodontists

Concerned with diseases of tissues affecting the vitality of teeth, such as nerve and pulp. They are especially trained in root canal therapy, as well as other traditional dental procedures.

General Dentistry

Account for the largest group of practicing dentists. Provide general dental care for their patients, and represent the traditional "family dentist" with whom most people are familiar.

Oral Pathologist

Specialize in the diagnosis and treatment of diseases of the mouth. This includes tumors and various other lesions.

Oral Surgeon

Specializes in performing surgery on the mouth and jaws. This includes the removal of teeth, tumors and other abnormal tissue growths. Oral surgeons often prepare a patient's mouth for dental prostheses, repair fractures of the jaws and correct abnormal jaw relations.

OUTLINE 113, cont'd

Orthodontists

Specialists in the prevention, diagnosis and treatment of abnormalities involved with the growth, development and position of teeth and other dental tissues. Orthodontic treatment includes the design and application of devices to adjust the position and relationship of teeth and jaws as required to maintain normal growth and function.

Pedodontists

Specialists in the prevention, diagnosis and treatment of children's dental disorders.

Periodontists

Specialists in the prevention, diagnosis and treatment of oral diseases and problems involving the gums.

Prosthodontists

Specialists in making, designing, and fitting artificial teeth, dentures, and associated oral structures. They are also involved in the correction of natural or acquired deformities of the mouth and jaw.

Public Health Dentists

Involved with dental health planning and programs through various public health agencies. This particularly involves the analysis of community dental health needs.

Naturopathic Doctors (Naturopaths)

Practitioners who are concerned with the prevention, diagnosis and treatment of a variety of disorders. Their practice finds its basis in the treatment of physiological functions and deviations of natural laws governing the human body. Their treatment includes therapies involving air, water, light, heat, earth, foods, herbs, electrotherapy, naturopathic manipulations, physical therapy, mechanical therapy, counseling and suggestive therapy, as well as other means. Their practice does not involve the use of major surgery, therapeutic use of X-rays or the use of drugs (other than natural medicines).

[NOTE: Many Chiropractors employ some naturopathic techniques]

OUTLINE 113, cont'd

Optometrists (O.D.)

Practitioners concerned with the prevention, diagnosis and treatment of visual problems, diseases and other abnormalities of the eyes. This includes testing the eyes for visual efficiency and performance, depth and color perception, and the ability to focus and coordinate the eyes. Most optometrists are also involved with prescription, fit and adjustment of eyeglasses and contact lenses. If disease is indicated, optometrists refer patients to appropriate physicians, since their practice does not involve ocular surgery. Optometrists are allowed to prescribe drugs in many states.

Pharmacists

Practitioners involved with the preparation of drugs for dispensing to patients. Many are becoming more actively involved with medical therapy and in patient counseling. Some practitioners who have earned a master or doctoral degree function in much the same way as a Physician's Assistant or Nurse Practitioner in certain clinical scenarios. Traditionally, pharmacists have been involved in the diagnosis and treatment of self-medicating consumers, and regarding the appropriate selection and use of nonprescription drug products. Many pharmacists serve as clinical consultants for nursing homes, hospitals and home health-care agencies.

Podiatrists (D.P.M.)

Practitioners who are trained in the prevention, diagnosis, and treatment of foot ailments. Their practice includes foot surgery and the use of prescription drugs. They refer patients to appropriate physicians when symptoms of the feet and legs indicate systemic or other diseases appropriate for other specialists.

Psychologists

Practitioners who are concerned with such mental functions as sensation, memory, thought, and the behavior and actions of individuals and groups in various situations and environments. May have earned an Ed.D., Ph.D. or Psy.D. Psychologists do not utilize prescription drugs in their practice. There are a number of specialties in psychology. The following are the two most commonly available to consumers:

OUTLINE 113, cont'd

Clinical Psychologists

Typically involved in the prevention, diagnosis and treatment of more severe adjustment problems and mental disorders. These include those associated with psychotic, neurotic and delinquent behaviors. However, their clients include many patients with relatively minor problems.

Counseling Psychology

Tends to deal more commonly with less severe problems. For example, these may involve patients with problems in adjusting to work, school and interpersonal relations.

Veterinarians (D.V.M.)

Practitioners trained in the prevention, diagnosis and treatment of diseases and disorders of animals. The profession involves many specialties, particularly those related to specific groups of animals.

[NOTE: Veterinarians may write prescriptions to be dispensed at a pharmacy for their animal patients. However, they may not legally write a prescription for a human]

OUTLINE 114

DOCTORS WHO CAN (OR CANNOT)) WRITE PRESCRIPTIONS

Doctors who **CAN** write prescriptions

Dentists (D.D.S. or D.M.D.)
Medical Doctors (i.e., Allopathic Physicians) (M.D.)
Optometrists (O.D.)*
Osteopathic Doctors (D.O.)
Podiatrists (D.P.M.)
Veterinarians (D.V.M.)

* Depends upon the state involved.

Doctors who **CANNOT** write prescriptions

Chiropractors (D.C.)
Doctor of Pharmacy (Pharm.D., Ph.D., or P.D.)**
Doctor of Philosophy (Ph.D.)
Naturopathic Doctors
Physician's Assistants***
Psychologist (Ph.D., Ed.D. or Psych. D.)

** Doctors of Pharmacy are sometimes employed by physicians and write prescriptions under the authority of a physician much as nurse practitioners or physician's assistants do. However, federal law does not currently allow nurses, physician's assistants or doctors of pharmacy to write prescriptions under their own authority.

*** Physician's Assistants are not doctors, since they do not earn a doctoral degree of any kind. However, they normally practice in clinic settings, often with doctors, and they are allowed to prescribe under the authority of a licensed physician. They are included here because of their close association with physicians.

38. SELECTING DRUG LITERATURE FOR THE HOME

As scarce as truth is, the supply is much greater than the demand.

— Saunder's Slant #1, John Peers

By 1980 there were already more than 5,500 self-help books available in American bookstores. One might assume that they were all credible or else they could not be sold. Unfortunately, many health books serve more as an example of wishful thinking than facts. Some authors make such exaggerated claims that one might argue they are more designed to promote personal fame and fortune than to promote good health practices.

On the other hand, some books are credible medical books, but they simply are not appropriate references for consumers (e.g., The Physician's Desk Reference or PDR), since they require technical knowledge beyond the expertise of the public. The average person who buys a PDR, for example, will have purchased information, but not understanding. There are many examples of people who made inappropriate health decisions after reading medical references that were not written for them. Health professionals *interpret* what they read based upon their training and experiences.

Evaluating and Selecting Health References for the Home

How does one go about selecting health and medical references for the home? Outline 115 summarizes some of the factors you should consider. The author is an appropriate place to begin. This is an important consideration, since anyone can write a book on any topic. There are no laws or regulations which require you to be an expert in a given field in order to write a book about it.

Begin by asking, "Is this author qualified to write this book?" This may seem a difficult question to answer, but there are clues for which you should look. For example, are the author's credentials and degrees congruent with the topic? What about professional accomplishments? Outline 116 summarizes degrees, titles and abbreviations that are often associated with health writers. This information can provide insight about the author. Books often include background information about the author on the cover materials or first few pages of the text. This information provides additional clues about the qualifications of the author (e.g., current vocation, honors, activities). If the author has no real credentials regarding the subject matter, you should question his/her ability to write a book on this topic.

It is ironic indeed that many authors promote their books on the basis that they are not experts in the topic, and therefore, they are better able to tell the "truth" to other nonexperts. There is a tremendous flaw in logic here, but it seems to have an appeal to many readers. Imagine someone writing a book on auto mechanics, who actually knows very little about automobile repair. Yet, this author insists that his book is more truthful because, like me, he drives a car but does not know what to do when it won't start! Sound absurd? It is!

Some authors actually have expertise that is related to the topic of the book, but then they extend their expertise to topics about which they are not experts. Consider, for example, a popular series of books about drugs and pharmacies written by a pharmacologist. Pharmacology is the study of how drugs work in the body. Pharmacists, doctors and nurses take courses in pharmacology. However, taking courses in pharmacology alone does NOT provide sufficient training to be a doctor or pharmacist. Even though this author has training in pharmacology, he is not a pharmacist, is not eligible to be licensed as a pharmacist and has never practiced pharmacy. His experience with pharmacy practice is the same as any other consumer. Yet, on a national radio show he was asked, "Just what is a pharmacologist?" He answered, "Well, basically it is someone who teaches pharmacists!" So are university history teachers! This author has implied that he has the expertise to write a book on pharmacy, the interaction between pharmacists and consumers, pharmacy as a profession and the practice of pharmacy. However, pharmacists have training in areas about which this author has no background or experience.

Another author (who is not a health professional) promotes a questionable medication in several places in his book and encourages all readers to request it from their physicians. He suggests that the way to obtain "desirable" drugs is to become knowledgeable about the drug (e.g., by reading PDR) and then impress the physician with your "knowledge" about the drug. This author asserts that this drug is underutilized because consumers and health professionals alike are uninformed about the true merits of the drug.

OUTLINE 115

FACTORS TO CONSIDER WHEN EVALUATING HEALTH AND MEDICAL REFERENCES FOR HOME

The Author

❦ Is the author actually qualified to write this book?

❦ What are the author's real interests?

❦ Is the author biased?

❦ Is the author merely selling opinions and wishful thinking, or facts?

❦ Is the author authoritative and reliable?

The Book

❦ Does the content have practical value?

❦ Does the content have value and interest?

❦ Does the content fit the actual qualifications of the author?

❦ Does the content fit the needs and expertise of the reader?

❦ Is the content factual, or is it merely relating opinions that people want to hear?

❦ Is the content accurate?

❦ Has the content been properly presented and evaluated?

❦ Is the material suitable for the intended reader?

❦ Does the information sound "too good to be true"?

❦ Are sources and references identified and competent?

❦ Is the format of the book "user friendly"?

The Publisher

❦ Is the publisher geared to professional or consumer audiences?

The Reader

❦ How significant and useful is the material to you?

❦ For what purposes do you intend to use the information?

❦ Are you being honest with yourself regarding your motives for purchasing the book? Are you truly able to understand the content?

In reality, ethical physicians do not prescribe drugs on demand. Drugs are prescribed if they are actually indicated and if they are effective (i.e., based upon the doctor's experiences with the drug in the treatment of patients and based upon the best available medical evidence). Therapy is based on sound reasoning and experience, not wishful thinking. The author of this questionable book seems not to understand this aspect of responsible professional care.

You should also consider the materials. What is it that you want to learn? There are books on drugs, first-aid, pregnancy, general health, family health, males, females, children and pets. Or, perhaps your interests involve physical fitness, dieting, nutrition, exercise or some other area. Books have been written on virtually every topic.

There are two very important clues to the materials contained in the book. First, consider the title. Titles are usually designed to attract your attention. However, they also provide you with initial clues to the content and objectives of the author.

A more informative source is the table of contents of the book. Scan this information to see if the book addresses topics of interest. You should also be able to gain a sense of whether or not the cover materials (e.g., title, book descriptions) accurately reflect the content.

Finally, review the materials to see if the book is written in a manner that you would enjoy reading and which presents the information in a "user friendly" format.

In addition to the book, you should also evaluate yourself! In what ways do you intend to use the information? Do you want specific, or more general information? The book you choose should address your needs and interests.

You should select books which you can easily read. In the same way that reading an auto mechanic's manual would seem foreign to most of us, medical literature written for health care professionals is not appropriate for most laymen. There are books written for consumers which have eliminated the medical jargon, and which are written at an appropriate level to be more easily understood.

Each of us should also be honest with ourselves about our level of expertise and understanding. Avoid advanced books as a beginning reference. Give yourself a chance to grow in knowledge and understanding.

In brief, the key to selecting medical literature for the home is to accurately and honestly evaluate books and yourself before you buy them. Learn to assess their content and credibility. Be honest with yourself about your needs and present levels of expertise regarding topics of interest.

Finally, ask for professional assistance. Nurses, physicians and pharmacists can often help you to evaluate references. Also, there are many organizations available which provide literature free of charge or for a nominal fee. These organizations include the American Cancer Society, American Heart Association, American Arthritis Association and others. Outline 117 lists sources from which you can obtain information from legitimate organizations.

Drug Monographs

Many drug references present their information in the form of a *drug monograph* which provides information on a single drug or a group of closely related drugs.

Not all monographs contain the same information. By knowing the types of information each publication contains, you can determine which reference to use when looking for specific information. Health professionals do the same thing. Doctors, pharmacists and nurses keep numerous references on hand which provide the information they normally need (e.g., *Drug Facts And Comparisons, USP DI, American Hospital Formulary Service*, PDR).

Topic headings and subheadings are used in monographs to indicate where certain information is located. So, you do not have to read an entire monograph in order to find specific information. However, you must be familiar with the terms used for headings in order to find the information you need. There are several important terms which are critical for drug use:

Absorption refers to the activities and processes involved in the transfer of a drug from its site of administration to its sites of action.

Action (or *Mechanism of Action*) describes how the drug works and what it does. These discussions tend to address how the drug works in the treatment of diseases for which it is prescribed. Discussions may be restricted to uses of the drug which have been approved by the FDA.

Administration and Dosage indicates the way in which the drug is taken or used, as well as information about how to prepare the product for administration (e.g., injections must often be diluted before they can be given). Dosage ranges are usually included for the more common uses of the drug.

Adverse Drug Reactions (also, *Side Effects* or *Toxicology*) tend to be used interchangeably as heading terms in drug monographs, even though these terms are not identical in meaning. This section refers to adverse drug reactions which are known to occur and have been reported to health authorities.

Monographs sometimes include information about how often side effects can be expected to occur. It is important to realize that ADRs are listed even if they occur only rarely. The fact that a particular ADR appears in the literature does not mean that it will actually occur in most people. It only means that it has been reported. Professional judgment is required to assess the risk for certain ADRs to occur in any given person.

Bioavailability is concerned with how much of the drug is transferred from one site to another (e.g., the site of administration to the circulation and then to its sites of action). Information may also be included about how long it takes for the drug to begin working.

Biopharmaceutics is the study of how dosage forms (e.g., tablets versus liquids) affect your therapy. For example, some tablets should not be taken with milk; some liquids may work more quickly than the same drug in a tablet form.

Biotransformation (or *metabolism*) considers the ways in which the body is able to alter a drug after it is taken. Your body considers all drugs to be a "foreign substance" and attempts to change them so that they can be excreted.

Chemistry describes the chemical characteristics of the drug (for example, chemical structure, melting points, boiling points, appropriate and inappropriate solvents, etc.).

Clinical pharmacology considers the effects of drugs on living cells, tissues, organs and organ systems, especially regarding the treatment of disease.

Contraindications are those conditions which normally discourage use of the drug. If a drug is used in the presence of these conditions, hazardous consequences may occur.

Distribution describes the processes involved in the transfer of a drug from one area of the body to another. This section may also indicate the cells, tissues, organs, and organ systems where the drug will not go. For example, some drugs can reach the brain, while others cannot.

Dosage forms provides a listing of the dosage forms available and the strengths of each of these dosage forms. Some monographs will only indicate the more commonly used dosage forms (especially in publications written for consumers).

Drug interactions may be listed that occur between a drug and some other entity (e.g., other drugs, foods, laboratory tests, activities, etc.) These typically list only those interactions which are clinically significant. However, some publications also list less significant interactions.

Duration of drug activity is the length of time that clinical effects may be observed in a patient. It is often expressed as a time range.

Excretion includes the processes, mechanisms and sites by which drugs are eliminated from the body.

Fate is generally concerned with what happens to a drug while in the body. Thus, it may include information about absorption, bioavailability, distribution, excretion, metabolism, the effects that a particular disease state has on the drug, other pharmacokinetic information, etc. This is a more general heading term which may include information found under more specific headings defined in this listing in other references.

History sections relate information regarding the discovery and development of the drug. This section may include significant events in the history of the drug from its discovery (or before) to the present.

Indications (or *Therapeutic Uses*) list the purposes for which the drug is used. Very often these refer only to those uses which have been approved by the FDA. However, some monographs also list "unofficial uses" or "investigational uses".

Onset of Action Time refers to the time it takes for the drug to begin working after you have taken it.

Overdosage is a listing of the symptoms of toxicity (i.e., more serious adverse drug reactions) which occur when too much of a drug has been taken. These sections sometimes include guidelines for treating the overdose (e.g., first aid).

Parameters to Monitor include laboratory tests and clinical signs which should be monitored in order to insure safe and effective therapy and how often monitoring should occur. This information may be found in the "precautions" or "warnings" sections of drug monographs which do not contain this particular heading.

Patient instructions include information which you should know in order to use the drug product in an appropriate, safe and effective way.

Pharmacogenetics is concerned with altered drug effects due to genetic differences between one individual and another. It is also concerned with detecting susceptible individuals before the drug is administered. This is not a common heading in most drug monographs. However, this information is sometimes included under other headings (e.g., "warnings," "precautions," etc.).

Pharmacognosy is concerned with the natural sources of drug products. It has been specifically concerned with drugs from plant sources, although it is not necessarily restricted to this category. Pharmacognosy considers the scientific basis of herbal therapeutics.

Pharmacokinetics is concerned with the rate of various processes (e.g., absorption, biotransformation, distribution and excretion). It is also concerned with drug concentration at the site of action and with the intensity of drug effects over time.

Pharmacology is defined as the science or knowledge of drugs. As a heading in drug monographs its use may be quite broad. In fact, it can logically include information found in many of the other headings considered in this listing. In most references, however, its use tends to be restricted to a few categories of information (e.g., actions, pharmacokinetics, absorption metabolism, excretion, etc.).

Pharmacotherapeutics includes information regarding the use of drugs in the prevention, treatment, or diagnosis of disease.

Plasma levels relates therapeutic blood levels of the drug. This is typically included only for drugs in which research has clearly identified correlations between blood levels and drug activity. Most often this information is included under other headings (e.g., pharmacology, actions, pharmacokinetics, etc.).

Precautions and Warnings are similar in meaning, and so are considered together. As used in drug monographs, *precautions* are situations in which the drug must be used with caution and may list parameters to monitor. By definition, *warnings* tell of a coming danger or misfortune, and therefore, caution about certain acts. As used in drug monographs, it lists conditions for which the drug is not absolutely contraindicated, but for which the drug must be used with great caution, and with a concern for potential risks and benefits.

Hierarchy of risk for these related terms:

- Contraindications: Most risky scenario
- Warnings: Less risky scenario than contraindications
- Precautions: Less risky scenario than warnings

In practice, the distinction between "warnings" and "precautions" can be subtle. When both are included in the same monograph, "precautions" are often more preventable and possibly less dangerous to your well-being than "warnings."

Sources provides information about the source from which the drug is derived. This information tends to be related to pharmacognosy considerations.

Structure/activity relationships correlate drug action and its chemical structure. This information is often included under the "chemistry" heading.

T 1/2 (or *half-life*) refers to the time required for 50% of a dose to be eliminated from the body. This is an indicator of how long the dose of a drug can be expected to be in the body.

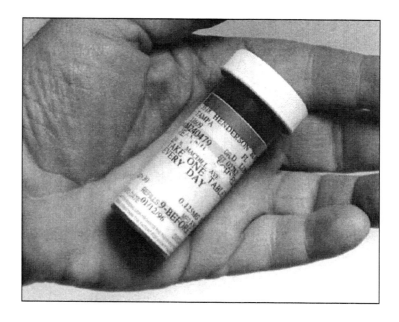

OUTLINE 116

EXAMPLES OF DEGREES, TITLES AND ABBREVIATIONS ASSOCIATED WITH HEALTH WRITERS

	Title or Degree	Comments
B.A.	Bachelor of Arts	Undergraduate academic degree which designates bachelor level training. Can be earned in many fields of study.
B.S.	Bachelor of Science	Undergraduate academic degree which designates bachelor level training. Can be earned in many fields of study.
D.C.	Doctor of Chiropractic	The professional degree of Chiropractors.
D.D.S. D.M.D.	Doctor of Dental Surgery Doctor of Dental Medicine	Professional degrees of Dentists.
D.O.	Doctor of Osteopathy	The professional degree of Osteopathic physicians.
D.Ph.	Doctor of Pharmacy	A title which is being used by some states as a replacement for R.Ph (i.e., Registered Pharmacist) It is not a degree.
D.P.H.	Doctor of Public Health	A professional degree designating doctoral level training in public health.
D.P.M.	Doctor of Podiatric Medicine	The professional degree of Podiatrists.
D.V.M.	Doctor of Veterinary Medicine	The professional degree of Veterinarians
D.Sc.	Doctor of Science	Either a professional degree (if earned), or an honorary degree awarded because of scholarly or noteworthy accomplishments.
Ed.D.	Doctor of Education	A professional degree which designates doctoral level training. May be obtained in various fields of study (e.g., education, counseling psychology, etc.).

OUTLINE 116, cont'd

M.A.	Master of Arts	A graduate degree which designates masters level training. May be earned in many fields of study.
M.D.	Doctor of Medicine	The professional degree of Medical Doctors.
M.S. or M.Sc.	Master of Science	A graduate degree in science which designates masters level training. May be earned in many fields of study.
P.A.	Physicians Assistant	These individuals assist physicians with a variety of patient assessment and care functions. They operate under the authority of a supervising physician.
P.D.	Doctor of Pharmacy	A title conferred by some organizations as a part of membership. It is not a degree.
Ph.D.	Doctor of Philosophy	Highest academic degree offered by American universities. Designates doctoral level training. May be earned in many fields of study.
Pharm.D.	Doctor of Pharmacy	The "new" Pharm.D. is being promoted as the entry level degree required to practice pharmacy (it replaces the B.S. in Pharmacy). Many clinical pharmacists hold the "old" Pharm.D. which required 2 to 3 years of advanced training beyond the B.S. in Pharmacy.
Psy.D.	Doctor of Psychology	A professional doctorate in Clinical Psychology training which indicates expertise in the field of mental health.
R.N.	Registered Nurse	A state licensing credential for Nurses
R.Ph.	Registered Pharmacist	A state licensing credential for pharmacists.

OUTLINE 117

EXAMPLES OF INFORMATION RESOURCES FOR CONSUMERS

❦ CENTER FOR THE STUDY OF AGING
706 Madison Ave.
Albany, NY 12208
Write for a publications listing.

❦ HEALTH ADVOCACY SERVICES — HEALTH CALENDAR
American Association of Retired Persons (AARP)
1909 K St., NW
Washington, DC 20049

❦ HEALTH PROMOTION FOR OLDER ADULTS
American Association of Retired Persons (AARP)
1909 K St., NW
Washington, DC 20049
A listing of organizations, publications, and other resources.

❦ HEALTHY PEOPLE 2000 — HEALTHY OLDER ADULTS
American Association of Retired Persons (AARP)
1909 K St., NW
Washington, DC 20049
Tips, techniques and resources for a longer, healthier life.

❦ HELP YOURSELF TO HEALTH
A marvelous book prepared by Dr. Art Ulene (if it is still available).
This book lists more than 3,500 nationwide health resources and
organizations that address myriad health problems and interests.

❦ NATIONAL COUNCIL ON THE AGING — HEALTH PROMOTION
INSTITUTE
Dept. 5087
Washington, DC, 20061-5087
The Health Promotion Institute is one of 8 constituent units of the
National Council on Aging. Write for information about services,
membership opportunities and benefits, and resources.

OUTLINE 117, cont'd

❦ NATIONAL HEALTH CLEARINGHOUSE
PO Box 1133
Washington, DC 20013
Write for their publication entitled, HEALTH INFORMATION
RESOURCES. This book lists addresses and information regarding a
great many health concerns and problems.

❦ NATIONAL HEART, LUNG AND BLOOD INSTITUTE
Information Center
7200 Wisconsin Ave.
Box 329
Bethesda, MD 20814-4820
Write for a publications listing.

❦ NUTRITION RESOURCE LIST
Division of Nutrition Research Coordination
National Institutes of Health
Building 31, Rm 4B63
9000 Rockville Pike
Bethesda, MD 20892
A listing of nutrition resources.

❦ STAYING WELL — HEALTH PROMOTION PROGRAMS FOR
OLDER PERSONS
American Association of Retired Persons (AARP)
Provides a listing of resources and programs on health promotion.

❦ STEP BY STEP — PLANNING WALKING ACTIVITIES
American Association of Retired Persons

❦ Superintendent of Documents
U.S. Government Printing Office
Washington, DC 20402
Write for the NATIONAL INSTITUTE ON AGING RESOURCE
DIRECTORY FOR OLDER PEOPLE. This is a valuable resource
regarding organizations, services and opportunities of interest to many
people, not just older individuals. Also, this source has listings of other
information sources and publications. Ask for a listing of information
available through this office.

CASE STUDY

LESSONS FROM REAL LIFE — WOULD YOU TAKE THIS PRESCRIPTION?

Suppose that you came to your pharmacist with minor aches and pains and asked, "What can you recommend for this?" The pharmacist provides you with a bottle of tablets and states, "Here take these. However, before you do, I want you to read the list of side effects for this product."

Here is the list of side effects for the product which you have just been given:

nausea	epigastric discomfort	coma
dyspepsia	anorexia	disturbances of acid/base balance
reflux esophagitis	gastrointestinal bleeding	increased bleeding time
dizziness	tinnitus	cardiovascular collapse
headache	lassitude	hemorrhagic disturbances
profuse sweating	thirst	depression
mental confusion	tremor	stupor
delirium	impaired hearing	convulsions
dimness of vision	tachycardia	respiratory failure
hyperventilation	skin eruptions	death
diarrhea		

Given this list of side effects . . . would you want to take this product? Although this example has been used in consumer drug education presentations hundreds of times . . . no one has ever indicated that they would be willing to take this product.

Yet, this is the list of side effects for ASPIRIN taken from standard medical references (including the PDR)!

Health professionals recognize that most of these adverse effects will only occur in cases of overdose. They also know which ones are more likely to occur with normal dosing, as well as those that indicate that more serious problems are developing.

39. PHARMACY SERVICES

"Health and happiness are the expression of the
manner in which the individual responds and
adapts to the challenges that he meets in everyday
life."

— Rene Dubos

A pharmacy is a unique business. It is a retail store. Yet, drugs are
the most regulated of all products available to us, and this places limitations on what pharmacists can do for the consumer. Because pharmacists are health care professionals, they may have problems balancing their professional responsibilities with the retail or business
demands of their practice environments.

Generally speaking, there are three types of services which pharmacies may offer: (1) general merchant services; (2) professional
health services; and (3) clinical services. Outline 118 summarizes
examples of these services. Some are quite familiar to the public,
while others may be less familiar to the average consumer. In defense
of pharmacies, it is not always possible or practical to offer some services. As with any retail store, pharmacies attempt to select services
that appeal to people and which represent their needs. Some services
are considerably more expensive to offer (e.g., delivery, soda fountains,
personal charge accounts). Like any retail store, pharmacies must
offer services that are profitable.

General Merchant Services are those which are common to any
retail setting. These include convenient hours of operation, acceptance
of major credit cards, personal charge accounts, and friendly personnel.
Almost all stores advertise the lowest prices in town regardless of what
they actually charge. The inclusion of "discount" in a store name actually has no meaning whatsoever. Convenient locations mean different
things to different people. Some people prefer stores that are closer to
home. Others prefer stores that are closer to work, or located near the
office of their physician.

Professional Health Services refer to a more general category of
services which are unique to pharmacies, but which do not necessarily require the expertise of the pharmacist. For example, most pharmacies will provide prescription records for income tax and insurance

purposes. Pharmacies may have waiting areas for their patients or a private counseling area (You should insist on the availability of an area where you can discuss issues of concern in private, and not in the middle of the deodorant aisle).

Clinical Services refer to those that require the expertise of the pharmacist. These typically refer to counseling and educational activities, but may also include drug interaction screening or other professional services (e.g., blood pressure screening).

The list of service examples included in Outline 118 illustrate the variety of possibilities which are available. You should inquire about the services which each pharmacy offers, then select a pharmacy which provides the services most relevant to your needs. Let your pharmacist know if there are other services which would be desirable.

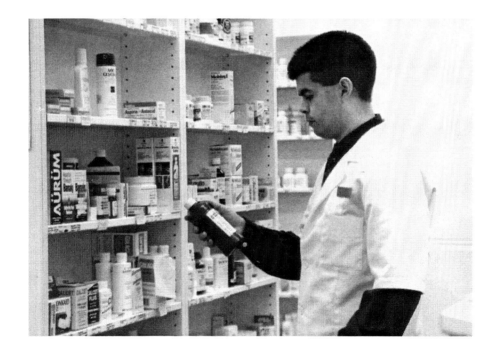

OUTLINE 118

EXAMPLES OF PHARMACY SERVICES WHICH YOU MAY WANT TO CONSIDER WHEN SELECTING A PERSONAL OR FAMILY PHARMACY

Business (General Merchant Services)

- Receipts for all purchases
- Charge accounts
- Accepting credit cards
- Delivery services
- Low (or reasonable) prices
- Convenient location
- Cheerful/friendly personnel
- Convenient hours
- Pleasant atmosphere

Professional Health Services (General)

- Explaining the pricing method used by the pharmacy
- Marking the number of refills left on each prescription
- Supplying year-end prescription purchase records for income tax records
- Patient profiles
- Mailing of prescriptions to out-of-town customers
- Patron waiting area
- Pharmacist contacts physician concerning possible drug/drug interactions
- Pharmacist contacts physician to obtain refill instructions
- 24-hour emergency prescription service
- Pharmacist's home phone number available for emergencies
- Surgical and sick room supplies available for sale or rent
- Availability of information regarding area physicians
- Availability of medical literature and information
- Names of drugs are included on prescription labels
- Patients are called regarding overdue renewals of prescriptions
- Auxiliary labels on prescriptions
- OTCs are included on the patient's profile

Professional Health Services (Clinical Services)

- Counseling services
- First aid services and/or first aid supplies
- Fitting room for surgical supplies
- Information provided to area physicians regarding new drugs
- Screenings (e.g., blood pressure)
- OTC counseling

40. HOW TO SELECT OTC PRODUCTS

"A thing not looked for is seldom found."

— Frenaz's Rule, John Peers

Because of the number of products available without a prescription, choosing from the various alternatives can be confusing. In many cases, advertisements influence our decicions. However, the quality of a product tends to be unrelated to the amount of advertising and promotion associated with it. In fact, many products of questionable quality are the most heavily advertised (and the most expensive of the alternatives).

In order to make the best choice, there are three guidelines to consider. By using these guidelines, it is possible to make economical purchases that provide optimal benefits and fewer problems.

1. Tailor the ingredients to the symptoms which you actually have.

Advertisements promote the idea that the more ingredients that a product contains, the better it is. This simply is not true. For example, one popular cold product advertises that it is designed to treat 12 cold symptoms. Yet, this is only an advantage if you happen to have all 12 cold symptoms! Most people rarely have this many symptoms at once, so there is little advantage to be gained from a product which is designed this way. Also, 6 of the 12 cold symptoms listed in this ad are treated by the aspirin contained in the product. Since most people already have aspirin at home, it makes little sense to purchase another aspirin-containing product.

In fact, it is much better to purchase products which contain only one or two ingredients. This limits the potential for side effects, and allows you to treat only those symptoms which you actually have. Since each product can be safely stored in the home for reasonable time periods and used to treat only those symptoms that you actually have, this practice is actually more cost effective than purchasing the more expensive "shotgun" products (i.e., products with several ingredients in them).

Moreover, side effects can occur with each ingredient included in a product, which is another reason to choose only those ingredients which you actually need. Taking ingredients to treat symptoms that do not exist can expose you to side effects that could have been avoided.

People often take medications to prevent certain symptoms or conditions (e.g., colds). While prevention is a realistic objective for some OTC therapy (e.g., motion sickness medications), it is an unrealistic objective in other cases. For example, OTC medications do not prevent colds, and in fact, can actually increase the likelihood of catching one. Finally, taking medications when they are not needed can result in the development of tolerance. If so, the medication may not work as well when you truly need it.

2. Make certain that the critical ingredients are present in sufficient quantities.

Many products contain minimal doses of their ingredients and some contain too little to really be effective. It makes little sense to take two tablets of one product, when one tablet of another is just as effective. With regard to most cold and allergy medications, it is probably best to take a full therapeutic dose. For example, the recommended therapeutic dose for the antihistamine chlorpheniramine is 2 to 4 mg. However, many products are formulated with only 1 or 2 mg. per tablet (you would have to take 2 to 4 tablets to get a full therapeutic dose). While this is beneficial for the manufacturer's profit margins, it is usually not as cost-effective for you.

Obviously there are some patients who are very sensitive to the side effects of medications. In such cases, taking a lower dose may be advisable. You may want to purchase lower-strength tablets initially just to see how the drug will affect you. If you do, purchase a package containing a minimal number of tablets. Then, if the product is not adequate, only a small amount would have been purchased.

3. In order to compare costs of products, compare the cost of therapy per day, and not the package cost.

When making price comparisons, most people simply compare package costs. More recently, many grocery stores have begun to compute costs per ounce, cost per tablet, etc. (unit cost system). This information is usually listed on the shelf along with the package cost. However, this is not an entirely accurate way of comparing the costs of medication products. Some products require that you must take up to eight to twelve tablets each day in order to obtain a full therapeutic dose. Other products only require that two tablets must be taken each day. In such cases, the package cost can be quite deceiving, as can the cost per tablet, capsule, teaspoonful, etc. You must calculate the cost of therapy per day in order to make accurate price comparisons. This can be easily done:

For tablets and capsules

(Cost per tablet) $\times$ (tablets taken per day)

= Cost of therapy per day

For liquids taken by teaspoon (tsp)

(Cost per tsp) $\times$ (tsp taken per day)

= Cost of therapy per day

For liquids taken by tablespoon (tbs)

(Cost per tbs) $\times$ (tbs taken per day)

= Cost of therapy per day

Note: 1 tsp = 5 ml; and 1 tbs = 15 ml.

41. DRUG STORAGE IN THE HOME

"Nature always sides with the hidden flaw."

— Murphy's 9th Law, John Peers

Proper drug storage in the home has not been a major health concern for most people, but it should be. This is because improperly stored medications can become useless or even toxic.

The primary issue of concern here is one of *stability*, which refers to the degree to which a drug retains the properties and characteristics it had when it left the manufacturer. Drug stability is affected by how drugs are stored at home. Improper storage, for example, can cause drugs to decompose. For many drugs, decomposition merely means that the drug will lose its effectiveness. While this does not always represent a serious health threat, it usually means that you're wasting your money.

Decomposition can threaten your health if drugs become toxic as they decompose. For example, decomposition of tetracycline antibiotics may result in a condition known as *Faconi Syndrome*, which is associated with potentially serious kidney, blood and intestinal problems. Tetracycline decomposition has also been associated with an unusual sensitivity to light, especially sunlight.

Another way in which decomposition can threaten your health is by a loss of the drug's potency. In such a case, the disease or health problem being treated can become worse. An example of this involves sublingual nitroglycerin (NTG) tablets, which are specially formulated to dissolve rapidly when placed under the tongue. Sublingual nitroglycerin is used by heart patients to treat a condition known as *angina pectoris*. If improperly stored, sublingual NTG tablets lose their potency and may not work in emergency situations.

Manufacturers take precautions to preserve the stability of their products (protective coatings, protective ingredients, protective packaging and storage conditions). So, drug products are manufactured in such a way that potency is guaranteed for a certain number of years. Eventually, the drug expires. Manufacturers indicate an expiration date on each container so that pharmacists receiving the drug will know when to remove the drug from their stock. This system works quite well for drug products *as long as they are being stored in a pharmacy*. Pharmacies provide for a constant room temperature (usually slightly to the cool side) with relatively low and constant humidity levels. Since prescription departments tend to be located away from doors and windows, sunlight is rarely a problem. The expiration date provided by a manufacturer is reasonably accurate because environmental factors are less likely to affect drugs in a pharmacy.

However, once a drug is taken home it becomes difficult to accurately predict expiration dates. The environmental factors of the home which are the greatest threat to drug stability are temperature, moisture and light. Studies indicate that most people store drugs in inappropriate locations in the home. Consumers are not entirely to blame for this, since health professionals have done a poor job of educating the public about proper storage.

Temperature

Drugs are especially susceptible to temperature extremes (room temperature is best for most drugs). Most people are aware that warmer temperatures are destructive to medications, so they may store all of their medications in the refrigerator. However, medications should not be stored there unless cool temperatures are specifically required to protect them. Since the moisture content is different for hot and cold air, removal of a prescription vial from a cold refrigerator to warmer room air causes moisture to condense on the bottle.

The damage from exposure to heat includes:

- High temperatures affect the moisture content of the air
- Chemical reactions
- Physical changes
- Losses of solvents from solutions (e.g., evaporation)
- Color fading
- Separation of liquids into layers
- Cracking of sugar-coated tablets
- Gelatin capsules may melt and stick together.

Damage from exposure to cold temperatures includes:

- Decreased drug solubility

❦ Separation of certain liquids into layers

❦ Cracking of sugar-coated tablets.

Moisture

Water vapor is a major problem for drug stability, and can affect drugs both chemically and physically. The results of drug exposure to moisture include:

❦ Increased decomposition

❦ Changes in drug potency

❦ Powders become caked and hard

❦ Loss of effervescence in effervescent powders

❦ Tablets fall apart, then cake together

❦ Mold and bacterial growth.

Heat and Moisture

Heat and moisture often occur together. This is a significant consideration, since the combination can cause drugs to deteriorate more quickly than exposure to either condition alone.

Light

Light is frequently overlooked as a source of problems, but may affect drug stability in various ways. One obvious example is color fading. Light can also generate certain types of degradation reactions, called photodecomposition (decomposition due to light). This process is more likely to occur in some drugs than others (e.g., the B vitamins), but the potential exists for most drug products.

Drug Storage At Home

In terms of home storage, the major problems are those sites where drug products are most likely to be exposed to environmental extremes (i.e., temperature, moisture and light). Of all the rooms in the home, the bathroom is the worst place to store medications since showers and tubs generate considerable heat and moisture. We tend to keep bathrooms at a higher temperature. Since bathrooms tend to be relatively small rooms, the heat and moisture generated tend to be more concentrated. Medicine cabinets (a misnomer) are neither temperature-proof or moisture-proof and do not protect drugs from deterioration.

The kitchen is another popular storage site for drugs. Kitchens may be better storage sites for drugs than bathrooms because they tend to be larger and more open. However, the appliances associated with food preparation can generate considerable heat and moisture.

Light is not usually a problem if your medications are not being stored on a window sill or area where they are directly exposed to light. Amber colored vials protect medications from some light, but they cannot protect medications stored in direct light for long periods of time. In addition, direct sunlight can generate a considerable amount of heat.

Medication storage tends to be based on convenience. It is an irony of home building that storage cabinets just happen to be located in places where medications should not be stored. The bathroom medicine chest is an American tradition, and it is easy to assume that if a builder has placed the "medicine" cabinet in the bathroom, then it must be an appropriate storage site. Actually, home builders know no more about drug storage than anyone else. They place the medicine cabinets in bathrooms because it has always been done this way, not because it is an appropriate storage site for medications. Kitchen cabinets are designed for the storage of food and food preparation items, not medications. Bathrooms and kitchens are no doubt popular drug storage sites because of the availability of water (and drinking glasses) with which to take medications.

It is a common misconception that prescription vials will protect the contents from environmental exposures. Most vials will protect medications from exposure to solid materials from outside the container (e.g., dust, dirt, lint, etc.) and they offer protection from light if the vial is not stored in direct sunlight. However, they offer limited protection from liquids, moisture and temperature extremes.

Medications in liquid form are usually dispensed in glass or plastic bottles. They are designed to protect their contents from exposure to other liquids, solids and vapors, from loss of the drug and from damage to effervescent type materials under normal handling situations.

Proper Drug Storage

Medication containers cannot protect medications from improper storage in the home. Rather, the containers (and contents) must also be protected from exposure to environmental extremes.

Ideally, drugs should be stored in special cabinets which are high enough from the floor to prevent easy access by children. Such a cabinet should be located in a closet or some other out-of-the way area, and should be locked to prevent unauthorized entry by children or others. Storage of drugs in purses, dressers and bedside tables is probably better than traditional medicine cabinets as far as environmental factors are concerned. However, they are more readily accessible to children in these locations.

Checking Home Storage Sites

Studies by one of the authors (GH) have been conducted in which people were asked how often they check their medication storage sites for outdated drugs or products. The results (see Outline 119) indicate that many people do not check their medication storage sites for storage problems on a regular basis. Medications stored in the home should be checked at least once each year. Outdated products, as well as medications which are no longer being used, should be thrown away. The availability of unnecessary drug products can pose an increased risk of accidental poisonings in small children. And, if you have forgotten why a certain medication was originally purchased . . . you probably do not need it!

People have a tendency to keep any medications that are left over after therapy "just in case they are ever needed again" and also because they tend to be expensive. Thus, it seems like throwing money away.

There is some rationale for keeping medications that can be used "whenever needed," but we also tend to keep medications which should not be reused. For example, antibiotics are popular items for our "home pharmacies." People reason that if they ever develop an infection of any kind, they will have a medication available to treat it. However, antibiotics are relatively specific for certain types of infections. An antibiotic used for one type of infection may prove useless, or even harmful, if used for another type of infection. We all have a tendency to self-diagnose and self-prescribe when medications are available in the home. This can be a hazardous practice. Additionally, we all enjoy being a neighborhood health authority, so it is tempting to offer medications from the "home pharmacy" to family and friends who "have the same symptoms." Not only is this is a hazardous practice, it is also illegal.

OUTLINE 119

HOW PEOPLE TEND TO STORE MEDICATIONS IN THEIR HOMES

Storage Site	Percent Responding*
Bathroom	
Medicine cabinet	62%
Other cabinets	18%
Kitchen	
Cabinets	34%
Refrigerator	11%
Window sill	3%
Bedroom	
Closet	2%
Chest of drawers/dressers	14%
Night stand	6%
Hall Closet	14%
Other	6%

*Responses add up to more than 100% because respondents were asked to check all sites where medications were stored.

How often do people check their medications stored at home?

Last Time Checked	Percent Responding
Within the last month	29%
Within the last 6 months	29%
Within the last year	17%
More than a year ago	7%
More than 2 years ago	3%
I can't remember the last time I checked it	16%

OUTLINE 120

GENERAL HOME STORAGE GUIDELINES FOR MEDICATIONS

❧ **Evaluate your home medicine chest at least once each year.**

It would probably be a good idea to set a time each year when these products will be examined. Establish a time that reoccurs each year (e.g., a holiday, summer vacation, spring break, etc.).

❧ **Discard medications that are no longer being used.**

Medications left at home are subject to self-diagnosis and self-prescribing. This is a risky practice. Medications left at home are also potentially available to children. If you cannot remember why the medication was purchased . . . chances are that you really don't need it. At the very least, check with your doctor, nurse, or pharmacist to see if you should keep it.

❧ **Probably all medications should be discarded after one year of storage.**

This reduces the risk that improperly stored medications will become toxic or lose potency.

❧ **Antibiotics should never be stored.**

Antibiotics lend themselves to self-diagnosing and self-prescribing. This is an extremely risky practice with this category of products. Every infection should be evaluated by a health professional.

❧ **Call your pharmacist regarding ANY questions about drug storage in the home.**

Expiration Dates on Prescription Labels

There seems to be a great deal of support for requiring pharmacists to provide an expiration date on prescription drug labels. This might seem to be reasonable, but there are also good reasons to question this practice.

Expiration dates are based on the assumption that the medication is being stored properly. The previous discussion and studies indicate ample reason to doubt this. It is important to emphasize that placing an expiration date on a prescription vial may suggest to people that the product is good until the expiration date *regardless of storage conditions!*

The major issue of concern here is the potential for these expiration dates to actually threaten your health. This is possible if you use a product until its expiration date, even though it has been improperly stored and has become toxic or has lost its potency.

Providing expiration dates on prescription drug labels cannot be viewed merely as a simple act of typing an additional line on a label. Rather, a major education effort is required to insure that people store medications properly. Otherwise, the expiration date is not valid. Even with major education efforts, there is no guarantee that people will actually store their medications properly.

OUTLINE 121

STORAGE TEMPERATURE INSTRUCTIONS AND WHAT THEY MEAN

Storage Instruction	°C	°F
Refrigerate	2° - 8°	35° - 46°
Cold	8° or less	46° or less
Cool	8° - 15°	46° - 59°
Room Temperature	15° - 30°	59° - 86°
Warm	30° - 40°	86° - 104°
Heat	40°+	104°+

42. CHILD RESISTANT CONTAINERS

"It is a mistake to allow any mechanical object to realize you are in a hurry."

— Ralph's Observation, John Peers

The Poison Prevention Packaging Act (PPPA) of 1970 (Public Law 91-601) is the law responsible for the childproof lids found on most prescription and nonprescription drugs, as well as many other household products. It requires that certain products must have special packaging that will make them difficult to open for children under the age of five.

However, formal government involvement in poison prevention actually began almost ten years earlier. Because of the efforts of a Missouri pharmacist, Homer A. George, and the profession of pharmacy, Congress passed a joint resolution on September 26, 1961 requesting that the President of the United States should designate the third week in March as National Poison Prevention Week each year. President John F. Kennedy proclaimed the first National Poison Prevention Week, which was observed in March of 1962.

Prior to 1970, the involvement of the government in poison prevention was centered on educational campaigns alerting adults to the hazards of household poisonings. These efforts increased public awareness of the use and storage of medicines and household items, and were probably responsible for the decline in fatal poisonings during the 1960's. Despite this progress, childhood poisoning still represented a major problem. Warning labels and educational campaigns offered little advantage to nonreading children, who were the usual victims.

With this in mind, the Poison Prevention Packaging Act was passed to provide additional protection for younger children. By requiring special packaging, children under the age of five were less likely to accidentally take medications and other hazardous substances. The FDA was initially responsible for this Act, but in 1973 the U.S. Consumer Product Safety Commission was established and the responsibility for the law was transferred to this agency.

Rationale and Intent

The original intent of this law was to require that potentially hazardous household items and drugs be placed in containers that would be difficult for small children to open, but easy for adults. Unfortunately, this is an idealistic concept. If a container is designed so that it is absolutely childproof, it will also be largely adult proof as well. Recognizing this delemma, a compromise was necessary.

Current Standards

Federal standards do not require that *all* children must be unable to open the containers, or that *all* adults must be able to open them. Under current regulations, a package fails the test if more than 20% of a representative group of children are able to gain access (after a visual demonstration of the proper way to open the container) or if more than 10% of a representative group of adults are unable to open the package. Unit-dose packages are tested differently. If a child is able to open more than 8 individual units, or the number of units representing a toxic amount (whichever is less), then the product fails.

More recent changes in testing procedures now require that older adults must also be included in the testing phase. The results of these studies are not known at the present time, but it is safe to say that they will lead to further improvement in our drug container laws.

Problems With the PPPA

Over the years the PPPA has been heavily criticized by many individuals. Although consumer acceptance was not considered to be absolutely necessary for success of the Act, it was desirable. Acceptance could affect the willingness of consumers and health professionals to comply with the Act, which in turn, could impact the number of childhood poisonings.

Despite testing procedures, there are many adults who have trouble opening child-resistant containers (CRCs). Container designs vary considerably and some containers are simply more difficult to open than others. Liquids and syrups may "gum-up" the mechanism of liquid containers making the lid difficult to open. Usually this problem can be corrected by running warm water on the lid. Also, it is advisable to keep the container and lid as clean as possible. After each dose, the lid and bottle should be checked for remaining liquid. The rim and inner lid areas can be cleaned with a wet cloth or rinsed off with water.

This serves to prevent problems later.

A more serious problem occurs when people transfer medications from the the original container to another container which is easier to open. Once the medication is removed from its original container, it is easy to forget the name of the medication, what it was used for, or other important information. Moreover, if the original container is thrown away, the prescription number is no longer available (although most pharmacies now use computer systems to locate prescription numbers). Still, the most serious problem with this scenario involves poisonings. If medications are involved in accidental poisonings, it may be difficult or impossible to identify which medications were actually taken.

The lids of virtually all CRCs deteriorate with repeated use. Pharmacists are supposed to change the CRCs with each refill, but this is not always done. In time the containers lose their protective ability, so that it becomes easier for children to accidentally get into them.

It is probably advisable to try and remove the lids before leaving the pharmacy. In this way, if problems arise the pharmacist or staff will be available to assist you and to provide any additional instructions. Also, if removing the lid is difficult, then the medication can be transferred to a conventional container by the pharmacist before you leave.

Destruction of the lid or the container can also pose several problems. To begin with, this may result in destruction of some of the medication. If the container is a glass bottle, bits of glass may contaminate the medication. Finally, destruction of the container will usually damage the label, which provides important information for the patient, and so, should be protected.

Because of difficulties opening these lids, many people leave them off, or they may leave the safety mechanism disengaged. Obviously, the lids cannot serve their intended purpose when this is done. The medication is more likely to be exposed to temperature, light and moisture extremes when the lid is off. Thus, the drug may deteriorate more quickly. Obviously, medications are more likely to spill when the lid is removed. This can result in lost or contaminated medications. For these reasons, it is far better to request conventional packaging than to leave the lid off altogether.

It is frequently reported that "children can open these lids better than adults." No doubt, this is true for children over five. However, it is important to remember that the lids were designed to target chil-

dren under the age of five, who are more likely to have problems opening these containers. Furthermore, because their attention span is
usually short, they are less likely to spend the time required to open
them. This is not to suggest that children under 5 cannot open them.
However, relative to other age groups, this group should have much
more trouble. In all likelihood, the belief on the part of many consumers that children can open these lids better than adults is based
on a misunderstanding. An adult can enlist the aid of a nine year old
child and declare, "Children can open these things better than I can!"
This misunderstanding on the part of adults is a concern to health
professionals, since negative attitudes mean that people are less likely to use child-resistant containers.

A potentially serious problem is that some patients may miss
doses of their medications if they cannot open these lids. Again, ask
for easy-open lids if this type of problem is likely to occur.

People sometimes complain that they spill or lose medications
while trying to open the containers. Some containers are designed so
that the lids snap off and it may be difficult to remove them without
jerky movements. Medications may spill out of the container and be
lost, which represents both an economic and therapeutic loss to the
consumer. Problems may also arise for non-English speaking patients, since the instructions on CRCs are usually in English.

No doubt problems such as these will continue to occur. Many
people are embarrassed to ask for help in opening CRCs. Often they
forget to ask for easy-open containers, or they are not aware that they
have the right to do so. Furthermore, pharmacists frequently forget
to ask if easy-open lids would be helpful. Pharmacists have a legal
and moral obligation to dispense medications in CRCs unless you
authorize them to use easy-open lids.

Success of Child-Resistant Containers

Many people believe that the PPPA was pointless and ineffective.
The facts, however, indicate otherwise. Some indication of this can be
seen by considering the impact that this law had on accidental poisonings due to aspirin alone, since this was the first drug to be affected by the Act. Aspirin had historically been the number one substance involved in childhood poisonings.

Within one year after the law was implemented, deaths among
children due to the accidental ingestion of aspirin declined by 43.5%,
and only 17.4% of the substances involved in accidental deaths were

due to aspirin. This was the lowest level ever observed!

Figures for the period from 1972 to 1976 indicated a 51% decline in aspirin fatalities and a 55% decline in aspirin ingestions. For the time period from 1968 to 1977, the decline in accidental poisonings in this age group was about 62%.

As of 1979, the agents involved in most poisonings were as follows:

1. House plants
2. Soaps / detergents
3. Vitamins / minerals
4. Aspirin products
5. Antihistamines

Thus, by 1979 aspirin had dropped to the #4 slot in terms of the frequency with which it was associated with childhood poisonings. Notice also that household plants, as well as many soaps and detergents, cannot be protected by CRCs. Thus, aspirin exists as a valuable indicator of the potential for CRCs to protect children under 5 from potentially fatal poisonings.

More recent statistics indicate that pain relievers are once again on the rise as agents involved in accidental childhood poisonings. This may be because there are increasing numbers of pain relief products which are being made available to the public in easy-open containers. It may also be due to apathy on the part of the American public regarding the use of safety lids. Many people simply refuse to use them, including parents and grandparents of small children.

New Regulations on CRCs

Pharmacists *must* dispense all prescription medication in child-resistant containers unless you authorize them to use an easy-open container. In the past, you were not allowed to give a "blanket" permission for all of your medications. This meant that pharmacists were required to obtain authorization *each time a prescription was dispensed*.

More recently, the U.S. Consumer Product Safety Commission (CPSC) has reversed this policy, largely because of protests from pharmacists and consumers. So, you can now give the pharmacist a "blanket" waiver requesting that all future medication be placed in easy-open containers. It is important to emphasize that this is your decision and not that of the pharmacist. Without authorization, the pharmacist cannot legally or ethically dispense medications in easy-open containers.

The major concern with this new policy is the fear that we may be sacrificing public welfare for simple convenience. At least one study has indicated that pharmacists have not uniformly complied with the law. A study of 60 pharmacies indicated that only 76% routinely dispensed medications in accordance with the law. Some pharmacists do not even stock CRCs, insisting that their patients "don't like them!" Again, this is not a decision which pharmacists can legitimately make. The decision is yours! Still, you are encouraged to use CRCs if small children may be around, even occasionally.

It is a sad, but all too frequent, scenario when an emergency team is working diligently to save the life of a child who has accidentally ingested a medication or household product, while the family cries in the hallway, "I thought my child knew better than that!"

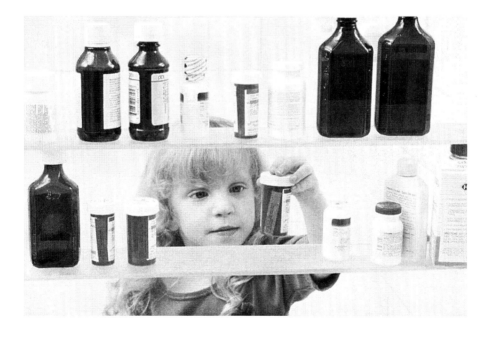

43. PRODUCT TAMPERING

"Health, as a vast societal enterprise, is too important
to be solely the concern of the providers of service."

— Rene Dubos

During the past decade or so there have been a number of cases of product tampering in which containers were opened, toxic substances introduced and the container resealed to make it appear that it was new. These incidents represent a serious concern for the drug industry, health professionals and the public at large. The drug industry has responded to these problems with packaging that discourages tampering, or which makes it more obvious to the purchaser if tampering has occurred. Still, no packaging can be 100% safe. For this reason all medication products should be carfully examined at the store before the purchase is made. Moreover the seal of the package should be examined again before taking the product. Outline 122 summarizes the signs that may indicate tampering. This information reflects guidelines developed by the United States Pharmacopeial Convention, Inc. in the interests of consumer welfare.

When considering the potential for tampering, it is important to ask (1) if it would be easy for someone to tamper with the product; and (2) if you can determine if tampering occurred.

The type of dosage form (e.g., tablets, capsules, liquids) provides some insight regarding the type of tampering that might occur. For example, if someone has poured a toxic liquid on tablets or capsules, they will probably be partially dissolved, discolored, or changed in some obvious way.

The product's label will usually describe its protective packaging features. If something is wrong with any of these features, do not buy the product. If you notice a problem *after* you have purchased the product, return it to the store and do not use it. Above all, never take any medications from packages that look suspicious in any way (i.e., that look like tampering might have occurred).

Finally, take medications in appropriate lighting. Never take medicines in areas of dark or poor lighting. Read labels and carefully note the dose before you take any medication.

OUTLINE 122

TAMPER-PROOFING GUIDELINES - - LOOK FOR THESE PROBLEMS!

Packaging

☙ Breaks, cracks or holes in outer or inner wrappings or protective seals.

☙ Package wrappings (outer or inner) that appear to have been disturbed in some way.

☙ The shrink band (i.e., the tight fitting wrap) around the top of the bottle appears to have been disturbed in some way (e.g., distorted; stretched; slit, then retaped), or is missing.

☙ A container bottom that has been disturbed in some way.

☙ The container does not appear to be as full as you would expect.

☙ The container cap is not on tight.

☙ Bits of paper or glue stuck on the rim of the container as if the container once had a protective seal (NOTE: Check to see if the outer package mentions a protective seal).

☙ The cotton plug or filler in the bottle is disturbed (e.g., torn, sticky, stained) or appears to have been removed and put back.

☙ An eye product that does not have a protective seal (NOTE: All eye drops must have a protective seal. If it is missing, do not use this product).

☙ Ointment tubes without a properly sealed bottom. These tubes are crimped up from the bottom like a tube of toothpaste and should be firmly sealed.

☙ Expiration dates that are different on the inner and outer container.

Liquids

☙ Unusual color, thickness, odor or other appearance (e.g., cloudy appearance).

☙ Particles in the bottom or floating in the solution (NOTE: Suspensions are special liquids in which floating particles may be normal. Check with your pharmacist if you are not sure).

Tablets

☙ Unusual appearance (e.g., unusual spots or markings, dull coatings instead of shiny coatings, unusual color).

☙ Lack of uniform shape or size.

☙ Printing or identifying marks that are different or missing.

☙ Unusual odor or taste.

OUTLINE 122 cont'd

Capsules

- Unusual appearance (e.g., cracks or dents, unusual size or color).
- A dull finish instead of a smooth, shiny finish (e.g., fingerprints, as if they had been handled).
- Fillings look different.
- Stuck together.
- Printing or identifying marks that are different or missing.
- Unusual odor or taste.

Ointments, Creams, Pastes

- Product container looks unusual or different in some way.
- Texture is gritty, not smooth, or appears unusual in some way.

44. HEALTH FRAUD

"There are always men starved for hope or greedy for sensation who will testify to the healing power of a spectacular surgical feat or of a new miracle drug. They provide the testimonies of the new religions for which scientists with theories unproved or incomplete are always ready to provide the mystic language."

— Rene Dubos

Fraudulent products and promoters tempt us with useless remedies that result in economic losses, discourage professional treatment and sometimes result in risks to health, including deaths. This trend will likely continue with the increasing availability of self-care products.

Unethical promoters find it particularly easy to exploit individuals with serious or incurable illnesses (e.g., arthritis, AIDS, cancer). When people opt for fraudulent remedies, their illnesses can progress to a point where no treatment offers any hope whatsoever. These products are also particularly attractive to individuals who are interested in miraculous transformations, such as bust developers among teenagers and anti-aging products among middle-aged adults.

The exact extent, nature and consequences of health fraud is not known. However, it is estimated that Americans may spend as much as $100 billion each year in the search for miracle agents. The promotion of fraudulent products occurs via the same media as legitimate products because most people are unable to discriminate between false versus valid advertising claims. In part, this occurs because the deceptive advertising practices of legitimate manufactureres can condition us in such a way that we are more likely to accept a fraudulent promotion as a "legitimate one."

The terms "quack," "quackery," and "health fraud" all refer to misinformation about health. They may refer to products, services or the people who promote them. Health fraud involves the promotion of a medical remedy, product or service for profit that does not work, or one which has not been proven to work. This latter concept is important, since many fraud promoters erroneously insist that their products are not "drugs," and therefore, do not have to be tested like drugs. In actuality, any product promoted for a drug purpose must be tested as a drug (i.e., it must be proven to be safe and effective for its stated claims).

The FDA categorizes quackery according to the type of hazard which it presents to the public or to the target audience. Direct health hazards involve products or therapies that can directly harm your health when used as directed. These demand priority attention by the FDA. Civil or criminal actions may be taken to remove these products and services from the market. Indirect health hazards involve products or services that can indirectly harm your health by replacing proper medical care at a time when it is really needed. The FDA will take action against these products if they are distributed on a nationwide basis, or if they are promoted for the treatment of a serious illness (AIDS, cancer, etc.). Economic fraud involves products and services which pose little health risk, but result in an economic loss to the consumer. The FDA will take legal action against these products if they are promoted on a nationwide basis, serve no legitimate medical purpose and are scientifically unsupported. The FDA fraud categories are:

- Cure-alls
- Diagnostics (i.e., items used to "diagnose" diseases or health problems)
- Figure enhancers
- Hair and scalp devices
- Pain relievers (e.g., arthritis)
- Respiratory, pure air and water devices
- Sex aids
- Sleep aids
- Youth prolongers / anti-aging

The largest single group of fraud products are those promoted as weight control agents, which is a subgrouping of the figure enhancer category.

Many of these products are successful because they appeal to our vanity (e.g., breast and penis enlargers, wrinkle removers), or more tragically, people may turn to fraud products at a time when they are seriously ill and desperately need help (e.g., cancer, AIDS).

It has been pointed out by officials with the National Council Against Health Fraud that most well-publicized scientific advances are quickly followed by copycat quack scams which are designed to bilk the public for profits. As we have said, it is difficult for most consumers to discriminate between a quack using scientific jargon and qualified scientists.

Similarly, many companies engage in questionable marketing practices. For example, shortly after Retin-A was reported in the medical literature to have some potential in reducing wrinkles, a product with a similar name appeared in many retail stores. The packages were similar in appearance, and the OTC product contained the following statement:

> Provides a beneficial environment for
> skin's natural renewal process.

No doubt, many consumers purchased the alternative product under the impression that they were getting the Retin A product.

Grace Monaco, a Washington attorney and health activist, emphasizes that quacks are convincing salespeople. Many of them appear on talk shows on television or radio, which invests them with an aura of authenticity. Since our constitution guarantees freedom of speech even to frauds and quacks, consumer education is the best weapon available for dealing with such claims.

In reality, we allow ourselves to be misled by the promise of quick and easy cures and unrealistic physical transformations. Health fraud is successful because so many of us are gullible and uninformed.

The Role of Advertising

Advertisments can serve useful functions. They inform us about new products and services and can serve to reinforce healthy behaviors and lifestyles. Unfortunately, many advertisements simply are not truthful, or promise results that cannot actually be achieved. In fact, it has been suggested that health fraud "lives and thrives . . . because of successful advertising."

Consumer surveys have indicated that many Americans believe that advertisements about medications and health products must be true or they would not be allowed. In reality, most media do not screen advertisements for accuracy or truth. Television and radio stations usually air virtually any product or service for which promoters are willing to pay the ad fee. Federal and state agencies do not screen advertisements before they are aired. Authorities can only take action after a questionable advertisement appears.

Ironically, most fraud advertisements are relatively easy to spot. The problem is simply that most people have not learned to watch for them (see Outline 124).

Legal Actions

The actions of the FDA and other agencies against fraudulent claims is based upon a number of factors (e.g., potential health hazards, extent of national distribution, manpower of the agencies to address the problem). When the problem is serious, the FDA may take immediate enforcement action. Unfortunately, the health fraud problem has become so large and complicated that no single agency can effectively address it.

Most government agencies do not have the manpower or resources to address all cases which come to their attention. Instead, they prioritize the problems that are reported and address those that pose the greatest health threats. Because an investigation can take years, a fraudulent promoter can earn millions of dollars in profits from an uninformed public during the interim. Or, they may change their name and address and start over again with the same health fraud scheme. And of course, our flawed legal system allows for quack promoters to appeal their convictions again and again, while their products remain on the market.

Fraud Prevention

There are several steps you can take to avoid being victimized. First, always investigate an advertiser's claims before purchasing medical or health products. This is particularly true regarding products distributed through the mail or some other package delivery service. Most fraud promotions are based upon the wishful thinking of consumers, and so they tell you what you want to hear, not what is actually true. These individuals will usually be aware of any new "miracle" products that have become available to the public.

Next, investigate products before you purchase. Check with a doctor or pharmacist. Health professionals will have heard about new products available to treat most conditions. If you want to, you can call pharmacists anonymously.

Avoid purchase of medical or health products from television, radio or newspaper advertisements. Reputable health products are simply not distributed in this manner.

Avoid products that promise "quick" and "easy" cures and physical changes. They know that people want simple and quick solutions to their problems. They will promise anything to make a sale.

Avoid products advertised as being good for a wide variety of problems. Most reputable products are formulated to address specific problems. "Shotgun" therapies (products that contain several ingredients) are not sound and usually result in increased risk of side effects. Health fraud products are often promoted for numerous problems in order to generate more sales. Since fraud promoters are not really concerned about curing anything, they can afford to make many claims.

Avoid products promoted for the treatment or cure of health problems for which medical science has had little success. It is ironic that we have the most advanced health care in the world, and yet we are easily led into believing that modern medicine has somehow missed something regarding the treatment of serious health problems. Health professionals and drug companies are very much interested in finding effective treatments for serious health problems. ANY significant advances in medicine will be made available to your physician.

Avoid products that are "only available" through the mail or UPS. Health fraud uses the mail and UPS to deliver their products. If it is only available by these routes, avoid it! Actually, many fraud products are delivered by UPS and similar services because it is against the law to commit a crime through the mail. Commercial delivery service companies tend to "ask no questions" about the packages which they ship.

Avoid products that require advance payment. This is especially true for products which must be ordered by mail, credit card, etc.

Avoid products promoted with case histories or testimonials from "satisfied" users. "Satisfied" users are easily purchased for promotional purposes. Some individuals may actually believe that they were helped by the product. This is especially true when the problem would have improved regardless of how it was treated.

Products are sometimes used along with other measures that are already known to be effective. For example, weight control products are typically used with a diet. The diet alone would be expected to result in weight loss. The product being promoted may have little to do with it.

Avoid products which promote ingredients using the following terms or descriptions:

- ❦ "Special" ingredients
- ❦ "Secret" ingredients
- ❦ "Ancient" ingredients
- ❦ "Natural" ingredients
- ❦ Ingredients "not available from other sources"
- ❦ "Foreign" ingredients
- ❦ A "scientific breakthrough"
- ❦ "Miracle cures" held back by the medical community.

There is very little that is not known by the medical community. Legitimate medical books currently list information about European drugs, herbs and almost every known substance with any medical potential. If the medical community is not impressed by a particular substance . . . you shouldn't be either. The jargon listed above is nothing more than hype to trick you into purchasing a product.

Products which sound too good to be true . . . usually are!

OUTLINE 123

WHO TO CONTACT IF YOU SUSPECT A HEALTH FRAUD

❦ State Agencies
-Local or State Health Department
-State Attorney General's Office
-State Consumer Protection Agency

❦ About False Advertising
Federal Trade Commission
6th St. and Pennsylvania Ave., NW
Washington, DC   20580

❦ About Quack Products Via the Mail
U.S. Postal Service
Chief Postal Inspector
475 L'Enfant Plaza
Washington, DC   20260

❦ FDA
Office of Consumer Affairs
5600 Fishers Lane
Rockville, MD   20857

OUTLINE 124

EXAMPLE OF A HEALTH FRAUD ADVERTISEMENT

Advertisement	*Comments*
Diet Pills Sweeping U.S.	1. The title is a common ploy, especially for fraud weight control products.
DOCTORS INVENT 'LAZY WAY' TO LOSE WEIGHT	While the concept is unrealistic, it is attractive to an uninformed public.
U.S. Government Approves Patent Claims for New Diet Pill	2. This gives the impression that the product has been "approved" for its

OUTLINE 124, cont'd

promoted use. This is not the case! Even if a patent has been granted, the manufacturer must still prove that the product is safe and effective for the drug purpose for which it is being promoted. The patent has nothing to do with the drug approval process.

An amazing new "lazy way" to lose weight has recently been developed and perfected by two prominent doctors at a world famous hospital in Metropolis that reportedly "guarantees" to help you steadily lose fat and reduce calories by simply taking their tested and proven new "fat-flusher" pill.

[NOTE: The name of the city and product have been changed for purposes of our example]

3. This is nothing but advertising hype. The concept is unrealistic, but attractive to an uninformed public. This rhetoric gives the impression that the product was "developed and perfected" at a "world famous hospital." This is NOT actually what the advertisement states (notice the wording carefully!), but is the impression that is given. And in fact, this advertisement was checked by one of the authors (GH). The hospital where these doctors supposedly practiced indicated that they had nothing to do with this study.

The U.S. government has just approved the doctors' claims for a hard-to-get patent that confirms "there has never been anything like their fat-bonding pill process before." It is a totally new major scientific breakthrough and is revolutionizing the weight loss industry.

4. Same as #2. All patents are "hard-to-get!" And, there is no "scientific breakthrough" here. The only thing particularly revolutionary in the weight loss industry is the degree to which disreputable promoters will go to get your money.

You can "eat normally." Best of all, "you can continue to eat your favorite foods and don't have to change your normal eating habits. You can start losing fat and reduce calories from the first day, until you achieve the ideal weight desire without exercising."

5. Sounds wonderful doesn't it? It's not true, of course, but it makes an attractive ad.

OUTLINE 124, cont'd

Flushes fat out of body. The new pill is appropriately called the "fat-flusher" pill because it breaks into thousands of particles, each acting like a tiny magnet, "attracting" and trapping many times its size in undigested fat particles and calories from food that you have just eaten. Then, all the trapped fat and calories are naturally "flushed" right out of your body, reducing the calories you absorb "before" they can turn into ugly bulging body fat and cellulite. Within 2 days you should notice a change in the color of your stool, caused by the fat particles being eliminated.

"Automatically" lose fat. According to one of the inventors, Dr. Robert Squill, heart specialist and associate professor of medicine at Metro medical school, the new fat bonding process is a "lazy way" to lose weight because the pills alone "automatically" reduce calories by eliminating dietary fat. It is 100% safe and not a drug.

[NOTE: The name of the doctor and medical school have been changed. Naturally, it is our hope that the doctor has decided to re-enter the legitimate practice of medicine. Or perhaps, he is now selling ink pens in the doctor's lounge!]

The fat-flusher pills are already sweeping the country with glowing reports of weight loss from formerly overweight people in all walks of life who are now slimmer, trimmer and more attractive.

6. Advertising hype. Utilizes pseudo-pharmacological and pseudo-clinical language which can mislead an uninformed public into believing that the product is legitimate. From a true scientific and medical perspective, this whole section has not actually explained a single thing in any rational way. Also, a color change in your stool does not necessarily indicate that you are losing fat. It could be a side effect of the product. Many drug products change stool color.

7. According to officials at the Medical school, Dr. Squill was NOT an Associate Professor there.

8. This product IS a drug according to federal guidelines because it is being promoted for a "drug" purpose. The FDA indicated that there were no clinical studies to support claims of safety and effectiveness for its labeled claims. It is ironic that this advertisement refers to this product as a "diet pill," but then suggests that it is not a "drug."

9. The "get on the bandwagon" approach. Yet, there is actually no substantiation for any of these claims. In all likelihood, the only thing "sweeping the country" was the advertising hype.

OUTLINE 124, cont'd

Now available to the public. If you are trying to lose 20, 50, 100 pounds or more, you can order your supply of these "no-risk" highly successful fat-magnet pills directly from the doctors' exclusive manufacturer only (includes optional calorie-reduction plan for even better results). Send $20 for a 90 pill supply, or $35 for a 180 pill supply [address supplied].

Unconditional money-back guarantee if not 100% satisfied.

For fastest service for credit card orders ONLY call anytime 24 hours, toll free [number supplied]

10. Of course, they're "only" available this way ... no reputable drug company or reputable health professionals would associate with this scam.

11. "Money-back guarantees" are a common ploy of health fraud products. Why not, most of them have no intention of refunding your money.

12. 800 numbers are also frequent ploys of health fraud promoters. Usually, the agency that takes the calls will only take orders. They will provide NO product information (including an address or phone number of the company that is promoting the product). This is another warning sign.

It is indeed unfortunate that phone companies have such little regard for the American public that they take no action to prevent fraud transactions over the phone (It IS illegal to transact fraud through the U.S. mail!). Basically, phone companies have the attitude that as long as fraud promoters pay their phone bill ... they can conduct any business they choose over the phone.

EPILOGUE

"Change is inevitable; Growth is optional."

— a student of Joan Halifax in *Healers on Healing*

The basic premise of this book is that health, however you choose to define it, is an outcome of our individual choices, commitments and values. We define our health more in terms of our behaviors and health care choices than we do in our words. *The road to a healthier you is a journey that cannot be delegated to someone else.*

The message is positive. Each of us can impact our quality and quantity of life . . . if we choose to! Prevention is always more effective than cures in terms of physical and fiscal health of both individuals and societies.

We very much need the availability of professional health care, but we must learn to reduce our dependency upon modern medicine as an antidote for unhealthy lifestyle choices. We must cease our search for "magic bullets" (e.g., "miracle" herbs) and "fountains of youth" as an alternative to healthy living. And, we must cease blaming medicine for its inability to undo the negative outcomes of years of lifestyle folly which we have selected for ourselves.

The inescapable reality is that each of us is responsible for our own well-being. Health is not an item of property which we can simply present to a "mechanic" for preservation or repair. Each of us must become an advocate of rational living. This is as it should be. No one else has the same vested interest in your health that you do.

What you do now to promote your personal and environmental health becomes the medium of exchange with which you purchase your future in terms of quality and quantity of life. Can you live to be 400? Probably not. Yet, you can live a life of meaning and one which frees you from the disabilities, premature disease and death associated with destructive lifestyles.

The Rule of Accuracy, as related by John Peers (in 1001 LOGICAL LAWS . . .) is:

> When working toward the solution of a problem . . .
> it helps if you know the answer.

OK, so here is the answer for maximizing your quantity and quality of life:

You!

APPENDICES

APPENDIX A

YOUR INDIVIDUALIZED LIFE EXTENSION PROGRAM

(Do these to improve your quality and quantity of life)
DAILY

❧ **General Health**
- ❏ Get 7-8 hours sleep each night
- ❏ Brush and floss your teeth
- ❏ Avoid excessive sun exposures
- ❏ Implement safety practices at home, work and play
- ❏ Look for ways to increase your activity levels
- ❏ Read and listen to music more often; watch TV less
- ❏ Prevention

❧ **Drug Use**
- ❏ Use ALL drug products appropriately (both prescription and nonprescription products)
- ❏ Read labels before using medication and health products

❧ **Nutrition**
- ❏ Eat breakfast
- ❏ Eat three meals daily at regular intervals
- ❏ Limit snacking
- ❏ Limit alcohol consumption
- ❏ Drink fluids (especially water)
- ❏ Eat a balanced diet
- ❏ Decrease cholesterol intake
- ❏ Decrease fat intake
- ❏ Decrease caffeine intake

APPENDIX A cont'd

❧ **Smoking**
- ❏ No tobacco use
- ❏ Avoid being around smokers

❧ **Stress**
- ❏ Reduce stress in your daily life (e.g., time management, breaks)
- ❏ Avoid taking on too much
- ❏ Practice relaxation techniques
- ❏ Exercise

WEEKLY

- ❏ Exercise
- ❏ Maintain an appropriate weight
- ❏ Play, hobbies
- ❏ Decrease stress (e.g., stress reduction activities)
- ❏ Healthy grocery shopping
- ❏ Quality family time

MONTHLY

- ❏ Breast self-exam
- ❏ Recreation, hobbies, play
- ❏ Get away weekends (leave your watch at home)

YEARLY

- ❏ Checkups
  - ○ dental   ○ medical   ○ vision
- ❏ Vocational assessments regarding stress and career satisfaction
- ❏ Check medications being stored at home

APPENDIX A cont'd

MISCELLANEOUS

- ❏ Communicate with health professionals
- ❏ Eat healthy when eating out
- ❏ Promote a healthy planet
- ❏ Get to know your doctor, pharmacist and other health professionals
- ❏ Learn how to evaluate health and medical literature
- ❏ Use child-resistant containers in ANY home where small children live or visit
- ❏ Screen for product tampering when buying food or drug products

To help you have

an expanded lifespan, qualified

with health and vigor,

we encourage you to check

each of the boxes in Appendix A

APPENDIX B

HOW TO PREPARE A PRACTICAL EMERGENCY KIT FOR HOME OR TRAVEL

First aid kits come in all shapes and sizes. Some contain myriad supplies, while others amount to little more than a collection of bandaids. Not everyone has the same needs. For example, people who participate in outdoor activities (e.g., boating, camping, fishing), or who travel a great deal, may need more supplies than people who do not participate in these activities. Regardless of your needs, an appropriate first aid kit can be prepared by collecting needed items from local pharmacies, outdoor and other stores.

The listing of items which follows can be modified to suit your individual needs or the needs of your family. You may choose to include or delete items listed or you may choose to add items not mentioned on the list. The listed is included merely to provide suggestions for preparing a personal first aid kit.

It is important to familiarize yourself with the items which have been included. All items should be used in an appropriate manner. Follow label instructions, where provided. It is also important to check for expiration dates on items that may deteriorate over time. And as always, consult with an appropriate health professional if you have questions about the selection and use of items to be included. Pharmacists are an easily accessible resource for this type of information and they will typically stock many of the items of interest.

Items for a personal first aid kit can be collected and organized in larger fishing tackle boxes. These kits can be conveniently stored at home or carried along for travel.

It is advisable for everyone to take a standard first aid course (e.g., Red Cross), including training in CardioPulmonary Resuscitation (CPR). The Red Cross also offers a variety of other training programs which may be of interest to some individuals who may encounter specific emergency situations (e.g., infant and child CPR, swimming and water safety, lifeguard training, canoeing, sailing, kayaking, babysitting, back injury prevention, etc.).

APPENDIX B cont'd

SUGGESTED SUPPLIES FOR A PERSONAL OR FAMILY FIRST AID KIT

Medications[1]

❑ Allergy / Itching
❑ Antidiarrheals
❑ Antihistamines
❑ Charcoal (activated)
❑ Eye drops / washes
❑ Laxatives
❑ Sunscreen
❑ Motion sickness / nausea
❑ Throat lozenges
❑ Water purification tablets[2]

❑ Antacids
❑ Anti-gas
❑ Antiseptics / antibiotics
❑ Decongestants
❑ Fever blister
❑ Sunburn
❑ Syrup of ipecac
❑ Pain medications
❑ Toothache drops

Supplies

❑ Bandages (Ace, Bandaids, Butterfly, Gauze, sterile pads)
❑ Cotton (sterile)
❑ Eye dropper
❑ Forceps (e.g. tweezers)
❑ Medicine glass or cup
❑ Scalpel blade (sterile) or sharp knife
❑ Tape (bandaging)
❑ Tongue depressors

❑ Bandage scissors
❑ Bulb syringe
❑ Dental floss
❑ Eye patches
❑ Ice bag
❑ Safety pins
❑ Snake bite kit[3]
❑ Sponge
❑ Thermometer
❑ Towels

Miscellaneous

❑ First Aid manual

APPENDIX B cont'd

1. Consult with a health professional regarding the appropriate selection and use of medication products. Realize that medications which are appropriate for one member of the family, may not be for others (e.g., children)

2. Water purification tablets may, or may not, be available. At the very least, water from natural sources should always be boiled for several minutes if it is to be used for drinking, to clean wounds, etc. Water from natural sources frequently carries bacteria and other organisms which can cause human diseases. Ideally, it is best to use bottled water for drinking and cooking, since boiling may not destroy all disease-causing organisms.

3. Snake bite kits are not routinely recommended as items to be included in first aid kits. This item should be considered only for cases in which there is no reasonable opportunity to transport the victim to a medical facility. Individuals who are likely to use this item should become completely familiar with its use prior to emergencies (e.g., consult with a physician).

REFERENCES

SECTION I
Introduction to a Healthier You

CHAPTERS 1 and 2

1.   Ardell, D.B. *The New Edition of High Level Wellness – an Alternative to Doctors, Drugs and Disease*. Ten Speed Press, Berkeley, CA, (1986).

2.   Banta, David. "What is Health Care?" *Health Care Delivery in the United States* (2nd ed.), Springer Publishing Co., (1981).

3.   *Bartlett's Familiar Quotations*, (1941).

4.   Brody, Howard and Sobel, David. "A Systems View of Health and Disease." *The Nation's Health* (Philip Lee, Nancy Brown and Ida Red, editors), Boyd & Frasier Publishing Co., San Francisco, (1981).

5.   Chapman, J.S. "Health and Medicine" in *The Nation's Health* (P.R. Lee et al., editors). Boyd and Fraser, San Francisco, CA, (1981).

6.   *Dimensions in Wholistic Healing* (Herbert Otto and James Knight, editors). Nelson-Hall, Chicago, (1979).

7.   Dubos, R. "Health and Creative Adaptation" in *The Nation's Health* (P.R. Lee et al., editors). Boyd and Fraser, San Francisco, CA, (1981).

8.   Dubos, R. *Man Adapting*. Yale University Press, New Haven, (1980).

9.   Eckholm, E.P. "Creating Better Health" in *The Nation's Health* (P.R. Lee, et al., editors). Boyd and Fraser, San Francisco, CA, (1981).

10.   Freymann, John G. *The American Health Care System: Its Genesis and Trajectory*. Robert E. Krieger Publishing Co., Malabar, Fl, (1980).

11.   Kleinman, A. "The Failure of Western Medicine" *The Nation's Health* (P.R. Lee, et al., editors). Boyd and Fraser, San Francisco, CA, (1981).

12.   Mayer, Jean. *Health*. D. Van Nostrand Co., NY, (1974).

CHAPTER 3.

1.   Allbutt, T. Clifford. *Greek Medicine in Rome*., Benjamin Blom, Inc., NY, (1970).

2. Barthell, Edward E., Jr. *Goddesses of Ancient Greece.* University of Miami Press, Coral Gables, FL, (1971).

3. Castiglioni, Arturo. "The Serpent as Healing God in Antiquity." Ciba Symposia, Vol. 3, No. 12, (March 1942).

4. Edelstein, Ludwig. *Ancient Medicine.* The Johns Hopkins Press, Baltimore, (1967).

5. "Swine Flue Vaccine Immunization Program." FDA Report, Micromedex, Inc., (1976)

6. Haggard, Howard W. *Mystery, Magic and Medicine.* Doubleday, Doran & Company, Inc., Garden City, NY, (1933).

7. Margotta, Roberto. *The Story of Medicine.* Golden Press, New York, (1968).

8. McLeish, Kenneth. *Children of the Gods.* Longman House, Burnt Mill, Harlow, Essex England, (1983).

9. Sigerist, Henry E. *A History of Medicine* (Vol. 1), Oxford University Press, NY, (1955).

CHAPTER 4.

1. Holt, Gary A. and Hall, Edwin L. "Potentials for Holism in Pharmacy." American Pharmacy, (January 1983), pp. 38 ff.

2. *Body, Mind and Spirit – the Journey Toward Health and Wholeness* (Peter Albright and Beth Albright, editors). The Stephen Greene Press, Brattleboro, VT, (1980).

3. *Health for the Whole Person* (Arthur Hastings, et al., editors). Westview Press, Boulder, CO, (1980).

4. Otto, Herbert A. and Knight, James W. "Wholistic Healing: Basic Principles and Concepts." *Dimensions in Wholistic Healing – New Frontiers in the Treatment of the Whole Person.* Nelson-Hall, Chicago, (1979).

5. Smuts, Jan. *Holism and Evolution.* Greenwood Press, Westport, Conn., (1973).

CHAPTER 5.

1. "Health for All — Pass it Along." American Association for World Health, Washington, D.C., (1989).

2. Lazlo, Ervin. *The Systems View of the World.* George Braziller, New York, (1972).

3.   *Systems and Medical Care* (Alan Sheldon, Frank Baker and Curtis McLaughlin, editors). The MIT Press, Cambridge, Mass., (1970).

CHAPTER 6.

1.   "A Study of Attitudes, Concerns and Information Needs for Prescription Drugs and Related Illnesses." The CBS Consumer Model, CBS Television Network, New York, (1984), p.8.

2.   "Abuse of Medicines — Part 1: Self-Medication." A Report by a Working Party, 1975, Council of Europe, European Public health Community. Drug Intelligence and Clinical Pharmacy, Vol. 10, (Jan. 1976), pp. 16-33.

3.   "Aging and Health — The Role of Self-Medication: Current Practices, Costs and Benefits, Importance of Information." Nonprescription Drug Manufacturers Association, Washington, D.C., (April 1991).

4.   Bloom, Marlene Z. "FDA's Kessler: A Prescription for Change." American Pharmacy, Vol. NS31, No. 12, (Dec. 1991), pp. 34-37.

5.   Boyce, Robert W. and Herrier, Richard N. "Obtaining and Using Patient Data." American Pharmacy, Vol. NS31, No. 7, (July 19910, pp. 65-70.

6.   "Communication with Patients Effectively." American Pharmacy, Vol. NS31, No. 7, (July 1991), pp. 9-10.

7.   Cousins, Norman. *Anatomy of an Illness – As Perceived by the Patient.* Bantam Books, New York, (1979).

8.   Davis, Joseph L. and Madhavan, Suresh. "Should Prescription Drugs Be Advertised to Consumers?" American Druggist, (May 1991), pp. 83-85.

9.   Doluisio, James T. "Rx-OTC: New Resources in Self-Medication." American Pharmacy, Vol. NS23, No. 1, (Jan. 1983), pp. 26-28.

10.   Donabedian, A., et al. *Medical Care Chartbook.* Health Administration Press, Ann Arbor, Mich., (1986).

11.   Dubos, Rene. *Mirage of Health.* Harper Torchbook, New York, (1980).

12.   Dubos, Rene. *The World of Rene Dubos – A Collection From His Writings.* Henry Holt and Co., New York, (1990).

13.   "FDA Spreads Anti-Tampering Message." Executive Newlestter of the Nonprescription Drug Manufacturers Association, Washington, D.C., (Oct. 11, 1991), p. 4.

14.   Feisullin, Sophia and Sause, Robert B. "Update on Direct-to-Consumer Advertising of Prescription Drugs." American Pharmacy, Vol. NS31, No. 7, (July 1991), pp. 47-52.

15. Fincham, Jack E. "An Overview of Adverse Drug Reactions." American Pharmacy, Vol. NS31, No. 6, (June 1991), pp. 47-52.

16. Gelb, Bruce S. "Self-Medication: From Here to 2001." Self-Medication — Making It Work Better for More People. Proceedings of the World Feveration of Proprietary Medicine Manufacturers 8th General Assembly, Washington, D.C., sponsored by the Nonprescription Drug Manufacturers Association, (Sept. 1986), pp. 54-58.

17. Hall, Edwin L.; Baker, Daniel; and Holt, Gary A. "Potentials for Holism in Pharmacy." California Pharmacist, Vol. 30, No. 12, (1983), p. 20.

18. Harris, T. George. "Questions and Answers — The Pharmacist as Information Sources." Self-Care, Self-Medication in America's Future — A Symposium. The Nonprescription Drug Manufacturers Association in Cooperation with the FDA, Washington, D.C., (Feb. 8, 1988), pp. 55-56.

19. Harris, T. George. "The Uses of Knowledge Regulation Versus Information." Self-Care, Self-Medication in America's Future — A Symposium. The Nonprescription Drug Manufacturer's Association in Cooperation with the FDA, Washington, D.C., (Feb. 8, 1988), pp. 51-54.

20. *Healers on Healing* (Richard Carlson and Benjamin Shield, editors). Jeremy P. Tarcher, Inc., Los Angeles, (1989).

21. "Health Care Practices and Perceptions — A Consumer Survey of Self-Medication." Prepared for the Nonprescription Drug Manufacturers Association by the Harry Heller Research Corp. (HHR #72792), Washington, D.C., (Feb. 1984).

22. Helm, DeWitt. "Advertising — An Essential Active Ingredient" and "Questions and Answers — Consumer Education." Self-Medication — Making It Work Better for More People. Proceedings of the World Federation of Proprietary Medicine Manufacturers 8th General Assembly, Washington, D.C., sponsored by the Nonprescription Drug Manufacturers Association, (Sept. 1986), pp. 86-92.

23. Holt, Gary A.; Beck, Doug; and Williams, M. Margaret. "Interview Analysis Regarding Health Status, Health Needs and Health Care Utilization of Ambulatory Elderly." Unpublished study sponsored by Warner Lambert and the National Council on the Aging, (Spring 1991).

24. Holt, Gary A. and Hall, Edwin L. "Potentials for Holism in Pharmacy." American Pharmacy, (January 1983), pp. 38 ff.

25. Holt, Gary; Hollon, James D.; Hughes, Scott E.; Coyle, Rebecca. "OTC Labels: Can Consumers Read and Understand Them?" American Pharmacy, Vol. NS30, No. 11, (November, 1990), pp. 51-54.

26. Holt, Gary A. and Hall, Edwin L. "The Pros and Cons of Self-Medicating." Journal of Pharmacy Technology, (Sept./Oct 1986), pp. 213-218.

26. Hutt, Peter B. "A Legal Framework for future Decisions on Transferring Drugs from Prescription to Nonprescription Status." Rx-OTC: New Resources in Self-Medication — A Symposium. The Nonprescription Drug Manufacturers Association, Washington, D.C., (Nov. 1, 1982), pp. 25-26.

28. "Improving Patient Compliance: Is There a Pharmacist in the House?" Schering Report XIV, Schering Laboratories, Kenilworth, NJ, (1992).

29. "Information Sources in Self-Medication." Self-Medication in Health Care — An International Perspective. World Federation of Proprietary Medicine Manufacturers, (April 1985).

30. "International Pharmacists Reveal Benefits of a Transition Class of Drugs." Pharmacy Today, Vol. 30, No. 20, (Sep. 27, 1991).

31. Kline, Charles H. "The Economic Benefits of Self-Medication." Self-Care, Self-Medication in America's Future: A Symposium, The Proprietary Association, 1988.

32. Kline, Charles H. "Nonprescription Drugs: From Folk Remedy to HighTech." Self-Medication — Making It Work Better for More People. Proceedings of the World Federation of Proprietary Medicine Manufacturers 8th General Assembly, Washington, D.C., sponsored by the Nonprescription Drug Manufacturers Association, (Sept. 1986).

33. Lawrence, Arthur J. "The Community RPh's Role in Health Promotion and Disease Prevention." Pharmacy Times, (March 1991).

34. Martin, Sara. "Exploring the Benefits of a Third Class." American Pharmacy, Vol. NS31, No. 12, (Dec. 1991).

35. Meade, Vicki. "Patients Need Advice As Array of Cold Products Grows." American Pharmacy, Vol. NS31, No. 12, (Dec. 1991).

36. Palumbo, Francis B. "The Impact of the Rx to OTC Switch on Practicing Pharmacists." American Pharmacy, Vol. NS31, No. 4, (April. 1991).

37. "Pharmacies Offer More Clinical Services." American Druggist, (February 1991).

38. *Pharmacy Law Digest* (J.L. Fink et al., editors), Facts and Comparisons Division, J.B. Lippincott, St. Louis, Mo., (1995).

39. Pray, W. Steven. "Quackery: A Deadly Threat to Health." U.S. Pharmacist, (May 1991).

40. "Prescription Drug Advertising — Issues and Perspectives." A CBS Television Network Presentation. CBS Television Network Sales/Marketing Service, New York.

41. "Responsible Self-Medication — What It Is, How It Helps, Who Benefits." Nonprescription Drug Manufacturers Association, Washington, D.C.

42. Rubin, Irvin. "A 10-Point Preview of Health Care in the Year 2000 — Part 2." Wellcome Trends in Pharmacy, Vol. 10, No. 9, (Oct. 1988).

43. Rupp, Michael T. and Parker, Jonathon M. "Drug Names: When Marketing and Safety Collide." American Pharmacy, Vol. NS33, No. 5, (May 1993).

44. Shepherd, Marvin D. "Pharmaceutical Care: Adding Value to the Future." American Pharmacy, Vol. NS31, No. 4, (April 1991).

45. Smith, Mickey; Juergens, John; and Jack, William. "Medication and the Quality of Life." American Pharmacy, Vol. NS31, No. 4, (April 1991).

46. "Talk About Prescriptions Month — Planning Guide" National Council on Patient Information and Education, Washington, D.C., (October 1991).

47. *Teaching Information for Management Educators.* Upjohn Company, (1990).

48. White, Arthur H. "The American Self-Care Movement." Self-Care, Self-Medication in America's Future — A Symposium. The Nonprescription Drug Manufacturers Association in cooperation with the FDA, Washington, D.C., (Feb. 8, 1988).

49. Young, F.E. "A Theme in Three Parts: Science, Society, the Economy." Self-Care, Self-Medication in America's Future — A Symposium. The Nonprescription Drug Manufacturers Association in cooperation with the FDA, Washington, D.C., (Feb 8, 1988).

SECTION 2
Aging

1. Bauer, KG. *Improving the Chances for Health: Lifestyle Change and Health Evaluation.* National Center for Health Education, San Francisco, CA.

2. "Developing Fall Prevention Programs for Older Adults." American Association of Retired Persons, Washington, DC, (1993).

3. Healthy People 2000 — Healthy Older Adults" from *Healthy People 2000 National Health Promotion and Disease Prevention Objectives*, U.S. Department of Health and Human Services, Public Health Service and the American Association of Retired Persons, Washington, DC.

4. Henig, Robin M., and the editors of *Esquire. How a Woman Ages.* New York: Ballantine, (1985).

5. Holt, Gary A.; Beck, Doug; and Williams, M. Margaret. "Interview Analysis Regarding Health Status, Health Needs and Health Care Utilization of Ambulatory Elderly." Unpublished study sponsored by Warner Lambert and the National Council on the Aging, (Spring 1991).

6.   Holt, Gary A. *Physical Aspects of Aging.* A nonpublished course packet, South Oklahoma City Junior College, Oklahoma City, OK, (1980).

7.   Institute of Medicine. *Extending Life, Enhancing Life: A National Research Agenda on Aging.* National Academy Press.

8.   Kimmel, D.C. *Adulthood and Aging* (2nd ed.). John wiley & Sons, New York, (1980).

9.   "Older and Wiser." The Baltimore Longitudinal Study of Aging. U.S. Dept. of Health and Human Services, Public Health Service, National Institutes of Health, (Sept. 1989).

10.   Pesman, Curtis, and the editors of *Esquire. How a Man Ages.* New York: Ballantine, (1984).

11.   *Priorities and Approaches for Improving Prescription Drug Use by Older Americans.* A Report to the National Council on Patient Information and Education, Washington, DC., (October, 1987).

12.   Newman, B.M. and Newman, P.R. *Understanding Adulthood.* Holt, Rinehart and Winston, New York, (1983).

13.   Schaie, K.W. and Geiwitz, J. *Adult Development and Aging.* Little, Brown and Co., Boston, (1982).

14.   Sherman, David S. "Managing Sleep Disturbances in the Elderly." Contemporary LTC, (September 1989), pp. 127 ff.

SECTION 3
Diseases and Interventions of the 20th Century

CHAPTER 11.

The American Heart Association has available numerous publications on the prevention, diagnosis and treatment of heart and vascular diseases (Toll Free Phone Number: 1-800-242-8721). These include the following publications used as references for this book:

1.   "1993 Heart and Stroke Facts Statistics."

2.   "A Guide to Losing Weight."

3.   "About High Blood Pressure."

4.   "About High Blood Pressure in African-Americans."

5.   "About High Blood Pressure in Children."

6.   "Cardiovascular Fitness — Facts to Know Before You Start an Exercise Program."

7. "Children and Smoking: A Message to Parents."

8. "Cigarette Smoking and Cardiovascular Disease — Special Report for the Public."

9. "Cholesterol and Your Heart."

10. "Controlling Your Risk Factors for Heart Attack."

11. "Cycling for a Healthy Heart."

12. "Dancing for a Healthy Heart."

13. "Dining Out — A Guide to Restaurant Dining."

14. "Doctors Answer Your Questions About Blood Pressure."

15. " 'E' is for Exercise."

16. "Eat Well, But Wisely to Reduce Your Risk of Heart Attack."

17. "Exercise and Your Heart."

18. "Fact Sheet on Heart Attack, Stroke and Risk Factors."

19. "Facts About Potassium."

20. "Facts About Stroke."

21. "Heart and Stroke Facts."

22. "Heart Attack."

23. "Heart Attack and Stroke: Signals and Action."

24. "High Blood Pressure."

25. "High Blood Pressure Fact Sheet."

26. "High Blood Pressure in Teenagers."

27. "How Stroke Affects Behavior."

28. "How to Avoid Weight Gain when Quitting Smoking."

29. "How to Choose a Nutrition Counselor for Cardiovascular Health — A Consumer Guide."

30. "How to Have Your Cake and Eat it Too — A Painless Guide to Low-Fat, Low-Cholesterol Eating."

31. "How to Make Your Heart Last A Lifetime."

32. "How to Quit — A Guide to Help You Stop Smoking."

33. "How to Read the New Food Label."

34. "How to Win at Losing — A Guide to Permanent Weight Loss."

35. "How You Can Help Your Doctor Treat Your High Blood Pressure."

36. "Now You're Cookin' — Helpful Recipes to Help Control High Blood Pressure."

37. "Nutrition for the Fitness Challenge."

38. "Nutrition Labeling — Food Selection Hints for Fat-Controlled Meals."

39. "Nutritious Nibbles — A Guide to Healthy Snacking."

40. "Recipes for Low-Fat, Low-Cholesterol Meals."

41. "Recovering from a Stroke."

42. "Risko — A Heart Hazard Appraisal."

43. "Running for a Healthy Heart."

44. "Salt, Sodium and Blood Pressure."

45. "Save Food Dollars and Help Your Heart."

46. "Signs of a Heart Attack."

47. "Signs of a Stroke."

48. "Six Important Facts for a Healthy Heart."

49. "Smoking and Heart Disease."

50. "Strokes: A Guide for the Family."

51. "Swimming for a Healthy Heart."

52. "Ten Commandments for the Patient with High Blood Pressure."

53. "The American Heart Association Diet — An Eating Plan for Healthy Americans."

54. "The Good Life — A Guide to Help You Stop Smoking."

55. "Walking for a Healthy Heart."

56. "Walking . . . Natural Fun, Natural Fitness."

57. "Weight Control Guidance in Smoking Cessation."

58. "What Every Woman Should Know about High Blood Pressure."

59. "What to Ask about High Blood Pressure."

60. "Why Exercise?"

61. "Winning for Life — A Guide to Staying at Your Best Weight."

62. "Your Heart and Cholesterol."

CHAPTER 12.

The American Cancer Society has available numerous publications on cancer prevention, diagnosis and treatment (Toll Free Phone Number: 1-800- ACS-2345). These include the following publications used as references for this book:

1. "Cancer Facts & Figures — 1993.".

2. "Cancer Facts for Men."

3. "Cancer Facts for Women."

4. "Cancer-Related Checkups."

5. "Cancer Risk Report — Prevention and Control — 1992."

6. "Diet, Nutrition & Cancer."

7. "Eat Smart — Reduce Your Cancer Risk."

8. "Eat Smart with Fresh Fruits and Vegetables."

9. "Eating Smart."

10. "Facts on Breast Cancer."

11. "Facts on Lung Cancer."

12. "Facts on Oral Cancer."

13. "Facts on Ovarian Cancer."

14. "Facts on Prostate Cancer."

15. "Facts on Skin Cancer."

16. "Facts on Testicular Cancer."

17. "For Men Only."

18. "Get a Fresh Start — Let Us Help You Quit Smoking."

19. "Guidelines for the Cancer-Related Checkup."

20. "How to do Breast Self Examination."

21. "How to Quit Cigarettes."

22. "Special Touch — A Personal Plan of Action for Breast Health."

23. "The Older You Get, the More You Need A Mammogram."

24. "The Smoke Around You"

25. "World Smoking & Health."

26. "You Can Protect Yourself Against Cancer! Here's How."

CHAPTER 13.

1. "Fact Sheet on Heart Attack, Stroke and Risk Factors."

2. "How to Make Your Heart Last A Lifetime."

3. "Diabetes Complications Fourth Leading Cause of Death." Pharmacy Times, (Feb. 15, 1995).

CHAPTER 14.

1. Carmichael, Jan. "Postmenopausal Hormone Replacement." Women's Health Issues Supplement to U.S. Pharmacist, (February 1992).

2. Rifee, J. M. "Osteoporosis: Prevention and Management." American Pharmacy, (August 1992).

3. Sagraves, Rosalie. "Prevention and Treatment of Osteoporosis in Women." Supplement to U.S. Pharmacist, (September, 1994).

4. *The Merck Manual* (15th ed.), Merck Sharp & Dohme Research Laboratories, Rahway, NJ, (1987).

5. "Therapeutic Options for Osteoporosis." APhA Special Report, American Pharmaceutical Association, (1993).

CHAPTER 15.

1. Larrat, Paul E. "Update on the Treatment of Alzheimer's Disease." American Pharmacy, (September 1992).

2.   *The Merck Manual* (15th ed.), Merck Sharp & Dohme Research Laboratories, Rahway, NJ, (1987).

CHAPTER 16.

1.   *Facts and Comparisons,* St. Louis, Mo., (1995).

2.   Pray, W. Steven. "Medications and Sexual Dysfunction." U.S. Pharmacist, (August 1993).

3.   *The Merck Manual* (15th ed.), Merck Sharp & Dohme Research Laboratories, Rahway, NJ, (1987).

CHAPTER 17.

1.   "AIDS and You." U.S. Dept. of Health and Human Services, Public Health Service, Centers for Disease Control.

2.   Aral, SO and Holmes, KK. "Sexual Transmitted Diseases in the AIDS Era." Scientific American, (February 1991).

3.   Bender, M. "Condoms and Other Devices / Techniques — Part 1: Condoms." in A Pharmacists Guide to AIDS Education, California Pharmacists Association, (December 1991).

4.   Berger, J. W. and Foster, E. "What about HIV Testing?" in A Pharmacists Guide to AIDS Education, California Pharmacists Association, (December 1991).

5.   *Care of the Patient with HIV Infection.* Glaxo, Inc., (1991)

6.   "Caregiver Training: Helpful Techniques for Working with the HIV Infected Patient." in A Pharmacists Guide to AIDS Education, California Pharmacists Association, (December 1991).

7.   "Common Questions and Answers about AIDS." Oklahoma State Department of Health, (April 1990).

8.   Denetclaw, Tina H; et al. "Questions People Ask." in A Pharmacists Guide to AIDS Education, California Pharmacists Association, (December 1991).

9.   Essex, M. and Kanki, PJ. "The Origins of the AIDS Virus." Scientific American, (October 1988).

10.   *Facts and Comparisons*, St. Louis, Mo., (1995).

11.   Falloon, J. "Current Therapy for HIV Infection and Its Infectious Complications." Postgraduate Medicine, (June 1992).

12.   Fineberg, H. "The Social Dimensions of AIDS." Scientific American, (October 1988).

13. Gallo, R. C. and Montagnier, L. "AIDS in 1988." Scientific American, (October 1988).

14. Gerberding, Julie Louise; et al. "HIV and the Health Care Worker." Glaxo, Inc., Research Triangle Park, NC, (July 1992).

15. Haseltine, William A and Wong-Staal, Flossie. "The Molecular Biology of the AIDS Virus." Scientific American, (October 1988).

16. "Health United States 1991 and Prevention Profile." U.S. Dept. of Health and Human Services, Public Health Service, Centers for Disease Control, National Center for Health Statistics, Hyattsville, Md, (May 1992).

17. Henry, W. keith. "Essential HIV / AIDS Facts." Postgraduate Medicine, (June 1992).

18. Henry, W. Keith. "HIV and AIDS — Challenges and Rewards for Primary Care Physcians." Postgraduate Medicine, (June 1992).

19. Heyward, William L. and Curran, Janes W. "The Epidemiology of AIDS in the U.S." Scientific American, (October American, (October 1988).

20. "HIVID (Zalcitabine)." Professional Monograph, Roche Laboratories, (June 1992).

21. Huls, C. E. "Managing, Treating and Prevending AIDS." Drug Store News, (May 18, 1992).

22. "IV Needle Use and AIDS (Part II)" in A Pharmacists Guide to AIDS Education, California Pharmacists Association, (December 1991).

23. Jones, Jeffrey M and De Muth, James E. "Outpatient Management of AIDS." U.S. Pharmacist, (November 1991), pp. H3-H22.

24. Jue, Sally. "Identifying and Meeting the Needs of Minority Clients with AIDS" in A Pharmacists Guide to AIDS Education, California Pharmacists Association, (December 1991).

25. Kanuha, Vali. "Women and AIDS: Considerations for Effective HIV and AIDS Education" in A Pharmacists Guide to AIDS Education, California Pharmacists Association, (December 1991).

26. Lawrence, Arthur J. "The Dynamics of the HIV Epidemic: Pharmacist-Initiated Prevention Interventions." Wellcome Programs in Pharmacy, (July 1991).

27. Mann, Jonathan M; Chin, James; Piot, Peter; and Quinn, Thomas. "The International Epidemiology of AIDS.." Scientific American, (October 1988).

28. Matthews, Thomas J. and Bolognesi, Dani P. "AIDS Vaccine." Scientific American, (October 1988).

29. Meng, Tze-Chiang; et al. "Combination Therapy with Zidovudine and Dideoxycytidine in Patients with Advanced HIV Infection." Annals of Internal Medicine, (January 1992).

30. Oksas, Richard M. "Current HIV Treatment and Therapies" in A Pharmacists Guide to AIDS Education, California Pharmacists Association, (December 1991).

31. Purdy, Bonnie D. and Plaisance, Karen I. "Infection with the Human Immunodeficiency Virus: Epidemiology, Pathogenesis, Transmission, Diagnosis and Manifestations." American Journal of Hospital Pharmacy, American Society of Hospital Pharmacists, (1989).

32. Quinn, Thomas C. "Screening for HIV Infection — Benefits and Costs." The New England Journal of Medicine, (August 13, 1992).

33. Redfield, Robert R. and Burke, Donald s. "HIV Infection: The Clinical Picture." Scientific American, (October 1988).

34. Rhame, Frank S. "Preventing HIV Transmission." Postgraduation Medicine, (June 1992).

35. Schulman, David. "AIDS / HIV Workplace Law and Policy" in A Pharmacists Guide to AIDS Education, California Pharmacists Association, (December 1991).

36. Thurn, Joseph R. "HIV Worldwide." Postgraduate Medicine, (June 1992).

37. Weber, Jonathan N. and Weiss, Robin A. "HIV Infection: The Cellular Picture." Scientific American, (October 1988).

38. Yarchoan, Robert; Mitsuya, Hiroaki; and Broder, Samuel. "AIDS Therapies." Scientific American, (October 1988).

CHAPTER 19.

1. "A Guide to Losing Weight." American Heart Association.

2. "Cardiovascular Fitness — Facts to Know Before You Start an Exercise Program." American Heart Association.

3. "Cholesterol and Your Heart." American Heart Association.

4. "Controlling Your Risk Factors for Heart Attack." American Heart Association.

5. "Diet, Nutrition & Cancer." American Cancer Society.

6. "Dining Out — A Guide to Restaurant Dining." American Heart Association.

7. *Drug Facts and Comparisons*, St. Louis, Mo, (1995).

8. "Eat Smart — Reduce Your Cancer Risk." American Cancer Society.

9. "Eat Smart with Fresh Fruits and Vegetables." American Cancer Society.

10. "Eating Smart." American Cancer Society.

11. "Eat Well, But Wisely to Reduce Your Risk of Heart Attack." American Heart Association.

12. *Goodman and Gilman's – The Pharmacological Basis of Therapeutics* Pergamon Press, Elmsford, NY, (1990).

13. Holt, G.A.; et al. Food and Drug Interactions: *A Health Care Professional's Guide*. Bonus Books, Chicago, (1992).

14. "How to Choose a Nutrition Counselor for Cardiovascular Health — A Consumer Guide." American Heart Association.

15. "How to Have Your Cake and Eat It Too — A Painless Guide to Low-Fat, Low-Cholesterol Eating." American Heart Association.

16. "How to Make Your Heart Last A Lifetime." American Heart Association.

17. "How to Read the New Food Label." American Heart Association.

18. "How to Win at Losing — A Guide to Permanent Weight Loss." American Heart Association.

19. "Now You're Cookin' — Helpful Recipes to Help Control High Blood Pressure." American Heart Association.

20. "Nutrition for the Fitness Challenge." American Heart Association.

21. "Nutrition Labeling — Food Selection Hints for Fat-Controlled Meals." American Heart Association.

22. "Nutritious Nibbles — A Guide to Healthy Snacking." American Heart Association.

23. "Recipes for Low-Fat, Low-Cholesterol Meals." American Heart Association.

24. "Salt, Sodium and Blood Pressure." American Heart Association.

25. "Save Food Dollars and Help Your Heart." American Heart Association.

26. "The American Heart Association Diet — An Eating Plan for Healthy Americans." American Heart Association.

27. "Winning for Life — A Guide to Staying at Your Best Weight." American Heart Association.

28. "You Can Protect Yourself Against Cancer! Here's How." American Cancer Society.

29. "Your Heart and Cholesterol." American Heart Association.

CHAPTER 19.

1. "About High Blood Pressure." American Heart Association.

2. "Cardiovascular Fitness — Facts to Know Before You Start an Exercise Program." American Heart Association.

3. "Controlling Your Risk Factors for Heart Attack." American Heart Association.

4. "Cycling for a Healthy Heart." American Heart Association.

5. "Dancing for a Healthy Heart." American Heart Association.

6. " 'E' is for Exercise." American Heart Association.

7. "Exercise and Your Heart." American Heart Association.

8. "Heart and Stroke Facts." American Heart Association.

9. "High Blood Pressure Fact Sheet." American Heart Association.

10. "How to Make Your Heart Last A Lifetime." American Heart Association.

11. "Running for a Healthy Heart." American Heart Association.

12. "Six Important Facts for a Healthy Heart." American Heart Association.

13. "Swimming for a Healthy Heart." American Heart Association.

14. "Walking for a healthy Heart." American Heart Association.

15. "Walking . . . Natural Fun, Natural Fitness." American Heart Association.

16. "Why Exercise?" American Heart Association.

CHAPTER 21.

1. Davis, M.D.; Exhelman, E.R. and McKay, M. *The Relaxation & Stress Reduction Workbook* (3rd ed.) New Harbinger Publications, Inc., (1988).

CHAPTER 22.

1. Hardin, Garrett and Baden, John. *Managing the Commons.* W.H. Freeman and Company, New York, (1977).

2. Odum, Eugene. *Fundamental of Ecology*. W.B. Saunders Company, Philadelphia, (1971).

3. Ehrlich, Paul; et al. *Ecoscience – Population, Resources, Environments*. W.H. Freeman & Co., San Francisco, (1977).

4. Vesilind, P. A.; and Peirce J. J. *Environmental Pollution and Control*. Butterworths, Boston, (1983).

5. ReVelle, Penelope and ReVelle, Charles. *The Environment – Issues and Choices for Society*. Jones and Bartlett Publishers, Boston, (1988).

6. Nadakavukaren, Anne. *Man & Environment— A Health Perspective* (3rd ed.). Waveland Press, Inc., Prospect Heights, Ill., (1990)

CHAPTERS 23-26.

1. *Blakiston's New Gould Medical Dictionary*, McGraw-Hill Book Company, New York, (1956).

2. Harvey, Stewart C. "Drug Absorption, Action, and Disposition." *Temington's Pharmaceutical Sciences*. Mack Publishing Co., (1980).

3. Holt, Gary A. *Food and Drug Interactions*, Precept Press, Chicago, (1992)

4. *Pharmacy Law Digest* (Joseph L. Fink III, Karl W. Marquardt, and Larry M. Simonsmeier, editors). Facts and Comparisons, St. Louis, MO., (1995).

CHAPTER 27.

1. Fincham, Jack E. "An Overview of Adverse Drug Reactions." American Pharmacy, (June 1991).

2. Goth, Andres. *Medical Pharmacology*, C.V. Mosby, Co., St. Louis, (1984).

3. "Improving Patient Compliance: Is There a Pharmacist in the House?" Schering Report XIV, Schering Laboratories, Kenilworth, NJ, (1992).

4. Holt, Gary; Dorcheus, Leona; Hall, Edwin L.; et al. "Patient Interpretation of Label Instructions." American Pharmacy, Vol. NS32, No. 3, (March1992).

5. "Talk About Prescriptions Month." National Council on Patient Information and Education, Washington, DC, (October 1990).

CHAPTER 28.

1. "Cancer Facts and Figures — 1994." American Cancer Society, Atlanta, GA, (1994).

2. "Cancer Risk Report — Prevention and Control, 1992." American Cancer Society, Atlanta, GA, (1992).

3. "Children and Smoking: A Message to Parents." American Heart Association, Dallas, TX, (1987).

4. "Cigarette Smoking and Cardiovascular Disease." American Heart Association, Dallas, TX, (1985).

5. "Facts on Oral Cancer." American Cancer Society, Atlanta, GA, (1989).

6. Galizia, Virginia J. and Sause, Robert B. "Smoking Cessation: Advice to Patients." U.S. Pharmacist, (June 1992).

7. Gossel, Thomas A. "The Physiological and Pharmacological Effects of Nicotine." U.S. Pharmacist, (February 1992).

8. Green, H.L.; Godbery, RJ; and Ockene, JK. "Cigarette Smoking: The Physician's Role in Cessation and Maintenance." Journal of General Internal Medicine, (1988).

9. "Heart and Stroke Facts." American Heart Association, Dallas, (1992).

10. "How to Avoid Weight Gain When Quitting Smoking." American Heart Association, Dallas, (1993).

11. "How to Quit — A Guide to Help You Stop Smoking." American Heart Association, Dallas, TX, (1984).

12. Novello, Antonia C. "Youth: An Urgent Challenge for Tobacco Control." Vol. 17, No. 3, American Cancer Society, Atlant, GA, (1992).

13. Ruby, Lisa A; Zarus, Stephanie A.; and Morris, Erick J. "Breaking the Barriers: A Review of Smoking Cessation Options." Philadelphia College of Pharmacy and Science and Marion Merrell Dow, (1991).

14. "The Good Life — A Guide to Help You Quit Smoking." American Heart Association, Dallas, TX (1984).

CHAPTER 30.

1. Rall, Theodore W. "Hypnotics and Sedatives; Ethanol." *Goodman and Gilman's the Pharmacological Basis of Therapeutics*, Pergamon Press, New York, (1990).

2. Reiss, Barry S. "Pharmacodynamics of Alcohol." U.S. Pharmacist, (February, 1992).

CHAPTER 31.

1. "A Useful Guide to Herbal Health Care." Health Center for Better Living, Inc., Naples, FL. (1995).

2. *The Lawrence Review of Natural Products*, Facts and Comparisons, St. Louis, (1995).

CHAPTER 33.

I.   Troetel, William M. "How New Drugs Win FDA Approval." U.S. Pharmacist, (November 1988).

2.   Young, Fran E. "From Test Tube to Patient: New Drug Development in the U.S." FDA Consumer, (November 1987).

CHAPTER 34.

I.   "NDMA Counters 'New' Third Class Push." Executive Newsletter (No. 33-91), Nonprescription Drug Manufacturers Association, Washington, DC, (September 6, 1991).

2.   Palumbo, Francis B. "The Impact of the Rx to OTC Switch on Practicing Pharmacists." American Pharmacy, (April 1991).

3.   Temin, Peter. "Costs and Benefits in Switching Drugs from Rx to OTC." Rx-OTC New Resources in Self-Medication — A Symposium. The Nonprescription Drug Manufacturers Association, Washington, DC, (November 1982).

4.   Waxman, Henry A. "Self-Care: The Legislative Perspective." Self-Care, Self-Medication in America's Future — A Symposium. The Proprietary Association in cooperation with the FDA, Washington, DC, (February 1988).

5.   Young, Frank E. "A Doctor's Advice on Self-Care." A pamphlet produced by the Nonprescription Drug Manufacturers Association in cooperation with the FDA.

CHAPTER 42.

I.   Biberdorf, Robert L. and Forbes, David S. "Child-Resistant Medicine Containers — Public Use, Preference and Storage." Journal of the American Pharmaceutical Association, (March 1977).

2.   Carter, Jimmy. Presidential Documents. Proclaimation 4683, (February 8, 1979).

3.   Dance, Betsy. "Child-Resistant Caps Keep Adults Out Too." American Pharmacy, (November 1990).

4.   "Poison Prevention Packaging: A Test for Pharmacists and Physicians." U.S. Consumer Product Safety Commission, Washington, DC, (1990).

5.   "Poison Prevention Packaging — Alternatives for Older Consumers and the Handicapped." Consumer Product Safety Commission, Washington, DC.

CHAPTER 43.

I.   Cramer, Tom. "Look Twice — How to Protect Yourself Against Drug Tampering." Executive Newsletter, Nonprescription Drug Manufacturers Association, (October 18, 1991), pp. 20 - 23.

CHAPTER 44.

1.   Cagle, Eldon. "The Billion Dollar Hoax." American Druggist, (January 1990).

2.   "Health Fraud Activities — Status Report," Office of Consumer Affairs, FDA, (February 1988).

3.   "Health, Information and the Use of Questionable Treatments: A Study of the American Public" (Study #833015) conducted by Louis Harris & Associates for the U.S. Dept. of Health & Human Services, (September 1987).

4.   Miller, Roger W. "Critiquing Quack Ads." FDA Consumer, (March 1985).

5.   Pray, Steven W. "Quackery: A Deadly Threat to Health." U.S. Pharmacist, (May 1991).

6.   "Quackery — The Billion Dollar Miracle Business" (HHS Publication No. 85-4200), U.S. Dept. of Health and Human Services, Public Health Service, FDA, HFI-40.

INDEX